O Lord,
let our prayer
come before you.
Listen, and answer us.

People's Prayer Book

Dedicated to

Saint Joseph

Patron of the

Universal Church

Lord Jesus, Master of prayer, the beginning and the end of all things, teach us to pray.

New Saint Joseph

People's Prayer Book

A NEW AND COMPLETE PRAYER BOOK

**WITH PRAYERS FROM
THE BIBLE AND THE LITURGY,
THE ENCHIRIDION OF INDULGENCES,
THE SAINTS AND SPIRITUAL WRITERS
AS WELL AS TRADITIONAL
AND CONTEMPORARY PRAYERS
FOR EVERY NEED AND ALL OCCASIONS**

General Editor
REV. FRANCIS EVANS

CATHOLIC BOOK PUBLISHING CO.
New York

NIHIL OBSTAT: Daniel V. Flynn, J.C.D.

Censor Librorum

IMPRIMATUR: Joseph T. O'Keefe

Vicar General, Archdiocese of New York

ACKNOWLEDGMENTS

We are grateful for permission to quote from the following copy-righted works:

LITURGICAL TEXTS: Excerpts from the English translation of the *Rite of Baptism for Children* © 1969, International Committee on English in the Liturgy, Inc. (ICEL); excerpts from the English translation of the *Roman Missal* © 1973, ICEL; excerpts from the English translation of *Holy Communion and Worship of the Eucharist Outside Mass* © 1974, ICEL; excerpts from the English translation of the *Rite of Penance* © 1974, ICEL; excerpts from the English translation of Morning and Evening Prayer from *The Liturgy of the Hours* © 1974, ICEL; excerpts from the English translation of the *Rite of Confirmation* © 1975, ICEL. All rights reserved.

Excerpts (only in nos. 143, 145, 153, 154) from *The Psalms: A New Translation* © The Grail, (England) 1963. The Complete Psalms first published in 1963 by and available through Wm. Collins Sons & Co., Limited — In North America through the Paulist Press Inc. and Collins-World.

BIBLICAL TEXTS: Excerpts from *The New American Bible* © 1970 by the Confraternity of Christian Doctrine, Washington, D.C. All rights reserved.

No. 545: Translated from Pierre Teilhard de Chardin, *La Messe sur le Monde* © by Editions du Seuil, 1956.

No. 552: Reprinted from *An Order of Worship for the Proclamation of the Word of God and the Celebration of the Lord's Supper,* © 1968 by Consultation on Church Union.

No. 553: Reprinted from the *Book of Common Prayer (Proprosed).* © 1977 by Charles Mortimer Guilbert as Custodian of the Standard Book of Common Prayer. All rights reserved. Used with permission.

No. 620: Reprinted from *"The Scarlet Muse": An Anthology of Polish Poems,* edited by Umadevi and Harischandra B. Bhatt, published by Nalanda Publications, Bombay.

Nos. 621-622: Reprinted from *A Minute of Prayer,* edited by Christopher Cross, published by Pocket Books (Simon and Schuster), 1954.

Note: If through inadvertence a copyright has failed to be acknowl-edged, sincere apologies are offered together with the assurance that this omission will be remedied in future editions.

(T-900)

PREFACE

A NOTHER book of prayers? Yes, and hopefully something much more. Seen in its totality this book is not just a collection of formulations. It is not merely anthology, not a sampler but rather an exemplar. It demonstrates the almost universal human need for communication with God. A need that expresses itself in many ways. An expression that speaks of inspiration.

You may see in this book examples of prayer from all over the world, even from those who have not received the gift of faith. Who, nonetheless, have been moved to praise and glorify, to acknowledge dependence, to worship and adore. In them we might find words that will inspire us.

Yet, we must guard against regarding these exemplars of prayer as magic formulae. They are examples and may move one or another by the beauty of expression or exalted concepts. They have been gathered in order to help us to build up a manner of being able to speak to God without fear and in love as to the One who loves us the most.

What then is prayer? Clearly it is not just a feeling, not a mood. It is much more. It involves the whole being of the person. In the classic definition it is a lifting of mind and heart to God. St. John Vianney tells us it is union with God and "in this union, God and soul are like two pieces of wax melted into one."[1] St. John Chrysostom affirms that prayer is not the result of external attitude but comes from the heart and "prayer, loving conversation with God,

---

[1] *Catechism on Prayer,* text compiled by A. Monchanin in *The Spirit of the Curé of Ars* (Tequi 1899), p. 87.

is the supreme good. It is union ... with him."[2] *John Cardinal Newman spoke of prayer being to the spiritual life what the pulse and breathing are to physical life.*[3]

If you are a prayerful person this book may help you to find better ways to express what is in your heart and what in its roots cannot be fully expressed in words. If you are merely curious may you be moved by something here to seek further and find union with God. The Gospels often mention that the Lord Jesus drew aside to pray. In the Garden his whole being became immersed in prayer. It was intense prayer and did not change anything in God. But through his words of submission, "Not my will, but yours be done,"[4] *it recognized the reality of what God willed at that moment to be the effect of the Lord's prayerful union.*

Reflecting on this scene consider these words from Thomas Merton, "Prayer and sacrifice work together; where there is no sacrifice, there will eventually turn out to be no prayer, and vice versa. When sacrifice is an infantile self-dramatization, prayer will also be false and operatic self-display, or maudlin self-pitying introspection. Serious and humble prayer, united with mature love, will unconsciously and spontaneously manifest itself in a habitual spirit of sacrifice and concern for others that is unfailingly generous, though perhaps we may not be aware of the fact."[5]

Rev. Francis Evans

---

[2] *Sixth Homily on Prayer: PG* 64, 462D.
[3] *Parochial & Plain Sermons* (Longmans Green & Co., 1917), Vol. VII, p. 209.
[4] Luke 22:42.
[5] *The Climate of Monastic Prayer* (Spencer, Mass.; Cistercian Publications, 1966), p. 102.

INTRODUCTION

This new prayerbook combines liturgical and non-liturgical prayers with communal and personal prayers of all types and for all occasions. It is the only single book that enables the reader to participate in any liturgical action and also to pray with the best prayers of the Bible, the Saints, the tradition of the Church, and the experience of contemporary life.

We present the outstanding prayers from the Bible, the very Word of God. Thus readers can pray in the words of the great personages of the faith, the universal and timeless sentiments of the psalms, the very prayers of Jesus, and the prayers of the early Church.

The Liturgy is the next source of countless prayers and dialogue with God. The faithful can thus take part in all the major liturgical celebrations of their lives and also utilize those same texts for personal prayer.

Another powerful source is the *Enchiridion of Indulgences,* which contains prayers that are time-tested and especially approved by the Church. These enable the readers to pray with the Church and to form within themselves the sentiments that are most Christ-like.

Closely allied to this source is the prayer-treasury of the Saints and spiritual writers of the Church, our brothers and sisters in Christ who preceded us and composed magnificent prayers in every circumstance of life. These can be of immense help to us as we encounter situations similar to those that faced them.

However, in line with the guidelines of the Church, Catholics are also called upon to pray with their "Separated Brethren" as well as their neighbors who profess the Jewish faith or other faiths. Hence, we have included a section of prayers from other religions.

The Church wants us to pray in accord with the Church Year. Hence, the next section includes prayers for every season as well as for every month and even every day of the week.

Ordinarily, the prayers of the Church are addressed to the Father through Jesus his Son in the unity of the Holy Spirit. However, there are times when we want to speak to one of the other Persons. Hence, there is a large selection of prayers to the Trinity.

Catholics also have a tradition of praying to others beside God—to the Mother of Jesus and all the Saints. Accordingly, there is a section of prayers to Saints and to patrons of professions and countries.

Again, prayer is used in all states of mind and circumstances of life. This calls for texts to be used on various occasions and for every need.

Prayers also stem from various relationships—world and country, church and parish, family and neighborhood, self and friends. A section provides many such prayers both traditional and contemporary.

Traditional Catholic devotions are provided in a totally new section with a modern biblical and liturgical slant as requested by Vatican II.

Finally, Catholics have a history of blessings to sanctify their world every day of their lives. A section of blessings brings the book to a close.

This volume is intended to be a veritable encyclopedia of prayer. It provides the best prayers possible in the most attractive format. And the text is adorned with inspiring illustrations.

The invaluable analytical Index will help the reader make optimum usage of the treasury of prayer texts.

CONTENTS

1

PRAYERS FROM THE BIBLE

MOSES — POWERFUL EXAMPLAR OF PRAYER

The prayer life of the Israelites was typified by leaders such as Moses. By communing with God in the burning bush and on the holy mountain (for forty days and nights), he set an example of how the individual Israelites should pray to God.

A) PRAYER IN THE HISTORY OF ISRAEL (OLD TESTAMENT)

MAN'S intercourse with God is so natural and spontaneous that it existed from the very beginning of the human race. The Old Testament writers acknowledged that God was infinitely superior to man and could not be compelled to answer human prayers by incantations, exorcisms, or magical formulas; so they forbade the use of such superstitious practices.

Thus, Israel surpassed all the ancient religions in its unique concept of God and its life of prayer. Prayer is directed to God alone in the Old Testament and every Israelite is encouraged to make prayer an essential part of his religious obligations.

The most characteristic element of Old Testament prayer is its relation to the saving plan of God: man prays, beginning with what has happened or with what is happening, so that something may happen and God's salvation may be granted to the earth. All of sacred history is marked by prayer; the high points are punctuated by the prayer of the mediators and the whole people, who depend on the knowledge of the plan of God to obtain his intervention in the present moment.

Public prayer is exercised by leaders and kings, such as Moses, David, and Solomon; prophets, like Elijah, Samuel, and Jeremiah; religious leaders, such as Ezra and Nehemiah; and freedom fighters, like Judas Maccabeus. Personal prayer is practiced by many different individuals, such as Jonah, Tobit, Judith, Esther, and Job.

The Church encourages us to make all these prayers our own, since they are found in her own book, the Bible, which is inspired by the Holy Spirit, and they can add much knowledge and devotion to our lives.

13

1   Prayer of Moses

Hymn of victory after the crossing of the Red Sea

I WILL sing to the Lord, for he is gloriously triumphant;
  horse and chariot he has cast into the sea.
My strength and my courage is the Lord,
  and he has been my savior.

He is my God, I praise him;
  the God of my father, I extol him.
The Lord is a warrior,
  Lord is his name!
Pharaoh's chariots and army he hurled into the sea.

At a breath of your anger the waters piled up,
  the flowing waters stood like a mound,
  the flood waters congealed in the midst of the sea.

The enemy boasted, "I will pursue and overtake them;
  I will divide the spoils and have my fill of them;
  I will draw my sword; my hand shall despoil them!"
When your wind blew, the sea covered them;
  like lead they sank in the mighty waters.

Who is like to you among the gods, O Lord?
  Who is like to you, magnificent in holiness?
O terrible in renown, worker of wonders,
  when you stretched out your right hand, the earth
    swallowed them!

In your mercy you led the people you redeemed;
  in your strength you guided them to your holy dwell-
    ing.

And you brought them in and planted them on the
    mountain of your inheritance—
  the place where you made your seat, O Lord,
  the sanctuary, O Lord, which your hands established.
The Lord shall reign forever and ever.

Exodus 15:1-4a, 8-13, 17-18

2

Prayer of Hannah

The humble find joy in God

MY HEART exults in the Lord,
my horn is exalted in my God.

I have swallowed up my enemies;
I rejoice in my victory.
There is no Holy One like the Lord;
there is no Rock like our God.

Speak boastfully no longer,
nor let arrogance issue from your mouths.
For an all-knowing God is the Lord,
a God who judges deeds.

The bows of the mighty are broken,
while the tottering gird on strength.
The well-fed hire themselves out for bread,
while the hungry batten on spoil.
The barren wife bears seven sons,
while the mother of many languishes.

The Lord puts to death and gives life;
he casts down to the nether world;
he raises up again.
The Lord makes poor and makes rich,
he humbles, he also exalts.

He raises the needy from the dust;
from the ash heap he lifts up the poor,
To seat them with nobles
and make a glorious throne their heritage. . . .

For the pillars of the earth are the Lord's,
and he has set the world upon them.
He will guard the footsteps of his faithful ones,
but the wicked shall perish in the darkness.
For not by strength does man prevail;
the Lord's foes shall be shattered.

The Most High in heaven thunders;
   the Lord judges the ends of the earth.
Now may he give strength to his king
   and exalt the horn of his anointed!

1 Samuel 2:1-10

Prayer of David

Glory and honor are due to God alone

BLESSED may you be, O Lord,
   God of Israel our father,
from eternity to eternity.

Yours, O Lord, are grandeur and power,
   majesty, splendor, and glory.

For all in heaven and on earth is yours;
   yours, O Lord, is the sovereignty:
   you are exalted as head over all.

Riches and honor are from you,
   and you have dominion over all.
In your hand are power and might;
   it is yours to give grandeur and strength to all.

Therefore, our God, we give you thanks
   and we praise the majesty of your name.

1 Chronicles 29:10-13

4   ## Prayer of Solomon

May God heed the petitions of his people

LORD, God of Israel,
   there is no God like you
in heaven above or on earth below;

You keep your covenant of kindness with your servants
   who are faithful to you with their whole heart.

Can it indeed be
   that God dwells among men on earth?
If the . . . highest heavens cannot contain you,
   how much less [can] this temple. . . !

Look kindly on the prayer and petition of your servant,
   O Lord, my God,
And listen to the cry of supplication
   which I, your servant, utter before you this day.

May your eyes watch night and day over this temple,
   the place where you have decreed you shall be hon-
      ored;
May you heed the prayer
   which I, your servant, offer in this place.

Thus may your eyes be open to the petition of your
      servant
   and to the petition of your people. . . .
Hear them whenever they call upon you,
   because you have set them apart
Among all the peoples of the earth
   for your inheritance.

1 Kings 8:23, 27-29, 52-53

5   Prayer of Tobit

God afflicts but only to heal

BLESSED be God who lives forever,
   because his kingdom lasts for all ages.

For he scourges and then has mercy;
   he casts down to the depths of the nether world,
   and he brings up from the great abyss.
No one can escape his hand.

Praise him, you Israelites, before the Gentiles,
  for though he has scattered you among them,
  he has shown you his greatness even there.

Exalt him before every living being,
  because he is the Lord our God,
  our Father and God forever.

He scourged you for your iniquities,
  but will again have mercy on you all.
He will gather you from all the Gentiles
  among whom you have been scattered.

When you turn back to him with all your heart,
  to do what is right before him,
Then he will turn back to you,
  and no longer hide his face from you.

So now consider what he has done for you,
  and praise him with full voice.
Bless the Lord of righteousness,
  and exalt the King of the ages.

In the land of my exile I praise him,
  and show his power and majesty to a sinful nation.

"Turn back, you sinners! do the right before him:
  perhaps he may look with favor upon you
  and show you mercy.

"As for me, I exalt my God
  and my spirit rejoices in the King of heaven.
Let all men speak of his majesty,
  and sing his praises in Jerusalem."

Tobit 13:1-8

6 **Prayer of Judith**

God who created the world takes care of his people

STRIKE up the instruments,
    a song to my God with timbrels,
  chant to the Lord with cymbals.
Sing to him a new song,
  exalt and acclaim his name.

A new hymn I will sing to my God.
  O Lord, great are you and glorious,
  wonderful in power and unsurpassable.

Let your every creature serve you;
  for you spoke, and they were made.
You sent forth your spirit, and they were created;
  no one can resist your word.

The mountains to their bases, and the seas, are
      shaken;
  the rocks, like wax, melt before your glance.
But to those who fear you,
  you are very merciful.

Judith 16:1, 13-15

7 **Prayer of Esther**

God alone has the power to save us

MY LORD, our King,
  you alone are God.
Help me, who am alone and have no help but you,
  for I am taking my life in my hand.

As a child I was wont to hear from the people
  of the land of my forefathers

That you, O Lord, chose Israel from among all peoples
   and our fathers from among all their ancestors,
   as a lasting heritage,
And that you fulfilled
   all your promises to them.

But now we have sinned in your sight,
   and you have delivered us into the hands of our
enemies,
   because we worshiped their gods.
You are just, O Lord.

Be mindful of us,
   O Lord.
Manifest yourself in the time of our distress
   and give me courage,
   King of gods and Ruler of every power.

Save us by your power, and help me,
   who am alone and have no one
   but you, O Lord.
Esther C: 14-18, 23, 25

8   # Prayer of Job

The living God who vindicates

OH, would that my words were written down!
   Would that they were inscribed in a record:
That with an iron chisel and with lead
   they were cut in the rock forever!

But as for me, I know that my Vindicator lives,
   and that he will at last stand forth upon the dust;
Whom I myself shall see:
   my own eyes, not another's, shall behold him,
And from my flesh I shall see God;
   my inmost being is consumed with longing.

I know that you can do all things,
　and that no purpose of yours can be hindered.
I have dealt with great things that I do not understand;
　things too wonderful for me, which I cannot know.
I had heard of you by word of mouth,
　but now my eye has seen you.
Therefore I disown what I have said,
　and repent in dust and ashes.

Job 19:23-26; 42:2-6

9　Prayer of the Sage for Wisdom

Lord, give me Wisdom

GOD of my fathers, Lord of mercy,
　you who have made all things by your word
And in your wisdom have established man
　to rule the creatures produced by you,
To govern the world in holiness and justice,
　and to render judgment in integrity of heart:

Give me Wisdom, the attendant at your throne,
　and reject me not from among your children:
For I am your servant, the son of your handmaid,
　a man weak and short-lived
　and lacking in comprehension of judgment and of
　　laws.

Indeed, though one be perfect among the sons of men,
　if Wisdom, who comes from you, be not with him,
　he shall be held in no esteem.

Now with you is Wisdom who knows your works
　and was present when you made the world;
Who understands what is pleasing in your eyes
　and what is conformable with your commands.

Send her forth from your holy heavens
and from your glorious throne dispatch her
That she may be with me and work with me,
that I may know what is your pleasure.

For she knows and understands all things,
and will guide me discreetly in my affairs
and safeguard me by her glory.

Wisdom 9:1-6, 9-11

10   Prayer of the Sage for Trust in God's Word

The Lord fed his people with the bread of angels

YOU nourished your people with food of angels
and furnished them bread from heaven, ready to
hand, untoiled-for,
endowed with all delights and conforming to every
taste.

For this substance of yours
revealed your sweetness toward your children,
And serving the desire of him who reecived it,
was blended to whatever flavor each one wished,

That your sons whom you loved might learn, O Lord,
that it is not the various kinds of fruits that nourish
man,
but it is your word that preserves those who believe
you!
For great are your judgments and hardly to be described.

Wisdom 16:20-21, 26; 17:1a

11   **Prayer of Sirach**

Prayer of entreaty for the holy city, Jerusalem

COME to our aid, O God of the universe,
    and put all the nations in dread of you!
Raise your hand against the heathen,
    that they may realize your power.

As you have used us to show them your holiness,
    so now use them to show us your glory.
Thus they will know, as we know,
    that there is no God but you.

Give new signs and work new wonders;
    show forth the splendor of your right hand and arm.

Gather all the tribes of Jacob,
    that they may inherit the land as of old.
Show mercy to the people called by your name;
    Israel, whom you named your first-born.

Take pity on your holy city,
    Jerusalem, your dwelling place.
Fill Zion with your majesty,
    your temple with your glory.

Sirach 36:1-5, 10-13

12   **Prayer of Isaiah in Thanksgiving**

Joy of God's ransomed people

I GIVE you thanks, O Lord;
    though you have been angry with me,
    your anger has abated, and you have consoled me.

God indeed is my savior;
    I am confident and unafraid.

My strength and my courage is the Lord,
and he has been my savior.

With joy you will draw water
at the fountain of salvation, and say on that day:

Give thanks to the Lord, acclaim his name;
among the nations make known his deeds,
proclaim how exalted is his name.

Sing praise to the Lord for his glorious achievement;
let this be known throughout all the earth.

Shout with exultation, O city of Zion,
for great in your midst
is the Holy One of Israel!

Isaiah 12:1-6

13 Prayer of Isaiah for God's Judgment

The divine vindicator

A STRONG city have we;
he sets up walls and ramparts to protect us.
Open up the gates
to let in a nation that is just,
one that keeps faith.

A nation of firm purpose you keep in peace;
in peace, for its trust in you.
Trust in the Lord forever!
For the Lord is an eternal Rock.

The way of the just is smooth;
the path of the just you make level.
Yes, for your way and your judgments, O Lord,
we look to you;
Your name and your title
are the desire of our souls.

My soul yearns for you in the night,
  yes, my spirit within me keeps vigil for you;
When your judgment dawns upon the earth,
  the world's inhabitants learn justice.

O Lord, you mete out peace to us,
  for it is you who have accomplished all we have
    done.

Isaiah 26:1-4, 7-9, 12

14 Prayer of Isaiah for Trust in God

Prayer of trust in need

O LORD, have pity on us, for you we wait.
  Be our strength every morning,
our salvation in time of trouble!

At the roaring sound, peoples flee;
  when you rise in your majesty, nations are scattered.
Men gather spoil as caterpillars are gathered up;
  they rush upon it like the onrush of locusts.

The Lord is exalted, enthroned on high;
  he fills Zion with right and justice.
That which makes her seasons lasting,
  the riches that save her, are wisdom and knowledge;
  the fear of the Lord is her treasure.

See, the men of Ariel cry out in the streets,
  the messengers of Shalem weep bitterly.
The highways are desolate,
  travelers have quit the paths,
Covenants are broken, their terms are spurned;
  yet no man gives it a thought.

The country languishes in mourning,
  Lebanon withers with shame;

Sharon is like the steppe,
    Bashan and Carmel are stripped bare.
Now will I rise up, says the Lord,
    now will I be exalted, now be lifted up.

Isaiah 33:2-10

15   Prayer of Hezekiah

Prayer in time of sickness

ONCE I said,
    "In the noontime of life I must depart!
To the gates of the nether world I shall be consigned
      for the rest of my years."

I said, "I shall see the Lord no more
    in the land of the living.
No longer shall I behold my fellow men
    among those who dwell in the world."

My dwelling, like a shepherd's tent,
    is struck down and borne away from me;
You have folded up my life, like a weaver
    who severs the last thread.

Day and night you give me over to torment;
    I cry out until the dawn.
Like a lion he breaks all my bones;
    [day and night you give me over to torment].

Like a swallow I utter shrill cries;
    I moan like a dove.
My eyes grow weak, gazing heavenward:
    O Lord, I am in straits; be my surety!

What am I to say or tell him?
    He has done it!
I shall go on through all my years
    despite the bitterness of my soul.

Those live whom the Lord protects;
  yours . . . the life of my spirit.
You have given me health and life;
  thus is my bitterness transformed into peace.

You have preserved my life
  from the pit of destruction,
When you cast behind your back all my sins.

For it is not the nether world that gives you thanks,
  nor death that praises you;
Neither do those who go down into the pit
  await your kindness.

The living, the living give you thanks,
  as I do today.
Fathers declare to their sons,
  O God, your faithfulness.

The Lord is our savior;
  we shall sing to stringed instruments
In the house of the Lord
  all the days of our life.   Isaiah 38:10-20

16   **Prayer of Jeremiah**

The lament of the people in war and famine

LET my eyes stream with tears
  day and night, without rest,
Over the great destruction which overwhelms
  the virgin daughter of my people,
  over her incurable wound.

If I walk out into the field,
  look! those slain by the sword;
If I enter the city,
  look! those consumed by hunger.
Even the prophet and the priest
  forage in a land they know not.

Have you cast Judah off completely?
  Is Zion loathsome to you?
Why have you struck us a blow
  that cannot be healed?

We wait for peace, to no avail;
  for a time of healing, but terror comes instead.
We recognize, O Lord, our wickedness,
  the guilt of our fathers;
    that we have sinned against you.

For your name's sake spurn us not,
  disgrace not the throne of your glory;
    remember your covenant with us, and break it
      not.   Jeremiah 14:17-21

17   **Prayer of an unknown prophet**

A prayer in time of distress

REMEMBER, O Lord, what has befallen us,
  look, and see our disgrace:
Our inherited lands have been turned over to strangers,
    our homes to foreigners.

We have become orphans, fatherless;
  widowed are our mothers.

The water we drink we must buy,
  for our own wood we must pay.

On our necks is the yoke of those who drive us;
  we are worn out, but allowed no rest.

To Egypt we submitted,
  and to Assyria, to fill our need of bread.

Our fathers, who sinned, are no more;
  but we bear their guilt.

The joy of our hearts has ceased,
  our dance has turned into mourning;

The garlands have fallen from our heads:
  woe to us, for we have sinned!

Over this our hearts are sick,
  at this our eyes grow dim:

You, O Lord, are enthroned forever;
  your throne stands from age to age.

Why, then, should you forget us,
  abandon us so long a time?

Lead us back to you, O Lord, that we may be restored:
  give us anew such days as we had of old.

Lamentations 5:1-7, 15-17, 19-21

18   Prayer of Daniel

Praise of God who has gifted us

BLESSED be the name of God for ever and ever,
  for wisdom and power are his.
He causes the changes of the times and seasons,
  makes kings and unmakes them.
He gives wisdom to the wise
  and knowledge to those who understand.
He reveals deep and hidden things
  and knows what is in the darkness,
  for the light dwells with him.

Daniel 2:20-22

19   Prayer of Azariah

Trust in God's power for deliverance

BLESSED are you, and praiseworthy,
  O Lord, the God of our fathers,
and glorious forever is your name.

For you are just in all you have done;
    all your deeds are faultless, all your ways right,
    and all your judgments proper.

For we have sinned and transgressed
    by departing from you,
    and we have done every kind of evil.

For your name's sake, do not deliver us up forever,
    or make void your covenant.

Do not take away your mercy from us,
    for the sake of Abraham, your beloved,
    Isaac your servant, and Israel your holy one,

To whom you promised to multiply their offspring
    like the stars of heaven,
    or the sand on the shore of the sea.

For we are reduced, O Lord, beyond any other nation,
    brought low everywhere in the world this day
    because of our sins.

We have in our day no prince, prophet, or leader,
    no holocaust, sacrifice, oblation, or incense,
    no place to offer first fruits, to find favor with you.

But with contrite heart and humble spirit
    let us be received;
As though it were holocausts of rams and bullocks,
    or thousands of fat lambs,
So let our sacrifice be in your presence today
    As we follow you unreservedly;
    for those who trust in you cannot be put to shame.

And now we follow you with our whole heart,
    we fear you and we pray to you.

Daniel 3:26, 27, 29, 34-41

20   **Doxological Prayer of the
Three Young Men**

Let all creatures praise the Lord

BLESSED are you, O Lord, the God of our fathers,
praiseworthy and exalted above all forever.

And blessed is your holy and glorious name,
praiseworthy and exalted above all for all ages.

Blessed are you in the temple of your holy glory,
praiseworthy and glorious above all forever.

Blessed are you on the throne of your kingdom,
praiseworthy and exalted above all forever.

Blessed are you who look into the depths
from your throne upon the cherubim,
praiseworthy and exalted above all forever.

Blessed are you in the firmament of heaven,
praiseworthy and glorious forever.

Bless the Lord, all you works of the Lord,
praise and exalt him above all forever.

Daniel 3:52-57

See also no. 144, p. 133.

21   **Prayer of Jonah**

Psalm of thanksgiving

OUT of my distress I called to the Lord,
and he answered me;
From the midst of the nether world I cried for help,
and you heard my voice.

For you cast me into the deep, into the heart of the sea,
  and the flood enveloped me;
All your breakers and your billows
  passed over me.

Then I said, "I am banished from your sight!
  yet would I again look upon your holy temple."
The waters swirled about me, threatening my life;
  the abyss enveloped me;
  seaweed clung about my head

Down I went to the roots of the mountains;
  the bars of the nether world
  were closing behind me forever,
But you brought up my life from the pit,
  O Lord, my God

When my soul fainted within me,
  I remembered the Lord;
My prayer reached you
  in your holy temple.

Those who worship vain idols
  forsake their source of mercy.
But I, with resounding praise,
  will sacrifice to you;
What I have vowed I will pay:
  deliverance is from the Lord.   Jonah 2:3-10

22   **Prayer of Habakkuk**

              God comes to judge

O LORD, I have heard your renown,
    and feared, O Lord, your work.
In the course of the years revive it,
    in the course of the years make it known;
    in your wrath remember compassion!

You come forth to save your people,
    to save your anointed one.

Decay invades my bones,
    my legs tremble beneath me.
I await the day of distress
    that will come upon the people who attack us.

For though the fig tree blossom not
    nor fruit be on the vines,
Though the yield of the olive fail
    and the terraces produce no nourishment,

Though the flocks disappear from the fold
    and there be no herd in the stalls,
Yet will I rejoice in the Lord
    and exult in my saving God.

God, my Lord, is my strength;
    he makes my feet swift as those of hinds
    and enables me to go upon the heights.

Habakkuk 3:2, 13a, 16b-19

THE PSALMS — PRAYERBOOK OF THE HOLY SPIRIT

The Psalms may be looked upon as the prayerbook of the Holy Spirit. Over the long centuries of Israel's existence, the Spirit of God inspired the psalmists (typified by David) to compose magnificent prayers and hymns for every religious desire and need, mood and feeling. Thus, the psalms have great power to raise minds to God, to inspire devotion, to evoke gratitude in favorable times, and to bring consolation and strength in times of trial.

B) THE PSALMS:
PRAYER OF THE ASSEMBLY

THE Psalms are the prayer of God's assembly, the public prayer par excellence of the people of God. No prayer of Israel is comparable to the Psalter because of its universal character. The idea of the unity of the chosen people's prayer guided its elaboration as well as its adoption by the Church.

In giving us the Psalter which sums up the major aspects of man's relationship to his Creator and Redeemer, God puts into our mouths the word he wishes to hear, and indicates to us the dimensions of prayer.

"The Psalms recall to mind the truths revealed by God to the chosen people, which were at one time frightening and at another filled with wonderful tenderness; they keep repeating and fostering the hope of the promised Redeemer which in ancient times was kept alive with song, either around the hearth or in the stately Temple; they show forth in splendid light the prophesied glory of Jesus Christ: first, his supreme and eternal power, then his lowly coming to this earthly exile, his kingly dignity and priestly power and finally his beneficent labors, and the shedding of his Blood for our redemption.

"In a similar way they express the joy, the bitterness, the hope and fear of our hearts and our desire of loving God and hoping in him alone, and our mystic ascent to divine tabernacles" (Pius XII: *Mediator Dei*, no. 148).

To help the reader use the Psalms in a Christian way (with a predominantly Christological meaning), psalm-prayers have been added. These were not part of the original text.

35

23   ## Prayer for True Happiness

The way of the just

HAPPY the man who follows not
the counsel of the wicked
Nor walks in the way of sinners,
    nor sits in the company of the insolent,
But delights in the law of the Lord
    and meditates on his law day and night.

He is like a tree
    planted near running water,
That yields its fruit in due season,
    and whose leaves never fade.
    [Whatever he does, prospers.]

The way of the sinner

Not so the wicked, not so;
    they are like chaff which the wind drives away.
Therefore in judgment the wicked shall not stand,
    nor shall sinners, in the asssembly of the just,
For the Lord watches over the way of the just,
    but the way of the wicked vanishes.

Psalm-prayer   Psalm 1

Lord, you brought us to the fountain of life,
like trees planted near running waters.
Grant that we may bear perpetual fruit
through the cross of your Son
and be admitted into the assembly of the just.

24   ## Prayer of Trust in God

A call for God's help

WHEN I call, answer me, O my just God,
    you who relieve me when I am in distress;
Have pity on me, and hear my prayer!

Sinner, repent

Men of rank, how long will you be dull of heart?
  Why do you love what is vain and seek after false-
    hood?
Know that the Lord does wonders for his faithful one;
  the Lord will hear me when I call upon him.
Tremble, and sin not;
  reflect, upon your beds, in silence.
Offer just sacrifices,
  and trust in the Lord.

Confidence in God

Many say, "Oh, that we might see better times!"
  O Lord, let the light of your countenance shine upon
    us!
You put gladness into my heart,
  more than when grain and wine abound.
As soon as I lie down, I fall peacefully asleep,
  for you alone, O Lord,
  bring security to my dwelling.

Psalm 4

Psalm-prayer

O Lord, in you alone we trust.
Have pity on us and hear our prayer.
Help us to repent for our sins
and to attain true peace with you.

25   Prayer for Divine Assistance

A call for help

HEARKEN to my words, O Lord,
  attend to my sighing.
Heed my call for help,
  my king and my God!

To you I pray, O Lord;
   at dawn you hear my voice;
   at dawn I bring my plea expectantly before you.

Hatred of evil

For you, O God, delight not in wickedness;
   no evil man remains with you;
   the arrogant may not stand in your sight.
You hate all evildoers;
   you destroy all who speak falsehood;
The bloodthirsty and the deceitful
   the Lord abhors.

Guidance

But I, because of your abundant kindness,
   will enter your house;
I will worship at your holy temple
   in fear of you, O Lord;
Because of my enemies, guide me in your justice;
   make straight your way before me.

Destruction of the wicked

For in their mouth there is no sincerity;
   their heart teems with treacheries.
Their throat is an open grave;
   they flatter with their tongue.
Punish them, O God;
   let them fall by their own devices;
For their many sins, cast them out
   because they have rebelled against you.

Protection of the just

But let all who take refuge in you
   be glad and exult forever.
Protect them, that you may be the joy
   of those who love your name.

For you, O Lord, bless the just man;
   you surround him with the shield of your good will.

Psalm 5

Psalm-prayer

God, the source of all justice and goodness,
you hate wickedness and abhor falsehood.
Guide the way of your servants in your service
and grant us true joy in your Church.

26   Prayer of Repentance

Sorrow for sin

O LORD, reprove me not in your anger,
   nor chastise me in your wrath.
Have pity on me, O Lord, for I am languishing;
   heal me, O Lord, for my body is in terror;
My soul, too, is utterly terrified;
   but you, O Lord, how long . . . ?

The mercy of God

Return, O Lord, save my life;
   rescue me because of your kindness,
For among the dead no one remembers you;
   in the nether world who gives you thanks?
I am wearied with sighing;
   every night I flood my bed with weeping;
   I drench my couch with my tears.
My eyes are dimmed with sorrow;
   they have aged because of all my foes.

Confidence in prayer

Depart from me, all evildoers,
   for the Lord has heard the sound of my weeping;
The Lord has heard my plea;
   the Lord has accepted my prayer.

All my enemies shall be put to shame in utter terror;
  they shall fall back in sudden shame.

Psalm 6

Psalm-prayer

God, lover of mercy and compassion,
you bestow life and command death.
Look upon your Church covered with wounds
and renew her by your Son's resurrection
that she may praise you with a new song.

27 Prayer in Time of Trouble

Plea for God's help

O LORD, my God, in you I take refuge;
  save me from all my pursuers and rescue me,
Lest I become like the lion's prey,
  to be torn to pieces, with no one to rescue me.

Cry of innocence

O Lord, my God, if I am at fault in this,
  if there is guilt on my hands,
If I have repaid my friend with evil,
  I who spared those who without cause were my foes—
Let the enemy pursue and overtake me;
  let him trample my life to the ground,
  and lay my glory in the dust.

Appeal to God's judgment

Rise up, O Lord, in your anger;
  rise against the fury of my foes;
  wake to the judgment you have decreed.
Let the assembly of the peoples surround you;
  above them on high be enthroned.
  [The Lord judges the nations.]

Do me justice, O Lord, because I am just,
   and because of the innocence that is mine.
Let the malice of the wicked come to an end,
   but sustain the just,
   O searcher of heart and soul, O just God.

Psalm 7:1-10

Psalm-prayer

God, you know the secrets of our hearts.
Save us from all our pursuers.
Forgive us if we have repaid good with evil.
Grant us the strength to return good for evil
and to give thanks to the Lord for his justice.

28 Prayer Extolling the Majesty of God and the Dignity of Man

Man's finite nature and God's infinite majesty

O LORD, our God;
   how glorious is your name over all the earth!
You have exalted your majesty above the heavens.
Out of the mouths of babes and sucklings
   you have fashioned praise because of your foes,
   to silence the hostile and the vengeful.
When I behold your heavens, the work of your fingers,
   the moon and the stars which you set in place—
What is man that you should be mindful of him,
   or the son of man that you should care for him?

Man accorded dignity and power by God

You have made him little less than the angels,
   and crowned him with glory and honor.
You have given him rule over the works of your hands,
   putting all things under his feet:

All sheep and oxen,
    yes, and the beasts of the field,
The birds of the air, the fishes of the sea,
    and whatever swims the paths of the seas.
O Lord, our Lord,
    how glorious is your name over all the earth!

Psalm 8

Psalm-prayer

How glorious you are, Maker of all things!
You have given us men dominion over all creation.
Help us to subject ourselves to you.

29   Prayer to God the Supreme Good

The Lord is my portion

I BLESS the Lord who counsels me;
    even in the night my heart exhorts me.
I set the Lord ever before me;
    with him at my right hand I shall not be disturbed.
Therefore my heart is glad and my soul rejoices,
    my body, too, abides in confidence;
Because you will not abandon my soul to the nether
    world,
    nor will you suffer your faithful one to undergo cor-
    ruption.

Joyous resurrection

You will show me the path to life,
    fullness of joys in your presence,
    the delights at your right hand forever.

Psalm 16:7-11

Psalm-prayer

God, who can fathom the mystery of your love!
You gave your Son the cup of death to drink

but did not let your holy one see corruption
and brought him home to heavenly glory.
Grant that we may seek happiness in you alone
and attain fullness of joys in your presence
in the glory of the resurrection.

30 **Prayer of Christ on the Cross**

Lament in suffering

MY GOD, my God, why have you forsaken me,
    far from my prayer, from the words of my cry?
O my God, I cry out by day, and you answer not;
    by night, and there is no relief for me.
Yet you are enthroned in the holy place,
    O glory of Israel!
In you our fathers trusted;
    they trusted, and you delivered them.
To you they cried, and they escaped;
    in you they trusted, and they were not put to shame.
But I am a worm, not a man;
    the scorn of men, despised by the people.
All who see me scoff at me;
    they mock me with parted lips, they wag their heads:
"He relied on the Lord; let him deliver him,
    let him rescue him, if he loves him."
You have been my guide since I was first formed,
    my security at my mother's breast.
To you I was committed at birth,
    from my mother's womb you are my God.
Be not far from me, for I am in distress;
    be near, for I have no one to help me.

Joy of the risen Savior

I will proclaim your name to my brethren;
    in the midst of the assembly I will praise you:

"You who fear the Lord, praise him;
    all you descendants of Jacob, give glory to him;
    revere him, all you descendants of Israel!
For he has not spurned nor disdained
    the wretched man in his misery,
Nor did he turn his face away from him,
    but when he cried out to him, he heard him."
So by your gift will I utter praise in the vast assembly;
    I will fulfill my vows before those who fear him.
The lowly shall eat their fill;
    they who seek the Lord shall praise him:
    "May your hearts be ever merry!"

Psalm 22:2-12, 23-27

Psalm-prayer

Father, as your Son hung on the cross
at the mercy of his executioners,
he cried out to you as if abandoned by you.
Let death be dead and life return.
In virtue of his resurrection
redeem the poor, lift up the lowly,
and loosen the fetters that shackle the nations.
Let the Church break out in Alleluias
joining the eternal praises of your Son.

31   Prayer to the Good Shepherd

Constant protector

THE Lord is my shepherd; I shall not want.
    In verdant pastures he gives me repose;
Beside restful waters he leads me;
    he refreshes my soul.

He guides me in right paths
    for his Name's sake.

Even though I walk in the dark valley
   I fear no evil; for you are at my side
With your rod and your staff
   that give me courage.

Considerate host

You spread the table before me
   in the sight of my foes;
You anoint my head with oil;
   my cup overflows.

Only goodness and kindness follow me
   all the days of my life;
And I shall dwell in the house of the Lord
   for years to come.

Psalm 23

Psalm-prayer

Lord Jesus Christ, good shepherd of your Church,
you anoint with the oil of salvation
all who are born again in the fount of baptism.
Give them repose in verdant pastures
and spread your table before them.

32   Prayer in Time of Fear

Trust in God

THE Lord is my light and my salvation;
   whom should I fear?
The Lord is my life's refuge;
   of whom should I be afraid?
When evildoers come at me
   to devour my flesh,
My foes and my enemies
   themselves stumble and fall.

Though an army encamp against me,
    my heart will not fear;
Though war be waged upon me,
    even then will I trust.

Secure refuge

One thing I ask of the Lord;
    this I seek:
To dwell in the house of the Lord
    all the days of my life,
That I may gaze on the loveliness of the Lord
    and contemplate his temple.
For he will hide me in his abode
    in the day of trouble;
He will conceal me in the shelter of his tent,
    he will set me high upon a rock.
Even now my head is held high
    above my enemies on every side.
And I will offer in his tent
    sacrifices with shouts of gladness;
I will sing and chant praise to the Lord.

                                                    Psalm 27:1-6

Psalm-prayer

God, you are the protector and source of power
of all who hope in you.
You accepted the sacrifice of your Son
in the day of trouble.
Receive us sinners also in our necessity
and show us your face in your kingdom.

33   **Prayer for God's Mercy**

Hope of the penitent

O LORD, in your anger punish me not,
    in your wrath chastise me not;

For your arrows have sunk deep in me,
  and your hand has come down upon me.
There is no health in my flesh because of your indignation;
  there is no wholeness in my bones because of my sin,
For my iniquities have overwhelmed me;
  they are like a heavy burden, beyond my strength.

Sorrow for sin

For I am very near to falling,
  and my grief is with me always.
Indeed, I acknowledge my guilt;
  I grieve over my sin.
But my undeserved enemies are strong;
  many are my foes without cause.
Those who repay evil for good
  harass me for pursuing good.
Forsake me not, O Lord;
  my God, be not far from me!
Make haste to help me,
  O Lord my salvation!

Psalm 38:1-5, 18-23

Psalm-prayer

Do not forsake us, Lord, our savior,
as you did not forget your Son's broken body
or his selfless love.
Shower your loving kindness
on your children weighed down by sin.

34   Prayer of Longing and Hope

Longing to see God

AS THE hind longs for the running waters,
  so my soul longs for you, O God.
Athirst is my soul for God, the living God.
  When shall I go and behold the face of God?

My tears are my food day and night,
    as they say to me day after day, "Where is your God?"
Those times I recall,
    now that I pour out my soul within me,
When I went with the throng
    and led them in procession to the house of God,
Amid loud cries of joy and thanksgiving,
    with the multitude keeping festival.
Why are you so downcast, O my soul?
    Why do you sigh within me?
Hope in God! For I shall again be thanking him,
    in the presence of my Savior and my God.

Hopeful of God's promises

Within me my soul is downcast;
    so will I remember you
From the land of the Jordan and of Hermon,
    from Mount Misar.
Deep calls unto deep
    in the roar of your cataracts;
All your breakers and your billows
    pass over me.
By day the Lord bestows his grace,
    and at night I have his song,
    a prayer to my living God.
I sing to God, my Rock:
    "Why do you forget me?
Why must I go about in mourning
    with the enemy oppressing me?"
It crushes my bones that my foes mock me,
    as they say to me day after day, "Where is your God?"
Why are you so downcast, O my soul?
    Why do you sigh within me?
Hope in God! For I shall again be thanking him,
    in the presence of my Savior and my God.

Psalm 42:2-12

Psalm-prayer

Lord, show us your face
that our spirits may not be downcast.
Turn away wrath and pardon us.
As the hind longs for the running waters,
so our souls long for you.
Grant that we may drink from the source
of life and happiness.

35   ## Prayer before Confession

Sincere sorrow for sin

HAVE mercy on me, O God, in your goodness;
     in the greatness of your compassion wipe out my
          offense.
Thoroughly wash me from my guilt
     and of my sin cleanse me.
For I acknowledge my offense,
     and my sin is before me always:

"Against you only have I sinned,
     and done what is evil in your sight"—
That you may be justified in your sentence,
     vindicated when you condemn.
Indeed, in guilt was I born,
     and in sin my mother conceived me;
Behold, you are pleased with sincerity of heart,
     and in my inmost being you teach me wisdom.
A clean heart create for me, O God,
     and a steadfast spirit renew within me.
Cast me not out from your presence,
     and your holy spirit take not from me.
Give me back the joy of your salvation,
     and a willing spirit sustain in me.

Praise of God for his mercy

I will teach transgressors your ways,
  and sinners shall return to you.
Free me from blood guilt, O God, my saving God;
  then my tongue shall revel in your justice.
O Lord, open my lips,
  and my mouth shall proclaim your praise.
For you are not pleased with sacrifices;
  should I offer a holocaust, you would not accept it.
My sacrifice, O God, is a contrite spirit;
  a heart contrite and humbled, O God, you will not
    spurn.

Psalm 51:3-8, 12-19

Psalm-prayer

Merciful God,
that we might become the very holiness of God,
you made your Son who did not know sin
to be sin.
Consider our repentance
and raise us up in your goodness,
that we may sing your praise and your glory
in the Holy Spirit before the nations.

36   **Prayer to End Wars**

Fortify us against the enemy

O GOD, you have rejected us and broken our defenses;
    you have been angry; rally us!
You have rocked the country and split it open;
  repair the cracks in it, for it is tottering.
You have made your people feel hardships;
  you have given us stupefying wine.
You have raised for those who fear you a banner
  to which they may flee out of bowshot

That your loved ones may escape;
help us by your right hand, and answer us!

Lead us to victory

Who will bring me into the fortified city?
Who will lead me into Edom?
Have not you, O God, rejected us,
so that you go not forth, O God, with our armies?

Give us aid against the foe,
for worthless is the help of men.
Under God we shall do valiantly;
it is he who will tread down our foes.

Psalm 60:3-7, 11-14

Psalm-prayer

Lord Jesus Christ, you have gone before us
as an exemplar of your people.
You rocked the earth and split it
and conquered death and Satan.
Help your Church by your right hand
and deliver your loved ones from all evil,
that they may tell of your wonders forever.

37 Prayer of Ardent Longing for God

Thirst for God

O GOD, you are my God whom I seek;
for you my flesh pines and my soul thirsts
like the earth, parched, lifeless and without water.
Thus have I gazed toward you in the sanctuary
to see your power and your glory,
For your kindness is a greater good than life;
my lips shall glorify you.

Union with God

Thus will I bless you while I live;
  lifting up my hands, I will call upon your name.
As with the riches of a banquet shall my soul be satisfied,
  and with exultant lips my mouth shall praise you.
I will remember you upon my couch,
  and through the night-watches I will meditate on you:
That you are my help,
  and in the shadow of your wings I shout for joy.
My soul clings fast to you;
  your right hand upholds me.

Psalm 63:2-9

Psalm-prayer

God, you are the source of eternal light.
We seek you from the dawn of day.
Enlighten us,
that we may glorify you in word and work
and that our whole life may sing your praises.

38   Prayer for Help against Enemies

Protection from enemies

HEAR, O God, my voice in my lament;
  from the dread enemy preserve my life.
Shelter me against the council of malefactors,
  against the tumult of evildoers,

Who sharpen their tongues like swords,
  who aim like arrows their bitter words,
Shooting from ambush at the innocent man,
  suddenly shooting at him without fear.

They resolve on their wicked plan;
  they conspire to set snares,
  saying, "Who will see us?"

They devise a wicked scheme,
  and conceal the scheme they have devised;
  deep are the thoughts of each heart.

God's punishment

But God shoots his arrows at them;
  suddenly they are struck.
He brings them down by their own tongues;
  all who see them nod their heads.

And all men fear and proclaim the work of God,
  and ponder what he has done.
The just man is glad in the Lord and takes refuge in him;
  in him glory all the upright of heart.

Psalm 64

Psalm-prayer

Father, you protected and rescued your Son
when he suffered from blasphemers.
Be also our refuge in all life's dangers,
and grant that with him and through him
we may overcome wickedness.

39   **Prayer of Thanks**

Gratitude

TO YOU we owe our hymn of praise
  O God, in Zion;
To you must vows be fulfilled,
  you who hear prayers.
To you all flesh must come
  because of wicked deeds.
We are overcome by our sins;
  it is you who pardon them.
Happy the man you choose, and bring
  to dwell in your courts.

May we be filled with the good things of your house,
   the holy things of your temple!

God's bountiful harvest

You have visited the land and watered it;
   greatly have you enriched it.
God's watercourses are filled;
   you have prepared the grain.
Thus have you prepared the land: drenching its furrows,
   breaking up its clods,
Softening it with showers,
   blessing its yield.
You have crowned the year with your bounty,
   and your paths overflow with a rich harvest;
The untilled meadows overflow with it,
   and rejoicing clothes the hills.
The fields are garmented with flocks
   and the valleys blanketed with grain.
They shout and sing for joy.

Psalm 65:1-6, 10-14

Psalm-prayer

God, you created all things through your Son,
not because you needed creatures
but because in your goodness you desired to favor us.
You have visited the land and watered it.
Remain with your Church and shower her with graces
that she may attain perfection in union with you.

40   **Prayer of a Grateful Heart**

Thanksgiving in love

I LOVE the Lord because he has heard
   my voice in supplication,

Because he has inclined his ear to me
    the day I called.

The cords of death encompassed me;
    the snares of the nether world seized upon me;
    I fell into distress and sorrow,
And I called upon the name of the Lord,
    "O Lord, save my life!"

Petition granted

Gracious is the Lord and just;
    yes, our God is merciful.
The Lord keeps the little ones;
    I was brought low and he saved me.

Psalm 116:1-6

Psalm-prayer

Almighty and merciful God,
your Son has freed our life from death,
our eyes from tears and our feet from stumbling.
May he accompany us on our pilgrimage
and lead us to you.

41   Prayer for Spiritual Need

Look to our heavenly helper

TO YOU I lift up my eyes
    who are enthroned in heaven.
Behold, as the eyes of servants
    are on the hands of their masters,
As the eyes of a maid
    are on the hands of her mistress,
So are our eyes on the Lord, our God,
    till he have pity on us.

Prayer of pity

Have pity on us, O Lord, have pity on us,
    for we are more than sated with contempt;
Our souls are more than sated
    with the mockery of the arrogant,
    with the contempt of the proud.

Psalm 123

Psalm-prayer

God, you are present everywhere.
To you we raise our eyes.
Crush our pride
and grant us your compassion.

42   Prayer for Home Life

Blessings of a good family

HAPPY are you who fear the Lord,
    who walk in his ways;
For you shall eat the fruit of your handiwork;
    happy shall you be and favored.
Your wife shall be like a fruitful vine
    in the recesses of your home;
Your children like olive plants
    around your table.
Behold, thus is the man blessed
    who fears the Lord.

Prosperity and long life

The Lord bless you from Zion:
    may you see the prosperity of Jerusalem
    all the days of your life;
May you see your children's children.
    Peace be upon Israel!

Psalm 128

Psalm-prayer

Lord, inspire us with fear of your name,
but also give us your love
that drives out fear.
Teach us to walk joyfully
in your path.

43   Prayer for Pardon and Peace

Plea to be heard

OUT of the depths I cry to you, O Lord;
   Lord, hear my voice!
Let your ears be attentive
   to my voice in supplication:

God's pardon

If you, O Lord, mark iniquities,
   Lord, who can stand?
But with you is forgiveness,
   that you may be revered.

Trust in God's mercy

I trust in the Lord;
   my soul trusts in his word.
My soul waits for the Lord
   more than sentinels wait for the dawn.

Hope in the Redemption

More than sentinels wait for the dawn,
   let Israel wait for the Lord,
For with the Lord is kindness
   and with him is plenteous redemption;
And he will redeem Israel
   from all their iniquities.   Psalm 130

Psalm-prayer

God, you are power and life.
In the incarnation of your Son
you stooped down to us sinners
and raised us from the depths of our sinfulness.
Strengthen your Church
that she may live with confidence in your salvation.

44   **Prayer for Fraternal Charity**

Holy unity

BEHOLD, how good it is, and how pleasant,
  where brethren dwell at one!
It is as when the precious ointment upon the head
  runs down over the beard, the beard of Aaron,
  till it runs down upon the collar of his robe.
It is a dew like that of Hermon,
  which comes down upon the mountains of Zion;
For there the Lord has pronounced his blessing,
  life forever.

Psalm 133

Psalm-prayer

Lord, fill your Church
with fraternal love and peace.
Strengthen her with your blessing.

45   **Prayer of Praise from All Creation**

Let all creation praise God

PRAISE the Lord in his sanctuary,
  praise him in the firmament of his strength.
Praise him for his mighty deeds,
  praise him for his sovereign majesty.

Praise him with the blast of the trumpet,
  praise him with lyre and harp,
Praise him with timbrel and dance,
  praise him with strings and pipe.
Praise him with sounding cymbals,
  praise him with clanging cymbals.
Let everything that has breath
  praise the Lord! Alleluia.

Psalm 150

Psalm-prayer

God, you have created heaven and earth.
You are the sanctification of the saints
and the justification of repentant sinners.
Receive us into the community of your saints
that we may eternally praise you.

JESUS — MAN OF ASSIDUOUS PRAYER

As a faithful Jew, Jesus undoubtedly recited those prayers which were commonly said by devout Jews of his day. Among these were the **Shema** ("Hear, O Israel") recited as a creed each morning and night, and the **Tefillah** (eighteen benedictions) recited at sunrise, midadfternoon, and sunset. He was also accustomed to taking part in the Sabbath day synagogue services (Luke 4:16).

C. THE PRAYERS OF JESUS

JESUS lived his entire life in communion with God, so that the attitude of prayer was for him a permanent one. Reference is made in the Gospels on several occasions to his withdrawal to desert places for refreshment and solace of spirit (see Matthew 14:13; Mark 6:32; Luke 4:42).

In addition, Jesus prayed at important occasions of his public ministry; before his baptism (Luke 3:21), before the call of his disciples (Luke 6:12-13), on the occasion of many of his miracles (Luke 9:16; see John 6:23; Mark 7:34; 9:29; John 9:30-33; 11:41f), before the Eucharistic promise (Matthew 14:23), before the promise of the primacy to Peter (Luke 9:38), at his transfiguration (Luke 9:28) and both before and during his passion (Luke 22:39-46; Matthew 27:46; Luke 22:32; 23:34; 23:46; John 17).

Jesus prayed for the glorification of his Father (John 2:27-28), and for his own glorification (John 17:1-5); he prayed for his apostles (John 17:6-19), and in particular for Peter (Luke 22:31-32); he prayed for all the faithful (John 17:20-26) and for his enemies (Luke 23:34). He also taught his disciples the Our Father (Matthew 6:9-13).

Thus, his whole life was one of prayer inasmuch as he was constantly offering acts of worship, praise, and thanksgiving to his heavenly Father.

Now seated at the right hand of God the Father, Jesus continues to pray for us. He intercedes for us (Romans 8:34), appears before God on our behalf (Hebrews 9:24), and is our Advocate with the Father (1 John 2:1).

The prayers of Jesus can be an inspiration to our prayer life, for we also have been given a task to do on this earth and have been sent by the Father to carry on the work of Jesus.

46   The Lord's Prayer

OUR Father in heaven,
   hallowed be your name,
your kingdom come,
your will be done
on earth as it is in heaven.
Give us today our daily bread,
and forgive us the wrong we have done
as we forgive those who wrong us.
Subject us not to the trial
but deliver us from the evil one.

Matthew 6:9-13

47   Jesus' Praise of the Father

FATHER,
   Lord of heaven and earth,
to you I offer praise;
for what you have hidden from the learned and the
   clever
you have revealed to the merest children.
Father, it is true;
you have graciously willed it so.

Matthew 11:25-26

48   Jesus' Prayer in the Garden

MY FATHER,
   if it is possible,
let this cup pass me by.
Still, let it be
as you would have it, not as I.

My Father,
if this cannot pass me by,
without my drinking it,
your will be done!

Matthew 26:39, 42

49 Jesus' Prayer on the Cross

MY GOD,
my God,
why have you
forsaken me?

Matthew 27:46

50 Jesus' Prayer for His Enemies

FATHER,
forgive them;
they do not know
what they are doing.

Luke 23:34

51 Jesus' Last Prayer

FATHER,
into your hands
I commend
my spirit.

Luke 23:46

52   **Jesus' Prayer at Lazarus' Tomb**

FATHER, I thank you for having heard me.
I know that you always hear me
but I have said this for the sake of the crowd,
that they may believe that you sent me.

John 11:41-42

53   **Jesus' Prayer**
for His Father's Glorification

MY SOUL is troubled now,
yet what should I say—
Father, save me from this hour?
But it was for this that I came to this hour.
Father, glorify your name!

John 12:27-28

54 **Jesus' Prayer for His Own Glorification**

FATHER, the hour has come!
Give glory to your Son
that your Son may give glory to you,
inasmuch as you have given him authority over all mankind,
that he may bestow eternal life on those you gave him.
(Eternal life is this:
to know you, the only true God,
and him whom you have sent, Jesus Christ.)
I have given you glory on earth
by finishing the work you gave me to do.
Do you now, Father, give me glory at your side,
a glory I had with you before the world began.

John 17:1-5

55   **Jesus' Prayer for His Disciples**

I HAVE made your name known
to those you gave me out of the world.
These men you gave me were yours;
they have kept your word.
Now they realize
that all that you gave me comes from you.
I entrusted to them
the message you entrusted to me,
and they received it.
They have known that in truth I came from you,
they have believed it was you who sent me.

For these I pray—
not for the world
but for these you have given me,
for they are really yours.
(Just as all that belongs to me is yours,
so all that belongs to you is mine.)
It is in them that I have been glorified.
I am in the world no more,
but these are in the world
as I come to you.

O Father most holy,
protect them with your name which you have given me
[that they may be one, even as we are one].
As long as I was with them,
I guarded them with your name which you gave me.
I kept careful watch,
and not one of them was lost,
none but him who was destined to be lost—
in fulfillment of Scripture.
Now, however, I come to you;

I say all this while I am still in the world
that they may share my joy completely.

I gave them your word,
and the world has hated them for it;
they do not belong to the world
[any more than I belong to the world].
I do not ask you to take them out of the world,
but to guard them from the evil one.
They are not of the world,
any more than I belong to the world.
Consecrate them by means of truth—
"Your word is truth."

As you have sent me into the world,
so I have sent them into the world;
I consecrate myself for their sakes now,
that they may be consecrated in truth.

John 17:6-19

56 Jesus' Prayer for All Believers

I DO not pray for them alone.
    I pray also for those who will believe in me through
        their word,
that all may be one
as you, Father, are in me, and I in you;
I pray that they may be [one] in us,
that the world may believe that you sent me.
I have given them the glory you gave me
that they may be one, as we are one—
I living in them, you living in me—
that their unity may be complete.
So shall the world know that you sent me,
and that you loved them as you loved me.

Father,
all those you gave me
I would have in my company
where I am,
to see this glory of mine
which is your gift to me,
because of the love you bore me before the world began.

Just Father,
the world has not known you,
but I have known you;
and these men have known that you sent me.
To them I have revealed your name,
and I will continue to reveal it
so that your love for me may live in them,
and I may live in them.

John 17:20-26

THE EARLY CHURCH — UNITED IN PRAYER

The early Christians devoted themselves to the apostolic instruction and the communal life, to the breaking of bread and the prayers. With exultant and sincere hearts they took their meals in common, praising God and winning the approval of all the people.

D) PRAYERS OF THE CHURCH

FROM the beginning the first Christians were conscious of being a people of prayer. This flowed from their Israelite origin as well as from the instructions and example of Jesus. While waiting for the coming of the Holy Spirit, who had been promised by Jesus, the apostles gathered in prayer with Mary and the other relatives of Jesus (Acts 1:14).

After the Spirit's coming and under his inspiration, the early Christians took part in communal prayer, including the Eucharist, and in temple worship (Acts 2:42-47). They prayed for boldness in proclaiming God's word (Acts 4:24-31) and elected ministers to leave the apostles free to do their primary work of prayer and preaching (Acts 6:4).

At first the Christians were led to sing and then to imitate the Psalms of the Old Testament. Soon, however, they began to compose prayers of their own—in keeping with the idea of their union with one another in Christ. This gave rise to the use of canticles and thanksgiving prayers in liturgical celebrations as well as in private prayers.

Some of the most famous examples of these are the so-called Gospel canticles—the Magnificat of Mary, the Benedictus of Zechariah, and the Nunc Dimittis of Simeon (Luke 1—2) as well as the canticles and thanksgivings found throughout Paul's Epistles (Ephesians 5:14; 1 Timothy 3:6; 2 Timothy 2:11) and the Book of Revelation (4:11; 5:12).

Christians are invited to make these prayers their own, so as to recover that fervent faith and singleminded outlook which were characteristic of the early days of the Church.

57   Canticle of Mary

The soul rejoices in the Lord

MY BEING proclaims the greatness of the Lord,
   my spirit finds joy in God my savior,
For he has looked upon his servant in her lowliness;
   all ages to come shall call me blessed.
God who is mighty has done great things for me,
   holy is his name;
His mercy is from age to age
   on those who fear him.

He has shown might with his arm;
   he has confused the proud in their inmost thoughts
He has deposed the mighty from their thrones
   and raised the lowly to high places.
The hungry he has given every good thing,
   while the rich he has sent empty away.
He has upheld Israel his servant,
   ever mindful of his mercy;
Even as he promised our fathers,
   promised Abraham and his descendants forever.

Luke 1:46-55

58   Canticle of Zechariah

The Messiah and his forerunner

BLESSED be the Lord the God of Israel
   because he has visited and ransomed his people.
He has raised a horn of saving strength for us
   in the house of David his servant,
As he promised through the mouths of his holy ones,
   the prophets of ancient times:
Salvation from our enemies
   and from the hands of all our foes.

He has dealt mercifully with our fathers
   and remembered the holy covenant he made,
The oath he swore to Abraham our father
   he would grant us:
   that, rid of fear and delivered from the enemy,
We should serve him devoutly and through all our days
   be holy in his sight.

And you, O child, shall be called
   prophet of the Most High;
For you shall go before the Lord
   to prepare straight paths for him,
Giving his people a knowledge of salvation
   in freedom from their sins.
All this is the work of the kindness of our God;
   he, the Dayspring, shall visit us in his mercy
To shine on those who sit in darkness
   and in the shadow of death,
   to guide our feet into the way of peace.

Luke 1:68-79

59   Canticle of Simeon

**Christ is the light of the nations
and the glory of Israel**

NOW, Master, you can dismiss your servant in peace;
   you have fulfilled your word.
For my eyes have witnessed your saving deed
   displayed for all the peoples to see:
A revealing light of the Gentiles,
   the glory of your people Israel.

Luke 2:29-32

60   **Prayer of Thanksgiving**

SOVEREIGN Lord, who made heaven and earth and
    sea
and all that is in them,
you have said by the Holy Spirit
through the lips of our father David your servant:
"Why did the Gentiles rage,
    the peoples conspire in folly?
The kings of the earth were aligned,
    the princes gathered together
    against the Lord and against his anointed."

Indeed, they gathered in this very city
    against your holy Servant,
Jesus, whom you anointed—
Herod and Pontius Pilate in league with the Gentiles
and the peoples of Israel.
They have brought about the very things
which in your powerful providence
you planned long ago.

But now, O Lord, look at the threats
they are leveling against us.
Grant to your servants,
even as they speak your words,
complete assurance by stretching forth your hand
in cures and signs and wonders
to be worked in the name of Jesus, your holy Servant.

Acts 4:24-30

61 ### Praise for God's Wisdom and Knowledge

HOW deep are the riches and the wisdom
and the knowledge of God!
How inscrutable his judgments,
how unsearchable his ways!

For who has known the mind of the Lord?
Or who has given him anything
so as to deserve return?

For from him
and through him
and for him
all things are.
To him be glory forever.

Romans 11:33-36

62 ### Praise of Divine Love

IF I SPEAK with human tongues
and angelic as well,
but do not have love,
I am a noisy gong, a clanging cymbal.
If I have the gift of prophecy
and, with full knowledge, comprehend all mysteries,
if I have faith great enough to move mountains,
but have not love,
I am nothing.
If I give everything I have to feed the poor
and hand over my body to be burned,
but have not love,
I gain nothing.

Love is patient;
love is kind.
Love is not jealous,
it does not put on airs,
it is not snobbish.
Love is never rude,
it is not self-seeking,
it is not prone to anger;
neither does it brood over injuries.
Love does not rejoice in what is wrong
but rejoices with the truth.
There is no limit to love's forbearance,
to its trust, its hope,
its power to endure.

Love never fails.
Prophecies will cease,
tongues will be silent,
knowledge will pass away.
Our knowledge is imperfect
and our prophesying is imperfect.
When the perfect comes,
the imperfect will pass away.
When I was a child
I used to talk like a child,
think like a child,
reason like a child.
When I became a man
I put childish ways aside.

Now we see indistinctly, as in a mirror;
then we shall see face to face.
My knowledge is imperfect now;
then I shall know even as I am known.

There are in the end three things that last:
faith, hope, and love,
and the greatest of these
is love.

1 Corinthians 13:1-13

63 Thanksgiving after Affliction

PRAISED be God,
the Father of our Lord Jesus Christ,
the Father of mercies,
and the God of all consolation!
He comforts us in our afflictions
and thus enables us to comfort those who are in trouble,
with the same consolation we have received from him.

2 Corinthians 1:3-4

64 Prayer to God Who Saves Us

PRAISED be the God and Father
of our Lord Jesus Christ,
who has bestowed on us in Christ
every spiritual blessing in the heavens.

God chose us in him
before the world began
to be holy
and blameless in his sight.

He predestined us
to be his adopted sons through Jesus Christ,
such was his will and pleasure,
that all might praise the glorious favor
he has bestowed on us in his beloved.

In him and through his blood, we have been redeemed,
and our sins forgiven,
so immeasurably generous
is God's favor to us.

God has given us the wisdom
to understand fully the mystery,
the plan he was pleased
to decree in Christ,

A plan to be carried out
in Christ, in the fullness of time,
to bring all things into one in him,
in the heavens and on earth.

Ephesians 1:3-10

65   Prayer for Others

THAT is why I kneel before the Father
      from whom every family in heaven and on earth
        takes its name;
and I pray that he will bestow on you gifts in keeping
with the riches of his glory.
May he strengthen you inwardly
through the working of his Spirit.
May Christ dwell in your hearts through faith,
and may charity be the root and foundation of your life.

Thus you will be able to grasp fully,
with all the holy ones,
the breadth and length and height and depth
of Christ's love,
and experience this love which surpasses all knowledge,
so that you may attain to the fullness of God himself.

To him whose power now at work in us
can do immeasurably more than we ask or imagine—
to him be glory in the church and in Christ Jesus
through all generations, world without end.

Ephesians 3:14-21

66   Prayer for Peace, Love, and Faith

MAY God the Father and the Lord Jesus Christ
grant the brothers peace and love and faith.
Grace be with all who love our Lord Jesus Christ
with unfailing love.

Ephesians 6:23-24

67   Praise to Christ the Lord

THOUGH he was in the form of God,
    Jesus did not deem equality with God
    something to be grasped at.

Rather, he emptied himself
    and took the form of a slave,
    being born in the likeness of men.

He was known to be of human estate,
    and it was thus that he humbled himself,
    obediently accepting even death,
    death on a cross!

Because of this,
    God highly exalted him
    and bestowed on him the name
    above every other name,

> So that at Jesus' name
>   every knee must bend
>   in the heavens, on the earth,
>   and under the earth,
>   and every tongue proclaim
>   to the glory of God the Father:
>   JESUS CHRIST IS LORD!

Philippians 2:6-11

68   Thanksgiving to the Father for Choosing Us

LET us give thanks to the Father
    for having made you worthy
to share the lot of the saints
in light.

He rescued us
from the power of darkness
and brought us
into the kingdom of his beloved Son.
Through him we have redemption,
the forgiveness of our sins.

He is the image of the invisible God,
the first-born of all creatures.
In him everything in heaven and on earth was created,
things visible and invisible.

All were created through him;
all were created for him.
He is before all else that is.
In him everything continues in being.

It is he who is head of the body, the church;
he who is the beginning,
the first-born of the dead,
so that primacy may be his in everything.

It pleased God to make absolute fullness reside in him
and, by means of him, to reconcile everything in his
    person,
both on earth and in the heavens,
making peace through the blood of his cross.

Colossians 1:12-20

69   Praise for the Glory of Jesus

WONDERFUL is the mystery of our faith,
    as we say in professing it:
Christ was manifested in the flesh,
    vindicated in the Spirit;
Seen by the angels;
    preached among the Gentiles,
Believed in throughout the world,
    taken up into glory.

1 Timothy 3:16

70   Praise of God, King of Kings

GOD is the blessed and only ruler,
    the King of kings and Lord of lords
who alone has immortality
and who dwells in unapproachable light,
whom no human being has even seen
or can see.

To him be honor
and everlasting rule!

1 Timothy 6:15-16

Praise of God for Giving Us New Birth

PRAISED be the God and Father
of our Lord Jesus Christ,
he who in his great mercy
gave us new birth;
a birth unto hope which draws its life
from the resurrection of Jesus Christ from the dead;
a birth to an imperishable inheritance,
incapable of fading or defilement,
which is kept in heaven for you
who are guarded with God's power through faith;
a birth to a salvation which stands ready
to be revealed in the last days.

1 Peter 1:3-5

Praise of Christ Who Suffered for Us

CHRIST suffered for you,
and left you an example
to have you follow in his footsteps.

He did no wrong;
no deceit was found in his mouth.
When he was insulted,
he returned no insult.

When he was made to suffer,
he did not counter with threats.
Instead he delivered himself up
to the One who judges justly.

In his own body
he brought your sins to the cross,

so that all of us, dead to sin,
could live in accord with God's will.

By his wounds you were healed.

1 Peter 2:21-24

73   Doxology

THERE is One who can protect you from a fall
and make you stand unblemished and exultant
in the presence of his glory.

Glory be to this only God our savior,
through Jesus Christ our Lord.

Majesty, too, be his,
might and power from ages past,
now and for ages to come.

Jude 24-25

74   Praise to Jesus Our Redeemer

O LORD our God, you are worthy
to receive glory and honor and power.

For you have created all things;
by your will they came to be and were made.

Worthy are you, O Lord,
to receive the scroll and break open its seals.

For you were slain;
with your blood you purchased for God
men of every race and tongue,
of every people and nation.

You made of them a kingdom,
and priests to serve our God,
and they shall reign on the earth.

Worthy is the Lamb that was slain
to receive power and riches,
wisdom and strength,
honor and glory and praise.

Revelation 4:11; 5-9, 10, 12

75   **Praise to God Our Judge**

WE PRAISE you, the Lord God Almighty,
who is and who was.
You have assumed your great power,
you have begun your reign.

The nations have raged in anger,
but then came your day of wrath,
and the moment to judge the dead:
The time to reward your servants the prophets
and the holy ones who revere you,
the great and the small alike.

Now have salvation and power come,
the reign of our God and the authority
of his Anointed One.
For the accuser of our brothers is cast out,
who night and day accused them before God.

They defeated him by the blood of the Lamb
and by the word of their testimony;

love for life did not deter them from death.
So rejoice, you heavens,
and you that dwell therein!

Revelation 11:17-18; 12:10b-12a

76   Praise to God Our Father

MIGHTY and wonderful are your works,
Lord God Almighty!
Righteous and true are your ways,
O King of the nations!

Who would dare refuse you honor,
or the glory due your name, O Lord?

Since you alone are holy,
all nations shall come
and worship in your presence.
Your mighty deeds are clearly seen.

Revelation 15:3-4

77   Joy on the Lamb's Wedding Day

ALLELUIA!
Salvation, glory and might belong to our God,
for his judgments are true and just!

Praise our God, all you his servants,
the small and the great, who revere him!

Alleluia!
The Lord is king,
our God, the Almighty!

Let us rejoice and be glad,
   and give him glory!

For this is the wedding day of the Lamb;
   his bride has prepared herself for the wedding.
She has been given a dress to wear
   made of finest linen, brilliant white.

Revelation 19:1, 5-7

77a   Angelic Salutation
(Hail Mary)

This prayer is added here as being substantially from the Bible, although it was put together by the Church which added the word Jesus at the end of the first part and the entire second part.

HAIL Mary,
   full of grace,
the Lord is with you.
Blessed are you among women
and blessed is the fruit of your womb,
Jesus.

Luke 1:28; 2:42

Holy Mary,
Mother of God,
pray for us sinners,
now and at the hour of our death.

2

PRAYERS FROM THE LITURGY

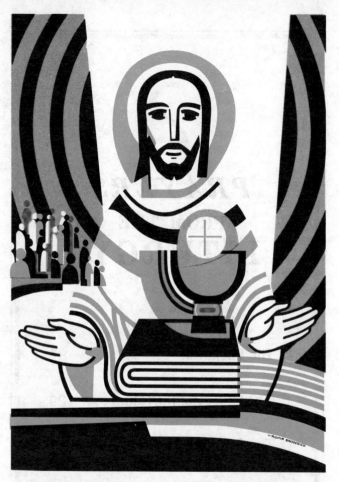

THE EUCHARIST — THE GREATEST PRAYER

The Eucharist is the greatest prayer we have. Through it we give thanks and praise to the Father for the wonderful future he has given us in his Son. We also ask forgiveness for our sins and beg the Father's blessing upon ourselves and our fellow human beings.

86

A) THE EUCHARIST

1) Celebrations

THE Jews celebrate their Exodus from bondage in Egypt, which is their birthday as a free nation, with the annual Passover. The remarkable thing is that they attribute their redemption expressly to the intervention of almighty God and celebrate it annually with a detailed ritual. Until the destruction of the Jewish temple in Jerusalem (70 A.D.) this ritual consisted of the Passover sacrifice (offering God a lamb as a symbol of appreciation) and a sacrificial repast (symbolizing both communion with God, to whom the victim was offered, and communion with fellow worshipers). Afterward the Jewish Passover became, what it still is, only a memorial meal.

Nevertheless, this celebration is not just a grateful remembrance of the past; rather past and present coincide. At the Passover, Jews identify themselves with those who actually did leave Egypt.

2) The Christian Passover

As a faithful Jew, Jesus celebrated the annual Passover. In the Gospels, we have detailed information about the last time he celebrated it with his disciples on the night before his death. This event is known as "The Last Supper." After the Passover lamb had been sacrificed to God in the temple, it was brought to the upper room where Jesus and his friends ate it as a sacrificial repast according to Jewish ritual.

At this Last Supper, Jesus did a remarkable thing. He gave this ancient sacrifice and sacred meal (the Jewish Passover) a new meaning. Referring to his cruel death

87

on the cross, he said in other words: "From now on I am that Passover lamb, sacrificed to deliver you figuratively from the slavery in Egypt and actually from all evil. Do this as a memorial of me." In meditating on our Lord's death on the cross, the early Church saw Jesus as a Jewish high priest offering sacrifice to God. This sacrifice, however, was not a lamb; it was his own body and blood, shed to set us free from the bondage of evil (Hebrews 9:10).

Following this trend of thought, we understand Paul when he says: "Christ, our Passover, has been sacrificed" (1 Corinthians 5:7). Our Eucharistic celebration is a Jewish Passover with a new meaning. The Jews celebrate Passover as a memorial of their redemption from bondage in Egypt, brought about by God's mighty hand. We Christians celebrate the Eucharist as a memorial of our redemption from the slavery of evil, brought about by Christ's death on the cross.

3) How To Celebrate

In celebrating the memorial of our redemption, the Eucharist [Mass], we do what our Lord has told us to do: "Do this as a remembrance of me" (Luke 22:19). Moreover, we look to the early Church of Jerusalem, closest to the source of Christianity. In Acts we read: "The community of believers were of one heart and one mind" (Acts 4:32). "They devoted themselves to the apostles' instruction and the communal life, to the breaking of the bread and the prayers" (Acts 2:42). These early Christians were very much aware of our Lord's promise: "Where two or three are gathered in my name, there am I in their midst" (Matthew 18:20).

In the celebration of Mass, which perpetuates the sacrifice of the cross, Christ is really present in the assembly itself, which is gathered in his name" (General

Instruction of the Roman Missal, *ch. II, no. 7). All Christians share in Christ's royal priesthood, which is a function of intercession for all fellowmen. Hence, the celebration of the Eucharist is the action of the whole Church. All should participate. However, through the sacrament of orders, some Christians are singled out to exercise a special ministry in this priestly people, whose "spiritual sacrifice to God is accomplished through the ministry of presbyters [priests], in union with the sacrifice of Christ, our one and only Mediator" (Ibid., no. 5).*

In summary, "the celebration of Mass is the action of Christ and the people of God hierarchically [in graded order] assembled" (Ibid., ch. I, no. 1), of one heart and mind, each playing his role in the great memorial drama of our redemption, the Eucharist.

4) Structure

Mass is made up of the Liturgy of the Word (Bible readings and Homily) and the Liturgy of the Eucharist. There are also introductory rites, which prepare us for both the table of God's word and the table of Christ's body and blood, and a concluding rite which consists of a final blessing and dismissal. Assembled "in graded order," we listen to the prayers assigned to the priest, actively take part in the dialogues, sing wholeheartedly, meditatively apply God's word to our own life situation, make Christ's sacrifice, present in the signs of bread and wine, a token of our own self-surrender to God, and make Communion an intimate encounter with our Lord.

There is no time for idle dreaming. If properly understood, participating in the Eucharist is exciting—even without the usual trappings we associate with excitement, such as a swinging band! Music at Mass is meaningful only if it underlines and fosters activities of heart and mind.

THE ORDER OF MASS

INTRODUCTORY RITES

Acts of prayer and penitence prepare us to meet Christ as he comes in Word and Sacrament. We gather as a worshiping community to celebrate our unity with him and with one another in faith.

STAND

Mass begins with an entrance procession of the ministers to the sanctuary, during which a hymn is sung or the Entrance Antiphon of the day is recited.

78 **GREETING** (3 forms)

Priest: **In the name of the Father, ✠ and of the Son, and of the Holy Spirit.**

People: **Amen.**

A

Priest: **The grace of our Lord Jesus Christ and the love of God and the fellowship of the Holy Spirit be with you all.**

People: **And also with you.**

B

Priest: **The grace and peace of God our Father and the Lord Jesus Christ be with you.**

90

People: **Blessed be God, the Father of our Lord Jesus Christ.**

or:

And also with you.

C

Priest: The Lord be with you.

People: **And also with you.**

79 **PENITENTIAL RITE (3 forms)**

A

Priest and **PEOPLE:**

> **I confess to almighty God,**
> **and to you, my brothers and sisters,**
> **that I have sinned through my own fault**

They strike their breast:

> **in my thoughts and in my words,**
> **in what I have done,**
> **and in what I have failed to do;**
> **and I ask blessed Mary, ever virgin,**
> **all the angels and saints,**
> **and you, my brothers and sisters,**
> **to pray for me to the Lord our God.**

B

Priest: Lord, we have sinned against you:
Lord, have mercy.

People: **Lord, have mercy.**

Priest: Lord, show us your mercy and love.

People: **And grant us your salvation.**

C

Priest or other minister:

> You were sent to heal the contrite:
> Lord, have mercy

People: **Lord, have mercy.**

Priest or other minister:

> You came to call sinners:
> Christ, have mercy.

People: **Christ, have mercy.**

Priest or other minister:

> You plead for us at the right hand of the
> Father:
> Lord, have mercy.

People: **Lord, have mercy.**

(Other invocations may be used.)

Absolution:

At the end of any of the forms of the penitential rite:

Priest: **May almighty God have mercy on us,**
> **forgive us our sins,**
> **and bring us to everlasting life.**

People: **Amen.**

80   **KYRIE**

*Unless included in the penitential rite, the Kyrie is sung or said
by all, with alternating parts for the choir or cantor and for the
people:*

℣. Lord, have mercy.   ℟. **Lord, have mercy.**

℣. Christ, have mercy.   ℟. **Christ, have mercy.**

℣. Lord, have mercy.   ℟. **Lord, have mercy.**

81 GLORIA

As the Church assembled in the Spirit, we praise and pray to the Father and the Lamb.

GLORY to God in the highest,
and peace to his people on earth.
Lord God, heavenly King,
almighty God and Father,
   we worship you, we give you thanks,
   we praise you for your glory.
Lord Jesus Christ, only Son of the Father,
Lord God, Lamb of God,
you take away the sin of the world:
   have mercy on us;
you are seated at the right hand of the Father:
   receive our prayer.
For you alone are the Holy One,
you alone are the Lord,
you alone are the Most High,
   Jesus Christ,
   with the Holy Spirit,
   in the glory of God the Father. Amen

82 OPENING PRAYER

Priest: Let us pray.

Priest and people pray silently for a while.
Then the priest says the opening prayer which gives the theme of the particular celebration and asks God to help us. Then he says:

WE ASK you this through our Lord Jesus Christ, your Son, who lives and reigns with you and the Holy Spirit, one God, for ever and ever.

People: Amen.

LITURGY OF THE WORD

The proclamation of God's Word is always centered on Christ, present through his Word. Old Testament writings prepare for him; New Testament books speak of him directly. All of scripture calls us to believe once more and to follow. After the reading we reflect upon God's words and respond to them.

SIT

83 READINGS AND RESPONSORIAL PSALM

At the end of the first reading:

Reader: This is the Word of the Lord.

People: **Thanks be to God.**

The people repeat the response sung by the cantor the first time and then after each verse.

At the end of the second reading:

Reader: This is the Word of the Lord.

People: **Thanks be to God.**

84 ALLELUIA (Gospel Acclamation)

STAND

The people repeat the alleluia after the cantor's alleluia and then after the verse.

During Lent one of the following invocations is used as a response instead of the alleluia:

A **Praise to you, Lord Jesus Christ, king of endless glory!**

B **Praise and honor to you, Lord Jesus Christ!**

C **Glory and praise to you, Lord Jesus Christ!**

D **Glory to you, Word of God, Lord Jesus Christ!**

85   GOSPEL

Deacon (or priest): **The Lord be with you.**

People: **And also with you.**

Deacon (or priest):

✠ **A reading from the holy gospel according to** N.

People: **Glory to you, Lord.**

At the end:

Deacon (or priest): **This is the gospel of the Lord.**
People: **Praise to you, Lord Jesus Christ.**

HOMILY   *SIT*

God's word is spoken again in the homily. The Holy Spirit
speaking through the lips of the preacher explains and applies
today's biblical readings to the needs of this particular congregation. He calls us to respond to Christ through the life we
lead.

STAND

86   PROFESSION OF FAITH (CREED)

As a people we express our acceptance of God's message in
the scriptures and homily. We summarize our faith by proclaiming a creed handed down from the early Church.

All say the profession of faith on Sundays.

86a   The Nicene Creed

WE BELIEVE in one God,
    the Father, the Almighty,
maker of heaven and earth,
  of all that is seen and unseen.

We believe in one Lord, Jesus Christ,
   the only Son of God,
  eternally begotten of the Father,
  God from God, Light from Light,

true God from true God,
begotten, not made, one in Being with the Father.
Through him all things were made.
For us men and for our salvation
he came down from heaven:

All bow at the following words up to: and became man.

by the power of the Holy Spirit
he was born of the Virgin Mary, and became
man.
For our sake he was crucified under Pontius Pilate;
he suffered, died, and was buried.
On the third day he rose again
in fulfillment of the Scriptures;
he ascended into heaven
and is seated at the right hand of the Father.
He will come again in glory to judge the living
and the dead,
and his kingdom will have no end.

We believe in the Holy Spirit, the Lord, the giver of
life,
who proceeds from the Father and the Son.
With the Father and the Son he is worshiped and
glorified.
He has spoken through the Prophets.
We believe in one holy catholic and apostolic
Church.
We acknowledge one baptism for the forgiveness
of sins.
We look for the resurrection of the dead,
and the life of the world to come. Amen.

86b   **The Apostles' Creed**

I BELIEVE in God, the Father almighty,
   creator of heaven and earth.

I believe in Jesus Christ, his only Son, our Lord.
   He was conceived by the power of the Holy Spirit
      and born of the Virgin Mary.
   He suffered under Pontius Pilate,
      was crucified, died, and was buried.
   He descended to the dead.
   On the third day he rose again.
   He ascended into heaven,
      and is seated at the right of the Father.
   He will come again to judge the living and the
      dead.

I believe in the Holy Spirit,
   the holy catholic Church,
   the communion of saints,
   the forgiveness of sins,
   the resurrection of the body,
   and the life everlasting. Amen.

87   **GENERAL INTERCESSIONS**
               (Prayer of the Faithful)

As a priestly people we unite with one another to pray for
today's needs in the Church and the world.

*After the priest gives the introduction the deacon or other
minister sings or says the invocations.*

People: **Lord, hear our prayer.**

(or other response, according to local custom)
At the end the priest says the concluding prayer:

People: **Amen.**

LITURGY OF THE EUCHARIST

Made ready by reflection on God's Word, we enter now into the eucharistic sacrifice itself, the Supper of the Lord. We celebrate the memorial which the Lord instituted at his Last Supper. We are God's new people, the redeemed brothers of Christ, gathered by him around his table. We are here to bless God and to receive the gift of Jesus' body and blood so that our faith and life may be transformed.

SIT

The bread and wine for the Eucharist, with our gifts for the Church and the poor, are gathered and brought to the altar. We prepare our hearts by song or in silence as the Lord's table is being set.

88   PREPARATION OF THE BREAD

Blessed are you, Lord, God of all creation.
Through your goodness we have this bread to offer,
which earth has given and human hands have made.
It will become for us the bread of life.

If there is no singing, the priest may say this prayer aloud, and the people may respond:

People: Blessed be God for ever.

89   PREPARATION OF THE WINE

By the mystery of this water and wine
may we come to share in the divinity of Christ,
who humbled himself to share in our humanity.

98

Blessed are you, Lord, God of all creation.
Through your goodness we have this wine to offer,
fruit of the vine and work of human hands.
It will become our spiritual drink.

*If there is no singing, the priest may say this prayer aloud,
and the people may respond:*

People: Blessed be God for ever.

90   INVITATION TO PRAYER

Priest: Pray, brethren, that our sacrifice may be acceptable to God, the almighty Father.

**People: May the Lord accept the sacrifice at your
hands,**

for the praise and glory of his name,

for our good, and the good of all his Church.

STAND

The priest, speaking in our name, says the proper Prayer over
the Gifts, asking the Father to bless and accept these gifts.

People: Amen.

EUCHARISTIC PRAYER

We begin the eucharistic service of praise and thanksgiving, the center of the entire celebration, the central prayer of worship. At the priest's invitation we lift our hearts to God and unite with him in the words he addresses to the Father through Jesus Christ. Together we join Christ in his sacrifice, celebrating his memorial in the holy meal and acknowledging with him the wonderful works of God in our lives.

91   INTRODUCTORY DIALOGUE

Priest: The Lord be with you.

People: **And also with you.**

Priest: Lift up your hearts.

People: **We lift them up to the Lord.**

Priest: Let us give thanks to the Lord our God.

People: **It is right to give him thanks and praise.**

92   PREFACE FOR
SUNDAYS IN ORDINARY TIME I (P 29)

FATHER, all-powerful and ever-living God,
   we do well always and everywhere to give you thanks
through Jesus Christ our Lord.

Through his cross and resurrection
he freed us from sin and death
and called us to the glory that has made us

a chosen race, a royal priesthood,
a holy nation, a people set apart.

Everywhere we proclaim your mighty works
for you have called us out of darkness
into your own wonderful light.

And so, with all the choirs of angels in heaven
we proclaim your glory
and join in their unending hymn of praise.

93   **ACCLAMATION**

Priest and **People:**

**Holy, holy, holy Lord, God of power and might,
heaven and earth are full of your glory.**
Hosanna in the highest.
Blessed is he who comes in the name of the Lord.
Hosanna in the highest.

KNEEL

*Then the priest continues with one of the following Eucharistic
Prayers.*

EUCHARISTIC PRAYER	Choice of four
1 *We come to you, Father*	p. 108
2 *Lord, you are holy indeed*	p. 113
3 *Father, you are holy indeed*	p. 119
4 *Father, we acknowledge your*	p. 124

Communion Rite

To prepare for the paschal meal, to welcome the Lord, we pray for forgiveness and exchange a sign of peace. Before eating Christ's body and drinking his blood, we must be one with him and with all our brothers in the Church.

STAND

94   LORD'S PRAYER

The priest asks the people to join him in the prayer that Jesus taught us.

Priest and **People:**

> **Our Father, who art in heaven,**
> **hallowed be thy name;**
> **thy kingdom come;**
> **thy will be done on earth as it is in heaven.**
> **Give us this day our daily bread;**
> **and forgive us our trespasses**
> **as we forgive those who trespass against us;**
> **and lead us not into temptation,**
> **but deliver us from evil.**

95   DOXOLOGICAL CONCLUSION
AND ACCLAMATION

Priest: Deliver us, Lord, from every evil,
and grant us peace in our day.
In your mercy keep us free from sin
and protect us from all anxiety
as we wait in joyful hope
for the coming of our Savior, Jesus Christ.

People: **For the kingdom, the power, and the glory**
are yours, now and forever.

96 SIGN OF PEACE

The priest says the prayer for peace:

Lord Jesus Christ, you said to your apostles:
I leave you peace, my peace I give you.
Look not on our sins, but on the faith of your Church,
and grant us the peace and unity of your kingdom
where you live for ever and ever.

People: Amen.

Priest: **The peace of the Lord be with you always.**
People: **And also with you.**

Deacon (or priest):

Let us offer each other the sign of peace.

The people exchange a sign of peace and love, according to local custom.

97 BREAKING OF THE BREAD

Then the following is sung or said:

People:

Lamb of God, you take away the sins of the world:
   have mercy on us.

Lamb of God, you take away the sins of the world:
   have mercy on us.

Lamb of God, you take away the sins of the world:
   grant us peace.

The hymn may be repeated until the breaking of the bread is finished, but the last phrase is always: "Grant us peace."

Meanwhile the priest breaks the host over the paten and places a small piece in the chalice, saying quietly:

May this mingling of the body and blood of our Lord Jesus Christ
bring eternal life to us who receive it.

KNEEL

The priest prays quietly before Communion

98   RECEPTION OF COMMUNION

The priest genuflects. Holding the host elevated slightly over the paten, the priest says:

Priest: **This is the Lamb of God**
who takes away the sins of the world.
Happy are those who are called to his supper.

Priest and **People** (once only):

Lord, I am not worthy to receive you,
but only say the word and I shall be healed.

He then gives communion to the people.

Priest: **The body of Christ:**

Communicant: **Amen.**

The Communion Psalm or other appropriate Song or Hymn is sung while Communion is given to the faithful. If there is no singing, the Communion Antiphon is said.

After communion there may be a period of silence, or a song of praise may be sung.

STAND

Then the priest prays in our name that we may live the life of faith since we have been strengthened by Christ himself. Our Amen makes his prayer our own.

Priest: **Let us pray.**

People: **Amen.**

Concluding Rite

We have heard God's Word and eaten the body of Christ. Now it is time for us to leave, to do good works, to praise and bless the Lord in our daily lives.

STAND

99   BLESSING AND DISMISSAL

After any brief announcements (sit), the blessing and dismissal follow:

Priest: **The Lord be with you.**

People: **And also with you.**

Priest: **May almighty God bless you, the Father, and the Son, ✠ and the Holy Spirit.**

People.   **Amen.**

Deacon (or priest):

A   Go in the peace of Christ.

B   The Mass is ended; go in peace.

C   Go in peace to love and serve the Lord.

People: **Thanks be to God.**

THE FOUR
EUCHARISTIC PRAYERS

A T A farewell party for a retiring employee most of
the time is taken up by speaking words of thanks
and appreciation for services rendered, and only at the
end is a token of appreciation offered, a gift which signifies whatever has been said.

The Eucharistic Prayer should be considered in a similar setting. Most of it consists of words of praise and
thanksgiving, and in that framework time and again we
offer Almighty God a token of our gratitude, namely,
the body and blood of Christ (Christ himself in the signs
of bread and wine), offered in sacrifice on the altar of
the cross "once for all" (Hebrews 10:10).

The Roman Missal offers a choice of many Prefaces
and four versions of the Eucharistic Prayer proper. All
contain the following elements.

a) Preface. We should wholeheartedly join in the
dialogue, in which we are invited to give thanks to God,
and the acclamation, the "Holy, holy . . .," said/sung in
union with all the angels of heaven.

b) Epiclesis (Invocation). These are the prayers before the Consecration in which the priest and we with
him invoke God's power and ask him that the gifts offered by men may be consecrated, that is, become the
body and blood of Christ and source of salvation for

those who partake. "[God] let your Spirit come upon these gifts to make them holy, so that they may become for us the body and blood of our Lord, Jesus Christ" (Eucharistic Prayer II).

c) Narrative of the Institution and Consecration. *We celebrate the sacrifice which Jesus Christ instituted at the Last Supper when in the signs of bread and wine he offered his body and blood (himself), gave them to the apostles, and told them to do the same "in memory" of him.*

d) Anamnesis *(a calling to mind). Calling to mind our Lord's death, resurrection, and ascension, we offer God in thanksgiving "this holy and living sacrifice," the body and blood of Christ, and in and with him ourselves "as an everlasting gift" to the Almighty (Eucharistic Prayer III).*

e) Intercessions, *which we should make our own.*

f) Final Doxology *(hymn of praise), which we should confirm with our acclamation "Amen" (So be it!).*

Eucharistic Prayer No. 1

THE Roman Canon is of ancient origin, going back to the fifth century and even beyond in its primitive form. From the eleventh or twelfth century on, it was the only Eucharistic Prayer used in the whole Western Church until the introduction of the three new Eucharistic Prayers in 1969.

This ancient Eucharistic Prayer was highly regarded because of its theological precision, sobriety of expression, biblical and Christian terminology, repetition of concepts in clusters of two or three, and its brevity.

In addition, this magnificent prayer contains a theology of offering that is well-exposed and easy to grasp. Following Christ's explicit example and command, bread and wine are chosen from among the gifts God has given us and are offered to him as a symbol of the offering of ourselves, of what we possess, and of the whole of material creation.

In this offering we ask God to accept them, bless them, and transform them through his Spirit into the body and blood of Christ. We then pray that they will be given back to us transformed in such a way that we may be united in the Spirit to Christ and to one another, sharing in the divine nature.

100   Praise to the Father

WE come to you, Father,
    with praise and thanksgiving,
through Jesus Christ your Son.
Through him we ask you to accept and bless
these gifts we offer you in sacrifice.

101   **Intercessions: For the Church**

WE OFFER them for your holy Catholic Church,
watch over it, Lord, and guide it;
grant it peace and unity throughout the world.
We offer them for N. our Pope,
for N. our bishop,
and for all who hold and teach the catholic faith
that comes to us from the apostles.

102 *Intercessions: For the Assembly and those*
united to it

REMEMBER, Lord, your people,
especially those for whom we now pray, N. and N.
Remember all of us gathered here before you.
You know how firmly we believe in you
and dedicate ourselves to you.
We offer you this sacrifice of praise
for ourselves and those who are dear to us.
We pray to you, our living and true God,
for our well-being and redemption.

103   **In Communion with the Saints**

IN UNION with the whole Church
we honor Mary,
the ever-virgin mother of Jesus Christ our Lord and
God.
We honor Joseph, her husband,
the apostles and martyrs
Peter and Paul, Andrew,
[James, John, Thomas,
James, Philip,
Bartholomew, Matthew, Simon and Jude;
we honor Linus, Cletus, Clement, Sixtus,
Cornelius, Cyprian, Lawrence, Chrysogonus,

John and Paul, Cosmas and Damian]
and all the saints.
May their merits and prayers
gain us your constant help and protection.
[Through Christ our Lord. Amen.]

104   *For the local community*

FATHER, accept this offering
from your whole family.
Grant us your peace in this life.
save us from final damnation,
and count us among those you have chosen.
[Through Christ our Lord. Amen.]

105   *Invocation before the Consecration*

BLESS and approve our offering;
make it acceptable to you,
an offering in spirit and in truth.
Let it become for us
the body and blood of Jesus Christ,
your only Son, our Lord.

106   **The Lord's Supper**

THE day before he suffered
he took bread in his sacred hands
and looking up to heaven,
to you, his almighty Father,
he gave you thanks and praise.
He broke the bread,
gave it to his disciples, and said:

Take this, all of you, and eat it:
this is my body which will be given up for you.

WHEN supper was ended,
he took the cup.

Again he gave you thanks and praise,
gave the cup to his disciples, and said:

Take this, all of you, and drink from it:
this is the cup of my blood,
the blood of the new and everlasting covenant.
It will be shed for you and for all men
so that sins may be forgiven.
Do this in memory of me.

107   Memorial Acclamation

Priest: Let us proclaim the mystery of faith.

People:

A **Christ has died,**
   Christ is risen,
   Christ will come again.

B **Dying you destroyed our death,**
   rising you restored our life.
   Lord Jesus, come in glory.

C **When we eat this bread and drink this cup,**
   we proclaim your death, Lord Jesus,
   until you come in glory.

D **Lord, by your cross and resurrection**
   you have set us free.
   You are the Savior of the world.

108   The Memorial Prayer

FATHER, we celebrate the memory of Christ, your
    Son.
We, your people and your ministers,
recall his passion,
his resurrection from the dead,
and his ascension into glory;
and from the many gifts you have given us
we offer to you, God of glory and majesty,

this holy and perfect sacrifice:
the bread of life
and the cup of eternal salvation.

109   *For God's acceptance of the sacrifice*

LOOK with favor on these offerings
and accept them as once you accepted
the gifts of your servant Abel,
the sacrifice of Abraham, our father in faith,
and the bread and wine offered by your priest Melchisedech.

110   *For God's grace and blessing*

ALMIGHTY God
we pray that your angel may take this sacrifice
to your altar in heaven.
Then, as we receive from this altar
the sacred body and blood of your Son,
let us be filled with every grace and blessing.
[Through Christ our Lord. Amen.]

111   **For the Dead**

REMEMBER, Lord, those who have died
and have gone before us marked with the sign of
faith,
especially those for whom we now pray, N. and N.
May these, and all who sleep in Christ,
find in your presence
light, happiness, and peace.
[Through Christ our Lord. Amen.]

112   *For the assembly*

FOR ourselves, too, we ask
    some share in the fellowship of your apostles and
    martyrs,
with John the Baptist, Stephen, Matthias, Barnabas,
[Ignatius, Alexander, Marcellinus, Peter,
Felicity, Perpetua, Agatha, Lucy,
Agnes, Cecilia, Anastasia]
and all the saints.
Though we are sinners,
we trust in your mercy and love.
Do not consider what we truly deserve,
but grant us your forgiveness.

113   *Blessing of God's gifts*

THROUGH Christ our Lord
    you give us all these gifts.
You fill them with life and goodness,
you bless them and máke them holy.

114   **Concluding Doxology**

THROUGH him,
    with him,
in him,
in the unity of the Holy Spirit,
all glory and honor is yours,
almighty Father,
for ever and ever.

All reply: Amen.

Continue with the Mass, as on p. 102.

Eucharistic Prayer No. 2

BECAUSE of its brevity, concise language, and clear concepts, this text should be particularly effective for weekday Masses, home Masses, Masses for the young, and Masses for small groups.

This is substantially the text of Hippolytus—a eucharistic prayer which has come down to us from the primitive Church and dates back to about 215 A.D. There have been several modifications of the original version —the addition of the Sanctus and intercessions, an alteration in the doxology, and the clarification of more obscure phrases. It is extremely brief, particularly when compared to the customary Roman Canon.

Simplicity and clarity characterize this eucharistic prayer. The overall theme is Christ, in a motif that is established as the prayer addresses the Father in praise and thanksgiving for all that Jesus is and has done for us by forming a new people of God through his death and rising.

PREFACE

115

Praise to the Father

FATHER, it is our duty and our salvation,
    always and everywhere
to give you thanks
through your beloved Son, Jesus Christ.
He is the Word, through whom you made the universe,
the Savior you sent to redeem us.
By the power of the Holy Spirit
he took flesh and was born of the Virgin Mary.
For our sake he opened his arms on the cross;
he put an end to death
and revealed the resurrection.

**In this he fulfilled your will
and won for you a holy people.
And so we join the angels and the saints
in proclaiming your glory
as we sing (say):**

Holy, holy holy . . .

KNEEL

116   Invocation of the Holy Spirit

L ORD, you are holy indeed,
the fountain of all holiness.
Let your Spirit come upon these gifts to make them
holy,
so that they may become for us
the body and blood of our Lord, Jesus Christ.

117   The Lord's Supper

B EFORE he was given up to death,
a death he freely accepted,
he took bread and gave you thanks.
He broke the bread,
gave it to his disciples, and said:

*Take this, all of you, and eat it:
this is my body which will be given up for you.*

W HEN supper was ended, he took the cup.
Again he gave you thanks and praise,
gave the cup to his disciples, and said:

*Take this, all of you, and drink from it:
this is the cup of my blood,
the blood of the new and everlasting covenant.
It will be shed for you and for all men
so that sins may be forgiven.
Do this in memory of me.*

[107]   **Memorial Acclamation**

Priest: Let us proclaim the mystery of faith.

People:

A   Christ has died,
Christ is risen,
Christ will come again.

B   Dying you destroyed our death,
rising you restored our life.
Lord Jesus, come in glory.

C   When we eat this bread and drink this cup,
we proclaim your death, Lord Jesus,
until you come in glory.

D   Lord, by your cross and resurrection
you have set us free.
You are the Savior of the world.

118   **The Memorial Prayer**

IN MEMORY of his death and resurrection,
we offer you, Father, this life-giving bread,
this saving cup.
We thank you for counting us worthy
to stand in your presence and serve you.

119   **Invocation of the Holy Spirit**

MAY all of us who share in the body and blood of
Christ
be brought together in unity by the Holy Spirit.

120   **Intercessions: For the Church**

LORD, remember your Church throughout the world;
make us grow in love,
together with N. our Pope,
N. our bishop, and all the clergy.*

121   **For the Dead**

R EMEMBER our brothers and sisters
    who have gone to their rest
in the hope of rising again;
bring them and all the departed
into the light of your presence.

122   **In Communion with the Saints**

H AVE mercy on us all;
    make us worthy to share eternal life
with Mary, the virgin mother of God,
with the apostles,
and with all the saints who have done your will through-
    out the ages.
May we praise you in union with them,
and give you glory
through your Son, Jesus Christ.

[114]   **Concluding Doxology**

T HROUGH him,
    with him,
in him,
in the unity of the Holy Spirit,
all glory and honor is yours,
almighty Father,
for ever and ever.

All reply: Amen.

Continue with the Mass, as on p. 102.

123

* In Masses for the Dead the following may be added:
Remember *N.,* whom you have called from this life.
In baptism he (she) died with Christ:
may he (she) also share his resurrection.

Eucharistic Prayer No. 3

THE key themes in this eucharistic prayer are *sacrifice* and the *Holy Spirit*—with an obvious connection between the two. The opening section mentions the work of the Spirit in forming a worshiping community which will offer a clean sacrifice to God's glory. A familiar ("from east to west . . .") quotation from the prophet Malachi, often used by the Fathers in writing of the Eucharist, concludes that section.

Just as the Spirit gathers together a people for worship, so we ask the Father in the consecratory invocation to make holy by the power of the Spirit the gifts offered so they may become Christ's body and blood.

A theology of sacrifice is developed in the memorial, offering, and communion invocation. What is being offered in sacrifice to God is the bread and wine—taken from among the gifts he has given us, and considered as symbols of ourselves and of all things—but also, and at the same time, it is Christ in person.

Offering Christ and his sacrifice to God means consciously uniting ourselves in heart and mind to the offering which Christ makes of himself, of us, and of the whole world to God.

We are one in the Spirit, one with Christ, one with ourselves, one with our neighbor. But it is "this sacrifice, which has made our peace with you," that brings about that oneness and enables us to be at peace, love and union with God, ourselves and the whole world. Quite naturally the prayer flows then into prayer for those others and for the world around us—asking that all God's children be united in mercy and love.

118

124 Praise to the Father

FATHER, you are holy indeed,
and all creation rightly gives you praise.
All life, all holiness comes from you
through your Son, Jesus Christ our Lord,
by the working of the Holy Spirit.
From age to age you gather a people to yourself,
so that from east to west
a perfect offering may be made
to the glory of your name.

125 Invocation of the Holy Spirit

AND so, Father, we bring you these gifts.
We ask you to make them holy by the power of
your Spirit,
that they may become the body and blood
of your Son, our Lord Jesus Christ,
at whose command we celebrate this eucharist.

126 The Lord's Supper

ON THE night he was betrayed,
he took bread and gave you thanks and praise.
He broke the bread, gave it to his disciples, and said:

Take this, all of you, and eat it:
this is my body which will be given up for you.

WHEN supper was ended, he took the cup.
Again he gave you thanks and praise,
gave the cup to his disciples, and said:

Take this, all of you, and drink from it:
this is the cup of my blood,
the blood of the new and everlasting covenant.
It will be shed for you and for all men

so that sins may be forgiven.
Do this in memory of me.

[107]   **Memorial Acclamation**

Priest: Let us proclaim the mystery of faith.
People:

A   **Christ has died,**
    Christ is risen,
    Christ will come again.

B   **Dying you destroyed our death,**
    rising you restored our life.
    Lord Jesus, come in glory.

C   **When we eat this bread and drink this cup,**
    we proclaim your death, Lord Jesus,
    until you come in glory.

D   **Lord, by your cross and resurrection**
    you have set us free.
    You are the Savior of the world.

127   **The Memorial Prayer**

FATHER, calling to mind the death your Son endured for our salvation,
his glorious resurrection and ascension into heaven,
and ready to greet him when he comes again,
we offer you in thanksgiving this holy and living sacrifice.
Look with favor on your Church's offering,
and see the Victim whose death has reconciled us to yourself.

128   **Invocation of the Holy Spirit**

GRANT that we, who are nourished by his body and blood,
may be filled with his Holy Spirit,
and become one body, one spirit in Christ.

129   **Intercessions: In Communion**
with the Saints

MAY he make us an everlasting gift to you
and enable us to share in the inheritance of your
saints,
with Mary, the virgin mother of God;
with the apostles, the martyrs,
(Saint N.) and all your saints,
on whose constant intercession we rely for help.

130   **For the Church**

LORD, may this sacrifice, which has made our peace
with you,
advance the peace and salvation of all the world.
Strengthen in faith and love your pilgrim Church on
earth:
your servant, Pope N., our bishop N.,
and all the bishops,
with the clergy and the entire people your Son has
gained for you.
Father, hear the prayers of the family you have gathered
here before you.
In mercy and love unite all your children
wherever they may be.*

131   * In Masses for the Dead the following is said:
Remember N.
In baptism he (she) died with Christ:
may he (she) also share his resurrection,
when Christ will raise our mortal bodies
and make them like his own glory.
Welcome into your kingdom our departed brothers and sisters,
and all who have left this world in your friendship.
There we hope to share in your glory
when every tear will be wiped away.
On that day we shall see you, our God, as you are.
We shall become like you
and praise you for ever through Christ our Lord,
from whom all good things come.
Through him, etc.,

132 **For the Dead**

WELCOME into your kingdom our departed brothers and sisters,
and all who have left this world in your friendship.
We hope to enjoy for ever the vision of your glory,
through Christ our Lord, from whom all good things come.

[114] **Concluding Doxology**

THROUGH him,
with him,
in him,
in the unity of the Holy Spirit,
all glory and honor is yours,
almighty Father,
for ever and ever.

All reply: Amen.

Continue with the Mass, as on p. 102.

Eucharistic Prayer No. 4

*T*HE *fourth eucharistic prayer—longest of the three,*
yet still considerably shorter than the Roman Canon
—is perhaps the most beautiful of the new texts. It con-
tains real possibilities for teaching since its specific
characteristic is a synthetic presentation of the total
movement of salvation history.

Every eucharistic prayer is essentially Trinitarian in
structure. It is addressed to the Father, centers on the
mystery of the Son, seeks extension into our lives and
into the world around us through the power of the Holy
Spirit. The fourth eucharistic prayer reflects this outline
in its text.

Uniquely, however, among the new texts, it gives a
complete picture of human history and a view of the
Trinity within the prayer itself. Following the Sanctus,
we speak of the Father creating man, of Christ saving
him, of the Spirit who will "complete his work on earth."

Then, logically continuing the text and the theme,
we ask the Father that "this Holy Spirit sanctify these
offerings" so they may become "the body and blood of
Jesus Christ our Lord."

The memorial, offering, and communion invocation
are terse and intertwined with the acclamation. They,
too, form an explicit Trinitarian prayer.

133 PREFACE

FATHER in heaven, it is right that we should give
   you thanks and glory:
you alone are God, living and true.
Through all eternity you live in unapproachable light.
Source of life and goodness, you have created all things,
   to fill your creatures with every blessing
and lead all men to the joyful vision of your light.
Countless hosts of angels stand before you to do your
   will;
they look upon your splendor
and praise you, night and day.
United with them, and in the name of every creature
   under heaven,
we too praise your glory as we sing (say):

Holy, holy, holy . . .

KNEEL

134 Praise to the Father

FATHER, we acknowledge your greatness:
   all your actions show your wisdom and love.
You formed man in your own likeness
and set him over the whole world
to serve you, his creator,
and to rule over all creatures.
Even when he disobeyed you and lost your friendship
you did not abandon him to the power of death,
but helped all men to seek and find you.
Again and again you offered a covenant to man,
and through the prophets taught him to hope for salvation.
Father, you so loved the world
that in the fullness of time you sent your only Son to be
   our Savior.
He was conceived through the power of the Holy Spirit,
   and born of the Virgin Mary,

a man like us in all things but sin.
To the poor he proclaimed the good news of salvation,
to prisoners, freedom,
and to those in sorrow, joy.
In fulfillment of your will
he gave himself up to death;
but by rising from the dead,
he destroyed death and restored life.
And that we might live no longer for ourselves but for him,
he sent the Holy Spirit from you, Father,
as his first gift to those who believe,
to complete his work on earth
and bring us the fullness of grace.

135   Invocation of the Holy Spirit

FATHER, may this Holy Spirit sanctify these offerings.
Let them become the body and blood of Jesus Christ our Lord
as we celebrate the great mystery
which he left us as an everlasting covenant.

136   The Lord's Supper

HE ALWAYS loved those who were his own in the world.
When the time came for him to be glorified by you, his heavenly Father,
he showed the depth of his love.
While they were at supper,
he took bread, said the blessing, broke the bread
and gave it to his disciples, saying:

Take this, all of you, and eat it:
this is my body which will be given up for you.

IN the same way, he took the cup filled with wine. He gave you thanks, and giving the cup to his disciples, said:

Take this, all of you, and drink from it:
this is the cup of my blood,
the blood of the new and everlasting covenant.
It will be shed for you and for all men
so that sins may be forgiven.
Do this in memory of me

[107]   **Memorial Acclamation**

Priest: Let us proclaim the mystery of faith.
People:

A   Christ has died,
     Christ is risen,
     Christ will come again.

B   Dying you destroyed our death,
     rising you restored our life.
     Lord Jesus, come in glory.

C   When we eat this bread and drink this cup,
     we proclaim your death, Lord Jesus,
     until you come in glory.

D   Lord, by your cross and resurrection
     you have set us free.
     You are the Savior of the world.

137   **The Memorial Prayer**

FATHER, we now celebrate this memorial of our redemption.
We recall Christ's death, his descent among the dead, his resurrection, and his ascension to your right hand; and, looking forward to his coming in glory, we offer you his body and blood,

the acceptable sacrifice which brings salvation to the whole world.
Lord, look upon this sacrifice which you have given to your Church;
and by your Holy Spirit, gather all who share this bread and wine
into the one body of Christ, a living sacrifice of praise.

138   Intercessions: For the Church

LORD, remember those for whom we offer this sacrifice,
especially N., our Pope,
N., our bishop, and bishops and clergy everywhere.
Remember those who take part in this offering,
those here present and all your people,
and all who seek you with a sincere heart.

139   For the Dead

REMEMBER those who have died in the peace of Christ
and all the dead whose faith is known to you alone.

140   In Communion with the Saints

FATHER, in your mercy grant also to us, your children,
to enter into our heavenly inheritance
in the company of the Virgin Mary, the mother of God,
and your apostles and saints.
Then, in your kingdom, freed from the corruption of sin and death,
we shall sing your glory with every creature through Christ our Lord,
through whom you give us everything that is good.

[114]   Concluding Doxology

See p. 122.

THE LITURGY OF THE HOURS —
THE PRAYER OF THE CHURCH

The Liturgy of the Hours is the public prayer of the whole Church. When it becomes the personal prayer of all Christians, it makes clear the relation that exists between the liturgy and the whole of Christian life.

The whole life of the faithful, hour by hour, during day and night, is a kind of **leitourgia** or public service, in which the faithful give themselves over to the ministry of love toward God and fellow human beings, identifying themselves with the action of Christ, who by his life and self-offering sanctified the life of all.

B) THE LITURGY OF THE HOURS

IN THE Holy Spirit Christ carries out through the Church "the work of man's redemption and God's perfect glorification," not only when the Eucharist is celebrated and the sacraments administered but also in other ways, and especially when the Liturgy of the Hours is celebrated. In it Christ himself is present, in the assembled community, in the proclamation of God's word, "in the prayer and song of the Church," and through it the Church consecrates to God the whole cycle of day and night and the whole range of human activity.

Man's sanctification is accomplished, and worship offered to God, in the Liturgy of the Hours in an exchange or dialogue between God and man in which God speaks to his people and his people reply to him in song and prayer.

Those taking part in the Liturgy of the Hours have access to holiness of the richest kind through the life-giving word of God, to which it gives such great importance. The readings are drawn from Sacred Scripture, God's words in the psalms are sung in his presence, and the intercessions, prayers and hymns are steeped in the inspired language of Scripture.

Gatherings of the laity—for prayer, apostolic work or any other reason—are encouraged to fulfill the Church's office by celebrating part of the Liturgy of the Hours. The laity must learn, especially in liturgical actions, how to adore God the Father in spirit and in truth.

(Cf. General Instruction of the Liturgy of the Hours,
nos. 13-14, 25-27.)

This Morning and Evening Prayer are taken from The Liturgy of the Hours for Sunday, Week I. The antiphons for the Canticles of Zechariah and Mary are those of Saturday, Week IV, and Tuesday, Week I, respectively. The concluding Prayers are those of the 16th and 8th Ordinary Sunday respectively.

Morning Prayer

MORNING Prayer, as is clear from many of the elements that make it up, is intended and arranged for the sanctification of the morning. Saint Basil the Great gives an excellent description of its character in these words:

"It is said in the morning in order that the first stirrings of our mind and will may be consecrated to God, and that we may take nothing in hand until we have been gladdened by the thought of God, as it is written: 'I was mindful of God and was glad' (Psalm 77:4), or set our bodies to any task before we do what has been said: 'I will pray to you, Lord, you will hear my voice in the morning; I will stand before you in the morning and gaze on you' (Psalm 5:4-5)."

This Hour, celebrated as it is as the light of a new day is dawning, also recalls the resurrection of the Lord Jesus, the true light enlightening all mankind (see John 1:9) and "the Sun of justice" (Malachi 4:2), "rising from on high" (Luke 1:78). Hence, we can well understand the advice of Saint Cyprian: "There should be prayer in the morning, so that the resurrection of the Lord may be celebrated by morning prayer."

(General Instruction of the Liturgy of the Hours, no. 38.)

141 **Introductory Dialogue**

L ORD, open my lips.
 And my mouth will proclaim your praise.
Glory to the Father, and to the Son, and to the Holy
 Spirit:
— **as it was in the beginning, is now, and will be
 for ever. Amen. Alleluia.**

Hymn

Ant. Come, let us sing to the Lord, and shout with
 joy to the Rock who saves us, alleluia.

142 **PSALM 95**

A call to praise God

Encourage each other daily while it is still today (Hebrews 3:13).

(The antiphon is recited and then repeated)

C OME, let us sing to the Lord
 and shout with joy to the Rock who saves us.
Let us approach him with praise and thanksgiving
 and sing joyful songs to the Lord.

(Antiphon repeated)

The Lord is God, the mighty God,
 the great king over all the gods.
He holds in his hands the depths of the earth
 and the highest mountains as well.
He made the sea; it belongs to him,
 the dry land, too, for it was formed by his hands.

(Antiphon repeated)

Come, then, let us bow down and worship,
 bending the knee before the Lord, our maker.
For he is our God and we are his people,
 the flock he shepherds.

(Antiphon repeated)

Today, listen to the voice of the Lord:
Do not grow stubborn, as your fathers did
    in the wilderness,
when at Meriba and Massah
    they challenged me and provoked me,
although they had seen all of my works.

(Antiphon repeated)

Forty years I endured that generation.
I said, "They are a people whose hearts go astray
    and they do not know my ways."
So I swore in my anger,
    "They shall not enter into my rest."

(Antiphon repeated)

Glory to the Father, and to the Son, and to the Holy
    Spirit:
as it was in the beginning, is now, and will be for ever.
    Amen.

(Antiphon repeated)

Ant. 1   As morning breaks I look to you, O God, to
be my strength this day, alleluia.

143   **PSALM 63:2-9**

A soul thirsting for God

Whoever has left the darkness of sin, yearns for God.

O GOD, you are my God, for you I long;
    for you my soul is thirsting.

My body pines for you
like a dry, weary land without water.
So I gaze on you in the sanctuary
to see your strength and your glory.

For your love is better than life,
my lips will speak your praise.

So I will bless you all my life,
in your name I will lift up my hands.
My soul shall be filled as with a banquet,
my mouth shall praise you with joy.

On my bed I remember you.
On you I muse through the night
for you have been my help;
in the shadow of your wings I rejoice.
My soul clings to you;
your right hand holds me fast.

Glory to the Father, and to the Son, and to the Holy
  Spirit:
as it was in the beginning, is now, and will be for ever.
  Amen.

Psalm-prayer

Father, creator of unfailing light, give that same light
to those who call to you. May our lips praise you; our
lives proclaim your goodness; our work give you honor,
and our voices celebrate you for ever.

Ant.   As morning breaks I look to you, O God, to be
        my strength this day, alleluia.

Ant. 2 From the midst of the flames the three young
        men cried out with one voice: Blessed be God,
        alleluia.

144   **CANTICLE: Daniel 3:57-88, 56**
        Let all creatures praise the Lord

All you servants of the Lord, sing praise to him (Revelation 19:5).

BLESS the Lord, all you works of the Lord.
    Praise and exalt him above all forever.

Angels of the Lord, bless the Lord.
You heavens, bless the Lord.
All you waters above the heavens, bless the Lord.
All you hosts of the Lord, bless the Lord.
Sun and moon, bless the Lord.
Stars of heaven, bless the Lord.

Every shower and dew, bless the Lord.
All you winds, bless the Lord.
Fire and heat, bless the Lord.

Cold and chill, bless the Lord.
Dew and rain, bless the Lord.
Frost and chill, bless the Lord.
Ice and snow, bless the Lord.
Nights and days, bless the Lord.
Light and darkness, bless the Lord.
Lightnings and clouds, bless the Lord.

Let the earth bless the Lord.
Praise and exalt him above all forever.
Mountains and hills, bless the Lord.
Everything growing from the earth, bless the Lord.
You springs, bless the Lord.
Seas and rivers, bless the Lord.
You dolphins and all water creatures, bless the Lord.
All you birds of the air, bless the Lord.
All you beasts, wild and tame, bless the Lord.
You sons of men, bless the Lord.

O Israel, bless the Lord.
Praise and exalt him above all forever.
Priests of the Lord, bless the Lord.
Servants of the Lord, bless the Lord.
Spirits and souls of the just, bless the Lord.
Holy men of humble heart, bless the Lord.
Hananiah, Azariah, Mishael, bless the Lord.
Praise and exalt him above all forever.

Let us bless the Father, and the Son, and the Holy Spirit.
Let us praise and exalt him above all forever.
Blessed are you, Lord, in the firmament of heaven.
Praiseworthy and glorious and exalted above all forever.

Ant.   From the midst of the flames the three young men cried out with one voice: Blessed be God, alleluia.

Ant. 3   Let the people of Zion rejoice in their King, alleluia.

145   **PSALM 149**

The joy of God's holy people

Let the sons of the Church, the children of the new people, rejoice in Christ, their King (Hesychius).

SING a new song to the Lord,
  his praise in the assembly of the faithful.
Let Israel rejoice in its maker,
let Zion's sons exult in their king.
Let them praise his name with dancing
and make music with timbrel and harp.

For the Lord takes delight in his people.
He crowns the poor with salvation.
Let the faithful rejoice in their glory,
shout for joy and take their rest.
Let the praise of God be on their lips
and a two-edged sword in their hand,

to deal out vengeance to the nations
and punishment on all the peoples;
to bind their kings in chains
and their nobles in fetters of iron;
to carry out the sentence pre-ordained;
this honor is for all his faithful.

Glory to the Father, etc.

Psalm-prayer

Let Israel rejoice in you, Lord, and acknowledge you as creator and redeemer. We put our trust in your faithfulness and proclaim the wonderful truths of salvation. May your loving kindness embrace us now and for ever.

Ant. **Let the people of Zion rejoice in their King, alleluia.**

146 **READING**

Revelation 7:9-12

AFTER this I saw before me a huge crowd which no one could count from every nation and race, people and tongue. They stood before the throne and the Lamb, dressed in long white robes and holding palm branches in their hands. They cried out in a loud voice, "Salvation is from our God, who is seated on the throne, and from the Lamb!" All the angels who were standing around the throne and the elders and the four living creatures fell down before the throne to worship God. They said: "Amen! Praise and glory, wisdom and thanksgiving and honor, power and might, to our God forever and ever. Amen!"

147 **RESPONSORY**

Christ, Son of the living God, have mercy on us.
—**Christ, Son of the living God, have mercy on us.**
You are seated at the right hand of the Father,
—**have mercy on us.**
Glory to the Father . . .
—**Christ, Son of . . .**

148   **CANTICLE OF ZECHARIAH**

Ant.   Lord, guide our feet into the way of peace.

The Messiah and his forerunner

BLESSED be the Lord, the God of Israel;
   he has come to his people and set them free.

He has raised up for us a mighty savior,
born of the house of his servant David.

Through his holy prophets he promised of old
   that he would save us from our enemies,
   from the hands of all who hate us.

He promised to show mercy to our fathers
and to remember his holy covenant.

This was the oath he swore to our father Abraham:
to set us free from the hands of our enemies,
free to worship him without fear,
holy and righteous in his sight
   all the days of our life.

You, my child, shall be called the prophet of the Most
   High;
for you will go before the Lord to prepare his way,
to give his people knowledge of salvation
by the forgiveness of their sins.

In the tender compassion of our God
the dawn from on high shall break upon us,
to shine on those who dwell in darkness and the shadow
   of death,
and to guide our feet into the way of peace.

Glory to the Father, and to the Son, and to the Holy
   Spirit:

as it was in the beginning, is now, and will be for ever.
   Amen.

Ant.   Lord, guide our feet into the way of peace.

149   **INTERCESSIONS**

CHRIST is the sun that never sets, the true light that
   shines on every man. Let us call out to him in
praise:
   Lord, you are our life and our salvation.
Creator of the stars, we thank you for your gift, the
   first rays of the dawn,
— and we commemorate your resurrection.
May your Holy Spirit teach us to do your will today,
— and may your Wisdom guide us always.
Each Sunday give us the joy of gathering as your people,
— around the table of your Word and your Body.
From our hearts we thank you,
— for your countless blessings.

Our Father . . .

150   **PRAYER**

GOD our Father,
   gifts without measure flow from your goodness
to bring us your peace.
Our life is your gift.
Guide our life's journey,
for only your love makes us whole.
Keep us strong in your love.
We ask this through Christ our Lord.

151 **DISMISSAL**

If a priest or deacon presides, he dismisses the people:

THE Lord be with you.
— **And also with you.**

May almighty God bless you,
the Father, and the Son, and the Holy Spirit.
— **Amen.**

Another form of the blessing may be used, as at Mass.

Then he adds:

Go in peace.
— **Thanks be to God.**

In the absence of a priest or deacon and in individual recitation, Morning Prayer *concludes:*

May the Lord bless us,
protect us from all evil
and bring us to everlasting life.
— **Amen.**

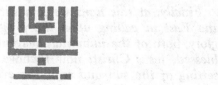

Evening Prayer

WHEN *evening approaches and the day is already far spent, Evening Prayer is celebrated in order that we may give thanks for what has been given us, or what we have done well, during the day. We also recall the redemption through the prayer which we send up like incense in the Lord's sight, and in which the raising up of our hands becomes an evening sacrifice.*

This may be understood also in a deeper spiritual sense of that true evening sacrifice which, as is handed down to us, was offered in the evening by the Lord and Savior, at supper with the apostles, when he instituted the most holy mysteries of the Church, or of the evening sacrifice, that is, the sacrifice at the end of the ages, in which on the next day he was offered to the Father as he raised up his hands for the salvation of the whole world.

Again, in order to fix our hope on the light that knows no setting, we pray and make petition for the light to come down on us anew and ask Christ to give us the grace of eternal light.

Finally, at this hour we join with the Churches of the East in calling upon the joy-giving light of holy glory, born of the immortal, heavenly Father, holy and blessed, Jesus Christ; now that we have come to the setting of the sun and seen the evening star, we sing in praise of the Father and the Son and the Holy Spirit as God.

(Cf. General Instruction of the Liturgy of the Hours, no. 39.)

152 **INTRODUCTORY DIALOGUE**

GOD, come to my assistance.
— **Lord make haste to help me.**

Glory to the Father, and to the Son, and to the Holy Spirit:
— **as it was in the beginning, is now, and will be for ever. Amen. Alleluia.**

Hymn

Ant. 1 The Lord will stretch forth his mighty scepter from Zion, and he will reign for ever, alleluia.

153 **PSALM 110:1-5, 7**

The Messiah, king and priest

Christ's reign will last until all his enemies are made subject to him (1 Corinthians 15:25).

THE Lord's revelation to my Master:
  "Sit on my right:
your foes I will put beneath your feet."

The Lord will wield from Zion
your scepter of power:
rule in the midst of all your foes.

A prince from the day of your birth
on the holy mountains;
from the womb before the dawn I begot you.

The Lord has sworn an oath he will not change.
"You are a priest for ever,
a priest like Melchizedek of old."

The Master standing at your right hand
will shatter kings in the day of his great wrath.

He shall drink from the stream by the wayside
and therefore he shall lift up his head.

Glory to the Father, and to the Son, and to the Holy Spirit:
as it was in the beginning, is now, and will be for ever. Amen.

Psalm-prayer

Father, we ask you to give us victory and peace. In Jesus Christ, our Lord and King, we are already seated at your right hand. We look forward to praising you in the fellowship of all your saints in our heavenly homeland.

Ant.   The Lord will stretch forth his mighty scepter from Zion, and he will reign for ever, alleluia.

Ant. 2   The earth is shaken to its depths before the glory of your face.

154   **PSALM 114**

The Israelites are delivered from the bondage of Egypt

You too left Egypt when, at baptism, you renounced that world which is at enmity with God (St. Augustine).

WHEN Israel came forth from Egypt,
Jacob's sons from an alien people,
Judah became the Lord's temple,
Israel became his kingdom.

The sea fled at the sight:
the Jordan turned back on its course,
the mountains leapt like rams
and the hills like yearling sheep.

Why was it, sea, that you fled,
that you turned back, Jordan, on your course?
Mountains, that you leapt like rams,
hills, like yearling sheep?

Tremble, O earth, before the Lord,
in the presence of the God of Jacob,
who turns the rock into a pool
and flint into a spring of water.

Glory to the Father, and to the Son, and to the Holy
  Spirit:
as it was in the beginning, is now, and will be for ever.
  Amen.

Psalm-prayer

Almighty God, ever-living mystery of unity and Trinity, you gave life to the new Israel by birth from water and the Spirit, and made it a chosen race, a royal priesthood, a people set apart as your eternal possession. May all those you have called to walk in the splendor of the new light render you fitting service and adoration.

Ant.   The earth is shaken to its depths before the glory of your face.

Ant. 3   All power is yours, Lord God, our mighty King, alleluia.

The following canticle is said with the Alleluia when Evening Prayer is sung; when the office is recited, the Alleluia may be said at the beginning and end of each strophe.

155 **CANTICLE**

See Revelation 19:1-7

The wedding of the Lamb

ALLELUIA.
  Salvation, glory, and power to our God:
(℟. **Alleluia.**)
his judgments are honest and true.
℟. **Alleluia. (alleluia.)**

Alleluia.
Sing praise to our God, all you his servants,
(℟.   Alleluia.)
all who worship him reverently, great and small.
℟.   Alleluia. (alleluia.)

Alleluia.
The Lord our all-powerful God is King;
(℟.   Alleluia.)
let us rejoice, sing praise, and give him glory.
℟.   Alleluia. (alleluia.)

Alleluia.
The wedding feast of the Lamb has begun,
(℟.   Alleluia.)
and his bride is prepared to welcome him.
℟.   Alleluia. (alleluia.)

Glory to the Father, and to the Son, and to the Holy
    Spirit:
as it was in the beginning, is now, and will be for ever.
    Amen.

Ant.   All power is yours, Lord God, our mighty King,
        alleluia.

156   **READING**

2 Corinthians 1:3-4

PRAISED be God, the Father of our Lord Jesus
    Christ, the Father of mercies and the God of all
consolation! He comforts us in all our afflictions and
thus enables us to comfort those who are in trouble,
with the same consolation we have received from him.

157   RESPONSORY

THE whole creation proclaims the greatness of your glory.
— **The whole creation proclaims the greatness of your glory.**
Eternal ages praise
— **the greatness of your glory.**
Glory to the Father . . .
— **The whole creation . . .**

158   CANTICLE OF MARY

Ant.   My spirit rejoices in God my Savior.

The soul rejoices in the Lord

MY SOUL proclaims the greatness of the Lord,
my spirit rejoices in God my Savior
for he has looked with favor on his lowly servant.

From this day all generations will call me blessed:
the Almighty has done great things for me,
and holy is his Name.

He has mercy on those who fear him
in every generation.

He has shown the strength of his arm,
he has scattered the proud in their conceit.

He has cast down the mighty from their thrones,
and has lifted up the lowly.

He has filled the hungry with good things,
and the rich he has sent away empty.

He has come to the help of his servant Israel
for he has remembered his promise of mercy,
the promise he made to our fathers,
to Abraham and his children for ever.

Glory to the Father, and to the Son, and to the Holy
    Spirit:
as it was in the beginning, is now, and will be for ever.
    Amen.

Ant.   My spirit rejoices in God my Savior.

159   **INTERCESSIONS**

CHRIST the Lord is our head; we are his members.
    In joy let us call out to him:
    Lord, may your kingdom come.
Christ our Savior, make your Church a more vivid
    symbol of the unity of all mankind,
— make it more effectively the sacrament of salvation
    for all peoples.
Through your presence, guide the college of bishops in
    union with the Pope,
— give them the gifts of unity, love and peace.
Bind all Christians more closely to yourself, their divine
    Head,
— lead them to proclaim your kingdom by the witness
    of their lives.
Grant peace to the world,
— let every land flourish in justice and security.
Grant to the dead the glory of resurrection,
— and give us a share in their happiness.

Our Father . . .

160   **PRAYER**

FATHER in heaven,
    form in us the likeness of your Son
and deepen his life within us.
Send us as witnesses of gospel joy
into a world of fragile peace and broken promises.

Touch the hearts of all men with your love
that they in turn may love one another.
We ask this through Christ our Lord.

[151] **DISMISSAL**

If a priest or deacon presides, he dismisses the people:

THE Lord be with you.
— **And also with you.**

May almighty God bless you,
the Father, and the Son, and the Holy Spirit.
— **Amen.**

Another form of the blessing may be used, as at Mass.

Then he adds:

Go in peace.
— **Thanks be to God.**

In the absence of a priest or deacon and in individual recitation, Evening Prayer *concludes:*

May the Lord bless us,
protect us from all evil
and bring us to everlasting life.
— **Amen.**

THE SACRAMENTS — Living Encounters with Christ

The Sacraments constitute living encounters with Christ. By means of words and actions they put us into contact with Jesus and enable us to receive his saving grace. As such, they provide excellent food for prayer and contemplation.

C) THE SACRAMENTS

Christer: Sacrament of God. *A sacrament is the visible action of God in man. Hence, Christ is the sacrament of God par excellence. He was seen, touched, and heard by men while he was on earth. By his passion, death, and resurrection he took away man's sin and brought life to the whole world. "God, in Christ, was reconciling the world to himself"* (2 Corinthians 5:19).

The Church: Sacrament of Christ. *After his ascension Jesus entered into the invisible world but he desired to continue to live visibly among men. He does so through the Church: "As the Father has sent me, so I send you. . . . Receive the Holy Spirit. If you forgive men's sins, they are forgiven them; if you hold them bound, they are held bound"* (John 20:21-23). *"He who welcomes you welcomes me"* (Matthew 10:40).

The Sacraments: Actions of Christ. *The Church prolongs herself by actions accompanied by words whose celebration has been entrusted to her by Christ. Thus, the sacraments are the actions of Christ, who administers them through men. Therefore, the sacraments are holy in themselves, and by the power of Christ, they pour grace into the soul when they touch the body. A sacrament is the symbol of a sacred reality and the visible form of an invisible grace*

The purpose of the sacraments is to sanctify men, to build up the body of Christ, and, finally, to give worship to God; because they are signs they also instruct. They not only presuppose faith, but by words and objects they also nourish, strengthen, and express it; that is why they are called "sacraments of faith." They do indeed impart grace, but, in addition, the very act of celebrating them

149

most effectively disposes the faithful to receive this grace in a fruitful manner, to worship God duly, and to practice charity.

For well-disposed members of the faithful, the liturgy of the sacraments and sacramentals sanctifies almost every event in their lives; they are given access to the stream of divine grace which flows from the paschal mystery of the passion, death, and resurrection of Christ, the font from which all sacraments and sacramentals draw their power. There is hardly any proper use of material things which cannot thus be directed toward the sanctification of men and the praise of God.

Fortified by so many and such powerful means of salvation, all the faithful, whatever their condition or state, are called by the Lord, each in his own way, to that perfect holiness whereby the Father himself is perfect.

In this section extracts from the full rites of the sacraments are provided for prayer and for study purposes in order to familiarize the user with the basic structure of the revised rite. Not all the options provided in the complete ritual are presented here inasmuch as this book is not intended for use by the celebrant during a celebration of the sacraments.

BAPTISM

BAPTISM is the door to life and to the kingdom of God. Christ offered this first sacrament of the new law to all men that they might have eternal life (John 3:5). He entrusted this sacrament and the gospel to his Church when he told his apostles: "Go, make disciples of all nations, and baptize them in the name of the Father, and of the Son, and of the Holy Spirit" (Matthew 28:19). Therefore baptism is, above all, the sacrament of that faith by which men and women, enlightened by the Spirit's grace, respond to the gospel of Christ. They are freed from the power of darkness and incorporated into Christ.

Further, baptism is the sacrament by which men and women are incorporated into the Church, built into a house where God lives, in the Spirit (Ephesians 2:22), into a holy nation and a royal priesthood (1 Peter 2:9). It makes us sharers in God's own life (2 Peter 1:4) and his adopted children (Romans 8:15; Galatians 4:5). Signed in the name of the Trinity, they are consecrated to it and enter into fellowship with the Father, the Son, and the Holy Spirit.

Baptism produces all these effects by the power of the mystery of the Lord's passion and resurrection. Those who are baptized are engrafted in the likeness of Christ's death (Romans 6:4f). They are buried with him, they are given life again with him, and with him they rise again (Ephesians 2:6).

161   **Reception of the Children**

The people may sing a psalm or hymn suitable for the occasion. Meanwhile the celebrating priest or deacon, accompanied by the ministers, goes to the entrance of the church or to that part of the church where the parents and godparents are waiting with those to be baptized.

The celebrant greets all present and especially the parents and godparents, reminding them briefly of the joy with which the parents welcomed their children as gifts from God, the source of life, who now wishes to bestow his own life on these little ones. Then he questions the parents of each child:

Celebrant: **What name do you give your child (each of these children)?**

Parents: **N. . . .**

Celebrant: **What do you ask of God's Church for N. . . . (your children)?**

Parents: **Baptism.**

Celebrant *(in these or similar words)*:   **You have asked to have your children baptized. In doing so you are accepting the responsibility of training them in the practice of the faith. It will be your duty to bring them up to keep God's commandments as Christ taught us, by loving God and our neighbor. Do you clearly understand what you are undertaking?**

Parents: **We do.**

Celebrant *(addressing the godparents in these or similar words)*:   **Are you ready to help these parents in their duty as Christian mothers and fathers?**

Godparents: **We are.**

Celebrant: N. . . . (My dear children), the Christian community welcomes you with great joy. In its name I claim you for Christ our Savior by the sign of his cross. I now trace the cross on your foreheads, and invite your parents (and godparents) to do the same.

He signs each child on the forehead, in silence. Then he invites the parents and (if it seems appropriate) the godparents to do the same.

Celebration of God's Word

One or two of the following gospel passages are read, during which all may sit if convenient.

John 3:1-6 *The meeting with Nicodemus.*
Matthew 28:18-20 *The apostles are sent to preach and baptize.*
Mark 1:9-11 *The baptism of Jesus.*
Mark 10:13-16 *"Let the little children come to me."*

162   **GOSPEL**

✠ A reading from the holy gospel according to John

The meeting with Nicodemus

A certain Pharisee named Nicodemus, a member of the Jewish Sanhedrin, came to Jesus at night. "Rabbi," he said, "we know you are a teacher come from God, for no man can perform signs and wonders such as you perform unless God is with him." Jesus gave him this answer:

"I solemnly assure you,
no one can see the rule of God
unless he is begotten from above."

"How can a man be born again once he is old?" retorted Nicodemus. "Can he return to his mother's womb and be born over again?" Jesus replied:

"I solemnly assure you,
no one can enter into God's kingdom
without being begotten of water and Spirit.
Flesh begets flesh,
Spirit begets spirit."

*After the reading the celebrant gives a short homily. This may
be followed by a period of silence and a suitable hymn.*

163 INTERCESSIONS (PRAYER OF THE FAITHFUL)

Celebrant: My brothers and sisters, let us ask our
Lord Jesus Christ to look lovingly on this child
(these children) who is (are) to be baptized, on
his/her (their) parents and godparents, and on the
baptized.

Reader: By the mystery of your death and resurrection,
bathe this child (these children) in light, give
him/her (them) the new life of baptism and welcome him/her (them) into your holy Church.

All: **Lord, hear our prayer.**

Reader: Through baptism and confirmation, make
him/her (them) your faithful follower(s) and
witness(es) to your gospel.

All: **Lord, hear our prayer.**

Reader: Lead him/her (them) by a holy life to the
joys of God's kingdom.

All: **Lord, hear our prayer.**

Reader: Make the lives of his/her (their) parents and
godparents examples of faith to inspire this child
(these children).

All: **Lord, hear our prayer.**

Reader: Keep his/her family (their families) always
in your love.

All: **Lord, hear our prayer.**

Reader: Renew the grace of our baptism in each one
of us.

All: **Lord, hear our prayer.**

164   INVOCATION OF THE SAINTS

The celebrant invites all present to invoke the saints

Holy Mary, Mother of God	**pray for us.**
Saint John the Baptist	**pray for us.**
Saint Joseph	**pray for us.**
Saint Peter and Saint Paul	**pray for us.**

*The names of other saints may be added, especially the patrons
of the children to be baptized, and of the church or locality.
The litany concludes:*

All holy men and women	**pray for us.**

165 Prayer of Exorcism and Anointing before Baptism

Celebrant: **Almighty and ever-living God,**
you sent your only Son into the world
to cast out the power of Satan, spirit of evil,
to rescue man from the kingdom of darkness,
and bring him into the splendor of your kingdom
of light.
We pray for this child (these children):
set him/her (them) free from original sin,
make him/her (them) temples of your glory,
and send your Holy Spirit to dwell within him/
her (them).
We ask this through Christ our Lord.

All: **Amen.**

Celebrant: We anoint you with the oil of salvation
in the name of Christ our Savior;
may he strengthen you
with his power,
who lives and reigns for ever and ever.

All: Amen.

He anoints each child on the breast with the oil of cate-
chumens.

166   Celebration of the Sacrament

All proceed to the baptistry. At the font the celebrant briefly
reminds the people of the wonderful work of God whose plan
it is to sanctify man, body and soul, through water. He may use
the following or similar words:

Celebrant: My dear brothers and sisters, we now ask
God to give this child (these children) new life in
abundance through water and the Holy Spirit.

167   BLESSING AND INVOCATION OF GOD OVER BAPTISMAL WATER

Celebrant: Father, you give us grace through sacramental signs, which tell us of the wonders of your
unseen power.

In baptism we use your gift of water, which you
have made a rich symbol of the grace you give us
in this sacrament.

At the very dawn of creation your Spirit breathed on the waters, making them the wellspring of
all holiness.

The waters of the great flood you made a sign of
the waters of baptism, that make an end of sin and
a new beginning of goodness.

Through the waters of the Red Sea you led Israel out of slavery, to be an image of God's holy people, set free from sin by baptism.

In the waters of the Jordan your Son was baptized by John and anointed with the Spirit.

Your Son willed that water and blood should flow from his side as he hung upon the cross.

After his resurrection he told his disciples: "Go out and teach all nations, baptizing them in the name of the Father, and of the Son, and of the Holy Spirit."

Father, look now with love upon your Church, and unseal for her the fountain of baptism.

By the power of the Spirit give to the water of this font the grace of your Son.

You created man in your own likeness: cleanse him from sin in a new birth to innocence by water and the Spirit.

He touches the water with his right hand and continues:

We ask you, Father, with your Son to send the Holy Spirit upon the water of this font. May all who are buried with Christ in the death of baptism rise also with him to newness of life. We ask this through Christ our Lord.

All: **Amen.**

168   **RENUNCIATION OF SIN AND PROFESSION OF FAITH**

Celebrant: Dear parents and godparents, you have come here to present this child (these children) for baptism. By water and the Holy Spirit they are to receive the gift of new life from God, who is love.

On your part, you must make it your constant care to bring them up in the practice of the faith. See that the divine life which God gives them is kept safe from the poison of sin, to grow always stronger in their hearts.

If your faith makes you ready to accept this responsibility, renew now the vows of your own baptism. Reject sin; profess your faith in Christ Jesus. This is the faith of the Church. This is the faith in which this child is (these children are) about to be baptized.

Celebrant: Do you reject Satan?

Parents & Godparents: **I do.**

Celebrant: And all his works?

Parents & Godparents: **I do.**

Celebrant: And all his empty promises?

Parents & Godparents: **I do.**

Celebrant: Do you believe in God, the Father almighty, creator of heaven and earth?

Parents & Godparents: **I do.**

Celebrant: Do you believe in Jesus Christ, his only Son, our Lord, who was born of the Virgin Mary, was crucified, died, and was buried, rose from the dead, and is now seated at the right hand of the Father?

Parents & Godparents: **I do.**

Celebrant: Do you believe in the Holy Spirit, the holy Catholic Church, the communion of saints, the forgiveness of sins, the resurrection of the body, and life everlasting?

Parents & **Godparents:** **I do.**

Celebrant: This is our faith. This is the faith of the Church. We are proud to profess it, in Christ Jesus our Lord.

All: **Amen.**

169   **BAPTISM**

Celebrant: It is your will that N. should be baptized in the faith of the Church, which we have all professed with you?

Parents & **Godparents:** **It is.**

The celebrant pours water over the child's head three times, saying:

Celebrant: N., I baptize you in the name of the Father, and of the Son, and of the Holy Spirit.

170   **ANOINTING WITH CHRISM**

Celebrant: God the Father of our Lord Jesus Christ has freed you from sin, given you a new birth by water and the Holy Spirit, and welcomed you into his holy people. He now anoints you with the chrism of salvation. As Christ was anointed Priest, Prophet, and King, so may you live always as members of his body, sharing everlasting life.

All: **Amen.**

The celebrant anoints each child on the crown of the head with sacred chrism in silence.

171   **CLOTHING WITH WHITE GARMENT**

Celebrant: N., you have become a new creation, and have clothed yourself in Christ. See in this white

garment the outward sign of your Christian dignity. With your family and friends to help you by
word and example, bring that dignity unstained
into the everlasting life of heaven.

All: **Amen.**

The white garments are put on the children.

172   LIGHTED CANDLE

The celebrant takes the Easter candle and says:

Celebrant: Receive the light of Christ.

*Someone from each family (e.g., the father or godfather) lights
the child's candle from the Easter candle.*

Parents and godparents, this light is entrusted to
you to be kept burning brightly. This child (these
children) of yours has (have) been enlightened by
Christ. He/she (they) is (are) to walk always as
a child (children) of the light. May he/she (they)
keep the flame of faith alive in his/her (their)
heart(s). When the Lord comes, may he/she
(they) go out to meet him with all the saints in
the heavenly kingdom.

173   EPHPHETHA OR PRAYER OVER
EARS AND MOUTHS

*The celebrant touches the ears and mouth of each child with
his thumb, saying:*

Celebrants   The Lord Jesus made the deaf hear and
the dumb speak. May he soon touch your ears to
receive his word, and your mouth to proclaim his
faith, to the praise and glory of God the Father.

All: **Amen.**

174 ## Conclusion of the Rite

*All proceed to the altar, unless the baptism was performed in
the sanctuary. The lighted candles are carried for the children.
A baptismal song is appropriate, e.g.:*

> You have put on Christ,
> in him you have been baptized.
> Alleluia, Alleluia.

175 ## LORD'S PRAYER

*The celebrant stands in front of the altar and addresses the
people:*

Celebrant: Dearly beloved, this child has (these children have) been reborn in baptism. He/she is (they are) now called the child (children) of God, for so indeed he/she is (they are). In confirmation he/she (they) will receive the fullness of God's Spirit. In holy communion he/she (they) will share the banquet of Christ's sacrifice, calling God his/her (their) Father in the midst of the Church. In the name of this child (their name), in the Spirit of our common sonship, let us pray together in the words that our Lord has given us.

All: **Our Father . . .**

176 ## BLESSING

*The celebrant blesses the mothers, who hold their children in
their arms.*

Celebrant: God the Father, through his Son, the Virgin Mary's child, has brought joy to all Christian mothers, as they see hope of eternal life shine on their children. May he bless the mother(s) of this child (these children). She (they) now thank(s) God for the gift of her child (their children). May she/they be one with him/her (them) in thanking him for ever in heaven, in Christ Jesus our Lord.

All: **Amen.**

177

The celebrant blesses the fathers, and afterward the entire assembly:

God is the giver of all life, human and divine. May he bless the father(s) of this child (these children). He and his wife (With their wives they) will be the first teachers of their child (children) in the ways of faith. May they be also the best teachers, bearing witness to the faith by what they say and do, in Christ Jesus our Lord.

All: **Amen.**

178

Celebrant: By God's gift through water and the Holy Spirit we are reborn to everlasting life. In his goodness, may he continue to pour out his blessings upon all present who are his sons and daughters. May he make them always, wherever they may be, faithful members of his holy People. May he send his peace upon all who are gathered here, in Christ Jesus our Lord.

All: **Amen.**

Celebrant: May Almighty God, the Father, and the Son, and the Holy Spirit, bless you.

All: **Amen.**

After the blessing all may sing a hymn which suitably expresses thanksgiving and Easter joy.

CONFIRMATION

THOSE who have been baptized continue on the path of Christian initiation through the sacrament of confirmation. In this sacrament they receive the Holy Spirit, whom the Lord sent upon the apostles at Pentecost.

This giving of the Holy Spirit conforms believers more perfectly to Christ and strengthens them so that they may bear witness to Christ for the building up of his body in faith and love. They are so marked with the character or seal of the Lord that the sacrament of confirmation cannot be repeated.

Ordinarily confirmation takes place within Mass in order to express more clearly the fundamental connection of this sacrament with the entirety of Christian initiation. The latter reaches its culmination in the communion of the body and blood of Christ. The newly confirmed should therefore participate in the eucharist which completes their Christian initiation.

Confirmation effects a more perfect and conscious configuration of baptized persons to Christ, associating them more intimately in his prophetic, priestly, and royal mission. Pouring forth on Christians the abundance of his Spirit, Christ enriches them with inner strength to continue his mission in the world, to proclaim his Gospel and accomplish salvation by an unreserved witness in word and deed.

This mission is completed in the Christian community: the Church. Hence, confirmation effects a fuller and more active incorporation into the Church. It is a consecration through an active celebration of divine worship and liturgical actions under the guidance of the ministerial priesthood.

179   Renewal of Baptismal Promises

The sacrament is usually celebrated during Mass. After the Gospel, the bishop stresses the important step the candidates for confirmation are about to take. Then one of the priests of the parish invites the candidates to come forward. Since confirmation is an endorsement of the promises made in baptism the bishop asks the candidates to renew the vows they then made.

Bishop: Do you reject Satan and all his works and all his empty promises?

Candidates: I do.

Bishop: Do you believe in God the Father Almighty, creator of heaven and earth?

Candidates: I do.

Bishop: Do you believe in Jesus Christ, his only Son, our Lord,
who was born of the Virgin Mary,
was crucified, died and was buried,
rose from the dead,
and is now seated at the right hand of the Father?

Candidates: I do.

Bishop: Do you believe in the Holy Spirit,
the Lord, the giver of life,
who came upon the apostles at Pentecost,
and today is given to you sacramentally in confirmation?

Candidates: I do.

Bishop: Do you believe in the holy Catholic Church,
the communion of saints, the forgiveness of sins?
the resurrection of the body, and life everlasting?

Candidates: I do.

The bishop confirms their profession of faith by proclaiming the faith of the Church:

Bishop: This is our faith. This is the faith of the
Church. We are proud to confess it in Christ Jesus
our Lord.

All: **Amen.**

180 The laying on of hands

The concelebrating priests stand near the bishop. He faces the people and, with hands joined, says:

Bishop: My dear friends:
in baptism God our Father gave the new birth of
eternal life
to his chosen sons and daughters.
Let us pray to our Father
that he will pour out the Holy Spirit
to strengthen his sons and daughters with his gifts
and anoint them to be more like Christ the Son
of God.

All pray in silence for a short time.
The bishop and the priests who will minister the sacrament with him lay hands upon all the candidates (by extending their hands over them).

Bishop:

All-powerful God, Father of our Lord Jesus Christ,
by water and the Holy Spirit
you freed your sons and daughters from sin
and gave them new life.
Send your Holy Spirit upon them
to be their Helper and Guide.

Give them the spirit of wisdom and understanding,
the spirit of right judgment and courage,
the spirit of knowledge and reverence.
Fill them with the spirit of wonder and awe in
    your presence.
We ask this through Christ our Lord.

All: **Amen.**

181 The anointing with chrism

*The deacon brings the chrism to the bishop. Each candidate
goes to the bishop. The one who presented the candidate places
his right hand on the latter's shoulder and gives the candidate's name to the bishop; or the candidate may give his own
name. The bishop dips his right thumb in the chrism and
makes the sign of the cross on the forehead of the one to be
confirmed, as he says:*

Bishop: N., be sealed with Gift of the Holy Spirit.

Candidate: Amen.

Bishop: Peace be with you.

Candidate: And also with you.

182 FINAL BLESSING

*The Mass now proceeds in the usual manner. At the end of
Mass the bishop gives this special blessing:*

Bishop: God our Father
made you his children by water and the Holy Spirit:
may he bless you
and watch over you with his fatherly love.

All: **Amen.**

Bishop: Jesus Christ the Son of God
promised that the Spirit of truth
would be with his Church for ever:

may he bless you and give you courage
in professing the true faith.

All: **Amen.**

Bishop: The Holy Spirit
came down upon the disciples
and set their hearts on fire with love:
may he bless you,
keep you one in faith and love
and bring you to the joy of God's kingdom.

All: **Amen.**

Bishop: May almighty God bless you,
the Father, and the Son, and the Holy Spirit.

All: **Amen.**

PENANCE

W E MERELY *have to look around us and within ourselves to see that something is not quite right in the world. There are so many injustices to eliminate, divisions and discriminations to overcome, oppressions and harassments to overthrow.*

Yet we also know that it is not enough to change things externally unless the heart of people is also changed. The root of every evil resides in the free and conscious person—and the name of it is sin. Since we have a relationship with both God and our neighbor, sin is anything that harms or breaks either relationship.

For those who go from unbelief to faith in Jesus, the sacrament of conversion, the sacrament which remits sin, is baptism—as we profess in the Creed. However, the combat between the carnal self and the self led by the Spirit of God, between love and egotism, is not ended for us with our baptism. It must perdure throughout our life in spite of defections and falls on our part. . .

Hence, the Lord offers us the sacrament of penance in which he holds out the possibility of renewing our baptismal covenant. This pardon reconciles us with God and fellow human beings (especially the community of the Church). This sacrament is one of reconciliation for those who have disrupted their friendship with God

168

and one of healing *for those who have injured it (venial sins)—to help them conform more closely to Christ and to follow the voice of the Spirit more attentively.*

This sacrament requires a real response from us—a desire to change. This is aided by hearing the Word of God. Through this Word, Christians receive light to recognize their sins and are called to conversion and to confidence in God's loving mercy.

Thus, this sacrament now contains a more communitarian dimension, showing that it is part of the Church's work of reconciling sinners to God. It also contains elements of thanksgiving and praise to God for salvation. Finally, it shines out with the paschal joy of those who have been redeemed by the Son of God.

RITE OF PENANCE

(Extracted from the Rite of Penance approved for use in the United States beginning January 1, 1976)

Texts for the Penitent

The penitent should prepare for the celebration of the sacrament by prayer, reading of Scripture, and silent reflection. The penitent should think over and should regret all sins since the last celebration of the sacrament.

183   RECEPTION OF THE PENITENT

The penitent enters the confessional or other place set aside for the celebration of the sacrament of penance. After the welcoming of the priest, the penitent makes the sign of the cross saying:

IN THE name of the Father, and of the Son, and of the Holy Spirit. Amen.

The priest invites the penitent to have trust in God, in these or similar words:

May the grace of the Holy Spirit
fill your heart with light,
that you may confess your sins with loving trust
and come to know that God is merciful.

The penitent answers:

Amen.

184　READING OF THE WORD OF GOD

The penitent then listens to a text of Scripture (such as the one below) which tells about God's mercy and calls man to conversion.

After John's arrest, Jesus appeared in Galilee proclaiming the good news of God: "This is the time of fulfillment. The reign of God is at hand! Reform your lives and believe in the gospel!"

Mark 1:14-15

CONFESSION OF SINS AND ACCEPTANCE OF SATISFACTION

The penitent speaks to the priest in a normal, conversational fashion. The penitent tells when he or she last celebrated the sacrament and then confesses his or her sins. The penitent then listens to any advice the priest may give and accepts the satisfaction from the priest. The penitent should ask any appropriate questions.

PRAYER OF THE PENITENT

Before the absolution is given, the penitent expresses sorrow for sins in these or similar words:

185　　PRAYER OF REPENTANCE

MY GOD,
　　I am sorry for my sins with all my heart.
In choosing to do wrong
and failing to do good,

I have sinned against you
whom I should love above all things.
I firmly intend, with your help,
to do penance,
to sin no more,
and to avoid whatever leads me to sin.
Our Savior Jesus Christ
suffered and died for us.
In his name, my God, have mercy.

186 PRAYER FOR PARDON OF PAST SINS

REMEMBER, Lord, your compassion and mercy
which you showed long ago.
Do not recall the sins and failings of my youth.
In your mercy remember me, Lord, because of your
goodness.

187 PRAYER TO BE CLEANSED

WASH me from my guilt
and cleanse me of my sin.
I acknowledge my offense;
my sin is before me always.

188 PRAYER FOR MERCY

FATHER, I have sinned against you
and am not worthy to be called your son.
Be merciful to me, a sinner.

189 PRAYER TO THE TRINITY

FATHER of mercy,
like the prodigal son
I return to you and say:
"I have sinned against you
and am no longer worthy to be called your son."

Christ Jesus, Savior of the world,
I pray with the repentant thief
to whom you promised Paradise:
"Lord, remember me in your kingdom."
Holy Spirit, fountain of love,
I call on you with trust:
"Purify my heart,
and help me to walk as a child of light."

190   PRAYER TO JESUS THE HEALER

LORD Jesus,
you opened the eyes of the blind,
healed the sick,
forgave the sinful woman,
and after Peter's denial confirmed him in your love.
Listen to my prayer,
forgive all my sins,
renew your love in my heart,
help me to live in perfect unity with my fellow
    Christians
that I may proclaim your saving power to all the
    world.

191   PRAYER TO JESUS, FRIEND OF SINNERS

LORD Jesus,
you choose to be called the friend of sinners,
By your saving death and resurrection
free me from my sins.
May your peace take root in my heart
and bring forth a harvest
of love, holiness, and truth.

192   PRAYER TO JESUS, THE LAMB OF GOD

LORD Jesus Christ,
you are the Lamb of God;

you take away the sins of the world.
Through the grace of the Holy Spirit
restore me to friendship with your Father,
cleanse me from every stain of sin
and raise me to new life
for the glory of your name.

193 PRAYER FOR AN UPRIGHT SPIRIT

LORD God,
in your goodness have mercy on me:
do not look on my sins,
but take away all my guilt.
Create in me a clean heart
and renew within me an upright spirit.

194 PRAYER TO JESUS, SON OF GOD

LORD Jesus, Son of God,
have mercy on me, a sinner.

195 ABSOLUTION

If the penitent is not kneeling, he or she bows his or her head as the priest extends his hands (or at least extends his right hand).

GOD, the Father of mercies,
through the death and resurrection of his Son
has reconciled the world to himself
and sent the Holy Spirit among us
for the forgiveness of sins;
through the ministry of the Church
may God give you pardon and peace,
and I absolve you from your sins
in the name of the Father, and of the Son,
and of the Holy Spirit. Amen.

196 PROCLAMATION OF PRAISE OF GOD AND DISMISSAL

Penitent and priest give praise to God.

Priest: Give thanks to the Lord, for he is good.

Penitent: **His mercy endures for ever.**

Then the penitent is dismissed by the priest.

Form of Examination of Conscience

This suggested form for an examination of conscience should be completed and adapted to meet the needs of different individuals and to follow local usages.

In an examination of conscience, before the sacrament of penance, each individual should ask himself these questions in particular:

197 RELATIONS TOWARD THE SACRAMENT

1. What is my attitude to the sacrament of penance? Do I sincerely want to be set free from sin, to turn again to God, to begin a new life and to enter into a deeper friendship with God? Or do I look on it as a burden, to be undertaken as seldom as possible?

2. Did I forget to mention, or deliberately conceal, any grave sins in past confessions?

3. Did I perform the penance I was given? Did I make reparation for any injury to others? Have I tried to put into practice my resolution to lead a better life in keeping with the Gospel?

Each individual should examine his life in the light of God's word.

198 RELATIONS TOWARD GOD

I. The Lord says: "You shall love the Lord your God with your whole heart."

1. Is my heart set on God, so that I really love him above all things and am faithful to his commandments, as a son loves his father? Or am I more concerned about the things of this world? Have I a right intention in what I do?

2. God spoke to us in his Son. Is my faith in God firm and secure? Am I wholehearted in accepting the Church's teaching? Have I been careful to grow in my understanding of the faith, to hear God's word, to listen to instructions on the faith, to avoid dangers to faith? Have I been always strong and fearless in professing my faith in God and the Church? Have I been willing to be known as a Christian in private and public life?

3. Have I prayed morning and evening? When I pray, do I really raise my mind and heart to God or is it a matter of words only? Do I offer God my difficulties, my joys, and my sorrows? Do I turn to God in time of temptation?

4. Have I love and reverence for God's name? Have I offended him in blasphemy, swearing falsely, or taking his name in vain? Have I shown disrespect for the Blessed Virgin Mary and the saints?

5. Do I keep Sundays and feast days holy by taking a full part, with attention and devotion, in the liturgy, and especially in the Mass? Have I fulfilled the precept of annual confession and of communion during the Easter season?

6. Are there false gods that I worship by giving them greater attention and deeper trust than I give to God: money, superstition, spiritism, or other occult practices?

199   RELATIONS TOWARD OTHERS

II. The Lord says: "Love one another as I have loved you."

1. Have I a genuine love for my neighbors? Or do I use them for my own ends, or do to them what I would not want done to myself? Have I given grave scandal by my words or actions?

2. In my family life, have I contributed to the well-being and happiness of the rest of the family by patience and genuine respect and giving them help in their spiritual and material needs? Have I been careful to give a Christian upbringing to my children, and to help them by good example and by exercising authority as a parent. Have I been faithful to my husband (wife) in my heart and in my relations with others?

3. Do I share my possessions with the less fortunate? Do I do my best to help the victims of oppression, misfortune, and poverty? Or do I look down on my neighbor, especially the poor, the sick, the elderly, strangers, and people of other races?

4. Does my life reflect the mission I received in confirmation? Do I share in the apostolic and charitable works of the Church and in the life of my parish? Have I helped to meet the needs of the Church and of the world and prayed for them: for unity in the Church, for the spread of the Gospel among the nations, for peace and justice, etc.?

5. Am I concerned for the good and prosperity of the human community in which I live, or do I spend my life caring only for myself? Do I share to the best of my ability in the work of promoting justice, morality, harmony, and love in human relations? Have I done my duty as a citizen? Have I paid my taxes?

6. In my work or profession am I just, hard-working, honest, serving society out of love for others? Have I paid a fair wage to my employees? Have I been faithful to my promises and contracts?

7. Have I obeyed legitimate authority and given it due respect?

8. If I am in a position of responsibility or authority, do I use this for my own advantage or for the good of others, in a spirit of service?

9. Have I been truthful and fair, or have I injured others by deceit, calumny, detraction, rash judgment, or violation of a secret?

10. Have I done violence to others by damage to life or limb, reputation, honor, or material possessions? Have I involved them in loss? Have I been responsible for advising an abortion or procuring one? Have I kept up hatred for others? Am I estranged from others through quarrels, enmity, insults, anger? Have I been guilty of refusing to testify to the innocence of another because of selfishness?

11. Have I stolen the property of others? Have I desired it unjustly and inordinately? Have I damaged it? Have I made restitution of other people's property and made good their loss?

12. If I have been injured, have I been ready to make peace for the love of Christ and to forgive, or do I harbor hatred and the desire for revenge?

200 RELATIONS TOWARD SELF

III. Christ our Lord says: "Be perfect as your Father is perfect."

1. Where is my life really leading me? Is the hope of eternal life my inspiration? Have I tried to grow in

the life of the Spirit through prayer, reading the word of God and meditating on it, receiving the sacraments, self-denial? Have I been anxious to control vices, my bad inclinations and passions, e.g., envy, love of food and drink? Have I been proud and boastful, thinking myself better in the sight of God and despising others as less important than myself? Have I imposed my own will on others, without respecting their freedom and rights?

2. What use have I made of time, of health and strength, of the gifts God has given me to be used like the talents in the Gospel? Do I use them to become more perfect every day? Or have I been lazy and too much given to leisure?

3. Have I been patient in accepting the sorrows and disappointments of life? Have I performed mortification to "fill up what is wanting to the sufferings of Christ"? Have I kept the precept of fasting and abstinence?

4. Have I kept my senses and my whole body pure and chaste as a temple of the Holy Spirit consecrated for resurrection and glory, and as a sign of God's faithful love for men and women, a sign that is seen most perfectly in the sacrament of matrimony? Have I dishonored my body by fornication, impurity, unworthy conversation or thoughts, evil desires or actions? Have I given in to sensuality? Have I indulged in reading, conversation, shows, and entertainments that offend Christian and human decency? Have I encouraged others to sin by my failure to maintain these standards? Have I been faithful to the moral law in my married life?

5. Have I gone against my conscience out of fear or hypocrisy?

6. Have I always tried to act in the true freedom of the sons of God according to the law of the Spirit, or am I the slave of forces within me?

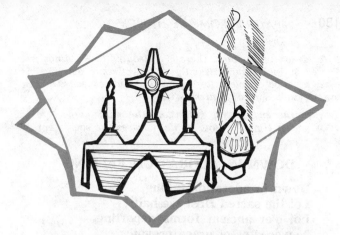

RITE OF EUCHARISTIC EXPOSITION
AND BENEDICTION

WHEN the faithful adore Christ present in the sacrament, they should remember that this presence derives from the sacrifice and is directed toward both sacramental and spiritual Communion.

In consequence, the devotion which leads the faithful to visit the Blessed Sacrament draws them into an ever deeper participation in the Paschal Mystery. It leads them to respond gratefully to the gift of him who through his humanity constantly pours divine life into the members of his body. Dwelling with Christ our Lord, they enjoy his intimate friendship and pour out their hearts before him for themselves and their dear ones, and pray for the peace and salvation of the world.

They offer their entire lives with Christ to the Father in the Holy Spirit, and receive in this wonderful exchange an increase of faith, hope, and charity. Thus they nourish those right dispositions which enable them with all due devotion to celebrate the memorial of the Lord and receive frequently the heavenly Bread, Christ truly present, given us by the Father.

After an opening Hymn, there is a Reading or Readings from Sacred Scripture and a Homily by the priest or deacon. Then after a period of Silent Reflection the minister leads the community in a series of intercessions.

Toward the end of the exposition, the minister goes to the altar, and a Hymn is sung as he incenses the sacrament.

201   **DOWN IN ADORATION FALLING**

> Down in adoration falling,
> Lo! the sacred Host we hail;
> Lo! o'er ancient forms departing,
> Newer rites of grace prevail;
> Faith for all defects supplying,
> Where the feeble senses fail.

> To the everlasting Father,
> And the Son who reigns on high,
> With the Holy Spirit proceeding
> Forth from each eternally,
> Be salvation, honor, blessing,
> Might and endless majesty. Amen.

℣.   You have given them bread from heaven,
℟.   **Having all sweetness within it.**

The minister then says the following Prayer (or a similar one):

202   **PRAYER**

LORD Jesus Christ,
    you gave us the eucharist
as the memorial of your suffering and death.
May our worship of this sacrament of your body and
    blood
help us to experience the salvation you won for us
and the peace of the kingdom

where you live with the Father and the Holy Spirit,
one God, for ever and ever.
℟. **Amen.**

The minister blesses the people with the sacrament; then he may say the Divine Praises together with the people.

203 **THE DIVINE PRAISES**

BLESSED be God
   Blessed be his holy name
Blessed be Jesus Christ, true God and true man
Blessed be the name of Jesus
Blessed be his most sacred heart
Blessed be his most precious blood
Blessed be Jesus in the most holy Sacrament of the altar
Blessed be the Holy Spirit, the Paraclete
Blessed be the great Mother of God, Mary most holy
Blessed be her holy and immaculate conception
Blessed be her glorious assumption
Blessed be the name of Mary, virgin and mother
Blessed be St. Joseph, her spouse most chaste
Blessed be God in his angels and in his saints.

THE RECEPTION OF HOLY
COMMUNION OUTSIDE MASS

BELIEVING in Jesus Christ, we should desire to receive him in Holy Communion, even when we cannot participate in the Mass. The sick and the aged especially should nourish themselves frequently on the Bread of Life.

Communion may be given outside Mass on any day and at any hour. . . . Nevertheless:

a) on Holy Thursday, communion may be given only during Mass; communion may be brought to the sick at any hour of the day;

b) on Good Friday communion may be given only during the celebration of the Passion of the Lord; communion may be brought to the sick who cannot participate in the celebration at any hour of the day;

c) on Holy Saturday, communion may be given only as viaticum.

The priest and deacon are the ministers of Holy Communion. Other special ministers too may be appointed by the bishop.

Preparations for Communion

A suitable table covered with a cloth and provided with candles should be available when communion is brought to a private home.

The Eucharist can be received under the appearance of wine by those who cannot receive the consecrated bread.

Eucharistic Fast

Communicants are not to receive the sacrament unless they have fasted for one hour from solid food and beverages, with the exception of water.

The period of the eucharistic fast, that is, abstinence from food or alcoholic drink, is reduced to about a quarter of an hour for: (1) the sick who are living in hospitals or at home, even if they are not confined to bed; (2) the faithful of advanced age, even if not bedridden, whether they are confined to their homes because of old age or live in a nursing home; (3) sick priests, even if not bedridden, or elderly priests, whether they are to celebrate Mass or to receive communion; (4) persons who care for the sick or aged, and the family of the sick or aged, who wish to receive communion with them, when they cannot conveniently observe the fast of one hour.

The Communion Service

The Communion Service begins with a short penitential rite, like that at Mass.

A celebration of the Word of God may then take place, comprising one or more readings, a psalm, a period of silence and some general intercessions.

After saying the Our Father together, the Sacrament is offered to the communicant. Presenting the Sacrament, the minister says "The Body of Christ." The communicant answers "Amen."

A short prayer and concluding rite follow.

A Sample Service

204   **EUCHARISTIC ANTIPHON**

BODY of Jesus, born of the Virgin Mary,
    body bowed in agony,
raised upon the cross
and offered for us in sacrifice,
body pierced and flowing with blood and water,
come at the hour of our death
as our living bread,
the foretaste of eternal glory:
come, Lord Jesus,
loving and gracious Son of Mary.

205   **GOSPEL OF JESUS AS THE TRUE VINE**

✠ A reading from the holy gospel according to John

JESUS said to his disciples:
    "I am the true vine
and my Father is the vinegrower.
He prunes away
every barren branch,
but the fruitful ones
he trims clean
to increase their yield.
You are clean already,
thanks to the word I have spoken to you.
Live on in me, as I do in you.
No more than a branch can bear fruit of itself
apart from the vine,
can you bear fruit
apart from me.

"I am the vine, you are the branches.

He who lives in me and I in him,
will produce abundantly,
for apart from me you can do nothing.
A man who does not live in me
is like a withered, rejected branch,
picked up to be thrown in the fire and burnt.
If you live in me,
and my words stay part of you,
you may ask what you will—
it will be done for you.
My Father has been glorified
in your bearing much fruit
and becoming my disciples."

John 15:1-8

This is the gospel of the Lord

R̷.   **Praise to you, Lord Jesus Christ.**

[94]   **LORD'S PRAYER**

The minister asks the people to join him in the prayer that Jesus taught us.

Minister and **People:**

O̶UR Father . . .

The minister may invite the people in these or similar words:

Let us offer each other the sign of peace.

All make an appropriate sign of peace, according to local custom.

[98]   **RECEPTION OF COMMUNION**

The minister genuflects. Holding the host elevated slightly over the paten, the priest says:

Minister: This is the Lamb of God
          who takes away the sins of the world.
          Happy are those who are called to his supper.

Minister and **People** (once only):
     **Lord, I am not worthy to receive you,
     but only say the word and I shall be healed.**

He then gives communion to the people.

Minister: The body of Christ.
Communicant: Amen.

206   **CONCLUDING PRAYER**

The minister then says the concluding prayer:

L ORD,
     we thank you for the nourishment you give us
through your holy gift.
Pour out your Spirit upon us
and in the strength of this food from heaven
keep us single-minded in your service.
We ask this in the name of Jesus the Lord.

People: Amen.

MATRIMONY

MARRIED Christians, in virtue of the sacrament of matrimony, signify and share in the mystery of that unity and fruitful love which exists between Christ and his Church; they help each other to attain to holiness in their married life and in the rearing and education of their children; and they have their own special gift among the people of God.

Marriage arises in the covenant of marriage, or irrevocable consent, which each partner freely bestows on and accepts from the other. This intimate union and the good of the children impose total fidelity on each of them and argue for an unbreakable oneness between them.

Christ the Lord raised this union to the dignity of a sacrament so that it might more clearly recall and more easily reflect his own unbreakable union with his Church.

Christian couples, therefore, nourish and develop their marriage by undivided affection, which wells up from the fountain of divine love, while in a merging of human and divine love, they remain faithful in body and in mind, in good times as in bad.

By their very nature, the institution of matrimony and wedded love are ordained for the procreation and education of children and find in them their ultimate

187

*crown. Therefore, married Christians, while not con-
sidering the other purposes of marriage of less account,
should be steadfast and ready to cooperate with the love
of the Creator and Savior, who through them will constantly enrich and enlarge his own family.*

(Rite of Marriage, nos. 1-4)

*This Sacrament is normally celebrated as part of the Mass.
After the Gospel the priest gives a homily drawn from the
sacred text. He speaks about the mystery of Christian marriage,
the nobility of married love, and the responsibilities of married
people.*

207   Declaration of Intentions

M Y dear friends, you have come together in this
church so that the Lord may seal and strengthen
your love in the presence of the Church's minister and
this community. Christ abundantly blesses this love. He
has already consecrated you in baptism and now he enriches and strengthens you by a special sacrament so
that you may assume the duties of marriage in mutual
and lasting fidelity. And so, in the presence of the
Church, I ask you to state your intentions.

*The priest then questions them about their freedom of choice,
faithfulness to each other, and the acceptance and upbringing
of children:*

N. and N., have you come here freely and without
reservation to give yourselves to each other in marriage?

Will you love and honor each other as man and
wife for the rest of your lives?

*The following question may be omitted if, for example, the
couple is advanced in years.*

Will you accept children lovingly from God, and
bring them up according to the law of Christ and his
Church?

Each answers the questions separately.

208 Consent

The priest invites the couple to declare their consent.

Since it is your intention to enter into marriage, join your right hands, and declare your consent before God and his Church.

They join hands.
The bridegroom says:

I, N., take you, N., to be my wife. I promise to be true to you in good times and in bad, in sickness and in health. I will love you and honor you all the days of my life.

The bride says:

I, N., take you, N., to be my husband. I promise to be true to you in good times and in bad, in sickness and in health. I will love you and honor you all the days of my life.

209 OR

In the dioceses of the United States
The bridegroom says:

I, N., take you, N., for my lawful wife, to have and to hold, from this day forward, for better, for worse, for richer, for poorer, in sickness and in health, until death do us part.

The bride says:

I, N., take you, N., for my lawful husband, to have and to hold, from this day forward, for better, for worse, for richer, for poorer, in sickness and in health, until death do us part.

210 Acceptance of Consent

Receiving their consent, the priest says:

YOU have declared your consent before the Church.
May the Lord in his goodness strengthen your
consent and fill you both with his blessings.
What God has joined, men must not divide.

℟. **Amen.**

211 Blessing of Rings

Priest:

MAY the Lord bless ✠ these rings
which you give to each other
as the sign of your love and fidelity.

℟. **Amen.**

212 OR

LORD, bless these rings which we bless ✠ in your
name.
Grant that those who wear them
may always have a deep faith in each other.
May they do your will
and always live together
in peace, good will, and love.
We ask this through Christ our Lord.

℟. **Amen.**

213 OR

LORD,
bless ✠ and consecrate N. and N.
in their love for each other.
May these rings be a symbol
of true faith in each other,

and always remind them of their love.
Through Christ our Lord.

℞. **Amen.**

214 Exchange of Rings

The bridegroom places his wife's ring on her ring finger.
He may say:

N., take this ring as a sign of my love and fidelity. In the name of the Father, and of the Son, and of the Holy Spirit.

The bride places her husband's ring on his ring finger. She may say:

N., take this ring as a sign of my love and fidelity. In the name of the Father, and of the Son, and of the Holy Spirit.

215 Nuptial Blessing

After the Lord's Prayer, the prayer Deliver us *is omitted. The priest faces the bride and bridegroom and says the following blessing over them.*

M Y dear friends, let us turn to the Lord and pray that
he will bless with his grace this woman (or N.)
now married in Christ to this man (or N.)
and that (through the sacrament of the body and blood
   of Christ)
he will unite in love the couple he has joined in this
   holy bond.

All pray silently for a short while. Then the priest extends his hands and continues:

Father, by your power you have made everything out
   of nothing.
In the beginning you created the universe
and made mankind in your own likeness.

You gave man the constant help of woman
so that man and woman should no longer be two, but
  one flesh,
and you teach us that what you have united
may never be divided.
Father, you have made the union of man and wife so
  holy a mystery
that it symbolizes the marriage of Christ and his Church.
Father,
by your plan man and woman are united,
and married life has been established
as the one blessing that was not forfeited by original sin
or washed away in the flood.
Look with love upon this woman, your daughter,
now joined to her husband in marriage.
She asks your blessing.
Give her the grace of love and peace.

May she always follow the example of the holy women
whose praises are sung in the scriptures.
May her husband put his trust in her
and recognize that she is his equal
and the heir with him to the life of grace.
May he always honor her and love her
as Christ loves his bride, the Church.

Father,
keep them always true to your commandments.
Keep them faithful in marriage
and let them be living examples of Christian life.
Give them the strength which comes from the gospel
so that they may be witnesses of Christ to others.
[Bless them with children
and help them to be good parents.
May they live to see their children's children.]
And, after a happy old age,

grant them fullness of life with the saints
in the kingdom of heaven.
We ask this through Christ our Lord.

℟.   **Amen.**

(Other Nuptial Blessings may be used)

216   **Solemn Blessing**

*Before blessing the people at the end of Mass, the priest
blesses the bride and bridegroom:*

God the eternal Father keep you in love with each other,
so that the peace of Christ may stay with you
and be always in your home.

℟.   **Amen.**

May (your children bless you,)
your friends console you
and all men live in peace with you.

℟.   **Amen.**

May you always bear witness to the love of God in this
     world
so that the afflicted and the needy
will find in you generous friends
and welcome you into the joys of heaven.
May almighty God bless you,
the Father, and the Son, ✠ and the Holy Spirit.

℟.   **Amen.**

(Other Solemn Blessings may be used)

217 **Additional Form of Final Blessing**

*An additional form of final blessing may be used in the dio-
ceses of the United States:*

MAY almighty God, with his Word of blessing, unite
your hearts in the never-ending bond of pure love.

℟.   **Amen.**

May your children bring you happiness, and may your generous love for them be returned to you, many times over.

℟.   **Amen.**

May the peace of Christ live always in your hearts and in your home.

May you have friends to stand by you, both in joy and in sorrow.

May you be ready and willing to help and comfort all who come to you in need.

And may the blessings promised to the compassionate be yours in abundance.

℟.   **Amen.**

May you find happiness and satisfaction in your work.

May daily problems never cause you undue anxiety, nor the desire for earthly possessions dominate your lives.

But may your hearts' first desire be always the good things waiting for you in the life of heaven.

℟.   **Amen.**

May the Lord bless you with many happy years together, so that you may enjoy the rewards of a good life.

And after you have served him loyally in his kingdom on earth, may he welcome you to his eternal kingdom in heaven.

℟.   **Amen.**

HOLY ORDERS

THE Son of God became man to call human beings to repentance and to announce the good news of salvation to them, to offer himself as a sacrifice to reconcile sinful humanity with God, and to become the head of a people whom he would lead to his Father. Christ is at the same time the Prophet, King (or Shepherd), and Priest of this new people of God, that is, the Church, which he founded with his blood.

Thus, the Church is a community of Prophets, Kings (or Shepherds), and Priests. All its members by their baptism and confirmation are associated with Christ in this threefold office. They form a prophetic, royal, and priestly people who must offer spiritual sacrifices to God, by the offering of their whole lives completed by the offering of Christ's sacrifice in the Eucharist. They must labor in the world to restore all things in Christ. And they are called to witness to their faith.

However, not everyone in the Church has the same function. The Spirit gives to each special gifts for the building up of Christ's Body. Accordingly, the Lord has established ministers among his faithful to unite them together in one body. These ministers in the society of the faithful are able by the sacred power of orders to offer sacrifice and to forgive sins, and they perform their priestly office publicly for men in the name of Christ.

Therefore, having sent the apostles just as he himself had been sent by the Father, Christ, through the apostles themselves, made their successors, the bishops, sharers in his consecration and mission. The office of their ministry has been handed down, in a lesser degree indeed, to the priests and deacons. Established in the order of the priesthood they can be co-workers of the episcopal order for the proper fulfillment of the apostolic mission entrusted to priests by Christ.

By the power of the sacrament of orders, in the image of Christ the eternal high Priest, they are consecrated to preach the Gospel and shepherd the faithful and to celebrate divine worship, so that they are true priests of the New Testament. Partakers of the function of Christ the sole Mediator, on their level of ministry, they announce the divine word to all.

They exercise their sacred function especially in the eucharistic worship or the celebration of the Mass by which acting in the person of Christ and proclaiming his Mystery they unite the prayers of the faithful with the sacrifice of their Head and renew and apply in the sacrifice of the Mass until the coming of the Lord the only sacrifice of the New Testament, namely that of Christ offering himself once for all a spotless Victim to the Father.

ORDINATION OF BISHOPS

THE ordination of a deacon, priest, or bishop is celebrated during Mass between the Liturgy of the Word and the Liturgy of the Eucharist. The rite for each of these orders follows an identical plan. However, three bishops form a minimum requirement for the ordination of a new bishop—to stress that he is being *added to the episcopal college, successors of the college of apostles.*

After the Gospel the principal consecrator enumerates the duties of the episcopal offices: to preach the Gospel, guard the trust of the faith, build the Church in unity, obey the successor of Peter, take fatherly care of the people of God, especially the poor, strangers, and the straying, and pray without ceasing for the Church.

After the new bishops promise to be faithful to these duties, the assembly prays for them with the litany of saints.

The principal consecrator then imposes his hands on the heads of the new bishops without saying anything, and the others do the same after him.

218   Prayer in Praise of God Who Gave Us Priests

The principal consecrator next places the open Book of the Gospels upon the heads of the new bishops. Then with his hands extended over the bishops-elect he says the consecratory prayer:

GOD the Father of our Lord Jesus Christ,
  Father of mercies and God of all consolation,
you dwell in heaven,
yet look with compassion on all that is humble.
You know all things before they come to be;
by your gracious word
you have established the plan of your Church.
From the beginning
you chose the descendants of Abraham to be your holy
    nation.
You established rulers and priests,

and did not leave your sanctuary without ministers to
serve you.
From the creation of the world
you have been pleased to be glorified
by those whom you have chosen.

219   **Prayer for the Holy Spirit**

The following part of the prayer is recited by all the conse-
crating bishops, with hands joined:

SO NOW pour out upon these chosen ones
    that power which is from you,
the governing Spirit
whom you gave to your beloved Son, Jesus Christ,
the Spirit given by him to the holy apostles,
who founded the Church in every place to be your
    temple
for the unceasing glory and praise of your name.

220   **Prayer for Episcopal Powers**

Then the principal consecrator continues alone:

FATHER, you know all hearts.
    You have chosen your servants for the office of
bishop.
May they be shepherds to your holy flock,
and high priests blameless in your sight,
ministering to you night and day;
may they always gain the blessing of your favor
and offer the gifts of your holy Church.

Through the Spirit who gives the grace of high priest-
    hood
grant them the power
to forgive sins as you have commanded,
to assign ministries as you have decreed,

and to loose every bond by the authority which you gave
   to your apostles.

May they be pleasing to you by their gentleness and
   purity of heart,
presenting a fragrant offering to you,
through Jesus Christ, your Son,
through whom glory and power and honor are yours
with the Holy Spirit
in your holy Church,
now and for ever.

℞. **Amen.**

*The complementary rites express what the new bishops have
received: the* anointing of the head with chrism *evokes the
overshadowing of the Holy Spirit who will render their ministry fruitful; the* giving of the Gospel *reminds them of their
mission to preach; the* giving of the ring *signifies their alliance
with the Church; and the* giving of the miter and the staff
symbolizes their pastoral office.

*Now that they have been added to the college of bishops,
the new bishops receive the kiss of peace from the ordaining
bishops and concelebrate the Eucharist with them.*

ORDINATION OF PRIESTS

A FTER *the Christian community has been consulted
concerning the worthiness of the candidates and
the priest responsible for their candidacy has given a
favorable response, the bishop calls the candidates. He
addresses the people and the candidates on the duties
of a priest: to be a co-worker of the bishop in the service
of the people of God. He is set apart for the Gospel
and for the sacraments..*

Sharing as much as possible in the life of other people, he has the task of announcing to them the Good News of salvation and of fostering an authentic and living faith in them by means of all forms of instruction (catechism, preaching, Christian reflection, etc.).

By baptism he brings men and women into the people of God. In the sacrament of penance he forgives sins in the name of Christ and the Church. By the sacrament of anointing he relieves and consoles the sick. In the celebration of the liturgy he offers thanks and praise to God throughout the day, praying not only for the people of God but for the whole world. Thus, as he presides over the Eucharist, the memorial of the Lord's death and resurrection, he must make every effort to die to sin and walk in the life of Christ. At the same time, he must instruct the people to offer to God the Father the divine Victim and offer their own lives as well.

The bishop next examines the candidates as to whether they accept the duties and responsibilities of their state and promise to live in obedience to him and his successors. Then, while the candidates prostrate themselves, the litany of saints is sung.

The bishop lays his hand on the head of each of the candidates as they come one by one to kneel before him. The other priests do the same as a sign of unity to receive these new brothers into their communion. The priests then remain on either side of the bishop until the end of the prayer of consecration.

221 ## Prayer of Consecration

With his hands extended over the candidates, the bishop sings or says the prayer of consecration, of which the essential part is the following:

ALMIGHTY Father,
grant to these servants of yours
the dignity of the priesthood.
Renew within them the Spirit of holiness.
As co-workers with the order of bishops
may they be faithful to the ministry
that they receive from you, Lord God,
and be to others a model of right conduct.

May they be faithful in working with the order of bishops,
so that the words of the Gospel may reach the ends of the earth,
and the family of nations,
made one in Christ,
may become God's one, holy people.

We ask this through our Lord Jesus Christ, your Son,
who lives and reigns with you and the Holy Spirit,
one God, for ever and ever.

℞. **Amen.**

222 ## Anointing of Hands

The bishop receives a linen gremial and anoints with chrism the palms of each new priest as he kneels before him. The bishop says:

THE Father anointed our Lord Jesus Christ
through the power of the Holy Spirit.
May Jesus preserve you to sanctify the Christian people
and to offer sacrifice to God.

223   **Presentation of the Gifts**

After receiving the stoles and chasubles, the new priests receive the paten with the bread and the chalice with the wine as the bishop says:

ACCEPT from the holy people of God the gifts to be offered to him.
Know what you are doing, and imitate the mystery you celebrate:
model your life on the mystery of the Lord's cross.

After receiving the kiss of peace from the bishop, the new priests join him and the other priests in concelebrating the Eucharist.

ORDINATION OF DEACONS

AS IN the case of the ordination of priests, the rite opens with a consultation of the people and a presentation of the candidates. The bishop then calls the candidates and reminds them of their task: to help the bishop and his body of priests as ministers of the word, of the altar, and of charity. They will bring God's word to believer and unbeliever alike, preside over public prayer, baptize, assist at marriages and bless them, give viaticum to the dying, and lead the rites of burial.

They must fulfill this duty after the example of Jesus —in faith, with a clear conscience, and with holy indifference.

The bishop goes on to examine the candidates as to whether they accept all the duties of their state and he asks them to promise to give him respect and obedience. The litany of the saints is then chanted while the candidates lie prostrate.

Afterward, the candidates kneel before the bishop who lays his hands on them one by one in silence.

224   **Prayer of Consecration**

Then with his hands extended over the kneeling candidates, the bishop says or sings the prayer of consecration, of which the following is the essential part:

L ORD,
    send forth upon them the Holy Spirit,
that they may be strengthened
by the gift of your sevenfold grace
to carry out faithfully the work of the ministry.

May they excel in every virtue:
in love that is sincere,
in concern for the sick and the poor,
in unassuming authority,
in self-discipline,
and in holiness of life.

May their conduct exemplify your commandments,
and lead your people to imitate their purity of life.
May they remain strong and steadfast in Christ,
giving to the world the witness of a pure conscience.
May they in this life imitate your Son,
who came, not to be served but to serve,
and one day reign with him in heaven.

We ask this through our Lord Jesus Christ, your Son,
who lives and reigns with you and the Holy Spirit,
one God, for ever and ever.

225 **Presentation of the Book of the Gospels**

After the deacons are invested with the stole and the dal-
matic, the bishop gives each the Book of the Gospels and says:

R ECEIVE the Gospel of Christ, whose herald you
now are.
Believe what you read,
teach what you believe,
and practice what you teach.
℞. **Amen.**

Lastly, the bishop gives each deacon the kiss of peace.

ANOINTING OF THE SICK

SICKNESS *and pain have always been a heavy burden for man and an enigma to his understanding. Christians suffer sickness and pain as do all other men; yet their faith helps them to understand better the mystery of suffering and to bear their pain more bravely. From Christ's words they know that sickness has meaning and value for their own salvation and for the world's; they also know that Christ loved the sick and that during his life he often looked upon the sick and healed them.*

Sickness, while it is closely related to man's sinful condition, cannot be considered a punishment which man suffers for his personal sins (see John 9:3). Christ himself was sinless, yet he fulfilled what was written in Isaiah: he bore all the sufferings of his passion and understood human sorrow (see Isaiah 53:4-5). Christ still suffers and is tormented in his followers whenever we suffer. If we realize that our sufferings are preparing us for eternal life in glory, then they will seem short and even easy to bear (see 2 Corinthians 4:17).

It is part of the plan laid down by God's providence that we should struggle against all sickness and carefully seek the blessings of good health, so that we can fulfill our role in human society and in the Church. Yet we should always be prepared to fill up what is lacking in Christ's sufferings for the salvation of the world as we look forward to all creation being set free in the glory of the sons of God (see Colossians 1:24; Romans 8:19-21).

Moreover, the role of the sick in the Church is to remind others not to lose sight of the essential or higher things and so to show that our mortal life is restored through the mystery of Christ's death and resurrection.

Not only the sick person should fight against illness; doctors and all who are dedicated to helping the sick should consider it their duty to do whatever they judge will help the sick both physically and spiritually. In doing so they fulfill the command of Christ to visit the sick, for Christ implied that they should be concerned for the whole man and offer both physical relief and spiritual comfort.

This sacrament provides the sick person with the grace of the Holy Spirit by which the whole man is brought to health, trust in God is encouraged, and strength is given to resist the temptations of the Evil One and anxiety about death. Thus the sick person is able not only to bear his suffering bravely, but also to fight against it. A return to physical health may even follow the reception of this sacrament if it will be beneficial to the sick person's salvation. If necessary, the sacrament also provides the sick person with the forgiveness of sins and the completion of Christian penance.

If it is possible, there should be by the bedside a crucifix, two blessed candles and a small glass of drinking water. The candles should be lit shortly before the priest is due; he should be met at the door and led to the sick room.

The priest approaches the sick person and greets him and the others present in a friendly manner.

226 **Introductory Rites**

Priest: Peace be to this house and to all who live in it.
All: **And also with you.**

He may then sprinkle the sick person and the room with holy water.

He may say these words:

Priest: **Let this water call to mind
your baptismal sharing
in Christ's redeeming passion and resurrection.**

Then he addresses those present in these or similar words:

Priest: **Dear brothers and sisters,
We have come together in the name of our Lord Jesus Christ, who restored the sick to health, and who himself suffered so much for our sake. He is present among us as we recall the words of the apostle James: "Is there anyone sick among you? Let him call for the elders of the Church, and let them pray over him and answer him in the name of the Lord. This prayer, made in faith, will save the sick man. The Lord will restore his health, and if he has committed any sins, they will be forgiven."**

Let us entrust our sick brother (sister) N. to the grace and power of Jesus Christ, that the Lord may ease his (her) suffering and grant him (her) health and salvation.

227   ## Penitential Rite and Reading

Then there follows a brief penitential rite, as at Mass (see p. 91), and a reading from Scripture.

The priest and others present may then say these or similar prayers.

Priest: My brothers and sisters, with faith let us ask the Lord to hear our prayers for our brother (sister) N.

Lord, through this holy anointing, come and comfort N. with your love and mercy.

All: **Lord, hear our prayer.**

Priest: Free N. from all harm.

All: **Lord, hear our prayer.**

Priest: Relieve the sufferings of all the sick [here present].

All: **Lord, hear our prayer.**

Priest: Assist all those dedicated to the care of the sick.

All: **Lord, hear our prayer.**

Priest: Free N. from sin and all temptation.

All: **Lord, hear our prayer.**

Priest: Give life and health to our brother (sister) N. on whom we lay our hands in your name.

All: **Lord, hear our prayer.**

Laying on of Hands

The priest then lays his hands on the head of the sick person in silence.

228   **Prayer of Thanksgiving**

The priest says the prayer of thanksgiving over the blessed oil that will be used for the anointing.

Priest: Praise to you, almighty God and Father.
You sent your Son to live among us
and bring us salvation.

All: **Blessed be God.**

Priest: Praise to you, Lord Jesus Christ,
the Father's only Son.
You humbled yourself to share in our humanity,
and desired to cure all our illnesses.

All: **Blessed be God.**

Priest: Praise to you, God the Holy Spirit, the Consoler.
You heal our sickness, with your mighty power.

All: **Blessed be God.**

Priest: Lord God,
with faith in you
our brother (sister)
will be anointed with this holy oil.
Ease his (her) sufferings and strengthen him (her)
in his (her) weakness.
We ask this through Christ our Lord.

All: **Amen.**

229   **Anointing**

Then the priest takes the oil and anoints the sick person on the forehead:

Priest: Through this holy anointing
may the Lord in his love and mercy help you
with the grace of the Holy Spirit.

All: **Amen.**

Then on the hands:

Priest: **May the Lord who frees you from sin**
save you and raise you up.

All: **Amen.**

230 **Prayer after Anointing**

Priest: **Let us pray.**
Lord Jesus Christ, our Redeemer,
by the power of the Holy Spirit,
ease the sufferings of our sick brother (sister)
and make him (her) well again in mind and body.
In your loving kindness forgive his (her) sins
and grant him (her) full health
so that he (she) may be restored to your service.
You are Lord for ever and ever.

All: **Amen.**

231 **Or**

When the sick person is suffering considerably:

Priest: **Lord Jesus Christ,**
you shared in our human nature
to heal the sick and save all mankind.
Mercifully listen to our prayers
for the physical and spiritual health of our sick
brother (sister)
whom we have anointed in your name.
May your protection console him (her)
and your strength make him (her) well again.
Help him (her) find hope in suffering,
for you have given him (her) a share in your
passion.
You are Lord for ever and ever.

All: **Amen.**

232 **Or**

When the illness is the result of advanced age:

Priest: **Lord,**
look kindly on our brother (sister)
who has grown weak under the burden of his (her)
years.
In this holy anointing
he (she) asks for the grace of health in body and
soul.
By the power of your Holy Spirit
make him (her) firm in faith and sure in hope,
so that his (her) cheerful patience
may reveal your love for us.
We ask this through Christ our Lord.

All: **Amen.**

[95] **Lord's Prayer**

The priest then introduces the Lord's prayer in these or similar
words:

Priest: Now let us pray to God as our Lord Jesus
Christ taught us:

All: **Our Father . . .**

[98] **Reception of Communion**

The priest takes the host and as at Mass says:

Priest: This is the Lamb of God
who takes away the sins of the world.
Happy are those who are called to his supper.

All: **Lord, I am not worthy to receive you**
but only say the word and I shall be healed.

As the priest gives the sick person communion, he says:

Priest: **The Body of Christ.**
Sick Person: **Amen.**

233 Prayer after Communion

After communion the priest may use one of the following prayers:

Priest: **Let us pray.**
God our Father, almighty and eternal,
we confidently call upon you,
that the body (and blood) of Christ
which our brother (sister) has received
may bring him (her)
lasting health in mind and body.
We ask this through Christ our Lord.
All: **Amen.**

234 Or

Priest: **Father,**
you brought to completion
the work of our redemption
through the paschal mystery of Christ your Son.
May we who faithfully proclaim
his death and resurrection
in these sacramental signs
experience the constant growth of your salvation
in our lives.
We ask this through Christ our Lord.
All: **Amen.**

235   **Or**

Priest: Lord,
          in the eucharist we share today
          you renew our life.
          Through your Spirit,
          make life grow strong within us and keep us faith-
              ful to you.
          We ask this in the name of Jesus our Lord.

All: **Amen.**

236   **Final Blessing**

The final blessing may take this form:

Priest: May God the Father bless you.

All: **Amen.**

Priest: May God the Son heal you.

All: **Amen.**

Priest: May God the Holy Spirit enlighten you.

All: **Amen.**

Priest: May God protect you from harm
          and grant you salvation.

All: **Amen.**

Priest: May he shine on your heart
          and lead you to eternal life.

All: **Amen.**

Priest: And may Almighty God,
          the Father and the Son and the Holy Spirit
          bless you all.

All: **Amen.**

RITE FOR THE COMMENDATION
OF THE DYING

CHARITY toward one's neighbor urges Christians to express fellowship with a dying brother or sister by praying with him or her for God's mercy and for confidence in Christ.

Prayers, litanies, aspirations, psalms, and readings from Scripture are provided in this section for the commendation of souls. Thus the dying person, if still conscious, may imitate Christ in the face of the anxiety about death that is common to all men and may accept suffering and death in the hope of heavenly life and resurrection, for Christ, by his power, destroyed our death by his own dying.

Those who are present may also draw consolation from these prayers even if the dying person is not conscious and so come to a better understanding of the paschal character of Christian death. This may be visibly expressed by making the sign of the cross on the forehead of the dying person, who was first signed with the cross of baptism.

Prayers and readings may be chosen freely from those which follow, and others may be added if the situation *demands. They should always be adapted to the spiritual and physical condition of the person as well as to other circumstances. They should be recited in a slow, quiet voice, alternated with periods of silence. Often it may be desirable to recite one or more of the brief formulas given below with the dying person and, if necessary, they may be softly repeated two or three times.*

SHORT TEXTS

237

WHAT can come between us and the love of Christ? *(Romans 8:35)*

238

WHETHER we live or die we are the Lord's. *(Romans 14:8)*

239

WE HAVE an everlasting home in heaven. *(2 Corinthians 5:1)*

240

WE SHALL be with the Lord for ever. *(1 Thessalonians 4:17)*

241

WE SHALL see God as he really is. *(1 John 3:2)*

242

WE HAVE passed from death to life because we love the brothers. *(1 John 3:14)*

243

TO YOU I lift up my soul. *(Psalm 24:1)*

244

THE Lord is my light and my salvation. *(Psalm 27:1)*

245

I BELIEVE that I shall see the goodness of the Lord in the land of the living. *(Psalm 27:13)*

246

MY SOUL thirsts for the living God. *(Psalm 42:3)*

247

THOUGH I walk in the shadow of death, I will fear no evil for you are with me. *(Psalm 23:4)*

248

ALL who believe in the Son, will have eternal life. *(John 6:40)*

249

TRULY I say to you:
   Today you will be with me in paradise,
says the Lord Jesus. *(Luke 23:43)*

250

IN MY Father's home
   there are many dwelling places,
says the Lord Jesus. *(John 14:2)*

251

THE Lord Jesus says,
   I go to prepare you a place,
and I will take you with me. *(John 14:3)*

252

I WISH that where I am,
they also may be with me,
says the Lord Jesus. *(John 17:24)*

253

COME, blessed of my Father,
says the Lord Jesus,
and take possession of the kingdom
prepared for you. *(Matthew 25:34)*

254

INTO your hands, Lord, I commit my spirit. *(Psalm 31:6a)*

255

LORD Jesus, receive my spirit. *(Acts 7:59)*

256

HOLY Mary, pray for me.

257

ST. JOSEPH, pray for me.

258

JESUS, Mary, and Joseph,
assist me in my last agony.

Readings from the Old Testament

259   **GOD HIMSELF WILL COME AND SAVE US**

A reading from the book of the prophet Isaiah

STRENGTHEN the hands that are feeble,
   make firm the knees that are weak,
Say to those whose hearts are frightened:
  Be strong, fear not!
Here is your God,
  He comes with vindication;
With divine recompense
  he comes to save you.
Streams will burst forth in the desert,
  and rivers in the steppe.
The burning sands will become pools,
  and the thirsty ground, springs of water;
The abode where jackals lurk
  will be a marsh for the reed and papyrus.
Those whom the Lord has ransomed will return
  and enter Zion singing,
  crowned with everlasting joy;
They will meet with joy and gladness,
  sorrow and mourning will flee. This is the Word
of the Lord. **Thanks be to God.**

Isaiah 35:3-4. 6c-7. 10

I Know That My Redeemer Lives, no. 8, p. 20.

Psalms

The Lord, Shepherd and Host, no. 31, p. 44.

260   **PRAYER FOR GUIDANCE AND HELP**

I TO YOU I lift up my soul,
   O Lord, my God.
Your ways, O Lord, make known to me;

teach me your paths,
Guide me in your truth and teach me,
   for you are God my savior,
   and for you I wait all the day.
Remember that your compassion, O Lord,
   and your kindness are from of old.
The sins of my youth and my frailties remember not;
   in your kindness remember me,
   because of your goodness, O Lord.

II Good and upright is the Lord;
   thus he shows sinners the way.
He guides the humble to justice,
   he teaches the humble his way.
All the paths of the Lord are kindness and constancy
   toward those who keep his covenant and his decrees.
For your name's sake, O Lord,
   you will pardon my guilt, great as it is.

Psalm 25:1, 4-11

Readings from the New Testament

261   **CHRIST'S RESURRECTION**

**A reading from the first letter of Paul
to the Corinthians**

BROTHERS, I want to remind you of the gospel I preached to you, which you received and in which you stand firm. You are being saved by it at this very moment if you hold fast to it as I preached it to you. Otherwise you have believed in vain. I handed on to you first of all what I myself received, that Christ died for our sins in accordance with the Scriptures; that he was buried and, in accordance with the Scriptures, rose on the third day. This is the Word of the Lord.

Thanks be to God.   1 Corinthians 15:1-4

262

GOD IS LOVE

A reading from the first letter of John

WE have come to know and to believe
in the love God has for us.
God is love,
and he who abides in love
abides in God,
and God in him.

1 John 4:16

This is the Word of the Lord.
Thanks be to God.

Gospels

263

JESUS' AGONY

✠ A reading from the holy gospel
according to Luke

JESUS went out and made his way, as was his custom,
to the Mount of Olives; his disciples accompanied
him. On reaching the place he said to them, "Pray that
you may not be put to the test." He withdrew from
them about a stone's throw, then went down on his
knees and prayed in these words: "Father, if it is your
will, take this cup from me; yet not my will but yours
be done." An angel then appeared to him from heaven
to strengthen him. In his anguish he prayed with all
the greater intensity, and his sweat became like drops
of blood falling to the ground. Then he rose from
prayer and came to his disciples, only to find them
asleep, exhausted with grief. He said to them, "Why
are you sleeping? Wake up, and pray that you may not
be subjected to the trial."

Luke 22:39-46

This is the gospel of the Lord.
Praise to you, Lord Jesus Christ.

264   **PROMISE OF PARADISE**

✠ A reading from the holy gospel
according to Luke

[ONE of the criminals said:] "Jesus, remember me
when you enter upon your reign." And Jesus replied,
"I assure you: this day you will be with me in paradise."

Luke 23:42-43

This is the gospel of the Lord.
Praise to you, Lord Jesus Christ.

265   **THE RESURRECTION AND THE LIFE**

✠ A reading from the holy gospel
according to John

MARTHA said to Jesus, "Lord, if you had been
here, my brother would never have died. Even
now, I am sure that God will give you whatever you
ask of him." "Your brother will rise again," Jesus assured her. "I know he will rise again," Martha replied,
"in the resurrection on the last day.' Jesus told her:
"I am the resurrection and the life:
whoever believes in me,
though he should die, will come to life;
and whoever is alive and believes in me
will never die.
Do you believe this?" "Yes, Lord," she replied. "I have
come to believe that you are the Messiah, the Son of
God: he who is to come into the world."

John 11:21-27

This is the gospel of the Lord.
Praise to you, Lord Jesus Christ.

266 **THE FATHER'S HOUSE**

✠ **A reading from the holy gospel
according to John**

[JESUS said to his disciples:]
"Do not let your hearts be troubled.
Have faith in God
and faith in me.
In my Father's house there are many dwelling places;
otherwise, how could I have told you
that I was going to prepare a place for you?
I am indeed going to prepare a place for you,
and then I shall come back to take you with me,
that where I am you also may be.
You know the way that leads where I go."

"Lord," said Thomas, "we do not know where you are
going. How can we know the way?" Jesus told him:

"I am the way, and the truth, and the life;
no one comes to the Father but through me.

"Anyone who loves me
will be true to my word,
and my Father will love him;
we will come to him
and make our dwelling place with him.

" 'Peace' is my farewell to you,
my peace is my gift to you;
I do not give it to you as the world gives peace.
Do not be distressed or fearful."

John 14:1-6. 23-27

This is the the gospel of the Lord.
Praise to you, Lord Jesus Christ.

If the dying person is not able to bear lengthy prayers, it is recommended that, according to the particular circumstances, those present pray for him reciting the litany of the saints, or at least some invocations from it, with the response "pray for him (her)." Special mention may be made of the patron saint or saints of the dying person or his family. Those present may also recite other customary prayers.

When the moment of death seems to be near, someone may say some of the following prayers which are in accord with the Christian disposition for death.

Prayers at the Moment of Death

267   ENCOURAGEMENT TO GO FORTH

IN THE name of God the almighty Father who created you,
in the name of Jesus Christ, Son of the living God, who suffered for you,
in the name of the Holy Spirit, who was poured out upon you,
go forth, faithful Christian.
May you live in peace this day,
may your home be with God in Zion,
with Mary the virgin Mother of God,
with Joseph, and all the angels and saints.

268   PRAYER FOR FORGIVENESS AND PEACE

MY BROTHER (sister) in faith,
I entrust you to God who created you.
May you return to the one
who formed you from the dust of this earth.
May Mary, the angels, and all the saints
come to meet you as you go forth from this life.
May Christ who was crucified for you

bring you freedom and peace.
May Christ, the Son of God, who died for you
take you into his kingdom.
May Christ, the Good Shepherd,
give you a place within his flock.
May he forgive your sins
and keep you among his people.
May you see your Redeemer face to face
and enjoy the sight of God for ever.

℟. **Amen.**

269   PRAYER FOR GOD'S FREEDOM

ACCEPT your servant, Lord,
into the place of salvation
for which he/she hopes.

℟. **Amen.**

Free your servant, Lord,
from every pain and suffering.

℟. **Amen.**

Free your servant, Lord,
as you freed Noah from the flood.

℟. **Amen.**

Free your servant, Lord,
as you freed Abraham from his enemies.

℟. **Amen.**

Free your servant, Lord,
as you freed Job from his sufferings.

℟. **Amen.**

Free your servant, Lord,
as you freed Moses from the hand of the Pharaoh.

℟. **Amen.**

Free your servant, Lord,
as you freed Daniel from the den of lions.

R̊. **Amen.**

Free your servant, Lord,
as you freed the three young men from the burning fire.

R̊. **Amen.**

Free your servant, Lord,
as you freed Susanna from false witness.

R̊. **Amen.**

Free your servant, Lord,
as you freed David from the attacks of Saul and Goliath.

R̊. **Amen.**

Free your servant, Lord,
as you freed Peter and Paul from prison.

R̊. **Amen.**

Free your servant, Lord,
through Jesus our Savior,
who suffered death for us
and gave us eternal life.

R̊. **Amen.**

270   **PRAYER AFTER DEATH**

Immediately after death, the following should be said:

SAINTS of God, come to his (her) aid!
    Come to meet him (her), angels of the Lord!

R̊. **Receive his (her) soul and present him (her)
to God the Most High.**

May Christ, who called you, take you to himself;
may angels lead you to Abraham's side.

℟.   **Receive his (her) soul and present him (her) to God the Most High.**

Give him (her) eternal rest, O Lord,
and may your light shine on him (her) for ever.

℟.   **Receive his (her) soul and present him (her) to God the Most High.**

271   **CONCLUDING PRAYER**

L ET us pray.

We commend our brother (sister) N. to you, Lord.
Now that he (she) has passed from this life,
may he (she) live on in your presence.
In your mercy and love,
forgive whatever sins he (she) may have committed
through human weakness.

We ask this through Christ our Lord.

℟.   **Amen.**

RITES FOR THE DEAD

CHRISTIANS look upon death of loved ones and friends with the eyes of faith. This does not eliminate the pain of separation but illumines it with the light of hope. We also know that through prayer we can remain in mysterious touch with our loved ones.

Today people call for great sacrifices to fight for justice, peace, and an end to hunger. Yet in the face of death this positive approach is forgotten. We must make a strong effort to view death as the beginning of a new life!

Although the mystery of death utterly beggars the imagination, the Church has been taught by divine revelation that human beings have been created by God for a blissful purpose beyond the reach of earthly misery. For God has called all people to be joined to him with their whole beings in an endless sharing of a divine life beyond corruption.

Thus, the most profound hopes of the human heart find their full response in the Risen Christ. He is the conqueror of death. In him death becomes a passover, a passage from this world to the Father. That is the reason why he is our hope, the ultimate and definitive meaning of our lives.

Prayers for the faithful departed will be found on pp. 989-1002.

FUNERAL VIGIL OR WAKE SERVICE

The relatives, friends, and acquaintances of the deceased person gather at the funeral parlor around the body of the deceased—which is sacred since it was the temple of God and is destined to rise again—for a vigil of prayer. This is a family liturgy that solidifies the bonds of affection existing among the participants and also expresses their common faith and hope in the resurrection.

[81]   ## Greeting

THE grace of our Lord Jesus Christ and the love of God and the fellowship of the Holy Spirit be with you all.

People: And also with you.

[31]   ## PSALM 23: THE LORD, SHEPHERD AND HOST

Ant.   **Lord, remember me in your kingdom.**

I

The Lord is my shepherd; I shall not want.
    In verdant pastures he gives me repose;
Beside restful waters he leads me;
    he refreshes my soul.
He guides me in right paths
    for his name's sake.
Even though I walk in the dark valley
    I fear no evil; for you are at my side
With your rod and your staff
    that give me courage.

II

You spread the table before me
    in the sight of my foes;
You anoint my head with oil;
    my cup overflows.

Only goodness and kindness follow me
    all the days of my life;
And I shall dwell in the house of the Lord
    for years to come.

272   Prayer

FOR THE DECEASED PERSON

ALMIGHTY Father,
    eternal God,
hear our prayers
for your son/daughter N.
whom you have called from this life to yourself.
Grant him/her light, happiness, and peace.
Let him/her pass in safety through the gates of death,
and live for ever with all your saints
in the light you promised to Abraham
and to all his descendants in faith.
Guard him/her from all harm
and on that great day of resurrection and reward
raise him/her up with all your saints.

Pardon his/her sins
and give him/her eternal life in your kingdom.
We ask this through Christ our Lord.

℟. **Amen.**

273   Reading

I TELL you truly:
    you will weep and mourn
while the world rejoices;
you will grieve for a time,
but your grief will be turned to joy.

When a woman is in labor
she is sad that her time has come.
When she has borne her child,
she no longer remembers her pain
for joy that a man has been born into the world.
In the same way, you are sad for a time,
but I shall see you again;
then your hearts will rejoice
with a joy no one can take from you.

John 16:20-22

A homily is then given.

274   General Intercessions

GOD, the almighty Father, raised Christ his Son from the dead; with confidence we ask him to save his people, living and dead.

Our brother/sister, N., was given the promise of eternal life in baptism; Lord, give him/her communion with your saints forever.

℟.   **Lord, hear our prayer.**

N. ate the bread of eternal life, the body of Christ; raise him/her up, Lord, at the last day.

℟.   **Lord, hear our prayer.**

(For a priest) Our brother, N., was a priest on earth; welcome him, Lord, into the sanctuary of heaven.

℟.   **Lord, hear our prayer.**

We pray for our brothers and sisters, our relatives, for all who were close to us and good to us; Lord, give them the reward of their goodness.

℟.   **Lord, hear our prayer.**

We pray for all who have died in the hope of rising again; welcome them, Lord, into the light of your presence.

℞.   **Lord, hear our prayer.**

We pray for all who have gathered here to worship in faith; Lord, make us one in your kingdom.

℞.   **Lord, hear our prayer.**

Then [the Lord's Prayer or] the following prayer is added:

275   Prayer

FOR THE DECEASED PERSON AND FOR MOURNERS

L ORD Jesus,
  our Redeemer,
you willingly gave yourself up to death
so that all people might be saved
and pass from death into a new life.
Listen to our prayers;
look with love on your people
who mourn and pray for their dead brother/sister.
Lord Jesus, you alone are holy and compassionate;
forgive our brother/sister his/her sins.

By dying you opened the gates of life
for those who believe in you:
do not let your brother/sister be parted from you,
but by your glorious power
give him/her light, joy, and peace in heaven
where you live for ever and ever.

℞.   **Amen.**

FUNERAL MASS

Rite at the Entrance of the Church

After a hymn, the celebrant greets the people and sprinkles the body with holy water, saying these or similar words:

276   SPRINKLING THE BODY

I BLESS the body of N., with the holy water that recalls his/her baptism of which Saint Paul writes: All of us who were baptized into Christ Jesus were baptized into his death. By baptism into his death we were buried together with him, so that just as Christ was raised from the dead by the glory of the Father, we too might live a new life. For if we have been united with him by likeness to his death, so shall we be united with him by likeness to his resurrection.

A white pall, in remembrance of the baptismal garment, may then be placed on the coffin by the pallbearers or others, and the priest may say these or similar words:

277   PLACING OF WHITE PALL

ON the day of his/her baptism, N. put on Christ. In the day of Christ's coming, may he/she be clothed with glory.

Liturgy of the Word

Human reflection has found words of wisdom to impart consolation in the face of death. However, it is only the death of Jesus, the God-Man, who is one with all his brothers and sisters in their entire destiny, which gives new meaning to our death. Christ's death was a passage from this world to the Father—and so is our death.

Pain and sorrow remain but in the depths of our heart reigns the peace of those who know and believe that death is conquered and present suffering is the prelude to a new world.

From the ample list of readings found in the Lectionary the relatives of the deceased can indicate their preference for those which best express their faith and hope, or the spiritual experience of the one who has left them.

Liturgy of the Eucharist

By celebrating the eucharist we enter more deeply into contact with the paschal mystery of Jesus. United, in him, with our deceased brother or sister, we proclaim the death of Jesus which saves us, as well as his resurrection and ours, in the expectation of his coming to us at our last hour in an encounter filled with light and everlasting joy.

278 EUCHARISTIC PRAYER (PREFACE)

FATHER, all-powerful and ever-living God,
    we do well always and everywhere to give you thanks
through Jesus Christ our Lord.
In him, who rose from the dead,
our hope of resurrection dawned.
The sadness of death gives way
to the bright promise of immortality.
Lord, for your faithful people life is changed, not ended.
When the body of our earthly dwelling lies in death
we gain an everlasting dwelling place in heaven.
And so, with all the choirs of angels in heaven
we proclaim your glory
and join in their unending hymn of praise:

Holy, holy, holy . . .

FINAL COMMENDATION AND FAREWELL AT THE GRAVE

On the way out of the church the following antiphons may be sung:

279 ANTIPHON

MAY the angels lead you into paradise;
may the martyrs come to welcome you
and take you to the holy city,
the new and eternal Jerusalem

280 Or

I AM the resurrection and the life.
The man who believes in me will live
even if he dies,
and every living person
who puts his faith in me
will never suffer eternal death.

The celebrant stands near the coffin with the ministers who have the holy water and incense. He faces the people and introduces the rite:

281 Introduction of Rite

WITH faith in Jesus Christ,
we reverently bring the body of our brother/
sister
to be buried in its human imperfection.

Let us pray with confidence to God,
who gives life to all things,
that he will raise up this mortal body
to the perfection and the company of the saints.

May God give him/her a merciful judgment
and forgive all his/her sins.
May Christ, the Good Shepherd,
lead him/her safely home
to be at peace with God our Father.

And may he/she be happy for ever
with all the saints
in the presence of the eternal King.

282   **Reading**

JESUS said:
    "The hour has come
for the Son of Man to be glorified.
I solemnly assure you,
unless the grain of wheat falls to the earth and dies,
it remains just a grain of wheat.
But if it dies,
it produces much fruit.
The man who loves his life
loses it,
while the man who hates his life in this world
preserves it to life eternal.
If anyone would serve me,
let him follow me;
where I am,
there will my servant be.
If anyone serves me,
him the Father will honor."

                                        John 12:23-26

283   **Responsorial Psalm**

PSALM 62: TRUST IN GOD ALONE

I

Ant.   **Only in God is my soul at rest;**
              from him comes my hope.

Only in God is my soul at rest;
    from him comes my salvation.
He only is my rock and my salvation,
    my stronghold; I shall not be disturbed at all.

How long will you set upon a man and all together beat
    him down
  as though he were a sagging fence, a battered wall?
Truly from my place on high they plan to dislodge me;
    they delight in lies;
They bless with their mouths,
    but inwardly they curse.

II

Only in God be at rest, my soul,
    for from him comes my hope.
He only is my rock and my salvation,
    my stronghold; I shall not be disturbed.

With God is my safety and my glory,
    he is the rock of my strength; my refuge is in God.
Trust in him at all times, O my people!
    Pour out your hearts before him;
    God is my refuge!

III

Only a breath are mortal men;
    an illusion are men of rank;
In a balance they prove lighter,
    all together, than a breath.

Trust not in extortion; in plunder take no empty pride;
 though wealth abound, set not your heart upon it.
One thing God said; these two things which I heard:
 that power belongs to God, and yours, O Lord, is
 kindness;
 and that you render to everyone according to his
 deeds.

[270] **Prayer of the Faithful**

The body is sprinkled with holy water and incensed, or this may be done after the song of farewell.

℣. Saints of God, come to his/her aid!
 Come to meet him/her, angels of the Lord!

℟. **Receive his/her soul and present him/her to God the Most High.**

℣. May Christ, who called you, take you to himself;
 may angels lead you to Abraham's side.

℟. **Receive his/her soul and present him her to God the Most High.**

℣. Give him/her eternal rest, O Lord,
 and may your light shine on him/her for ever.

℟. **Receive his/her soul and present him/her to God the Most High.**

Then the priest says:

[271]

WE COMMEND our brother/sister N. to you, Lord.
 Now that he/she has passed from this life,
may he/she live on in your presence.
In your mercy and love,
forgive whatever sins he/she may have committed
through human weakness.
We ask this through Christ our Lord. ℟. **Amen.**

The prayer on p. 231, no. 275, is also said.

VOTIVE PRAYERS — PRAYING WITH THE CHURCH

The votive prayers provide us with model prayers to use in many life situations. They are permeated by the Scriptures and the centuries-long experience of the Church. In this sense many liturgists consider them to have been composed under the inspiration of the Holy Spirit.

D) VOTIVE PRAYERS

THE new Sacramentary contains some 2,000 prayers to be used at the eucharistic liturgy—about twice as many as the pre-Vatican II Roman Missal. These prayers (including the Prefaces) give this Sacramentary its proper character.

These prayers are taken from the thousand-year history of the Roman liturgy as well as other Latin liturgies and are adapted to present-day requirements and conditions, or they are created to respond to new needs. Many of them were composed by St. Leo the Great or St. Gregory the Great and others were the direct result of their guiding spirit. A good deal of the newer prayers bear the stamp of the Second Vatican Council—in some cases utilizing the very words of the Council Fathers.

All the prayers speak the language of the Scriptures. In some cases, the words are taken directly from the sacred writings while in others the ideas are totally biblical. In this way, this entire treasury of liturgical prayer is pervaded by the Bible.

Thus, the prayers of the Sacramentary constitute an inexhaustible treasury of genuine piety for all Christians. They can serve as helps for our prayer life and can provide valuable orientations for our devotion. The following section gives a few of the prayers found therein.

PRAYERS FROM THE
PROPER OF THE SEASON

284 To Bring Christ's Peace to the World

GOD our Father,
  your Word, Jesus Christ, spoke peace to a sinful
    world
and brought mankind the gift of reconciliation
by the suffering and death he endured.

Teach us, the people who bear his name,
to follow the example he gave us:
may our faith, hope, and charity
turn hatred to love, conflict to peace, death to eternal
  life.

(4th Sun of Lent)

285 For Courage to Embrace the World

FATHER in heaven,
  the love of your Son led him to accept the suf-
    fering of the cross
that his brothers might glory in new life.
Change our selfishness into self-giving.
Help us to embrace the world you have given us,
that we may transform the darkness of its pain
into the life and joy of Easter.

(5th Sun of Lent)

286   For the Jewish People

ALMIGHTY and eternal God,
long ago you gave your promise to Abraham and
    his posterity.
Listen to your Church as we pray
that the people you first made your own
may arrive at the fullness of redemption.

(Good Friday)

287 For Those Who Do Not Believe in Christ

ALMIGHTY and eternal God,
enable those who do not acknowledge Christ
to find the truth
as they walk before you in sincerity of heart.
Help us to grow in love for one another,
to grasp more fully the mystery of your godhead,
and to become more perfect witnesses of your love
in the sight of men.

(Good Friday)

288 For Those Who Do Not Believe in God

ALMIGHTY and eternal God,
you created mankind
so that all might long to find you
and have peace when you are found.
Grant that, in spite of the hurtful things
that stand in their way,
they may all recognize in the lives of Christians
the tokens of your love and mercy,
and gladly acknowledge you
as the one true God and Father of us all.

(Good Friday)

289   For Those in Special Need

ALMIGHTY, ever-living God,
  you give strength to the weary
and new courage to those who have lost heart.
Hear the prayers of all who call on you in any trouble
that they may have the joy of receiving your help in
    their need.

(Good Friday)

290   To Follow Christ Our Shepherd

GOD and Father of our Lord Jesus Christ,
  though your people walk in the valley of darkness,
no evil should they fear;
for they follow in faith the call of the shepherd
whom you have sent for their hope and strength.

Attune our minds to the sound of his voice,
lead our steps in the path he has shown,
that we may know the strength of his outstretched arm
and enjoy the light of your presence for ever.

(4th Sun of Easter)

291   To Receive the Holy Spirit

FATHER of light, from whom every good gift comes,
  send your Spirit into our lives
with the power of a mighty wind,
and by the flame of your wisdom
open the horizons of our minds.

Loosen our tongues to sing your praise
in words beyond the power of speech,
for without your Spirit
man could never raise his voice in words of peace
or announce the truth that Jesus is Lord.

(Pentecost)

292 **To God Who Brings Good Out of Evil**

ALMIGHTY and ever-present Father,
your watchful care reaches from end to end
and orders all things in such power
that even the tensions and the tragedies of sin
cannot frustrate your loving plans.

Help us to embrace your will,
give us the strength to follow your call,
so that your truth may live in our hearts
and reflect peace to those who believe in your love.

(2nd Ord. Sun)

293 **For Openness to God**

ALMIGHTY God,
Father of our Lord Jesus Christ,
faith in your word is the way to wisdom,
and to ponder your divine plan is to grow in the truth.

Open our eyes to your deeds,
our ears to the sound of your call,
so that our every act may increase our sharing
in the life you have offered us.

(7th Ord. Sun)

294 **For Faith and Trust**

GOD our Father,
teach us to cherish the gifts that surround us.
Increase our faith in you
and bring our trust to its promised fulfillment
in the joy of your kingdom.

(9th Ord. Sun)

295   **For the Strength to Repent**

FATHER in heaven,
   the light of Jesus
has scattered the darkness of hatred and sin.
Called to that light
we ask for your guidance.
Form our lives in your truth, our hearts in your love.

(13th Ord. Sun)

296   **For God's Continued Blessing**

FATHER,
   let the gift of your life
continue to grow in us,
drawing us from death to faith, hope, and love.
Keep us alive in Christ Jesus.
Keep us watchful in prayer
and true to his teaching
till your glory is revealed in us.

(16th Ord. Sun)

297   **To Recognize God's Presence in the World**

GOD our Father,
   open our eyes to see your hand at work
in the splendor of creation,
in the beauty of human life.
Touched by your hand our world is holy.
Help us to cherish the gifts that surround us,
to share your blessings with our brothers and sisters,
and to experience the joy of life in your presence.

(17th Ord. Sun)

298 **To Overcome Prejudice**

A LMIGHTY God, ever-loving Father,
your care extends beyond the boundaries of race
and nation
to the hearts of all who live.

May the walls, which prejudice raises between us,
crumble beneath the shadow of your outstretched arm.

(20th Ord. Sun)

299 **To Be Free from Fear**

L ORD our God,
in you justice and mercy meet.
With unparalleled love you have saved us from death
and drawn us into the circle of your life.

Open our eyes to the wonders this life sets before us,
that we may serve you free from fear
and address you as God our Father.

(23rd Ord. Sun)

300 **For Courage to Stand before God's Truth**

A LMIGHTY and eternal God,
Father of the world to come,
your goodness is beyond what our spirit can touch
and your strength is more than the mind can bear.
Lead us to seek beyond our reach
and give us the courage to stand before your truth.

(27th Ord. Sun)

301   For God's Continued Providence

FATHER in heaven,
   the hand of your loving kindness
powerfully yet gently guides all the moments of our day.

Go before us in our pilgrimage of life,
anticipate our needs and prevent our falling.
Send your Spirit to unite us in faith,
that sharing in your service,
we may rejoice in your presence.

(28th Ord. Sun)

302   For Faith in Discouragement

FATHER in heaven, God of power and Lord of
   mercy,
from whose fullness we have received,
direct our steps in our everyday efforts.
May the changing moods of the human heart
and the limits which our failings impose on hope
never blind us to you, source of every good.

Faith gives us the promise of peace
and makes known the demands of love.
Remove the selfishness that blurs the vision of faith.

(31st Ord. Sun)

303   To Bring Christ's Eucharistic Love
to the World

LORD Jesus Christ,
   we worship you living among us
in the sacrament of your body and blood.

May we offer to our Father in heaven
a solemn pledge of undivided love.

May we offer to our brothers and sisters
a life poured out in loving service of that kingdom
where you live with the Father and the Holy Spirit,
one God, for ever and ever.

(Corpus Christi)

304 For the Coming of Christ's Kingdom

FATHER all-powerful, God of love,
    you have raised our Lord Jesus Christ from death
        to life,
resplendent in glory as King of creation.
Open our hearts,
free all the world to rejoice in his peace,
to glory in his justice, to live in his love.
Bring all mankind together in Jesus Christ your Son,
whose kingdom is with you and the Holy Spirit,
one God, for ever and ever.

(Christ the King)

PRAYERS FROM MASSES AND
PRAYERS FOR VARIOUS NEEDS
AND OCCASIONS

305   **For the Universal Church**

GOD our Father,
  by the promise you made
in the life, death, and resurrection of Christ your Son,
you bring together in your Spirit, from all the nations,
a people to be your own.
Keep the Church faithful to its mission:
may it be a leaven in the world
renewing us in Christ,
and transforming us into your family.

306   **For the Local Church**

GOD our Father,
  in all the churches scattered throughout the world
you show forth the one, holy, catholic and apostolic
    Church.
Through the gospel and the eucharist
bring your people together in the Holy Spirit
and guide us in your love.
Make us a sign of your love for all people,
and help us to show forth
the living presence of Christ in the world,
who lives and reigns with you and the Holy Spirit,
one God, for ever and ever.

307   For the Pope

LORD,
    source of eternal life and truth,
give to your shepherd N.
a spirit of courage and right judgment,
a spirit of knowledge and love.
By governing with fidelity those entrusted to his care
may he, as successor to the apostle Peter and vicar of
    Christ,
build your Church into a sacrament of unity, love, and
    peace for all the world.

308   For a Bishop

LORD our God,
    you have chosen your servant N.
to be a shepherd of your flock
in the tradition of the apostles.
Give him a spirit of courage and right judgment,
a spirit of knowledge and love.
By governing with fidelity those entrusted to his care
may he build your Church as a sign of salvation for the
    world.

309   For a Council or Synod

GOD our Father,
    you judge your people with kindness
and rule us with love.
Give a spirit of wisdom
to those you have entrusted with authority
in your Church
that your people may come to know the truth more fully
and grow in holiness.

310   For Priests

LORD our God,
  you guide your people by the ministry of priests.
Keep them faithful in obedient service to you
that by their life and ministry
they may bring you glory in Christ.

We ask this through our Lord Jesus Christ, your Son,
who lives and reigns with you and the Holy Spirit,
one God, for ever and ever.

311   For the Ministers of the Church

FATHER,
  you have taught the ministers of your Church
not to desire that they be served but to serve their
  brothers and sisters.
May they be effective in their work
and persevering in their prayer,
performing their ministry with gentleness and concern
  for others.

312   For Priestly Vocations

FATHER,
  in your plan for our salvation you provide shep-
    herds for your people.
Fill your Church with the spirit of courage and love.
Raise up worthy ministers for your altars
and ardent but gentle servants of the gospel.

313   For Religious

FATHER,
  you inspire and bring to fulfillment every good
    intention.

Guide your people in the way of salvation
and watch over those who have left all things
to give themselves entirely to you.
By following Christ and renouncing worldly power and
   profit,
may they serve you and their brothers faithfully
in the spirit of poverty and humility.

314   For Religious Vocations

FATHER,
   you call all who believe in you to grow perfect in
      love
by following in the footsteps of Christ your Son.
May those whom you have chosen to serve you as religious
provide by their way of life
a convincing sign of your kingdom
for the Church and the whole world.

315   For the Laity

GOD our Father,
   you send the power of the gospel into the world
as a life-giving leaven.
Fill with the Spirit of Christ
those whom you call to live in the midst of the world
and its concerns;
help them by their work on earth
to build up your eternal kingdom.

316   For Unity of Christians

ALMIGHTY and eternal God,
   you keep together those you have united.
Look kindly on all who follow Jesus your Son.

We are all consecrated to you by our common baptism;
make us one in the fullness of faith
and keep us one in the fellowship of love.

317 For the Spread of the Gospel

GOD our Father,
you will all men to be saved
and come to the knowledge of your truth.
Send workers into your great harvest
that the gospel may be preached to every creature
and your people, gathered together by the word of life
and strengthened by the power of the sacraments,
may advance in the way of salvation and love.

318 For Persecuted Christians

FATHER,
in your mysterious providence,
your Church must share in the sufferings of Christ your
Son.
Give the spirit of patience and love
to those who are persecuted for their faith in you
that they may always be true and faithful witnesses
to your promise of eternal life.

319 For Pastoral or Spiritual Meetings

GOD our Father,
your Son promised to be with all who gather in
his name.
Make us aware of his presence among us
and fill us with his grace, mercy, and peace,
so that we may live in truth and love.

320   For the Nation, (State) or City

GOD our Father,
you guide everything in wisdom and love.
Accept the prayers we offer for our nation;
by the wisdom of our leaders and integrity of our
    citizens,
may harmony and justice be secured
and may there be lasting prosperity and peace.

321   For Those Who Serve in Public Office

ALMIGHTY and eternal God,
you know the longings of men's hearts
and you protect their rights.
In your goodness,
watch over those in authority,
so that people everywhere may enjoy
freedom, security, and peace.

322   For the Assembly of National Leaders

FATHER,
you guide and govern everything with order and
    love.
Look upon the assembly of our national leaders
and fill them with the spirit of your wisdom.
May they always act in accordance with your will
and their decisions be for the peace and well-being of
    all.

323   For the King or Head of State

GOD our Father,
all earthly powers must serve you.
Help your servant N. (our King N.)

to fulfill his responsibilities worthily and well.
By honoring and striving to please you at all times,
may he secure peace and freedom
for the people entrusted to him.

324   For the Progress of Peoples

FATHER,
you have given all peoples one common origin,
and your will is to gather them as one family in yourself.
Fill the hearts of all men with the fire of your love
and the desire to ensure justice for all their brothers
    and sisters.
By sharing the good things you give us
may we secure justice and equality for every human
    being,
an end to all division,
and a human society built on love and peace.

325   For Peace and Justice

LORD,
you guide all creation with fatherly care.
As you have given all men one common origin,
bring them together peacefully into one family
and keep them united in brotherly love.

326   In Time of War or Civil Disturbance

GOD of power and mercy,
you destroy war and put down earthly pride.
Banish violence from our midst and wipe away our tears
that we may all deserve to be called your sons and
    daughters.

327 **For the Blessing of Man's Labor**

GOD our Father,
by the labor of man you govern and guide to perfection
the work of creation.
Hear the prayers of your people
and give all men work that enhances their human dignity
and draws them closer to each other
in the service of their brothers.

328 **For Productive Land**

GOD our Father,
we acknowledge you as the only source of growth and abundance.
With your help we plant our crops
and by your power they produce our harvest.
In your kindness and love
make up for what is lacking in our efforts.

329 **After the Harvest**

FATHER, God of goodness,
you give man the land to provide him with food.
May the produce we harvest sustain our lives,
and may we always use it for your glory and the good of all.

330 **In Time of Famine**

ALL-POWERFUL Father,
God of goodness,
you provide for all your creation.

Give us an effective love for our brothers and sisters
who suffer from lack of food.
Help us do all we can to relieve their hunger,
that they may serve you with carefree hearts.

331   **For Refugees and Exiles**

LORD,
no one is a stranger to you
and no one is ever far from your loving care.
In your kindness watch over refugees and exiles,
those separated from their loved ones,
young people who are lost,
and those who have left or run away from home.
Bring them back safely to the place where they long to
be
and help us always to show your kindness
to strangers and to those in need.

332   **For Those Unjustly Deprived of Liberty**

FATHER,
your Son came among us as a slave
to free the human race from the bondage of sin.
Rescue those unjustly deprived of liberty
and restore them to the freedom you wish for all men
as your sons.

333   **For Prisoners**

FATHER of mercy,
the secrets of all hearts are known to you alone.
You know who is just and you forgive the unjust.
Hear our prayers for those in prison.
Give them patience and hope in their sufferings,
and bring them home again soon.

334 For the Sick

FATHER,
your Son accepted our sufferings
to teach us the virtue of patience in human illness.
Hear the prayers we offer for our sick brothers and
sisters.
May all who suffer pain, illness or disease
realize that they are chosen to be saints,
and know that they are joined to Christ
in his suffering for the salvation of the world,
who lives and reigns with you and the Holy Spirit,
one God, for ever and ever.

335 For the Dying

GOD of power and mercy,
you have made death itself
the gateway to eternal life.
Look with love on our dying brother/sister,
and make him/her one with your Son in his suffering
and death,
that, sealed with the blood of Christ,
he/she may come before you free from sin.

336 In Time of Earthquake

GOD our Father,
you set the earth on its foundation.
Keep us safe from the danger of earthquakes
and let us always feel the presence of your love.
May we be secure in your protection
and serve you with grateful hearts.

337   **For Rain**

LORD God,
    in you we live and move and have our being.
Help us in our present time of trouble,
send us the rain we need,
and teach us to seek your lasting help
on the way to eternal life.

338   **For Fine Weather**

ALL-POWERFUL and ever-living God,
    we find security in your forgiveness.
Give us the fine weather we pray for
so that we may rejoice in your gifts of kindness
and use them always for your glory and our good.

339   **To Avert Storms**

FATHER,
    all the elements of nature obey your command.
Calm the storms that threaten us
and turn our fear of your power
into praise of your goodness.

340   **For Any Need**

GOD our Father,
    our strength in adversity,
our health in weakness,
our comfort in sorrow,
be merciful to your people.
As you have given us the punishment we deserve,
give us also new life and hope as we rest in your kind-
    ness.

341 In Thanksgiving

FATHER of mercy,
you always answer your people in their sufferings.
We thank you for your kindness
and ask you to free us from all evil,
that we may serve you in happiness all our days.

342 For Forgiveness of Sins

LORD,
hear the prayers of those who call on you,
forgive the sins of those who confess to you,
and in your merciful love
give us your pardon and your peace.

343 For Charity

LORD,
fill our hearts with the spirit of your charity,
that we may please you by our thoughts,
and love you in our brothers and sisters.

344 For Promoting Harmony

GOD our Father,
source of unity and love,
make your faithful people one in heart and mind
that your Church may live in harmony;
be steadfast in its profession of faith,
and secure in unity.

345 For the Family

FATHER,
we look to your loving guidance and order
as the pattern of all family life.

By following the example of the holy family of your
    Son, in mutual love and respect,
may we come to the joy of our home in heaven.

346 **For Relatives and Friends**

FATHER,
    by the power of your Spirit
you have filled the hearts of your faithful people
with gifts of love for one another.
Hear the prayers we offer for our relatives and friends.
Give them health of mind and body
that they may do your will with perfect love.

347 **For Our Oppressors**

FATHER,
    according to your law of love
we wish to love sincerely all who oppress us.
Help us to follow the commandments of your new
    covenant,
that by returning good for the evil done to us,
we may learn to bear the ill-will of others out of love
    for you.

348 **For a Happy Death**

FATHER,
    you made us in your own image
and your Son accepted death for our salvation.
Help us to keep watch in prayer at all times.
May we be free from sin when we leave this world
and rejoice in peace with you for ever.

3

PRAYERS
FROM THE
ENCHIRIDION
OF
INDULGENCES

INDULGENCES — SPIRITUAL TREASURY
OF THE CHURCH

From her spiritual treasury made up of Christ's merits (as well as those of Mary and the Saints), the Church grants the remission of the temporal punishment due to sin already forgiven—through indulgences attached to works and prayers.

A) THREE GENERAL GRANTS
OF INDULGENCES

FROM the Council of Trent to the beginning of Vatican II, many Catholics had a particular fondness for prayers that were indulgenced by the Church. Undoubtedly, they felt that in reciting such prayers they were guarded from praying fruitlessly, so to speak. However, the precise nature of indulgences often escaped the faithful and abuses crept into the practice, so that they came to be used by some in an almost magical way.

On January 1, 1967, Pope Paul VI promulgated new norms regarding the discipline of indulgences in the Church. The document dealt with the nature of sin, the punishment due to sin, the solidarity of all human beings in Adam and in Christ, the Communion of Saints, and the treasury of the expiations and merits of Christ, of the Blessed Virgin, and of the Saints—a treasury which has been given to the Church to be placed by her at the disposition of the faithful.

It also stressed how salutary is the use of indulgences, since they promote through charity the union of all the faithful with Christ and with the pastors of the Church, his representatives. At the same time it called for a revision of the indulgenced prayers and practices. This became a reality on June 29, 1968 when a revised and revamped Enchiridion of Indulgences was published.

The key idea of this new volume is the preeminent value of charity. The faithful are urged to look first of all to the worthy performance of their duties, with the assurance of obtaining, not only greater merit, but also a proportionate remission of temporal punishment for *their sins already forgiven, this by virtue of both their personal effort and of the gift of the Church.*

This section presents all the new indulgenced prayers and grants as well as many of the practices, so that the faithful can make use of them at opportune times and derive the greatest benefit from them.

For the complete list of practices as well as a more complete treatment of indulgences, the reader is referred to the source of this entire section: the *Enchiridion of Indulgences,* authorized English edition, published 1969 by Catholic Book Publishing Co.

Introduction

1) An indulgence is the remission before God of the temporal punishment due for sins already forgiven as far as their guilt is concerned. This remission the faithful with the proper dispositions and under certain determined conditions acquire through the intervention of the Church which, as minister of the Redemption, authoritatively dispenses and applies the treasury of the satisfaction won by Christ and the Saints.

2) An indulgence is partial or plenary, according as it removes either part or all of the temporal punishment due for sin.

3) No one, acquiring indulgences, can apply them to other living persons.

4) Partial as well as plenary indulgences can always be applied to the departed by way of suffrage.

5) The grant of a partial indulgence is designated only with the words "partial indulgence," without any determination of days or years.

6) The faithful, who at least with contrite heart perform an action to which a partial indulgence is attached, obtain, in addition to the remission of temporal punishment acquired by the action itself, an

equal remission of punishment through the intervention of the Church,

7) The faithful, who devoutly use an *article of devotion* (crucifix or cross, rosary, scapular or medal) properly blessed by any priest, obtain a partial indulgence.

But if the *article of devotion* has been blessed by the Sovereign Pontiff or by any bishop, the faithful, using it devoutly, can also gain a plenary indulgence on the feast of the Holy Apostles, Peter and Paul, provided they also make a profession of faith according to any legitimate formula.

8) To be capable of gaining an indulgence for oneself, it is required that one be baptized, not excommunicated, in the state of grace at least at the completion of the prescribed works, and a subject of the one granting the indulgence.

9) In order that one who is capable may actually gain indulgences, one must have at least a general intention to gain them and must in accordance with the tenor of the grant perform the enjoined works at the time and in the manner prescribed.

10) A plenary indulgence can be acquired once only in the course of a day. But one can obtain the plenary indulgence *for the moment of death*, even if another plenary indulgence had already been acquired on the same day. A partial indulgence can be acquired more than once a day, unless otherwise expressly indicated.

11) The work prescribed for acquiring a plenary indulgence connected with a church or oratory consists in a devout visit and the recitation during the visit of one *Our Father* and the *Creed*.

12) To acquire a plenary indulgence it is necessary to perform the work to which the indulgence is attached

and to fulfill the following three conditions: sacramental confession, eucharistic Communion, and prayer for the intention of the Sovereign Pontiff. It is further required that all attachment to sin, even venial sin, be absent.

13) The three conditions may be fulfilled several days before or after the performance of the prescribed work; it is, however, fitting that Communion be received and the prayer for the intention of the Sovereign Pontiff be said on the same day the work is performed.

14) A single sacramental confession suffices for gaining several plenary indulgences; but Communion must be received and prayer for the intention of the Sovereign Pontiff must be recited for the gaining of each plenary indulgence.

15) The condition of praying for the intention of the Sovereign Pontiff is fully satisfied by reciting one *Our Father* and one *Hail Mary*; nevertheless, each one is free to recite any other prayer according to his piety and devotion.

16) To gain an indulgence attached to a prayer, it is sufficient to recite the prayer alternately with a companion or to follow it mentally while it is being recited by another.

First General Grant

A PARTIAL indulgence is granted to the faithful who, in the performance of their duties and in bearing the trials of life, raise their mind with humble confidence to God, adding—even if only mentally—some pious invocation.

This first grant is intended to serve as an incentive to the faithful to put into practice the commandment of Christ that "they must always pray and not lose

heart" (Luke 18:1) and at the same time as a reminder
so to perform their respective duties as to preserve and
strengthen their union with Christ.

349 IMPORTUNATE PRAYER

ASK, and it shall be given you;
seek, and you shall find;
knock, and it shall be opened.
For everyone who asks receives,
and he who seeks finds,
and to him who knocks it shall be opened.

Matthew 7:7-8

350 DO ALL FOR THE GLORY OF GOD

THEREFORE, whether you eat or drink,
or do anything else,
do all for the glory of God.

1 Corinthians 10:31

351 DO ALL IN THE NAME OF JESUS

WHATEVER you do in word or in work,
do all in the name of the Lord Jesus,
giving thanks to God the Father
through him.

Colossians 3:17

See also Matthew 26:41; Luke 21:34-36; Acts 2:42; Romans
12:12; Ephesians 6:18; Colossians 4:2; 1 Thessalonians 5:17-18.

352 HARMONIZING ALL THINGS FOR GOD'S GLORY

THE split between the faith which many profess
and their daily lives
deserves to be counted among the more serious errors

of our age. . . .
Therefore, let there be no false opposition
between professional and social activities on the one
  hand,
and religious life on the other. . . .
Christians should rather rejoice that,
following the example of Christ who worked as an
  artisan,
they are free to give proper exercise
to all their earthly activities
and to their humane, domestic, professional,
social and technical enterprises
by gathering them into one vital synthesis with religious
  values,
under whose supreme direction
all things are harmonized unto God's glory.

Constitution on the Church in the Modern World, no. 43.

See also: *Constitution on the Church,* no. 41, and *Decree on the Apostolate of the Laity,* no. 4.

Second General Grant

A PARTIAL indulgence is granted to the faithful, who in a spirit of faith and mercy give of themselves or of their goods to serve their brothers in need.

This second grant is intended to serve as an incentive to the faithful to perform more frequent acts of charity and mercy, thus following the example and obeying the command of Christ Jesus (John 13:15; Acts 10:38).

However, not all works of charity are thus indulgenced, but only those which "serve their brothers in need," in need, for example, of food or clothing for the body or of instruction or comfort for the soul.

353   SERVING CHRIST IN OTHERS

FOR I was hungry and you gave me to eat;
I was thirsty and you gave me to drink;
I was a stranger and you took me in;
naked and you covered me;
sick and you visited me;
I was in prison and you came to me. . . .
Amen I say to you,
as long as you did it for one of these,
the least of my brethren,
you did it for me (Matthew 25:35-36, 40).

See also Tobit 4:7-8 and Isaiah 58:7.

354   TRUE RELIGION

RELIGION pure and undefiled before God the
Father is this:
to give aid to orphans and widows in their tribulation,
and to keep oneself unspotted from this world.

(James 1:27)

See also James 2:15-16; John 13:34f; Romans 12:8, 10f, 13;
1 Corinthians 13:3; Galatians 6:10; Ephesians 5:2; 1 Thessalo-
nians 4:9; Hebrews 13:1; 1 Peter 1:22; 3:8f; 2 Peter 1:5, 7.

355   LOVE IN ACTION

HE WHO has the goods of this world
and sees his brother in need and closes his heart
to him,
how does the love of God abide in him?
My dear children,
let us not love in word,
neither with the tongue,
but in deed and in truth (1 John 3:17-18).

356   **SERVICE OF OTHERS FOR CHRIST**

MINDFUL of the Lord's saying:
  "By this will all men know that you are my
    disciples,
if you have love for one another" (John 13:35),
Christians cannot yearn for anything more ardently
than to serve the men of the modern world
with mounting generosity and success. . . .
Now the Father wills that in all men
we recognize Christ our brother
and love him effectively, in word and in deed.

Constitution on the Church in the Modern World, no. 93.

See also Decree on the Apostolate of the Laity, nos. 8 and 31c.

Third General Grant

A PARTIAL indulgence is granted to the faithful,
who in a spirit of penance voluntarily deprive
themselves of what is licit and pleasing to them.

This third grant is intended to move the faithful to
bridle their passions and thus learn to bring their bodies
into subjection and to conform themselves to Christ
in his poverty and suffering. (See Matthew 8:20 and
16:24.)

But self-denial will be more precious, if it is united
to charity, according to the teaching of St. Leo the
Great: "Let us give to virtue what we refuse to self-
indulgence. Let what we deny ourselves by fast—be
the refreshment of the poor."

357   **FOLLOWING OF CHRIST**

IF ANYONE wishes to come after me,
  let him deny himself,

and take up his cross daily,
and follow me (Luke 9:23).

358 CHRISTIAN TRAINING

AND everyone in a contest abstains from all things,
and they indeed to receive a perishable crown,
but we an imperishable.
I, therefore, so run as not without a purpose;
I so fight as not beating the air;
but I chastise my body and bring it into subjection.

(1 Corinthians 9:25-27)

359 DEATH AND GLORY WITH CHRIST

THIS saying is true:
If we have died with him,
we shall also live with him;
if we endure,
we shall also reign with him (2 Timothy 2:11-12).

*See also Matthew 10:30; Luke 13:5, 13; 14:27; Romans 8:13,
17; 2 Corinthians 4:10; Titus 2:12; 1 Peter 4:13.*

360 THREE WAYS OF DOING PENANCE

THE Church urges all the faithful
to live up to the divine commandment of penance
by afflicting their bodies by some acts of chastisement,
over and above the discomforts and annoyances of
everyday life. . . .
There are three principal ways
of satisfying the commandment to do penance,
handed down from ancient times—
prayer, fasting and works of charity—
even though abstinence from meat and fasting have
received special stress.

Paul VI: *Apostolic Constitution on Penance, no. III, e*
*See also Decree on Priestly Training, no. 9, and Dogmatic
Constitution on the Church, nos. 10 and 41.*

INDULGENCED WORKS AND PRAYERS

Indulgenced works and prayers ultimately have as their purpose to bring the faithful into a closer union with Christ and the Church through charity. This should also be the basic reason for us to do the work or say the prayer graced with indulgences.

B) OTHER GRANTS OF INDULGENCES

TO THE *three general grants of indulgences con-sidered above, a few others are here added. These it has seemed beneficial to include, either because of traditional esteem in the case of the old, or because appropriate to the needs of the present in the case of the new.*

All these grants complement one another and, while by the offer of an indulgence they move the faithful to perform works of piety, charity and penance, they at the same time bring them into an ever closer union through charity with Christ the Head and with the Church his body.

The individual works, described in the following pages, are each enriched with indulgences. The grant of a partial indulgence is sometimes expressly stated; very often, however, it is merely indicated by the words: Partial indulgence.

If a particular work, when performed in special cir-cumstances, is enriched with a plenary indulgence, this fact, as well as the special circumstances in which the work must be performed, is expressly noted each time; but other requirements for the gaining of a plenary in-dulgence are, for the sake of brevity, left understood.

Wherever a text of a prayer is given, it must be said to gain the indulgence. When a text is not given, any text can be used including the optional text given in the Supplement section, pp. 311-343.

For the complete list of grants, consult the *Enchiridion of Indulgences* mentioned on p. 264.

361   Direct, We Beg You, O Lord

DIRECT, we beg you, O Lord,
    our actions by your holy inspirations,
and carry them on by your gracious assistance,
that every prayer and work of ours may begin always
    with you,
and through you be happily ended. Amen.

Partial indulgence.

362-365   Acts of the Theologal Virtues and of Contrition

A partial indulgence *is granted to the faithful, who
recite devoutly, according to any legitimate formula,
the acts of the theologal virtues (faith, hope, charity)
and of contrition. Each act is indulgenced.* [See p. 312.]

366   Adoration of the Most Blessed Sacrament

A partial indulgence *is granted to the faithful, who
visit the Most Blessed Sacrament to adore it; a plenary
indulgence is granted, if the visit lasts for at least one
half an hour.* [See p. 334.]

367   Hidden God

HIDDEN God, devoutly I adore you,
    Truly present underneath these veils:
All my heart subdues itself before you,
Since it all before you faints and fails.

Not to sight, or taste, or touch be credit,
Hearing only do we trust secure;
I believe, for God the Son has said it—
Word of Truth that ever shall endure.

On the cross was veiled your Godhead's splendor,
Here your manhood lies hidden too;
Unto both alike my faith I render,
And, as sued the contrite thief, I sue.

Though I look not on your wounds with Thomas,
You, my Lord, and you, my God, I call:
Make me more and more believe your promise,
Hope in you, and love you over all.

O memorial of my Savior dying,
Living Bread, that gives life to man;
Make my soul, its life from you supplying,
Taste your sweetness, as on earth it can.

Deign, O Jesus, Pelican of heaven,
Me, a sinner, in your Blood to lave,
To a single drop of which is given
All the world from all its sin to save.

Contemplating, Lord, your hidden presence,
Grant me what I thirst for and implore,
In the revelation of your essence
To behold your glory evermore.

*A partial indulgence is granted to the faithful, who recite
devoutly the above hymn.*

368   We Have Come

WE HAVE come,
O Lord, Holy Spirit,
we have come before you,
hampered indeed by our many and grievous sins,
but for a special purpose gathered together in your
    name.

Come to us
and be with us
and enter our hearts.

Teach us what we are to do
and where we ought to tend;
show us what we must accomplish,
in order that, with your help,
we may be able to please you in all things.

May you alone be the author and the finisher of our
    judgments,
who alone with God the Father and his Son
possess a glorious name.

Do not allow us to disturb the order of justice,
you who love equity above all things.
Let not ignorance draw us into devious paths.
Let not partiality sway our minds
or respect of riches or persons pervert our judgment.

But unite us to you effectually
by the gift of your grace alone,
that we may be one in you and never forsake the
    truth;
inasmuch as we are gathered together in your name,
so may we in all things hold fast to justice tempered
    by mercy,
so that in this life
our judgment may in no wise be at variance with you
and in the life to come
we may attain to everlasting rewards for deeds well
    done.
Amen.

*This prayer, usually recited at the opening of a meeting to
discuss matters of common interest, is enriched with a partial
indulgence.*

369   ## To You, O Blessed Joseph

TO YOU, O blessed Joseph,
   do we come in our tribulation,
and having implored the help of your most holy
   spouse,
we confidently invoke your patronage also.
Through that charity which bound you
to the immaculate Virgin Mother of God
and through the paternal love
with which you embraced the Child Jesus,
we humbly beg you graciously to regard
the inheritance which Jesus Christ has purchased by
   his Blood,
and with your power and strength to aid us in our
   necessities.

O most watchful Guardian of the Holy Family,
defend the chosen children of Jesus Christ;
O most loving father,
ward off from us every contagion of error and cor-
   rupting influence;
O our most mighty protector,
be propitious to us and from heaven assist us
in our struggle with the power of darkness;
and, as once you rescued the Child Jesus from deadly
   peril,
so now protect God's Holy Church
from the snares of the enemy and from all adversity;
shield, too, each one of us by your constant protection,
so that, supported by your example and your aid,
we may be able to live piously,
to die holily,
and to obtain eternal happiness in heaven. Amen.

Partial indulgence.

370   We Give You Thanks

WE GIVE you thanks, Almighty God,
     for all your blessings:
who live and reign for ever and ever. Amen.

Partial indulgence.

371   Angel of God

ANGEL of God, my guardian dear,
     to whom his love commits me here,
enlighten and guard,
rule and guide me. Amen.

Partial indulgence.

372   The Angel of the Lord

a) During the year (outside of Paschal Season)

℣.   The Angel of the Lord declared unto Mary,
℞.   **And she conceived of the Holy Spirit.**

Hail Mary.

℣.   Behold the handmaid of the Lord,
℞.   **Be it done unto me according to your word.**

Hail Mary.

℣.   And the Word was made flesh,
℞.   **And dwelt among us.**

Hail Mary.

℣.   Pray for us, O holy Mother of God,
℞.   **That we may be made worthy of the promises
of Christ.**

Let us pray. Pour forth, we beg you, O Lord,
your grace into our hearts:
that we, to whom the Incarnation of Christ your Son
was made known by the message of an Angel,
may by his Passion and Cross
be brought to the glory of his Resurrection.
Through the same Christ our Lord. Amen.

373 Queen of Heaven

b) During Paschal Season

QUEEN of Heaven, rejoice, alleluia:
For he whom you merited to bear, alleluia,
Has risen, as he said, alleluia.
Pray for us to God, alleluia.

℣. Rejoice and be glad, O Virgin Mary, alleluia.

℟. **Because the Lord is truly risen, alleluia.**

Let us pray. O God, who by the Resurrection of your
   Son,
our Lord Jesus Christ,
granted joy to the whole world:
grant, we beg you,
that through the intercession of the Virgin Mary, his
   Mother,
we may lay hold of the joys of eternal life.
Through the same Christ our Lord. Amen.

A partial indulgence is granted to the faithful, who devoutly recite the above prayers according to the formula indicated for the time of the year.

It is a praiseworthy practice to recite these prayers in the early morning, at noon, and in the evening.

374   Soul of Christ

SOUL of Christ, sanctify me.
   Body of Christ, save me.
Blood of Christ, inebriate me.
Water from the side of Christ, wash me.
Passion of Christ, strengthen me.
O good Jesus, hear me.
Within your wounds, hide me.
Separated from you let me never be.
From the malignant enemy, defend me.
At the hour of death, call me.
To come to you, bid me,
That I may praise you in the company
Of your Saints, for all eternity. Amen.
   Partial indulgence.

375   Papal Blessing

A plenary indulgence is granted to the faithful, who piously and devoutly receive, even by radio transmission, the Blessing of the Sovereign Pontiff, when imparted to Rome and the World.[*See p. 334.*]

376   Act of Spiritual Communion

An act of spiritual Communion, according to any pious formula, is enriched with a partial indulgence. [*See p. 313.*]

[86b]   I Believe in God

See Creed for Mass, no. 86b, p. 97.

[43]   **Out of the Depths**

A partial indulgence *is granted to the faithful, who piously recite the psalm* Out of the depths, (Psalm 130). [*See no.* [43], p. 57.]

377   **Christian Doctrine**

A partial indulgence *is granted to the faithful, who take part in teaching or in learning christian doctrine.*

N.B.: *One who in a spirit of faith and charity teaches christian doctrine can gain a* partial indulgence *according to the second of the three general grants of indulgences; see above* (p. 268).

This new grant confirms the partial indulgence *in favor of the teacher of christian doctrine and extends it to the learner.* [*See p.* 335.]

378   **Lord God Almighty**

L ORD, God Almighty,
  you have brought us safely to the beginning of
this day.
Defend us today by your mighty power,
that we may not fall into any sin,
but that all our words may so proceed
and all our thoughts and actions be so directed,
as to be always just in your sight.
Through Christ our Lord. Amen.

Partial indulgence.

379   Look Down Upon Me, Good and Gentle Jesus

LOOK down upon me,
   good and gentle Jesus,
while before your face I humbly kneel,
and with burning soul pray and beseech you
to fix deep in my heart
lively sentiments of faith, hope and charity,
true contrition for my sins,
and a firm purpose of amendment,
while I contemplate with great love and tender pity
your five wounds,
pondering over them within me,
calling to mind the words which David, your prophet,
said of you, my good Jesus:
"They have pierced my hands and my feet;
they have numbered all my bones" (Psalm 22:17-18).

A plenary indulgence *is granted on each Friday of Lent and Passiontide to the faithful, who after Communion piously recite the above prayer before an image of Christ crucified; on other days of the year the indulgence* is partial.

380   Eucharistic Congress

A plenary indulgence *is granted to the faithful, who devoutly participate in the customary solemn eucharistic rite at the close of a Eucharistic Congress.* [*See p.* 335.]

381   Hear Us

HEAR us,
   Lord, holy Father, almighty and eternal God;
and graciously send your holy angel from heaven
to watch over, to cherish, to protect,

to abide with, and to defend
all who dwell in this house.
Through Christ our Lord. Amen.

Partial indulgence.

382   **Spiritual Exercises**

A plenary indulgence *is granted to the faithful, who
spend at least three whole days in the spiritual exercises of a retreat.* [See p. 336.]

383   **Most Sweet Jesus—Act of Reparation**

MOST sweet Jesus,
     whose overflowing charity for men is requited
by so much forgetfulness, negligence and contempt,
behold us prostrate before you,
eager to repair by a special act of homage
the cruel indifference and injuries
to which your loving Heart is everywhere subject.

Mindful, alas! that we ourselves have had a share
in such great indignities,
which we now deplore from the depths of our hearts,
we humbly ask your pardon
and declare our readiness to atone by voluntary expia-
     tion,
not only for our own personal offenses,
but also for the sins of those, who,
straying far from the path of salvation,
refuse in their obstinate infidelity to follow you,
their Shepherd and Leader,
or, renouncing the promises of their baptism,
have cast off the yoke of your law.

We are now resolved to expiate
each and every deplorable outrage committed against
     you;

we are now determined to make amends
for the manifold offenses against Christian modesty
in unbecoming dress and behavior,
for all the foul seductions laid
to ensnare the feet of the innocent,
for the frequent violations of Sundays and holydays,
and the shocking blasphemies uttered against you
and your Saints.

We wish also to make amends for the insults
to which your Vicar on earth and your priests are subjected,
for the profanation,
by conscious neglect or terrible acts of sacrilege,
of the very Sacrament of your divine love,
and lastly for the public crimes of nations
who resist the rights and teaching authority of the
Church
which you have founded.

Would that we were able
to wash away such abominations with our blood.
We now offer,
in reparation for these violations of your divine honor,
the satisfaction you once made
to your Eternal Father on the cross
and which you continue to renew daily on our altars;
we offer it in union with the acts of atonement
of your Virgin Mother and all the Saints
and of the pious faithful on earth;
and we sincerely promise to make recompense,
as far as we can with the help of your grace,
for all neglect of your great love
and for the sins we and others have committed in the
past.
Henceforth, we will live a life of unswerving faith,
of purity of conduct,

of perfect observance of the precepts of the Gospel
and especially that of charity.
We promise to the best of our power
to prevent others from offending you
and to bring as many as possible to follow you.

O loving Jesus,
through the intercession of the Blessed Virgin Mother,
our model in reparation,
deign to receive the voluntary offering we make
of this act of expiation;
and by the crowning gift of perseverance
keep us faithful unto death
in our duty and the allegiance we owe to you,
so that we may all one day come to that happy home,
where with the Father and the Holy Spirit
you live and reign, God,
forever and ever. Amen.

*A partial indulgence is granted to the faithful, who piously
recite the above act of reparation. A plenary indulgence is
granted if it is publicly recited on the feast of the Most Sacred
Heart of Jesus.*

384 Most Sweet Jesus, Redeemer—
Act of Dedication of the Human Race to
Jesus Christ King

MOST sweet Jesus,
Redeemer of the human race,
look down upon us humbly prostrate before you.
We are yours, and yours we wish to be;
but to be more surely united with you,
behold, each one of us freely consecrates himself today
to your Most Sacred Heart.
Many indeed have never known you;
many, too, despising your precepts,

have rejected you.
Have mercy on them all, most merciful Jesus,
and draw them to your Sacred Heart.

Be King, O Lord,
not only of the faithful who have never forsaken you,
but also of the prodigal children who have abandoned
    you;
grant that they may quickly return to their Father's
    house,
lest they die of wretchedness and hunger.

Be King of those who are deceived by erroneous opin-
    ions,
or whom discord keeps aloof,
and call them back to the harbor of truth
and the unity of faith,
so that soon there may be but one flock and one
    Shepherd.

Grant, O Lord, to your Church
assurance of freedom and immunity from harm;
give tranquility of order to all nations;
make the earth resound from pole to pole with one cry:
Praise to the divine Heart that wrought our salvation;
to it be glory and honor for ever. Amen.

*A partial indulgence is granted to the faithful, who piously
recite the above Act of Dedication of the Human Race to
Jesus Christ King. A plenary indulgence is granted, if it is
recited publicly on the feast of our Lord Jesus Christ King.*

385   The Moment of Death

*To the faithful in danger of death, who cannot be
assisted by a priest to bring them the sacraments and
impart the Apostolic Blessing with its plenary indulgence (see can. 468, §2 of Code of Canon Law), Holy
Mother Church nevertheless grants a plenary indulgence*

to be acquired at the point of death, provided they are properly disposed and have been in the habit of reciting some prayers during their lifetime. The use of a crucifix or a cross to gain this indulgence is praiseworthy.

The condition: provided they have been in the habit of reciting some prayers during their lifetime *supplies in such cases for the three usual conditions required for the gaining of a plenary indulgence.*

The plenary indulgence at the point of death can be acquired by the faithful, even if they have already obtained another plenary indulgence on the same day. [See p. 336.]

386-391   Litanies

The following Litanies are each enriched with a partial indulgence: *the Most Holy Name of Jesus, the Most Sacred Heart of Jesus, the Most Precious Blood of our Lord Jesus Christ, the Blessed Virgin Mary, St. Joseph, All Saints,* [See p. 314.]

[57]   Magnificat

A partial indulgence *is granted to the faithful, who piously recite the canticle of the Magnificat.* [See no. 57, p. 70.]

392   Mary, Mother of Grace

MARY, Mother of grace,
  Mother of mercy,
Shield me from the enemy
And receive me at the hour of my death.

Partial indulgence.

393   Remember, O Most Gracious Virgin Mary

REMEMBER, O most gracious Virgin Mary,
that never was it known
that anyone who fled to your protection,
implored your help or sought your intercession,
was left unaided.
Inspired with this confidence,
I fly to you, O Virgin of virgins, my Mother;
to you do I come,
before you I stand, sinful and sorrowful.
O Mother of the Word Incarnate,
despise not my petitions,
but in your mercy hear and answer me. Amen.

Partial indulgence.

[35]   Have Mercy on Me

See Psalm 51, p. 49.

394   Novena Devotions

A partial indulgence is granted to the faithful, who devoutly take part in the pious exercises of a public novena before the feast of Christmas or Pentecost or the Immaculate Conception of the Blessed Virgin Mary.
[*See pp.* 337 *and* 937ff.]

395   Use of Articles of Devotion

The faithful, who devoutly use an article of devotion *(crucifix or cross, rosary, scapular or medal) properly blessed by any priest, obtain a partial indulgence.*

But if the article of devotion has been blessed by the Sovereign Pontiff or by any Bishop, the faithful, using it, can also gain a plenary indulgence on the feast of the Holy Apostles, Peter and Paul, provided they also make a profession of faith according to any legitimate formula. [See p. 337.]

396 Prayer for Sacerdotal or Religious Vocations

A partial indulgence *is granted to the faithful, who recite a prayer, approved by ecclesiastical Authority, for the above intention.* [See pp. 330 and 905-906.]

397 Mental Prayer

A partial indulgence *is granted to the faithful, who piously spend some time in mental prayer.* [See p. 337.]

398 Let Us Pray for Our Sovereign Pontiff

℣. Let us pray for our Sovereign Pontiff N.

℟. **The Lord preserve him and give him life, and make him blessed upon the earth, and deliver him not up to the will of his enemies.**

Partial indulgence.

399 O Sacred Banquet

O SACRED banquet,
in which Christ is received,
the memory of his Passion is renewed,
the mind is filled with grace,
and a pledge of future glory is given to us.

Partial indulgence.

400   **Assistance at Sacred Preaching**

A partial indulgence *is granted to the faithful, who assist with devotion and attention at the sacred preaching of the Word of God.*

A plenary indulgence *is granted to the faithful, who during the time of a Mission have heard some of the sermons and are present for the solemn close of the Mission.* [*See p. 338.*]

401   **First Communion**

A plenary indulgence *is granted to the faithful, when they receive Communion for the first time, or when they assist at the sacred ceremonies of a First Communion.* [*See p. 338.*]

402   **First Mass of Newly-Ordained Priests**

A plenary indulgence *is granted to a priest on the occasion of the first Mass he celebrates with some solemnity and to the faithful who devoutly assist at the same Mass.* [*See p. 339.*]

403   **Prayer for Unity of the Church**

A LMIGHTY and merciful God,
    you willed that the different nations
should become one people through your Son.
Grant in your kindness
that those who glory in being known as Christians
may put aside their differences
and become one in truth and charity,
and that all men, enlightened by the true faith,

may be united in fraternal communion in the one
Church.
Through Christ our Lord. Amen.

Partial indulgence.

404   Monthly Recollection

A partial indulgence *is granted to the faithful, who
take part in a monthly retreat.* [*See p.* 339.]

405   Eternal Rest

ETERNAL rest grant to them,
    O Lord,
and let perpetual light shine upon them.
May they rest in peace.

Partial indulgence, *applicable only to the souls in purgatory.*
See also pp. 989ff.

406   May It Please You, O Lord

MAY it please you,
    O Lord,
to reward with eternal life
all those who do good to us for your Name's sake.
Amen.

Partial indulgence.

407   Recitation of the Marian Rosary

A plenary indulgence *is granted, if the Rosary is
recited in a church or public oratory or in a family
group, a religious Community or pious Association; a
partial indulgence is granted in other circumstances.*

*Now the Rosary is a certain formula of prayer, which
is made up of fifteen decades of "Hail Marys" with an
"Our Father" before each decade, and in which the*

recitation of each decade is accompanied by pious meditation on a particular mystery of our Redemption.

The name "Rosary," however, is commonly used in reference to only a third part of the fifteen decades.

The gaining of the plenary indulgence is regulated by the following norms:

1) The recitation of a third part only of the Rosary suffices; but the five decades must be recited continuously.

2) The vocal recitation must be accompanied by pious meditation on the mysteries.

3) In public recitation the mysteries must be announced in the manner customary in the place; for private recitation, however, it suffices if the vocal recitation is accompanied by meditation on the mysteries.

[See pp. 331 and 962.]

408   Jubilees of Sacerdotal Ordination

A plenary indulgence is granted to a priest, who on the 25th, 50th and 60th anniversary of his Ordination renews before God his resolve to fulfill faithfully the duties of his vocation.

If the priest celebrates a jubilee Mass in some solemn manner, the faithful, who assist at it, can acquire a plenary indulgence. [See p. 340.]

409   Reading of Sacred Scripture

A partial indulgence is granted to the faithful, who with the veneration due the divine word make a spiritual reading from Sacred Scripture. A plenary indulgence is granted, if this reading is continued for at least one half an hour. [See p. 341.]

410 **Hail, Holy Queen**

HAIL, holy Queen, Mother of mercy;
hail, our life, our sweetness and our hope.
To you do we cry,
poor banished children of Eve.
To you do we send up our sighs,
mourning and weeping in this valley of tears.
Turn then, most gracious Advocate,
your eyes of mercy toward us.
And after this our exile
show unto us the blessed fruit of your womb, Jesus.
O clement, O loving, O sweet Virgin Mary.

Partial indulgence.

411 **Holy Mary, Help the Helpless**

HOLY Mary,
help the helpless,
strengthen the fearful,
comfort the sorrowful,
pray for the people,
plead for the clergy,
intercede for all women consecrated to God;
may all who keep your sacred commemoration
experience the might of your assistance.

Partial indulgence.

412 **Holy Apostles Peter and Paul**

HOLY Apostles Peter and Paul,
intercede for us.
Guard your people,
who rely on the patronage of your apostles Peter and
Paul,

O Lord,
and keep them under your continual protection.
Through Christ our Lord. Amen.

Partial indulgence.

413   Veneration of the Saints

A partial indulgence *is granted to the faithful, who on the feast of any Saint recite in his honor the oration of the Missal or any other approved by legitimate Authority.* [See p. 342.]

414   Sign of the Cross

A partial indulgence *is granted to the faithful, who devoutly sign themselves with the sign of the cross, while saying the customary words.*

IN THE name of the Father,
and of the Son,
and of the Holy Spirit. Amen.

415   We Fly to Your Patronage

WE FLY to your patronage,
O holy Mother of God;
despise not our petitions in our necessities,
but deliver us always from all dangers,
O glorious and blessed Virgin.

Partial indulgence.

416   Diocesan Synod

A plenary indulgence *is granted to the faithful, who during the time of the diocesan Synod devoutly visit the church, in which the Synod is being held, and there recite one Our Father and the Creed.* [See p. 342.]

[201-202] **Down in Adoration Falling**

A partial indulgence is granted to the faithful, who devoutly recite the above hymn. But a plenary indulgence is granted on Holy Thursday and on the feast of Corpus Christi, if it is recited in a solemn manner.
[*See nos. 201-202, p. 180.*]

417 **The Te Deum**

YOU are God: we praise you;
You are the Lord: we acclaim you;
You are the eternal Father:
All creation worships you.

To you all angels, all the powers of heaven,
Cherubim and Seraphim, sing in endless praise:
Holy, holy, holy, Lord, God of power and might,
heaven and earth are full of your glory.

The glorious company of apostles praise you.
The noble fellowship of prophets praise you.
The white-robed army of martyrs praise you.

Throughout the world the holy Church acclaims you:
Father, of majesty unbounded,
your true and only Son, worthy of all worship,
and the Holy Spirit, advocate and guide.

You, Christ, are the king of glory,
the eternal Son of the Father.

When you became man to set us free
you did not spurn the Virgin's womb.

You overcame the sting of death,
and opened the kingdom of heaven to all believers.

You are seated at God's right hand in glory.
We believe that you will come, and be our judge.

Come then, Lord, and help your people,
bought with the price of your own blood,
and bring us with your saints
to glory everlasting.

℣.   Save your people, Lord, and bless your inheritance.

℟.   **Govern and uphold them now and always.**

℣.   Day by day we bless you.

℟.   **We praise your name for ever.**

℣.   Keep us today, Lord, from all sin.

℟.   **Have mercy on us, Lord, have mercy.**

℣.   Lord, show us your love and mercy;

℟.   **for we put our trust in you.**

℣.   In you, Lord, is our hope:

℟.   **and we shall never hope in vain.**

A partial indulgence is granted to the faithful, who recite the Te Deum in thanksgiving. But a plenary indulgence is granted, if the hymn is recited publicly on the last day of the year.

418   Come, Holy Spirit, Creator Blest

COME, Holy Spirit, Creator blest,
    And in our souls take up your rest;
Come with your grace and heavenly aid
To fill the hearts which you have made.

O Comforter, to you we cry,
O heavenly gift of God Most High,
O fount of life and fire of love,
And sweet anointing from above.

You in your sevenfold gifts are known;
You, finger of God's hand we own;
You, promise of the Father, you
Who do the tongue with power imbue.

Kindle our senses from above,
And make our hearts o'erflow with love;
With patience firm and virtue high
The weakness of our flesh supply.

Far from us drive the foe we dread,
And grant us your peace instead;
So shall we not, with you for guide,
Turn from the path of life aside.

Oh, may your grace on us bestow
The Father and the Son to know;
And you, through endless times confessed,
Of both the eternal Spirit blest.

Now to the Father and the Son,
Who rose from death, be glory given,
With you, O holy Comforter,
Henceforth by all in earth and heaven. Amen.

A partial indulgence is granted to the faithful, who devoutly recite the hymn Come, Holy Spirit, Creator Blest. *But a* plenary indulgence *is granted, if the hymn is recited publicly on the 1st of January and on the feast of Pentecost.*

419   Come, Holy Spirit

COME, Holy Spirit,
     fill the hearts of your faithful
and kindle in them the fire of your love.

Partial indulgence.

420   Exercise of the Way of the Cross

A plenary indulgence *is granted to the faithful, who make the pious exercise of the* Way of the Cross.

In the pious exercise of the Way of the Cross *we recall anew the sufferings, which the divine Redeemer*

endured, while going from the praetorium of Pilate, where he was condemned to death, to the mount of Calvary, where he died on the cross for our salvation.
[*See pp.* 332 *and* 952.]

421 Visit to the Parochial Church

A plenary indulgence *is granted to the faithful, who devoutly visit the parochial church:*

—on the titular feast;
—on the 2nd of August, when the indulgence of the "Portiuncula" occurs.

Both indulgences can be acquired either on the day designated above or on some other day designated by the Ordinary for the benefit of the faithful.

The same indulgences apply to the Cathedral church and, where there is one, to a Co-Cathedral church, even if they are not parochial churches; they apply to quasi-parochial churches also. [*See p.* 342.]

422 Visit to a Church or an Altar on the Day of Its Consecration

A plenary indulgence *is granted to the faithful, who visit a church or an altar on the day itself of its consecration, and there recite one* Our Father *and the* Creed.
[*See p.* 343.]

423 Visit to a Church or Oratory on All Souls Day

A plenary indulgence, *applicable only to the Souls in Purgatory, is granted to the faithful, who on the day dedicated to the Commemoration of all the faithful*

departed piously visit a church, a public oratory or—
for those entitled to use it—a semipublic oratory. [See p. 343.]

424 Visit to a Church or Oratory of Religious on the Feast of the Holy Founder

A plenary indulgence *is granted to the faithful, who devoutly visit a church or oratory of Religious on the Feast of the canonized Founder, and there recite one* Our Father *and the Creed.* [See p. 344.]

424a Renewal of Baptismal Promises

A partial indulgence *is granted to the faithful, who renew their baptismal promises according to any formula in use; but a* plenary indulgence *is granted, if this is done in the celebration of the Paschal Vigil or on the anniversary of one's baptism.* [See p. 332.]

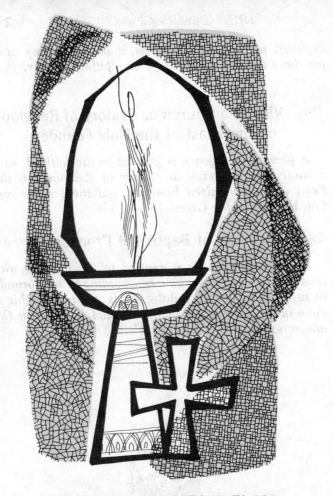

INVOCATIONS — DIRECT LINE TO GOD

Pious invocations are like our own private line to
God. We can get in touch with him at any time and
in any circumstance, simply by raising our hearts
and minds to him. The invocation can help us tune
into God, but the actual encounter must come from
deep within us.

C) PIOUS INVOCATIONS

IN REGARD to any invocation, the following observations are to be noted:

1) An invocation, as far as indulgences are concerned, is no longer considered a work, distinct and complete in itself, but as complementing an action, by which the faithful raise their heart and mind with humble confidence to God in performing their duties or bearing the trials of life. Hence, a pious invocation perfects the inward elevation; both together are as a precious jewel joined to one's ordinary actions to adorn them, or as salt added to them to season them properly.

2) That invocation is to be preferred which is best suited to the particular situation and one's personal dispositions, whether it is one that comes spontaneously to mind or is chosen from those approved through long-standing use by the faithful and brought together in the following brief list.

3) An invocation can be of the briefest kind, expressed in one or few words or only thought of mentally.

The following have been taken from pp. 81-84 of the Enchiridion of Indulgences.

Examples of Very Brief Invocations

425 (1)

MY God.

425 (2)

FATHER *(see Romans 8:15 and Galatians 4:6).*

425 (3)

MAY Jesus Christ be praised.

425 (4)

LORD, I believe in you.

425 (5)

I ADORE you.

425 (6)

I PLACE my trust in you.

425 (7)

I LOVE you.

425 (8)

ALL for you.

425 (9)

I THANK you.

425 (10)

T HANKS be to God.

425 (11)

MAY God be blessed.

425 (12)

LET us bless the Lord.

425 (13)

YOUR kingdom come.

425 (14)

YOUR will be done.

425 (15)

AS THE Lord wills (*see Job 1:21*).

425 (16)

O GOD, help me.

425 (17)

COMFORT me.

425 (18)

GRACIOUSLY hear me.

425 (19)

HEAR my prayer.

425 (20)

SAVE me.

425 (21)

HAVE mercy on me.

425 (22)

O LORD, spare me.

425 (23)

DO NOT permit me to be separated from you.

425 (24)

DO NOT abandon me.

425 (25)

HAIL, Mary.

425 (26)

GLORY to God in the highest.

425 (27)

GREAT are you, O Lord (*Judith* 16:16; *see Psalm* 86:10).

Examples of Invocations in Customary Use

425a (1)

WE ADORE you, O Christ,
and we bless you;
because by your holy Cross
you have redeemed the world.

425a (2)

MAY the Holy Trinity be blessed.

425a (3)

CHRIST conquers!
Christ reigns!
Christ commands!

425a (4)

O HEART of Jesus,
burning with love for us,
inflame our hearts with love for you.

425a (5)

O HEART of Jesus,
I place my trust in you.

425a (6)

O HEART of Jesus,
all for you.

425a (7)

MOST Sacred Heart of Jesus,
have mercy on us.

425a (8)

MY GOD
and my all.

425a (9)

O GOD,
have mercy on me, a sinner *(Luke 18:13)*.

425a (10)

GRANT that I may praise you,
O sacred Virgin;
give me strength against your enemies.

425a (11)

TEACH me to do your will,
because you are my God *(Psalm 143:10)*.

425a (12)

O LORD,
increase our faith *(Luke 17:5)*.

425a (13)

O LORD,
may we be of one mind in truth
and of one heart in charity.

425a (14)

O LORD,
save us, we are perishing *(Matthew 8:25)*.

425a (15)

MY LORD
and my God (*John* 20:28).

425a (16)

SWEET Heart of Mary,
be my salvation.

425a (17)

GLORY be to the Father,
and to the Son,
and to the Holy Spirit.

425a (18)

JESUS, Mary, Joseph.

425a (19)

JESUS, Mary, Joseph, I give you my heart and my soul.
Jesus, Mary, Joseph, assist me in my last agony.
Jesus, Mary, Joseph, may I sleep and rest in peace with
you.

425a (20)

JESUS, meek and humble of heart,
make my heart like your Heart.

425a (21)

MAY the Most Blessed Sacrament
be praised and adored forever.

425a (22)

STAY with us,
O Lord (*Luke* 24:29).

425a (23)

MOTHER of Sorrows,
   pray for us.

425a (24)

MY Mother,
   my Hope.

425a (25)

SEND, O Lord,
   laborers into your harvest (*see Matthew* 9:38).

425a (26)

MAY the Virgin Mary together with her loving Child
   bless us.

425a (27)

HAIL, O Cross,
   our only hope.

425a (28)

ALL you holy men and women of God,
   intercede for us.

425a (29)

PRAY for us, O Holy Mother of God,
   that we may be made worthy of the promises of
      Christ.

425a (30)

FATHER, into your hands
   I commend my spirit (*Luke* 23:46; *see Psalm* 31:6).

425a (31)

M ERCIFUL Lord Jesus,
grant them everlasting rest.

425a (32)

Q UEEN conceived without original sin,
pray for us.

425a (33)

H OLY Mother of God, Mary ever Virgin,
intercede for us.

425a (34)

H OLY Mary,
pray for us.

425a (35)

Y OU are the Christ,
the Son of the living God (*Matthew 16:16*).

425a (36)

M Y JESUS,
mercy.

425a (37)

V IRGIN Mary, Mother of God,
make us saints.

THE VALUE OF INDULGENCED PRAYERS

All prayers enable us to carry on a dialogue with God. Indulgenced prayers have an added value because they have been time-tested by the Church and found to be very effective in helping people talk with God or the Saints. They also inculcate spiritual sentiments that work to lessen or do away with temporal punishment due to sin.

SUPPLEMENT OF PRAYERS

THIS section of the part on prayers from the Enchiridion of Indulgences contains prayer texts that can be used to obtain the indulgences already mentioned. However, these are not the only texts that can be used to gain such indulgences. Others that have the same content can also be used.

The first group is made up of prayer texts found in the Supplement of the Enchiridion itself. As such they can be said to be official texts for gaining the indulgences specified by the bracketed number above them.

The second group is made up of prayer texts not found in the Supplement. They are given as unofficial but approved texts that can aid in the positing of the work to which the indulgence is attached.

The value of indulgenced prayers, besides the fact of indulgences themselves, is that they provide us with the mind of the Church. When praying such texts we can be sure that they reproduce sentiments that the Church wants the faithful to cultivate and possess. In such cases, we need never worry that we are praying for the wrong thing.

Optional Texts
From the Supplement

[362]   **Act of Faith**

O MY God,
     who are infallible Truth and can neither deceive
  nor be deceived,
I firmly believe all that you have revealed
and propose to my belief through your holy Church,
because you have revealed it.

I believe that you are
one in nature and three in Persons:
the Father, the Son, and the Holy Spirit.
I believe that you are the Creator of all things
and that you reward the just for all eternity in heaven
and punish the wicked for all eternity in hell.

I believe that Jesus Christ is the Son of God made man,
that he suffered and died for my sins
and rose from the dead in glory,
and that it is only in him through the Holy Spirit
that eternal life is given to men.

I believe in fine all that your holy Church believes.
I thank you for having called me to the true faith,
and I protest that with the help of your grace
I will live and die in this holy faith.

[363]   **Act of Hope**

O MY God,
     trusting in your promises
and because you are faithful, powerful and merciful,
I hope,
through the merits of Jesus Christ,
for the pardon of my sins,
final perseverance and the blessed glory of heaven.

[364]   **Act of Love**

O MY God,
   because you are infinite goodness
and worthy of infinite love,
I love you with my whole heart above all things,
and for love of you I love my fellowmen as myself.

[365]   **Act of Contrition**

O MY God,
   I repent with my whole heart of all my sins,
and I detest them,
because I have deserved the loss of heaven
and the pains of hell,
but most of all because I have offended you,
infinite Goodness.
I firmly purpose with the help of your grace,
which I pray you to grant me now and always,
to do penance
and rather to die than offend you again.
I purpose also to receive the holy Sacraments
during my life and at my death.

[376]   **An Act of Spiritual Communion**

MY Jesus,
   I believe that you are in the Blessed Sacrament.
I love you above all things,
and I long for you in my soul.
Since I cannot now receive you sacramentally,
come at least spiritually into my heart.
As though you have already come,
I embrace you and unite myself entirely to you;
never permit me to be separated from you.

[386] Litany of the Most Holy Name of Jesus

LORD, have mercy.
Christ, have mercy.
Lord, have mercy.
Jesus, hear us.
Jesus, graciously hear us.
God, the Father of heaven, *have mercy on us.*[*]
God the Son, Redeemer of the world,
God, the Holy Spirit,
Holy Trinity, one God,
Jesus Son of the living God,
Jesus, splendor of the Father,
Jesus, brightness of eternal light,
Jesus, king of glory,
Jesus, sun of justice,
Jesus, Son of the Virgin Mary,
Jesus, most amiable,
Jesus, most admirable,
Jesus, the mighty God,
Jesus, Father of the world to come,
Jesus, angel of great counsel,
Jesus, most powerful,
Jesus, most patient,
Jesus, most obedient,
Jesus, meek and humble of heart,
Jesus, lover of chastity,
Jesus, our lover,
Jesus, God of peace,
Jesus, author of life,
Jesus, model of virtues,

Jesus, zealous for souls,
Jesus, our God,
Jesus, our refuge,
Jesus, father of the poor,
Jesus, treasure of the faithful,
Jesus, good shepherd,
Jesus, true light,
Jesus, eternal wisdom,
Jesus, infinite goodness,
Jesus, our way and our life,
Jesus, joy of the angels,
Jesus, king of the patriarchs,
Jesus, master of the apostles,
Jesus, teacher of the evangelists,
Jesus, strength of martyrs,
Jesus, light of confessors,
Jesus, purity of virgins,
Jesus, crown of all saints,
Be merciful, *spare us, O Jesus!*
Be merciful, *graciously hear us, O Jesus!*
From all evil, *deliver us, O Jesus.*[**]
From all sin,
From your wrath,
From the snares of the devil,
From the spirit of fornication,
From everlasting death,
From the neglect of your inspirations,
Through the mystery of your holy incarnation,

[*] Have mercy on us *is repeated after each invocation.*

[**] Deliver us, O Jesus, *is repeated after each invocation.*

Through your nativity,
Through your infancy,
Through your most divine life,
Through your labors,
Through your agony and passion,
Through your cross and dereliction,
Through your sufferings,
Through your death and burial,
Through your resurrection,
Through your ascension,
Through your institution of the most holy Eucharist,
Through your joys,
Through your glory,

Lamb of God, you take away the sins of the world; *spare us, O Jesus!*

Lamb of God, you take away the sins of the world; *graciously hear us, O Jesus!*

Lamb of God, you take away the sins of the world, *have mercy on us, O Jesus!*

Jesus, hear us.
Jesus, graciously hear us.

[386a]

LET us pray.
O Lord Jesus Christ, you have said,
"Ask and you shall receive;
seek, and you shall find;
knock, and it shall be opened to you";
mercifully attend to our supplications,
and grant us the grace of your most divine love,
that we may love you with all our hearts,
and in all our words and actions,
and never cease to praise you.

Make us, O Lord,
to have a perpetual fear and love of your holy name,
for you never fail to govern
those whom you solidly establish in your love.
You, who live and reign forever and ever.

℟. **Amen.**

[387] ## Litany of the Most Sacred Heart of Jesus

LORD, have mercy.
Christ, have mercy.
Lord, have mercy.
Christ, hear us.
Christ, graciously hear us.
God, the Father of heaven, *have mercy on us.**
God the Son, Redeemer of the world,
God, the Holy Spirit,
Holy Trinity, one God,
Heart of Jesus, Son of the eternal Father,
Heart of Jesus, formed by the Holy Spirit in the womb of the Virgin Mother,
Heart of Jesus, substantially united to the Word of God,
Heart of Jesus, of infinite majesty,
Heart of Jesus, sacred temple of God,
Heart of Jesus, tabernacle of the Most High,
Heart of Jesus, house of God and gate of heaven,
Heart of Jesus, burning furnace of charity,
Heart of Jesus, abode of justice and love,
Heart of Jesus, full of goodness and love,
Heart of Jesus, abyss of all virtues,

Heart of Jesus, most worthy of all praise,
Heart of Jesus, king and center of all hearts,
Heart of Jesus, in whom are all the treasures of wisdom and knowledge,
Heart of Jesus, in whom dwells the fullness of divinity,
Heart of Jesus, in whom the Father was well pleased,
Heart of Jesus, of whose fullness we have all received,
Heart of Jesus, desire of the everlasting hills,
Heart of Jesus, patient and most merciful,
Heart of Jesus, enriching all who invoke you,
Heart of Jesus, fountain of life and holiness,
Heart of Jesus, propitiation for our sins,
Heart of Jesus, loaded down with opprobrium,
Heart of Jesus, bruised for our offenses,
Heart of Jesus, obedient to death,
Heart of Jesus, pierced with a lance,
Heart of Jesus, source of all consolation,

* Have mercy on us *is repeated after each invocation.*

Heart of Jesus, our life and resurrection,

Heart of Jesus, our peace and reconciliation,

Heart of Jesus, victim for our sins,

Heart of Jesus, salvation of those who trust in you,

Heart of Jesus, hope of those who die in you,

Heart of Jesus, delight of all the saints,

Lamb of God, you take away the sins of the world; *spare us, O Lord.*

Lamb of God, you take away the sins of the world; *graciously hear us, O Lord.*

Lamb of God, you take away the sins of the world; *have mercy on us.*

℣. Jesus, meek and humble of heart.

℟. *Make our hearts like to yours.*

[387a]

LET us pray.
    Almighty and eternal God,
look upon the Heart of your most beloved Son
and upon the praises and satisfaction
which he offers you in the name of sinners;
and to those who implore your mercy,
in your great goodness, grant forgiveness
in the name of the same Jesus Christ, your Son,
who lives and reigns with you forever and ever.

℟. **Amen.**

[388]   **Litany of the Most Precious Blood of Jesus**

LORD, have mercy.
    Christ have mercy.
Lord, have mercy.
Christ, hear us.
Christ, graciously hear us.
God, the Father of heaven,
    have mercy on us.

God the Son, Redeemer of the world,
    have mercy on us.
God, the Holy Spirit,
    have mercy on us.
Holy Trinity, one God,
    have mercy on us.

Blood of Christ, only-begotten Son of the eternal Father, *save us.* *

Blood of Christ, incarnate Word of God,

Blood of Christ, of the new and eternal Testament,

Blood of Christ, falling upon the earth in the agony,

Blood of Christ, shed profusely in the scourging,

Blood of Christ, flowing forth in the crowning with thorns,

Blood of Christ, poured out on the cross,

Blood of Christ, price of our salvation,

Blood of Christ, without which there is no forgiveness,

Blood of Christ, Eucharistic drink and refreshment of souls,

Blood of Christ, stream of mercy,

Blood of Christ, victor over demons,

Blood of Christ, courage of martyrs,

Blood of Christ, strength of confessors,

Blood of Christ, bringing forth virgins,

Blood of Christ, help of those in peril,

Blood of Christ, relief of the burdened,

Blood of Christ, solace in sorrow,

Blood of Christ, hope of the penitent,

Blood of Christ, consolation of the dying,

Blood of Christ, peace and tenderness of hearts,

Blood of Christ, pledge of eternal life,

Blood of Christ, freeing souls from purgatory,

Blood of Christ, most worthy of all glory and honor,

Lamb of God, you take away the sins of the world; *spare us, O Lord!*

Lamb of God, you take away the sins of the world; *graciously hear us, O Lord!*

Lamb of God, you take away the sins of the world; *have mercy on us.*

℣. You have redeemed us, O Lord, in your Blood.

℟. *And made us, for our God, a kingdom.*

* *Save us is repeated after each invocation.*

[388a]

L ET us pray.
   Almighty and eternal God,
you have appointed your only-begotten Son
the Redeemer of the world,
and willed to be appeased by his Blood.
Grant, we beg of you,
that we may worthily adore this price of our salvation,
and through its power
be safeguarded from the evils of the present life,
so that we may rejoice in its fruits forever in heaven.
Through the same Christ our Lord. ℟. **Amen.**

[389] Litany of the Blessed Virgin Mary

L ORD, have mercy.
   Christ, have mercy.
Lord, have mercy.
Christ, hear us.
Christ, graciously hear us.
God, the Father of heaven,
   have mercy on us.
God the Son, Redeemer of
   the world,
   have mercy on us.
God the Holy Spirit,
   have mercy on us.
Holy Trinity, one God,
   have mercy on us.
Holy Mary, *pray for us.* *
Holy Mother of God,
Holy Virgin of virgins,
Mother of Christ,
Mother of divine grace,
Mother most pure,

Mother most chaste,
Mother inviolate,
Mother undefiled,
Mother most amiable,
Mother most admirable,
Mother of good counsel,
Mother of our Creator,
Mother of our Savior,
Virgin most prudent,
Virgin most venerable,
Virgin most renowned,
Virgin most powerful,
Virgin most merciful,
Virgin most faithful,
Mirror of justice,
Seat of wisdom,
Cause of our joy,
Spiritual vessel,
Vessel of honor,
Singular vessel of devotion,

* *Pray for us is repeated after each invocation.*

Mystical rose,
Tower of David,
Tower of ivory,
House of gold,
Ark of the covenant,
Gate of heaven,
Morning star,
Health of the sick,
Refuge of sinners,
Comforter of the afflicted,
Help of Christians,
Queen of angels,
Queen of patriarchs,
Queen of prophets,
Queen of apostles,
Queen of martyrs,
Queen of confessors,
Queen of virgins,
Queen of all saints,
Queen conceived without original sin,

Queen assumed into heaven,
Queen of the most holy Rosary,
Queen of peace,

Lamb of God, you take away the sins of the world; *spare us, O Lord!*

Lamb of God, you take away the sins of the world; *graciously hear us, O Lord!*

Lamb of God, you take away the sins of the world; *have mercy on us.*

℣. Pray for us, O holy Mother of God.

℟. *That we may be made worthy of the promises of Christ.*

[389a]

LET us pray.
Grant, we beg you, O Lord God,
that you your servants
may enjoy lasting health of mind and body,
and by the glorious intercession
of the Blessed Mary, ever Virgin,
be delivered from present sorrow
and enter into the joy of eternal happiness.
Through Christ our Lord.

℟. **Amen.**

During Advent   [389b]

L ET us pray.
O God,
you willed that, at the message of an angel,
your Word should take flesh
in the womb of the Blessed Virgin Mary;
grant to your suppliant people,
that we, who believe her to be truly the Mother of God,
may be helped by her intercession with you.
Through the same Christ our Lord.

℟. **Amen.**

[389c] **From Christmas to the Purification**

L ET us pray.
O God,
by the fruitful virginity of Blessed Mary,
you bestowed upon the human race
the rewards of eternal salvation;
grant, we beg you,
that we may feel the power of her intercession,
through whom we have been made worthy
to receive the Author of life,
our Lord Jesus Christ your Son,
who lives and reigns with you forever and ever.

℟. **Amen.**

[389d]   **During Paschaltime**

L ET us pray.
O God,
who by the Resurrection of your Son,
our Lord Jesus Christ,
granted joy to the whole world,

grant, we beg you,
that through the intercession of the Virgin Mary, his
Mother,
we may attain the joys of eternal life.
Through the same Christ our Lord.

℞. **Amen.**

[390]   ## Litany of St. Joseph

LORD, have mercy.
Christ, have mercy.
Lord, have mercy.
Christ, hear us.
Christ, graciously hear us.
God, the Father of Heaven,
   have mercy on us.
God the Son, Redeemer of
   the world,
   have mercy on us.
God the Holy Spirit,
   have mercy on us.
Holy Trinity, one God,
   have mercy on us.
Holy Mary, *pray for us.* *
St. Joseph,
Renowned offspring of David,
Light of patriarchs,
Spouse of the Mother of God,
Chaste guardian of the Virgin,
Foster father of the Son of
   God,
Diligent protector of Christ,
Head of the Holy Family,
Joseph most just,
Joseph most chaste,

Joseph most prudent,
Joseph most strong,
Joseph most obedient,
Joseph most faithful,
Mirror of patience,
Lover of poverty,
Model of artisans,
Glory of home life,
Guardian of virgins,
Pillar of families,
Solace of the wretched,
Hope of the sick,
Patron of the dying,
Terror of demons,
Protector of Holy Church,
Lamb of God, you take away
   the sins of the world; *spare
   us, O Lord!*
Lamb of God, you take away
   the sins of the world; *graciously hear us, O Lord!*
Lamb of God, you take away
   the sins of the world; *have
   mercy on us.*
℣. He made him the lord of
   his household.
℞. *And prince over all his
   possessions.*

* Pray for us *is repeated after each invocation.*

[390a]

L ET us pray.
    O God,
in your ineffable providence
you were pleased to choose Blessed Joseph
to be the spouse of your most holy Mother;
grant, we beg you,
that we may be worthy
to have him for our intercessor in heaven
whom on earth we venerate as our Protector:
you who live and reign forever and ever.
℟.   **Amen.**

[391]   ## Litany of the Saints

L ORD, have mercy.
    Christ, have mercy.
Lord, have mercy.
Christ, hear us.
Christ, graciously hear us.
God the Father of Heaven,
    have mercy on us.
God the Son, Redeemer of
    the world,
    have mercy on us.
God the Holy Spirit,
    have mercy on us.
Holy Trinity, one God,
    have mercy on us.
Holy Mary, *pray for us.**
Holy Mother of God,
Holy Virgin of virgins,
St. Michael,
St. Gabriel,

St. Raphael,
All you holy angels and
    archangels,
All you holy orders of blessed
    spirits,
St. John the Baptist,
St. Joseph,
All you holy patriarchs and
    prophets,
St. Peter,
St. Paul,
St. Andrew,
St. James
St. John,
St. Thomas,
St. James,
St. Philip,
St. Bartholomew,
St. Matthew,

* Pray for us *is repeated after each invocation down to* All
you holy Virgins and Widows.

St. Simon,
St. Thaddeus,
St. Matthias,
St. Barnabas,
St. Luke,
St. Mark,
All you holy apostles and
    evangelists,
All you holy disciples of the
    Lord,
All you holy Innocents,
St. Stephen,
St. Lawrence,
St. Vincent,
Sts. Fabian and Sebastian,
Sts. John and Paul,
Sts. Cosmas and Damian,
Sts. Gervase and Protase,
All you holy martyrs,
St. Sylvester,
St. Gregory,
St. Ambrose,
St. Augustine,
St. Jerome,
St. Martin,
St. Nicholas,
All you holy bishops and con-
    fessors,
All you holy doctors,
St. Anthony,
St. Benedict,
St. Bernard,
St. Dominic,
St. Francis,
All you holy priests and
    levites,

All you holy monks and her-
    mits,
St. Mary Magdalene,
St. Agatha,
St. Lucy,
St. Agnes,
St. Cecilia,
St. Catherine,
St. Anastasia,
All you holy virgins and wid-
    ows,
All you holy men and women,
    saints of God, *make inter-
    cession for us.*
Be merciful, *spare us, O Lord.*
Be merciful, *graciously hear
    us, O Lord.*
From all evil, *O Lord, deliver
    us.***
From all sin,
From your wrath,
From sudden and unprovided
    death,
From the snares of the devil,
From anger, and hatred, and
    all ill-will,
From the spirit of fornication,
From lightning and tempest,
From the scourge of earth-
    quake,
From plague, famine and
    war,
From everlasting death,
Through the mystery of your
    holy incarnation,

** O Lord, deliver us *is repeated down to* In the day of judgment.

Through your coming,

Through your nativity,

Through your baptism and holy fasting,

Through your cross and passion,

Through your death and burial,

Through your holy resurrection,

Through your admirable ascension,

Through the coming of the Holy Spirit, the Paraclete,

In the day of judgment,

We sinners, *we beseech you, hear us.* ***

That you would spare us.

That you would pardon us,

That you would bring us to true penance,

That you would deign to govern and preserve your holy Church,

That you would deign to preserve our Apostolic Prelate, and all orders of the Church in holy religion,

That you would deign to humble the enemies of Holy Church,

That you would deign to princes, peace and deign to Christian people,

That you would deign to call back to the unity of the Church all who have strayed from the truth and lead all unbelievers to the light of the Gospel,

That you would deign to confirm and preserve us in your holy service,

That you would lift up our minds to heavenly desires,

That you would render eternal blessings to all our benefactors,

That you would deliver our souls and the souls of our brethren, relations and benefactors, from eternal damnation,

That you would deign to give and preserve the fruits of the earth,

That you would deign to grant eternal rest to all the faithful departed,

That you would deign graciously to hear us,

Son of God,

Lamb of God, you take away the sins of the world, *spare us, O Lord.*

Lamb of God, you take away the sins of the world; *graciously hear us, O Lord.*

Lamb of God, you take away the sins of the world; *have mercy on us.*

*** *We beseech you, hear us is repeated down to* Son of God.

Christ, hear us.
Christ, graciously hear us.
Lord, have mercy.
Christ, have mercy.
Lord, have mercy.

Our Father, etc. (*inaudibly*).
℣. And lead us not into temptation.
℟. *But deliver us from evil.*

PSALM 70

DEIGN, O God, to rescue me;
O Lord, make haste to help me.
Let them be put to shame and confounded
who seek my life.
Let them be turned back in disgrace
who desire my ruin.
Let them retire in their shame
who say to me, "Aha, aha!"
But may all who seek you
exult and be glad in you,
And may those who love your salvation
say ever, "God be glorified!"
But I am afflicted and poor;
O God, hasten to me!
You are my help and deliverer;
O Lord, hold not back!
Glory be to the Father, and to the Son,
and to the Holy Spirit.
As it was in the beginning, is now, and ever shall be,
world without end. Amen.

℣. Save your servants,
℟. *Who trust in you, O my God.*

℣. Be a tower of strength for us, O Lord,
℟. *Against the attack of the enemy.*

℣. Let not the enemy prevail against us.
℟. *And let not the son of evil dare to harm us.*

℣. O Lord, deal not with us according to our sins.
℟. *Neither requite us according to our iniquities.*

℣. Let us pray for our Sovereign Pontiff N.
and *preserve him,
the earth, and
him not up to the and
of his enemies.*

℣. Let us pray for our benefactors.

℟. *Deign, O Lord, for your name's sake, to reward with eternal life all those who do us good. Amen.*

℣. Let us pray for the faithful departed.

℟. *Eternal rest give to them, O Lord; and let perpetual light shine upon them.*

℣. May they rest in peace.

℟. *Amen.*

℣. For our absent brethren.

℟. *Save your servants, who trust in you, my God.*

℣. Send them help, O Lord, from your sanctuary.

℟. *And sustain them from Zion.*

℣. O Lord, hear my prayer.

℟. *And let my cry come to you.*

℣. The Lord be with you.

℟. *And with your spirit.*

[391a]

LET us pray.
O God,
whose property is always to have mercy and to spare,
receive our petition, that we,
and all your servants who are bound by the chains of sin,
may, by the compassion of your goodness,
be mercifully absolved.

[391b]

GRACIOUSLY hear,
we beg you, O Lord,
the prayers of your suppliants,
and pardon the sins of those who confess to you,
that in your bounty
you may grant us both pardon and peace.

[391c]

IN YOUR clemency, O Lord,
show us your ineffable mercy,
that you may both free us from all our sins,
and deliver us from the punishments
which we deserve for them.

[391d]

O GOD,
who by sin are offended and by penance pacified,
mercifully regard the prayers of your suppliant people,
and turn away the scourges of your anger,
which we deserve for our sins.

[391e]

ALMIGHTY, everlasting God,
have mercy upon your servant N., our Sovereign
Pontiff,
and direct him according to your clemency
into the way of everlasting salvation,
that by your grace
he may desire those things that are pleasing to you,
and perform them with all his strength.

[391f]

O GOD,
from whom are holy desires,
good counsels, and just works,
give to your servants
that peace which the world cannot give,
that our hearts may be set to keep your commandments,
and that, being removed from the fear of our enemies,
we may pass our time in peace under your protection.

[391g]

BURN our desires and our hearts
with the fire of the Holy Spirit,
O Lord,
that we may serve you with a chaste body,
and with a clean heart be pleasing to you.

[391h]

O GOD, the Creator and Redeemer of all the faithful,
grant to the souls of your servants and handmaids
the remission of all their sins,
that, through devout prayers,
they may obtain the pardon which they always desired.

[391i]

DIRECT, we beg you, O Lord,
our actions by your holy inspirations,
and carry them on by your gracious assistance,
that every prayer and work of ours
may begin always with you,
and through you be happily ended.

[391j]

ALMIGHTY and everlasting God,
you have dominion over the living and the dead,
and you are merciful to all who you foreknow
will be yours by faith and good works;
we humbly beg you
that those for whom we intend to pour forth our prayers,
whether this present world still detain them in the flesh,
or the world to come has already received them
out of their bodies,

may, through the intercession of all your Saints,
by the clemency of your goodness,
obtain the remission of all their sins.
Through Christ our Lord.

℟. **Amen.**

℣. O Lord, hear my prayer.
℟. **And let my cry come to you.**

℣. May the almighty and merciful Lord graciously
hear us.
℟. **Amen.**

℣. And may the souls of the faithful departed,
through the mercy of God, rest in peace.
℟. **Amen.**

[396]   **Prayer for Sacerdotal or
Religious Vocations**

O LORD,
send workers for your harvest,
so that the commands of your only-begotten Son
may always be obeyed
and his sacrifice be everywhere renewed.

Look with favor upon your family,
and ever increase its numbers.
Enable it to lead its sons/daughters
to the holiness to which they are called
and to work for the salvation of others.
Through Christ our Lord.

℟. **Amen.**

[407]   The Mysteries of the Rosary

THE JOYFUL MYSTERIES

1. The Annunciation of the Archangel Gabriel to the Virgin Mary
2. The Visitation of the Virgin Mary to the Parents of St. John the Baptist
3. The Birth of Our Lord at Bethlehem
4. The Presentation of Our Lord in the Temple
5. The Finding of Our Lord in the Temple

THE SORROWFUL MYSTERIES

1. The Agony of Our Lord in the Garden of Gethsemane
2. The Scourging of Our Lord at the Pillar
3. The Crowning of Our Lord with Thorns
4. The Carrying of the Cross by Our Lord to Calvary
5. The Crucifixion and Death of Our Lord

THE GLORIOUS MYSTERIES

1. The Resurrection of Our Lord from the Dead
2. The Ascension of Our Lord into Heaven
3. The Descent of the Holy Spirit upon the Apostles
4. The Assumption of Our Blessed Lady into Heaven
5. The Coronation of Our Blessed Lady as Queen of Heaven and Earth

[420]   The Stations of the Cross

1. Jesus is condemned to death
2. Jesus bears his cross
3. Jesus falls the first time
4. Jesus meets his mother
5. Jesus is helped by Simon
6. Veronica wipes the face of Jesus
7. Jesus falls a second time
8. Jesus speaks to the women
9. Jesus falls a third time
10. Jesus is stripped of his garments
11. Jesus is nailed to the Cross
12. Jesus dies on the Cross
13. Jesus is taken down from the Cross
14. Jesus is placed in the tomb

[424a] Renewal of Baptismal Promises

I, N.N.,
who through the tender mercy of the Eternal Father
was privileged to be baptized
"in the name of the Lord Jesus" (Acts 19:5)
and thus to share in the dignity of his divine Sonship,
wish now in the presence of this same loving Father
and ot his only-begotten Son
to renew in all sincerity the promises I solemnly made
at the time of my holy Baptism.

I, therefore, now do once again renounce Satan;

I renounce all his works;
I renounce all his allurements.

I believe in God, the Father almighty,
Creator of heaven and earth.
I believe in Jesus Christ, his only Son, our Lord,
who was born into this world
and who suffered and died for my sins
and rose again.
I believe in the Holy Spirit,
the Holy Catholic Church,
the communion of Saints,
the forgiveness of sins,
the resurrection of the body and life everlasting.

Having been buried with Christ unto death
and raised up with him unto a new life,
I promise to live no longer for myself
or for that world which is the enemy of God
but for him who died for me and rose again,
serving God, my heavenly Father,
faithfully and unto death in the holy Catholic Church.

Taught by our Savior's command
and formed by the word of God,
I now dare to say:

Our Father,
who art in heaven,
hallowed be thy name;
thy kingdom come;
thy will be done on earth as it is in heaven.
Give us this day our daily bread;
and forgive us our trespasses
as we forgive those who trespass against us;
and lead us not into temptation,
but deliver us from evil. Amen.

Additional Optional Texts

[366] **Adoration of the Blessed Sacrament**

MY JESUS,
    I thank you for having bestowed on me so many
       graces:
for having created me,
redeemed me by your blood,
made me a Christian by the Sacrament of Baptism,
and borne with me for so long
when I was under your displeasure.
How unhappy should I be
if I had died in the state of mortal sin!
I should now be lost forever,
O my God,
and I could no longer love you.

I thank you
for having pardoned me in your mercy,
as I confidently hope.
I thank you especially
for having remained with us in the Blessed Sacrament,
for giving yourself so often to me in Holy Communion,
becoming my food,
and for admitting me now into your presence.
I thank you for all these favors,
and I hope one day
to thank you more perfectly for them in heaven,
and to celebrate without ceasing your ineffable mercy
for all eternity.

[375] **Papal Blessing**

MAY the blessing of almighty God:
    Father,

Son,
and Holy Spirit,
descend upon you
and remain forever.

℟. **Amen.**

[377]   **Prayer for Those Who Study
or Teach Christian Doctrine**

LORD Jesus Christ,
by your Holy Spirit
you give to some the word of wisdom,
to others the word of knowledge,
and to still others the word of faith.
Grant us a knowledge of the Father
and of yourself.

Help us to cling steadfastly
to the Catholic faith.
In our studies and in our teaching
make us seek only the extension of your kingdom
and your holy Church
both in ourselves and in others.

[380] **Prayer for a Eucharistic Congress**

O JESUS,
you are really present in the Blessed Sacrament
to be our spiritual food and drink.
Bless and bring to a successful issue
all Eucharistic congresses,
especially this one.

Enkindle the hearts of priests and faithful
so that frequent and daily Communion may be held in
    honor

in all the countries of the world.
May your kingship over human society
be everywhere acknowledged.

[382] Prayer for the Success of Spiritual Exercises

O JESUS,
our Redeemer and our King,
during these spiritual exercises
your representatives will break for us
the bread of God's Word
and bring us the joy of forgiveness.
Help all who make this retreat
to be faithful to your grace
and respond generously to your mercy.
Let the preaching of your eternal truths
enlighten our minds
and move our hearts
so that we may realize our shortcomings
and sincerely repent of them.

For a prayer after a retreat, see no. [404], p. 339.

[385] Prayer for a Good Death

O JESUS,
while I adore your dying breath,
I beg you to receive mine.
Since I do not know
whether I shall have command of my senses
when I depart from this world,
I offer you even now my last agony
and all the sorrows of my passing.
I give my soul into your hands
for you are my Father and my Savior.
Grant that the last beat of my heart
may be an act of perfect love for you.

[394]   Prayer for Novena Devotions (Christmas)

GOD of love, Father of all,
the darkness that covered the earth
has given way to the bright dawn
of your Word made flesh.
Make us a people of this light.
Make us faithful to your Word,
that we may bring your life
to the waiting world.

[395]   Blessing of an Article of Devotion

FATHER in heaven,
we give you thanks for sending your Spirit
to teach us to pray.
Bless this article of devotion
and let it become for us
an aid to sincere and devout prayer.
May we become daily more proficient in prayer
and more pleasing to you.

[397]   Prayer before Mental Prayer

O MY God,
I offer up to you once more
my thoughts, words, and actions
in union with those of Jesus Christ,
that they may be worthy of being received by you.
And I renounce every other intention
but such as Jesus would have,
were he upon earth and in my place.

I unite myself,
O my God,

with the divine Spirit of Jesus,
who causes you to be loved and adored
by all the angels and saints
who fill heaven and earth with your holy praise.
Through Jesus
may I join with all those creatures that honor you,
and especially with those who honor you
by mental prayer.

[400]   **Prayer before**
Hearing the Word of God Preached

O LORD,
   grant to your preacher
a truly mild and judicious eloquence.
Through your Holy Spirit,
place on his lips
words of consolation, edification, and exhortation.
Enable him to encourage the good to be better,
and to recall to the path of righteousness
those who have strayed.

Enlighten the minds of his listeners
with greater knowledge of you
and fill their hearts
with deeper love for you.

[401]   **Prayer for First Communicants**

O JESUS,
   you loved us so much
that you bequeathed to us the ineffable gift
of the Holy Eucharist.
Look graciously on the young children
who are about to receive you for the first time.

Protect them from the assaults of evil,
strengthen their faith,
increase their love,
and endow them with all the virtues
that will make them worthy to receive you.

[402] **Prayer for a Priest at His First Mass**

O HOLY Spirit,
your servant who is about to celebrate this Mass
shares the holy priesthood of Jesus
and your apostolate.
Enkindle in his heart the flames
that transformed the disciples in the Upper Room.
Let him be no longer an ordinary man
but a man living to transfuse the divine life
into the souls of others.

Give him an ardent desire for the inner life
as well as your consolation and strength.
Enable him to see that even here below
there is no true happiness
unless his life partakes of yours
and that of the Heart of Jesus
in the bosom of the Father.

[404] **Prayer after a Monthly Day of Recollection**

O JESUS,
I thank you for all the benefits of your love
which you bestowed upon me this day.
I offer you my whole life
and in particular my labors and sufferings.

Help me to carry out diligently
all the duties of my state
and to direct my entire life
in accord with your divine plans for me.

Grant me all the graces I need
to serve you faithfully on earth
and attain everlasting joy with you in heaven.

[408] Prayer on the Anniversary of Sacerdotal Ordination

MOST loving Jesus,
today is the anniversary of the day on which,
despite my unworthiness and through your goodness,
you conferred on me the dignity of the priesthood.
You made me not only your minister
but the voice of your sublime wisdom as well,
and the dispenser of your mysteries.
My soul is filled with joy, love, and gratitude
for this singular privilege which I have received.
At the same time I am sad and troubled
for having so often, and without reason,
failed to respond as I ought
to your great generosity.

I beg the continual assistance of your infinite goodness
which will enable me to accomplish the sublime work
for which you have commissioned me.
With your light in my mind
and your strength in my heart
I shall daily dispense in greater abundance
the fruits of your redemption to all people.

[409] **Prayer before Reading Scriptures**

COME, Holy Spirit,
    fill the hearts of your faithful
and enkindle in them the fire of your love.

℣.   Send forth your Spirit and they shall be created.
℟.   **And you shall renew the face of the earth.**

Let us pray.
O God, you instructed the hearts of the faithful
by the light of the Holy Spirit.
Grant us by the same Spirit
to have a right judgment in all things
and ever to rejoice in his consolation.
Through Christ our Lord.

[409a]   **Prayer after Reading the Scriptures**

LET me not,
    O Lord,
be puffed up with worldly wisdom,
which passes away.
Grant me that love which never abates,
that I may not choose to know anything among men
but Jesus, and him crucified.

I pray you, loving Jesus,
that as you have graciously given me
to drink in with delight the words of your knowledge,
so you would mercifully grant me
to attain one day to you,
the Fountain of all wisdom,
and to appear forever before your face.

[413] Prayer for the Veneration of the Saints

GOD our Father,
you alone are holy;
without you nothing is good.
Trusting in the prayers of St. N.
we ask you to help us
to become the holy people you call us to be.
Never let us be found undeserving
of the glory you have prepared for us.

(Common of Holy Men and Women)

[416] Prayer for a Diocesan Synod

GOD our Father,
you judge your people with kindness
and rule us with love.
Give a spirit of wisdom
to those you have entrusted with authority
in your Church
that your people may come to know the truth more fully
and grow in holiness.

(Mass for a Council or Synod)

[421] Prayer for a Visit to a Parochial Church

GOD our Father,
in all the churches scattered throughout the world
you show forth the one, holy, catholic and apostolic
Church.
Through the gospel and the Eucharist
bring your people together in the Holy Spirit
and guide us in your love.

Make us a sign of your love for all people,
and help us to show forth
the living presence of Christ in the world.

(Mass for the Local Church)

[422] Prayer for a Visit to a Church or an Altar on the Day of Its Consecration

ALL-POWERFUL, ever-living God,
fill this church with your love
and give your help to all who call on you in faith.
May the power of your word and sacraments in this place
bring strength to the people gathered here.

(Mass for the Dedication of a Church)

[423] Prayer for a Visit to a Church or Oratory on All Souls Day

LORD God,
you are the glory of believers
and the life of the just.
Your Son redeemed us
by dying and rising to life again.
Since our departed brothers and sisters
believed in the mystery of our resurrection,
let them share the joys and blessings
of the life to come.

(Mass of November 2)

[424] **Prayer for a Visit to a Church or Oratory of Religious on the Feast of the Holy Founder**

FATHER,
     each year we recall the dedication of this church
to your service.
Let our worship always be sincere
and help us to find your saving love
in this church.

(Mass for Anniversary of Dedication)

4

PRAYERS
FROM THE
SAINTS
AND SPIRITUAL WRITERS

345

ST. AUGUSTINE — RELIGIOUS GENIUS

One of the most towering figures in the first five centuries of the Church was the Bishop of Hippo. He was a man of intellectual brilliance, countless friendships, pastoral concern, religious greatness, and deep prayerful spirit. He more than adequately stands for all the Saints of this period whose prayers are still an inspiration for us today.

346

A) FIRST TO FIFTH CENTURIES

I N THE *beginning the Church was obliged to live in a pagan and alien world, and concentrated on keeping its members away from pagan errors and vices. Hence, the prayers of the first two centuries show this defensive attitude toward the world.*

After Christianity became the religion of Rome, it had to assimilate the culture of the Empire in all its diverse forms. The prayers from the third century on demonstrate this quality of the Church to adapt itself to the different cultures.

The prayers found in this first section are thus among the oldest in the Church—yet some of them sound as if they were written yesterday. They form a precious legacy of the prayer life of the Church and the spiritual treasury that is our heritage.

Some of them have been popular throughout the ages—such as those of St. Augustine—because of the universality of the sentiments they express. Others are not so well known but are also perfectly geared to nourish the prayer life of people today. All of them are filled with insights that can be of immense help in our spiritual life.

426   ## Prayer in the Name of the Whole Christian People

WE BEG you, Master,
be our help and strength.
Save those among us who are oppressed,
have pity on the lowly, and lift up the fallen.
Heal the sick, bring back the straying,
and feed the hungry.
Release those in prison, steady those who falter,
and strengthen the fainthearted.
Let all nations come to know you the one God,
with your Son Jesus Christ,
and us your people and the sheep of your pasture.

Do not keep count of the sins of your servants
but purify us through the bath of your truth
and direct our steps.
Help us to walk in holiness of heart,
and to do what is good and pleasing in your eyes
and in the eyes of our rulers.

Master, let your face shine on us
to grant us every good in peace,
to protect us by your powerful hand,
to deliver us from every evil by the might of your arm,
and to save us from the unjust hatred of our enemies.
Grant to us and to all who dwell on this earth
peace and harmony, O Lord.

St. Clement I (c. 38–c. 101)
Roman Missionary and Fourth Pope

427   ## Prayer for Martyrdom

I AM the wheat of God,
and am ground by the teeth of the wild beasts,
that I may be found the pure bread of God. . . .

I long after the Lord,
the Son of the true God and Father,
Jesus Christ.
Him I seek,
who died for us and rose again. . . .

I am eager to die for the sake of Christ.
My love has been crucified,
and there is no fire in me that loves anything.
But there is living water springing up in me,
and it says to me inwardly:
Come to the Father.

St. Ignatius of Antioch (c. 50–117)
Bishop and Martyr

428 **Prayer before Martyrdom**

LORD God almighty,
Father of Jesus Christ,
your dear Son through whom we have come to know
    you,
God of the angels and powers,
God of all creation,
God of those who live in your presence,
the race of the just:
I bless you.

You have considered me to be worthy of this day and
    hour,
worthy to be numbered with the martyrs
and to drink the cup of your Anointed One,
and thus to rise and live forever,
body and soul,
in the incorruptibility of the Holy Spirit.

St. Polycarp of Smyrna (c. 69-166)
Bishop and Martyr

429 **Prayer in Praise of Christ**

BORN as a son,
  led forth as a lamb,
sacrificed as a sheep,
buried as a man,
he rose from the dead as a God,
for he was by nature God and man.

He is all things:
he judges, and so he is Law;
he teaches, and so he is Word;
he saves, and so he is Grace;
he begets, and so he is Father,
he is begotten, and so he is Son;
he suffers, and so he is Sacrifice;
he is buried, and so he is man;
he rises again, and so he is God.
This is Jesus Christ,
to whom belongs glory for all ages.

St. Melito of Sardis (c. 100–c. 180)
Bishop and Martyr

430 **Prayer for Various Types of Christians**

FATHER,
  give perfection to beginners,
understanding to the little ones,
and help to those who are running their course.
Give sorrow to the negligent,
fervor to the lukewarm,
and a good consummation to the perfect.

St. Irenaeus of Lyons (c. 125–202)
Bishop, Defender of the Faith, and Martyr

431 **Prayer to Practice What Jesus Taught**

O LORD Jesus Christ,
  grant us a measure of your Spirit.
Help us to obey your teaching,
soothe anger,
cultivate pity,
overcome desire,
increase love,
cast off sorrow,
shun vainglory,
renounce revenge,
and not be afraid of death.
Let us ever entrust our spirit to the everlasting God
who with you and the Holy Spirit
lives and rules forever and ever.

St. Apollonius of Rome (? – 185)
Senator, Apologist, and Martyr

432 **Prayer for Prisoners and Correction Officers**

MOST gracious Father,
  bless with your special care
all penitentiaries and homes of refuge.
Look with pity on those who are housed there.
Guide and protect those who have returned to the
  world.
Grant all of them true contrition for past sins
and strengthen them in their good resolutions.
Lead them along from grace to grace,
so that by the help of the Holy Spirit
they may persevere in the ways of obedience and humility,
and in the struggle against evil thoughts and desires.

Grant the Holy Spirit
to those engaged in teaching and training them,
that they might have a right judgment
with respect to those entrusted to them.
May they labor for love of you
with deep humility and singleness of purpose,
purity of heart and life,
and true zeal for your glory and the salvation of souls.
Give them faith and love to sustain them in disappointment,
love and patience toward those under them,
and in your own good time
crown their work with an eternal recompense.

St. Cyprian of Carthage (200–258)
Bishop, Martyr, and Doctor

433   Prayer to Follow Christ and See the Father

O EDUCATOR [Jesus],
be favorable to your children. . . .
Grant that we who follow your command
may attain the likeness of your image
and in accord with our strength find in you
both a good God
and a judge who is not severe.

Clement of Alexandria (c. 150–c. 215)
Greek Convert and Theologian

434   Prayer for True Spiritual Vision

M AY the Lord Jesus place his hands on our eyes
that we may begin to catch sight of
the things that are not seen
more than the things that are seen.

May he open our eyes
that they will alight on the things to come
more than on the things of this age.
May he unveil the vision of our heart
that it may contemplate God in spirit.
We ask this through our Lord Jesus Christ
to whom belong glory and power for ever.

Origen (185–253)
Theologian and Educator

435   **Prayer for Harmony**

GOD the Father,
source of everything divine,
you are good surpassing everything good
and just surpassing everything just.
In you is tranquility,
as well as peace and harmony.
Heal our divisions
and restore us to the unity of love,
which is similar to your divine nature.

Let the bond of love
and the ties of divine affection
make us one in the Spirit
by your peace
which renders everything peaceful.
We ask this through the grace, mercy, and compassion
of your only Son, our Lord Jesus Christ.

St. Dionysius of Alexandria (190–264)
Bishop and Educator

436   **Prayer to Practice the Golden Rule**

MAY I be an enemy to no one
and the friend of what abides eternally.
May I never quarrel with those nearest me,

and be reconciled quickly if I should.
May I never plot evil against others,
and if anyone plot evil against me
may I escape unharmed
and without the need to hurt anyone else.

May I love, seek, and attain only what is good.
May I desire happiness for all
and harbor envy for none.
May I never find joy in the misfortune
of one who has wronged me.
May I never wait for the rebuke of others,
but always rebuke myself until I make reparation. . . .

May I gain no victory that harms me or my opponent. . . .
May I reconcile friends who are mad at each other.
May I, insofar as I can,
give all necessary help to my friends
and to all who are in need.
May I never fail a friend in trouble.
When visiting the grief-stricken,
may I be able to soften their pain
with comforting words.

May I respect myself. . . .
May I always maintain control of my emotions. . . .
May I habituate myself to be gentle,
and never be angry with others
because of circumstances.
May I never discuss the wicked
or what they have done,
but know good people
and follow in their footsteps.

Eusebius of Caesarea (263-339)
Bishop and Ecclesiastical Historian

437   **Prayer to Mary, Mother of Grace**

I T BECOMES you to be mindful of us,
   as you stand near him who granted you all graces,
for you are the Mother of God
and our Queen.
Help us for the sake of the King,
the Lord God and Master who was born of you.
For this reason you are called full of grace.

Remember us,
most holy Virgin,
and bestow on us gifts from the riches of your graces,
Virgin full of grace.

St. Athanasius (295–373)
Bishop and Doctor

438   **Prayer of Gratitude
for God's Blessings**

O LORD and Vivifier,
   your grace has achieved for us
all that you had spoken and promised.
Grant us access to the place of your peace.
For you are our Vivifier,
you are our Consoler,
you are our life Remedy,
you are our Standard of victory.

Blessed are we, O Lord, because we have known you!
Blessed are we, because we have believed in you!
Blessed are we, because we bear your wounds
and the sign of your blood on our countenances!
Blessed are we, because you are our great hope!
Blessed are we, because you are our God forever!

Acts of Thomas (3rd century addition)

439   Praise of God for His Goodness to Us Sinners

LORD, from you flows true and continual kindness.
    You had cast us off and justly so,
but in your mercy you forgave us.
You were at odds with us,
and you reconciled us.
You had set a curse on us,
and you blessed us.
You had banished us from the garden,
and you called us back again.

You took away the fig leaves
that had been an unsuitable garment,
and you clothed us in a cloak of great value.
You flung wide the prison gates,
and you gave the condemned a pardon.
You sprinkled clean water on us,
and you washed away the dirt.

St. Gregory of Nyssa (c. 300–394)
Priest, Writer, and Doctor

440   Prayer for Strength in Weakness

LORD Jesus Christ, King of kings,
    you have power over life and death.
You know even things
that are uncertain and obscure,
and our very thoughts and feelings
are not hidden from you.
Cleanse me from my secret faults,
for I have done wrong and you saw it. . . .

You know how weak I am, both in soul and in body.
Give me strength, O Lord, in my frailty
and sustain me in my sufferings. . . .

Grant me a prudent judgment, dear Lord,
and let me always be mindful of your blessings. . . .
Let me retain until the end
your grace that has protected me till now.

St. Ephrem of Syria (306-375)
Deacon, Poet, and Doctor

441 **Prayer in Honor of Christ's Passion**

I GIVE you glory, O Christ,
because you, the Only-begotten,
the Lord of all, . . .
underwent the death of the Cross
to free my sinful soul from the bonds of sin.

What shall I give to you, O Lord,
in return for all this kindness?

Glory to you, O Lord,
for your love,
for your mercy,
for your patience.

Glory to you
for forgiving us all our sins,
for coming to save our souls,
for your incarnation in the Virgin's womb.

Glory to you
for your bonds,
for receiving the cut of the lash,
for accepting mockery.

Glory to you
for your crucifixion,
for your burial,
for your resurrection.

Glory to you
for your resurrection,
for being preached to men,
for being taken up to heaven.

Glory to you
who sit at the Father's right hand
and will return in glory. . . .

Glory to you
for willing that the sinner be saved
through your great mercy and compassion.

St. Ephrem of Syria (306-375)
Deacon, Poet, and Doctor

442 Prayer toward the End of One's Life

L ORD, . . .
be merciful
now that my life is approaching its end,
and the evening awaits me.
There is not enough time
for me to cleanse myself of my sins,
for they are so many. . . .

Heal me while I am still on earth,
and I shall truly be healthy.
In your mercy, move me to repent
so that I shall not be ashamed
when I encounter you in heaven.

St. Macarius of Egypt (309-390)
Hermit and Mystic

443 Prayer to Remain Steadfast in Faith

O LORD,
deliver us from futile battles of words,
and assist us in professing the truth.

Keep us steadfast in faith,
a genuine and unadulterated faith.
Enable us to remain faithful
to what we promised when we were baptized
in the name of the Father,
the Son,
and the Holy Spirit.
Let us have you as our Father,
and continue ever to live in your Son
and in the fellowship of the Holy Spirit.

St. Hilary of Poitiers (315–368)
Bishop and Doctor

444 **Prayer Acknowledging That God Is in His Creation**

WHEN I look at your heavens,
according to my own lights,
with these weak eyes of mine,
I am certain that they are your heavens
without any qualification whatever.

I note that the stars circle about them
and reappear year after year . . . ,
each with a different function and service
to fulfill.
And though I do not understand them,
I come to the realization that you, O God,
are in them.

St. Hilary of Poitiers (315–368)
Bishop and Doctor

445 **Prayer to Continue to Do Battle for God**

LORD,
if your people still have need of my services,
I will not avoid the toil.
Your will be done.

Indeed, I have fought the good fight long enough.
Yet if you bid me continue to hold the battle line
in defense of your camp,
I will never beg to be excused
on account of failing strength.
I will diligently perform the tasks
that you entrust to me.
And as long as you command
I will continue to do battle under your banner.

St. Martin of Tours (315–397)
Italian Soldier, Hermit, and Bishop

446 **Prayer for a Deeper Sense
of Fellowship with All Living Things**

O GOD,
    grant us a deeper sense of fellowship
with all living things,
our little brothers and sisters,
to whom in common with us
you have given this earth as home.

We recall with regret that in the past
we have acted high-handedly and cruelly
in exercising our domain over them.
Thus, the voice of the earth
which should have risen to you in song
has turned into a groan of travail.

May we realize that all these creatures also live
for themselves and for you—
not for us alone.
They too love the goodness of life,
as we do,
and serve you better in their way
than we do in ours.

St. Basil of Caesarea (329–379)
Bishop and Doctor

447 Prayer to the All-Transcendent God

O ALL-TRANSCENDENT God
(what other name describes you?),
what words can hymn your praises?
No word does you justice.
What mind can probe your secret?
No mind can encompass you.
You are alone beyond the power of speech,
yet all that we speak stems from you.
You are alone beyond the power of thought,
yet all that we can conceive springs from you.

All things proclaim you,
those endowed with reason and those bereft of it.
All the expectation and pain of the world
coalesces in you.
All things utter a prayer to you,
a silent hymn composed by you.

You sustain everything that exists,
and all things move together to your orders.
You are the goal of all that exists.
You are one and you are all,
yet you are none of the things that exist—
neither a part nor the whole.
You can avail yourself of any name;
how shall I call you, the only unnameable? . . .
All-transcendent God!

St. Gregory of Nazianzen
Bishop and Doctor (329–390)

448 Prayer That We May Seek God and Find Him

L ORD, teach me to seek you,
and reveal yourself to me when I seek you.
For I cannot seek you
unless you first teach me,

nor find you
unless you first reveal yourself to me.

Let me seek you in longing,
and long for you in seeking.
Let me find you in love,
and love you in finding.

St. Ambrose of Milan (340–397)
Bishop, Writer, and Doctor

449   Prayer for Christ's Mercy

O LORD, show your mercy to me
and gladden my heart,
I am like the man on the way to Jericho
who was overtaken by robbers,
wounded, and left half-dead:
O Good Samaritan, come to my aid.
I am like the sheep that went astray:
O Good Shepherd, seek me out
and bring me home in accord with your will.
Let me dwell in your house all the days of my life
and praise you for ever and ever
with those who are there.

St. Jerome (342–420)
Priest, Writer, and Doctor

450   Prayer to Jesus before Holy Communion

O LORD, my God,
I am not worthy that you should come into my
soul,
but I am glad that you have come to me
because in your loving kindness
you desire to dwell in me.
You ask me to open the door of my soul,
which you alone have created,
so that you may enter into it

with your loving kindness
and dispel the darkness of my mind.

I believe that you will do this
for you did not turn away Mary Magdalene
when she approached you in tears.
Neither did you withhold forgiveness
from the tax collector who repented of his sins
or from the good thief
who asked to be received into your kingdom.
Indeed, you numbered as your friends
all who came to you with repentant hearts.
O God, you alone are blessed
always, now, and forever.

St. John Chrysostom (344–407)
Bishop, Orator, and Doctor

451 **Prayer on Finding God
after a Long Search**

TOO late have I loved you,
   O Beauty so ancient, O Beauty so new,
too late have I loved you!
You were within me but I was outside myself,
and there I sought you!
In my weakness
I ran after the beauty
of the things you have made.
You were with me,
and I was not with you.
The things you have made kept me from you—
the things which would have no being
unless they existed in you!

You have called,
you have cried out,
and you have pierced my deafness.
You have radiated forth,

you have shined out brightly,
and you have dispelled my blindness.
You have sent forth your fragrance,
and I have breathed it in,
and I long for you.
I have tasted you,
and I hunger and thirst for you.
You have touched me,
and I ardently desire your peace.

St. Augustine of Hippo (354–430)
Bishop, Writer, and Doctor

452 Prayer to Center One's Life on Jesus

LORD Jesus, let me know myself;
    let me know you,
and desire nothing else but you.
Let me hate myself and love you,
and do all things for the sake of you.
Let me humble myself and exalt you,
and think of nothing else but you.
Let me die to myself and live in you,
and take whatever happens as coming from you.
Let me forsake myself and walk after you,
and ever desire to follow you.

Let me flee from myself and turn to you,
that so I may merit to be defended by you.
Let me fear for myself, let me fear you,
and be among those that are chosen by you.
Let me distrust myself and trust in you,
and ever obey for the love of you.
Let me cleave to nothing but you,
and ever be poor because of you.
Look upon me that I may love you,
call me, that I may see you,
and forever possess you, for all eternity.

St. Augustine of Hippo (354–430)
Bishop, Writer, and Doctor

453 **Prayer of Trust in God's Heavenly Promise**

MY GOD,
let me know and love you,
so that I may find my happiness in you.
Since I cannot fully achieve this on earth,
help me to improve daily
until I may do so to the full.
Enable me to know you ever more on earth,
so that I may know you perfectly in heaven.
Enable me to love you ever more on earth,
so that I may love you perfectly in heaven.
In that way my joy may be great on earth,
and perfect with you in heaven.

O God of truth,
grant me the happiness of heaven
so that my joy may be full
in accord with your promise.
In the meantime,
let my mind dwell on that happiness,
my tongue speak of it,
my heart pine for it,
my mouth pronounce it,
my soul hunger for it,
my flesh thirst for it,
and my entire being desire it
until I enter through death
into the joy of my Lord forever.

*St. Augustine of Hippo (354–430)
Bishop, Writer, and Doctor*

454 **Prayer in Honor of Mary, Mother of God**

HAIL, Mary, Mother of God,
venerable treasure of the whole universe,

lamp that is never extinguished,
crown of virginity,
support of the true faith,
indestructible temple,
dwelling of him whom no place can contain,
O Mother and Virgin!

Through you
all the holy Gospels call blessed
the one who comes in the name of the Lord.

Hail, Mother of God;
you enclosed under your heart the infinite God
whom no space can contain.
Through you
the Most Holy Trinity is adored and glorified,
the priceless cross is venerated
throughout the universe.

Through you
the heavens rejoice,
and the angels and archangels are filled with gladness.
Through you
the demons are banished,
and the tempter fell from heaven.
Through you
the fallen human race is admitted to heaven.

Hail, Mother of God;
through you
kings rule,
and the only-begotten Son of God
has become a star of light
to those who were sitting in darkness
and in the shadow of death.

St. Cyril of Alexandria (374–444)
Bishop and Doctor

455   **Prayer for Pardon of Faults**

I HAVE consecrated my entire self to you,
   and taking me by your right hand
you have led me with your counsel.
But in my human frailty
I have sinned both in word and deed
many times against you,
who alone are pure and without sin.

Therefore, accept my prayer
together with the tears I offer you
through your holy ones, the victors in the arena.
Purify me, this poor handmaid of yours,
so that on departing toward you
my passage may be hastened.

St. Melania the Younger (383–439)
Roman Patrician and Ascetic

456   **Prayer for God's Protection
and Christ's Presence**

A S I arise today,
   may the strength of God pilot me,
the power of God uphold me,
the wisdom of God guide me.
May the eye of God look before me,
the ear of God hear me,
the word of God speak for me.
May the hand of God protect me,
the way of God lie before me,
the shield of God defend me,
the host of God save me.

May Christ shield me today . . .
Christ with me, Christ before me,
Christ behind me,

Christ in me, Christ beneath me,
Christ above me,
Christ on my right, Christ on my left,
Christ when I lie down, Christ when I sit,
Christ when I stand,
Christ in the heart of everyone
who thinks of me,
Christ in the mouth of everyone
who speaks of me,
Christ in every eye that sees me,
Christ in every ear that hears me.

St. Patrick of Ireland (385–461)
Bishop and Missionary

457 Prayer to Christ Who Influences the Whole World

LORD, . . .
kings are guided by your cross,
and queens follow the way of your love.
The world is held in the palm of your hand,
and the universe rests in your love.
Your song is found in the mouths of children,
and your psalms are on the lips of women.
Your feasts are filled with praises
by the world and its children who please you.

Lord, let your wrath be dissipated
for our necks are too frail to sustain your sword.
Bring all wars to an end,
and fill the earth with peace and tranquility.
Put a halt to earthquakes,
and give the just peaceful and contrite hearts.

In your mercy, grant us good harvests,
and let all rejoice in the products of their work.

May we enjoy a pleasant summer
and be blessed with a mild winter.
Turn away your wrath,
and pour down your mercy on us.

Cyrillona (d. 4th century)
Mesopotamian Deacon and Bishop

458 Prayer for the Gifts to Seek God and Live in Him

FATHER,
   in your goodness grant me
the intellect to comprehend you,
the perception to discern you,
and the reason to appreciate you.

In your kindness endow me with
the diligence to look for you,
the wisdom to discover you,
and the spirit to apprehend you.

In your graciousness bestow on me
a heart to contemplate you,
ears to hear you,
eyes to see you,
and a tongue to speak of you.

In your mercy confer on me
a conversation pleasing to you,
the patience to wait for you,
and the perseverance to long for you.
Grant me a perfect end—
your holy presence.

St. Benedict of Nursia (480-547)
Monk and Founder of Benedictines

459   **Prayer in Praise of God's Greatness**

ALMIGHTY, true, and incomparable God,
you are present in all things,
yet in no way are you limited by them.
You remain unaffected by place,
untouched by time,
unperturbed by years,
and undeceived by words.
You are not subject to birth
and in no need of protection.
You are beyond all corruption,
above all change,
and immutable by nature.

You live in unapproachable light
and are invisible,
yet you are known to all those
who seek you with hope and love.
You are the God of Israel,
and of all who hope in Christ.

Apostolic Constitutions (4th-5th Century)

460   **Prayer for a Heavenly Feast**

I WISH I had a great lake of ale
for the King of kings,
and the family of heaven to drink it
through time eternal.

I wish I had
the meats of belief and genuine piety,
the flails of penance,
and the men of heaven in my house.
I would like keeves of peace to be at their disposal,
vessels of charity for distribution,

caves of mercy for their company,
and cheerfulness to be in their drinking.

I would want Jesus also to be in their midst,
together with the three Marys of illustrious renown,
and the people of heaven from all parts.
I would like to be a rent-payer to the Lord,
so that if I should suffer distress
he would confer on me a good blessing.

St. Brigid of Kildare (453–523)
Nun and Founder of Monasteries

461 **Prayer for Help to Contemplate God**

FATHER,
  enable our minds to rise
to your ineffable dwelling-place.
Let us find the light
and direct the eyes of our soul to you.
Dispel the mists and the opaqueness
of the earthly mass,
and shine out with your splendor.

You are the serene and tranquil abode
of those who persevere in their goal
of seeing you.
You are at the same time
the beginning,
the vehicle,
the guide,
the way,
and the goal.

St. Severinus Boethius (475–525)
Philosopher and Writer

**ST. GREGORY THE GREAT —
POPE AND LITURGIST**

St. Gregory the Great was a man of many interests and extraordinary talents. He enriched the fields of moral, liturgy, and music while at the same time administering the Church during a dark period of history. He is a fine representative for the Saints of this period whose prayers still speak to us today.

B) SIXTH TO TENTH CENTURIES

THIS period, technically known as the Dark Ages, was a time of turmoil, wars, and little social stability. Nations were being forged and so were the Churches in developing cultures. While the Roman base of the Church was being eroded by the Barbarian invasions and it was undergoing setbacks, it was also experiencing a revitalization and expanding into the emerging peoples and nations.

One of the principal means by which the Church was held together and flourished during this time was the office of the episcopate. The preponderance of the bishop is the great social fact of the Dark Ages. The calendar is filled with the saint-bishops of the sixth to eighth centuries, their personalities haloed by a thousand outstanding miracles.

The bishop was the all-around leader of the community. He was the sole lawgiver of the diocese and the administrator of all property. He was in charge of all social work taken on by the Church—hospitals, schools, and prisons. He was the principal judge and a kind of fiscal adviser to the great. He was the only one who could stand up to the king.

This general preeminence of the bishop is reflected in the prayers which have come down to us from the period.

462   **Prayer for God's Light**

O LORD,
      grant us that love which can never die,
which will enkindle our lamps
but not extinguish them,
so that they may shine in us
and bring light to others.

Most dear Savior,
enkindle our lamps
that they may shine forever in your temple.
May we receive unquenchable light from you
so that our darkness will be illuminated
and the darkness of the world will be made less.

                                    St. Columba of Ireland (521–597)
                                    Abbot and Founder of Monasteries

463   **Prayer for Forgiveness**

O GOD,
      mercy and forgiveness are yours
by nature and by right.
Receive our humble petitions.
Though we are bound tightly
by the chain of our sins,
set us free
by the power of your great mercy.

                                    St. Gregory the Great (540–604)
                                    Pope, Writer, and Doctor

464   **Prayer to the Holy Spirit for Guidance**

O HOLY Spirit,
      we are here before you
conscious of our many sins,

but united in a special way in your holy name.
Come and abide with us,
and deign to penetrate our hearts.

Be the guide of our actions,
indicate the path we should follow
and show us what we must do,
so that, with your help,
our work may be wholly pleasing to you.

May you be our only inspiration
and the overseer of our intentions,
for you alone possess a glorious name
with the Father
and the Son.

May you, who are infinite justice,
never permit us to be disturbers of justice.
Let not our ignorance induce us to evil,
nor flattery sway us,
nor moral and material interest corrupt us.

Unite our hearts to you alone,
and do it strongly,
so that with the gift of your grace
we may be one in you
and may in nothing depart from the truth.

Thus, united in your name,
may we in our every action
follow the dictates of your mercy and justice,
so that today and always
our judgments may not be alien to you
and in eternity we may obtain
the unending reward of our actions.

St. Isidore of Seville (560-636)
Bishop and Encyclopedist

465   **Prayer to Remain Faithful to God**

LEAD me in your way,
and I will walk in your truth.
Let my heart rejoice
that it may fear your name.
My God,
save me from the clutches of the sinner
who works against your law:
for you are the one I await.

St. Helier of Jersey (6th century)
Hermit and Martyr

466   **Prayer to Christ for Protection**

O LORD,
give me that fire
which you sent forth when coming on earth. . . .
Enable me to be aflame with the ardor of charity,
to glow with the splendor of obedience,
and to grow ardent with love.

Help me to be saved from destruction amid dangers,
to escape all perils,
and to hasten toward your goodness.
Grant me to come peacefully into your presence,
to be satiated forever by its manifestation,
and to praise you unceasingly
for all eternity.

St. Ildephonsus of Toledo (c. 607–667)
Bishop, Writer, and Mystic

467   **Prayer for a Holy Death**

O CHRIST,
  let me confess your name with my last breath.
In your great mercy receive me
and do not disappoint me in my hope.
Open the gates of life for me,
and let the prince of darkness
have no power over me.
Protect me by your kindness,
shield me with your might,
and lead me by your right hand
to the place of refreshment,
the tabernacle you have prepared
for your servants
and for those who revere you.

St. Eligius of France (?–660)
Bishop and Founder of Churches

468   **Prayer in Praise of the Creator**

L ET us praise the Creator of heaven,
  the might of the Maker,
the deeds of the Father,
and the thought of his heart.
As everlasting Lord,
he established of old the source of all wonders.
As all-holy Creator,
he spread the bright heavens,
a roof high above the children of man.
The King of mankind then created for mortals
the world in its beauty,
the earth spread beneath them—
the Lord everlasting and almighty God!

St. Caedmon (?–685)
Monk and Poet

469   **Prayer to Remain Faithful to One's Vow**

L ORD,
     by your grace,
may I your servant
find favor in your eyes.
Help me to do what I ought
in my trouble.
You are my benefactor,
my leader,
my ruler,
and my protector.
Enable me to render to you
the vow which my lips have made.

St. Begga of Ireland (650–693)
Princess and Solitary Wanderer

470   **Prayer to Christ to Receive the Holy Spirit**

O KING of glory
     and Lord of all power,
on this day you triumphed
and ascended above the heavens.
Do not leave us as orphans,
but send down on us,
from the Father,
the Spirit of truth
whom you have promised.

St. Bede the Venerable (673–735)
Monk, Historian, and Doctor

471   **Prayer for God's Help**

O ETERNAL Light,
     shine into our hearts.

O eternal Goodness,
deliver us from evil.
O eternal Power,
be our strength.
O eternal Wisdom,
dispel the darkness of our ignorance.
O eternal Pity,
show mercy to us.

Grant that we may ever seek your countenance
with all our hearts, minds, and strength.
And in your infinite mercy
enable us to reach your holy presence.

Alcuin (735–804)
Priest, Educator, and Liturgist

472   Prayer for God's Ministers

MOST gracious God,
lovingly heed our prayers
and enlighten the hearts
of those whom you have called. . . .
Enable them to minister worthily to your mysteries,
to love you with an everlasting love,
and to attain joys without end.

Charlemagne (742–814)
Western Emperor

473   Prayer to Christ against Evil

CHRIST our Lord,
you suffered and were tempted.
You are powerful to come to the aid
of those who are assailed by the devil,
for you are the support of Christian people.

O Lord,
protect with your right hand
those who trust in your name.
Deliver them from the evil one,
and grant them everlasting joy.

St. Gregory of Khandzta (759-861)
Abbot and Scholar

474   Prayer of Repentance

O LORD,
    you know how many and how great are my failings.
You know how often I sin,
from day to day,
from hour to hour,
in what I do
and in what I fail to do.

O Lord my God,
I resolve no more to provoke you,
and to desire nothing more than you,
for you are alone truly lovable.
If I should offend you again,
please grant me the strength
to find favor anew in your eyes
and to lead a life more pleasing to you.

St. Theodore of Studium (759-826)
Abbot and Scholar

475   Prayer for Help in Seeking God

O LORD,
    you are the eternal Essence of things.
You span space and time,
and yet you are within them.

You transcend all things,
and yet you pervade everything.

Manifest yourself to us
who grope toward you
and seek you in the shadows of ignorance.
Extend your hand to guide us,
for we cannot come to you without your help.
Reveal yourself to us,
for we desire nothing else but you.

John Scotus Erigena (810-880)
Philosopher and Theologian

476   Prayer for an End to Discord

GOD the Father,
origin of divinity,
good beyond all good,
and fair beyond all fair,
you are the abode
of calmness, peace, and concord.
Put an end to the discord
that separates us from one another,
and lead us back to a unity of love
that may show some similarity
to your divine nature.

As you are above all things,
unite us by the unanimity of a good mind,
so that through the embrace of love
and the bonds of affection
we may become spiritually one—
both in ourselves and in each other—
by means of your peace
which renders all things peaceful.

St. Dionysius the Syrian (818-848)
Patriarch and Historian

477   **Prayer to Jesus Our Redeemer**

PEACE comes from you alone
for only you can atone for our sins;
put aside your wrath
and trace out a path to heaven for us.
O holy Lord and God,
eternal Christ of God,
heed our faltering breath
and spare us from everlasting death.

Bl. Notker Balbulus (840-912)
Swiss Monk and Hymnist

478   **Prayer in Celebration of God's Perfections**

WE PRAY to you, O Lord,
who are the supreme Truth,
and all truth is from you.
We beseech you, O Lord,
who are the highest Wisdom,
and all the wise depend on you for their wisdom.
You are the supreme Joy,
and all who are happy owe it to you.
You are the highest Good,
and all goodness comes from you.
You are the Light of minds,
and all receive their understanding from you. . . .

We love you—
indeed we love you above all things.
We seek you,
follow you,
and are prepared to serve you.

We desire to dwell under your power,
for you are the King of all.

Alfred the Great (849–901)
King of England

479 **Prayer to the Ineffable Trinity**

O BLESSED Trinity,
you are the Universal One
and the Light.
There never was a name for you
and there never will be.
You are the Being with so many names
based on your works. . . .

You are the only Glory,
the Origin, the Might, and the Kingdom.
You are the Light,
and all is one in you—
Will, Word, and Command,
Strength and Virtue.
Have mercy on me
in my lowliness.

Simeon the New Theologian (949–1022)
Eastern Abbot and Mystic

ST. THOMAS AQUINAS — THE ANGELIC DOCTOR

St. Thomas Aquinas is the logical man to represent this period because of his vast influence on those who have come after him. Among the many writings that he has left us are the beautiful prayers and hymns in honor of the Blessed Sacrament that have been repeated by thousands over the years. He was a man of action but also a man of prayer.

C) ELEVENTH TO FIFTEENTH CENTURIES

THIS *period spans the centuries that have come to be known as the Middle Ages—when society was almost wholly Christian-oriented. It was a time of prodigious growth in countless fields of human endeavor—establishment of law, development of cities, and promotion of culture.*

This epoch prepared for the Modern Age a legacy of Christian life, art, architecture, literature, philosophy, education, and law (growing out of sacred customs and Roman law). It promoted the dignity of womanhood, economic activity, and political thought, organization of governments, peace, and unity of Christendom.

We might say that this period harbored and developed all the most saving elements of civilization—an independent papacy, a celibate clergy, elimination of slavery, protection of the rights of the individual, establishment of charitable institutions, and the rise of mendicant orders together with a new monasticism.

These centuries were characterized by feudalism in transition, guilds, markets, military religious orders, Crusades, pilgrimages, brotherhoods, troubadours, wandering scholars, the rise of universities, the Inquisition, and the codification of liturgical rites. Known as the Ages of Faith, they have bequeathed to us many prayers of faith like the ones found herein.

480   Prayer for All Classes of People

O LORD,
  we bring before you
the distress and dangers of peoples and nations,
the pleas of the imprisoned and the captive,
the sorrows of the grief-stricken,
the needs of the refugee,
the impotence of the weak,
the weariness of the despondent,
and the diminishments of the aging.
O Lord,
stay close to all of them.

St. Anselm of Canterbury (1033-1109)
Bishop, Writer, and Doctor

481   Prayer to God Who Loves Himself in Us

O LOVING Lord,
  you love yourself *in yourself*
when from the Father and the Son there proceeds
the Holy Spirit,
the love of the Father for the Son
and of the Son for the Father.
So sublime is this love that it is a unity,
and so profound is this unity
that Father and the Son have one substance.

And you love yourself *in us*
when the Spirit of your Son is sent into our hearts . . .
and you enable us to love you out of love.
Even more, you love yourself in us
in order that we might hope in you
and cherish your name. . . .

We love you,
or better, *you love yourself in us—*

we with affection
and you with efficacy—
making us one with your own unity,
that is, by your Spirit given us. . . .

Adorable, Awe-inspiring, and Blessed Spirit—
loving Lord, give him to us!
Send forth your Spirit and all shall be created,
and you shall renew the face of the earth.

William of Saint-Thierry (1085-1148)
Abbot and Spiritual Writer

482 **Prayer in Praise of Jesus**

JESUS,
    your loving memory rejoices our hearts,
but your presence is sweeter than honey
and all things.
Nothing is more melodious to sing,
nothing more joyful to hear,
nothing more pleasing to ponder—
than Jesus, Son of God! . . .

Jesus,
you are the happiness of every heart,
the source of all life,
and the light of every mind—
far beyond every joy and all desire. . . .

Lord,
stay with us,
and enlighten us with your light.
Dispel the darkness of our minds,
and fill the world with your sweetness.
Let praise and honor of your name
be in the kingdom of the blessed.

St. Bernard of Clairvaux (1090-1153)
Abbot, Writer, and Doctor

483 Prayer of a Person in Authority

O LORD,
let me learn at the school of your Spirit
to comfort the grieving,
to steady the faltering,
and to lift up the fallen.
Teach me to be weak with those who are weak,
to be indignant with those who are indignant,
and to be all things to all
so that I may gain all. . . .

You know that I love them with all my heart
and all my compassion is directed toward them.
I do not lead them out of a spirit of domination
but I desire to serve them
rather than lord it over them,
for humility prompts me to be submissive to them,
and affection makes me one of them.

You know the needs of every one of them.
Strengthen those who are feeble,
do not reject those who are weak,
heal those who are sick,
calm those who are troubled,
refresh those who are weary,
and reassure those who are unstable.
Let all experience your grace
in their every necessity and trial.

Aelred of Rievaulx (1110-1176)
Abbot and Mystical Writer

484 Prayer That Jesus Will Come As Our Savior

COME, O Lord,
but in swaddling clothes,
not with your hosts!

Come,
but in lowliness,
not in splendor!

Come,
but on the donkey,
not on the cherubim!

Come,
but in the stable,
not on the clouds of heaven!

Come,
but toward us,
not against us!

Come,
but to save,
not to judge!

Come,
but on the heart of your Mother,
not on the throne of your majesty!

Come,
but to visit us in peace,
not to accuse us in anger!
If you come in this manner—
far from fleeing from you—
we will fly to you!

> Peter of Celle (?-1187)
> *Bishop and Mystical Writer*

485 Prayer Offering the Day to God

O LORD,
   into your hands,
and into the hands of your holy angels,
I commit and entrust this day
myself,
my relatives,

my benefactors,
my friends and enemies,
and all your Christian people.

By the intercession of the Blessed Virgin Mary,
and of all your saints,
keep us this day
from all evil and unruly desires,
from all sins and temptations of the devil,
from sudden and unprovided death,
and from the pains of hell.

Enlighten my heart
with the grace of your Holy Spirit.
Grant that I may ever be obedient
to your commandments
and never let me be separated from you.

St. Edmund of Abingdon (1180-1246)
Bishop, Writer, and Ascetic

486 Prayer for the Grace to Help Others

LORD, make me an instrument of your peace.
   Where there is hatred, let me sow love.
Where there is injury, let me sow pardon.
Where there is friction, let me sow union.
Where there is error, let me sow truth.
Where there is doubt, let me sow faith.
Where there is despair, let me sow hope.
Where there is darkness, let me sow light.
Where there is sadness, let me sow joy.

O Divine Master,
grant that I may not so much seek
to be consoled as to console,
to be understood as to understand,
to be loved as to love.

For it is in giving that we receive.
It is in pardoning that we are pardoned.
It is in dying that we are born to eternal life.

St. Francis of Assisi (1182-1226)
Religious and Mystic

487 **Prayer in Praise of God
for All His Creatures**

MOST high, most powerful and good Lord,
to you be given praise, glory, honor,
and every blessing;
to you alone they are due, Most High,
and no man is worthy to call your name.

Blest be you, my Lord, with all your creatures,
especially my lord and brother Sun,
who makes the day and by whom you give us light;
he is beautiful, radiant with great splendor:
of you, Most High, he is the symbol.

Blest be you, my Lord, for sister Moon and the Stars;
in heaven you formed them,
clear, precious, and beautiful.

Blest be you, my Lord, for brother Wind,
and for the air and the clouds,
for the calm azure and all times
by which you give sustenance to your creatures.

Blest be you, our Lord, for sister Water,
which is very useful and humble
and precious and chaste.

Blest be you, my Lord, for brother Fire
by which you give light to the night:
it is beautiful and joyful,
unconquerable and strong.

Blest be you, my Lord, for our sister and mother Earth
which carries and feeds us,
which produces a variety of fruits,
and variegated flowers and herbs.

Blest be you, my Lord, for those
who give pardon for love of you;
who bear trials and illnesses;
blest are they when they preserve peace
for by you, Most High, they will be crowned.

Blest be you, my Lord, for our sister bodily Death,
from whom no living man can escape;
but woe to those who die in mortal sin.
Blest those whom she will find in your most holy will,
for the second death will not be able to harm them.

Praise and bless my Lord,
render thanks to him and serve him
with great humility!

St. Francis of Assisi (1182-1226)
Religious and Mystic

488 Prayer in Praise of God's Ineffable Greatness

YOU are holy,
  O Lord and only God,
you who work wonders.

You are strong, great, and sovereign,
you are almighty,
O Father most holy,
King of heaven and earth.
You are Triune and One at the same time,
Lord God,
and all good.
You are good, all good, and the supreme good,

O Lord God,
living and true.

You are charity and wisdom,
humility and patience,
security and tranquility,
gaiety and joy.

You are justice and temperance,
riches that surpass all sufficiency,
beauty and goodness.

You are a protector, a guardian, and a defender.
You are strength.
You are our refreshment and our courage.

You are our faith, hope, and charity.
You are our great tenderness.
You are our eternal life,

O great and wonderful Lord,
God almighty,
and dear Savior,
full of mercy.

St. Francis of Assisi (1182-1226)
Religious and Mystic

489 Prayer for the Help of the Holy Spirit

O GOD,
   send forth your Holy Spirit
into my heart that I may perceive,
into my mind that I may remember,
and into my soul that I may meditate.

Inspire me to speak with piety,
holiness, tenderness, and mercy.
Teach, guide, and direct my thoughts and senses
from the beginning to the end.

May your grace ever help and correct me,
and may I be strengthened now
with wisdom from on high,
for the sake of your infinite mercy.

St. Anthony of Padua (1195-1231)
Priest and Doctor

490 Prayer in Praise of God's Greatness

O FLAMING Mountain,
   O chosen Sun,
O full Moon,
O bottomless Well,
O unattainable Height,
O Brightness beyond compare,
O Wisdom without measure,
O Mercy unsurpassed,
O Might irresistible,
O Crown of all glory:
your lowly creature sings your praises.

Mechtild of Magdeburg (1210-1282)
Religious and Mystical Writer

491 Prayer to Be Centered on Christ

L ORD Jesus Christ, . . .
   may my soul always revolve around you,
seek you,
and find you.
Help it to turn to you,
and reach you.
Let its every thought and word be centered
on you.

Grant that my soul may sing your praise
and the glory of your holy name

with humility and reserve,
with love and joy,
with ease and gentleness,
with patience and tranquility,
with success and persistence
to the very end.

St. Bonaventure (1221-1274)
Bishop, Writer, and Doctor

492 Prayer for a Faithful and Upright Heart

O LORD my God,
   help me to be obedient without reserve,
poor without servility,
chaste without compromise,
humble without pretense,
joyful without depravity,
serious without affectation,
active without frivolity,
submissive without bitterness,
truthful without duplicity,
fruitful in good works without presumption,
quick to revive my neighbor without haughtiness,
and quick to edify others by word and example
without simulation.

Grant me, O Lord, an ever-watchful heart
that no alien thought can lure away from you;
a noble heart
that no base love can sully;
an upright heart
that no perverse intention can lead astray;
an invincible heart
that no distress can overcome;
an unfettered heart
that no impetuous desires can enchain.

O Lord my God,
also bestow upon me
understanding to know you,
zeal to seek you,
wisdom to find you,
a life that is pleasing to you,
unshakable perseverance,
and a hope that will one day take hold of you.

May I do penance here below
and patiently bear your chastisements.
May I also receive the benefits of your grace,
in order to taste your heavenly joys
and contemplate your glory.

St. Thomas Aquinas (1225-1274)
Priest, Theologian, and Doctor

493   **Prayer to the Lord of Joy**

LORD,
    you have put so much joy in my heart
that I beg you to extend it to my entire body.
Let my face and my eyes,
my mouth and my hands
manifest my joy.

Lord,
when I dwell on eternal life,
I am filled to overflowing with joy. . . .
So great is this joy
that neither anger nor distress can harm me,
nor even approach me. . . .

Lord,
I owe my joy and my strength to you,
and it would be useless
for me to take credit for them.

May you thus be pleased, O Lord,
that I consider every good as coming from you,
my Creator and my God.

Bl. Raymond Lull (1235-1315)
Scholar, Poet, and Martyr

494 **Prayer before Departing on a Trip**

O GOD,
you called Abraham your servant out of Ur
and kept him safe and sound in all his wanderings.
If it is your will,
protect your servants.
Be for us a support when setting out,
friendship along the way,
a little shade from the sun,
a mantle against cold and rain,
a crutch on slippery paths,
and a haven in shipwreck.

Bear us up in fatigue,
and defend us under attack.
Under your protection,
let us fulfill the purpose for our trip
and return safe and sound to our home.

Durandus of Mende (c. 1237-1296)
Canonist and Liturgist

495 **Prayer of Longing for Christ**

O CHRIST,
in you I find
everything that I desire.
I see nothing
that one could seek outside of you.
It is you yourself
that we receive from you.

You have become my sole tenderness,
my delight,
the exultation of my soul,
the joy of my spirit,
and the consoling music of my chant of love.

O beloved and sovereign Goodness,
for you alone I long,
to you alone I pray,
you alone I implore.
Do not refuse me this favor:
heal me,
for you are the help of the afflicted!

Richard Rolle (1290-1349)
Hermit and Spiritual Writer

496   Prayer in Praise of God's Infinite Goodness

O GOD, unlimited Goodness,
   when I desire to praise you,
no words can express
all that is contained in my heart.
The most beautiful creatures,
the most sublime spirits,
the most pure beings—
everything is infinitely beneath you.
But if I plunge into the abyss of your goodness,
O Master,
all praise is so small that it disappears.

I traverse the firmament and the earth,
the surface and the deep,
forests and prairies,
mountains and valleys:
all in unison cause to resound in my ears
the symphony of your glory without limit.

When I think of you,
the Good that merits praise,
you are the one that my soul has chosen
as the unique object of its love.
And my heart wishes to praise you
until death.

Bl. Henry Suso (1296-1366)
Religious, Writer, and Mystic

497 Prayer to Hear the Words of the Spirit

MY LORD and God,
the words of your Spirit are laden with delights.
As often as I hear them,
my soul seems to absorb them
and they enter the heart of my body
like the most delicious food,
bringing unbounded joy and ineffable comfort.

After hearing your words,
I remain both satisfied and hungry—
satisfied, for I desire nothing else;
but hungry, for I crave more of your words.

St. Bridget of Sweden (1302-1373)
Noblewoman and Religious

498 Prayer in Praise of the Holy Name of Jesus

O TRIUMPHANT Name,
O joy of angels and of the just,
O fear of hell:
in you
lies all hope of pardon, grace, and glory.
O most sweet Name,
you give pardon to sinners.

You renew us,
fill our hearts with divine delight,
and cast out our fears.

O Name full of grace,
through you
your faithful gain insight into great mysteries,
become aflame with divine grace,
receive strength in their combats,
and are delivered from all evil.

St. Bernardine of Siena (1380-1444)
Religious Preacher and Reformer

499 Prayer That God May Manifest Himself to All Who Seek Him

O LORD,
  help us,
for only you can do so.
It is really you whom people are imploring
when they invoke the various Divinities.
No matter what they seem to desire,
it is none other than the Supreme Good—
and you are that Good.
In their mental searchings
it is really your Truth which they seek.
For a living being longs only for life,
and a person endowed with existence
seeks only for being.

Hence, it is you,
giver of life and being,
who are sought in various ways
in different rites,
you who are called by different names—
for what you are

you remain for all:
unknown and ineffable. . . .

Almighty God, invisible to every spirit,
you can manifest yourself to each
according to his capacity.
Do not hide yourself, O Lord.
Be gracious and show your face,
and your people will be saved.

Nicholas of Cusa (1401-1464)
Cardinal and Scholar

500 Prayer of Self-Offering to God

MY LORD and my God,
remove far from me
whatever keeps me from you.

My Lord and my God,
confer upon me
whatever enables me to reach you.

My Lord and my God,
free me from self
and make me wholly yours.

St. Nicholas of Flue (1417-1487)
Soldier and Hermit

501 Prayer to Receive God's Mercy

HAVE mercy on me, O God,
in your goodness.
Not according to the mercy of human beings,
which is small,
but according to your mercy,
which is great, immense, and incomprehensible,
and which infinitely exceeds all sins:
according to that mercy

through which you have so loved the world
as to give your only Son for it.

Have mercy on me, O God,
but not according to your small mercy.
Your small mercy alleviates
the corporal miseries of people,
while your great mercy consists in remitting sins
and raising people
above all the grandeurs of the earth
by means of your grace.
Have mercy on me, O Lord,
according to that great mercy,
in order to convert me to you,
to destroy my sins,
and to justify me by your grace.

Girolamo Savonarola (1452-1498)
Religious Prophet and Reformer

502   Prayer for the Unity of the Church

O GOD,
you are the Friend of the human race
and you willed to grant us the gift of tongues
by which you once divinely instructed your apostles
so that they might preach the Gospel.
Through the ministry of your Holy Spirit,
grant that all people
in all places and in all tongues
may proclaim the glory of your Son Jesus.

Confound the tongues of false prophets
who have united to construct
the impious tower of Babel
so as to obscure your glory and enhance their own.
To you alone belongs all glory,
with Jesus your Son, our Lord,

and the Holy Spirit,
for all ages.

Desiderius Erasmus (1469-1536)
Priest and Humanist

503 Prayer to Love God Completely

MOST loving Father,
  you command me to love you
with all my heart and soul, mind, and strength.
But I am sure that I do not do so.
I know this by reflecting on how I loved others:
I loved them to the point of rarely forgetting them.
They were constantly present to my memory,
my heart dwelt on them almost all the time,
and their image ran through my head
in their presence as well as in their absence.

O loving Father,
I regret to say that I do not act this way
toward you.
I do not keep you in my memory,
nor do I have you present in my thoughts,
nor is my heart sufficiently occupied with you.
As soon as the merest trifle enters my head,
I drop you and lose sight of you.
As soon as the slightest whim enters my heart,
I discard you and quickly forget you. . . .

So with all the fervor of my being
I ask you to grant me your Holy Spirit
who will deliver me from this weakness of mine.
Your Holy Spirit will enable me to love you
with all my heart and soul, mind and strength,
for he is the origin of all true love.

St. John Fisher (1469-1535)
Bishop, Educator, and Martyr

504   **Prayer to Work for the Things
                We Pray For**

O LORD,
     give us a mind that is
humble, quiet, peaceable, patient, and charitable,
and a taste of your Holy Spirit
in all our thoughts, words, and deeds.
O Lord,
give us
a lively faith,
a firm hope,
a fervent charity,
a love of you.

Take from us
all lukewarmness in meditation
and dullness in prayer.
Give us fervor and delight
in thinking of you,
your grace,
and your tender compassion toward us.
Give us,
good Lord,
the grace to work for
the things we pray for.

                              St. Thomas More (1478-1535)
                              Statesman, Humanist, and Martyr

505   **Prayer for Health, Wisdom,
                and a Sense of Humor**

O LORD,
     give me a good digestion
as well as something to digest.

Give me health of body
as well as the sense to keep it healthy.
Give me a holy soul,
O Lord,
which keeps its eyes on beauty and purity,
so that it will not be afraid on seeing sin.

Give me a soul that knows nothing
of boredom, groans, and sighs.
Never let me be overly concerned
for this inconstant thing that I call me.
Lord,
give me a sense of humor,
so that I may take some happiness from this life,
and share it with others.

St. Thomas More (1478-1535)
Statesman, Humanist, and Martyr

506   Prayer of Self-Offering to God

TAKE, O Lord,
    and receive my entire liberty,
my memory, my understanding, and my whole will.
All that I am and all that I possess
you have given me.
I surrender it all to you
to be disposed of according to your will.
Give me only your love and your grace;
with these I will be rich enough
and will desire nothing more.

St. Ignatius of Loyola (1491-1556)
Religious and Founder

ST. TERESA OF AVILA — A MODERN SAINT

St. Teresa nicely symbolizes the modern times with which this section is concerned. She was a forerunner of the modern woman and she combined a keen practical understanding of life with a deep spiritual life. Her many gifts have earned her the title of "the Great," and her learned writings on the Faith have entitled her to be called a "Doctor of the Church."

D) SIXTEENTH TO TWENTIETH CENTURIES

THIS period, known broadly as Modern Times, has undergone a multiplicity of new influences. Some of these are: the outbreak of the Protestant Reformation, the discovery and exploration of the New World, the end of feudalism, the birth of the industrial revolution, the eruption of the French Revolution, the rise of democracy, the onset of the social sciences, the advance of technology, and the knowledge explosion.

The Church discovered new peoples to convert and became more conscious of the immense task of bringing the Gospel to the whole world, giving rise to the great missionary movement spurred on by the emergence of many new religious orders. The Church also gave birth to new forms of worship and devotion, such as the Sacred Heart, the Blessed Sacrament, Christ the King, and true devotion to Mary.

During this time, the emphasis on education impelled the Church to begin scientifically teaching the Faith to its members and bringing Christianity to the marketplace. In this task, the Church has been aided immeasurably by the rise of the Liturgical Movement, the Biblical Renewal, and the Catholic Action Movement which catapulted the laity into the active promulgation of the Faith to the masses. Our day has seen an emphasis on social consciousness and on building the world for Christ in conjunction with all other men.

On the other hand, the Church has been assailed on all sides by Rationalists, Pseudo-Scientists, and Atheistic Humanists. At the same time, however, the Church has been blessed with outstanding men and women who have labored zealously to live their Faith and convert others both by their inspiring example and by their powerful words. Much of this is reflected in the prayers presented here—which can be of great help to us.

507 Prayer for the Conversion of Unbelievers

O GOD of all peoples on the earth,
    be mindful of the many unbelievers.
They have been created in your image,
yet they do not know you
or your Son Jesus Christ,
their Savior who died for them.
By the prayers and labors
of your Church,
may they be freed from all ignorance and unbelief
and led to worship you.
We ask this through Jesus Christ,
your Son, our Lord,
whom you sent to be the resurrection and the life
of all human beings.

St. Francis Xavier (1506-1552)
Priest, Missionary, and Martyr

508 Prayer to Do Always the Will of God

O LORD,
    regulate all things by your wisdom,
so that I may always serve you
in the manner that you will
rather than in the manner that I will.
Do not punish me
by granting what I will
if it offends against your love,
for I want your love to live always in me.
Help me to deny myself
in order that I may serve you.
Let me live for you—
who in yourself are the true life.

St. Teresa of Avila (1515-1584)
Religious, Mystic, and Doctor

509 **Prayer That We Will Possess All Things in Christ**

MY GOD,
you will not take away what you have given me
in your only Son, Jesus Christ.
In him, you have given me all that I desire.
You will, therefore, no longer delay—
and this is my joy—
provided that I wait for you.

So, my heart, why do you delay?
Why do you procrastinate?
From this moment on you can love your God!

Mine are the heavens,
mine is the earth and mine are the peoples;
mine are the just and mine are the sinners;
mine are the angels;
mine is the mother of God—
God himself is mine, for me—
for mine is Christ
and everything is for me.

What do you ask, what do you seek, my soul?
Everything is for you and everything is yours!

Do not think of yourself as little
nor pay attention to the scraps that fall
from the table of your Father.

Rise on the great day
and take your glory in his!
Hide yourself in it
and be joyful:
everything which your heart desires
shall be yours.

St. John of the Cross (1549-1591)
Priest, Mystic, and Doctor

510 **Prayer for a Strong Virtue of Hope**

O LORD,
   give me a strong hope,
for I cannot attain salvation
without that virtue being deeply rooted in me.
This hope is necessary
so that I may ask you to pardon my sins
and reach my supernatural end.

How greatly this hope gladdens me,
making me firmly expect
that I will reach heaven, my homeland.
Even in this life it gives me
a foretaste of relishing, understanding, and possessing
   you,
my God.

St. Mary Magdalene de Pazzi (1566-1607)
Religious and Mystic

511 **Prayer of Consecration to the Trinity**

O GOD,
   I vow and consecrate to you
all that is in me:
my memory and my actions
to God the Father;
my understanding and my words
to God the Son;
my will and my thoughts
to God the Holy Spirit;
my heart and my body,
my tongue, my senses, and all my sorrows
to the sacred humanity of Jesus Christ,
who was content to be betrayed

into the hands of wicked men
and to suffer the torment of the Cross.

St. Francis de Sales (1567-1622)
Bishop and Doctor

512 Prayer to Know the Will of God

LORD,
    what is your will that I do?
I am completely open to your plan for me.
I desire to live only in you
and to be guided by you forever.
Grant that your holy will
may be carried out perfectly in me.

St. Jane Frances de Chantal (1572-1641)
Religious and Foundress

513 Prayer for Unity of Will with God

O GOD,
    my spiritual and corporal existence is yours
since you are my Creator.
But my will is mine
because you have created it as free
and want it to remain such.
However, I am free
to offer it in homage to you
and to make it a sacrifice of praise and honor
to you.
Hence, I give my will entirely to you,
so that it no longer belongs to me.

Henceforth I must be careful
to let nothing proceed from my heart
that would be unworthy of a God.
I must exert constant vigilance over my will

to avoid taking away from God
what is now truly his.

St. Louise de Marillac (1591-1660)
Religious and Foundress

514   Prayer of Longing for God Alone

O BELOVED Father,
   it appears that you withdraw from me.
I run,
I soar,
I seek you,
although I know you are in me;
for you have a dwelling there that is unknown to me.
When I open my arms to embrace you,
my failings get in the way
and put an obstacle between us.
I lose sight of you.
Where are you, my Beloved?
O Father, give me your Son.
Look with pity on my groanings.

It is not the saints that I desire,
neither is it the angels that I request,
nor is it paradise and its delights that I want.
It is you and you alone that I seek,
O my Beloved.
Give yourself to me
and heal this wound that you have inflicted on me,
or let it lead to my death.

Ven. Mary of the Incarnation (1599-1672)
Religious, Widow, and Mystic

515   Prayer to Be Clothed with All the Virtues

O MY GOD,
   I magnify you a thousand times

for all your mercies toward me.
Extend your mercies to all the poor
and take care of their needs.

You have provided me
with clothing for my body.
Grant me also clothing for my soul—
your very self, O Lord.
Let me be clothed
with your spirit and your love,
your charity, humility, and meekness,
your patience and obedience,
and all your other virtues.

St. John Eudes (1601-1680)
Religious, Spiritual Writer, and Founder

516 Prayer That God Will Speak Inwardly

SPEAK, speak, O Lord,
    for your servant is listening.
I say, your servant, because at last I am such.
I am your servant and I want to be;
I want to walk in your way
all the days and nights of my life.

Fill me with a spirit to understand
what your holy plans are for me.
And reduce my desires to the single desire
to understand your sublime truths. . . .

Speak, in order to console my anxious soul.
Speak, in order to lead it to repentance.
Speak, so that your glory,
thus more exalted,
will grow eternally.

Pierre Corneille (1606-1684)
Writer and Dramatist

517   **Prayer in Praise of the Incomparable God**

O MY GOD,
  I adore you in all your beauty and perfection,
such as you possess in yourself.
I adore your splendor,
a thousand times more beautiful than the sun.
I adore your fecundity,
a thousand times more wonderful than that of the stars.
I adore your life,
a thousand times more pleasing than that of the flowers.
I adore your activity,
infinitely more active than that of fire.
I adore your stability,
infinitely more fixed and solid than that of earth.
I adore your pervasiveness,
infinitely more delicate than that of air.
I adore your gentleness,
a thousand times more peaceful than that of our rivers.
I adore your expanse,
a thousand times more vast than that of the ocean. . . .
I adore your height,
a million times more sublime than the mountains I
  know. . . .
My God, in your works,
nothing is comparable to you.

> Jean Jacques Olier (1608-1656)
> *Priest and Founder*

518   **Prayer of Peace and Joy in God**

GOD of Abraham, God of Isaac, God of Jacob,
  not of the philosophers and the learned.
Certitude, certitude, sentiment, joy peace,
God of Jesus Christ.

"My God and your God" (Ruth 1:16).
Your God shall be my God.
Forgetfulness of the world and everything else
outside of God.
He can be found only in the ways taught in the Gospel.
Greatness of the human soul.
Just Father, the world has not known you,
but I have known you.
Joy, joy, joy, and tears of joy.

I have separated myself from you.
"They have gone away from me, the fountain of life"
    (Jeremiah 2:13).
My God, will you leave me?
Let me not be eternally separated from you.
This is eternal life,
that they may know you, the true God,
and the one whom you have sent—
Jesus Christ.
Jesus Christ—
I have separated myself from him.
I have fled from, renounced, and crucified him.
May I never be separated from him.

He is kept only by the ways taught by the Gospel.
Complete and contented renunciation.
Total submission to Jesus Christ
and to my spiritual director.
Eternal joy in exchange for
one day's exertion on earth.
"I will never forget your words" (Psalm 118:16).

Blaise Pascal (1623-1662)
Philosopher and Mystical Writer

519 **Prayer of Complete Trust in God**

O KIND and merciful God,
   in your hands I place my hopes and fears,
my likes and dislikes,
my happiness and unhappiness,
my joys and sorrows.
I offer you the needs of my perishable body
and the more important ones of my imperishable soul.
I do not have to be afraid for my soul
as long as I leave it in your loving care.

Great are my failings and my wretchedness,
but even greater is my hope in you.
It is stronger than my weakness,
greater than my difficulties,
and mightier than death.

Though assailed by temptation,
I will hope in you.
Though I may falter because of weakness,
I will continue to trust in you.
Though I may not live up to my promises,
I will confidently seek grace from you
to renew and keep them.
Though you may take away my earthly life,
even then I will maintain my hope in you.

You are my Father and my God,
the ground of my salvation.
You are my gracious and loving Father,
and I am your beloved child.
I cast myself in your arms
and ask for your blessing.
I place all my trust in you
and I know that I will not be confounded.

Bl. Claude de la Colombière (1641-1682)
Priest, Spiritual Director, and Educator

520 **Prayer of Trust in the Sacred Heart**

O HEART of love,
  I place all my trust in you.
I fear all things
from my own weakness,
but I hope for all things
from your goodness.

St. Margaret Mary Alacoque (1647-1690)
Religious and Mystic

521 **Prayer for All Things Necessary to Salvation**

I BELIEVE, Lord, but may I believe more firmly.
  I hope, but may I hope more securely.
I love, but may I love more ardently.
I grieve, but may I grieve more deeply.

I adore you as my first beginning.
I aspire after you as my last end.
I praise you as my perpetual benefactor.
I invoke you as my merciful protector.

Direct me by your wisdom.
Keep me in your grace.
Console me with your mercy.
Protect me with your power.

I offer you, O Lord,
my thoughts, that they may be about you;
my words, that they may be spoken for your glory;
my actions, that they may accord with your will;
my sufferings, that they may be accepted for your sake.

I desire whatever you desire.
I desire it because you desire it.

I desire it insofar as you desire it.
I desire it for as long as you desire it.

I pray, O Lord, that you will enlighten my mind,
inflame my will,
cleanse my heart,
and sanctify my soul.

May I repent of past sins,
repel future temptations,
correct wicked tendencies,
and cultivate virtuous ideals.

Good Lord, grant that I may love you,
renounce myself,
do good to my neighbor,
and be detached toward the world.

May I strive to obey my superiors,
support my inferiors,
aid my friends,
and spare my enemies.

Help me to overcome sensuality by self-denial,
avarice by liberality,
anger by meekness,
and tepidity by devotion.

Make me prudent in counsel,
steadfast in danger,
patient in adversity,
and humble in prosperity.

Grant, Lord, that I may be attentive at prayer,
temperate at meals,
diligent at work,
and constant in resolutions.

Let my conscience be upright,
my outward appearance be modest,

my conversation be edifying,
and my whole life be ordered.

Help me to labor to overcome nature,
to cooperate with your grace,
to keep your commandments,
and to further my salvation.

Teach me the futility of earthly things,
the greatness of divine things,
the shortness of temporal things,
and the length of eternal things.

Grant that I may be prepared for death,
fear judgment,
avoid hell,
and obtain paradise—
through Christ our Lord.

Clement XI (1649-1721)
Pope and Scholar

522 **Prayer to the God Who Is Always with Us**

M Y GOD,
   I understand you,
and you understand me better
than do all your creatures.
You are more than simply present here;
you are in me more than I am in myself.
I reside only in a finite manner
in the place where I exist.
You are there in an infinite manner,
and your infinite action is on me.
You have no limits,
and I find you everywhere.
You are there before I come,
and I only come there because you take me there.

I leave you in the place from which I set out,
I find you in every place I pass along the way,
and you are waiting for me at the place to which I come.
O my God,
see what my great affection makes me say,
or rather what it makes me stammer!

Francis Fenelon (1651-1715)
Archbishop and Theologian

523   Prayer to God Present Everywhere in the World

O MY God,
    you are in heaven,
and you are there in all your immensity.
You are also in the world,
which is entirely permeated with you,
because it contains you—
or rather because you contain it.

O my God,
I believe that wherever I go I will find you
and that there is no place
which you do not honor with your presence.

St. John Baptist de la Salle (1651-1719)
Religious, Educator, and Founder

524   Prayer for the Church of God

O LORD,
    remember your Church.
You possessed her in your mind from all eternity,
thinking of her from the beginning.
You possessed her in your hands
when you created the universe out of nothing
at the beginning.

You possessed her in your heart
when your dear Son died on the cross
and watered her with his blood
and consecrated her by his death,
entrusting her to his holy Mother.

Heed, O Lord,
the designs of your mercy.
Raise up new workers from your right hand,
as you have done in the past,
in giving prophetic qualities
to some of your greatest servants:
give us another St. Francis de Paul, St. Vincent Ferrer,
or St. Catherine of Siena.

St. Louis-Marie de Montfort (1673-1716)
Religious and Founder

525   **Prayer of Thanksgiving to Jesus**

LORD,
I give you thanks
for dying on the cross
for my sins.

St. Paul of the Cross (1694-1775)
Religious and Founder

526   **Prayer at the End of the Day**

JESUS Christ my God,
I adore you
and I thank you for all the graces
you have given me this day.
I offer you my sleep
and all the moments of this night,
and I implore you to keep me safe from sin.

To this end I place myself in your sacred side
and under the mantle of our Lady, my Mother.
Let your holy angels surround me
and keep me in peace;
and let your blessing be upon me.

St. Alphonsus Liguori (1696-1787)
Priest, Theologian, and Founder

527 Prayer to Attain Happiness in God

ALMIGHTY Giver of all mercies,
Father of all,
who know my heart
and pity its weakness and errors,
you know the desire of my soul
is to do your will.
It struggles to wing its flight to you,
its Creator,
and sinks again in sorrow for that imperfection
which draws it back to earth.
How long shall I contend with sin and mortality!
When will that hour arrive
which shall free the troubled spirit from its prison,
and change the sadness of this life
for immortality and endless happiness!

I bow to you, my God,
in cheerful hope,
that confiding in your infinite mercy
and assisted by your powerful grace
I shall soon arrive at that hour
of unspeakable joy.
But if it is your will
that the spirit shall yet contend with its dust,
assist me so to conduct myself through this life
as not to render it an enemy

but a conductor to that happy state
where all mortal contentions are done away
and where your eternal presence
will bestow eternal felicity.

St. Elizabeth Ann Seton (1774-1821)
Religious and Founder

528   Prayer of Those in Distress

LIKE travelers lost in a hot and arid desert,
   we cry out to you, O Lord,
Like those shipwrecked on a barren coast,
we cry out to you, O Lord.
Like a father robbed of a loaf of bread
that he was bringing home to his starving children,
we cry out to you, O Lord.
Like a prisoner cast into a dank and dark dungeon
by an unjust potentate,
we cry out to you, O Lord.
Like a slave lacerated by his master's lash,
we cry out to you, O Lord.
Like an innocent person led to execution,
we cry out to you, O Lord.
Like all the nations of the earth
who do not yet see the dawn of deliverance,
we cry out to you, O Lord.
Like Christ on the cross when he said:
"My God, my God, why have you forsaken me?"
we cry out to you, O Lord.

Felicité de Lamennais (1782-1854)
Priest and Founder

529   **Prayer for a New Coming
of the Holy Spirit**

O HOLY Spirit,
    we ask you to come anew. . . .
Send a comforting and beneficent breeze
on unfortunate souls who torment themselves.
Wreak havoc on the pride that wants to dominate all:
a doubt should make us incline toward kindness.

The humble lift up their eyes:
heaven is their inheritance.
Let them rejoice, knowing whose image they are!
Let those who receive much give with joy:
modesty uniting those who give and those who receive.

Be present in the incomparable laughter of children,
and in the charming blush of wise young women;
give consecrated virgins tranquil joys
and endow spouses with the love that triumphs over
    time.

Temper somewhat the ardor of haughty youths;
help virile plans to achieve fruition;
adorn white hair with joyous holy desires.
Be the hope of the dying
and shine forth in the depths of their eyes.

                        Alexander Manzoni (1785-1873)
                        Writer and Poet

530 **Prayer for God's Continued Protection**

O LORD,
    support us all the day long of this troublous life
until the shadows lengthen and the evening comes,
and the busy world is hushed,
and the fever of life is over,

and our work is done.
Then in your mercy
grant us a safe lodging
and a holy rest,
and peace at the last.

John Henry Newman (1801-1890)
Cardinal, Writer, and Educator

531   Prayer of Unswerving Fidelity to God

MY GOD,
   I am told in your name
that you want me here.
I will remain here
for love of you—
even if I am destined to perish.

Ven. Francis Libermann (1802-1852)
Priest, Spiritual Director, and Founder

532   Prayer to the Undying Christ

THERE is a man—flogged, killed, and crucified—
   whom an ineffable resurrection raises up
from the dead and from infamy,
in order to place him in the glory of a love that is un-
   dying,
and find in him peace, honor, joy, and even ecstasy.

There is a man pursued in his execution and his grave
by an inextinguishble hatred,
who asks for and finds apostles and martyrs
in the midst of all generations.

There is a man, finally,
who alone founded his love on earth,
and that man is you,

O Jesus,
you who kindly willed to baptize me,
anoint me, and consecrate me in your love.
Indeed, at this very moment,
your name alone opens my heart
and removes from it whatever was troubling me
even though I did not know it.

Henri Lacordaire (1802-1861)
Priest, Writer, and Orator

533 Prayer to Avoid Evil and Do Good

O MY GOD,
    I give myself to you,
with all my liberty,
all my intellect, heart, and will.
O holy spirit of God,
take me as your disciple:
guide me, illuminate me, sanctify me.
Bind my hands, that I may not do evil,
cover my eyes that I may see it no more,
sanctify my heart that evil may not rest within me.

Be my God and my guide.
Wherever you lead me I will go;
whatever you forbid I will renounce,
and whatever you command,
in your strength I will do.

Henry Manning (1808-1892)
Cardinal and Writer

534 Prayer for Undivided Love of God

YOU have made us for yourself,
    O God.
If we want to divide our heart

between God and creatures,
God will certainly get the smaller part.
Therefore, O my God,
take all my heart,
for it is not really very large.

St. Pierre Julian Eymard (1811-1868)
Religious and Founder

535 Prayer after Mass

O LORD Jesus Christ,
let your passion be my strength
to sustain, guard, and protect me.
Let your wounds be my food and drink
to nourish, fill, and invigorate me.
Let the shedding of your blood
cleanse me of all my sins.
Let your death obtain eternal life for me
and your cross lead me to everlasting glory.
Let these constitute for me
refreshment and joy,
health and uprightness of heart.

St. Pius X (1835-1914)
Pope and Reformer

536 Prayer That God May Not Abandon Us in Affliction

O MY God,
I beg you,
by your loneliness,
not that you may spare me affliction,
but that you may not abandon me in it.
When I encounter affliction,

teach me to see you in it
as my sole comforter.
Let affliction strengthen my faith,
fortify my hope,
and purify my love.
Grant me the grace
to see your hand in my affliction,
and to desire no other comforter but you.

St. Bernadette of Lourdes (1843-1879)
Religious and Mystic

537 Prayer to Love God As Much As We Can

O JESUS,
I love you very much.
I am being consumed by my love for you,
so that I am languishing and dying for you.
But despite such intense ardor,
I see and feel that my love is only a pale shadow
compared to the flame of your love for me.

Give me a heart as vast as the universe
so that I may love you—
if not as much as you deserve—
at least as much as I can!

St. Frances Xavier Cabrini (1850-1917)
Religious and Founder

538 Prayer for Christians of the East

L ORD,
you have brought together different peoples
in the profession of your name.
We pray for the Christian peoples of the East.
Calling to mind the privileged place
they once held in your Church,

we ask you to inspire in them the desire
to take their place with us once again—
one flock under one shepherd.
May they attain with us a greater knowledge
of the teachings of their holy Fathers—
who are our Fathers in the Church as well.

Do not let us widen the breach
that divides us.
By the Spirit of love and peace,
the sign of your presence among the faithful,
let the day come soon
when we will pray together,
and all peoples of every tongue
will acknowledge and glorify
the Lord Jesus Christ, your Son.

Benedict XV (1854-1922)
Pope and Humanitarian

539 **Prayer for the Faith That Overcomes All**

O LORD,
grant us faith,
the faith that removes the mask from the world
and manifests God in all things;
the faith that enables everything to be seen
in another light:
that shows us the greatness of God
and lets us see our own littleness;
that shows us Christ
where our eyes see only a poor person;
that shows us the Savior
where we feel only pain.

O Lord,
grant us the faith

that inspires us to undertake
everything that God wants
without hesitation,
without shame,
without fear,
and without ever retreating;
the faith that fears
neither danger, nor sorrow, nor death;
the faith that knows how to go through life
with calm, peace, and profound joy,
and that makes the soul completely indifferent
to everything that is not you.

Charles Foucauld (1858-1916)
Religious, Hermit, and Founder

540 Prayer of Our Love for God Alone

MY GOD,
you know that I have always desired
to love you alone.
I seek no other glory.
Your love has preceded me
from the time of my childhood,
become greater with my youth,
and is presently an abyss
whose depth I cannot fathom.

St. Theresa of Lisieux (1873-1897)
Religious and Mystic

541 Prayer for Humility

GREAT God, that bowest sky and star,
Bow down our towering thoughts to thee,
And grant us in a faltering war
The firm feet of humility.

Lord, we that snatch the swords of flame,
Lord, we that cry about thy ear,
We too are weak with pride and shame,
We too are as our foemen are.

Yea, we are mad as they are mad,
Yea, we are blind as they are blind,
Yea, we are very sick and sad
Who bring good news to all mankind.

The dreadful joy thy Son has sent
Is heavier than any care;
We find, as Cain his punishment,
Our pardon more than we can bear.

Lord, when we cry thee far and near
And thunder through all lands unknown
The gospel into every ear,
Lord, let us not forget our own.

Cleanse us from ire of creed or class,
The anger of the idle kings;
Sow in our souls, like living grass,
The laughter of all lowly things.

Gilbert Keith Chesterton (1874-1936)
Apologist, Novelist, and Poet

542 Prayer at the Beginning of a New Year

HEAVENLY Father,
you assist all things,
and you search for the best guide
for human hearts.
Make us responsive
in this time of grief and disintegration.
May this new year be for all of us
a year of edification and sanctification,
of interior life and reparation,
a year of great return
and of great pardon.

May your grace enkindle in all people
a love for the many unfortunate ones
whom poverty and misery reduce
to a condition of life
that is unworthy of human beings.
Arouse in the hearts
of those who call you Father
a hunger and thirst for social justice
and for fraternal charity
in deed and in truth.

O Lord,
grant peace in our days:
peace to our souls,
peace to our families,
peace to our country,
and peace among nations.

Pius XII (1876-1958)
Pope, Statesman, and Scholar

543   Prayer for Forgiveness of Sins

M Y JESUS,
  I place all my sins before you.
In my estimation they do not deserve pardon,
but I ask you . . .
to close your eyes to my want of merit
and open them to your infinite merit.
Since you willed to die for my sins,
grant me forgiveness for all of them.
Thus, I may no longer feel the burden of my sins,
a burden that oppresses me beyond measure.

Assist me, dear Jesus,
for I desire to become good
no matter what the cost.
Take away, destroy, and utterly root out

whatever you find in me that is contrary
to your holy will.
At the same time,
dear Jesus,
illumine me so that I may walk
in your holy light.

St. Gemma Galgani (1878-1903)
Religious and Stigmatic

544 Prayer to the Blessed Trinity

O ETERNAL Word of my God,
  I want to spend my life in heeding you.
I want to be wholly teachable
so that I may learn everything from you.
Then throughout all the nights,
all the emptinesses,
and all the powerlessnesses,
I want to concentrate on you alone
and dwell beneath your great light. . . .

O consuming Fire, Spirit of love,
inundate me so that my soul will become
like an incarnation of the Word. . . .

And you, O Father,
bend down toward your creature.
See in her only your Beloved
in whom you have placed all your good pleasure.

O my Threesome,
my All and my Beatitude,
infinite Solitude,
and Immensity in whom I lose myself,
I give myself to you as a prize.
Bury yourself in me
so that I may bury myself in you,

while waiting to contemplate in your light
the abyss of your greatness.

Elizabeth of the Trinity (1880-1906)
Religious and Mystical Writer

545   **Prayer to Christ, Lord of the World**

O GLORIOUS Christ,
  influence secretly diffused in the heart of matter,
and dazzling center
in which the countless number of fibers
of the multiple come together,
power as implacable as the world
and as warm as life.
Your forehead is of snow and your eyes are of fire,
your feet more sparkling than gold in fusion
and your hands imprison the stars.
You are the first and the last,
the one who died,
the one who lives,
and the one who rose again.
You gather together in your exuberant unity
all charms and all tastes,
all forces and all states.
It is you to whom my being called out
with a desire as vast as the universe.
You are truly
my Lord and my God.

Pierre Teilhard de Chardin (1881-1955)
Religious, Mystic, and Scientist

546 **Prayer That Jesus Will Pervade
Our Society**

O JESUS,
pervade our society,
our family life,
and our souls—
and rule as our peaceful Leader.
Let those who labor for the good of your people
and the poor
be enlightened with the radiance of faith
and the love of your kind heart.

Infuse them with your own spirit,
the spirit of discipline, order, and mildness,
and let the flame of enthusiasm burn ever brightly
in their hearts. . . .
May we soon see the day
when you are once more the center of civic life
and carried aloft by your joyful people.

John XXIII (1881-1963)
Pope and Ecumenist

547 **Prayer to Play Fair in the Game of Life**

DEAR Lord, in the struggle that goes on through life
we ask for a field that is fair,
a chance that is equal with all the strife,
the courage to strive and to dare;
and if we should win, let it be by the code,
with our faith and our honor held high;
and if we should lose, let us stand by the road
and cheer as the winners go by.

Knute Rockne (1888-1931)
Coach and Educator

548 **Prayer to Achieve Inner Peace**

SLOW me down, Lord.
Ease the pounding of my heart
by the quieting of my mind.
Steady my hurried pace
with a vision of the eternal reach of time.
Give me, amid the confusion of the day,
the calmness of the everlasting hills.
Break the tensions of my nerves and muscles
with the soothing music of the singing streams
that live in my memory.

Help me to know
the magical, restoring power of sleep.
Teach me the art of taking minute vacations—
of slowing down to look at a flower,
to chat with a friend,
to pat a dog,
to read a few lines from a good book.

Remind me each day of the fable
of the hare and the tortoise,
that I may know
that the race is not always to the swift—
that there is more to life
than increasing its speed.
Let me look upward
into the branches of the towering oak
and know that it grew great and strong
because it grew slowly and well.

Slow me down, Lord,
and inspire me to send my roots deep
into the soil of life's enduring values

that I may grow toward the stars
of my greater destiny.

Richard Cushing (1895-1968)
Cardinal and Founder

549 **Prayer for Peace**

O LORD,
God of peace,
you have created us
and poured out your love on us
so that we might share your glory.

We praise you and we thank you
for sending us Jesus,
your beloved Son.
Through the paschal mystery
you have made him
the architect of all salvation,
the source of all peace,
and the bond of all fraternity.

We thank you
for the desires, efforts, and accomplishments
which your Spirit of peace
has effected in our day,
to replace rancor with love,
distrust with understanding,
and indifference with solidarity.

Open our minds and hearts even more
to the concrete requirements
of the love of our brothers and sisters
so that we may be ever better workers for peace.
Remember, O Father of mercy,
all who are laboring, suffering, and dying
to create a more fraternal world.

May your kingdom of justice, peace, and love
come for all people of every race and tongue.
And may the earth be filled
with your glory.

Paul VI (1897-1978)
Pope, Statesman, and Scholar

550   Prayer to the Virgin of Guadalupe

VIRGIN of Guadalupe,
   Mother of the Americas . . . ,
grant to our homes the grace
of loving and respecting life in its beginnings,
with the same love
with which you conceived in your womb
the life of the Son of God.
Blessed Virgin Mary, Mother of Fair Love,
protect our families, so that they may always be united,
and bless the upbringing of our children.

We beg you to grant us a great love
for all the holy Sacraments,
which are, as it were, the signs
that your Son left us on earth.

Thus, Most Holy Mother,
with the peace of God in our conscience,
with our hearts free from evil and hatred,
we will be able to bring to all
true joy and true peace,
which come to us from your Son, our Lord Jesus Christ,
who with God the Father and the Holy Spirit,
lives and reigns for ever and ever.

John Paul II
Pope, Scholar, and Pastor

5

PRAYERS FROM OTHER RELIGIONS

439

PRAYERS OF OUR SEPARATED BRETHREN

It is obvious that the prayers of other Christians will be most like our own Catholic prayers. Since they have much in common with us, their prayers can be prayed with the least amount of adaptation on our part.

440

A) PROTESTANT AND ORTHODOX CHRISTIANS

THE Fathers of the Second Vatican Council acknowledged the things we have in common with our "separated Brethren" and urged all Catholics to esteem the Christian riches found in them:

"The Church recognizes that in many ways she is linked with those who, being baptized, are honored with the name of Christian, though they do not profess the faith in its entirety or preserve unity of communion with the successor of Peter. For there are many who honor Sacred Scripture, taking it as a norm of belief and a pattern of life, and who show a sincere zeal.

"They lovingly believe in God the Father Almighty and in Christ, the Son of God and Savior. They are consecrated by baptism, in which they are united with Christ. They also accept other sacraments within their Churches or ecclesiastical communities. Many of them rejoice in the episcopate, celebrate the Eucharist and cultivate devotion toward the Virgin Mother of God.

"They also share with us in prayer and other spiritual benefits. And we can say that in some real way they are joined with us in the Holy Spirit, for to them too he gives his gifts" (Constitution on the Church, no. 14).

"We should not forget that anything wrought by the grace of the Holy Spirit in the hearts of our separated brethren can be a help to our own edification. Whatever is truly Christian is never contrary to what genuinely belongs to the faith; indeed, it can always bring a deeper realization of the mystery of Christ and the Church" (Decree on Ecumenism, no. 4).

It is with these sentiments as well as in the interest of ecumenical gatherings that the following prayers have been gathered and included herein.

441

Prayers of Various Churches

551 Prayer of Thanksgiving for the Gifts of the Various Christian Churches

LET us give thanks for the gifts and graces of each great division of Christendom:

For the *Roman Catholic Church:* its glorious traditions, its disciplines in holiness, its worship, rich with the religious passion of the centuries; its noble company of martyrs, doctors, and saints;

We thank you, O Lord, and bless your holy name.

For the *Eastern Orthodox Church:* its secret treasure of mystic experience; its marvelous liturgy; its regard for the collective life and its common will as a source of authority;

We thank you, O Lord, and bless your holy name.

For the great *Protestant communions;*

We thank you, O Lord, and bless your holy name.

For the *Congregationalist* jealousy for the rightful independence of the soul and of the group;

We thank you, O Lord, and bless your holy name.

For the stress in the *Baptist Churches* upon personal regeneration and upon the conscious relation of the mature soul to its Lord;

We thank you, O Lord, and bless your holy name.

For the power of the *Methodists* to awaken the conscience of Christians to our social evils; and for their emphasis upon the witness of personal experience, and upon the power of the disciplined life;

We thank you, O Lord, and bless your holy name.

For the *Presbyterian* reverence for the sovereignty of God and their confidence in his faithfulness to his covenant; for their sense of the moral law, expressing itself in constitutional government;

We thank you, O Lord, and bless your holy name.

For the witness to the perpetual real presence of the inner light in every human soul borne by the Religious *Society of Friends* and for their faithful continuance of a free prophetic ministry;

We thank you, O Lord, and bless your holy name.

For the *Lutheran Church*: its devotion to the grace of God and the word of God, enshrined in the ministry of the word and sacraments;

We thank you, O Lord, and bless your holy name.

For the *Anglican Church*: its reverent and temperate ways, through its Catholic heritage and its Protestant conscience; its yearning concern over the divisions of Christendom, and its longing to be used as a house of reconciliation.

We thank you, O Lord, and bless your holy name.

(*Federal Council of Churches, U.S.A.*)

552   **Prayer of the Faithful**

I N PEACE, in the peace of God from above, let us pray to the Lord:

For the peace of the whole world; and for the peace, unity, and faithful service of the churches of God in this and every land.

℞.   **Hear us, O Lord.**

For all Christian people, their ministers and teachers, that by word and example they may bring many to faith and obedience in Christ.

℟. **Hear us, O Lord.**

For those in authority among the nations (and especially for the President, the Congress, and the Supreme Court of the United States), that they may govern with justice and promote peace and unity among all men.

℟. **Hear us, O Lord.**

For all on whose labor we depend, especially those whose duty brings them into danger, that they may have courage and strength to serve the common good.

℟. **Hear us, O Lord.**

For those who seek out knowledge, and guide our thought: for those who help us laugh and play, that truth and beauty may give joy to daily life.

℟. **Hear us, O Lord.**

For all who suffer: the poor and lonely, the sick and afflicted, the tempted and the bereaved; for prisoners, and those who are oppressed, or persecuted, that they may be strengthened and delivered.

℟. **Hear us, O Lord.**

For those who are enemies of the gospel of Christ, and who wrong their fellowmen, that they may be reconciled.

℟. **Hear us, O Lord.**

For the dying, that they may rise to eternal life; and for the departed, that they may rest in peace.

℟. **Hear us, O Lord.**

Here may be given the opportunity for members of the congregation to ask the prayers of the people for any special needs.

The minister may proceed:

Let us commit ourselves, one with another, to our God.

℟. **Lord, have mercy.**

Let us ask of the Lord brotherly love by the help of his Holy Spirit, and for each one of us the grace of a holy life.

℟. **Lord, have mercy.**

Let us remember before God all who are near and dear to us, those present and those absent, that we may love and serve one another in the bond of Christ.

℟. **Lord, have mercy.**

Let us pray for our community (and nation), that in all things we may be honest and just, and free from prejudice, bitterness, strife, and fear.

Let us recall in thanksgiving those who have died in the faith. May God give them the crown of life in the day of resurrection, and judge them worthy with the righteous to enter into the joy of their Lord.

℟. **Lord, have mercy.**

Let us give thanks for all his servants and witnesses of times past:

> Abraham, the father of believers,
> Moses, Samuel, Isaiah and all the prophets,
> John the Baptist, the forerunner,
> Mary, the mother of our Lord,
> Peter and Paul and all the apostles,
> Stephen the first martyr and all the martyrs and
> saints, in every age and in every land.

℟. **Lord, have mercy.**

May the Lord God in his mercy give us with them hope in his salvation, and in the promise of eternal life in his kingdom.

℟.   **Lord, have mercy.**

The minister may conclude·

Heavenly Father, you have promised to· hear what
we ask in the name of your Son. We pray you, accept
and fulfill our petitions, not as we ask in our ignorance
and unworthiness, nor as we deserve in our sinfulness,
but as you know and love us in your Son, Jesus Christ
our Lord.

℟.   **Amen.**   An Order of Worship (Protestant)
Consultation on Church Union

553   **Prayer to Walk in Holiness**

ALMIGHTY God, Father of all mercies,
   we your unworthy servants give you humble thanks
for all your goodness and loving-kindness
to us and to all whom you have made.
We bless you for our creation, preservation,
and all the blessings of this life;
but above all for your immeasurable love
in the redemption of the world
by our Lord Jesus Christ;
for the means of grace,
and for the hope of glory.

And, we pray,
give us such an awareness of your mercies,
that with truly thankful hearts
we may show forth your praise,
not only with our lips,
but in our lives,
by giving up our selves to your service,
and by walking before you
in holiness and righteousness all our days;
through Jesus Christ our Lord,

to whom, with you and the Holy Spirit,
be honor and glory throughout all ages.

The Episcopal Church
Proposed Book of Common Prayer, p. 101

554 **Prayer for the Blessings of Redemption**

O LORD,
you are God from eternity
yet man for our sakes.
Grant us, your unworthy servants,
what you have promised to all alike:
that your passion may be our deliverance,
your wounds our healing,
your Cross our redemption,
your death our life;
and that as you were raised upon the Cross
we may be lifted up to your Father
with whom you live and reign
in the unity of the Holy Spirit,
one God.   Lutheran Church

555 **Prayer for the Unity of All Christians**

WE ASK to be delivered from everything
that impedes the coming of unity in us:
from our lack of readiness to abandon past behavior;
from our sectarian spirit;
from the pride that transforms prejudices into principles;
from our tendency to sacrifice convictions for opportunity;
from our pessimism, defeatism, impatience, and laziness.
May we never place human hopes and fears
before the will of God.

Help us to serve the cause of unity
in accord with the gifts that are in us.
Let us not compromise the right cause
by lack of charity,
but honor the conviction of others
and seek the truth in love.
May the Church be more turned toward others
and look ahead,
so that vivified and renewed,
she may advance in her missionary task
toward all people.

Methodist Church

556 **Prayer in Union with the First Christians**

WITH John the Baptist we say:
"Behold the lamb of God
who takes away the sin of the world."
With Mary, the Mother of Jesus:
"Do whatever he tells you."
With Andrew:
"We have found the Messiah!"
With Nathaniel:
"You are the Son of God;
you are King of Israel!"

With the father of the possessed boy:
"I believe! Help my unbelief."
With Peter:
"You are the Messiah,
the Son of the living God!"
With the Samaritans:
"We know that he is truly the Savior of the world!"
With the Twelve:
"You have the words of eternal life;
and we know that you are the Holy One of God!"

With the centurion:
"Truly, this man was the Son of God!"
With Paul:
"He is the image of the invisible God,
the first-born of all creation!"
With John:
"He is the true light
that enlightens everyone."
With Thomas:
"My Lord and my God!"

French Reformed Church

557 Prayer That Christ May Come to Us

ALMIGHTY God,
Father of our Lord Jesus Christ,
we give you thanks
that in the fullness of time
the Light dawned on a dark world
and your Son was born in Bethlehem.
We praise you that he came
and that he shall come again.
We confess that the doors of our hearts
are too low to receive
the King of glory.
We are too indifferent
to go to meet him.

Come, we pray you,
and by your Holy Spirit
banish from us
all that resists his entrance
in our hearts.
Make us,
O God,
a people who watch and pray

for the day of his appearing.
Even so, come,
Lord Jesus;
come quickly!

Reformed Church in America

558 **Prayer in Thanksgiving for the Church**

O ETERNAL God,
   we give you thanks
for founding your holy and universal Church
on Jesus Christ
and for gathering into her
members of every age and race,
every nation and people,
that she may be a community of saints
for the establishment of your kingdom.
Endow her with your Spirit
and animate her with your might
that she may gladly proclaim
your Word and your Truth.

Guard her from the infatuation of vainglory,
and let her be the salt of the earth
and the light of the world.
By your grace
help her to live in the unity
of faith, hope, and love,
so that her sheep who have strayed
may be brought into the one fold
under the one shepherd,
Jesus Christ.

Swiss Reformed Church

559 Prayer at the Beginning of a New Day

O MASTER,
  holy and incomprehensible God,
you bid light to shine out of darkness.
After giving us rest in the sleep of night,
you have raised us up to glorify you
and petition your goodness.
Receive us who now worship you
and render you what thanks we can.
Grant all our requests
that will advance our salvation.
Make us children of light and day
and heirs of your eternal good things.

O Lord,
in your great mercy,
be mindful of all here present
praying with us
as well as all our brothers and sisters
in need of your love and help
on land,
at sea,
or in any place of your dominion,
and grant them your great mercy.
Thus, saved in soul and body,
we may use the free speech of friends
to glorify forever your wondrous and blessed Name.

Byzantine Liturgy

560 Prayer of Thanks for Sharing in God's Mysteries

O LORD, our God,
  our mouth has been filled with gladness
and our tongue with exultation

because we share in your immortal mysteries.
For what no eye has seen,
what no ear has heard,
what has not entered into the human heart
you have prepared
for those who love your holy name.

You were pleased to reveal it
to the lowly of your Church.
Yes, Father, it pleased you to do this
because you are merciful.
May honor, glory, and adoration be yours,
O Father,
with the Son
and the Holy Spirit
now and forever.

Coptic Liturgy

561 Prayer for the Blessings of the Gospel

O LORD God,
grant us the knowledge of your divine words,
and fill us
with the understanding of your holy Gospel,
the riches of your divine gifts,
and the indwelling of your Holy Spirit.

Help us
to keep your commandments with joy
and to accomplish them
and so fulfill your will.
Thus we may be accounted worthy
of the blessings and the mercies
that are from you
now and forever.

Jacobite Church

562 Prayer to Be Delivered from All Evil

O LORD,
  sanctify our souls, minds, and bodies
and touch our apprehensions.
Search out our consciences
and cast out of us
every evil thought and base desire,
all envy, pride, and hypocrisy,
all falsehood and deceit,
all worldly anxiety,
all covetousness, vainglory, and sloth,
all malice,
all wrath and anger,
all remembrance of injuries,
all blasphemy,
and every movement of flesh and spirit
that is contrary to your holy will.

O Lord,
lover of all people,
enable us to turn to you,
our holy God
and Father who are in heaven,
and to call upon you boldly,
with freedom and without condemnation,
with a pure heart and a contrite soul,
without confusion of face,
and with sanctified lips.

Liturgy of St. James

563   Prayer of Thanks
      for God's Many Blessings to Us

O GOD,
  you are ineffable and incomprehensible
invisible and imperceptible,

always existing yet never the same,
together with your only Son,
and the Holy Spirit.

You brought us into existence out of nothingness,
you raised us up after the fall,
and you will never cease to do whatever is needed
to lead us to heaven
and give us your kingdom which is to come.

For all these reasons
we give thanks to you,
to your only Son,
and to your Holy Spirit.
We give thanks for all that we know
and all that we do not know.
We give thanks for all your benefits to us,
those that are known to us
as well as those that remain hidden from us.

(Eastern) Liturgy of St. John Chrysostom

564 Prayer for the Spread of the Gospel

O LIGHT and desire of all nations,
    watch over your messengers
both by land and by sea.
Prosper the works of all your servants
to spread the Gospel among the nations.
Accompany the word of their testimony
concerning your atonement
with the demonstration of your spirit and power.

Bless our congregations
gathered from among the non-believers.
Keep them as the apple of your eye.
Have mercy on the ancient people of the covenant—
the Jews—
and deliver them from their blindness.

And bring all nations to the saving knowledge of you:
"Let the posterity of Israel praise the Lord;
let all the nations praise him."
Give your people open doors to preach the Gospel
and let them proclaim your praises on earth.

Moravian Church

565 Prayer to Remain Ever-Pleasing to God

O LORD,
  perfect your grace in us. . . .
May the mercy and compassion of your godhead
be on us
and on the people whom you have chosen
for yourself.
In your compassion,
grant that all the days of our lives
we may all be well-pleasing
to your godhead
in good works of righteousness
which appease and reconcile the glorious will
of your majesty.
May we be accounted worthy
by the help of your grace
to raise to you
praise, honor, confession, and worship
at all times,
O Lord of all,
Father, Son, and Holy Spirit,
forever.

Nestorian Liturgy

566   **Prayer to the God of Peace**

O GOD,
   you are the ineffable Ocean of love,
the unfathomable Abyss of peace,
the Source of all goodness,
and the Dispenser of affection.
You send peace to those
who are receptive to it.
Open for us today
the sea of your love,
and water us with the plenteous streams
from the riches of your grace.

Make us children of tranquility
and heirs of peace.
Enkindle in us the flame of your love,
and sow in us reverence for you.
Firm up our weakness by your strength,
and unite us closely with you
and with one another
in a bond of indissoluble unity
and firm accord.

Syrian Clementine Liturgy

567   **Prayer in Honor of Christ's Cross**

CHRIST our God, . . .
   we adore your holy cross
while we say:
the cross is a weapon which does not fail;
the cross is a stronghold which does not fall;
the cross dispersed the people of the Jews;
the cross gathered together the nations;
the cross put to shame the unbelievers;

the cross crowned the martyrs;
the cross reconciled those in heaven
with those on earth.

Therefore, Lord,
by your cross pardon our offenses;
by your cross forgive our faults;
by your cross guard our churches;
by your cross exalt our monasteries.
Make us and our departed brothers and sisters
worthy to worship you
on the day of your manifestation,
that we may be protected
beneath the wings of your cross.
And we will offer praise and thanksgiving
to you and your Father and your Holy Spirit
now and forever.

Syrian Orthodox Church

Prayers of Various Individuals

568   Prayer for the Honor of God's Name

O LORD,
    all-powerful God,
through your Spirit
you have made us your body
in the unity of faith.
You have commanded us
to give you thanks and praise
for the gift of grace
which you have given us
in the person of your only Son,
our Lord Jesus Christ,
who was delivered to death for our sins. . . .

Grant that I may never disgrace
your body, your family, or your children
so that even those who do not believe
may acknowledge your name and your glory.
Defend us, O Lord.
Help us to uphold your glory
and never shame your name
by the conduct of our lives.
O Lord,
give us greater faith and hope
in you.

> Ulrich Zwingli (1481-1531)
> *Minister and Reformer*

569 Prayer That God May Strengthen Our Weakness

O LORD,
   I come before you
as an empty vessel that needs filling.
My faith is weak;
make it strong.
My love is cold;
grant me ardor and warmth
that I may love my neighbor.

I lack a vibrant and unshakable faith;
sometimes I even have doubts
and I cannot trust completely in you.
O Lord,
come to my aid.
Increase my faith and hope in you.
I have placed in you
all the riches that I possess.

I am poor
but you are rich,

and you came to show mercy
to the poor.
I am a sinner
but you are just.
I am filled with sin
but you are full of justice.
Hence, I will remain with you
and receive from you
although I can give you nothing.

Martin Luther (1483-1546)
Minister and Reformer

570 Prayer for Unity in Body and Mind

O MERCIFUL God,
grant us love
that we may seek not our own honor
but the profit of our neighbor
and your glory in all things.
Expel out of us
all disdain, greediness, ungentleness,
headiness, and flattering of ourselves.

Preserve us from discord and division;
bind us together in uniform love,
that we may be one body,
and of one mind.
Establish also our faith,
that our minds may be always comforted
in the resurrection of your Son,
and in the immortal life purchased by him.

Myles Coverdale (1488-1568)
Bible Translator and Reformer

571 **Prayer for Spiritual Union with God**

O EVERLASTING God,
  have mercy upon us.
Through your Holy Spirit
unite us with yourself
Illumine us with true light
and inflame us with righteousness.

Your Son's words manifest to us
your loving-kindness,
the gift of your Holy Spirit,
and your ardent desire to assist us:
"How much more will the heavenly Father
give the Holy Spirit
to those who ask him" (Luke 11:13).

Hence we know that you are willing
to give us this good gift
provided we ask for it.
This makes us confident
that you will hear our prayers and petitions.

Philipp Melanchthon (1495-1560)
Educator and Reformer

572   **Prayer of Thanksgiving
for All God's Benefits**

O LORD our God,
  we give you praise and honor
for all your kind mercies
that have been bestowed on us
through another week.
We offer you continual gratitude
for creating us after your own likeness . . .
for your help and care in our needs,
for your protection in countless dangers of body and
soul

for your consolation in our sorrows,
for sparing us in life,
and for giving us time to repent.

O most merciful Father,
we thank you
for all the benefits
which we have received from your goodness alone.
And we beg you
to grant us always your Holy Spirit
that we may grow in grace,
in unshakable faith,
and in perseverance in all good works.

> John Knox (1505-1572)
> *Minister and Reformer*

573 Prayer That We May Be Guided by God's Word

ALMIGHTY God,
you have borne witness
by the law and the prophets
to what is right
so that we may live
in obedience to your will.
You have also given us
by your Gospel
a fuller knowledge of perfect righteousness.

Let us be governed by your Spirit
and give ourselves to you.
Help us to be guided by your Word . . .
and never deviate from it—
neither to the right
nor to the left.

Enable us to acknowledge our folly and vanity
and consent to be taught by your Word.

May we prove to be truly obedient to you
to the end of this life.
Then we will reach that heavenly rest
which has been obtained for us
by the blood of your only Son.

> John Calvin (1509-1564)
> *Theologian and Reformer*

574 Prayer That We May Live Uprightly in Our Calling

GOOD Father, . . .
grant also that I may join with all my travails,
labors, affections, desires, and endeavors:
faith,
with faith knowledge,
with knowledge temperance,
with temperance patience,
with patience godliness,
with godliness brotherly kindness,
and with brotherly kindness love;
that I may not be unfruitful in my calling,
but may acknowledge your Son, Christ Jesus,
and in him have peace of conscience.

May I be patient in troubles,
long-suffering in wrongs,
meek in trials,
rejoicing in heart.
quieted in mind,
in the hope to enjoy at your hands,
and in your good time,
whatever contributes to the true comfort
of my soul
and the relief of my body;
that in all truth

and inward feeling of your aid
my calling may be made perfect
and sealed with the seal
of your own spiritual approbation.

John Norden (1548-1625)
English Religious Writer

575   **Prayer of All the Hours**

YOU have placed the times and seasons
    in your own power;
grant that we may make our prayer to you
in an acceptable time when you may be found
—and save us!

You were born *in the dead of night*
for us and for our salvation;
renew us each day by the Holy Spirit
until you attain perfect manhood in us
—and save us!

At the *first hour* in the morning (6 a.m.)
while the sun was still rising,
you rose from the dead;
raise us up daily to new life
by showing us the paths of repentance
—and save us!

At the *third hour* (9 a.m.)
you sent the Holy Spirit on the apostles;
do not take this Holy Spirit from us
but renew him daily within us
—and save us!

At the *sixth hour* (noon) on the sixth day
you nailed to the cross
the sins of the world together with yourself;
blot out the handwriting of our sins

which is against us
_ and save us!

At the *sixth hour (noon)*
you sent to the apostle Peter
a great sheet from heaven,
symbolizing your Church;
receive into it the sinners that we are,
gathered from among the nations,
and with it receive us up into heaven
_ and save us!

At the *ninth hour (3 p.m.)*
you experienced death
for us and for our sins;
put to death in our earthly members
everything that is contrary to your will
_ and save us!

At *eventide*
you willed to be taken down from the cross
and buried in a tomb;
take away our sins from us
and bury them in your tomb,
covering with good works the evil we have done
_ and save us!

At the *supper hour*
you willed to institute the most sacred mysteries
of your body and blood;
help us to be mindful and partake of them,
never for judgment but for remission of sins
and for acquiring the bequests of the New Testament
_ and save us!

At *midnight*
you awakened David your prophet
and Paul the apostle
so that they might praise you;

enable us also to sing your praises at night
and to remember you upon our beds
— and save us!

With your own lips you have assured us
that at *midnight* the Bridegroom will return;
grant that our ears may ever resound with the cry:
"Here is the Bridegroom,"
so that we may always be ready to meet him
— and save us!

By the *crowing of a cock*
you admonished your apostle
and helped him repent;
grant us also at the same admonition
to follow his example
and to weep bitterly for the things
in which we have sinned against you
— and save us!

You have foretold that you will come to judge us
on a day when we do not expect it
and *at an hour which we do not know*;
make us prepared every day and every hour
to greet your coming
— and save us!

Lancelot Andrewes (1555-1626)
Bishop and Spiritual Writer

576 Prayer for Fitness in Our Vocation

O LORD,
make me worthy of the place
to which you have raised me
in your Church,
that all my endeavors may be
to make truth and peace meet together.
In this course

give me understanding to discover my enemies
and wisdom to thwart them;
a heart to love my friends
and a demeanor that may bind them.

Lord,
make me love your Church
and the place where your honor dwells;
that as you have honored me . . . ,
so I may honor you above all,
and spend whatever is acceptable
in the poor remainder of my life
to serve you
in your Church.

William Laud (1573-1645)
Archbishop and Spiritual Writer

577 Prayer to Be a True Servant of God

SPEAK to your servant
and permit me to hear you.
Tell me what you desire
and let me find it agreeable.
Give me the burden you judge to be fitting
and assist me to bear it.
Use me for whatever purpose you choose
and help me not be found wanting.
Command me to act in accord with your will
and grant me the grace to do so.
Let me be nothing
that you may be everything.

Jon Amos Komensky (1592-1670)
Moravian Bishop

578 Prayer for the Good Seed of the Word

O HOLY Jesus,
 you are the fountain of all blessing
and the Word of the eternal Father.
Be pleased to sow the good seed of your Word
in our hearts
and water it with the dew of your divine Spirit.
While we exercise in it day and night
may we be like a tree planted by the water side,
bringing forth in all times and seasons
the fruits of a holy conversation.

May we never walk in the way of sinners,
nor have fellowship
with the unfruitful works of darkness.
Then when this life is ended,
may we have our portion
in the congregation of the righteous
and be able to stand upright in the judgment
through the supporting arm of your mercy,
O blessed Savior and Redeemer.

Jeremy Taylor (1613-1667)
Bishop and Spiritual Writer

579 Prayer to Recover God's Image in Us

O LORD,
 you have breathed into me the breath of life,
and imbued me with an immortal spirit
which looks up to you
and remembers it is made after your own image.
Behold with grace and favor
the ardent desires which are in my heart
to recover a perfect likeness of you.
Endow me

with more contentedness in what is present
and less solicitude about what is future;
with a patient mind to submit
to any loss of what I have
or to any disappointment of what I expect.

Fill me,
O Lord,
with the knowledge of your will,
in all wisdom and spiritual understanding.
Fill me with goodness
and the fruits of righteousness.
And fill me with all joy and peace
in believing that you will never leave me
nor forsake me,
but make me perfect,
establish, strengthen, settle me,
and be my God forever and ever.

Patrick Symon (1626-1707)
Minister and Religious Writer

580   **Prayer in Time of Sorrow**

O LORD,
    when I am in sorrow I think of you.
Listen to the cry of my heart
and to my sad complaint.
Yet I would not prescribe for you,
O Father,
when and how your help should come.
I will patiently wait for the time
which you yourself have appointed
for my relief.

Strengthen me
in faith, hope, and trust.
Grant me the patience and resolution

to bear my trouble.
And let me at last behold the time
when you will gladden me
with your grace.

Johann Friedrich Stark (1680-1756)
Minister and Writer

581   Prayer to the Great Physician for Relief

O MOST blessed and gracious God,
    who alone can heal a wounded spirit
and quiet a troubled mind:
to you do I cry for help.

O great Physician of body and soul,
uphold and comfort my weak and dejected spirit.
Since you alone can relieve me,
to you do I call for relief.
O hear my most earnest supplication,
and make me possess
an easy, quiet, and cheerful spirit,
for my trust is in you.

John Wesley (1703-1791)
Evangelist and Founder of Methodism

582   Prayer When Beginning Study

A LMIGHTY God,
    the giver of wisdom,
without your help resolutions are vain
and without your blessings study is ineffectual.
Enable me, if it be your will,
to attain such knowledge
as may qualify me to direct the doubtful,
and instruct the ignorant;
to prevent wrongs and terminate contentions.

And grant that I may use that knowledge
which I shall attain
for your glory
and my own salvation,
for Jesus Christ's sake.

Samuel Johnson (1709-1784)
English Poet and Author

583   Prayer That God May Read Our Heart

FOUNTAIN of mercy,
    whose pervading eye can look within
and read what passes there,
accept my thoughts for thanks—
I have no words.
My soul,
over-fraught with gratitude,
rejects the aid of language.
Lord, behold my heart.

Hannah More (1745-1835)
Founder of the Religious Tract Society

584   Prayer for Cheerfulness amid Trials

O GOD,
    animate us to cheerfulness.
May we have a joyful sense of our blessings,
learn to look on the bright circumstances
of our lot,
and maintain a perpetual contentedness
under your allotments.
Fortify our minds
against disappointment and calamity.
Preserve us from despondency,
from yielding to dejection.

Teach us that no evil is intolerable
but a guilty conscience;
and that nothing can hurt us,
if, with true loyalty of affection,
we keep your commandments
and take refuge in you.

William Elery Channing (1780-1842)
Unitarian Minister and Author

585 Prayer for the Acceptance of God's Will

O LORD,
I do not know what to ask you.
You alone know my real needs,
and you love me more
than I even know how to love.
Enable me to discern my true needs
which are hidden from me.
I ask for neither a cross nor a consolation
but simply wait in patience for you.
My heart is open to you.

For your great mercy's sake,
come to me and help me.
Put your mark on me and heal me,
cast me down and raise me up.
I silently adore your holy will
and your inscrutable ways.
I offer myself in sacrifice to you
and put all my trust in you.
I desire only to do your will.
Teach me how to pray,
and pray in me yourself.

Vasily Drosdov Philaret (1782-1867)
Orthodox Metropolitan of Moscow

586 **Prayer to Get Along with Others**

O LORD,
   bless my dealings
with all those I encounter this day.
Teach me to greet everything that occurs
with peace of soul
and with the firm conviction
that your will governs everything.

Instruct me to act with firmness and wisdom,
without embittering others
or embarrassing them.
Grant me the strength to endure
the weariness of the approaching day
and all that comes with it.
Teach me to pray.

Vasily Drosdov Philaret (1782-1867)
Orthodox Metropolitan of Moscow

587 **Prayer for the Community**

F ATHER most kind, . . .
   grant that, mindful of our corruption and im-
      potence,
we may taste the happiness prepared for those
who purify themselves ever more of every defect
by faith in your Christ.
To this end
instill in our renewed community
a deeper attachment to the common meditation of your
   Word
and increase our fervor on receiving the sacraments.
Never let those who need help
lose the thirst for that living water
which your Son has caused to spring up
for all of us.

By your goodness and mercy
may that fount never be dried up or polluted.

Strengthen among us
the spirit of true concord and fraternal love.
Enable us to surpass all pettiness
and concentrate on what is important.
Let us direct everything on earth
toward the Kingdom.
Help us to possess earthly goods
and use them solely as a means
for each of us to have at heart
the salvation of all
and for all to have at heart
the salvation of each.
May all of us work together for our happiness
in truth and love.

> Friedrich Schleiermacher (1786-1834)
> *Reform Minister and Theologian*

588   **Prayer for Union with God
through the Day**

TEACH us, O Father,
    how to ask you each moment silently
for your help.
If we fail,
teach us at once to ask you to forgive us.
If we are disquieted,
enable us, by your grace,
quickly to turn to you.
May nothing come between us and you.
May we will, do, and say
just what you, our living and tender Father,
will us to will, do, and say.

Work your holy will in us, and through us,
this day.

Protect us,
guide us,
bless us within and without—
that we may do something this day
for love of you;
and that we may this evening be nearer to you,
though we see it not,
nor know it.

Edward B. Pusey (1800-1882)
Theologian and Leader of the Oxford Movement

589 **Prayer to Attain Equanimity in Our Lives**

O FATHER,
calm the turbulence of our passions,
quiet the throbbing of our hopes,
repress the waywardness of our wills,
direct the motions of our affections,
and sanctify the varieties of our lot.
Be all in all to us.
And may all things earthly,
while we bend them to our growth in grace
and to the work of blessing,
dwell lightly in our hearts,
so that we may readily,
or even joyfully,
give up whatever you ask.

Mary Carpenter (1807-1877)
Philanthropist and Writer

590 **Prayer for Brightening the Lives of Others**

O GOD,
who cover yourself with light as with a garment,
shine in us,

putting to flight all the forces
of darkness and guilt,
of sin and selfishness.
Shine also through us
to any that live in shadow,
and so fill us with your radiant spirit
that we may be a lamp unto a neighbor's feet,
and a light unto his path.
And when this day is done,
may every face we have met
be the brighter for our meeting,
and every heart braver,
with new joy and cheer and grace and strength.

Theodore Parker (1810-1860)
Unitarian Minister and Writer

591 Prayer That God Will Be Patient with Us

HEAVENLY Father,
be a little patient with us.
Often we sincerely intend to speak with you
but we speak so foolishly.
Sometimes we judge that good has befallen us
and we do not have the words to thank you enough—
just as mistaken children are thankful
for getting their own way.
Sometimes we judge that things are so bad
that we call upon you;
we even complain and cry out to you—
just as irrational children are afraid of something
that is good for them.

Yet even though we are childish,
we are far from being true children of yours,
who are our Father—
as if an animal were to pretend that man
was his father.

How childish we are
and both our language and our requests
fall far short of those
that we should direct to you.
We do at least realize that it should not be so
and that we should be different.
Therefore, be a little patient with us!

Soren Kierkegaard (1813-1855)
Lutheran Theologian and Philosopher

592   Prayer in Praise of God's Transcendence

O LORD,
    you are greater than our thoughts of you.
You are to us more than we can speak.
You also transcend our utmost conception.
All of your name that we can frame into words
is but little;
and all of you that we can frame into emotions
is still but little;
and all that we can conceive of you
by the imagination
is yet but very little.

Beyond our thoughts and feelings and conceptions
you stretch endlessly and boundlessly.
We look toward you
as people look toward the morning.
You are our sun;
you are our light;
you are our life.

Henry Ward Beecher (1813-1887)
Congregational Minister and Orator

593 **Prayer of Pardon for Our Frailties**

LORD,
   I am no hero.
I have been careless, cowardly
sometimes all but mutinous.
Punishment I have deserved,
I deny it not.
But a traitor I have never been;
a deserter I have never been.
I have tried to fight on your side,
in your battle against evil.
I have tried to do the duty
which lay nearest me;
and to leave whatever you committed to my charge
a little better than I found it.
I have not been good,
but I have at least tried to be good.

Take the will for the deed,
good Lord.
Strike not my unworthy name off the roll-call
of the noble and victorious army,
which is the blessed company of all faithful people;
and let me, too, be found written
in the book of life:
even though I stand the lowest and last
upon its list.

Charles Kingsley (1819-1875)
Canon and Novelist

594 **Prayer That God Will Bless Us**

O LORD,
   whose gifts are beyond words,
in whose loving fatherhood we are content to abide,
help us to know that you are near us today

and every day of our life on earth.
Give us,
we pray you,
that faith in the conquering power
of good deed and purposes
which may enable us to contend successfully
against the infirmities and temptations
to which our nature is subject.

May a sense of the true values of life
keep us in the faith appointed for us.
May we seek the patience of your saints
and the wisdom of your prophets
and the self-devotion of your martyrs.
May our worship give us a place
in the great church universal
of love and service forever.

Julia Ward Howe (1819-1910)
Composer and Suffragette

595 Prayer in Time of New Teachings

IN TIMES of doubts and questionings,
    when our belief is perplexed
by new learning, new teaching, new thought;
when our faith is strained
by creeds, by doctrines, by mysteries
beyond our understanding—
give us the faithfulness of learners,
and the courage of believers in you.

Give us boldness to examine,
and faith to trust all truth;
patience and insight to master difficulties;
stability to hold fast our traditions
with enlightened interpretations;
to admit all fresh truth made known to us,
and in times of trouble,

to grasp new knowledge
and to combine it loyally and honestly
with the old.
Save us and help us,
we humbly beseech you,
O Lord.

George Ridding (1828-1905)
Bishop of Southwell

596   **Prayer That Everything
            May Lead Us to God**

O LORD,
   by all your dealings with us,
whether of joy or pain,
of light or darkness,
let us be brought to you.
Let us value no treatment of your grace
simply because it makes us happy
or because it makes us sad,
or because it gives us or denies us
what we want.

But may all that you send us
bring us to you,
that knowing your perfectness
we may be sure in every disappointment
that you are still loving us,
and in every darkness
that you are still enlightening us,
and in every enforced idleness
that you are still using us,
yes, in every death,
that you are giving us life.

Phillips Brooks (1835-1893)
Episcopalian Minister and Composer

597 **Prayer to Lead a Good Life**

LORD,
behold our family here assembled.
We thank you for this place in which we dwell;
for the love that unites us;
for the peace accorded us this day;
for the hope with which we expect the morrow;
for the health, the work, the food,
and the bright skies
that make our lives delightful;
and for our friends in all parts of the earth.

Give us the grace and strength to persevere.
Give us courage, gaiety, and the quiet mind.
Spare us to our friends,
soften us to our enemies.
Bless us, if it may be,
in all our innocent endeavors.
If it may not,
give us the strength to encounter
that which is to come,
that we may be brave in peril,
constant in tribulation,
temperate in wrath,
and in all changes of fortune,
and down to the gates of death,
loyal and loving to one another.

Robert Louis Stevenson (1850-1894)
Novelist, Essayist, and Poet

598 **Prayer for Animals and Their Masters**

HEAR our humble prayer,
O God,
for our friends, the animals,

especially for animals who are suffering:
for animals that are over-worked,
under-fed, and cruelly treated;
for all wistful creatures in captivity
that beat their wings against bars;
for any that are hunted or lost or deserted
or frightened or hungry;
for all that must be put to death.

We entreat for them all
your mercy and pity,
and for those who deal with them
we ask a heart of compassion
and gentle hands and kindly words.
Make us, ourselves,
to be true friends to animals
and so to share the blessings of the Merciful.

> Albert Schweitzer (1875-1965)
> *Theologian and Humanitarian*

PRAYERS FROM OUR JEWISH HERITAGE

Catholics have been called spiritual Semites for our
roots lie in that direction. Accordingly, we can pray
with the prayers of the Old Testament, and we can
also make use of other prayers of the Jewish religion, adapting wherever necessary.

B) JEWISH RELIGION

THE Second Vatican Council set forth the spiritual patrimony that Christians have in common with members of the Jewish religion and took pains to stress that there should be mutual understanding and respect which is the fruit of biblical and theological studies as well as of fraternal dialogues.

"The Church of Christ acknowledges that, according to God's saving design, the beginning of her faith and her election are found already among the Patriarchs, Moses, and the Prophets. She professes that all who believe in Christ—Abraham's sons according to faith (cf. Gal 3:7)—are included in the same Patriarch's call, and that the salvation of the Church is mysteriously foreshadowed by the chosen people's exodus. . . .

"The Church, therefore, cannot forget that she received the revelation of the Old Testament through the people with whom God in his inexpressible mercy concluded the Ancient Covenant. Nor can she forget that she draws sustenance from the root of that well-cultivated olive tree onto which have been grafted the wild shoots, the Gentiles (cf. Rom 11:17-24). Indeed, the Church believes that by his cross Christ, our Peace, reconciled Jews and Gentiles, making both one in himself.

"The Church keeps ever in mind the words of the Apostle about his kinsmen: 'Theirs are . . . the fathers and from them is the Christ according to the flesh' (Rom 9:4-5), the Son of the Virgin Mary" (Decl. on the Relation of the Church to Non-Christian Religions, no. 4).

It is our hope that the prayers found in this section will aid spiritual growth, foster understanding, and bring about common projects.

Prayers from Religious Services

599   **Early Morning Blessings**

BLESSED are you,
O Lord our God, King of the universe:
you have given the mind understanding
to distinguish between day and night.

Blessed are you,
O Lord our God, King of the universe:
you have not made me a heathen.

Blessed are you,
O Lord our God, King of the universe:
you have not made me a bondman. . . .

Blessed are you,
O Lord our God, King of the universe:
you have made me according to your will.

Blessed are you,
O Lord our God, King of the universe:
you open the eyes of the blind.

Blessed are you,
O Lord our God, King of the universe:
you clothe the naked.

Blessed are you,
O Lord our God, King of the universe:
you set free those who are bound.

Blessed are you,
O Lord our God, King of the universe:
you lift up those who are bowed down.

Blessed are you,
O Lord our God, King of the universe:
you spread out the earth above the waters.

Blessed are you,
O Lord our God, King of the universe:
you provide for my every want.

Blessed are you,
O Lord our God, King of the universe:
you have made firm the steps of human beings.

Blessed are you,
O Lord our God, King of the universe:
you surround Israel with might.

Blessed are you,
O Lord our God, King of the universe:
you crown Israel with glory.

Blessed are you,
O Lord our God, King of the universe:
you give strength to the weary.

Blessed are you,
O Lord our God, King of the universe:
you take away sleep from my eyes
and slumber from my eyelids.

600 The Prayer Known as "The Shema"

(First Part)

HEAR, O Israel!
The Lord is our God,
the Lord alone!
Blessed be his name
whose glorious kingdom is forever and ever.

Therefore, you shall love the Lord, your God,
with all your heart,
and with all your soul,
and with all your strength.
Take to heart these words which I enjoin on you today.

Drill them into your children.
Speak of them at home and abroad,
whether you are busy or at rest.
Bind them at your wrist as a sign
and let them be as a pendant on your forehead.
Write them on the doorposts of your houses
and on your gates. (Deuteronomy 6:4-9)

Who is like you, O Lord, among the mighty,
who is like you glorious in holiness,
inspiring in praises, working wonders?

601 Prayer in Praise of the Almighty Father (The "Kaddish")

MAGNIFIED and sanctified
be the Name of the Most High
in the world that he has created
according to his will.
May he establish his kingdom
during your life and during your days,
and during the days of the whole house of Israel,
even speedily and at a near time!
And say Amen!

Blessed be the Name of the Most High forever,
and for all eternity!

Blessed, praised, and glorified,
exalted, extolled, and honored,
magnified and lauded be the Name of the Holy One,
blessed be he—
high above all blessings and hymns,
all praises and consolations
that we pronounce in this world!
And say: Amen!

May there come from heaven abundant peace,

and life for us and for all Israel!
And say: Amen!

May the Artisan of Peace in the highest heavens
also be the Artisan of Peace
for us and for all Israel!
And say: Amen!

602   **Prayer in Praise of God,
Worker of Wonders**

O LORD,
you are almighty forever,
you give perpetual life to the dead,
and you are mighty to save.
You graciously sustain the living,
mercifully revive the dead,
support the weak,
cure the sick,
free captives,
and remain faithful to those who sleep in the dust.

Who is like you,
O Lord of wondrous deeds,
and who can compare with you,
O King who order death,
restore life,
and grant salvation!

We will sanctify your Name in the world
even as it is sanctified in the highest heavens. . . .
For all generations we will declare your greatness,
and for all eternity we will proclaim your holiness;
and your praise, O our God,
shall not depart from our mouths forever,
for you are a great and holy God and King.

603 **Prayer for Help and Forgiveness**

O LORD our God,
   give us understanding to know your ways.
Open our hearts to fear you,
and forgive us so that we may be redeemed.
Keep us far from sorrow,
satisfy our needs on the produce of your land,
and gather our dispersed people
from the four corners of the earth.
Let those who go astray
be judged according to your will
and lay your hand upon the wicked. . . .
Blessed are you, O Lord,
who hearken to our prayer.

604 **Prayer of Thanksgiving for God's Unfailing Mercies**

WE GIVE you thanks,
   for you are the Lord our God
and the God of our fathers forever and ever.
You are the Rock of our lives,
the Shield of our salvation through every generation
We give thanks to you and declare your praise
for our lives which are committed into your hand,
for our souls which are in your care,
for your miracles which are with us daily,
and for your wonders and benefits
which are wrought at all times,
morning, noon, and night.

O merciful Being,
who are all good,
whose mercies never fail
and whose loving kindnesses never cease—
we have always placed our hope in you.

605 **Prayer to God the Creator
of Day and Night**

BLESSED are you,
O Lord our God, King of the universe.
You bring on the evening twilight at your word,
open the gates of the heavens with wisdom,
change times and vary seasons with understanding,
and arrange the stars in their watches in the sky,
according to your will.

You create day and night;
you roll away the light from before the darkness
and the darkness from before the light.
You make the day pass
and the night approach,
and you divide the day from the night.

The Lord of hosts is your name;
you are a God living and enduring continually,
and may you reign over us forever and ever.
Blessed are you, O Lord,
who bring on the evening twilight.

606 **Evening Prayer**

OUR Father and King,
grant that we may lie down to rest with a quiet
mind,
and rise again in health and strength.
Spread your shelter of peace over us
and direct us with your wise guidance.
Save us speedily for the sake of your Name.
Protect us and turn away from us
the stroke of enmity and the sword,
pestilence and famine,

misery and every form of grave calamity
and ruinous catastrophe.

Dilute the power of the wicked instigation
that assails us on every side
and take it away from us.
Shelter us in the shadow of your wings.
Guard our departings and our returnings
that our life may be happy and peaceful
from now on and forever.
For you are God,
our guardian and deliverer from every evil
and from fear in the darkness of night.
Blessed are you, O Lord,
who guard your people Israel.

607   Prayer That All Nations May Adore God

LET all the inhabitants of the world know and understand
that every knee must bow before you
and every tongue must swear you allegiance.
Let them bow and worship before you,
O Lord our God,
and let them give honor to your glorious Name.
May they all embrace the yoke of your kingdom
and may you rule over them speedily
and forever.

For yours is the kingdom
and you will reign in glory for all eternity,
as it is written in your law:
"The Lord shall reign forever and ever" (Exodus 15:18),
and "The Lord shall become king over the whole earth;
on that day the Lord shall be the only one,
and his name the only one" (Zechariah 14:9).

608 Prayer That All People Will Praise God's Name

O ETERNAL God,
  may all people praise your Name!
And may every life forever glorify and exalt
the remembrance of you!
You are and will eternally be the All-powerful;
you alone are our king, liberator, and protector.
You deliver, save, and sustain us.
You have mercy on us in our distress,
for you alone are our Master and our King.

God of past and future generations,
Sovereign of all creation,
and Lord of Nature,
all praises are addressed to you,
for you govern the world with your grace,
and your creatures with your mercy.

The Eternal One neither slumbers nor sleeps;
he awakens the sleeping and refreshes the weary,
he makes the dumb speak and sets captives free,
he upholds the wavering and sustains those bowed
  down. . . .

O God,
almighty, great, powerful, and redoubtable,
supreme Being, and Master of heaven and earth,
we praise, glorify, and exalt you.
And with David we bless you.
"May my soul bless the Eternal One,
and may my innermost being bless his holy Name!"

609   Prayer for Peace Among All Peoples

WE PRAY for all people.
     They are divided into nations and races,
but all are your children.
They draw life and being from you,
and are commanded to obey your laws,
according to each person's capacity
to know and understand them.

Put an end to hatred and conflict,
that lasting peace may pervade the earth
and all people may be blessed with the fruit of peace.
Thus the fraternal spirit among people
will manifest their faith
that you are the Father of all.

610   Prayer to Live a Full Life Cycle

O GOD,
     do not snatch us away in the midst of our days,
but let us complete the number of our years in peace.
Indeed, we are aware that our life is frail
and our days are like a hand-span.
Help us,
O God of our salvation,
to be truthful and upright in your sight --
over the course of our pilgrimage.
And be with us
when it pleases you to take us from the earth.
Then may our souls share the bond of life
with the souls of our parents
and of the just
who stand before you in heaven.

Prayers of Various Individuals

611 Prayer for a Gift That We Will Not Abuse

O LORD,
  because there are countless good things in nature,
grant me the one which is most suited to me,
even though it may be the most trivial of all.
I ask you to insure only one thing—
that I may not be subverted by it,
like a reprobate,
but rather that I may make use of it
with peace of mind.

> Philo (20 B.C.-40 A.D.)
> *Greek Jewish Philosopher*

612 Prayer in Praise of God Who Aids All

B LESSED are you, my God,
  for you open your servant's heart to knowledge,
render all his actions just,
and accomplish for the son of your handmaid
the plan that you have formed
with respect to those whom you have chosen.
May he remain unceasingly in your presence!

How can one walk a straight path without your help?
What can one accomplish without your accord?
From you alone comes all knowledge.
Nothing takes place except in accord with your will.
No one but you can make answer to you,
unravel the skein of your sacred designs,
scrutinize your unfathomable mysteries,
or meditate on your astounding works
and the munificence of your power.

> Dead Sea Scrolls (20 B.C.-70 A.D.)

613   **Prayer to Be in Tune with God**

O GOD,
     bring our hearts into harmony
in reverence for your holy Name.
Lead us far away from all that you hate,
guide us close to all that you love,
and be merciful to us
for the sake of your holy Name.

Hiyya ben Abba (3rd century)
Palestinian Writer

614   **Prayer of Utter Submission to God**

O GOD,
     I come before you
with full awareness of all my weaknesses
and in total awe of your greatness and majesty.
But you want me to pray to you
and to revere your exalted Name
in accord with the limits of my understanding.

You have the best knowledge
of the things that are for my good.
I give expression to my needs
not to recall them to you,
but solely to get a better understanding
of my utter dependence on you.

Therefore if I petition you
for something that is not good for me,
it is only out of ignorance.
You are in a far better position than I am
to choose what to grant me.
I submit myself completely to your ineffable decisions
and to your guidance which knows no equal.

Bachya ibn Pakudah (c. 1000-1080)
Spanish Philosopher and Religious Judge

615 Prayer of Those Who Care for the Sick

O LORD,
in your everlasting providence
you have assigned me
to care for the life and health of your creatures.
May I be motivated at all times
by love for my art.
May my mind be swayed
by neither greed nor stinginess,
nor desire for glory or great renown.
For those hostile to truth and philanthropy
could easily delude me
into forgetting my noble purpose
to help your children.

May I always regard patients
as fellow creatures who are in pain.
Give me the strength, the time, and the opportunity
ever to perfect the skill I have attained
and ever to enlarge its sphere of influence.
For the field of knowledge is vast,
and the human spirit can span infinite horizons
to become enriched daily with new exigencies.

O God,
you have assigned me
to care for the life and death of your creatures.
I am ready for my calling,
and I attend to the practice of my profession.

Moses Maimonides (1135-1204)
Spanish Rabbi, Physician, and Philosopher

616 Prayer in Praise for God's Greatness

O LORD,
your works are wonderful
as my soul knows with certainty.

To you belong greatness and might,
beauty, triumph, and splendor.
To you belongs the kingdom,
and you rule over it with exaltation.
To you belong riches and honor.
To you belong the creatures of the heights
as well as of the depths.
They give testimony that they perish
whereas you perdure.
To you belongs that mysterious power
which our thoughts cannot fathom
because you are so far above us.

Solomon ben Judah, Ibn Gabirol (1021-1058)
Poet and Philosopher

617   **Prayer to Avoid Envy**

O LORD,
  guard us from wicked tendencies and arrogant ways,
from anger and temper,
from depression and gossiping,
and from every other evil inclination.
Keep our hearts from envying others
and the hearts of others from envying us.
In its stead,
inspire our hearts
to discern the virtues of others
and to overlook their faults.

Elimelekh of Lizhensk (1716-1786)
Polish Rabbi and Hasidic Master

618   **Prayer to Discern
           the Meaning of Suffering**

O MASTER of the world,
  I am not asking you
to show me the secret of your ways,
for it would be too much for me.

But I am asking you
to show me one thing:
what is the meaning of the suffering
that I am presently enduring,
what this suffering requires of me,
and what you are communicating to me through it,
O Master of the world.
I want to know
not so much why I am suffering
but whether I am doing so for your sake.

Levi Isaac of Berdichev (1740–1809)
Galician Hasidic Rabbi and Moralist

619 Prayer That We May Bring God to Others

O LORD,
let me be a chariot
for your divine Presence.
Let me never depart from the Sanctity
by as much as a hair breadth.
Let me have no foreign thoughts
but continually cleave to you
and to your holy Law,
so that I will be enabled to bring others
to know the truth of your divinity.
Let me proclaim to all people
your mighty power
and the glorious honor of your kingdom.

Nahman of Bratzlav (1772–1810)
Rabbi, Mystic, and Hasidic Leader

620 Prayer for All Who Are in Need

I PRAY you, O Lord,
from all my heart, O Lord, I pray to you,
with fervor and zeal,
for the sufferings of the humiliated,
for the uncertainty of those who wait;

for the non-return of the dead;
for the helplessness of the dying;
for the sadness of the misunderstood,
for those who request in vain;
for all those abused, scorned, and disdained;
for the silly, the wicked, the miserable;
for those who hurry in pain to the nearest physician;
for those who return from work with trembling and an-
    guished hearts;
for those who are roughly treated and pushed aside,
for those who are kissed on the stage;
for all who are clumsy, ugly, tiresome, and dull,
for the weak, the beaten, the oppressed,
for those who cannot find rest during long sleepless
    nights;
for those who are afraid of death,
for those who wait in pharmacies;
for those who have missed the train;
for all the inhabitants of our earth
with all their pains and troubles,
their worries, sufferings, disappointments,
all their griefs, afflictions, sorrows,
longings, failures, defeats;
for everything which is not joy,
comfort, happiness, bliss—
let these shine for ever upon them
with tender love and brightness,
I pray you, O Lord, most fervently—
I pray you, O Lord, from the depths of my heart.

> Julian Tuwim (1894-)
> *Poet, Playwright, and Translator*

621 Prayer for Generosity to Others

TEACH us, O Lord, to understand
    that generosity consists
not only in providing material help

but in every act of helpfulness
toward those who stand in need of it,
and that every human being stands in need
of friendliness, sympathy, and understanding.
Teach us to be generous in thought as well as in act.
Teach us to know
that in the measure in which we give
we also receive,
that every worthy thing we do
brings its own reward,
and that seeking any other kind of reward
we spoil the grace of what we do.

Israel Goldstein (1896-   )
Rabbi and Founder of Brandeis University

622   Prayer in Time of Sickness

HEAVENLY Father:
     you who are our support in the hours of our trial,
in you alone do we find the everlasting arms
which uphold us in our grief and sorrow.
Teach us, we pray you,
to learn the deeper lessons of our loss.
For you come not with the hand of punishment,
but with the handclasp of peace.
Though our hearts be numb and our minds disquieted
by the shock we have known,
we know that you bring the balm of healing
upon the wings of time.
Give us patience to endure our pain,
perseverance to ennoble our portion,
and peace to enlarge our perspective.
Weeping tarries but for the night:
grant that on the morrow we shall find the light
in the dawning of memory.

Albert A. Goldman (1896-1960)
American Rabbi

VALUES OF THE EASTERN PRAYERS

The outstanding features of Eastern prayers is their emphasis on the overwhelming transcendence of God and on our total dependence on him for all things. We can fully enter into such sentiments and complete them by recalling that God stooped down to human beings by speaking to them through his chosen people and made himself known to us through his Son Jesus Christ.

C) RELIGIONS OF THE EAST

"FROM ancient times down to the present, there is found among various peoples a certain perception of that hidden power which hovers over the course of things and over the events of human history; at times some indeed have come to the recognition of a Supreme Being, or even of a Father. . . .

"Thus in Hinduism, people contemplate the divine mystery and express it through an inexhaustible abundance of myths and through searching philosophical inquiry. They seek freedom from the anguish of our human condition through either ascetical practices or profound meditation or a flight to God with love and trust.

"Again, Buddhism, in its various forms, realizes the radical insufficiency of this changeable world. It teaches a way by which people may in a devout and confident spirit be able either to acquire the state of perfect liberation, or attain supreme illumination by their own efforts or through higher help. . . .

"The Church regards with esteem also the Moslems. They adore the one God, living and subsisting in himself, merciful and powerful, the Creator of heaven and earth, who has spoken to human beings. . . . Finally, they value the moral life and worship God especially through prayer" (Declaration on the Relation of the Church to Non-Christian Religions, nos. 2-3).

The Council stressed that "the Church rejects nothing which is true and holy in these religions. She regards with sincere reverence . . . those teachings which, though differing in many respects from the ones she holds and sets forth, nonetheless often reflect a ray of that Truth which enlightens all people" (Ibid., no. 2).

501

Prayers of Various Religions

623   ## Prayer for Forgiveness

O LORD,
do not turn your servant away.
I am sunk in the mire—
grasp my hand.
Grant your mercy
in exchange for the sin I have committed.
Let the wind sweep away
the evil I have done.
Tear off my many transgressions
as one tears off a garment.
My God,
my sins number seven times seven;
forgive all of them.

Babylonian Psalm

624   ## Prayer for God's Favor and Pardon

O LORD,
look with favor on us.
In everything that we may hear or see,
and in everything that we may say or do,
look with favor on us.

I ask the great God for pardon.
I ask for pardon at sunset,
when sinners all turn to him.
I ask God for pardon now and forever.

O Lord,
save us from our sins,
protect our children,
and take care of those friends of ours
who are not very strong.

Bedouin Prayer

625   **Prayer of Self-Offering to God**

FOR the sake of all sentient beings on earth,
    I aspire for the abode of enlightenment
which is the Most High;
in all-embracing love awakened
and with heart steadily firm,
even my life I will sacrifice,
dear as it is.

Buddhist Religion
(Bodhisattva Vow)

626   **Prayer to God Our Sun**

O SUN,
    I have invoked you
in the midst of the high heavens.
You are in the shadow of the cedar,
and your feet rest on the heights.
The countries have eagerly called out to you;
they have turned their gaze toward you.

O Friend,
your brilliant light illumines every land,
overwhelming whatever impedes you.
Gather together the countries,
for you know their boundaries,
O Sun.

I have taken refuge in your presence
for you destroy falsehood,
dispel the wicked influence of wonders and omens,
sorceries, dreams, and malevolent apparitions,
bring evil plans to a good end,
and chastise nations addicted to deadly sorceries.

Chaldean Incantation

627 ## Prayer for God's Presence and Inspiration

UNITED in spirit,
    we call upon you.
Come down and be present with us,
O merciful Teacher
and great Father.
Draw near and receive our offerings,
O perfect compassionate Heart.
While we speak these divine thoughts
may your all-powerful and all-knowing holy spirit
come to us.   Chinese Liturgy

628 ## Prayer That God May Visit Us

YOU are the Being
    in whom countless creatures put their faith,
the Being who vanquishes the hosts of evil,
the Being who is all-wise:
come down to our world. . . .

Cast your glance upon us
and pour out blessings on all creatures,
for it is time to be gracious toward us
from your throne in your heavenly world.
You are the everlasting redemption of all creatures.
Stoop down to us
with all your unsullied heavenly societies.

                    Hindu Liturgy

629 ## Prayer for God's Guidance and Help

O SUPREME Director,
    you are the Lord of warmth and light,
life and consciousness,

and you know all things.
Guide us along the right path to happiness
and endow us with the strength and willingness
to battle against the sins
that seethe within us and lead us astray.
We bow down in reverence before you
and we pray to you.

Hindu Religion
(Atharva Veda)

630 Prayer to Serve God and Avoid Sin

O TOWERING God,
I want to promise myself to you
like a slave to a master.
May I be untouched by any fault!
O God of abundance,
you enable fools to reflect;
and you allow the greedy to enrich themselves,
O Inspired One.

Let my praise gain access to your heart,
O God mighty by your own laws!
May we be lucky in peace and lucky in war!
Protect us always with your blessings!

Hindu Religion

631 Prayer in Praise of God's Greatness

LORD of fire and death,
of wind, moon, and waters,
Father of the born,
and Father of the father of this world:
hail, all hail to you—
a thousand greetings.

O Lord,
take our salutations from every side.
You are infinite in power
and limitless in glory;

you are everything that is,
and we find you everywhere. . . .

You are the Author of this world,
the Unmoved and the Mover;
you alone are fitting to receive worship,
for you are the Most High.
Where can your equal be found? . . .

Therefore I prostrate myself before you
and ask for forgiveness.
Forgive me, O God,
as a person forgives a friend,
as a father forgives a child,
and as a loved one forgives a beloved.

Hindu Religion
(From the Bhagavad-Gita)

632   **Prayer of Repentance for Sins**

O ALL-POWERFUL Lord,
  I turn away from all sin.
I repent for every bad thought,
every evil word,
and every wicked act
that I might have intended
to entertain, say, or commit.
I am sorry for all the evil
that I might have initiated
and from all the evil that I have committed.

I turn aside from these sins
of thought, word, and deed,
concerning my body or my soul,
concerning this world or the world of the spirit.
I humbly ask your forgiveness
and I repent three times over.

Iranian Religion B.C.
(Religion of Zarathustra)

633   **Prayer of Thanksgiving**

O LORD,
      we are especially grateful to you
for the ripe golden corn
and for the hundreds of red fruits.
Where do they come from?
The farmers who store them in their barns
regard them as the products of their labor.
But they are yours,
O Lord.
To sustain our lives
you have bestowed on us
the necessary sunshine and the suitable rain;
these give sustenance to our lives,
and we thank you for it.

Following the law of nature,
the farmers diligently sow at the right time
so that they may reap.
May we also follow the rules you have established
and sow righteousness day after day

Korean Prayer

634   **Prayer to Walk Uprightly before God**

P RAISE be to God,
      Lord of the worlds,
the compassionate and merciful One,
and the King of the day of judgment.
It is you alone that we worship
and you alone that we invoke for help.

Guide us on the straight path,
the path of all those
to whom you have been gracious,
with whom you are not angry,
and in whom there is no falling away.

Moslem Prayer (From the Koran)

635   **Prayer of the 99 Names of God**

GOD possesses the most beautiful Names;
pray to him with these Names:

Benefactor	Seer
Merciful One	Attentive One
King	Judge
Beautiful One	Just One
Peace	Artful One
Faithful One	Observer
Protector	Clement One
Mighty One	Magnanimous One
Restorer	Agreeable One
Great One	Glorified One
Creator	Magnificent One
Worker	Guardian
Organizer	Nourisher
Kind One	Steward
Dominator	Majestic One
Giver	Generous One
Dispenser	Watchman
Victor	The One Who Exhorts
Knowledge	Sage
The One Who Opens Hearts	Proud One
The One Who Closes Hearts	Most Loving One
The One Who Abases	All-Powerful One
The One Who Lifts Up	Witness
The One Who Gives Dignity	Truth
The One Who Takes It Away	Strong One
Unshakable One	Law
Holy One	Pardon

The One Worthy of Praise	Magistrate
Omniscient One	Good
The Beginning	Amiable One
The One Who Will Raise His Creatures	Master of the Kingdom
Creator of Life	Lord of Majesty and Generosity
Creator of Death	Equitable One
Living One	Gatherer
Opulent One	Sufficient Unto Himself
Inventor	Rich One
Immutable One	The One Who Holds Goods
Unique One	The One Who Assigns Them
Eternal One	The One Who Distributes Them
Compassionate One	Light
Charitable One	Eternal One
Prudent One	Glorious One
Producer	Universal One
Prevenient One	Guide
The First	Immanent One
The Last	Perfect One
Manifested One	Sublime One
Hidden One	Patient One
Refresher	Sweet One
Worthy One	

The 100th Name remains ineffable,
known only to those to whom God communicates it.

Moslem Prayer
(From the Koran)

636   Prayer for Obedience to God

MY GOD,
inspire us to be obedient

and keep us away from rebelling.
Help us to desire what pleases you
and let us dwell in your gardens of abundance.
Dispel far from our minds the clouds of doubt,
and take from our hearts the veil of contestation.
Remove from our souls whatever is vain
and confirm truth in our innermost beings.

My God,
sweep us away in the breath of your salvation
and let us enjoy conversation with you.
Enable us to drink from the fountains of your love
and let us taste the sweetness of your friendship
and your presence.
May our struggle be for you
and may our concern be to obey you.
Purify our intentions
so that we may act toward you in sincerity.
We exist through you and for you,
and we have no other means of coming toward you
than you yourself.

Moslem Prayer
(Shiite)

637 **Prayer of Praise of the Ineffable God**

SOUL of the soul!
Neither thought nor reason grasps your essence,
and no one knows your attributes.
Souls have no idea of your being,
and even the prophets sink in the dust of your road.
Although the mind exists by you,
has it ever yet found the path of your existence?
O you who are in the interior and exterior
of the soul—
you are
and you are not
what I say you are.

In your presence reason becomes dizzy
and loses the thread that would lead it
in your path.
I perceive clearly the universe in you
and yet do not find you in the world.
All beings bear the trace of your imprint.
but you yourself have no visible imprint.
You hold back the secret of your existence.

Moslem Prayer

638   **Prayer of Thanks and Resolve
to Lead a Good Life**

IN THE Name of God,
    the Giver and Forgiver,
rich in love. . . ,
the God with the Name "Who always was,
always is,
and always will be";
the Heavenly among the heavenly,
with the Name "From whom alone is derived rule."

I offer thanks to you
with all my strength.

O God,
I accept all good at your command,
and think, speak, and do it.
I believe in the pure law;
and I seek forgiveness of all sins
by every good work.
I keep pure the six powers:
thought, speech, and work,
memory, mind, and understanding.
I am able to do all this
according to your will.

Persian Invocation

Prayers of Various Individuals

639   **Prayer to Live by God's Spirit**

I SHALL breathe the sweet breath
   that issues from your mouth
and daily see your beauty.
I desire to hear your gentle voice
even in the north wind,
that my limbs may be revivified
by love for you.
Let me take your hands which hold your spirit
that I may receive it
and live by it.
Call my name throughout eternity
and it shall never fail.

Amenhotep IV (c. 1370-c. 1350 B.C.)
King of Egypt

640   **Prayer to Love God above All**

O LORD,
   enable us to love you.
Grant that we may love those who love you
and that we may do those actions
that gain your love.
May our love for you
be more important to us
than ourselves,
our families,
all riches,
and even fresh water.

Mohammed (570-632)
Founder of Islam

641 **Prayer in Acknowledgment
of God's Greatness**

YOU are far above
all thought,
all conception,
all guess,
and all imagination.
Indeed you are far above
all we have spoken,
all we have heard,
or all we have read in books.
These deal with objects
but you are the universal Subject!

Sankara (c. 788–c. 820)
Indian Brahman Religious Teacher

642 **Prayer That We May Be Fools for God**

O GOD,
you are my sole companion,
my well-being and my happiness.
My heart refuses to love anyone
other than you—
O my Beloved,
you whom I call
with ardent longing,
you my passionate desire,
object of such a long expectation.

When will I attain
the hour of my meeting with you?
My mendicant supplication
does not stem from my folly;
it is not in this folly
that it has grown.

But I willingly accept this folly
so that I may guard the hope
of contemplating you.

Rihana "the Foolish" (8th cent.)
Moslem Woman Mystic

643 **Prayer to Know the Will of God Who Transcends All**

O MY God,
      never do I stoop to hear the cry of a beast,
the rustling of tree branches,
the gurgling of brooks,
or the pleasant chirping of birds;
and never do I lend an ear to
the delightful invitation of the shade,
the whistling of the wind,
or the rumbling of thunder—
without reflecting that they all bear witness
to your Oneness
and demonstrate that nothing in the world
is comparable with you.

O my God,
between me and your most distant desire
let there be no veil that you have not removed,
no barrier that you have not torn down,
no infection that you have not cured,
no door that you have left unopened,
so that you may place my heart
within the radiance of your knowledge
and make me taste the fragrance of your love.

Dhu 'l-Nun
Egyptian Moslem

644   Prayer of Thanks for God's Gifts

O GOD,
   glory be to your Name.
You have freed me
from the things that most people need
in this troubled life of transit.
Almighty Lord,
I thank you for enlightening me
concerning the way to faith and wisdom
and for opening to me the door of grace.

Nasir-i-Khusraw (c. 1003–c. 1070)

645   Prayer in Praise of God's Greatness

PRAISE to you,
   O eternal Life and Light,
praise to you,
O infinite Wisdom,
O radiant Mercy,
as clear and unlimited as air.
You give sight to the blind
and show mercy to all.
Praise to you,
O delight-imparting Light;
praise to you,
O munificent Power.
Your peace encompasses us like the sea
and immerses us in infinity.

Shinran Shonin (1175–1265)
Japanese Buddhist Reformer

646   Prayer to the Invisible
But Ever-Present God

O GOD,
   you are my hope—
how can I be disappointed!

You are my trust—
how can I ever despair!
Our eyes cannot discern you,
hidden as you are in the cloak of your glory.
But our hearts perceive your majesty,
visible as it is in the perfection of your splendor.

You are ever manifest—
how can you be hidden!
You are ever present
and constantly watch over us—
how can you be absent!

Ibn Atta Allah (c. 1240-1309)
Moslem Religious Leader

647   Prayer to Ask Pardon of the Transcendent God

O LORD,
    forgive the evil I have committed,
for my plight is sad indeed.
O Lord most high,
works of good and works of evil
are both under your control.
The world can never see you as you are—
even if it were obedient for a thousand years.
Neither can one jot of your worthiness be damaged—
even by a thousand years of sinfulness.

As for me,
I can do nothing of myself.
How then could I succeed in being obedient
to you, O Lord!
Yet I believe in your unity
and with a sincere heart keep your law!

Mohammed Fasli (c. 1500-1563)
Turkish Poet

648   Prayer to God Who Is All in All

O LORD,
    you are a soldier in battle array
and at the same time you are Supreme Peace.
You are man, woman, and child,
and you are God.
You are the flute player,
the cowherd leading his cows to pasture.

I love you
in all the forms you assume
and in all the places you inhabit—
for you yourself are in all of them!
You are my beginning and my end.

Govind Singh (1666–1708)
Sikh Spiritual Leader

649   Prayer to God Our Constant Companion

WHEREVER I go,
    you are my constant companion,
holding my hand and leading me on.

You are the sole support
along the path that I tread,
carrying my burden by my side.

If I stray along the way,
you set me right again.
You have overcome my resistance,
O God,
and you nudged me onward.

All things and all people
have become my beloved brothers.
Now your joy pervades and encircles me;
I am like a child at play
during a celebration.

Tukuram (17th cent.)
Hindu Mystic and Poet

**PRAYERS FROM THE AMERICAS —
NATURE AND DAILY LIFE**

The prayers from the religions of the Americas stress the real everyday activity in nature and in people and assign it to God. They start from life and carry us to the Almighty Spirit. They can give us good insights and are easy to adapt to our beliefs.

518

D) RELIGIONS OF THE AMERICAS

"NON-CHRISTIANS *who are deprived of explicit knowledge of Christ nevertheless benefit by the universal Providence of God. They are called upon to recognize the evidence which he gives them of his presence in created things and they receive, moreover, the light which the Eternal Word pours out on all people. Although seriously exposed to sin which afflicts the whole human race, they can count on the efficacious help of God . . . , and on the hope of salvation promised to human beings from the beginning of history.*

"God's action reaches human beings in the very experiences of life and of their conscience, all divine grace is grace of Christ through the Church, and it ordains non-Christians to take their place at the end of time among the People of God.

"The 'good and just,' the 'true and holy' things to be found in non-Christian religions can be at the same time the fruit and the occasion of this grace and consequently may be regarded as 'seeds of the Word' and 'preparation for the Gospel,' providentially arranged by God" (Vatican Secretariat for Non-Christians: *Towards the Meeting of Religions,* 9-21-67, nos 2-3).

Pope Paul VI summed it all up when he said: *"Immense portions of humanity practice non-Christian religions which the Church respects and esteems for they are the living expression of soul of vast human groups. They bear within them the echo of a thousands-of-years search for God, a search that is incomplete but often carried out with sincerity and rectitude of heart. They possess an impressive patrimony of profoundly religious texts. They have taught generations to pray. And they are all strewn with countless 'seeds of the Word' "* (12-8-75).

650 Prayer to Live By and For God

I PRAY for a long life.
   I pray for your fine appearance.
I pray for good breath.
I pray for propitious speech.
I pray that I may possess feet like yours
to conduct me through a long life.
I pray that I may have a life like yours.
I walk with people
and ahead of me all is well.
I pray that people will smile
as long as I live.

I pray that I will live a long time.
I pray that I will have a long life
to live with you
where the good people are.
I live in poverty.
I pray that the people there will speak of goodness
and talk to me.
I pray that like a brother
you will divide your good things with me.
Goodness lies ahead of me—
lead me on.

Apache Prayer

651 Prayer That God's Chastisement Will Aid Us

O LORD of mercy,
   grant that the chastisement
which you have sent us
will deliver us from evil
and from all foolishness.

Aztec Inscription

652 **Prayer to Walk Along Straight Paths**

O GREAT Spirit,
      pour down your blessings
on our children, friends, and guests
and give all of us happy lives.
Make all the trails we follow
lie straight and smooth before us,
and let us live to a grand old age.
For we are all your children,
and we make our requests
with sincerity of heart.

Blackfoot Prayer

653 **Prayer for Victory**

O GREAT Spirit on high,
      take pity on my wife and children.
Let them not be called upon
to mourn over me.
Enable me to be successful in my mission,
overcome my enemy,
and return home safely—
there to feast together
with my family and friends.
Take pity on me
and guard my life.

Delaware Indian Prayer

654 **Prayer in Time of Death**

O NOBLE Creator,
      do not forget me.
You who pervade my dreams—
will you forget me
now that I am on the verge of death!

Will you ignore my prayer
or will you reveal who you are!

You may well be what I thought you were
or you may even be a phantom,
something that inspires dread.
If only I might know for sure,
or if only it could be revealed to me!

You made me out of earth,
and you formed me out of clay.
Look upon me,
for you are my Creator.
Let me know who you are,
for I am very old.

Incan Prayer

655   **Prayer to the Creator at Dawn**

THE earthly dawn
   clothes itself with light
to give homage to
the Creator of all!

The sky itself
causes clouds to disperse
and bows down before
the Creator of all!

The lord of the stars,
our father, the Sun,
unfurls his tresses at the feet of
the Creator of all!

In its turn, the wind
stirs the treetops,
snaps off branches
and plummets them to earth.

In the midst of the trees
the birds chirp away

to give homage to
the Lord of the earth! . . .

So does my heart
at each dawn
render homage to you,
my Father and my Creator!

Incan Prayer

656   Prayer for a Prosperous New Year

WE THANK you for the growth of the earth—
for the rivers and streams,
for the sun and moon.
We thank you
for the herbs and plants
that heal the sick,
and for everything
that yields good and happiness.

We pray that we will have
a prosperous new year.
O Creator and Ruler,
we give you thanks,
for all things that exist in you.

We believe that you do all things
for our good and our happiness—
and indeed that you can do no evil.
Do not act severely toward us
when we disobey your commands.
Show us your kindness,
as you manifested it to our fathers
in times past.

Iroquois Prayer

657   Prayer for Recovery of Mind and Body

RESTORE to me
        my feet,
my body,
my mind,
and
my voice.
Take away your spell from me today,
remove your spell from me today.

You have taken it away from me!
It has departed far from me—
you have taken it far away from me.

I recover in a magnificent fashion.
My eyes regain their strength;
happily the spell is removed.
I walk without pain,
I walk with light within.
Thus happily you accomplish your works.

With happiness
the aged will regard you
and the children will look toward you.
They will regard you with happiness
as they return home.
May their trials homeward be pervaded with peace,
and may all of them return.

                                        Navajo Prayer

658   Prayer of Longing for God

O RULER and Lord of the universe,
        whether male or female,
you are Lord of reproduction
no matter where you may be.
Where are you,

O Lord of divination?
You may be above,
you may be below,
or you may be around your majestic throne and scepter.
Heed my prayer
from the sky above where you may be
or from the sea below where you may be.

Creator of the world,
Maker of all people,
Lord of all lords,
my eyes grow dim
out of the longing to see you
and out of the desire to know you.

O God,
you do not regulate
sun and moon,
day and night,
spring and winter
in vain.
They all traverse their given route
and all reach their assigned destination
in accord with your good pleasure.

You hold your royal scepter.
Heed my call and choose me.
Let it not be that I should grow weary
or die.

Peruvian Prayer

659   Prayer for Unity among Nations

ALMIGHTY and eternal God,
   you have called all people
to be members of one another,
and to lift their spirits to you as Father.
You alone are the Source

of our confidence,
our strength,
and our hope
during these perilous times. . . .

Strike from our hearts
the national self-righteousness that causes hatred and
   division
between persons and countries.
Teach us to love one another
as you have loved us.
Consecrate each of us anew,
that in our dealings
with one another and with other nations
we may do justly,
love mercy,
and walk humbly with you.

United Nations Prayer

6

PRAYERS IN ACCORD WITH CHURCH YEAR

ADVENT-CHRISTMAS — GOD COMES TO US

The prayers of this time of year emphasize God's goodness in deciding to make himself accessible to human beings, so that we might come to share in his life. They revolve around his Son Jesus who became one of us, by being born in a stable and leading a life of poverty and goodness.

A) ADVENT - CHRISTMAS

THE Second Vatican Council pointed out that "liturgy is the summit toward which the activity of the Church is directed; at the same time it is the font from which all her power flows" (Constitution on the Sacred Liturgy, no. 10). Accordingly, "prayers and devotions of the Christian people are to be so drawn up that they harmonize with the liturgical seasons, accord with the sacred liturgy, are in some fashion derived from it, and lead the people to it" (Ibid., no. 13).

In other words, no private prayer is ever entirely estranged from liturgical prayer. The mystery of the Church is also the mystery of each believer. Baptized in the Spirit of Christ, we have been baptized in the Church and by the Church. The Church bears within it the fullness of life and gives it to us. The Church continues the prayer of our Lord, and we pray in the Church.

The liturgical year is the periodic celebration of the mystery of Christ; the community actualizes this mystery, rendering it present through the liturgical actions. Thus while we "recall" the story of our salvation, we discover that we are involved in it—it is a story for today, one that concerns us.

Advent is the time of more than usual eager longing for Christ's coming in grace on Christmas Day while recalling his historical coming in the flesh and looking forward to his final coming in glory.

Christmas recalls Christ's visible coming into the world to bring light, life, and joy to a mankind lying in the darkness of ignorance and sin. It invites us to be born again through a more vital union with Jesus and to manifest him to others.

Communal Prayer Services
for Advent

I. Longing for God

660 ### INTRODUCTORY PRAYER
FOR ENLIGHTENMENT

O LORD,
     in this time of Advent
help us to be aided by the Church
so that we will grasp the true meaning
of the perpetual longing
that lies at the heart of all people.
May we be aided in this quest
by the great figures of the Advent liturgy—
Mary your Mother,
John your precursor,
and Isaiah your prophet.
Enable us to discover whom and what we expect
and to be resolved to do whatever is needed
to have our expectation fulfilled.

661 ### DIALOGUED PRAYER RECALLING
JESUS' LIFE

O JESUS, during your life on earth
     you satisfied both the natural and the spiritual
          hunger
of all who came to you.
— You instructed Nicodemus who visited you by night.
You gave the crowds who flocked to you by day
material food to satisfy their hunger
and spiritual food to satisfy their spiritual hunger.
— You promised the Samaritan woman
water that would quench her thirst forever.

662 JOINT PRAYER TO HUNGER FOR CHRIST

O LORD,
    enlighten our minds,
deliver us from all fear,
and make us totally open to your grace.
Let us grasp the deep meaning of our existence
and of our lifelong hunger.
Help us to see that we hunger for you
who are the living bread
and the fountain of perpetual life.
Aid us to overcome the desires
that may obscure this true hunger
so that we may run to meet you
as you come again in your grace
and in every person we encounter
along our life's journey to you.

II. Our Savior Comes

O UR help is in the name of the Lord.
    —Who made heaven and earth.

663 DIALOGUED PRAYER FORETELLING
CHRIST'S COMING

T HE desert and the parched land will exult;
    the steppe will rejoice and bloom.
They will bloom with abundant flowers,
    and rejoice with joyful song.
The glory of Lebanon will be given to them,
    the splendor of Carmel and Sharon;
They will see the glory of the Lord,
    the splendor of our God.

Strengthen the hands that are feeble,
    make firm the knees that are weak,

Say to those whose hearts are frightened:
Be strong, fear not!
Here is your God,
he comes with vindication;
With divine recompense
he comes to save you.

Then will the eyes of the blind be opened,
the ears of the deaf be cleared;
Then will the lame leap like a stag,
then the tongue of the dumb will sing.
Streams will burst forth in the desert,
and rivers in the steppe.

Go up onto a high mountain,
Zion, herald of glad tidings;
Cry out at the top of your voice,
Jerusalem, herald of good news!
Fear not to cry out
and say to the cities of Judah:
Here is your God!

Here comes with power
the Lord God,
who rules by his strong arm;
Here is his reward with him,
his recompense before him.
Like a shepherd he feeds his flock;
in his arms he carries the lambs,
Carrying them in his bosom,
and leading the ewes with care.

I am the Lord, there is no other;
I form the light, and create the darkness,
I make well-being and create woe;
I, the Lord, do all these things.

Let justice descend, O heavens, like dew from above,
like gentle rain let the skies drop it down.

Let the earth open and salvation bud forth;
   let justice also spring up!

Isaiah 35:1f; 40:9-11; 45:6-8

664   DIALOGUED PRAYER: THE GREAT "O" ANTIPHONS

O WISDOM,
   holy Word of God,
you rule all creation with power and true concern.
—Come to teach us the way of salvation.

O sacred Lord,
and Leader of ancient Israel,
you communicated with Moses at the burning bush
and gave him the law on Mount Sinai.
—Come to set us free by your mighty arm.

O Root of Jesse,
raised up as a sign of all peoples,
in your presence kings become mute
and the nations worship before you.
—Come to deliver us and do not delay.

O Key of David,
and Royal Power of Israel,
you open what no one can shut,
and you shut what no one can open.
—Come and deliver your people
imprisoned by darkness and the shadow of death.

O Radiant Dawn,
you are the Brightness of eternal light
and the Sun of justice.·
—Come to enlighten those who sit in darkness
and in the shadow of death.

O King of the Gentiles
and the longed-for Ruler of the nations,

you are the cornerstone who make all one.
— Come and save those whom you have created.

O Emmanuel,
our King and our Lawgiver,
you are the Desired of the nations
and the Savior of all people.
— Come to save us, O Lord our God!

Individual Prayers for Advent

665   Prayer to Help Others Find Christ

O LORD Jesus,
I thank you for the gift of faith
and for the continual grace you give me
to nourish and strengthen it.
Enable me to cultivate the genuine desire for you
that lies beyond the zealous search
for justice, truth, love, and peace
found in our contemporaries.
Encourage these searchings, O Lord,
and grant that all true seekers
may look beyond the present moment
and catch sight of your countenance in the world.
Come to the aid of those
who are weary and disillusioned
in their searching,
and inspire them with renewed hope
during this season of Christian hope.

666   Prayer for Christ's Triple Coming

L AMB of God,
you once came to rid the world of sin;
cleanse me now of every stain of sin.

Lord, you came to save what was lost;
come once again with your salvific power
so that those you redeemed will not be punished.
I have come to know you in faith;
may I have unending joy
when you come again in glory.

667 Prayer for Christ's Coming in Grace

O LORD Jesus,
    during this Advent
come to us in your grace.
Come to prepare our hearts, minds, and bodies
to welcome you on Christmas Day.
Come to comfort us in sadness,
to cheer us in loneliness,
to refresh us in weariness,
to buttress us in temptations,
to lead us in doubt,
and to exult with us in joy.

668 Prayer to Build Up the Body of Christ

O LORD Jesus,
    sometimes I become impatient
while waiting for the coming of your grace,
the coming of your peace,
the coming of your justice,
and the coming of your love.
I forget that you also are waiting—
for my efforts
to build up your Body in the world.

It is true, O Lord,
that unless you build the house
all who labor will come to nought.

But it is also true that
unless I join all people
in working for the coming of your Kingdom,
that Kingdom of justice, love, and peace
will delay in coming.

Help me to realize
that you need my poor efforts,
and hence to apply myself
with body, heart, and mind
to whatever task you may give me.

Prayer Services for Christmas

I. New Birth in Christ

669   **INTRODUCTORY PRAYER
TO BEGIN A NEW LIFE**

O LORD,
    we desire to live the birth of your Son
in all its truth and riches.
We want to welcome the God who comes
to pitch his tent among us.
We wish to give thanks for so great a gift
and to begin a new life—
the life that you bestow on us
for our true happiness.
Help us to throw off all fear,
all laziness,
and all infidelity.
Everything is possible for us now,
since Jesus is born with and for us.

670 DIALOGUED PRAYER TO DISCERN CHRIST'S COMING

LORD Jesus, you appear in our world,
and a whole group of people comes to life.
—The shepherds, astrologers, Simeon, and Anna.

You appear, O Lord,
but human sight sees nothing extraordinary.
—Just a little babe in its young mother's arms.

You perform no miracles, speak no words,
and no prodigy marks you out.
—But the Holy Spirit awakens humble hearts
with divine light.

This is how you also come into our lives today,
as discreetly as Mary's steps
on her way to the temple with the infant in her arms.
—Help us to discern your coming.

671 JOINT PRAYER FOR UNION WITH CHRIST

LORD Jesus,
open our hearts to your renewed coming.
Help us to be conformed to you
in a new birth.
Cast out all fear
which shuts us up within ourselves,
suffocates your gifts,
and prevents you from working in us
your perennial newness.
Grant that we may always discern your coming
so that we may remain united with you
and work out our salvation
and the salvation of the world.

II. God's Love for Us

OUR help is in the name of the Lord.
   —Who made heaven and earth.

672   INTRODUCTORY MEDITATION ON GOD'S LOVE

GOD'S love was revealed in our midst in this way:
   he sent his only Son to the world
that we might have life through him.
Love, then, consists in this:
not that we have loved God
but that he has loved us
and has sent his Son as an offering for our sins.
Beloved,
if God has loved us so,
we must have the same love for one another.
No one has ever seen God.
Yet if we love one another
God dwells in us,
and his love is brought to perfection in us.
The way we know we remain in him
and he in us
is that he has given us of his Spirit.
We have seen for ourselves, and can testify,
   that the Father has sent the Son as savior of the world.
                                             1 John 4:9-14

673   DIALOGUED PRAYER TO PROCLAIM CHRIST

SON of God,
   from the beginning you were with the Father;
now you are seen as man.
   —Grant us a love for all human beings.

You took the form of a slave
so that by your humility
we might rise to share the effect of your glory.
— Make us faithful ministers of your gospel.

We were without hope and without God;
you have given us grace upon grace from your fullness.
— Enable us to bring your hope
to our brothers and sisters in this world.

Give us an upright and sincere heart to hear your word;
show forth in us and in the world
the fruit of your glorification.
— Put the seeds of truth in our hearts.

674 **JOINT PRAYER TO SHARE
CHRIST'S DIVINITY**

H EAVENLY Father,
you established the dignity of human nature
in an admirable fashion,
and you restored it in a more admirable fashion.
Grant that we may come to share
the divinity of your Son
who chose to share our humanity.

III. Christ's Manifestation to the World

O UR help is in the name of the Lord.
— Who made heaven and earth.

675 **INTRODUCTORY MEDITATION:
THE LIGHT OF THE WORLD**

I WILL make you a light to the nations
that my salvation may reach to the ends of the earth.

When kings see you, they shall stand up,
     and princes shall prostrate themselves
Because of the Lord who is faithful,
     the Holy One of Israel who has chosen you.

Isaiah 49:6-7

676   DIALOGUED PRAYER TO BE IMBUED WITH CHRIST

KING of the nations,
     you summoned the Magi to adore you
as the first representatives of the Gentiles.
—Give us the spirit of adoration and service.

King of glory,
you judge the people with justice.
—Grant all people
the fulfillment of their desire for peace.

King of the ages,
you perdure for all generations.
—Send your word into our hearts
like drops of refreshing rain.

King of justice,
you desire to free the poor who are helpless.
—Comfort the suffering and the oppressed.

677   JOINT PRAYER TO BRING GOD TO OTHERS

HEAVENLY Father,
     on this day
you revealed your only Son
to the Gentiles.
Grant that we who already know you by faith
may be your witnesses with non-believers
and one day contemplate your sublime beauty.

Individual Prayers for Christmas

678 Prayer of Joy at the Birth of Jesus

LET the just rejoice,
  for their Justifier is born.
Let the sick and infirm rejoice,
for their Savior is born.
Let captives rejoice,
for their Redeemer is born.
Let slaves rejoice,
for their Master is born.
Let free people rejoice,
for their Liberator is born.
Let all Christians rejoice,
for Jesus Christ is born.

St. Augustine of Hippo

679 Prayer to Jesus, God's Greatest Gift

O JESUS,
  I believe that the greatest proof of God's love
is his gift to us of you,
his only Son.
All love tends to become like that which it loves.
You love human beings;
therefore you became Man.
Infinite love and mercy caused you,
the Second Person of the Blessed Trinity,
to leave the Kingdom of eternal bliss,
to descend from the throne of your majesty,
and to become a helpless babe.
Eventually you even suffered and died
that we might live.

You wished to enter the world as a child
in order to show that you were true Man.

But you become man
also that man may become like God.
In exchange for the humanity which you take from us
you wish to make us share in your divinity
by sanctifying grace,
so that you may take sole possession of us.
Grant me the grace to love you in return
with a deep, personal, and productive love.

680   Prayer to Know and Love Jesus

MY LORD Jesus,
I want to love you
but you cannot trust me.
If you do not help me,
I will never do any good.
I do not know you;
I look for you but I do not find you.
Come to me, O Lord.
If I knew you,
I would also know myself.
If I have never loved you before,
I want to love you truly now.
I want to do your will alone;
putting no trust in myself,
I hope in you,
O Lord.   St. Philip Neri

681   Prayer for Christ's Rebirth in the Church

O LORD Jesus Christ,
we do not ask you to renew for us
your birth according to the flesh.
We ask you
to incarnate in us your invisible divinity.

What you accomplished corporally in Mary
accomplish now spiritually in your Church.
May the Church's sure faith conceive you,
its unstained intelligence give birth to you,
and its soul united with the power of the Most High
preserve you forever.

682 Prayer That Christ May Be Known to All

O LORD,
    give us a new Epiphany
when you will be manifested to the world:
to those who do not know you,
to those who do not want you,
to those who vilify your name,
to those who oppress your Mystical Body,
to those who deny you,
and to all those who unconsciously long for you.

Bring the day closer
when all people will know and love you
together with the Father
and the Holy Spirit—
and the Kingdom of God will have arrived.

683 Prayer to the Infant King

O JESUS,
    the Magi offered you revealing gifts:
gold, because you are our King;
frankincense, because you are our God;
and myrrh, because you are our Redeemer.
Like the Magi,
I offer you my gifts:
the gold of my earnest love as your faithful subject;
the frankincense of frequent prayer as your creature;
and the myrrh of a generous self-sacrifice as a sinner.

LENT-EASTER — WE ALL RISE IN JESUS

The prayers of this time of year stress penance (death to self with Christ) and joy (resurrection to a new person with Christ). They enable us to take a greater part in the mystery of God's redeeming plan for the whole universe.

B) LENT - EASTER

CHRISTIANS *prepare themselves to celebrate the paschal mystery of our Lord's death and resurrection by a penitential season of forty days. Penance is the inner aversion from the evil existing in and around us and a generous conversion in love to God.*

Traditionally the Lenten practices of prayer, almsgiving, and fasting were the means for achieving this aversion-conversion. And they are still valid when they are not seen as ends in themselves. But there are many other forms of penance that one may use—for example, working for social or individual justice, performing corporal and spiritual works of mercy, and a renewed interest in the mysteries by which we are reborn to the children of God.

Easter is the highlight of all Christian celebrations. With Ascension-Pentecost as its completion, it lasts fifty days. Its lesson is that in Christ who rose from the dead and ascended into glory all will be made to live. Through our baptism, we now share in Christ's glorious resurrection, but we will share it fully by partaking in his ascension into heaven. The feast of Pentecost commemorates the outpouring of the pledge of our inheritance made to us at our confirmation.

We should recall at this time of the year that we are an Easter people; hence we should also be a joyous people. Death (both spiritual and corporal) has lost its sting. There is no longer any reason for prolonged sadness at life's defeats or at the end of our earthly existence. United with Christ, we will live forever.

Communal Prayer Services for Lent

I. Renewal of Life in Christ

684   INTRODUCTORY PRAYER FOR OPENNESS

L ORD Jesus,
   open our ears and hearts today
to your message
so that through the power
of your death and resurrection
we may walk in newness of life.
in accord with the teachings of your Gospel.

685   DIALOGUED PRAYER
ON THE BEATITUDES

O LORD Jesus, you said:
   "Blessed are the poor in spirit,
for theirs is the kingdom of heaven."
—Keep us from being preoccupied with money
and worldly goods
and trying to increase them at the expense of justice.

O Lord Jesus, you said:
"Blessed are the gentle,
for they shall inherit the earth."
—Help us not to be ruthless with one another,
and to eliminate the discord and violence
that exists in the world around us.

O Lord Jesus, you said:
"Blessed are those who mourn,
for they shall be comforted."
—Let us not be impatient under our own burdens
and unconcerned about the burdens of others.

O Lord Jesus, you said:
"Blessed are those who hunger and thirst for justice,
for they shall be filled."
— Make us thirst for you,
the fountain of all holiness,
and actively spread your influence
in our private lives and in society.

O Lord Jesus, you said:
"Blessed are the merciful,
for they shall receive mercy."
— Grant that we may be quick to forgive
and slow to condemn.

O Lord Jesus, you said:
"Blessed are the clean of heart,
for they shall see God."
— Free us from our senses and our evil desires,
and fix our eyes on you.

O Lord Jesus, you said:
"Blessed are the peacemakers,
for they shall be called children of God."
— Aid us to make peace in our families,
in our country, and in the world.

O Lord Jesus; you said:
"Blessed are those who are persecuted
for the sake of justice,
for the kingdom of heaven is theirs."
— Make us willing to suffer for the sake of right
rather than to practice injustice;
and do not let us discriminate against our neighbors
and oppress and persecute them.

686   JOINT PRAYER TO FOLLOW CHRIST

O LORD Jesus,
     gentle and humble of heart,
full of compassion and maker of peace,
you lived in poverty
and suffered persecution for the cause of justice.
You chose the Cross as the path to glory
to show us the way of salvation.
May we receive the word of the Gospel joyfully
and live by your example
as heirs and citizens of your kingdom.

II. Repentance for Sin

687   INTRODUCTORY PRAYER FOR PARDON

O LORD,
     the hour of your favor draws near,
the day of your mercy and our salvation—
when death was destroyed and eternal life began.
We acknowledge our sins
and our offenses are always before us.
Blot out all our wrongdoings
and give us a new and steadfast spirit.
Restore us to your friendship
and number us among the living
who share the joy of your Son's risen life.

688   DIALOGUED MEDITATION ON SIN

MY SON, if you have sinned, do so no more,
     and for your past sins pray to be forgiven.

Flee from sin as from a serpent,
     that will bite you if you go near it;

Its teeth are lion's teeth,
    destroying the souls of men.

Every offense is a two-edged sword;
    when it cuts there can be no healing.

He who hates correction walks the sinner's path,
    but he who fears the Lord repents in his heart.

The path of sinners is smooth stones
    that end in the depths of the nether world.
He who keeps the law controls his impulses;
    he who is perfect in the fear of the Lord has wisdom.

Sirach 21:1-3, 6, 10-11

689   JOINT PRAYER FOR AVOIDING SIN

HEAR, Lord, the prayers we offer from contrite
    hearts.
Have pity on us as we acknowledge our sins.
Lead us back to the way of holiness.
Protect us now and always
from the wounds of sin.
May we ever keep safe in all its fullness
the gift your love once gave us
and your mercy now restores.

Individual Prayers for Lent

690   Prayer To Be Freed of the Seven Deadly Sins

O MEEK Savior and Prince of Peace,
    implant in me the virtues
of gentleness and patience.
Let me curb the fury of *anger*
and restrain all resentment and impatience

so as to overcome evil with good,
attain your peace,
and rejoice in your love.

O Model of humility,
divest me of all *pride and arrogance.*
Let me acknowledge my weakness and sinfulness,
so that I may bear mockery and contempt
for your sake
and esteem myself as lowly in your sight.

O Teacher of abstinence,
help me to serve you rather than our appetites.
Keep me from *gluttony*—
the inordinate love of food and drink
and let me hunger and thirst for your justice.

O Lover of purity,
remove all *lust* from my heart,
so that I may serve you with a pure mind
and a chaste body.

O Father of the poor,
help me to avoid all *covetousness* for earthly goods
and give me a love for heavenly things.
Inspire me to give to the needy,
just as you gave your life
that I might inherit eternal treasures.

O Exemplar of love,
keep me from all *envy* and ill-will.
Let the grace of your love dwell in me
that I may rejoice in the happiness of others
and bewail their adversities.

O zealous Lover of souls,
keep me from all *sloth* of mind or body.
Inspire me with zeal for your glory,
so that I may do all things for you
and in you.

691   **Prayer of Contrition**

MERCIFUL Father,
    I am guilty of sin.
I confess my sins before you
and I am sorry for them.
Your promises are just;
therefore I trust that you will forgive me my sins
and cleanse me from every stain of sin.
Jesus himself is the propitiation
for my sins and those of the whole world.
I put my hope in his atonement.
May my sins be forgiven through his name,
and in his blood may my soul be made clean.

692   **Prayer to Know Jesus Christ**

O LORD Jesus,
    like St. Paul,
may I count everything as loss
in comparison with the supreme advantage
of knowing you.
I want to know you
and what your passion and resurrection can do.
I also want to share in your sufferings
in the hope that if I resemble you in death
I may somehow attain to the resurrection
from the dead.

Give me grace to make every effort
to supplement faith with moral courage,
moral courage with knowledge,
knowledge with self-control,
self-control with patience,
patience with piety,
piety with brotherly affection,

and brotherly affection with love.
May these virtues keep me both active and fruitful
and bring me to the deep knowledge of you,
Lord Jesus Christ.

(Holy Thursday)

693   Prayer to Appreciate the Mass

O LORD Jesus,
in order that the merits of your sacrifice
on the Cross
might be applied to every soul of all time,
you willed that it should be renewed
upon the altar.
At the Last Supper, you said:
"Do this in remembrance of me."
By these words
you gave your apostles and their successors
the power to consecrate
and the command to do what you yourself did.

I believe that the Mass is
both a sacrifice and a memorial—
reenacting your passion, death, and resurrection.
Help me to realize that the Mass
is the greatest gift of God to us
and our greatest gift to God.

(Good Friday)

694   Prayer of Love for the Crucified Lord

O JESUS,
it is not the heavenly reward you have promised
which impels me to love you;
neither is it the threat of hell
that keeps me from offending you.

It is you, O Lord,
it is the sight of you
affixed to the Cross and suffering insults;
it is the sight of your broken body,
as well as your pains and your death.

There is nothing you can give me
to make me love you.
For even if there were no heaven and no hell
I would still love you as I do!

(Holy Saturday)

695 **Prayer to Be Joined with Christ in Death**

O LORD,
your sorrowing Mother stood by your Cross;
help us in our sorrows
to share your sufferings.
Like the seed buried in the ground,
you have produced the harvest of eternal life for us;
make us always dead to sin and alive to God.
Shepherd of all,
in death you remained hidden from the world;
teach us to love our hidden spiritual life
with you and the Father.

In your role as the new Adam,
you went down among the dead
to release all the just there since the beginning;
grant that all who are dead in sin
may hear your voice and rise to new life.
Son of the living God,
you have allowed us through baptism
to be buried with you;
grant that we may also rise with you in baptism
and walk in newness of life.

Communal Services for the Easter Season

I. New Life and Renewed Hope

OUR help is in the name of the Lord.
—Who made heaven and earth.

696 INTRODUCTORY PRAYER OF PRAISE

PRAISED be the God and Father
    of our Lord Jesus Christ,
he who in his great mercy
gave us new birth;
a birth unto hope which draws its life
from the resurrection of Jesus Christ
from the dead;
a birth to an imperishable inheritance,
incapable of fading or defilement,
which is kept in heaven for you
who are guarded with God's power through faith;
a birth to a salvation which stands ready
to be revealed in the last days.   1 Peter 1:3-5

697   DIALOGUED PRAYER FOR THE FRUITS OF CHRIST'S RESURRECTION

GOD, the Father of lights,
    you have glorified the world
by the light of the risen Christ.
—Brighten our hearts today
with the light of your faith.

Through your risen Son
you opened the gate of eternal life

for all human beings.
—Grant to us who work out our salvation daily
the hope of eternal life.

You accepted the sacrifice of your Son
and raised him from the dead.
—Accept the offering of our work
which we perform for your glory
and the salvation of all people.

Open our minds and hearts
to our brothers and sisters.
—Help us to love and serve one another.

Your Son rose to lift up the downtrodden,
comfort the sorrowful,
cure the sick,
and bring joy to the world.
—Help all people to cast off sin and ignorance
and enjoy your Son's paschal victory.

698   **JOINT PRAYER FOR THE
EASTER VIRTUES**

O LORD,
    the resurrection of your Son
has given us new life and renewed hope.
Help us to live as new people
in pursuit of the Christian ideal.
Grant us the wisdom to know what we must do,
the will to want to do it,
the courage to undertake it,
the perseverance to continue to do it,
and the strength to complete it.

(Ascension)
II. Jesus' Exaltation
Foreshadows Our Own

699 **INTRODUCTORY PRAYER TO LIVE
A FULL LIFE**

O LORD,
your ascension into heaven
marks the culmination of the Paschal Mystery,
and it contains an important teaching for us.
We may live life as an earthly reality
and develop our human potential to its fullest.
We may make use of the results of science
to achieve a better life on this planet.
But in our best moments
we know that there must be more than all of this,
a transcending Reality.
As Christians, we know that this Reality
is your loving Father
who awaits us with you and the Holy Spirit.
Where you have gone,
we ultimately will come—if we are faithful.

700 **DIALOGUED PRAYER TO LIVE
IN UNION WITH CHRIST**

K ING of glory,
you took away the frailty of our flesh.
—Scrape away the decay of our guilt
and grant us the dignity of new life

We believe that you truly ascended into heaven
and are the forerunner for us.
—Never let any of us be separated

from your mystical body,
so that we may join you in glory at our death.

Eternal priest and minister of the new covenant,
you live forever to make intercession for us.
—Save your people who cry to you
in the throes of their earthly passage.

King of glory,
from your heavenly seat in glory,
you make perfect those whom you have sanctified.
—Unite us more closely to you by faith, hope, and love,
so that we may already be with you in heaven.

701   JOINT PRAYER TO DO GOD'S WILL

GOD, our Father,
help us not to lose sight of heavenly realities
while we apply ourselves diligently
to the circumstances of our earthly lives.
Enable us to hear your voice,
follow your will,
pursue your purpose,
and accept your judgments.
Help us to act to please you
rather than ourselves or others.
And after our earthly lives are over,
let us be united with your Son
in the unity that you share with him
and the Holy Spirit.

(Pentecost)

III. Come, Holy Spirit

702 **INTRODUCTORY PRAYER
TO RECEIVE THE SPIRIT**

HOLY Spirit,
powerful Consoler,
sacred Bond of the Father and the Son,
Hope of the afflicted,
descend into our hearts
and establish in them your loving dominion.
Enkindle in our tepid souls
the fire of your love,
so that we may be wholly subject to you.

703 **DIALOGUED PRAYER
FOR THE GRACE OF THE SPIRIT**

LORD and vivifying Spirit,
you moved over the primeval waters.
—Move our hearts to follow your inspirations.

You led your people out of bondage
and gave them the freedom of God's people.
—Free us from the bondage of our sins.

You came upon the Virgin Mary
and enabled her to become the Mother of God.
—Come upon us and make us children of God.

You raised Jesus from the dead
and manifested his divine power and glory.
—Infuse the divine life of grace in us
and help us never to lose it.

You came down on the first Christians
in tongues of fire

to establish your Church.
—Help us to remain ever faithful members.

You came to renew the face of the earth.
—Make us true witnesses to our faith
before the world.

704 **JOINT PRAYER FOR THE
GIFTS OF THE SPIRIT**

HOLY Spirit, Sanctifier blest,
 deign to grant us:
the gift of fear
which makes us shun all sin;
the gift of piety
which makes us respect and love
the Three Divine Persons,
our parents and children,
as is proper for true children of God;
the gift of knowledge
which makes us judge eternal and temporal things
as God judges them;
the gift of fortitude
which makes us bear all hardships
for the love and greater glory of God;
the gift of counsel
which makes us be guided, and guide others,
in the Way of Truth, of Christlike Life;
the gift of understanding
which makes us penetrate deeply into
what you, Holy Spirit, have deigned to reveal;
the gift of wisdom
which makes us relish all that is right
and is in line with Eternal Wisdom.
This we ask you to grant us,
Gift of God Most High,
who live in perfect unity of Love
with the Father and the Son.

Individual Prayers for the Easter Season

705 Appointment with the Resurrection

LORD, it is rather uncomfortable
    to believe
that you have really risen from death.
After all, to limit myself to knowing
that God exists
is less compromising:
it eliminates doubts,
compensates for some tensions,
grants a passport for the beyond.
To believe in you in such fashion
gives us also the right
to be unhappy
if you don't provide
for our well-being,
if you don't grant
our requests.

Today, Lord,
I have an appointment with your
resurrection.
To believe you risen
is to accept passing with you
from death to life,
from time to infinity,
from selfishness to love.
    And I do die every day
in my routine things,
in my routine contacts,
in my every situation.

To believe you have risen
is to spring out and live, free:
because we are, and feel that we are,
children of God,
able to love with your love;
because we are responding to you;
because we are sharing in others
and with others, with our brothers,
this liberation.

Lord,
to have risen
is to become new in you,
to experience and express
the deep joy
of your coming in love
among us.

Anna Teresa Ciccolini

706 Prayer in Praise of Christ's Humanity

O RISEN Lord,
your body was part of your power,
rather than you a part in its weakness.
For this reason you could not but rise again,
if you were to die—
because your body,
once taken by you,
never was or could be separated from you
even in the grave.

I keep your most holy body before me
as the pledge of my own resurrection.
Though I die,
as I certainly shall die,
it only means that my life is changed,
for I shall rise again.

Teach me so to live as one who believes
the great dignity and sanctity of the material frame
in which I am lodged.

707   Prayer to Christ Ascended into Heaven

O LORD Jesus,
    I adore you,
Son of Mary,
my Savior and my Brother,
for you are God.
I follow you in my thoughts,
O first-fruits of our race,
as I hope one day by your grace
to follow you in my person
into heavenly glory.

In the meantime,
do not let me neglect the earthly task
which you have given me.
Let me labor diligently all my life
with a greater appreciation for the present.
Let me realize that only by accomplishing
true human fulfillment
can I attain divine fulfillment
and ascend to you at the completion of my work.

708   Prayer to the Holy Spirit

H OLY Spirit of light and love,
    you are the substantial love
of the Father and the Son;
hear my prayer.

Bounteous bestower of most precious gifts,
grant me a strong and living faith,
which makes me accept all revealed truths
and shape my conduct in accord with them.
Give me a most confident hope in all divine promises
which prompts me to abandon myself unreservedly
to you and your guidance.

Infuse into me a love of perfect goodwill,
that makes me accomplish God's will in all things
and act according to God's least desires.
Make me love not only my friends but my enemies as
   well
in imitation of Jesus Christ
who through you
offered himself on the Cross
for all people.
Holy Spirit,
animate, inspire, and guide me,
and help me to be always
a true follower of you.

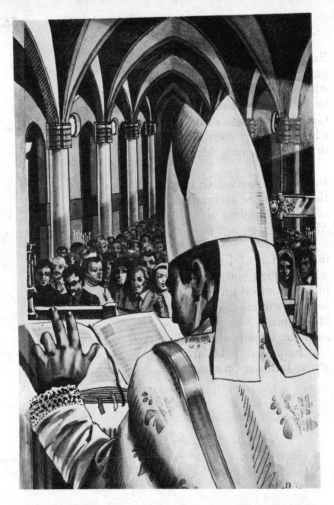

ORDINARY TIME — GROWTH IN THE SPIRIT

The prayers during this period stress growth, service, prayer, and God's Word. They enable us to work out our salvation through the Holy Spirit who has been given us by Jesus and the Father.

C) ORDINARY TIME

ORDINARY Time is the name given to that part of liturgical year which does not fall within one of the major seasons—Advent, Christmas, Lent, or Easter. During this season, the Church continues to celebrate the Lord's resurrection—but in its application to our earthly lives.

This season numbers thirty-three or thirty-four weeks and is assigned to two parts of the year. The first part occurs from Epiphany to Lent and is concerned with the beginning of the Lord's preaching, his baptism, and his first manifestation.

The second part of the season occurs after Pentecost and runs to Advent. During this time the Church presents Jesus in his public ministry of healing and preaching.

Ordinary time is a time of growth in the faith of all who follow the liturgy. It is a time for the accentuation of the Christian virtues, prayer, ministry of service to others, and meditation on God's word. The themes are endless. The sole unity is provided by the idea of spiritual growth symbolized by the green vestments that are worn.

During this time one may also concentrate on the major feasts that occur, such as the Trinity, Corpus Christi, Sacred Heart, Assumption, and Christ the King.

The following prayer services and individual prayers are only indicative. By a judicious use of the detailed Index, many more themes and prayers can be located and used.

Communal Prayer Services
for Ordinary Time

I. For Spiritual Growth

709   **INTRODUCTORY PRAYER
TO GROW INTO CHRIST**

HEAVENLY Father,
you are the One from whom
every family derives its origin.
Grant that, in keeping with your glorious riches,
we may be strengthened with power
through the Spirit
for the development of our inner selves.
Help us to develop our natural potentialities
to the full
while at the same time growing in likeness
to your Son, Jesus Christ.

710   **DIALOGUED PRAYER TO BE
PERFECTED IN LOVE**

LORD,
may we have Christ dwelling in our hearts
through faith.
—And may we be rooted and grounded in love.

Enable us to grasp more fully,
together with all the Saints,
the mystery of Christ's grace.
—Let us grasp its breadth and length,
its height and depth.

Grant us the power to know Christ's love
which surpasses all knowledge.
—In this way we may be perfected
in our love for you.

Teach us to pray always,
to be ever on the alert against evil,
and to persevere in our growth.
—Help us to find strength in your Son
and in his almighty power.

711 JOINT PRAYER TO REMAIN STEADFAST

BY YOUR grace,
O Lord,
make us stick to our resolutions,
act with courage,
remain constant in our devotion,
extend forgiveness without measure,
love without ceasing,
and live ever in your friendship.
Enable us,
with your help,
to put on Christ,
and manifest him to others
and bear witness to him to the world.

II. A Spirit of Service

712 INTRODUCTORY PRAYER TO LEARN TO SERVE

O LORD Jesus Christ,
you said that you came
not to be served
but to serve.
Your whole life bore witness to this
since from your birth to your death
you manifested a total self-surrender
on behalf of all people.

Teach us to follow your example
and to cultivate a spirit of service
toward all others.

713   DIALOGUED PRAYER
OF "USELESS SERVANTS"

LORD, may we develop the earth
by the work of our minds and hands
and by the aid of technology,
—so that it can bear fruit
and become a dwelling
worthy of the whole human family.

May we consciously take part in the life
of social groups,
—so that we may carry out the design of God
on our behalf.

This design is that we should subdue the earth,
bring creation to perfection,
and develop ourselves to the full.
—We will then be obeying the great commandment
to place ourselves at the service of our brothers.

Some of us are also called to give witness
to the human desire for a heavenly home.
—Others are called to dedicate ourselves
to the earthly service of others
and to make ready the material of the heavenly realm
by this ministry

In both cases let us understand
that we are useless servants.
—We are simply doing what we must do,
and only with God's unfailing help.

714   **JOINT PRAYER FOR TRUE SERVICE**

HEAVENLY Father,
help us to be true servants
after the example of your Son.
Send forth your Spirit
to give us a genuine spirit of service
of others.
Help us to realize that we are called
neither to run away from the world
nor to become slaves to its laws.
Rather our task is
to let ourselves be guided
by your Spirit of love, freedom, and service.
In this way we will be able
to build fraternal and praying communities
at the very heart of the world.

III. The Gift of Prayer

715   **INTRODUCTORY PRAYER
TO PRAY ALWAYS**

HEAVENLY Father,
your Son taught us to pray with confidence
when he said:
"Ask, and you will receive;
seek, and you will find;
knock, and you will gain admission."
Teach us how we are to pray
in order that we may fulfill
the command of Jesus
that we are to pray always and never lose heart.

Grant us the gift of prayer
that is our line of communication
with you and your Son in the Holy Spirit.

716   DIALOGUED PRAYER TO LEARN
HOW TO PRAY

LORD, you have fashioned us in such a way
that our lives are enriched by person-to-person
contact.
—Help us to realize that this applies to an encounter
that may take place between us and you.

This encounter may take place through Bible reading,
a good sermon,
or the Eucharistic celebration.
—But it may also take place
through contact with others
or through any event of our lives.

Most of all it may take place
through our prayer,
which is a dialogue
between us and you.
—Through prayer we get to know you
and we also get to know ourselves.

Help us to learn how to pray—
by praying and by using formal prayers
as well as informal prayers.
—Let us make use of communal prayer
as well as personal prayer.

717   JOINT PRAYER FOR OPENNESS
IN PRAYER

HEAVENLY Father,
we thank you for your gift of prayer.

Help us to use it frequently in our lives.
Let your ears be attentive
to the words of our lips
and the desires of our hearts.
Open our minds and our hearts
to be open to your plans for us
and strengthen our wills
to accept the answer you give to our prayers.
Above all, let us come to know you
and him whom you have sent, Jesus Christ—
for in this lies eternal life.

IV. The Power of God's Word

718 **INTRODUCTORY PRAYER
FOR TRUE WISDOM**

O HEAVENLY Father,
every day of our lives
we are bombarded with words of wisdom
from all sides.
We are told how to do our job,
how to keep our health,
how to take our leisure,
how to attain happiness,
and how to live every aspect of our lives.
We are in desperate need
of maintaining our balance
amid the flow of such constant earthly wisdom.
Help us to measure everything against the wisdom
of your Son Jesus Christ.

719   DIALOGUED PRAYER TO TAKE HOLD OF GOD'S WORD

THE wisdom of Jesus is found in two main sources:
— the Holy Bible
and the Sacred Tradition
of the Church.

But it can also reach us in hundreds of ways, such as:
encounters with other human beings,
meditation on good reading,
and the ordinary events of daily life.
— The sole requirement is
that we be open to this wisdom.

The Bible is transmitted to us in human words
written in a time and culture different from our own.
— It requires some effort on our part
so that it will be understood.

But if we persevere,
we will reach through the human word.
— We will take hold of the word of God
which has the power to change the world
beginning with our own lives.

720   JOINT PRAYER TO PROCLAIM GOD'S WORD

HEAVENLY Father,
you have spoken to the world
through your prophets in ancient times
and then through your only Son.
Your message is in the Scriptures
and your word is living and dynamic.
It is more penetrating than a two-edged sword,
reaching the very depths of human beings.

Help us to listen for your word
in the Bible,
in the Church,
and in the world.
Let us be transformed by its power
and bring it to others in our turn.

Individual Prayer
for Ordinary Time

721   Prayer for a Productive Faith

O LORD,
  increase my faith
and let it bear fruit in my life.
Let it bind me fast to other Christians
in the common certitude
that our Master is the God-Man
who gave his life for all.
Let me listen in faith
to the divine word that challenges me.

Help me to strive wholeheartedly
under the promptings of my faith
in the building of a world ruled by love.
Enable me to walk in faith
toward the indescribable future
that you have promised
to all who possess a productive faith in you.

722   Prayer to Grow with the Church Year

O LORD Jesus,
  I know that all human relations take time
if they are to grow and deepen.
This is also true of my relations

with you, the Father, and the Holy Spirit,
which must grow over the course of my life.
However, this growth is not automatic;
time alone means nothing
unless I add my earnest efforts to it.

You have inspired your Church to set aside special times
when this growth can develop more intensely—
the special seasons of the Church year.
If I fail to move toward you during these times,
I waste precious opportunities
and endanger my spiritual life.
Help me to take them seriously
and make a real attempt to use them well,
so that I may grow into the person
you want me to be.

723　　Prayer to Christ in the World

LORD Jesus,
let us realize
that every action of ours
no matter how small or how secular
enables us to be in touch with you.
Let our interest lie in created things—
but only in absolute dependence
upon your presence in them.
Let us pursue you and you alone
through the reality of created things.
Let this be our prayer—
to become closer to you
by becoming more human.

Let us become a tree branch on the vine
that is you,
a branch that bears much fruit.

Let us accept you in our lives
in the way it pleases you to come into them:
as Truth, to be spoken,
as Life, to be lived,
as Light, to be lighted,
as Love, to be followed,
as Joy, to be given;
as Peace, to be spread about;
as Sacrifice, to be offered;
among our relatives and friends,
among our neighbors and all people.

724 Prayer for Hope amid Despair

O LORD,
the world we live in
is particularly plagued with the curse of despair.
We are confronted daily with countless reasons—
of a physical, mental, or technological nature—
that urge personal or communal despair.
It is only natural that there will be moments
when we are in danger of giving in to this despair.

At such times, let us look to you,
O Jesus,
as our light, guide, and exemplar,
as our sign of encouragement
on the journey to salvation.
You are the Lord of the world
and the goal of the universe
toward whom everything and everyone is moving.
How then can we despair?
If you are with us, who is against us?
In you all problems can be worked out!

725   **Prayer to Turn Authority into Service**

LORD Jesus,
    let me realize that authority is conferred on us
not for ourselves but for others—
it is not a privilege but a service.
More often than not
it consists in a call to suffering and trials.
A leader must bear the burdens of others
in order to be able to understand them
and to walk at their head—
as you did.

Help us to realize that
no matter what kind of authority we hold,
whether as parents and teachers over children,
or children over other children,
or workers over other workers,
it constitutes a share in your own authority
which is a duty of love and service.
Enable us to act on this knowledge
and turn our authority into service.

726   **Prayer to Share Our Faith with Others**

O LORD Jesus,
    you manifested yourself to the world
when you lived among human beings
in the days of your earthly life.
Today, it is only through your members—
such as myself—
that you are manifested to the world.
Help me to realize that we live in
what has aptly been termed a "global village,"
where all feel the need to share their experiences
and enrich one another.

In such a world
let me regard your truth
not as something to be hoarded
but as something to be shared with others
by my actions as well as my words.
Help me to share my faith
with all whom I encounter—
not ostentatiously but quietly,
not with pride but with humility,
not out of fear but out of love,
not to overwhelm them but to inspire them,
not for my gain but for your glory.

727 Prayer to Show True Hospitality to Others

LORD Jesus,
  help me to grasp the true notion of hospitality
and practice it toward others.
Most people are very willing
to welcome into their midst
their parents and friends
as well as those with whom
they have professional or social contacts.
But the Christian notion of hospitality
goes far beyond this
and is based on a supernatural attitude.
The welcome extended may be of a material nature,
called a corporal work of mercy;
or it may be of a spiritual nature,
called a spiritual work of mercy.

Lord,
never let me limit my welcome
only to those who can do the same for me.
Let me focus on the fact

that it is you yourself that I welcome
when I show true hospitality to others,
especially those who are in need.
And a visit from you
is always a revelation of salvation.

728   Prayer to Be Generous in Giving

LORD Jesus,
   you came to tell us
that the meaning of life consists in giving.
You told us that those who cling too tightly
to what they have—
without thought for others—
end up by losing everything.
You gave us new values
by which to measure the worth of a person's life.

Help me to realize it is not
temporal success or riches or fame
that necessarily gives life meaning.
Rather it is the service rendered to others
in your Name
that brings fulfillment
and makes my life worthwhile.
May all my activity help build God's kingdom:
my suffering bear genuine fruit,
my obedience bring true freedom,
and my death lead to eternal life.

729   Prayer to Encounter God Frequently in Prayer

HEAVENLY Father,
   let me realize that, like all prayer,
prayer of petition is primarily

a means of encountering you
and being sustained by you.
You know what we need
because you are a loving Father
who watches over us at every moment.
Yet you respect our freedom
and wait for us to express our needs to you.

Let me have frequent recourse to you in prayer
so that I will purify my intentions
and bring my wishes into conformity with your own.
Let me pray with fixed formulas
as well as in my own words—
whether they be long or short.
Above all, let me come before you
with a heart moved by your Spirit
and a will ready to conform
to your holy will.

730 Prayer to Work and Pray for Our Salvation

HEAVENLY Father,
while I wait patiently for the Day
when Jesus will return in my life,
help me to steer clear of two erroneous attitudes
in working out my salvation.
Let me avoid an abandonment to your action
that will make me do nothing myself
and lead to the sin of presumption.
Let me also avoid a confidence in my own actions
that will make me do everything myself
and lead to the sin of despair when I fail.

Instead, let me blend these two attitudes:
praying as if everything depended on you

but working as if everything depended on me.
In this way I will bear witness
that salvation comes from you
but requires our generous collaboration.

731   Prayer to Jesus the Final Word of God

O LORD Jesus,
you are the Word of God in human form
who come to us at the end of a long dialogue
conducted by the Creator with his creatures.
You are God's final communication to us,
a communication in Word and Act.
The Word is the announcement
of the Good News of salvation
preached to the lowly and the sinful,
the Good News that is you yourself.
The Act is your Passion which bears witness
that the Father loves us to the end,
that his word is true and faithful,
and that all his promises are fulfilled in you.

Help us to receive this Word
at the hands of your Church,
and let it awaken our faith
and explain our rites.
Most of all, let it give sight to our eyes,
enabling us to see all of life
with the eyes of God.

732   Prayer to Discern God's Call

H EAVENLY Father,
your call never comes to us in a vacuum;
it comes to us in the circumstances
of our ordinary lives.

Therefore, our response cannot be given
only in the privacy of our own minds;
it must overflow into our daily lives.
You call us through our family,
through our community or Church,
and through the world.

Help me to see that when I say No
to the legitimate requests of my family,
my community, or my world,
I say No to you.
You have ordained that
whatever advances the true progress
of self,
of the Church,
and of the world
is my way of saying Yes to your call.
May I take advantage of the daily opportunities
which you place at my disposal
to answer your call affirmatively.

PRAYERS FOR SPECIFIC MONTHS AND DAYS

The good part about prayers assigned to specific days and months is that we will be assured of making the major mysteries of Church teaching part of our prayer life. However, we must guard against turning this type of praying into a mere formality.

D) MONTHLY AND DAILY PRAYERS

IN ADDITION to the pattern of praying throughout the year in tune with the liturgical seasons, another pattern of prayer exists in the Church. It is the pattern of assigning a mystery of Christ to each month of the year as well as each day of the week. This enables Christians to meditate on the pertinent aspect of their faith as they pray day by day.

Since there is nothing really official about the assignment of any mystery to a particular month or day, there is bound to be a difference in the mysteries assigned, depending on the source followed. Some are time-tested like the devotion to Mary during May, to the Blessed Sacrament during June, to the Rosary during October, and to the souls of the faithful departed during November. The same is true of the mysteries of the weekdays: devotion to St. Joseph on Wednesdays, to the Sacred Heart on Fridays, and to the Blessed Virgin on Saturdays.

The method followed in this section is to take those that accord best with the liturgical orientation of each month and day of the week. In this way one can continue to pray with the Church while using the prayers found therein.

Only one prayer is provided for each month and each day of the week. However, any number of prayers on the same subject can be found simply by using the detailed Index. Thus, readers can take advantage of the wealth of prayers and choose the one which best harmonizes with their internal states at any given time.

Prayers for Each Month of the Year

733   **January — The Holy Name of Jesus**

MOST merciful Jesus,
    you began your office of Savior
by shedding your blood
and assuming for us
that Name which is above all names.
I thank you for such early proofs
of your infinite love.
I venerate your sacred Name
in union with the deep respect of the angel
who first announced it to the earth.
I also unite my affections
to the sentiments of tender devotion
which your adorable Name has in all ages enkindled
in the hearts of your servants.

Jesus, you said:
"If you ask the Father anything in my Name,
he will give it to you" (John 16:23).
I earnestly ask the Father in your Name
for an increase of faith, hope, and love,
and the grace to lead a good life
and die a happy death.

Jesus,
your Name means "Savior."
Be my Savior.
Through your adorable Name
which is the joy of heaven,
the terror of hell,
the consolation of the afflicted,
and the solid ground of my unlimited confidence,
grant me all the petitions I make in this prayer.

734   **February — The Sacred Passion**

DEAR Lord Jesus,
     by your Passion and Resurrection
you brought life to the world.
But the glory of the Resurrection
came only after the sufferings of the Passion.

You laid down your life willingly
and gave up everything for us.
Your body was broken and fastened to a Cross,
your clothing became the prize of soldiers,
your blood ebbed slowly but surely away,
and your Mother was entrusted to the beloved disciple.

Stretched out on the Cross,
deprived of all earthly possessions and human aid,
racked with pain and burning with fever,
you cried out to your Father
that the end had come.
You had accomplished the work given you,
and you committed into his hands,
as a perfect gift.
the little life that remained to you.

Lord,
teach me to accept all afflictions
after the example you have given.
Let me place my death in yours
and my weakness in your abandonment.
Take hold of me with your love—
that same "foolish" love that knew no limits—
and let me offer myself to the Father with you
so that I may rise with you to eternal life.

March — St. Joseph

O GLORIOUS St. Joseph,
   you were chosen by God
to be the foster father of Jesus,
the most pure spouse of Mary ever Virgin,
and the head of the holy family.
You have been chosen by Christ's Vicar
as the heavenly patron and protector
of the Church founded by Christ.
Therefore it is with great confidence
that I implore your powerful assistance
for the whole Church on earth.
Protect in a special manner,
with true fatherly love,
the Pope and all bishops and priests
in communion with the See of Peter.
Be the protector of all who labor for souls
amid the trials and tribulations of this life,
and obtain that all the nations of the earth
may docilely follow that Church
out of which there is no salvation.

Dear St. Joseph,
accept the offering of myself
which I now make to you.
I dedicate myself to your service,
that you may ever be my father,
my protector, and my guide
in the way of salvation.
Obtain for me great purity of heart
and a fervent love for the interior life.
May all my actions,
after your example,
be directed to the greater glory of God,
in union with the divine Heart of Jesus,

the immaculate heart of Mary,
and your own paternal heart.
Finally, pray for me
that I may share in the peace and joy
of your holy death.

736 **April — The Holy Eucharist**

LORD Jesus,
I believe that in the Holy Eucharist
you give us the graces
to enter into the mystery of your redemptive sacrifice
and to cooperate in the formation of the whole Christ.
Grant me the grace of the spirit of sacrifice,
a willingness to do whatever you ask of me,
no matter what the cost.

With you I want to adore, love, and thank
the heavenly Father
from whom comes every good gift.
With you I beg the Supreme Judge to pardon
my sins and those of your people.
With you I present my requests confidently
because you have promised that the Father
will give me whatever I ask in your Name.

Jesus,
help me to live the Mass,
to bring its fruits into my everyday life.
Give me the courage to be a Christ-bearer.
Bearing you to my work and my leisure,
I can make my daily tasks my Mass,
and my whole life my thanksgiving.
Help me to live out the Sacrifice of the Mass
and carry you to the world.

737   May — The Blessed Virgin Mary

HOLIEST Virgin,
with all my heart I venerate you
above all the angels and saints in heaven
as the daughter of the Eternal Father,
and I consecrate to you
my soul with all its powers.

Holiest Virgin,
with all my heart I venerate you
above all the angels and saints in heaven
as the Mother of the only-begotten Son,
and I consecrate to you
my body with all its senses.

Holiest Virgin,
with all my heart I venerate you
above all the angels and saints in heaven
as the beloved Spouse of the Holy Spirit,
and I consecrate to you
my heart with all its affections.

Holiest Virgin,
intercede for me with the Holy Trinity
that I may obtain the graces I need
for my salvation.
To you I entrust all my worries and miseries,
my life and the end of my life,
so that all my actions may be directed
by the divine plan.

738   June — The Sacred Heart of Jesus

O LOVING Heart of our Lord Jesus Christ,
you move hearts that are harder than rock,
you melt spirits that are colder than ice,

and you reach souls that are more impenetrable
than diamonds.
Touch my heart with your sacred wounds
and permeate my soul with your precious Blood,
so that wherever I turn
I will see only my divine Crucified Lord,
and everything I see
will appear colored with your blood.

Lord Jesus,
let my heart never rest until it finds you,
who are its center, its love, and its happiness.
By the wound in your heart,
pardon the sins that I have committed
whether out of malice or out of evil desires.
Place my weak heart in your own divine Heart,
continually under your protection and guidance,
so that I may persevere in doing good
and in fleeing evil until my last breath.

Heart of Jesus, save me.
Heart of my Creator, perfect me.
Heart of my Savior, deliver me.
Heart of my Judge, forgive me.
Heart of my Father, govern me.
Heart of my Spouse, love me.
Heart of my Master teach me.

Heart of my King, crown me.
Heart of my Benefactor, enrich me.
Heart of my Pastor, defend me.
Heart of my Friend, embrace me.
Heart of my infant Jesus, draw me.

Heart of Jesus dying on the cross, pray for me.
Heart of Jesus, I greet you in all your states.
Give yourself to me.

St. Margaret Mary Alacoque

739   July — The Precious Blood

PRECIOUS Blood of Jesus,
    infinite price of our redemption
and both the drink and the laver of our souls,
you continually plead the cause of all people
before the throne of infinite mercy.
From the depths of my heart I adore you.
Jesus,
insofar as I am able
I want to make reparation for the insults and outrages
which you receive from human beings,
especially from those who blaspheme you.

Who would not venerate this Blood of infinite value!
Who does not feel inflamed with love for Jesus
who shed it!
What would have become of me
had I not been redeemed
by this divine Blood!
Who has drained it all from the veins of my Savior?
Surely this was the work of love!

O infinite love,
which has given us this saving balm!
O balm beyond all price,
welling up from the fountain of infinite love!
Grant that every heart and every tongue
may render you praise and thanks
now and forever!

740   **August — The Immaculate Heart of Mary**

MARY, Mother of God,
  your heart is a shrine of holiness
in which the demon of sin has never entered.
After the Heart of Jesus,
never was there a heart more pure and more holy.
Your heart is a counterpart of the Heart of Jesus.
His Heart is a loving Heart.
Your heart is also the most affectionate of hearts
after that of Jesus.
You love as a mother loves her children.
Your eyes ever watch over us;
your ears constantly listen to our cries;
your hands are always extended over us
to help us and impart heavenly gifts;
above all, your heart is full of tenderest care for us.

The heart of Jesus was a suffering Heart.
Your heart was also a suffering heart.
Its martyrdom began with Simeon's prophecy in the
    Temple
and was completed on Calvary.
When the hands and feet of Jesus were pierced with
    nails
the sound of each blow of the hammer
inflicted a wound in your heart.
When his side was opened with a lance,
a sword of sorrow also pierced your heart.

The Heart of Jesus was a pure Heart.
Your heart was also a pure heart,
free from the stain of original sin,
and from the least stain of actual sin.
Your heart is pure and spotless

because it was sanctified beyond all other hearts
by the indwelling of the Holy Spirit,
making it worthy to be the dwelling place
of the sacred Heart of Jesus.

The Heart of Jesus was a generous Heart.
Your heart is also a generous heart.
full of love, abounding in mercy.
All people may find a place there as your children
if only they choose to heed your loving appeal.
Your heart is a refuge for sinners,
for you are the Mother of Mercy,
who have never been known to turn away
anyone who came to seek your aid.

I consecrate myself entirely to your immaculate heart.
I give you my very being and my whole life:
all that I have,
all that I love,
all that I am.
I desire that all that is in me and around me
may belong to you
and may share in the benefits of your motherly blessing.

741   **September — Our Lady Queen
of Martyrs**

MARY, most holy Virgin,
    and Queen of Martyrs,
accept the sincere homage of my childlike love.
Welcome my poor soul
into your heart pierced by so many sorrows.
Receive it as the companion of your sorrows
at the foot of the cross,
on which Jesus died
for the redemption of the world.

Sorrowful Virgin,
in union with you I will gladly suffer
all the trials, misunderstandings, and pains
which our Lord lets me endure.
I offer them all to you in memory of your sorrows,
so that every thought of my mind
and every beat of my heart
may be an act of compassion and love for you.

Loving Mother,
have pity on me
and reconcile me to your divine Son.
Keep me in his grace
and assist me in my last agony,
so that I may be able to meet you in heaven
and sing your glories.

Mary most sorrowful,
Mother of Christians,
pray for us.
Mother of love, of sorrow, and of mercy,
pray for us.

742 October — The Most Holy Rosary

MOST holy Virgin,
you have revealed the treasures of graces
hidden in the recitation of the Rosary.
Inspire my heart with a sincere love
for this devotion,
so that by meditating on the mysteries
of our redemption
that are recalled in it,
I may gather the fruits
and obtain the special graces I ask of you,
for the greater glory of God,

for your honor,
and for the good of my soul.

O Virgin Mary,
grant that the recitation of the Rosary
may be for me each day,
amid my manifold duties,
a bond of unity in my actions,
a tribute of filial piety,
a delightful refreshment,
and an encouragement to walk joyfully
along the path of my state in life.
Let the mysteries of your Rosary
form in me little by little
a luminous atmosphere,
pure, strengthening, and fragrant,
which may penetrate my understanding and will,
my heart and memory,
my imagination and my whole being,
so that I shall acquire the habit
of praying while I work.

Most holy Virgin,
obtain for me the grace of imitating
the purity of your Annunciation,
the charity of your Visitation,
the tenderness of your love for Jesus
born in a stable,
the humility and obedience of your Presentation,
so that we may merit also to find Jesus
in the temple of glory
after having sought him eagerly on earth.

Sorrowful Virgin,
teach me the divine patience that associated you
with the Passion of Jesus
and made you co-redemptrix of the human race.

Let me learn from you
the way of Calvary,
Christian resignation,
and love of the Cross of your divine Son.

Glorious Virgin,
obtain for me
that by meditating on the mysteries
of your glorious and triumphant life,
I may merit to be in heaven one day,
among the ranks of your blessed servants,
to render to you
joint and eternal homage of filial love.

743 November — The Faithful Departed

CHRIST Jesus,
    Lord of life
and Redeemer of the world,
grant eternal rest to all the faithful departed.
Let my relatives and friends
whom you have called from this life
attain their eternal home.
Reward our departed benefactors
with eternal blessedness.
Grant your departed priests and religious
the recompense for their work in your vineyard.

O Lord,
receive into your peace
the souls of our brothers and sisters
who labored for peace and justice on earth.
Accept the sacrifices of those who gave their lives
out of love for you and their fellow human beings.
Look with mercy on all who showed good will
to others,
and grant them the peace they deserve.

O Lord,
through the bloody sweat
which you suffered in the garden of Gethsemani;
through the pains which you suffered
while carrying your Cross to Calvary;
through the pains which you suffered
in your most painful crowning with thorns;
through the pains which you suffered
during your most cruel Crucifixion;
through the pains which you suffered
in your most bitter agony on the Cross;
through the immense pain which you suffered
in breathing forth your blessed soul;
grant eternal rest to all the faithful departed.

744   December — The Holy Infancy

ADORABLE Child Jesus,
in you
wisdom resides,
divinity dwells,
and all eternal riches are found.
You are the beauty of heaven,
the delight of the angels,
and the salvation of mankind.
Here I am prostrated at your feet,
O Source of innocence, purity, and holiness.
Although I am a slave of sin,
I belong to you by the undeniable right
of your sovereignty.

I hereby render to you as my Lord—
my King and my dignified and most adorable Savior—
my faith and my homage with the shepherds,
and my act of adoration with the Magi.
I give myself entirely and without restriction

into your powerful hands,
which drew all the universe from nothingness
and preserved it in the admirable order
that we see.

O lovable Child,
grant that as a result of my total devotion
to honoring the mystery of your divine Childhood,
I may have the happiness—
through the mediation of your holy Mother
and St. Joseph, your foster father—
to live all the rest of my life
in the same manner as you.
May I live in you,
for you,
and under the direction of your divine Spirit,
so that not one moment of my life
deviates from your will,
or forestalls it in any respect,
but listens to it
and faithfully follows it in every way.

Prayers for Every Day of the Week

745 Sunday — The Most Holy Trinity

MOST blessed Trinity,
  Father, Son, and Holy Spirit,
behold us kneeling in your divine presence.
We humble ourselves deeply
and beg of you the forgiveness of our sins.

We adore you,
almighty Father,
and with all our hearts

we thank you for having given us
your divine Son Jesus to be our Redeemer.
He gave himself to us in the Holy Eucharist
even to the ends of the earth,
and thus revealed to us
the wondrous love of his heart
in this mystery of faith and love.

We adore you,
Word of God,
dear Jesus our Redeemer,
and with all our hearts we thank you
for having taken human flesh upon yourself
and having become priest and victim
for our redemption
in the sacrifice of the Cross,
a sacrifice which,
through the great love of your Sacred Heart,
you renew upon our altars at every moment.

Give us the grace to honor your Eucharistic Mystery
with the devotion of Mary most holy
and your entire Church in heaven and on earth.
We offer ourselves entirely to you.
Accept it through your infinite goodness and mercy;
unite it to your own
and grant us your blessing.

We adore you,
Divine Spirit,
and with all our hearts we thank you
for having worked the unfathomable mystery
of the Incarnation of the Word of God
with such great love for us,
a blessing which is being continually extended
and increased in the Sacrament of the Eucharist.

By this adorable mystery
grant us and all poor sinners
your holy grace.
Pour forth your sacred gifts upon us
and upon all redeemed souls.

746   **Monday — The Holy Spirit**

O HOLY Spirit,
   divine Paraclete,
Father of the poor,
Consoler of the afflicted,
and Sanctifier of souls,
behold us prostrate in your presence.
We adore you with deepest submission
and we repeat
with the seraphim who stand before your throne:
"Holy, holy, holy!"

You filled the soul of Mary with immense graces
and inflamed the hearts of the apostles with holy zeal;
enkindle our hearts with your love.
You are a divine spirit;
fortify us against evil spirits.
You are a spiritual fire;
set our hearts on fire with your love.
You are a supernatural light;
enlighten us that we may understand eternal things.
You appeared as a dove;
grant us purity of life.
You came as a wind full of sweetness;
disperse the storms of passion which rise in us.
You appeared as a tongue;
teach us to sing your praises without ceasing.
You came forth in a cloud;
cover us with the shade of your protection.

O Bestower of heavenly gifts,
vivify us by your grace,
sanctify us by your love,
and govern us by your infinite mercy,
so that we may never cease
blessing, praising, and loving you
now during our earthly lives
and later in heaven for all eternity.

747   Tuesday — All Angels and Saints

HEAVENLY Father,
    in praising your angels and saints
we praise your glory,
for by honoring them
we honor you
who are their Creator.
Their splendor shows us your greatness
which surpasses that of all creation.

In your loving providence,
you saw fit to send your angels
to watch over us.
Grant that we may always be under their protection
and one day enjoy their company in heaven.

Heavenly Father,
you are glorified in your saints,
for their glory is the crowning of your gifts.
You provide an example for us
by their lives on earth,
you give us their friendship
by our communion with them,
you grant us strength and protection
through their prayer for the Church,
and you spur us on to victory over evil

and the prize of eternal glory
by this great company of witnesses.
Grant that we who aspire to take part in their joy
may be filled with the Spirit
that blessed their lives,
so that, after sharing their faith on earth,
we may also experience their peace in heaven.

Help us to realize that there are saints
with whom we work day after day,
with whom we live and take our leisure,
with whom we come into contact every day.
For whoever follows your teachings faithfully
and corresponds with your grace
is a living saint.
Help us to live in such a way
as to attain this sanctity.

748   **Wednesday — St. Joseph**

HOLY Joseph,
   you were always most just;
make us relish what is right.
You sustained Jesus and Mary
in time of trial;
sustain us by your help.
You provided for all the needs of Jesus and Mary;
help the needy of the whole world.
You rescued Jesus from Herod
when he sought to kill your child;
save us from our many sins.

You were the foster father of Christ,
the priest-victim;
make priests faithful to their calling.
You were the foster father of Christ,

the divine physician;
sustain the sick and obtain relief for them.
You died the holiest of deaths
in the arms of Jesus and Mary;
intercede for the dying.
You were the intrepid guardian
of the Holy Family;
protect all Christian families.

You cared for Jesus
with true fatherly love;
protect all children in the world.
You were a dedicated and honest worker
in your trade as a carpenter;
teach us to labor for Jesus.
You were the faithful and chaste spouse
of the Blessed Virgin Mary;
preserve in all hearts
a love of fidelity and purity.
You were a model single person
and a model father later on;
help all men to imitate your virtues.

749 Thursday — The Blessed Sacrament

LORD Jesus,
at the Last Supper
as you sat at table with your apostles,
you offered yourself to the Father
as the spotless lamb,
the acceptable gift that renders perfect praise
to him.
You have given us the memorial of your Passion
to bring us its saving power until the end of time.
In this great sacrament

you feed your people
and strengthen them in holiness,
so that the human family
may come to walk in the light of one faith,
and in one communion of love.
We are fed at your table
and grow into your risen likeness.

Lord Jesus,
you are the eternal and true priest
who established this unending sacrifice.
You offered yourself as a victim
for our deliverance
and you taught us to offer it throughout time
in memory of you.
As we eat your Body which you gave for us,
we grow in strength.
As we drink your Blood which you poured out for us,
we are washed clean.

Lord Jesus,
let the power of your Eucharist
pervade every aspect of our daily lives.
Let your consecration transform all our actions
and all the events of each day
into supernatural agents that form your Mystical Body.
Accept the bread of our efforts
and the wine of our sufferings and sorrows.
Transform all life that will spring up,
grow, and flower this day
and all death that will emerge to decrease and spoil.
Grant that we may carry out
the work you have given us to do
and thus be united with you
at every moment of our day.

750   **Friday — The Holy Cross**

LORD Jesus,
     from the height of your throne of suffering
you reveal the depth of your love for us.
Lifted up from the world on the Cross,
you draw everyone to yourself.
The Cross is both the symbol and the act
by which you raised up the world
from all its sin and weakness.
But you also ask for our cooperation.

Help us to die to self
so that we may live for you
and our fellow human beings.
Set us free from the slavery
of our passions,
our prejudices,
and our selfishness.
Enable us to endure the pains and trials of this life
and really help to change the world
in our own small way.

Keep before our minds the conviction
that in the Cross is salvation and life
as well as defense against our enemies.
Through the Cross
heavenly grace is given us,
our minds are strengthened,
and we experience spiritual joy.

In the Cross is the height of virtue
and the perfection of all sanctity.
Let us take up our Cross,
and follow you through earthly sorrow
into eternal happiness in heaven.

751 **Saturday — The Blessed Virgin Mary**

O VIRGIN Mother of God,
   most august Mother of the Church,
we commend the whole Church to you.

You bear the sweet name of "Help of Bishops";
keep the bishops in your care,
and be at their side and at the side
of the priests, religious, and laity
who offer them help in sustaining the difficult work
of the pastoral office.

From the Cross,
the Divine Savior, your Son,
gave you as a most loving Mother
to the disciple whom he loved;
remember the Christian people who commit themselves
   to you.

Be mindful of all your children;
join to their prayers
your special power and authority with God.
Keep their faith whole and lasting,
strengthen their hope,
and enkindle their love.

Be mindful of those who find themselves
in hardship, in need, in danger
and especially those who are suffering persecution
and are kept in chains
because of their Christian faith.
Ask for strength of soul for them,
O Virgin Mother,
and hasten the longed-for day of their liberation.

Turn your eyes of mercy
toward our separated brethren,
and may it please you
that one day we be joined together once again—
you who gave birth to Christ,
the bridge and the artisan of unity
between God and human beings.

We commend the whole human race
to your immaculate heart,
O virgin Mother of God.
Lead it to acknowledge Jesus
as the one true Savior.
Drive far from it
all the calamities provoked by sin.
Bring it peace,
which consists in truth, justice, liberty, and love.

7

PRAYERS
TO THE
BLESSED TRINITY

THE TRINITY — ONE GOD IN THREE PERSONS

Our prayer life should manifest the fact that the Blessed Trinity constitutes the central reality for Christians. Our entire lives are lived in the loving embrace of Father, Son, and Holy Spirit.

A) THE BLESSED TRINITY

THE Mystery of the Blessed Trinity constitutes the central doctrine of the Catholic Church. A Christian's entire life is marked "in the Name of the Father, and of the Son, and of the Holy Spirit." All life begins in the Trinity and is destined to end in the Trinity.

God has been pleased to reveal this Mystery to us: "In his goodness and wisdom, God chose to reveal himself and to make known to us the hidden purpose of his will by which through Christ the Word made flesh, we have access to the Father in the Holy Spirit and come to share in the divine nature" (Vatican II: Constitution on Divine Revelation, no. 2).

There are three distinct Persons in one God—and they exist only in relation to one another. They are co-equal, co-eternal, and consubstantial. The Son proceeds from the Father by generation, and the Holy Spirit proceeds from the Father and the Son by spiration.

God the Father is the Creator, God the Son is the Redeemer, and God the Holy Spirit is the Sanctifier—but not in such a way that the Son and the Holy Spirit are excluded from creation, or the Father and the Holy Spirit from redemption, or the Father and the Son from sanctification.

All of us want to know about God. But it is more important for us to know God, the way two beloved know one another—as the result of an intimate person-to person relationship. The prayers found in this section are intended to help us attain such a knowledge of the three Persons of the Trinity.

752   **Prayer of Consecration**

O EVERLASTING and Triune God,
     I consecrate myself wholly to you today.
Let all my days offer you ceaseless praise,
my hands move to the rhythm of your impulses,
my feet be swift in your service,
my voice sing constantly of you,
my lips proclaim your message,
my eyes perceive you everywhere,
and my ears be attuned to your inspirations.
May my intellect be filled with your wisdom,
my will be moved by your beauty,
my heart be enraptured with your love,
and my soul be flooded with your grace.
Grant that every action of mine be done
for your greater glory
and the advancement of my salvation.

753   **Prayer in Praise of the Trinity**

I VENERATE and glorify you,
     O most Blessed Trinity,
in union with that ineffable glory
with which God the Father,
in his omnipotence,
honors the Holy Spirit forever.

I magnify and bless you,
O most Blessed Trinity,
in union with that most reverent glory
with which God the Son,
in his unsearchable wisdom,
glorifies the Father and the Holy Spirit forever.

I adore and extol you,
O most Blessed Trinity,

in union with that most adequate and befitting glory
with which the Holy Spirit,
in his unchangeable goodness,
extols the Father and the Son forever.

753a The Glory Be

GLORY to the Father,
and to the Son,
and to the Holy Spirit.
As it was in the beginning,
is now, and will be forever.

754 Litany of the Most Holy Trinity

(For Private Devotion)

LORD, have mercy.
Christ, have mercy.
Lord, have mercy.
Blessed Trinity, hear us.
*Adorable Unity, graciously
hear us.*
God the Father of heaven,
have mercy on us.
God the Son, Redeemer of
the world,*
God the Holy Spirit,
Holy Trinity, one God,
Father, from whom are all
things,
Son, through whom are all
things,
Holy Spirit, in whom are all
things,
Holy and undivided Trinity,
Father everlasting,
Only-begotten Son of the
Father,

Spirit, who proceed from the
Father and the Son,
Co-eternal Majesty of Three
Divine Persons,
Father the Creator,
Son the Redeemer,
Holy Spirit the Comforter,
Holy, holy, holy Lord God
of hosts,
Who are, who were, and who
are to come,
God, Most High, who inhab-
it eternity,
To whom alone are due all
honor and glory,
Who alone do great wonders,
Power infinite,
Wisdom incomprehensible,
Love unspeakable,
Be merciful.
Spare us, O Holy Trinity.
Be merciful.

* *Have mercy on us* is repeated after each invocation.

Graciously hear us, O Holy Trinity.

From all evil, *deliver us, O Holy Trinity.*

From all sin,**

From all pride,

From all love of riches,

From all uncleanness,

From all sloth,

From all inordinate affection,

From all envy and malice,

From all anger and impatience,

From every thought, word, and deed, contrary to your holy law,

From your everlasting malediction,

Through your almighty power,

Through your plenteous loving-kindness,

Through the exceeding treasures of your goodness and love,

Through the depths of your wisdom and knowledge,

Through all your ineffable perfections,

We sinners,

we beseech you, hear us.

That we may ever serve you alone,***

That we may worship you in spirit and in truth,

That we may love you with all our heart, with all our soul, and with all our strength,

That, for your sake, we may love our neighbor as ourselves,

That we may faithfully keep your holy commandments,

That we may never defile our bodies and our souls with sin,

That we may go from grace to grace, and from virtue to virtue,

That we may finally enjoy the sight of you in glory,

That you would hear us,

O blessed Trinity,

we beseech you, deliver us.

O blessed Trinity,

we beseech you, save us.

O blessed Trinity,

have mercy on us.

Lord, have mercy.

Christ, have mercy.

Lord, have mercy.

℣. Blessed are you, O Lord, in the firmament of heaven.

℟. And worthy to be praised, and glorious, and highly exalted forever.

** *Deliver us, O Holy Trinity* is repeated after each invocation.

*** *We beseech you, hear us* is repeated after each invocation.

754a   **PRAYER OF PETITION TO THE TRINITY**

L ET us pray.
   Almighty and everlasting God,
you have given us your servants
grace by the profession of the true faith
to acknowledge the glory of the eternal Trinity
and in the power of your divine majesty
to worship the Unity.
We beg you to grant that,
by our fidelity in this same faith,
we may always be defended from all dangers.

755   **Prayer of Self-Offering to the Trinity**

O MY God,
   in order that I may be a living act
of perfect love,
I offer myself as a whole burnt offering
to your tender love.
Consume me continually,
letting my soul overflow
with the floods of infinite tenderness
which are found in you,
so that I may become a martyr
of your love.

Let this martyrdom make me ready to appear
before you
and at last cause me to expire.
Let my soul cast itself without delay
into the everlasting arms of your merciful love.
O my beloved,
with every beat of my heart
I desire to renew this offering
an infinite number of times,

until that day when the shadows shall vanish
and I shall be able to retell my love
in an eternal face-to-face with you.

St. Theresa of Lisieux

756 Prayer to Be Conformed to the Divine Will

MOST holy Trinity,
Godhead indivisible,
Father, Son, and Holy Spirit,
our first beginning and our last end,
you have made us
in accord with your own image and likeness.
Grant that all the thoughts of our minds,
all the words of our tongues,
all the affections of our hearts,
and all the actions of our being
may always be conformed to your holy will.
Thus, after we have seen here below in appearances
and in a dark manner by means of faith,
we may come at last to contemplate you
face-to-face
in the perfect possession of you
forever in heaven.

757 Prayer in Praise of the Living Trinity

FATHER,
enable me to praise you,
and to sing to you,
my Lord and my Master,
through whom are the ages without end,
the light of the sun and the beauty of the stars. . . .
You have created all things,

assigning to each a place,
and you govern them with your providence.
You spoke a word and your work was accomplished.

Your Word is God the Son,
equal to you in substance and in dignity.
He rules over the world.

The Holy Spirit,
who is God,
envelops all things
and watches over and protects them.

I proclaim that you are the living Trinity,
unique and sole Ruler;
immutable Nature, and without beginning;
ineffable Essence;
Intelligence whose wisdom is inaccessible;
unshakable Power with no beginning or end;

Light whom no one can see,
but who sees all things.
You are not ignorant of anything.
You know even the most profound things
from the earth to the nether world.

Father, be gracious toward me.
Enable me to serve you in all your majesty,
remove my sins far from me,
purify my conscience,
so that I may glorify your divinity
while lifting up toward you pure hands,
so that I may bless Christ
and, bending the knee,
beg him to accept me as his servant
when he comes as Judge in glory.

Father, be gracious toward me.
May I find mercy and grace.

For yours are the glory and praise
until the endless ages.

Gregory Nazianzen

758   **Prayer to Seek God Continually**

O LORD my God,
  I believe in you,
Father, Son, and Holy Spirit. . . .
Insofar as I can,
insofar as you have given me the power,
I have sought you.
I became weary and I labored.

O Lord my God,
my sole hope,
help me to believe
and never to cease seeking you.
Grant that I may always and ardently
seek out your countenance.
Give me the strength to seek you,
for you help me to find you
and you have more and more given me
the hope of finding you.

Here I am before you
with my firmness and my infirmity.
Preserve the first and heal the second.

Here I am before you
with my strength and my ignorance.
Where you have opened the door to me,
welcome me at the entrance;
where you have closed the door to me,
open to my cry;
enable me to remember you,
to understand you,
and to love you.

St. Augustine of Hippo

759   **Prayer to Live in Union with the Trinity**

OMNIPOTENCE of the Father,
    help my weakness
and save me from the depths of misery.
Wisdom of the Son,
direct all my thoughts, words, and deeds.
Love of the Holy Spirit,
be the source
of all the activity of my mind,
that it may be conformed to the divine will.

760   **TO GOD THE FATHER**

O MY God, who have created me
    and redeemed me by your beloved Son,
I thank you for it with all my heart.
O my God, who bestowed on me the Christian faith
and adopted me as your child on the day of my baptism,*
O my God, who have surrounded me
with so many means of salvation,*
O my God, who have given me
a wonderful angel to protect me,*
O my God, who have given me
a sound intelligence, a just judgment, a loving heart,*
O my God, who have given me eyes which see,
ears which hear, a tongue which speaks,
and limbs which move,*
O my God, who have created
the beautiful sun to give me light,
the waters to refresh me,
and the flowers to delight me with their fragrance.*
O my God, who make fruits and crops to ripen,
and increase the animals to nourish and clothe us,*

For all the benefits which you will give me
up to my death,*
For the grace of final perseverance
which I hope from your mercy
through the merits of Jesus Christ,*
For the infinite happiness
with which you will crown me in heaven
as you have commanded me to hope,*

761   **TO GOD THE SON**

O JESUS, who for love of me consented to become
    man,
* *I thank you with all my heart.*
O Jesus, who for love of me
passed nine months in the bosom of a Virgin,*
O Jesus, who for love of me
willed to be born in a poor stable,*
O Jesus, who for love of me
worked in the sweat of your brow,*
O Jesus, who for love of me
suffered a painful passion,*
O Jesus, who for love of me
hung on the Cross for three hours
and died in ignominy on it,*
O Jesus, who from the Cross gave me Mary to be my
    Mother,*
O Jesus, who ascended to heaven, to prepare a place
    for me
and to make yourself my advocate with the Father,*
O Jesus, who for love of me
reside day and night in the tabernacle,*
O Jesus, who for love of me
immolate yourself every morning on the altar,*

O Jesus, who come so often into my heart
by Holy Communion,*
O Jesus, who in the holy tribunal
so often wash me in your precious Blood,*

762 TO GOD THE HOLY SPIRIT

O DIVINE Spirit, who have so often enlightened
my soul
with the light of your beams,
I thank you with all my heart.
O Divine Spirit, who have sent me
so many holy inspirations and good desires,*
O Divine Spirit, who sustain my weakness
by your sovereign virtue,*
For the acts of virtue which you have made me accomplish
and which are due to your salutary assistance,*
For the little good which I have been able to do
by your help,*

763 TO THE TRINITY

THANKS be rendered to the Father, Son, and Holy
Spirit
for all the graces with which I have been laden in the
past.

Thanks be rendered to the Father, Son, and Holy Spirit
for the graces with which I am laden now.

Thanks be rendered to the Father, Son, and Holy Spirit
for the graces with which the Supreme Goodness will
crown me
in the future.

Invocations to the Trinity

764

WITH all our hearts and voices
 we acknowledge, praise, and thank you,
God the Father unbegotten,
God the only-begotten Son,
God the Holy Spirit, the Paraclete,
O holy and undivided Trinity!

765

I BELIEVE in you,
 I hope in you,
I love you,
I adore you,
O blessed Trinity, one God.
Have mercy on me
now and at the hour of my death,
and save me.

766

MOST holy Trinity,
 we adore you
and through Mary
we implore you to give all mankind
unity in the faith
and courage faithfully to profess it.

767

HOLY God,
 Holy Strong One,
Holy Immortal One,
have mercy on us.

768

TO YOU be praise,
    to you be glory,
to you be thanksgiving
through endless ages,
O Blessed Trinity.

769

BLESSING and glory,
    wisdom and thanksgiving,
honor, might, and power
be to our God forever.

770

HOLY Trinity,
    one God,
have mercy on us.

GOD THE FATHER — OUR CREATOR AND LORD

God the Father is our Creator and Lord as well as
our loving Father. Prayer to him enables us to
balance his supreme perfections and transcendence
with his loving concern for the slightest thing he
has made.

B) GOD THE FATHER

TRADITIONALLY, God the Father is known as the first Person of the Blessed Trinity. He is truly Father as he begets a coeternal and coequal Son, to whom he imparts the fullness of his nature and in whom he contemplates his own perfect image.

By nature God is our Creator and Lord, and we are his creatures and subjects. As a result of sin, however, we have become his enemies and deserve his chastisements. Yet, through the grace of Christ, the Father lovingly pardons us, adopts us as his children, and destines us to share in the life and beatitude of that same Christ, his only-begotten Son.

Thus, by divine adoption God is our Father and we are his children. This adoption is effected through sanctifying grace, a divine quality or supernatural habit infused into the soul by God, which blossoms into the vision of glory in eternal life.

Catholics have a tendency to address all prayer to the Father's august majesty even when they do not name him directly. In the New Testament, the word "God" as naming someone always means the heavenly Father. Liturgical prayer is almost always addressed to the Father through the Son in the Holy Spirit. By such prayer we acknowledge the presence of the Spirit inspiring us to pray and we also acknowledge that our prayer would be valueless except for the love the Father has for his eternal Son.

Thus, besides the special prayers found in this section, we could make use of any of the liturgical prayers found in part II to honor the Father.

771 **Prayer of Adoration to the Father**

O GOD,
 I adore you,
and I count myself as nothing
before your divine majesty.
You alone are
Being, Life, Truth, Beauty, and Goodness.
Helpless and unworthy as I am,
I honor, praise, and thank you,
and I love you in union with your Son,
Jesus Christ, our Savior and our Brother,
in the merciful kindness of his Heart
and through his infinite merits.

I desire
to serve, please, obey, and love you always
in union with Mary Immaculate,
Mother of God and our Mother.
I also desire to love my neighbor
for the love of you.
Give me your Holy Spirit
to enlighten, correct, and guide me
in the way of your commandments and holiness,
while I strive for the happiness of heaven
where I shall glorify you forever.

772 **Prayer of Praise and Petition**

WE PRAISE you,
 invisible Father,
giver of immortality,
and source of life and light.
You love all human beings,
especially the poor.
You seek reconciliation with all of them

and you draw them to yourself
by sending your beloved Son to visit them.

Make us really alive
by giving us the light to know you,
the only true God,
and Jesus Christ whom you have sent.
Grant us the Holy Spirit
and enable us to speak volumes
about your ineffable mysteries.

St. Serapion of Thmuis

773   **Prayer of Petition to the Father**

FATHER of mercies,
from whom comes all that is good,
I offer you my humble prayers
through the most Sacred Heart of Jesus,
your most beloved Son,
our Lord and Redeemer,
in whom you are always well pleased
and who loves you so much.

In your goodness,
grant me the grace of a lively faith,
a firm hope,
and an ardent love for you
and for my neighbor.
Grant me also the grace
to be truly sorry for all my sins
with a firm purpose of never offending you again.
May I thus be able to live always
according to your divine good-pleasure,
to do your most holy will in all things
with a generous and willing heart,
and to persevere in your love to the end of my life.

774   Prayer to the Father for Spiritual Growth

HOLY Lord,
  Father almighty,
Eternal God,
for the sake of your generosity
and that of your Son
who endured suffering and death for me;
for the sake of the wonderful holiness of his Mother
and the merits of all the Saints,
grant to me,
a sinner unworthy of your blessings,
that I may love you alone
and ever thirst for your love.
Let me ever have in my heart
the remembrance of the benefits of the Passion.
May I recognize my own sinfulness
and desire to be humbled and deprecated by all.
Let nothing grieve me except sin.

                              St. Bonaventure

775   Prayer to the Father for the Benefits of Christ's Redemption

ETERNAL Father,
  I offer you the infinite satisfaction
which Jesus rendered to your justice
in behalf of sinners
on the tree of the Cross.
I ask that you would make available
the merits of his Precious Blood
to all guilty souls
to whom sin has brought death.
May they rise again to the life of grace
and glorify you forever.

Eternal Father,
I offer you the fervent devotion
of the Sacred Heart of Jesus
in satisfaction for the lukewarmness and cowardice
of your chosen people.
By the burning love which made him suffer death,
may you be pleased to rekindle their hearts
which are now so lukewarm in your service,
and to set them on fire with your love
that they may love you forever.

Eternal Father,
I offer you
the submission of Jesus to your will.
Through his merits
may I receive the fullness of all grace
and accomplish your will entirely.
Blessed be God!

St. Margaret Mary Alacoque

776 Prayer of Thanksgiving to the Father

GOD and Father of our Lord
Jesus Christ,
I thank you
because in Christ your Son
you have blessed us
with every manner of spiritual blessing
in the heavenly realm.
These blessings correspond
to your choice of us in Christ
before the foundation of the world,
that we should be holy and without blemish
in your sight.

You have filled us
with the grace of your Son

by imparting to us
all manner of wisdom and practical knowledge,
making known to us—
in keeping with your good pleasure—
the mystery of your will.
For this I thank you.

777 **Prayer of Thanks
for the Father's Revelation in Christ**

ETERNAL Father,
you are a mystery for us
that if left to ourselves
we would never have discovered.
Your living Word,
your Son, Jesus of Nazareth,
came among us
to reveal the way that leads to you.

O Father,
may you be thanked and praised
for this way which is discovered
by all who come together in Jesus' Name
to pray to you with one heart.
For in that case
you listen to them
as if your Son himself were asking you
to listen to us and respond.
Praise to you for this great assurance
which you have granted us.

778 **Prayer of Thanks for the Father's Love**

ETERNAL Father,
we thank you for your great love.
You give the world the best of yourself,

the mirror of your perfect transparency,
the splendor of your very being—
your Son Jesus.

We thank you for giving him to us
not as a judge but as a Savior;
not as a tyrant but as a friend,
not as a commander but as a relative,
not as a superior but as a brother.

Help us to open our hearts
to his light
without fear of being overwhelmed
but exultant with the joy that comes from this light
upon all who accept it with gladness.

779   Prayer for Liberty and Life

ETERNAL Father,
    I give you thanks
for setting me free from the law
of sin and death
by giving me the Spirit of life,
in Christ Jesus.
By sending your Son as an offering
in the likeness of sinful flesh,
you have empowered me
to live not according to the flesh
but according to the Spirit.

You have thereby made it possible
for me to attain eternal life
for your Spirit dwells in me.
The Spirit himself gives witness
with my spirit
that I am your child.
And I am also an heir with Christ,

if only I suffer with him
so as to be glorified with him.

780   **Prayer to the Father for Reconciliation**

HEAVENLY Father,
in the death and resurrection
of Jesus Christ your Son
you willed to reconcile all mankind
to yourself
and so to reconcile all human beings
with each other in peace.
Hear the prayer of your people.
Let your spirit of life and holiness renew us
in the depths of our being
and unite us throughout our life
to the risen Christ:
for he is our brother and Savior.

With all Christians
we seek to follow the way of the Gospel.
Keep us faithful to the teachings of the Church
and alive to the needs of our neighbors.
Give us strength to work
for reconciliation, unity, and peace.
May those who seek the God they do not yet know
discover in you the source of light and hope.
May those who work for others
find strength in you.
May those who already know you
seek even further
and experience the depths of your love.

Forgive us our sins,
deepen our faith,
kindle our hope,
and enliven our hearts with love.

May we walk in the footsteps of Jesus
as your beloved sons and daughters.
With the help of Mary, our Mother,
may your Church be the sign and sacrament
of salvation for all people,
that the world may believe in
your love and your truth.

781   **Prayer to the Father,
Our Creator and Liberator**

FATHER,
    you are a living person.
You are not an impersonal Owner
but a Father,
and your glory is a person who is fully human.

You created us and gave us creativity;
you are responsible for our being here,
and you endowed us with responsibility.
You are eternally new
and you inspire us to seek ever new fulfillment
in accord with your divine plan.

You are the liberating God of the Exodus
who inspire us to seek true freedom constantly.
You help us to free ourselves from all selfishness
and to go out of ourselves to others
and to you.

You are infinite Love
and you invite us to be new persons
and bring your love to others.
Grant us the power to labor in the world
with true freedom,
with honest creativity,

with ungrudging responsibility,
with complete selflessness,
and with unfeigned love for all.

781a Invocations to God the Father

ETERNAL Father,
I offer you the most Precious Blood
of Jesus Christ
in atonement for my sins,
in supplication for the faithful departed,
and for the needs of the holy Church.

781b

O GOD,
come to my assistance;
O Lord,
make haste to help me.

781c

TEACH me, O Lord,
to do your Will,
for you are my God.

781d

O GOD,
since you are all-powerful,
make me a saint,

781e

O LORD,
keep us without sin this day.

GOD THE SON —
OUR REDEEMER
AND BROTHER

Our knowledge of God is communicated to us primarily by God the Son made Man, Jesus Christ. In him we have access to the Father. By entrusting ourselves to him in prayer we attain our true goal in life.

C) GOD THE SON

JESUS Christ is the center of the Father's work of salvation because he is the Son of God made Man so that as perfect man he might save all people and sum up all things in himself. He summed up in himself the mysteries of our salvation by his death and his resurrection; he had received all power in heaven and on earth; he founded his Church as a means for our salvation. Hence, in Christ our Redeemer we are joined to all human beings.

By becoming Man, Jesus consecrated human experience; God, now one of us, can be found in human loving, striving, and hoping. The risen Jesus is the first-fruits which includes the entire harvest of mankind, having died to a world where sin is at home and risen to the full humanity of the new creation.

Jesus poured out on his people the Spirit of adoption by making us children of God. He made for himself a new people, filled with the grace of God. United with Jesus, this new people of God constitutes "the whole Christ." He offers them to his Father and gives him glory. This is the aim of his Father's plan for the salvation of all people.

As we have seen, many of our prayers are directed to the Father through Jesus in the Holy Spirit. However, we also should pray directly to Jesus since he is the image of the unseen God (Colossians 1:15). As we pray, we can form a picture of him in our minds—something that we cannot easily do concerning God the Father.

PRAYERS TO JESUS,
TRUE GOD AND TRUE MAN

Prayer to Jesus, True Man

O JESUS,
you are true Man.
You took upon yourself a human body and soul,
you thought with a human mind,
and you acted through a human will.

But you are far above every other human.
No one ever spoke like you,
with such authority, freedom, and gentleness,
indicating the paths of love, justice, and sincerity,
and no one ever matched your teachings.
You spoke about the mystery of God
in a way so elevated above others
that you make it possible for us
to have a sublime experience of God,
to come to know him
and achieve a living love for him.

O Jesus,
no one ever acted like you, either.
You left us an example of the perfect human life:
by your preference for poverty,
by your love for the poor and the sick,
by your concern for the suffering,
by your liberating message of salvation,
by your espousal of peace and service,
by your obedience to the Father—
even to the death of the Cross.

O Jesus,
help us to know you more
so that we may know ourselves more.
Help us to live with you
so that we may live fully human lives.
Satisfy our human hunger with yourself,
who are the Man for others and for God,
the Man with others and with God,
perfect Love,
the Man-who-is-Love,
and the God-who-is-Love.

783   Prayer to Jesus, True God

O JESUS,
you are the Son of God.
Hence, not only do you resolve our problems
and respond to our aspirations.
You also do so with unexpected fullness.

As the Son sent to us by the Father,
you are the God who comes to meet us
and manifests for us
the God whom we seek in groping fashion.

You are the revelation of God for us—
the full, perfect, and definitive revelation—
God in person.

In you
the God-who-is-far-off
becomes the God-who-is-near,
the God-with-us,
and the God-who-is-one-of-us,
our companion on life's journey.
You alone, O Lord,
are the Way, the Truth, and the Life,
the Messiah,
and the Son of the living God.

784   **Invocations to Christ**

WE adore you,
    the Most Holy One.
You abased yourself and have lifted us up,
you humbled yourself and have honored us,
you became poor and have enriched us.

You were born and have given us life,
you received baptism and have cleansed us,
you fasted and have filled us,
you fought and have given us strength.

You sat on a donkey
and have taken us into your cortege,
you appeared before the tribunal
and have offered us,
you were led as a prisoner before the high priest
and have set us free,
you were subjected to questioning

and have let us sit as judges,
you kept silence
and have instructed us,
you were whipped like a slave
and have given us freedom,
you were deprived of your clothing
and have clothed us.

You were tied to a column
and have loosed our bonds,
you were crucified
and have saved us,
you tasted the vinegar
and have given us delightful drink,
you were crowned with thorns
and have made us kings.

You died and have made us live,
you were placed in a tomb and have revived us,
you rose in glory and have given us joy,
you clothed yourself in glory
and have filled us with admiration,
you ascended to heaven and have taken us with you,
you are seated in glory and have elevated us,
you sent us the Holy Spirit and have sanctified us.

Blessed be you who come
all radiant with goodness!

Maronite Rite

785   Prayer to "Learn Christ"

TEACH me,
    Lord,
to be mild and gentle in all the events of life—
in disappointments,
in the thoughtlessness of others,

in the insincerity of those I trusted,
in the unfaithfulness of those on whom I relied.

Let me put myself aside,
to think of the happiness of others,
to hide my little pains and heartaches,
so that I may be the only one to suffer from them.

Teach me to profit by the suffering
that comes across my path.
Let me so use it that it may mellow me,
not harden or embitter me;
that it may make me patient, not irritable;
that it may make me broad in my forgiveness,
not narrow, haughty, and overbearing.

May no one be less good
for having come within my influence;
no one less pure, less true, less kind, less noble
for having been a fellow-pilgrim
on our journey toward eternal life.

As I go my rounds from one distraction to another,
let me whisper from time to time a word of love to you.
May my life be lived in the supernatural,
full of power for good,
and strong in its purpose of sanctity.

786   Petitions to Jesus

O GOOD Jesus:
    Word of the eternal Father, convert me.
Son of Mary, take me as her child.
My Master, teach me.
Prince of peace, give me peace.
My Refuge, receive me.
My Shepherd, feed my soul.
Model of patience, comfort me.

Meek and humble of heart, help me to become like you.
My Redeemer, save me.
My God and my All, possess me.
The true Way, direct me.
Eternal Truth, instruct me.
Life of the saints, make me live in you.
My Support, strengthen me.
My Justice, justify me.
My Mediator with the Father, reconcile me.
Physician of my soul, heal me.
My Judge, pardon me.
My King, rule me.

My Sanctification, sanctify me.
Abyss of goodness, pardon me.
Living Bread from heaven, nourish me.
Father of the prodigal, receive me.
Joy of my soul, be my only happiness.
My Helper, assist me.
Magnet of love, draw me.
My Protector, defend me.
My Hope, sustain me.
Object of my love, unite me to yourself.
Fountain of life, refresh me.
My Divine Victim, atone for me.
My Last End, let me possess you.
My glory, glorify me.

PRAYERS TO THE INFANT JESUS

787 **Prayer of Adoration**

JESUS,
Son of the glorious Virgin Mary
and only Son of the living God,
I adore you
and acknowledge you as my God,
the only true God, one and infinitely perfect.
You have made out of nothing
all things that are outside of you.
You preserve and govern them
with infinite wisdom, sovereign goodness,
and supreme power.

By the mysteries that were fulfilled
in your sacred Humanity
cleanse me in your Blood
from all my past sins.
Pour forth abundantly upon me
your Holy Spirit,
together with his grace, virtues, and gifts.
Make me believe in you,

642

hope in you,
love you,
and labor to merit the possession of you
through each of my actions.
Give yourself to me some day
in the brightness of your glory,
in the company of all your Saints.

788   Prayer to the Miraculous Infant of Prague

DEAR Jesus,
    Little Infant of Prague,
how tenderly you love us!
Your greatest joy is to dwell among us
and to bestow your blessing upon us.
So many who turned to you with confidence
have received graces
and had their petitions granted.
I also come before you now
with this special request (*mention it*).

Dear Infant,
rule over me
and do with me and mine as you will,
for I know that in your divine wisdom and love
you will arrange everything for the best.
Do not withdraw your hand from me,
but protect and bless me forever.

Dear Infant,
help me in my needs.
Make me truly happy with you
in time and in eternity,
and I shall thank you forever
with all my heart.

789   # Litany of the Infant Jesus

(For Private Devotion)

LORD, have mercy.
   Christ, have mercy.
Lord, have mercy.
Jesus, hear us.
Jesus, graciously hear us.
God the Father of heaven,
   have mercy on us.
God, the Son, Redeemer of
   the world,*
God, the Holy Spirit,
Holy Trinity, one God,
Infant, Jesus Christ,
Infant, true God,
Infant, Son of the living God,
Infant, Son of the Virgin
   Mary,
Infant, strong in weakness,
Infant, powerful in tender-
   ness
Infant, treasure of grace,
Infant, fountain of love,
Infant, renewer of the heav-
   ens,
Infant, repairer of the evils of
   earth,
Infant, head of the angels,
Infant, root of the patriarchs
Infant, speech of prophets,
Infant, desire of the Gentiles,
Infant, joy of shepherds,
Infant, light of the Magi,
Infant, salvation of infants,

Infant, expectation of the
   just,
Infant, instructor of the wise,
Infant, first-fruits of all saints,
Be merciful, *spare us, O
   Infant Jesus.*
Be merciful, *graciously hear
   us, O Infant Jesus.*
From the slavery of the chil-
   dren of Adam, *Infant Jesus,
   deliver us.*
From the slavery of the dev-
   il,**
From the evil desires of the
   flesh,
From the malice of the world,
From the pride of life,
From the inordinate desire of
   knowing,
From the blindness of spirit,
From an evil will,
From our sins,
Through your most pure
   Conception,
Through your most humble
   Nativity,
Through your tears,
Through your most painful
   Circumcision,
Through your most glorious
   Epiphany,

---

* *Have mercy on us* is repeated after each invocation.
** *Infant Jesus, deliver us* is repeated after each invocation.

Through your most pious Presentation,

Through your most divine life,

Through your poverty,

Through your many sufferings,

Through your labors and travels,

Lamb of God, you take away the sins of the world; *have mercy on us, O Infant Jesus.*

Lamb of God, you take away the sins of the world; *graciously hear us, O Infant Jesus.*

Lamb of God, you take away the sins of the world; *have mercy on us.*

℣. Jesus, Infant, hear us.

℟. *Jesus, Infant, graciously hear us.*

789a PRAYER TO THE INFANT JESUS

LET us pray.
O Lord Christ,
you were pleased so to humble yourself
in your incarnate Divinity
and most sacred Humanity,
as to be born in time
and become a little child.
Grant that we may acknowledge
infinite wisdom in the silence of a child,
power in weakness,
and majesty in humiliation.
Adoring your humiliations on earth,
may we contemplate your glories in heaven,
who with the Father and the Holy Spirit
live and reign forever.

790   Invocations to the Infant Jesus

JESUS, friend of children,
     bless the children of the whole world.

791

JESUS, son of the living God,
     have mercy on us.
Jesus, Son of the Virgin Mary,
have mercy on us.
Jesus, king and center of all hearts,
grant that peace may be in your kingdom.

792

JESUS,
     with all my heart I cling to you.

793

LORD Jesus,
     through your infant cries
when you were born for me in a manger;
through your love
as you live for me in the tabernacle—
have mercy on me and save me.

THE MOST HOLY NAME OF JESUS

794   **Prayer of Praise**

O GLORIOUS Name of Jesus,
   gracious Name,
Name of love and of power!
Through you sins are forgiven,
enemies are vanquished,
the sick are freed from illness,
the suffering are made strong and cheerful.
You bring honor to those who believe,
instruction to those who preach,
strength to those who toil,
and sustenance to those who are weary.

Our love for you is ardent and glowing,
our prayers are heard,
the souls of those who contemplate you
are filled to overflowing,
and all the blessed in heaven
are filled with your glory.
Grant that we too may reign with them
through this your most holy Name.

795   Prayer of Petition

O JESUS,
   your Name means "Savior."
Be my Savior,
dear Lord.
Your adorable Name is the joy of heaven,
the terror of hell,
the consolation of the afflicted,
and the solid basis for my unlimited confidence.
Through this glorious Name,
mercifully grant all the petitions
which I make in this prayer.

796   Prayer for Devotion to the Holy Name

O JESUS,
   grant to me and those I love
as well as to all the faithful
the grace of eternal salvation
through your holy Name.
Bestow on us a most ardent love for you
that will imprint your sacred Name upon our hearts.
May it be always in our minds
and frequently on our lips,
that it may be our defense in temptation,
our refuge in danger,
and our consolation and support
in the hour of our death.

797   Invocations to the Holy Name

D EAR Jesus,
   be not my judge but my Savior.

798

JESUS, my God,
   I love you above all things.

799

JESUS,
   for you I live;
Jesus, for you I die;
Jesus, I am yours in life and in death.

800

LORD Jesus Christ,
   you alone are holy,
you alone are Lord,
you alone are most high.

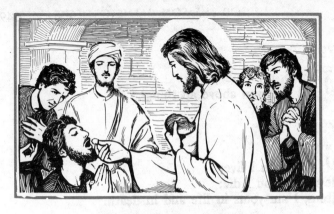

PRAYERS TO JESUS
IN THE BLESSED SACRAMENT

Prayers before Holy Communion
(1st Series)

801   **Prayer of St. Ambrose**

LORD Jesus Christ,
    I approach your banquet table
in fear and trembling,
for I am a sinner,
and dare not rely on my own worth
but only on your goodness and mercy.
I am defiled by many sins in body and soul,
and by my unguarded thoughts and words.

Gracious God of majesty and awe,
I seek your protection,
I look for your healing.
Poor troubled sinner that I am,
I appeal to you, the fountain of all mercy.
I cannot bear your judgment,

but I trust in your salvation.
Lord, I show my wounds to you
and uncover my shame before you.
I know my sins are many and great,
and they fill me with fear,
but I hope in your mercies,
for they cannot be numbered.

Lord Jesus Christ, eternal king, God and man,
crucified for mankind,
look upon me with mercy and hear my prayer,
for I trust in you.
Have mercy on me,
full of sorrow and sin,
for the depth of your compassion never ends.

Praise to you, saving sacrifice,
offered on the wood of the cross for me and for all mankind.
Praise to the noble and precious blood,
flowing from the wounds of my crucified Lord Jesus Christ
and washing away the sins of the whole world.
Remember, Lord, your creature,
whom you have redeemed with your blood.
I repent my sins,
and I long to put right what I have done.
Merciful Father, take away all my offenses and sins;
purify me in body and soul,
and make me worthy to taste the holy of holies.

May your body and blood,
which I intend to receive, although I am unworthy,
be for me the remission of my sins,
the washing away of my guilt,
the end of my evil thoughts,
and the rebirth of my better instincts.

May it incite me to do the works pleasing to you
and profitable to my health in body and soul,
and be a firm defense
against the wiles of my enemies.

802   **Prayer of St. Thomas Aquinas**

ALMIGHTY and ever-living God,
I approach the sacrament of your only-begotten Son,
our Lord Jesus Christ.
I come sick to the doctor of life,
unclean to the fountain of mercy,
blind to the radiance of eternal light,
and poor and needy to the Lord of heaven and earth.
Lord, in your great generosity,
heal my sickness, wash away my defilement,
enlighten my blindness, enrich my poverty,
and clothe my nakedness.

May I receive the bread of angels,
the King of kings and Lord of lords,
with humble reverence,
with the purity and faith,
the repentance and love, and the determined purpose
that will help to bring me to salvation.
May I receive the sacrament
of the Lord's body and blood,
and its reality and power.

Kind God,
may I receive the body of your only-begotten Son,
our Lord Jesus Christ,
born from the womb of the Virgin Mary,
and so be received into his mystical body
and numbered among his members.
Loving Father,
as on my earthly pilgrimage

I now receive your beloved Son
under the veil of a sacrament,
may I one day see him face to face in glory,
who lives and reigns with you for ever.

Prayers after Holy Communion
(1st Series)

803   **Prayer of St. Thomas Aquinas**

LORD, Father all-powerful and ever-living God,
   I thank you,
for even though I am a sinner,
your unprofitable servant,
not because of my worth
but in the kindness of your mercy,
you have fed me
with the precious body and blood of your Son,
our Lord Jesus Christ.
I pray that this holy communion
may not bring me condemnation and punishment
but forgiveness and salvation.

May it be a helmet of faith
and a shield of good will.
May it purify me from evil ways
and put an end to my evil passions.
May it bring me charity and patience,
humility and obedience,
and growth in the power to do good.
May it be my strong defense
against all my enemies, visible and invisible,
and the perfect calming of all my evil impulses,
bodily and spiritual.
May it unite me more closely to you,
the one true God,

and lead me safely through death
to everlasting happiness with you.

And I pray that you will lead me, a sinner,
to the banquet where you,
with your Son and Holy Spirit,
are true and perfect light,
total fulfillment, everlasting joy,
gladness without end,
and perfect happiness to your saints.
Grant this through Christ our Lord.

804   Prayer to Our Redeemer

SOUL of Christ, make me holy.
    Body of Christ, be my salvation.
Blood of Christ, let me drink your wine.
Water flowing from the side of Christ, wash me clean.
Passion of Christ, strengthen me.
Kind Jesus, hear my prayer;
hide me within your wounds
and keep me close to you.
Defend me from the evil enemy.
Call me at my death
to the fellowship of your saints,
that I may sing your praise with them
through all eternity.

805   Prayer of Self-Dedication to Jesus Christ

LORD Jesus Christ,
    take all my freedom,
my memory, my understanding, and my will.
All that I have and cherish
you have given me.
I surrender it all to be guided by your will.

Your grace and your love
are wealth enough for me.
Give me these, Lord Jesus,
and I ask for nothing more.

Prayers before Holy Communion
(2nd Series)

806   **Act of Faith**

LORD Jesus Christ,
   I firmly believe that you are present
in this Blessed Sacrament
as true God and true Man,
with your Body and Blood,
Soul and Divinity.
My Redeemer and my Judge,
I adore your divine majesty
in union with the angels and Saints.
I believe, O Lord;
increase my faith.

807   **Act of Hope**

GOOD Jesus,
   in you alone I place all my hope.
You are my salvation and my strength,
the source of all good.
Through your mercy,
through your Passion and death,
I hope to obtain the pardon of my sins,
the grace of final perseverance,
and a happy eternity.

808   Act of Love

JESUS, my God,
   I love you with my whole heart
and above all things,
because you are the one supreme Good
and an infinitely perfect Being.
You have given your life for me, a poor sinner,
and in your mercy
you have even offered yourself
as food for my soul.
My God,
I love you.
Inflame my heart
so that I may love you more.

809   Act of Contrition

O MY Savior,
   I am truly sorry for having offended you
because you are infinitely good
and sin displeases you.
I detest all the sins of my life
and I desire to atone for them.
Through the merits of your precious Blood,
wash me of all stain of sin,
so that entirely cleansed
I may worthily approach
the most holy Sacrament of the altar.

810   Act of Desire

JESUS,
   my God and my all,
my soul longs for you.

My heart yearns to receive you
in Holy Communion.
Come, Bread of heaven and Food of angels,
to nourish my soul
and rejoice my heart.
Come, most lovable Friend of my soul,
to inflame me with such love
that I may never again be separated from you.

Prayers after Holy Communion
(2nd Series)

811   Act of Faith

JESUS,
I firmly believe that you are present within me
as God and Man,
to enrich my soul with graces
and to fill my heart
with the happiness of the blessed.
I believe that you are Christ,
the Son of the living God.

812   Act of Adoration

WITH deepest humility,
I adore you,
my Lord and my God;
you have made my soul your dwelling place.
I adore you as my Creator
from whose hands I came
and with whom I am to be happy forever.

813 ## Act of Love

DEAR Jesus,
    I love you with my whole heart,
with my whole soul,
and with all my strength.
May the love of your own Sacred Heart
fill my soul and purify it
so that I may die to the world
for love of you,
as you died on the Cross
for love of me.
My God,
you are all mine;
grant that I may be all yours
in time and in eternity.

814 ## Act of Thanksgiving

DEAR Lord,
    I thank you from the depths of my heart
for your infinite kindness in coming to me.
With your most holy Mother
and all the angels,
I praise your mercy and generosity
toward me, a poor sinner.
I thank you for nourishing my soul
with your Sacred Body and Precious Blood.
I will try to show my gratitude to you
in the Sacrament of your love,
by obedience to your holy commandments,
by fidelity to my duties,
by kindness to my neighbor,
and by an earnest endeavor
to become more like you
in my daily conduct.

Prayers before Holy Communion
(3rd Series)

815   **Act of Faith**

O JESUS,
    my light and sanctification,
open the eyes of my mind,
and fill my soul with your grace
that I may know the importance of the action
which I am about to perform.
Let me consider how sacred and exalted
is he whom I am about to receive.

I am about to receive within my heart and soul
my God, my Creator, my Savior,
my sovereign Lord, my Jesus.
I am about to receive within my breast
really and truly
that same Jesus
who is the life, glory, treasure,
the love and delight of the eternal Father;
that same Jesus
whom so many patriarchs, prophets, and just
of the Old Testament
desired to see and did not see;
that same Jesus
who lived and walked on earth,
eating and drinking in the company of sinners;
that same Jesus
who was nailed to the Cross,
whose Body was bruised, wounded, and immolated
for me and all human beings.
I am about to receive that same Savior
who ascended gloriously into heaven,
who sits at the right hand of the Father,

and who will come again at the end of time,
clothed in power and majesty,
to judge the world.
O my God,
how unworthy I am of such a great favor.
I acknowledge this in the presence
of both heaven and earth. St. John Eudes (adapted)

816 **Act of Contrition**

O GOD,
loose, remit, and forgive my sins against you,
whether in word, in deed, or in thought;
and whether they are willingly or unwillingly,
knowingly or unknowingly committed,
forgive them all.
For you are good
and you love all human beings.
And through the prayers
of your most holy Mother,
or your heavenly servants and holy spirits,
and all the Saints who have found favor with you,
enable me to receive without condemnation
your holy Body and your Precious Blood.
Let my soul and body be thus healed
and my evil imaginings be driven away,
for yours is the kingdom, the power, and the glory:
Father, Son, and Holy Spirit,
now and forever. St. John Chrysostom (adapted)

817 **Act of Petition**

G IVE me yourself,
O my God,
give yourself to me.

Behold, I love you,
and if my love is too weak a thing,
grant me to love you more strongly.
I cannot measure my love to know
how much it falls short of being sufficient,
but let my soul hasten to your embrace
and never be turned away
until it is hidden in the secret shelter
of your presence.

This only do I know,
that it is not good for me
when you are not with me,
when you are only outside me.
I want you in my very self.
All the plenty in the world
which is not my God
is utter want.

St. Augustine of Hippo

Prayers after Holy Communion
(3rd Series)

818   **Act of Offering**

O KIND Father,
    I offer you this holy Sacrament
with all the merits and virtues of your beloved Son
for me, your poor creature,
with such love and fidelity
as Christ himself offered it
for the salvation of the world.
I offer it for all benefits
which you have showered on me
from my birth until this day.
You created me by your goodness,

redeemed me by your Son,
sanctified me by your Holy Spirit,
endowed me with imperishable goods by your grace,
and guarded me from many misfortunes
and countless sins.

As an adequate return for these favors,
I offer you all the praise and thanks
which your beloved Son, Jesus, ever gave
while he yet lived on earth,
and which he still renders to you in heaven.
I offer you this holy Sacrament
in compensation for all the virtues
which I ought to possess, yet do not,
and for obtaining all the necessary graces
of which I stand in need for your holy service.

I also offer it for the pardon of all the sins
which I have committed,
and in satisfaction for all the negligence and remissness
into which I have fallen.
Because I have deserved so much and such heavy punish-
    ment
that I can never be in a position
to satisfy for everything,
I have recourse to the immeasurable treasure
of the merits of your dear Son,
whom I now bear in my heart.
I wish to pay my debt honorably and fully
by this means.   Sts. Gertrude and Mechtild

819   **Act of Admiration**

O JESUS,
    my God, my Creator, my Savior, and my Lord,
what a wonderful thing it is for me

to possess you really at this moment!
The one who dwells from all eternity
in the bosom of the Father
has come into my innermost being. . . .
Even the Divinity,
the most Holy Trinity,
all that is most admirable in God
and in all heaven
has come down to me,
a poor and unworthy creature.

O God,
how good and merciful you are.
What can I say or what can I do
in the presence of things so great and marvelous?
Lord Jesus,
let all my faculties render homage and adoration
to you.
But, my God,
what temerity on my part
to have received you—you, the holy of holies—
into an abode so impure
and with so little love and preparation!
I ask your forgiveness for this
and for all sins and ingratitude of my past life.

St. John Eudes

820   Act of Hope

FOR your mercies' sake,
    O Lord my God,
tell me what you are to me.
Say to my soul: "I am your salvation."
So speak that I may hear,
O Lord;
my heart is listening;

open it that it may hear you,
and say to my soul: "I am your salvation."
After hearing this word,
may I come in haste to take hold of you.
Hide not your face from me.
Let me see your face even if I die,
lest I die with longing to see it.

The house of my soul is too small to receive you;
let it be enlarged by you.
It is all in ruins;
do you repair it.
There are things in it—
I confess and I know—
that must offend your sight.
But who shall cleanse it?
Or to what other besides you shall I cry out?
From my secret sins cleanse me,
O Lord,
and from those of others spare your servant.

St. Augustine of Hippo

821   Prayer to Be a Victim of Love

DIVINE Word,
        worthy of all admiration and all love,
you draw me continually to yourself.
You came into this world of exile
ready to suffer and die,
so as to bring souls within their true orbit,
the bosom of the Blessed Trinity.
And now, reascended into that inaccessible light
which is evermore your dwelling place,
you still frequent this valley of tears,
hidden under the appearance of the Sacred Host.
You are still ready to feed my soul
with your own divinity—

my poor soul which would sink back into nothingness
at any moment
if you did not give it life with a simple glance!

O Jesus,
my gratitude bids me say that you love me fondly;
and when I meet with such fondness from you,
how can my heart fail to go out to you—
how can any heart fail to go out to you—
and how can my trust in you have any limits? . . .
One day, I hope, you will come down
to carry off this poor creature of yours,
to carry it up to the very center of love,
and consume it in love's furnace,
to which it has offered itself as a victim.

St. Theresa of Lisieux

822   Act of Desire to Proclaim Christ

DEAR Jesus,
help me to spread your fragrance everywhere I go.
Flood my soul with your Spirit and Life.
Penetrate and possess my whole being so utterly
that my life may only be a radiance of yours.
Shine through me and be so in me
that every soul I come in contact with
may feel your presence in my soul.

Let them look up,
and see no longer me,
but only Jesus!
Stay with me
and then I will begin to shine as you shine,
so to shine as to be a light to others.

The light,
O Jesus,

will be all from you;
none of it will be mine.
It will be you, shining on others through me.
Let me thus praise you
in the way which you love best,
by shining on those around me.
Let me preach you without preaching,
not by words but by example,
by the catching force,
the sympathetic influence of what I do,
the evident fullness of the love
my heart bears for you.

Cardinal Newman

Prayers before Holy Communion
(4th Series)

823   **Act of Faith**

JESUS,
I believe that Holy Communion
gives me claim to all the actual graces
which I need to be holy
and to imitate you,
my divine Master.
With your grace I can live as a sincere Christian—
in some way as "another Christ"
among my fellow human beings.
Every act of virtue is derived from your grace.

You are not only the model of all virtues,
but one who merited for us
the grace to practice them.
You are the source of spiritual perfection.
Help me to foster a lively faith
in the mystery of grace

through which you will act in me,
because without your grace I can do nothing.
Your grace will help me
to maintain the spirit of devotion
which should underlie my Christian life.

824 **Act of Preparation**

LORD, I am preparing to meet you
at Mass.
I am coming as I am,
no change of feelings or of thoughts,
just as I am living my life today,
every day.
I am coming to meet you;
I know you are present in the Mass,
that you are the Christ
—born, dead, risen, ascended to the Father.
I am coming to measure my life in you,
to change myself;
you invite us to the "new,"
or we will not be Christians.

I am coming to bring you
what I am every day,
what I have every day;
in me are present at this moment
my dear ones, my friends,
all the people of the world;
the people I meet,
with whom I speak and work,
with whom I discuss and argue;
all my usual gestures,
all the things I use and deal with,
all the realities and situations
in which I am involved.

I am coming to be saved by you,
the Paschal mystery,
because I, too, a "lay person,"
"co-celebrate" the Mass
whenever I am with you, Christ,
and strive to bring all back to the Father;
I work in you, with you, and for you,
my "passing"
from mine to your life,
from yours to my life,
from mine to your love,
from yours to my love:
every day, every instant.

Lord, I am coming to Mass to understand
and to renew my place in the world,
in my family,
in my job,
in the Church,
in my encounters with others.

Lord, I am coming to learn that this
possibility
of love, life, salvation,
is a gift from you.
I am coming because I am not able
to love truly.

Anna Teresa Ciccolini

Prayers after Holy Communion
(4th Series)

825   **Prayer to Be Renewed**

L ORD, it makes no sense
to speak of Eucharist,
Mass,

Communion,
Encounter,
if I don't let myself
be "made new" by you.

To become truly
and continuously
new in love,
a love
which I am not able to retain
consistently,
but which I often replace
with a surrogate,
or an educated selfishness.

Lord, I have met with you
in this Mass;
to become new
means to discover
that this old man,
this coughing, clumsy bundle,
is my brother;
that this silly looking little woman
mumbling and fingering her rosary
is my sister;
really and truly.
I am going to move closer
and smile
and exchange a word.

It means to open the door
of the church
to start a new way
of loving,
as lovers of God
and human beings.
Exactly
like "lovers."

Anna Teresa Ciccolini

826   **Prayer to See Jesus in Others**

THROUGH this Holy Communion,
    I beg you, O Lord Jesus,
for the grace ever to love you
in my neighbor.
Let me see in every human being
your own dear self—disguised but really there.
Since every human being is a potential member
of your mystical Body,
I want to make my every act
a personal service rendered to you.

Your new law demands that I avoid
not only bodily injury to my neighbor
but also angry and uncharitable words and emotions.
Let me never put limits to my forgiveness,
so that your Father may forgive me my offenses.
Through this Communion
make me a living example
of your great commandment of love.

Prayers before
the Blessed Sacrament

Act of Desire

JESUS,
   I come to you.
You are the *Way*
that I want to follow
in obedience to your commandments,
your counsels, and your example.
Let me walk after you
in the way of obedience, self-denial, and sacrifice
which leads to heaven and to you.

Jesus,
you are the *Truth*.
You are the true Light which enlightens
everyone who comes into the world.
I believe in you.
I believe in your Gospel.
I want to know you that I may love you.
I want to make you known
in order to make you loved.

Jesus, you are the *Life*,
through your sanctifying grace
which is the life of our souls;
through your words
which are "the words of everlasting life";
through your Eucharist
which is "the living Bread that has come down from
    heaven";
through your Heart
which is the fountain of life
for individual souls and for society.

I cling to your Word
with all my heart.
I hunger for the living Bread
of your Eucharist.
I open my heart eagerly to the life-giving streams
from your Sacred Heart.
I unite myself inwardly to all its intentions.
May this divine Heart reign universally
over the children of the Church
and over all humanity.

828 Prayer without Words

HERE I am, Lord, in front of you
    without words.

No words: this is not
because I am overcome
at this moment
by your ineffable
mystery:
nor is it because I am distracted
by my lively imagination,
and the million fancies

of my mind
and heart.

I am without words
as a naked reality,
because I don't know what to tell you.
It is of no value
the little theology I know
and all the things of faith
I have heard
and accepted with enthusiasm.

I feel like running, but will stay,
without words, without a thought.
Formulated prayers
run
through my mind.
Incoherence,
extreme poverty,
God only knows.

Anna Teresa Cicollini

829 Prayer of Adoration and Petition

I ADORE you,
  O Jesus,
true God and true Man,
here present in the Holy Eucharist,
as I humbly kneel before you
and unite myself in spirit
with all the faithful on earth
and all the Saints in heaven.
In heartfelt gratitude for so great a blessing,
I love you,
my Jesus,
with my whole soul,
for you are infinitely perfect

and all worthy of my love.
Give me the grace
nevermore in any way to offend you.
Grant that I may be renewed
by your Eucharistic presence here on earth
and be found worthy to arrive with Mary
at the enjoyment
of your eternal and blessed presence in heaven.

830   Prayer of Reparation

WITH that deep and humble feeling
which the Faith inspires in me,
O my God and Savior, Jesus Christ,
true God and true Man,
I love you with all my heart,
and I adore you who are hidden here.

I do so in reparation
for all the irreverences, profanations, and sacrileges
which you receive
in the most august Sacrament of the altar.

I adore you,
O my God,
not so much as you are worthy to be adored,
nor so much as I am bound to do,
but at least as much as I am able.
Would that I could adore you
with that perfect worship
which the angels in heaven are able to offer you.

O Jesus,
may you be known, adored, loved, and thanked
by all people at every moment
in this most holy and divine Sacrament.

831 **Prayer of Thanksgiving and Petition**

WE GIVE you thanks,
O Christ, our God;
in your goodness
you have given us your Body in this Sacrament
to enable us to live holy lives.
Through your grace
keep us pure and without stain.
Remain in us to protect us.
Direct our steps in the way
of your holy and benevolent will.

Strengthen our souls
against the seductions of the devil
so that we may heed only your voice
and follow you alone,
O omnipotent and truthful Shepherd,
and attain the place prepared for us
in the kingdom of heaven:
O our God and Lord,
Redeemer Jesus Christ,
who are blessed
with the Father and the Spirit
now and forever.

832 **Prayer for Today's Needs**

LORD, for tomorrow and its needs I do not pray;
keep me, my God, from stain of sin, just for today.
Let me both diligently work and duly pray;
let me be kind in word and deed, just for today.

Let me be slow to do my will, prompt to obey;
help me to mortify my flesh, just for today.
Let me no wrong or idle word unthinking say;
set a seal upon my lips, just for today.

Let me in season, Lord, be grave, in season gay;
let me be faithful to your grace, just for today.
And if today my tide of life should ebb away,
give me your Sacraments divine, sweet Lord, today.
So for tomorrow and its needs, I do not pray;
but keep me, guide me, love me, Lord, just for today.

Sister M. Xavier, S.N.D.

833 Prayer to Bring Christ into Our Day

L ORD Jesus,
    present before me in the Blessed Sacrament
of the altar,
help me to cast out from my mind
all thoughts of which you do not approve
and from my heart
all emotions which you do not encourage.

Enable me to spend my entire day
as a co-worker with you,
carrying out the tasks that you have entrusted to me.
Be with me at every moment of this day:
during the long hours of work,
that I may never tire or slacken from your service;
during my conversations,
that they may not become for me
occasions for meanness toward others;
during the moments of worry and stress,
that I may remain patient and spiritually calm;
during periods of fatigue and illness,
that I may disregard self and think of others;
during times of temptation,
that I may take refuge in your grace.

Help me to remain generous and loyal to you this day
and so be able to offer it all up to you
with its successes which I have achieved by your help

and its failures which have occurred
through my own fault.
Let me come to the wonderful realization
that life is most real
when it is lived with you as the Guest
of my soul.

834 Litany of the Blessed Sacrament

(For Private Devotion)

LORD, have mercy.
Christ, have mercy.
Lord, have mercy.
Christ, hear us.
Christ, graciously hear us.
God the Father of heaven,
have mercy on us.*
God the Son, Redeemer of the world,
God the Holy Spirit,
Holy Trinity, one God,
Living Bread, that came down from heaven,
Hidden God and Savior,
Corn of the elect,
Wine whose fruit are virgins,
Bread of fatness, and royal Dainties,
Perpetual Sacrifice,
Clean Oblation,
Lamb without spot,
Most pure Feast,
Food of Angels,
Hidden Manna,
Memorial of the wonders of God,
Super-substantial Bread,

Word made flesh, dwelling in us,
Sacred Host,
Chalice of benediction,
Mystery of faith,
Most high and adorable Sacrament,
Most holy of all sacrifices,
True Propitiation for the living and the dead,
Heavenly Antidote against the poison of sin,
Most wonderful of all miracles,
Most holy Commemoration of the Passion of Christ,
Gift transcending all fullness,
Special Memorial of divine love,
Affluence of divine bounty,
Most august and holy Mystery,
Medicine of immortality,
Tremendous and life-giving Sacrament,
Bread made flesh by the omnipotence of the Word,

* Have mercy on us *is repeated after each invocation.*

Unbloody Sacrifice,
Our Feast at once and our Fellow-guest,
Sweetest Banquet, at which Angels minister,
Sacrament of piety,
Bond of charity,
Priest and Victim,
Spiritual Sweetness tasted in its proper source,
Refreshment of holy souls,

Viaticum of such as die in the Lord,
Pledge of future glory,
Be merciful,
spare us, O Lord.
Be merciful,
graciously hear us, O Lord.
From an unworthy reception of your Body and Blood,
O Lord, deliver us. **
From the lust of the flesh,
From the lust of the eyes,
From the pride of life,
From every occasion of sin,
Through the desire, by which you desired to eat this Passover with your disciples,
Through that profound humility, by which you washed their feet,
Through that ardent charity, by which you instituted this divine Sacrament,
Through your precious Blood, which you have left us on our altars,

Through the Five Wounds of this your most holy Body, which you received for us,
We sinners,
we beseech you, hear us. ***
That you would preserve and increase our faith, reverence, and devotion toward this admirable Sacrament,
That you would conduct us, through a true confession of our sins, to a frequent reception of the holy Eucharist,
That you would deliver us from all heresy, perfidy, and blindness of heart,
That you would impart to us the precious and heavenly fruits of this most holy Sacrament,
That at the hour of death you would strengthen and defend us by this heavenly Viaticum,
Son of God,
Lamb of God you take away the sins of the world;
spare us, O Lord.
Lamb of God, you take away the sins of the world;
graciously hear us, O Lord,
Lamb of God, you take away the sins of the world;
have mercy on us.
Christ, hear us.
Christ, graciously hear us.

** O Lord, deliver us *is repeated after each invocation.*
*** We beseech you, hear us *is repeated after each invocation.*

℣. You gave them Bread from heaven,
℟. *Containing in itself all sweetness.*

834a

L ET us pray.
O God,
in this wonderful Sacrament
you left us a memorial of your Passion.
Grant us so to venerate the sacred mysteries
of your Body and Blood
that we may ever continue to feel within us
the blessed fruit of your redemption.
You live and reign for ever and ever.

835 Invocations to Jesus in the Blessed Sacrament

L ORD Jesus,
through your infant cries
when you were born for me in the manger;
through your tears
when you died for me on the Cross;
through your love
as you live for me in the tabernacle,
have mercy on me and save me.

836

W E adore you,
most holy Lord Jesus Christ,
here and in all your churches in the world,
and we praise you,
because by your holy Cross
you have redeemed the world.

837

JESUS in the Blessed Sacrament,
have mercy on us.

838

PRAISE and adoration ever more be given
to the most Holy Sacrament.

839

O SACRAMENT most holy,
O Sacrament divine!
All praise and all thanksgiving
be every moment thine!

840

I ADORE you every moment,
O living Bread from heaven,
great Sacrament.

PRAYERS TO JESUS CRUCIFIED

841 Prayer for the Grace of the Passion

O LORD,
   for the redemption of the world,
you willed to be born among human beings,
subjected to the rite of circumcision,
rejected by the people,
betrayed by Judas with a kiss,
bound with cords,
led like an innocent lamb to slaughter,
shamelessly exposed to the gaze of Annas
as well as Caiaphas, Pilate, and Herod,
accused by false witnesses,
tormented by scourges and insults,
spat upon and crowned with thorns,
struck with blows of hand and reed,
blindfolded and stripped of your garments,
affixed to the wood and lifted high on the Cross,
numbered among thieves,
given gall and vinegar to drink,
and pierced by a lance.

Lord,
by these most holy sufferings
which we, your unworthy servants,
devoutly call to mind,
and by your holy Cross and death
deliver us from the pains of hell,
and be pleased to take us
where you took the penitent thief
who was crucified with you.
You live and reign
with the Father and the Holy Spirit,
one God, forever.

842 **Prayer of Acclaim to the Suffering Christ**

O LORD,
you received affronts without number
from your blasphemers,
yet each day you free captive souls
from the grip of the ancient enemy.

You did not avert your face
from the spittle of perfidy,
yet you wash souls in saving waters.

You accepted your scourging without murmur,
yet through your mediation
you deliver us from endless chastisements.

You endured ill-treatment of all kinds,
yet you want to give us a share
in the choirs of angels in glory everlasting.

You did not refuse to be crowned with thorns,
yet you save us from the wounds of sin.

In your thirst you accepted the bitterness of gall,
yet you prepare yourself
to fill us with eternal delights.

You kept silence under the derisive homage
rendered you by your executioners,
yet you petition the Father for us
although you are his equal in divinity.

You came to taste death,
yet you were the Life
and had come to bring it to the dead.

St. Gregory the Great (adapted)

843   **Prayer to Jesus on the Cross**

O JESUS,
   for how many ages have you been on the Cross
and yet people pass by in utter disregard of you
except to pierce once again your Sacred Heart.
How often have I myself passed you by,
heedless of your overwhelming sorrow,
your countless wounds,
and your infinite love!
How often have I myself stood before you,
not to comfort and console you,
but to offend you by my conduct
or neglect you,
and to scorn your love!

You have stretched out your hands to comfort me,
and I have seized those hands—
that might have consigned me to hell—
and have bent them back upon the Cross,
nailing them rigid and helpless to it.
Yet I have only succeeded in imprinting my name
on your palms forever.
You have loved me with an infinite love
and I have taken advantage of that love
to sin all the more against you.

Yet my ingratitude has only succeeded
in piercing your Sacred Heart
and causing your Precious Blood to flow forth upon me.

O Jesus,
let your Blood be upon me
not for a curse
but for a blessing.
Lamb of God,
you take away the sins of the world;
have mercy on me.

844   **Prayer of Sorrow for Sin**

LORD Jesus hanging on the Cross,
I raise sorrowful and shameful eyes
to you.
You have granted me untold blessings
and I have repaid you
by contributing to your Passion and death.
My hands took part in your scourging,
my voice was among those who denied you
and called for your death,
my thoughts brought about
your crowning with thorns,
my sins drove the nails into your hands and feet,
and the lance into your side.

Dear Lord,
forgive me for all these sins.
You are great, glorious, and infinitely good;
I am insignificant, selfish, and hopelessly sinful.
But I am sorry for all my sins,
and by the Blood shed in your Passion
I beg for forgiveness
and for a share in your love and grace.

845 **Prayer of the Seven Last Words**

O DIVINE Jesus,
   incarnate Son of God,
for our salvation you consented
to be born in a stable,
to spend your whole life
amid poverty, trials, and misery,
and to die surrounded by sufferings on the Cross.
At the hour of my death,
please say to your Father:
Father, forgive him/her.
Say to your beloved Mother:
Behold your son/daughter.
Say to my soul:
This day you shall be with me in paradise.

My God, my God,
do not forsake me in that hour.
I thirst,
yes, my soul thirsts for you
who are the fountain of living waters.
My life passes away like a shadow;
in a short while
everything will be accomplished.
Therefore, my adorable Savior,
from this moment and for all eternity
into your hands I commend my spirit.
Lord Jesus,
receive my soul.

846 **Prayer for Pardon to Jesus Crucified**

O MY crucified Lord Jesus,
   I kneel at your feet.
Do not cast me out,
although I come to you as a sinner.

I have offended you much in the past
but I resolve no longer to do so in the future.

O my God,
I place all my sins before you;
I have considered them and concluded
that they do not deserve pardon.
But I beg you to be mindful of your sufferings
which show the value of the Precious Blood
that flows from your veins.

Close your eyes to my lack of merit
and open them to the abundance of your infinite merit.
Since you deigned to die for my sins,
graciously grant me forgiveness of all of them,
so that I may no longer feel their burden
which oppresses me beyond measure.

Help me, dear Lord,
for I desire to become good at any cost.
Uproot, take away, and destroy in me
everything that is contrary to your will.
Enlighten me that I may be enabled
to walk in your holy light all the days of my life.

847 Prayer in the Steps of the Passion

MOST dear Jesus,
filled with sorrow during the agony in the garden,
covered with a sweat of blood while praying:
have mercy on us, O Lord (repeated after every asterisk).

Most dear Jesus,
delivered into the hands of the wicked by a kiss,
bound like a robber, and abandoned by your disciples:*

Most dear Jesus,
condemned to death by an unjust Council,
taken as an evildoer before Pilate,
and ridiculed by the wicked Herod:*

Most dear Jesus,
publicly shorn of your garments
and most cruelly scourged at the pillar: *

Most dear Jesus,
crowned with thorns, beaten and blindfolded,
clothed in rich purple and mocked: *

Most dear Jesus,
likened to the infamous Barabbas,
rejected by your people,
and unjustly sentenced to death: *

Most dear Jesus,
burdened with the weight of the Cross
and led to the place of execution
like a lamb to the slaughter: *

Most dear Jesus,
reckoned with the wicked, blasphemed, and derided,
and given gall to drink to mitigate your pain: *

Most dear Jesus,
dying on the Cross in the presence of Mary,
pierced with a lance
that drew blood and water from your side: *

Most dear Jesus,
taken down and placed in the arms of your Sorrowful
 Mother: *

Most dear Jesus,
horribly bruised and marked with five wounds,
anointed for burial and placed in a tomb: *
(Here no. 841, p. 681, is said.)

My Jesus,
I thank you for dying on the Cross for my sins.
Have mercy on us, O Lord.

848

Litany of the Passion

(For Private Devotion)

LORD, have mercy.
Christ, have mercy.
Lord, have mercy.
Christ, hear us.
Christ, graciously hear us.
God the Father of heaven,
have mercy on us.
God the Son, Redeemer of
the world,*
God the Holy Spirit,
Holy Trinity, one God,
Jesus, the eternal Wisdom,
Jesus, conversing with men,
Jesus, hated by the world,
Jesus, sold for thirty pieces of
silver,
Jesus, prostrate in prayer,
Jesus, strengthened by an
angel,
Jesus, agonizing in a bloody
sweat,
Jesus, betrayed by Judas with
a kiss,
Jesus, bound by the soldiers,
Jesus, forsaken by your disci-
ples,
Jesus, before Annas and
Caiaphas.
Jesus, struck by a servant on
the face,
Jesus, accused by false wit-
nesses,
Jesus, declared worthy of
death,

Jesus, spit upon in the face,
Jesus, blindfolded,
Jesus, smitten on the cheek,
Jesus, thrice denied by Peter,
Jesus, delivered up to Pilate,
Jesus, despised and mocked
by Herod,
Jesus, clothed in a white gar-
ment,
Jesus, rejected for Barabbas,
Jesus, torn with scourges,
Jesus, bruised for our sins,
Jesus, regarded as a leper,
Jesus, covered with a purple
robe,
Jesus, crowned with thorns,
Jesus, struck with a reed,
Jesus, demanded for cruci-
fixion,
Jesus, condemned to death,
Jesus, given up to your ene-
mies,
Jesus, laden with the Cross,
Jesus, led as a lamb to the
slaughter,
Jesus, stripped of your gar-
ments,
Jesus, fastened with nails to
the Cross,
Jesus, wounded for our ini-
quities,
Jesus, praying for your mur-
derers,
Jesus, reputed with the wick-
ed.

* *Have mercy on us* is repeated after each invocation.

Jesus, blasphemed on the Cross,

Jesus, reviled by the malefactor,

Jesus, giving Paradise to the thief,

Jesus, commending St. John to your Mother as her son,

Jesus, forsaken by your Father,

Jesus, given gall and vinegar to drink,

Jesus, testifying that all things written concerning you were accomplished,

Jesus, commending your spirit into the hands of your Father,

Jesus, obedient even unto death,

Jesus, pierced with a lance,

Jesus, made a propiation for us,

Jesus, taken down from the Cross,

Jesus, laid in the sepulcher,

Jesus, rising gloriously from the dead,

Jesus, ascending into heaven,

Jesus, our Advocate with the Father,

Jesus, sending down the Holy Spirit,

Jesus, exalting your Mother,

Jesus, who shall come to judge the living and the dead,

Be merciful, *spare us, O Lord.*

Be merciful, *graciously hear us, O Lord.*

From all evil, *deliver us, O Jesus.*

From all sin, **

From anger, hatred, and every evil will,

From war, famine, and pestilence,

From all dangers of mind and body,

From everlasting death,

Through your most pure conception,

Through your miraculous nativity,

Through your humble circumcision,

Through your baptism and fasting,

Through your labors and watchings,

Through your cruel scourging and crowning,

Through your thirst, and tears, and nakedness,

Through your precious death and Cross,

Through your glorious resurrection and ascension,

Through your sending forth the Holy Spirit, the Paraclete,

On the day of judgment,

we sinners, *we beseech you, hear us.*

** *Deliver us, O Jesus* is repeated after each invocation.

That you would spare us, ***
That you would pardon us,
That you would bring us to true penance,
That you would pour into our hearts the grace of the Holy Spirit,
That you would defend and propagate your Church.
That you would preserve and increase all societies assembled in your holy Name,
That you would bestow upon us true peace, humility, and charity,
That you would give us perseverance in grace and in your holy service,
That you would deliver us from unclean thoughts, the temptations of the devil, and everlasting damnation,
That you would unite us to the company of your Saints,
That you would graciously hear us,

Lamb of God, you take away the sins of the world; *spare us, O Lord.*

Lamb of God, you take away the sins of the world; *graciously hear us, O Lord!*

Lamb of God, you take away the sins of the world; *have mercy on us.*

Christ, hear us.
Christ, graciously hear us.
Lord, have mercy.
Christ, have mercy.
Lord, have mercy.

℣. We adore you, O Christ, and we bless you.
℟. Because by your holy Cross you have redeemed the world.

*** *We beseech you, hear us* is repeated after each invocation.

Prayer no. 841, p. 681.

849 Prayer to Imitate the Suffering Christ

O JESUS,
    you have called me to suffer
because you on your part suffered for me,
leaving me an example that I might follow.
When you were insulted,
you did not return the insult.
When you were mistreated,
you did not counter with threats

but entrusted yourself to the One who judges justly.
By your wounds we are healed.

Help me to imitate you in suffering.
Let me break with sin
by means of my sufferings,
so that I may no longer live
according to the lusts of sinners
but according to the will of the Father.

Since you yourself have suffered and been tempted,
I know that you are able to bring aid
to all who suffer and are tempted.
I entrust myself to you
and to the Father, my Creator,
knowing that you will never fail me.

850 Invocations to Jesus Crucified

THE Cross is my sure salvation.
The Cross it is that I always worship.
The Cross of our Lord is with me.
The Cross is my refuge.

851

BY THE sign of the Cross,
deliver us from our enemies,
O our God.

852

HAIL, O Cross,
our only hope.

853

ASSIST us, O Lord our God,
and defend us always
by the power of your holy Cross,
in whose honor you make us rejoice.

PRAYERS IN HONOR
OF THE PRECIOUS BLOOD OF JESUS

[388]   **Litany of the Precious Blood**

See p. 317.

854   **Prayer of Offering of the Precious Blood**

ETERNAL Father,
    you have given your only Son
to be the Redeemer of the world
and willed that he should shed—
even to the last drop—
his Precious Blood for love of all persons.

I offer you
the effusion of the Precious Blood
which flowed beneath the knife of the circumcision,
which watered the Garden of Olives,
which flooded the pretorium and streets of Jerusalem,
which was shed in torrents at the Crucifixion,
and whose last drops reddened the steel
of the lance.

692

In the name of this adorable Blood,
grant to sinners the grace of salvation,
to the just an increase of love,
and to all human beings a large share
in the merits which it has assured us.
Pardon us in the name of this divine Blood.
Heed its pleading voice.
Remember that it is the Blood of your Son
in whose Name you have promised to hear
our every prayer.

855 Petitions in Honor of the Precious Blood

PRECIOUS Blood of Jesus,
    shed in the circumcision,
make me pure of mind, heart, and body.

Precious Blood, oozing from every pore of Jesus
in the Agony,
enable me to love God's holy will above all.

Precious Blood,
flowing abundantly in the scourging at the pillar,
inspire me with a keen sorrow for my sins,
and a high-level tolerance of suffering.

Precious Blood,
falling in profusion from the crown of thorns,
grant me a ready acceptance of humiliations.

Precious Blood,
shed so profusely in the crucifixion of our Lord,
make me die entirely to self-love.

Precious Blood,
shed to the very last drop
by the opening of Christ's Sacred Heart,
give me that generous love
which sacrifices all for God.

Precious Blood,
sacred price of my redemption,
apply to me your infinite merits.

Precious Blood of Jesus,
I adore you from the depths of my heart;
I invoke you ardently
for you are my salvation,
and by you I hope to obtain the joys of heaven.

856   **Prayer of Intercession**

ETERNAL Father,
I offer you the merits of the Precious Blood
of your beloved Son Jesus,
my Savior and my God,
for the spread and exaltation of the Church,
the welfare of her visible Head, the Pope,
the Bishops and pastors of souls,
and all the ministers of the sanctuary.

Blessed and praised for evermore be Jesus,
who saved us with his Blood.

Eternal Father,
I offer you the merits of the Precious Blood
of your beloved Son Jesus,
my Savior and my God,
for peace and concord among nations,
the humbling of the enemies of the Faith,
and the welfare of all Christian people.

Blessed and praised for evermore be Jesus,
who saved us with his Blood.

Eternal Father,
I offer you the merits of the Precious Blood
of your beloved Son Jesus,

my Savior and my God,
for the conversion of unbelievers,
the elimination of all heresies,
and the return of sinners.

Blessed and praised for evermore be Jesus,
who saved us with his Blood.

Eternal Father,
I offer you the merits of the Precious Blood
of your beloved Son Jesus,
my Savior and my God,
for all my relatives, friends, and enemies,
for all in need, sickness, or tribulation,
for all those for whom you know I am bound to pray,
for all those for whom you know and desire
that I should pray.

Blessed and praised for evermore be Jesus,
who saved us with his Blood.

Eternal Father,
I offer you the merits of the Precious Blood
of your beloved Son Jesus,
my Savior and my God,
for all who are to depart from life this day,
that you would deliver them from the pains of hell,
and admit them speedily to the possession
of your glory.

Blessed and praised for evermore be Jesus,
who saved us with his Blood.

Eternal Father,
I offer you the merits of the Precious Blood
of your beloved Son Jesus,
my Savior and my God,
for all who love this great treasure
and who join me in adoring and glorifying it
and who labor to spread this devotion.

Blessed and praised for evermore be Jesus,
who saved us with his Blood.

Eternal Father,
I offer you the merits of the Precious Blood
of your beloved Son Jesus,
my Savior and my God,
for all my needs both temporal and spiritual,
as an intercession for the faithful departed,
and in an especial manner for those
who were most devoted to this price of our redemption,
and to the sorrows and sufferings of our Mother,
Mary most holy.

Blessed and praised for evermore be Jesus,
who saved us with his Blood.

Glory to the Blood of Jesus
both now and forevermore
and through the everlasting ages.

857   Invocations in Honor of the Precious Blood

ETERNAL Father,
I offer you the most Precious Blood of Jesus
in atonement for my sins,
in supplication for the faithful departed,
and for the needs of holy Church.

858

BE MINDFUL, O Lord, of your creature,
whom you have redeemed by your Precious Blood.

859

HAIL, Precious Blood,
    flowing from the wounds
of our crucified Lord Jesus Christ
and washing away the sins of the whole world!

860

PRECIOUS Blood of Jesus,
    cleanse and purify all sinners.

861

PRECIOUS Blood of Jesus,
    may your powerful voice drive far from us
all the scourges that threaten us.

862

PRECIOUS Blood of Jesus,
    by you may reparation be offered
to the outraged glory of God.

863

BLESSED be the Precious Blood of Jesus,
    which renders bearable the thorns of earth,
redeems our souls,
purifies them from their inequities,
and prepares them for an eternal crown.

THE MOST SACRED HEART OF JESUS

[387] **Litany of the Sacred Heart**

See p. 316.

See also no. 383, p. 283, and no. 734, p. 588.

864 **Prayer of Union with the Sacred Heart**

HAIL, Sacred Heart of Jesus,
living and strengthening source of eternal life,
infinite treasury of the Divinity,
and burning furnace of divine love!
You are my refuge and sanctuary.

My loving Savior,
consume my heart in that burning love
with which your own Heart is inflamed.
Pour out upon me those graces
which flow from your love.
Let my heart be so united with yours
that our wills may be one,
and my will may in all things be conformed
with your Will.
May your Will be the guide and rule
of my desires and of my actions.

St. Gertrude

865 **Prayer of Self-Offering
to the Sacred Heart**

O JESUS,
    reveal your Sacred Heart to me
and show me its attractions.
Unite me to it forever.
Grant that all my desires and every beat of my heart,
which does not cease even while I sleep,
may be a witness to you of my love
and may say to you:
Yes, Lord, I am yours!
The pledge of my loyalty to you
rests ever in my heart
and shall never cease to be there.

Accept the little good that I do
and be pleased to make up for all my wrongdoing,
so that I may be able to praise you in time
as well as in eternity.

866 **Prayer for Peace of Heart**

O MOST sacred, most loving Heart of Jesus,
    you are concealed in the Holy Eucharist,
and you beat for us still.
Now, as then, you say:
"With desire I have desired."
I worship you, then,
with all my best love and awe,
with fervent affection,
with my most subdued, most resolved will.
You for a while take up your abode within me.
O make my heart beat with your Heart!

Purify it of all that is earthly,
all that is proud and sensual,

all that is hard and cruel,
of all perversity,
of all disorder,
of all deadness.
So fill it with you,
that neither the events of the day,
nor the circumstances of the time,
may have the power to ruffle it;
but that in your power and your fear,
it may have peace.

Cardinal Newman

867 Prayer of Thanksgiving to the Father for Giving Us the Heart and Mind of Jesus

O MY God,
    how great is your love for us!
You are infinitely worthy
of being loved, praised, and glorified!
We have neither heart nor spirit worthy of doing so.
But your Wisdom and Goodness
have given us a way of carrying it out.
You have given us the Spirit and Heart of your Son,
to be our own heart and spirit,
in accord with the promise you made through your
    Prophet:
"I will give them a new heart,
I will put a new spirit in your midst" (Ezekiel 36:26).
In order that we may know
what this new heart and new spirit might be
you added:
"I will place my Spirit, which is my Heart,
in your midst."
Only the Spirit and Heart of a God
are worthy of loving and praising a God,

of blessing and loving him as much as he deserves.
Thus you have given us your Heart,
the Heart of your Son Jesus,
as well as the heart of his holy Mother
and the heart of the Saints,
and angels who together are only one heart,
as the Head and members form one single Body.

St. John Eudes

868 Prayer of Trust in the Sacred Heart

IN ALL my temptations, I place my trust in you,
    O Sacred Heart of Jesus.
In all my weaknesses, I place my trust in you,
O Sacred Heart of Jesus.
In all my difficulties, I place my trust in you,
O Sacred Heart of Jesus.
In all my trials, I place my trust in you,
O Sacred Heart of Jesus.
In all my sorrows, I place my trust in you,
O Sacred Heart of Jesus.

In all my work, I place my trust in you,
O Sacred Heart of Jesus.
In every failure, I place my trust in you,
O Sacred Heart of Jesus.
In every discouragement, I place my trust in you,
O Sacred Heart of Jesus.
In life and in death, I place my trust in you,
O Sacred Heart of Jesus.
In time and in eternity, I place my trust in you,
O Sacred Heart of Jesus.

869 Petitions to the Sacred Heart of Jesus

LOVE of the Sacred Heart of Jesus,
    embrace my heart.

Fire of the Heart of Jesus,
inflame my heart.
Charity of the Heart of Jesus,
fill my heart.
Strength of the Heart of Jesus,
sustain my heart.
Mercy of the Heart of Jesus,
pardon my heart.
Patience of the Heart of Jesus,
do not forsake my heart.
Reign of the Heart of Jesus,
establish yourself in my heart.
Wisdom of the Heart of Jesus,
teach my heart.
Will of the Heart of Jesus,
guide my heart.
Zeal of the Heart of Jesus,
consume my heart.

870 Prayer of Adoration and Petition

MOST holy Heart of Jesus,
fountain of every blessing,
I love you.
With a lively sorrow for my sins
I offer you this poor heart of mine.
Make me humble, patient, and pure,
and perfectly obedient to your Will.

Good Jesus,
grant that I may live in you
and for you.
Protect me in the midst of danger
and comfort me in my afflictions.
Bestow on me
health of body,

assistance in temporal needs,
your blessing on all that I do,
and the grace of a holy death.

871 **Prayer for Response to Christ's Love**

HEAVENLY Father,
we find joy in the gifts of love
that have come to us
from the Heart of Jesus, your Son.
Open our hearts to share his life
and continue to bless us
with his love.

Heavenly Father,
we honor the Heart of your Son
wounded by the cruelty of human beings.
That Heart is the symbol of love's triumph
and the pledge of all that human beings
are called to be.
Help us to see Christ in all whom we encounter,
and to offer him living worship
by rendering loving service to others.

872 **Prayer for Perseverance**

O SACRED Heart of Jesus,
living and life-giving fountain of eternal life,
infinite treasure of the Divinity,
and glowing furnace of love,
you are my refuge and my sanctuary.
O adorable and glorious Savior,
consume my heart with that burning fire
that ever inflames your Heart.
Pour down on my soul those graces
which flow from your love.
Let my heart be so united with yours

that our wills may be one,
and mine may in all things be conformed to yours.
May your Will be the rule
both of my desires and my actions.

St. Alphonsus Liguori

873 Contemporary Prayer of Reparation

LORD Jesus Christ,
   we look at the Cross,
and we—your pilgrim Church—can see
what sin has done to the Son of Mary,
to the Son of God.

But now you are risen and glorified.
You suffer no more in the flesh.
Sin can no longer expose you
to the agony of the garden,
to the scourging,
to death on a Cross.

But it can reach you through your Mystical Body.
This part of you, your Church on earth,
still feels the strength of sin.
For this we make our act of reparation.

We who have sinned in the past
now consecrate ourselves
to the healing of your Mystical Body,
to our part in the mystery
of its well-being and its growth.
Sanctify us for this task.

May your Sacred Heart be the symbol,
not of one love but two—
your love for us and ours for you.
Accept our love,
and help us make it real

by serving you in our brothers and sisters,
so that love and concern may lead all people
"to know the one true God
and Jesus Christ whom he has sent."

Apostleship of Prayer

874   **Prayer of Consecration**

I, N..., give myself
    to the Sacred Heart of our Lord Jesus Christ,
and I consecrate to him
my person and my life,
my actions, pains, and sufferings,
so that henceforth I shall be unwilling
to make use of any part of my being
except for the honor, love, and glory
of the Sacred Heart.

My unchanging purpose is to be all his
and to do all things for the love of him
while renouncing with all my heart
whatever is displeasing to him.

I take you,
O Sacred Heart,
as the only object of my love,
the guardian of my life,
the assurance of my salvation,
the remedy of my weakness and inconstancy,
the atonement for all my faults,
and the sure refuge at my death.

O Heart of goodness,
be my justification before God the Father,
and turn away from me
the strokes of his righteous anger.

O Heart of love,
I place all my trust in you,
for I fear everything
from my own wickedness and frailty,
but I hope for all things
from your goodness and bounty.

Consume in me all that can displease you
or resist your holy Will.
Let your pure love imprint you
so deeply upon my heart
that I shall nevermore be able to forget you
or be separated from you.
May I obtain from all your loving kindness
the grace of having my name written in you,
for I desire to place in you
all my happiness and all my glory,
living and dying in virtual bondage to you.

St. Margaret Mary Alacoque

875   Charismatic Prayer of Consecration

LOVING Father in heaven,
    we come to give ourselves to you in love.
We ask you to fulfill your promise
to give each of us a new heart.
We ask you to create in your people
this new heart.
We praise you, Father,
for having already fulfilled this promise
in Jesus Christ, your Son.
He is the new Heart for each of us
and for your Church.
He is the new Heart for all people.

We ask you, Father,
to fashion our hearts after his Heart.

Give to your Church his Heart as her new heart:
a heart alive and nourished by your Spirit.
May this new heart throb with new life
throughout the Church,
as if in a new Pentecost.

May this heart beat with compassion and love
for your poor,
for your alienated,
for the stranger,
for the little ones.

May this heart beat with outrage for sin
and with love for the sinner.
May this heart reach out to fashion you a people,
born of the spirit:
a people who will not shirk from the cross,
even laying down their lives,
from sacrificing themselves.

Let your people believe enough in love,
to pour themselves out for the brotherhood,
so that your love may indeed become visible
for all to see.
May every beat of this heart
bring forth your kingdom.
We ask this of you,
through Christ our Lord.

Rev. J. Faber MacDonald, Pastor of St. Pius X,
Charlottetown, P.E.I.

876   Prayer of Family Consecration

SACRED Heart of Jesus,
you revealed to St. Margaret Mary
your desire to reign over Christian families.
To fulfill this desire we today proclaim

your complete dominion over our family.
From now on we wish to live your life,
to cultivate in our home
those virtues which bring them your peace,
and avoid that worldliness which you have condemned.
You will rule over our minds by simple faith
and over our hearts by a love
kept aflame by frequent Holy Communion.

Divine Heart of Jesus,
be pleased to preside over our family,
to bless all we do,
to dispel our troubles,
sanctify our joys,
lighten our sufferings.
If one of us should ever offend you by sin,
remind him/her,
merciful Jesus,
of your goodness and mercy to the penitent sinner.
And when the hour of separation strikes,
when death brings its griefs into our midst,
those of us who go and those who must stay
will be submissive to what you have decreed.

Then it will be our consolation to remember
that the day will come when our entire family,
reunited in heaven,
will be able to sing forever
of your glory and your mercy.

May the Immaculate Heart of Mary
and the glorious patriarch St. Joseph
present to you this Consecration of ours
and keep us ever mindful of it
all the days of our life.
All glory to the Sacred Heart of Jesus,
our King and our Father!

American Apostleship of Prayer

877   **Traditional Morning Offering**

O JESUS,
    through the Immaculate Heart of Mary,
I offer you my prayers, works, joys, and sufferings
of this day
in union with the Holy Sacrifice of the Mass
throughout the world.
I offer them
for all the intentions of your Sacred Heart:
the salvation of souls,
reparation for sins,
the reunion of all Christians.

I offer them for the intentions of our Bishops
and of all the Apostles of Prayer,
and in particular for those
recommended by our Holy Father for this month.

Apostleship of Prayer

878   **Contemporary Morning Offering**

E TERNAL Father,
    I offer you everything I do this day:
my work, my prayers, my apostolic efforts;
my time with family and friends;
my hours of relaxation;
my difficulties, problems, distress
which I shall try to bear with patience.

Join these my gifts to the unique offering
which Jesus Christ, your Son, renews today
in the Eucharist.

Grant, I pray, that,
vivified by the Holy Spirit
and united to the Sacred Heart of Jesus,

my life this day may be of service
to you and to your children
and help consecrate the world to you.

Apostleship of Prayer

879   Invocations in Honor of the Sacred Heart

MAY the Sacred Heart of Jesus
be loved everywhere.

880

SWEET Heart of my Jesus,
grant that I may ever love you more.

881

SACRED Heart of Jesus,
your kingdom come!

882

DIVINE Heart of Jesus,
convert sinners,
save the dying,
and deliver the holy souls in purgatory.

883

SACRED Heart of Jesus,
I believe in your love for me.

884

GLORY, love and thanksgiving
be to the Sacred Heart of Jesus!

885

O HEART of love,
   I put all my trust in you;
for I fear all things from my weakness,
but I hope for all things from your goodness.

886

SACRED Heart of Jesus,
   have mercy on us
and on our erring brothers and sisters.

887

SACRED Heart of Jesus,
   may you be known, loved, and imitated!

888

SACRED Heart of Jesus,
   protect our families.

889

SACRED Heart of Jesus,
   strengthened in your agony by an angel,
strengthen us in our agony.

890

SACRED Heart of Jesus,
   let me love you and make you loved.

891

SACRED Heart of Jesus,
   grant that peace,
the fruit of justice and charity,
may reign throughout the world.

**GOD THE HOLY SPIRIT — OUR SANCTIFIER
AND GUIDE**

The Holy Spirit guides us in the way of sanctification and salvation. As he descended on Jesus at his baptism by John, so he descends on us at baptism and inspires us to a loving union with God through actions and prayer.

712

D) GOD THE HOLY SPIRIT

THE Holy Spirit is the Third Person of the Blessed Trinity, really God just as the Father and the Son are really God. He is the Love of the Father and the Son. As Jesus is the center of the history of salvation so the mystery of God is the center from which this history takes its origin and to which it is ordered as to its last end. The risen Jesus leads human beings to the Father by sending the Holy Spirit upon the People of God.

By his new and deeper coming into the world at Pentecost, the Spirit was to accomplish the salvation of humanity. He came to sanctify the Church forever, giving life to all people because he is the Spirit of life. He is the very soul of the Church.

The Spirit prays and bears witness in the faithful that they are adopted children of God. He guides the Church into the fullness of truth and gives her a unity of fellowship and service, furnishes and directs her with various gifts, and adorns her with the fruits of his grace. By the power of the Gospel he makes the Church grow, renews her constantly, and leads her to perfect unity with her Spouse, Jesus Christ.

Every Christian receives the Holy Spirit in Baptism and Confirmation. Through him we share in the life of grace, God's life in our souls. By his presence we are continually moved to have communion with God and our fellow human beings and to fulfill our duties.

The Spirit has always been something of a "forgotten" Person. The prayers found in this section are intended to enable all Catholics to love and adore this wondrous Spirit who dwells within us constantly.

892 **Prayer to Receive the Holy Spirit**

O KING of glory,
   send us the Promised of the Father,
the Spirit of Truth.
May the Counsellor who proceeds from you
enlighten us
and infuse all truth in us,
as you have promised.

893 **Prayer for the Seven Gifts of the Spirit**

O LORD Jesus,
   through you I humbly beg the merciful Father
to send the Holy Spirit of grace,
that he may bestow upon us his sevenfold gifts.

May he send us the gift of *wisdom*
which will make us relish the Tree of Life
that is none other than yourself;
the gift of *understanding*
which will enlighten us;
the gift of *counsel*
which will guide us in the way of righteousness;
and the gift of *fortitude*
which will give us the strength to vanquish
the enemies of our sanctification and salvation.

May he impart to us the gift of *knowledge*
which will enable us to discern your teaching
and distinguish good from evil;
the gift of *piety*
which will make us enjoy true peace;
and the gift of *fear*
which will make us shun all iniquity
and avoid all danger of offending your Majesty.

To the Father
and to the Son
and to the Holy Spirit
be given all glory and thanksgiving forever.

St. Bonaventure

894 **Prayer for the Twelve Fruits of the Spirit**

HOLY Spirit,
eternal Love of the Father and the Son,
kindly bestow on us
the fruit of *charity*,
that we may be united to you by divine love;
the fruit of *joy*,
that we may be filled with holy consolation;
the fruit of *peace*,
that we may enjoy tranquility of soul;
and the fruit of *patience*,
that we may endure humbly
everything that may be opposed to our own desires.

Divine Spirit,
be pleased to infuse in us
the fruit of *benignity*,
that we may willingly relieve our neighbor's necessities;
the fruit of *goodness*,
that we may be benevolent toward all;
the fruit of longanimity,
that we may not be discouraged by delay
but may persevere in prayer;
and the fruit of *mildness*,
that we may subdue every rising of ill temper,
stifle every murmur,
and repress the susceptibilities of our nature
in all our dealings with our neighbor.

Creator Spirit,
graciously impart to us
the fruit of *fidelity*,
that we may rely with assured confidence
on the word of God;
the fruit of *modesty*,
that we may order our exterior regularly;
and the fruits of *continence* and *chastity*,
that we may keep our bodies in such holiness
as befits your temple,
so that having by your assistance
preserved our hearts pure on earth,
we may merit in Jesus Christ,
according to the words of the Gospel,
to see God eternally
in the glory of his kingdom.

895   **Prayer for Union with the Holy Spirit**

O HOLY Spirit of Light and Love,
   to you I consecrate my heart, mind, and will
for time and eternity.
May I be ever docile to your divine inspirations
and to the teachings of the holy Catholic Church
whose infallible guide you are.

May my heart be ever inflamed
with the love of God and love of neighbor.
May my will be ever in harmony with your divine Will.
May my life faithfully imitate the life and virtues
of our Lord and Savior Jesus Christ.
To him,
with the Father,
and you, divine Spirit,
be honor and glory forever.

St. Pius X

896 Prayer for the Indwelling of the Spirit

HOLY Spirit,
powerful Consoler,
sacred Bond of the Father and the Son,
Hope of the afflicted,
descend into my heart
and establish in it your loving dominion.
Enkindle in my tepid soul
the fire of your Love
so that I may be wholly subject to you.

We believe that when you dwell in us,
you also prepare a dwelling
for the Father and the Son.
Deign, therefore, to come to me,
Consoler of abandoned souls,
and Protector of the needy.
Help the afflicted,
strengthen the weak,
and support the wavering.

Come and purify me.
Let no evil desire take possession of me.
You love the humble and resist the proud.
Come to me,
glory of the living,
and hope of the dying.
Lead me by your grace
that I may always be pleasing to you.

St. Augustine of Hippo

897 Prayer to the Holy Spirit for Unbelievers

HOLY Spirit,
on the first Pentecost,

through your inspiration many were transformed,
becoming adopted children of God
and faithful disciples of Jesus Christ.
They were animated by the love of God
that is poured into us
by you, Holy Spirit,
who are given to us.

Enlighten the minds of unbelievers,
incline their wills to accept the Good News,
and prompt them to be obedient
to the Teachers of the Church
about whom Christ said:
"He who hears you, hears me;
he who rejects you, rejects me" (Luke 10:16).
Teach them how to pray
and prepare their minds and hearts
for your coming into their souls.

898 Prayer for the Propagation of the Faith

O HOLY Spirit,
you desire the salvation of all human beings
and for that purpose you want all of them
to acquire the knowledge of your Truth.
Grant to all of them
your powerful Light and your Love of Goodwill
that they may give glory to God
in unity of faith, hope, and love.

Send laborers into the harvest
who are truly animated by you
who are the Soul of the missionary Church.

899 **Prayer of Spouses to the Spirit**

O HOLY Spirit,
    Spirit of *unity*,
Love and Goodwill of Father and Son,
you have made us one in the sacred union of marriage.
Grant that—like the first Christians—
we may be one heart and one mind.

Make us respect one another,
help one another in our striving for holiness,
and support one another.
Be our Guide,
our Counsellor,
and our Consoler.
Make us bear one another's burdens
during our journey to heaven
where we hope to live forever
as adopted children of the Triune God.

900 **Litany of the Holy Spirit**
(For Private Devotion)

L ORD, have mercy.
    Christ, have mercy.
Lord, have mercy.
Holy Spirit, hear us.
Holy Spirit, graciously hear us.
God, the Father of heaven, *have mercy on us.*
God, the Son, Redeemer of the world, *

God, the Holy Spirit,
Holy Trinity, one God,

Holy Spirit, who proceed from the Father,
Holy Spirit, co-equal with the Father and the Son,
Promise of the Father, most bounteous,
Gift of God most high,
Ray of heavenly Light,
Author of all good,
Source of living Water,
Consuming Fire,
Burning Love,

* *Have mercy on us* is repeated after each invocation.

Spiritual Unction,

Spirit of truth and power,

Spirit of wisdom and understanding,

Spirit of counsel and fortitude,

Spirit of knowledge and piety,

Spirit of fear of the Lord,

Spirit of compunction,

Spirit of grace and prayer,

Spirit of charity, peace, and joy,

Spirit of patience,

Spirit of longanimity and goodness,

Spirit of benignity and mildness,

Spirit of fidelity,

Spirit of modesty and continence,

Spirit of chastity,

Spirit of adoption of sons of God,

Holy Spirit, comforter,

Holy Spirit, sanctifier,

You through whom spoke holy men of God,

You who overshadowed Mary,

You by whom Mary conceived Christ,

You who descend upon men at Baptism,

You who, on the Day of Pentecost, appeared through fiery tongues,

You by whom we are reborn,

You who dwell in us as in a temple,

You who govern and animate the Church,

You who fill the whole world,

That you may renew the face of the earth, *we beseech you, hear us.*

That you may shed your Light upon us,**

That you may pour your Love into our hearts,

That you may inspire us to love our neighbor,

That you may teach us to ask for the graces we need,

That you may enlighten us with your heavenly inspirations,

That you may guide us in the way of holiness,

That you may make us obedient to your commandments,

That you may teach us how to pray,

That you may always pray with us,

That you may inspire us with horror for sin,

That you may direct us in the practice of virtue,

That you may make us persevere in a holy life,

That you may make us faithful to our vocation,

That you may grant us good priests and Bishops,

That you may give us good Christian families,

** *We beseech you, hear us* is repeated after each invocation.

That you may grant us a spiritual renewal of the Church,

That you may guide and console the Holy Father,

Lamb of God, you take away the sins of the world; *spare us, O Lord.*

Lamb of God, you take away the sins of the world, *graciously hear us, O Lord.*

Lamb of God, you take away the sins of the world; *have mercy on us.*

Holy Spirit, hear us.

Holy Spirit, graciously hear us.

Lord, have mercy.

Christ, have mercy.

Lord, have mercy.

℣. Create a clean heart in us.

℟. Renew a right spirit in us.

900a

LET us pray.
O merciful Father,
grant that your divine Spirit
may cleanse, inflame, and enlighten our minds and hearts.
Enable us to be fruitful in good works
for the glory of your Majesty
and the spiritual and material well-being of all people.
We ask this through Jesus Christ your Son
and the Holy Spirit.

901 Archconfraternity Prayer to the Holy Spirit

HOLY Spirit, Lord of Light,
from your clear celestial height,
your pure beaming radiance give.

Come, O Father of the Poor,
come with treasures which endure,
come, O Light of all that live.

You of all Consolers best,
and the soul's delightsome Guest,
do refreshing Peace bestow.

You in toil are Comfort sweet,
pleasant Coolness in the heat,
solace in the midst of woe.

Light immortal, Light Divine,
visit now this heart of mine,
and my inmost being fill.

If you take your grace away,
nothing pure in men will stay,
all their good is turned to ill.

Heal our wounds, our strength renew,
on our dryness pour your Dew,
wash the stains of guilt away.

Bend the stubborn heart and will,
melt the frozen, warm the chill,
guide the steps that go astray.

On all those who evermore
you confess and you adore,
in your *Sevenfold Gifts* descend.

Give them *Comfort* when they die.
Give them Life with you on high,
give them Joys which never end.

902   Prayer of Consecration to the Holy Spirit

BEFORE the multitude of heavenly witnesses,
I offer myself, soul and body,
to you, eternal Spirit of God.
I adore the brightness of your purity,
the unerring keenness of your justice,
and the power of your love.

You are the strength and light of my soul.
In you I live and move and have my being.

I desire never to grieve you by infidelity to your grace,
and I pray wholeheartedly to be preserved
from the slightest sin against you.
Make me faithful in my every thought,
and grant that I may always listen to your voice,
watch for your light,
and follow your gracious inspirations.
I cling to you,
and beg you, in your compassion,
to watch over me in my weakness.

Holding the pierced feet of Jesus,
gazing at his five wounds,
trusting to his Precious Blood,
and adoring his open side and stricken Heart,
I implore you, adorable Spirit,
so to keep me in your grace
that I may never sin against you.
Grant me the grace,
O Holy Spirit of the Father and the Son,
to say to you always and everywhere:
"Speak, Lord, for your servant is listening."

903   Prayer to the Spirit
for Universal Renewal

HOLY Spirit,
fulfill in us the work begun by Jesus.
Let our prayer on behalf of the whole world
be fruitful and unwavering.
Hasten the time when each of us
will attain a genuine spiritual life.

Enliven our work
that it may reach all human beings,
all who have been redeemed by the blood of Christ
and all his inheritance.

Take away our natural presumption
and uplift us with a holy humility,
with reverence for God
and selfless courage.

Let no vain attachment
impede the work of our state in life,
nor personal interest
divert us from the demands of justice.

May no scheming on our part
reduce love to our own petty dimensions.
May all be noble in us:
the quest and the respect for truth,
and the willingness to sacrifice
even to the cross and death.

And may all be accomplished
in accord with the final prayer
of the Son
to his heavenly Father
and in accord with the grace
which Father and Son give
through you, the Spirit of love,
to the Church and to its institutions,
to every soul and to all peoples.
Amen, amen. Alleluia, alleluia.

Pope John XXIII

904 ## Prayer to Be Sensitive
to the Spirit's Promptings

O Holy Spirit,
   you sanctify the people of God
through ministry and the Sacraments.
For the exercise of the Christian apostolate,
you give the faithful special gifts also,
allotting them to everyone according as you will
in order that individuals,
administering grace to others just as they have received it,
may also be good stewards of the manifold grace of God,
to build up the whole body in charity.

From the acceptance of these charisms,
including those which are more elementary,
there arise for each believer the right and duty
to use them in the Church and in the world
for the good of human beings
and the building up of the Church
in the freedom given by you
who breathe where you will.

Help us to learn especially how to perform
the mission of Christ and the Church
by basing our lives on belief
in the divine mystery of Creation and Redemption
and by being sensitive to your movement,
O Divine Spirit,
who give life to the People of God
and who urge all to love the Father
as well as the world and human beings in him.

Based on Vatican II

905   Prayer for the Freedom of the Spirit

DIVINE Spirit,
   your gifts are diverse.
You call some to give clear witness
to the desire for a heavenly home
and to keep that desire green among the human family.
You summon others to dedicate themselves
to the earthly service of human beings
and to make ready the material of the celestial realm
by this ministry of theirs.

Grant all of us your freedom
so that by putting aside love of self
and bringing all earthly resources
into the service of human life,
we can devote ourselves to that future
when humanity itself will become an offering
accepted by God.

                              Based on Vatican II

906   Invocations to the Holy Spirit

HOLY Spirit, Spirit of truth,
   come into our hearts;
shed the brightness of your light upon the nations,
so that they may please you in unity of faith.

907

HOLY Spirit,
   divine Guest of my soul,
abide in me
and grant that I may ever abide in you.

908

G OD the Holy Spirit,
have mercy on us.

909

H OLY Spirit,
Lord and source of life,
dispenser of the seven gifts,
sanctify us.

910

H OLY Spirit,
Divine Comforter,
comfort me in all my sorrows.

911

H OLY Spirit,
Giver of all good gifts,
grant me your seven gifts
and let your twelve fruits ripen in me.

912

H OLY Spirit,
substantial Goodwill of Father and Son,
teach me goodwill.

913

H OLY Spirit,
Instructor of the faithful,
help me to understand Christ's words.

914

HOLY Spirit,
   Sanctifier blest,
guide me on the way to holiness.

915

HOLY Spirit,
   Guest of my soul,
help me to pray well.

8

PRAYERS
TO
FAVORITE SAINTS

8

MARY — MOTHER, QUEEN, AND MEDIATRIX

Of all the Saints, Mary the Mother of Our Lord is by far the favorite of all Christians. She has been invoked throughout the centuries by all classes of Christians for all types of requests, and her clients have invariably been heard. Her intercession with her Son began at the Marriage Feast of Cana and continues to this day from her heavenly seat.

A) THE BLESSED VIRGIN MARY

I N A *magnificent Apostolic Exhortation of February 2, 1974, Pope Paul VI set down the basis for prayer to Mary:*

"*The Church's norm of faith requires that her norm of prayer should everywhere blossom forth with regard to the Mother of Christ. Such devotion to the Blessed Virgin is firmly rooted in the revealed Word and has solid dogmatic foundations. It is based on the singular dignity of Mary, Mother of the Son of God, and therefore beloved daughter of the Father and Temple of the Holy Spirit—Mary who, because of this extraordinary grace, is far greater than any other creature on earth or in heaven.*" (Devotion to the Blessed Virgin Mary, no. 56).

The Bishops of the United States gave further details in a splendid Pastoral Letter of November 21, 1973:

"*When Mary is honored, her Son is duly acknowledged, loved and glorified, and His commandments are observed. To venerate Mary correctly means to acknowledge her Son, for she is the Mother of God. To love her means to love Jesus, for she is always the Mother of Jesus.*

"*To pray to our Lady means not to substitute her for Christ, but to glorify her Son who desires us to have loving confidence in his Saints, especially in his Mother. To imitate the 'faithful Virgin' means to keep her Son's commandments*" (Behold Your Mother, no. 82).

The prayers in this section are intended to help us pray to Mary in the way the Church wants: in line with the Bible, in harmony with the Liturgy, in an ecumenical spirit, and in accord with the latest anthropological studies. (See Paul VI, Devotion . . . , nos. 29-39).

TRADITIONAL PRAYERS

[389]   **Litany of the Blessed Virgin Mary**

See p. 319.
Hail Mary, see no 77a, p. 84.

916   **Prayer of Veneration**

HOLIEST Virgin,
with all my heart I venerate you
above all the angels and Saints in Paradise
as the Daughter of the Eternal Father,
and I consecrate to you
my soul with all its powers.
Hail Mary . . . .

Holiest Virgin,
with all my heart I venerate you
above all the angels and Saints in Paradise
as the Mother of the only-begotten Son,
and I consecrate to you
my body with all its senses.
Hail Mary . . . .

Holiest Virgin,
with all my heart I venerate you
above all the angels and Saints in Paradise
as the beloved Spouse of the Holy Spirit,
and I consecrate to you
my heart and all its affections,
praying you to obtain for me from the Most Holy Trinity
all the graces I need for my salvation.
Hail Mary . . . .

917   **Prayer of Consecration to Mary**

O MY Queen and Mother,
I give myself entirely to you.

To show my devotion to you
I consecrate to you this day
my eyes, ears, mouth, heart,
and whole being without reserve.

Therefore, good Mother,
since I am your own,
keep me and guard me
as your property and possession.

918 Prayer of Self-Commendation to Mary

O HOLY Mary,
my Lady,
into your blessed trust and safe keeping
and into the depths of your mercy
I commend my soul and body
this day,
every day of my life,
and at the hour of my death.

To you I entrust
all my hopes and consolations,
all my trials and miseries,
my life and the end of my life.
By your most holy intercession
and by your merits,
may all my actions be directed and disposed
according to your will
and the Will of your divine Son.

St. Aloysius Gonzaga

919 Prayer in Praise of the Mother of God

M ARY, our Mother,
the whole world reveres you
as the holiest shrine of the living God,

for in you the salvation of the world dawned.
The Son of God was pleased
to take human form from you.
You have broken down the wall of hatred,
the barrier between heaven and earth
which was set up by man's first disobedience.
In you heaven met earth
when divinity and humanity were joined in one person,
the God-Man.

Mother of God, we sing your praises,
but we must praise you even more.
Our speech is too feeble to honor you
as we ought,
for no tongue is eloquent enough
to express your excellence.
Mary, most powerful, most holy,
and worthy of all love!
Your name brings new life,
and the thought of you inspires love
in the hearts of those devoted to you. St. Bernard

920 **Prayer of Dedication to Mary**

VIRGIN full of goodness,
    Mother of mercy,
I entrust to you my body and my soul,
my thoughts and my actions,
my life and my death.
O my Queen,
come to my aid
and deliver me from the snares of the devil.
Obtain for me the grace of loving
my Lord Jesus Christ, your Son,
with a true and perfect love,
and after him,

O Mary,
of loving you with all my heart
and above all things.

St. Thomas Aquinas

921   **Prayer of Offering to Mary**

MOST Holy Mary
Virgin Mother of God,
I am unworthy to be your servant.
Yet moved by your motherly care for me
and longing to serve you,
I choose you this day
to be my Queen, my Advocate, and my Mother.
I firmly resolve ever to be devoted to you
and to do what I can
to encourage others to be devoted to you.

My loving Mother,
through the Precious Blood of your Son shed for me,
I beg you to receive me as your servant forever.
Aid me in my actions
and beg for me the grace
never by thought, word, or deed,
to be displeasing in your sight
and that of your most holy Son.
Remember me, dearest Mother,
and do not abandon me at the hour of death.

St. Francis de Sales

922   **Prayer for the Spirit of Mary**

MY POWERFUL Queen,
you are all mine through your mercy,
and I am all yours.
Take away from me all that may displease God
and cultivate in me all that is pleasing to him.

May the light of your faith
dispel the darkness of my mind,
your deep humility
take the place of my pride,
your continual sight of God
fill my memory with his presence;
may the fire of the charity of your heart
inflame the lukewarmness of my own heart;
may your virtues take the place of my sins;
may your merits be my enrichment
and make up for all
that is wanting in me before God.

My beloved Mother,
grant that I may have no other spirit but your spirit,
to know Jesus Christ and his divine Will
and to praise and glorify the Lord,
that I may love God with burning love like yours.

St. Louis de Montfort

923   Prayer for the Grace to Love Jesus

MARY, my dear Mother,
how much I love you—
and yet in reality how little!
You teach me what I should know,
for you instruct me in
what Jesus is for me
and what I should be for him.

O my beloved Mother,
how close to God you are,
and how completely filled with him!
To the extent that we know God,
we are reminded of you.
Mother of God,

obtain for me the grace of loving my Jesus
and the grace of loving you.

924 Prayer to See Jesus through Mary

MOST holy and Immaculate Virgin,
my Mother!
You are the Mother of my Lord,
the Queen of the universe,
the advocate, hope, and refuge of sinners.
I, the most miserable of sinners,
have recourse to you today.
I venerate you, great Queen,
and I thank you for the many graces
you have bestowed on me until now.
I thank you especially for having saved me from hell
which I have so often deserved by my many sins.

Most lovable Lady,
I love you,
and by the love I have for you
I promise to serve you always
and to do all I can to make you loved by others.
I place in you all my hope of salvation.
Mother of mercy,
receive me as your servant
and cover me with the mantle of your protection.
Since you are so powerful with God,
deliver me from all temptations
or rather obtain for me the grace
to overcome them until death.

I ask of you a true love for Jesus Christ.
Through you I hope to die a good death.
My dear Mother,
by the love you have for almighty God

738   PRAYERS TO FAVORITE SAINTS

I beg you to help me always
and especially at the last moment of my life.
Do not leave me until you see me safe in heaven,
where I hope to thank and praise you forever.

CONTEMPORARY PRAYERS

925   **Biblical Litany of Our Lady**

*It is possible to compose a long list of praises of the Virgin
Mary by using God's own Word. They are concrete titles, attributed to her and emphasizing the Most Blessed Virgin's
"function" in the mystery of the Word made flesh and the
Mystical Body. When we call upon Mary by these titles we are
praying with the Word of God which has been from time to
time interpreted by the Church's tradition in a clearly Marian
sense. The litany which follows here was composed by A. M.
Roguet, and was published by La Vie Spirituelle, n. 553, pp. 213-
217.*

G REETED by the angel Gabriel: Lk 1:28.
    Full of Grace: *ibid.*
Mother of Jesus: Lk 1:31.
Mother of the Son of the Most High: Lk 1:32.
Mother of the son of David: *ibid.*
Mother of the King of Israel: Lk 1:33.
Mother by act of the Holy Spirit: Lk 1:35; Mt 1:20.
Handmaid of the Lord: Lk 1:38.
Virgin, Mother of Emmanuel: Mt 1:23, citing Is 7:14;
    cf Mt 5:2.
You in whom the Word became flesh: Jn 1:14.
You in whom the Word dwelt amongst us: *ibid.*
Blessed amongst all women: Lk 1:41; cf Jdt 13:18.
Mother of the Lord: Lk 1:43.
Happy are you who have believed in the words uttered
    by the Lord: Lk 1:43.
Lowly handmaid of the Lord: Lk 1:48.

Called blessed by all generations: *ibid.*

You in whom the Almighty worked wonders: *ibid.*

Heiress of the promises made to Abraham: Lk 1:55.

Mother of the new Isaac: Lk 1:37 (Gn 18:14).

You who gave birth to your firstborn at Bethlehem: Lk 2:7.

You who wrapped your child in swaddling clothes and laid him in a manger: *ibid.*

Woman from whom Jesus was born: Gal 4:4; Mt 1:16, 21.

Mother of the Savior: Lk 2:11; Mt 1:21.

Mother of the Messiah: Lk 2:11; Mt 1:16.

You who were found by the shepherds with Joseph and the newborn child: Lk 2:16.

You who kept and meditated all things in your heart: Lk 2:19.

You who offered Jesus in the Temple: Lk 2:22.

You who put Jesus into the arms of Simeon: Lk 2:28.

You who marvelled at what was said of Jesus: Lk 2:33.

You whose soul a sword should pierce: Lk 2:35.

Mother who were found together with the child by the Wise Men: Mt 2:11.

Mother whom Joseph took into refuge in Egypt: Mt 2:14.

You who took the child Jesus to Jerusalem for the Passover: Lk 2:42.

You who searched for Jesus for three days: Lk 2:46.

You who found Jesus again in his Father's house: Lk 2:46-49.

Mother whom Jesus obeyed at Nazareth: Lk 2:51.

Model of widows: cf Mk 6:3.

Jesus' companion at the marriage feast at Cana: Jn 2:1-2.

You who told the servants, "Do as he shall tell you": Jn 2:5.

You who gave rise to Jesus' first miracle: Jn 2:11.

Mother of Jesus for having done the will of the Father in heaven: Mt 12:50.

Mary who chose the better part: Lk 10:42.

Blessed for having heard the word of God and kept it: Lk 11:28.

Mother standing at the foot of the cross: Jn 19:25.

Mother of the disciple whom Jesus loved: Jn 19:26-27.

Queen of the Apostles, persevering in prayer with them: Acts 1:14.

Woman clothed with the sun: Rv 12:1.

Woman crowned with twelve stars: *ibid.*

Sorrowful Mother of the Church: Rv 12:2.

Glorious Mother of the Messiah: Rv 12:5.

Image of the new Jerusalem: Rv 21:2.

River of living water, flowing from the throne of God and the Lamb: Rv 22:1. Cf Ps 45:5.

926   **Prayer to Mary, Mother of the Church**

O BLESSED Virgin Mary,
the basic reason why you are Mother of the Church
is that you are the Mother of God
and the associate of Christ in his saving work.
Another reason is that you shine as the model of virtues
for the whole community of the elect.
You exemplified in your own life
the beatitudes preached by your divine Son.
Hence, you are the perfect model
for the imitation of Christ
on the part of all human beings.

Obtain for us the graces we need
to follow your example.
Teach us to practice the beatitudes proper to our state
and to rejoice in being known as your children
who are members of the Church of God.

Let us work for the unity of the Church
which your Son desired on earth
and which you now pray for in heaven.
Lead the whole human race
to acknowledge Christ Jesus, the one true Savior.
Drive from it all the calamities provoked by sin,
and bring it peace which consists
in truth, justice, liberty, and love.

927 **Prayer to Emulate Mary's Faith**

MARY our Mother,
   you consented in faith
to become the Mother of Jesus.
At the angel's announcement
you received the Word of God in your heart
as well as in your body,
and you brought Life to the world.
You conceived in your heart, with your whole being,
before you conceived in your womb.

Obtain for us
a faith similar to your own
which will enable us to hear the Word of God
and carry it out.
Let us imitate your motherhood by our faith,
bringing Christ to birth in others
who have desperate need of him.

928 **Prayer to Mary Assumed into Heaven**

O BLESSED Virgin Mary,
   united to the victorious Christ in heaven,
you are the image and first-flowering of the Church
as she is to be perfected in the world to come.
You shine forth as a sign of sure hope and solace

for the pilgrim People of God.
In your assumption,
you manifest the fullness of redemption
and appear as the spotless image of the Church
responding in joy to the invitation of the Bridegroom,
your Son
who is the first fruits of those who have fallen asleep.

Grant that we may follow your example on earth
thereby imitating your Son as well
and being enabled to share your glory
with him for all eternity.

929   Prayer to Mary, Queen of the Home

O BLESSED Virgin Mary,
       you are the Mother and Queen of every Christian
   family.
When you conceived and gave birth to Jesus,
human motherhood reached its greatest achievement.
From the time of the Annunciation
you were the living chalice
of the Son of God made Man.
You are the Queen of the home.
As a woman of faith,
you inspire all mothers to transmit faith
to their children.

Watch over our families.
Let the children learn free and loving obedience
inspired by your obedience to God.
Let parents learn dedication and selflessness
based on your unselfish attitude.
Let all families honor you
and remain devoted to you

so that they may be held together
by your example and your intercession.

930 Prayer to Mary the Christ-Bearer

O MARY,
you are a mystery
of faithfulness,
of light,
of perfection.
I love to think of you
as bearer of Christ
for all others.
Every child is for God
and for others.

I feel compelled
as I carry Christ
to others
to remain in the background like you
so that only he may be seen.
I am not running away,
or being detached,
but I am lending him
my voice,
my face,
my living,
my environment
so that he
may speak
and save
and love
all people of today.

Anna Teresa Ciccolini

Hail, Mary, full of grace

THE IMMACULATE CONCEPTION

931   Prayer for a Holy Life

VIRGIN Immaculate,
   Mother of God and my Mother,
from your throne in heaven
turn your merciful eyes upon me.
With full confidence in your goodness and power,
I beg you to help me in this journey of life,
which is strewn with dangers for my soul.

I entrust myself completely to you,
that I may never be the devil's slave through sin,
but may always live a humble and pure life.
I consecrate my heart to you forever,
since my sole desire is to love your divine Son Jesus.
O Mary,
since none of your devoted servants has ever perished,
let me too attain salvation.

932   In Praise of Mary Immaculate

YOU are all fair, O Mary;
   the original stain is not in you.
You are the glory of Jerusalem,
the joy of Israel,

the great honor of our people,
and the great advocate of sinners.
O Mary, Virgin most prudent,
Mother most merciful,
pray for us;
intercede for us with our Lord Jesus Christ.

933 Invocations in Honor of Mary Immaculate

MARY, conceived without sin,
pray for us who have recourse to you.

934

O MARY,
who entered the world without stain of sin,
obtain for me from God
that I may leave it without sin.

935

BLESSED be the holy and Immaculate Conception
of the Blessed Virgin Mary,
Mother of God.

936

BY YOUR Immaculate Conception,
O Mary,
make my body pure and my soul holy.

937

VIRGIN Mother,
you were never touched by any spot
of original or actual sin.

THE SORROWFUL MOTHER

938 Prayer to Grow in Grace through Sorrows

MOST holy Virgin and Mother,
your soul was pierced by a sword of sorrow
in the Passion of your divine Son,
and in his glorious Resurrection
you are filled with never-ending joy at his triumph.
Obtain for us who call upon you
the grace to partake in the trials of the Church
and the sorrows of the Pope
so that we may be found worthy to grow in grace
and rejoice with them in the consolations
for which we pray,
in the love and peace of the same Christ our Lord.

939 At the Cross Her Station Keeping

AT THE Cross her station keeping,
Stood the mournful Mother weeping,
Close to Jesus to the last.
    ough her heart, his sorrow sharing,
All his bitter anguish bearing,
Lo, the piercing sword has passed!

O, how sad and sore distressed,
Was that Mother highly blessed
Of the sole-begotten One.

Christ above in torment hangs,
She beneath beholds the pangs
Of her dying glorious Son.

Is there one who would not weep
'Whelmed in miseries so deep
Christ's dear Mother to behold?
Can the human heart refrain
From partaking in the pain
In that Mother's pain untold?

Bruised, derided, cursed, defiled,
She beheld her tender Child,
All with bloody scourges rent.
For the sins of his own nation
Saw him hang in desolation
Till his Spirit forth he sent.

O sweet Mother! fount of love,
Touch my spirit from above,
Make my heart with yours accord.
Make me feel as you have felt.
Make my soul to glow and melt
With the love of Christ, my Lord.

Holy Mother, pierce me through.
In my heart each wound renew
Of my Savior crucified.
Let me share with you his pain,
Who for all our sins was slain,
Who for me in torments died.

Let me mingle tears with you
Mourning him who mourned for me,
All the days that I may live.
By the Cross with you to stay,
There with you to weep and pray,
Is all I ask of you to give.

Virgin of all virgins blest!
Listen to my fond request:
Let me share your grief divine.
Let me, to my latest breath,
In my body bear the death
Of your dying Son divine.

Wounded with his every wound,
Steep my soul till it has swooned
In his very Blood away.
Be to me, O Virgin, nigh,
Lest in flames I burn and die,
In his awe-full judgment day.

Christ, when you shall call me hence,
Be your Mother my defense,
Be your Cross my victory.
While my body here decays,
May my soul your goodness praise,
Safe in heaven eternally.
Amen. Alleluia.

940   Invocations to the Sorrowful Mother

MARY most sorrowful,
Mother of Christians,
pray for us.

941

VIRGIN most sorrowful,
pray for us.

942

MOTHER of love, of sorrow, and of mercy,
pray for us.

THE IMMACULATE HEART OF MARY

943   **Prayer of Confidence
in the Immaculate Heart**

MARY Immaculate,
our Mother and Consolation,
with confidence I take refuge in your most loving heart.
You shall be the dearest object
of my love and veneration.
I shall always have recourse to you
who are the dispenser of the treasures of heaven,
that I may have peace in my sorrows,
light in my doubts,
protection in dangers,
and help in all my needs.

Be therefore my refuge, strength, and consolation,
O Mary the Consoler.
At the hour of my death,
graciously receive the last sighs of my heart
and obtain for me a place in your heavenly home,
where all hearts will praise with one accord
the adorable Heart of Jesus
as well as your most lovable heart forever.
Our tender Mother,
Comforter of the afflicted,
pray for us who have recourse to you.

749

944   Prayer of Consecration

O MARY,
Virgin most powerful and Mother of mercy,
Queen of heaven and Refuge of sinners,
we consecrate ourselves to your immaculate heart.

We consecrate to you our very being and our whole life:
all that we have,
all that we love,
all that we are.
We give you our bodies, hearts, and souls,
our homes, families, and countries.
We desire that everything in and around us
may belong to you
and share in the benefits of your motherly blessing.

In order that this act of consecration
may be truly efficacious and lasting,
we today renew at your feet
the promises made at Baptism and First Communion.
We pledge that we will courageously and unceasingly
    profess
the truths of our holy Faith,
and live as befits Catholics who are duly submissive
to the direction of the Pope
and the Bishops who are in communion with him.

We pledge ourselves to keep
the commandments of God and the Church,
in particular to keep holy the Lord's day.
We also pledge ourselves
to make consoling practices of the Christian religion,
especially Holy Communion,
an integral part of our lives,
insofar as we shall be able to do so.

Finally, we promise you,
O glorious Mother of God
and loving Mother of all human beings,
to dedicate ourselves with all our hearts
to the service of devotion to you.
Through the sovereignty of your immaculate heart,
may we thus hasten and assure the coming
of the kingdom of the Sacred Heart
of your adorable Son
in our own hearts as well as those of all people,
in our own country as well as in the whole world,
on earth as in heaven.

Invocations in Honor of the Immaculate Heart

945

SWEET heart of Mary,
be my salvation.

946

MOST pure heart of the Blessed Virgin Mary,
obtain for me from Jesus
a pure and humble heart.

947

HOLY Mary,
make my heart and my body pure.

THE BLESSED VIRGIN
UNDER VARIOUS TITLES

948 Our Lady of the Blessed Sacrament

O VIRGIN Mary,
  our Lady of the Blessed Sacrament,
you are the glory of the Christian people,
the joy of the universal Church,
and the salvation of the whole world.
Pray for us,
and awaken in all believers a vibrant devotion
for the most Holy Eucharist,
so that they may be worthy to partake daily
of this holy Sacrament of the Altar.

949 Our Lady of the Cenacle

M OST holy Virgin of the Cenacle,
  obtain for us the gifts of the Holy Spirit.
May we live in love and perseverance
united in prayer under your guidance and teaching
for the greater glory of God.
May we labor both by word and by work
for the salvation of souls
and so deserve to enter everlasting life.

Graciously be near us,
in our present needs,
and comfort us by your power.
By your intercession
may almighty God be pleased to grant us
the favor for which we earnestly pray.

950 Our Lady of Fatima

O MOST holy Virgin Mary,
Queen of the most holy Rosary,
you were pleased to appear to the children of Fatima
and reveal a glorious message.
We implore you,
inspire in our hearts a fervent love
for the recitation of the Rosary.
By meditating on the mysteries of the redemption
that are recalled therein
may we obtain the graces and virtues
that we ask,
through the merits of Jesus Christ,
our Lord and Redeemer.

951 Our Lady of Good Counsel

MOST glorious Virgin,
you were chosen by the eternal Counsel
to be the Mother of the eternal Word made flesh.
You are the treasurer of divine graces
and the advocate of sinners.
I who am your most unworthy servant
have recourse to you.
Graciously be my guide and counselor
in this valley of tears.

Obtain for me,
through the Precious Blood of your divine Son,
the forgiveness of my sins,
the salvation of my soul,
and the means necessary to obtain it.
In like manner, obtain for holy Church
victory over her enemies
and the spread of Jesus' kingdom
over the whole earth.

952   **Our Lady of Guadalupe**

OUR Lady of Guadalupe,
   mystical rose,
intercede for the Church,
protect the holy Father,
help all who invoke you in their necessities.
Since you are the ever Virgin Mary
and Mother of the true God,
obtain for us from your most holy Son
the grace of a firm faith and a sure hope
amid the bitterness of life,
as well as an ardent love
and the precious gift of final perseverance.

953   **Our Lady, Help of Christians**

MARY, powerful Virgin,
   you are the mighty and glorious protector
of the Church.
You are the marvelous help of Christians.
You are awe-inspiring as an army in battle array.
You eliminated heresy in the world.
In the midst of our anguish, struggle, and distress,
defend us from the power of the enemy,
and at the hour of our death
receive our soul in heaven.   St. John Bosco

954 **Our Lady, Hope of Christians**

HAIL Mary,
 hope of Christians,
hear the prayer of a sinner who loves you tenderly,
honors you in a special manner,
and places in you the hope of his salvation.
I owe you my life,
for you obtain for me the grace of your Son
and you are the sure pledge of my eternal happiness.

I entreat you,
deliver me from the burden of my sins,
take away the darkness of my mind,
destroy the earthly affections of my heart,
defeat the temptations of my enemies,
and rule all the actions of my life.
With you as my guide
may I arrive at the eternal happiness of heaven.

St. John Damascene

955 **Our Lady of Lourdes**

O IMMACULATE Virgin Mary,
 you are the refuge of sinners,
the health of the sick,
and the comfort of the afflicted.
By your appearances at the Grotto of Lourdes
you made it a privileged sanctuary
where your favors are given to people
streaming to it from the whole world.
Over the years countless sufferers
have obtained the cure of their infirmities—
whether of soul, mind, or body.

Therefore I come with limitless confidence
to implore your motherly intercession.

Loving Mother,
obtain the grant of my requests.
Let me strive to imitate your virtues on earth
so that I may one day share your glory in heaven.

956   **Our Lady, Mother of Mercy**

BLESSED Virgin Mary,
  who can worthily repay you with praise and thanks
for having rescued a fallen world
by your generous consent!
Receive our gratitude
and by your prayers obtain the pardon of our sins.
Take our prayers into the sanctuary of heaven
and enable them to make our peace with God.

Holy Mary,
help the miserable,
strengthen the discouraged,
comfort the sorrowful,
pray for your people,
plead for the clergy,
intercede for all women consecrated to God.
May all who venerate you
feel now your help and protection.

Be ready to help us when we pray,
and bring back to us the answers to our prayers.
Make it your continual concern
to pray for the people of God,
for you were blessed by God
and were made worthy
to bear the Redeemer of the world,
who lives and reigns forever.

St. Augustine of Hippo (adapted)

957   ## Our Lady of Perpetual Help

O MOTHER of Perpetual Help,
    grant that I may ever invoke your powerful name
which is the safeguard of the living
and the salvation of the dying.
O pure Virgin Mary,
let your name be henceforth ever on my lips.
Whenever I call on you by name,
hasten to help me.
When I speak your sacred name
or even think of you,
what consolation and confidence,
what sweetness and emotion fill my soul!

I thank God
for having given you
so sweet, powerful, and lovely a name
for my good.
Let my love for you prompt me ever to greet you
as Mother of Perpetual Help.

958   ## Our Lady, Queen of Peace

M OST holy Virgin,
    by your divine maternity you merited
to share in your divine Son's prerogative of universal
    Kingship,
and to be called Queen of Peace.
May your powerful intercession guard your people
from all hatred and discord among themselves
and direct their hearts in the way of peace.
Your Son came to teach us this way
for the good and well-being of all
and your Church continues to guide our steps
along that same way.

Look kindly upon the efforts of Christ's Vicar
to call together and unite nations
around the only center of saving faith.
Enlighten the rulers of our country
and of all countries on earth
to follow this path to peace.
Grant that there may be peace
in our hearts,
in our families,
and in our world.

959   **Our Lady of the Trinity**

HOLY Virgin Mary,
there is none like you among women
born in the world.
Daughter and handmaid of the heavenly Father,
the almighty King,

Mother of our most high Lord Jesus Christ,
and Spouse of the Holy Spirit,
pray for us to your most holy Son,
our Lord and Master.

Hail, holy Lady,
most noble Queen,
Mother of God, and Mary ever Virgin.
You were chosen by the heavenly Father,
who has been pleased to honor you
with the presence of his most holy Son
and the Divine Paraclete.

You were blessed with the fullness
of grace and goodness.

Hail, Temple of God,
his dwelling-place, his masterpiece, his handmaid.
Hail, Mother of God.
I venerate you for the holy virtues which—
through the grace and light of the Holy Spirit—
you bring into the hearts of your clients
to change them from unfaithful Christians
to faithful children of God.

St. Francis of Assisi

ST. JOSEPH — PATRON OF THE CHURCH

During his earthly life, St. Joseph was the foster father and protector of Jesus and Mary his Mother. Accordingly, Christians have called upon his aid unceasingly, and he has been named Patron of the Church of Jesus. He is the object of a devotion in the Church which has as its motto: "Go to Joseph."

B) FREQUENTLY INVOKED SAINTS

IN ADDITION to the Blessed Virgin Mary, there are a host of other Saints that are customarily invoked by Christians in time of trial or need—or even in time of joy and plenty. This is completely in line with the words of Vatican II on the subject:

"It is not by the title of example only that we cherish the memory of those in heaven, but still more in order that the union of the whole Church may be strengthened in the Spirit by the practice of fraternal charity. For just as Christian communion among wayfarers brings us closer to Christ, so our companionship with the Saints joins us to Christ, from whom as from a Fountain and Head issues every grace and the very life of the people of God" (Constitution on the Church, no. 50).

The Council text goes on to say that it is fitting for us to invoke our brothers and sisters in heaven who are our benefactors before God. And for centuries the members of the Church have been calling upon the Saints in private as well as in public prayer.

Some Saints have even become known as patrons of special circumstances, such as St. Anthony for help in finding lost articles and St. Jude for desperate cases. Such patronage is sometimes the result of a special decision of the Church, as in the case of St. Joseph being named Patron of the Universal Church. Most of the time, however, it is the result of popular tradition. The prayers in this section are intended to show how Catholics can make use of this patronage of the Saints—both to obtain help in time of need and to get closer to God in Christ.

Prayers to St. Joseph
Patron of the Universal Church

[390]   **Litany of St. Joseph**
See no. 390, p. 322.

[369]   **"To You, O Blessed Joseph"**
See no. 369, p. 277.

960   Prayer for the Whole Church

O GLORIOUS St. Joseph,
    you were chosen by God to be
the foster father of Jesus,
the most pure spouse of Mary, ever Virgin,
and the head of the Holy Family.
You have been chosen by Christ's Vicar
as the heavenly Patron and Protector
of the Church founded by Christ.

Protect the Sovereign Pontiff
and all bishops and priests united with him.
Be the protector of all who labor for souls
amid the trials and tribulations of this life;
and grant that all peoples of the world
may be docile to the Church
without which there is no salvation.

Dear St. Joseph,
accept the offering I make to you.
Be my father, protector, and guide
in the way of salvation.
Obtain for me purity of heart
and a love for the spiritual life.
After your example.

let all my actions be directed
to the greater glory of God,
in union with the Divine Heart of Jesus,
the Immaculate Heart of Mary,
and your own paternal heart.
Finally, pray for me
that I may share in the peace and joy
of your holy death.

961   **Prayer for the Spirit of Work**

GLORIOUS St. Joseph,
model of all who pass their life in labor,
obtain for me the grace to work in a spirit of penance
to atone for my many sins;
to work conscientiously,
putting the call of duty above my own inclinations;
to work with gratitude and joy,
considering it an honor to use and develop by my labor
the gifts I have received from God;
to work with order, peace, moderation, and patience,
without ever recoiling before weariness or difficulties.

Help me to work, above all, with purity of intention
and with detachment from self,
having always before my eyes the hour of death
and the accounting which I must render
of time lost, talents wasted, good omitted,
and vain complacency in success,
which is so fatal to the work of God.
All for Jesus,
all for Mary,
all after your example,
O Patriarch Joseph!
This shall be my watchword in life and in death.

962   **Prayer to Know One's Vocation**

O GREAT St. Joseph,
    you were completely obedient
to the guidance of the Holy Spirit.
Obtain for me the grace to know the state of life
that God in his providence has chosen for me.
Since my happiness on earth,
and perhaps even my final happiness in heaven,
depends on this choice,
let me not be deceived in making it.

Obtain for me the light to know God's Will,
to carry it out faithfully,
and to choose the vocation
which will lead me to a happy eternity.

963   **Prayer for a Happy Death**

O BLESSED Joseph,
    you gave forth your last breath
in the loving embrace of Jesus and Mary.
When the seal of death shall close my life,
come with Jesus and Mary to aid me.
Obtain for me this solace for that hour—
to die with their holy arms around me.
Jesus, Mary, and Joseph,
I commend my soul, living and dying,
into your sacred arms.

964   **Invocations to St. Joseph**

S T. JOSEPH,
    help us to lead an innocent life,
and keep it ever safe under your patronage.

965

ST. JOSEPH,
   foster father of our Lord Jesus Christ,
and true spouse of the Virgin Mary,
pray for us.

966

JESUS, Mary, and Joseph,
   bless us now and in death's agony.

Prayers to the Twelve Apostles

967 **Prayer to St. Peter**

O GLORIOUS St. Peter,
   because of your vibrant and generous faith,
sincere humility and flaming love
our Lord honored you with singular privileges
and especially leadership of the whole Church.
Obtain for us the grace of a living faith,
a sincere loyalty to the Church,
acceptance of all her teachings,
and obedience to all her precepts.
Let us thus enjoy an undisturbed peace on earth
and everlasting happiness in heaven.

968 **Prayer to St. Andrew**

O GLORIOUS St. Andrew,
   you were the first to recognize and follow
the Lamb of God.
With your friend St. John
you remained with Jesus for that first day,

for your entire life,
and now throughout eternity.

As you led your brother St. Peter to Christ
and many others after him,
draw us also to him.
Teach us to lead others to Christ
solely out of love for him
and dedication in his service.
Help us to learn the lesson of the Cross
and to carry our daily crosses without complaint
so that they may carry us to Jesus.

969   Prayer to St. John the Evangelist

O GLORIOUS St. John,
you were so loved by Jesus that you merited
to rest your head upon his breast,
and to be left in his place as a son to Mary.
Obtain for us an ardent love for Jesus and Mary.
Let me be united with them now on earth
and forever after in heaven.

970   Prayer to St. James the Greater

O GLORIOUS St. James,
because of your fervor and generosity
Jesus chose you to witness
his glory on the Mount
and his agony in the Garden.
Obtain for us strength and consolation
in the unending struggles of this life.
Help us to follow Christ constantly and generously,
to be victors over all our difficulties,
and to receive the crown of glory in heaven.

971 **Prayer to St. Philip**

O GLORIOUS St. Philip,
at the Last Supper you said to Jesus:
"Lord, show us the Father
and it will be enough for us."
Help us to make this our prayer also
and to seek God in all things.
Obtain for us the grace to know the Father
and Jesus Christ whom he has sent—
for in this does eternal life consist.

972 **Prayer to St. Bartholomew**

O GLORIOUS St. Bartholomew,
Jesus called you a person without guile
and you saw in this word a sign
that he was the Son of God and King of Israel.
Obtain for us the grace to be ever guileless
and innocent as doves.
At the same time, help us to have your gift of faith
to see the Divine hand in the events of daily life.
May we discern the signs of the times
that lead to Jesus on earth
and will eventually unite us to him forever in heaven.

973 **Prayer to St. Thomas**

O GLORIOUS St. Thomas,
your grief for Jesus was such
that it would not let you believe he had risen
unless you actually saw him and touched his wounds.
But your love for Jesus was equally great
and it led you to give up your life for him.
Pray for us that we may grieve for our sins

which were the cause of Christ's sufferings.
Help us to spend ourselves in his service
and so earn the title of "blessed"
which Jesus applied to those
who would believe in him without seeing him.

974   **Prayer to St. Matthew**

O GLORIOUS St. Matthew,
    in your Gospel you portray Jesus
as the longed-for Messiah
who fulfilled the Prophets of the Old Covenant
and as the new Lawgiver
who founded a Church of the New Covenant.
Obtain for us the grace to see Jesus
living in his Church
and to follow his teachings in our lives on earth
so that we may live forever with him in heaven.

975   **Prayer to St. James the Less**

O GLORIOUS St. James,
    you were our Lord's cousin
and at the same time his friend and follower.
You wrote that every good and perfect gift
comes to us from the Father of lights,
and that faith without works is useless.
You preached the divinity of Jesus
until your death as a martyr.
Obtain for us from the Father of lights
the great gift of a living faith in Jesus' divinity
which will inspire us to unstinting labor
in the service of God and our fellow human beings
and enable us to reach our heavenly destiny.

976   **Prayer to St. Jude**

O GLORIOUS St. Jude,
     you were honored to be a cousin
as well as a follower of Jesus,
and you wrote an Epistle in which you said:
"Grow strong in your holy faith
through prayer in the Holy Spirit."
Obtain for us the grace of being people of faith
and people of prayer.
Let us be so attached to the three Divine Persons
through faith and prayer on earth
that we may be united with them
in the glory of the beatific vision in heaven.

977   **Prayer to St. Simon**

O GLORIOUS St. Simon,
     you were a cousin of Jesus
and a devoted follower as well.
You were called "the Zealot,"
indicating that you were willing
to give your life for your religion
and your freedom as a human person.
Obtain for us the grace
to be willing to give our lives for Christ
and to labor for the freedom and peace
that only God can give.
Help us to spend ourselves for God on earth
and be received by him in eternal bliss in heaven.

978   **Prayer to St. Matthias**

O GLORIOUS St. Matthias,
     in God's design it fell upon you
to take the place of the unfortunate Judas

who betrayed his Master.
You were selected by the twofold sign
of the uprightness of your life
and the call of the Holy Spirit.

Obtain for us the grace
to practice the same uprightness of life
and to be called by that same Spirit
to wholehearted service of the Church.
Then after a life of zeal and good works
let us be ushered into your company in heaven
to sing forever the praises
of Father, Son, and Holy Spirit.

979   Prayer to St. Paul

O GLORIOUS St. Paul,
    after persecuting the Church
you became by God's grace its most zealous Apostle.
To carry the knowledge of Jesus, our divine Savior,
to the uttermost parts of the earth
you joyfully endured prison,
scourgings, stonings, and shipwreck,
as well as all manner of persecutions
culminating in the shedding of the last drop
of your blood
for our Lord Jesus Christ.

Obtain for us the grace to labor strenuously
to bring the faith to others
and to accept any trials and tribulations
that may come our way.
Help us to be inspired by your Epistles
and to partake of your indomitable love for Jesus,
so that after we have finished our course
we may join you in praising him in heaven
for all eternity.

Prayers to Other Saints

980 **Prayer to One's Guardian Angel**
Daily Protector throughout Life

DEAR Angel,
in his goodness
God gave you to me
to guide, protect, and enlighten me,
and to bring me back to the right way
when I go astray.
Encourage me when I am disheartened,
and instruct me when I err in my judgment.
Help me to become more Christlike,
and so some day to be accepted
into the company of Angels and Saints in heaven.

981 **Prayer to St. Anthony of Padua**
Patron of Seekers of Lost Articles

DEAR St. Anthony,
you are the patron of the poor
and the helper of all who seek lost articles.
Help me to find the object I have lost
so that I will be able to make better use
of the time that I will gain
for God's greater honor and glory.
Grant your gracious aid to all people
who seek what they have lost—
especially those who seek to regain God's grace.

982 **Prayer to St. Benedict**
Patron against Poisoning

A DMIRABLE Saint and Doctor of Humility,
   you practiced what you taught,
assiduously praying for God's glory
and lovingly fulfilling all work
for God and the benefit of all human beings.
You know the many physical dangers
that surround us today
often caused or occasioned by human inventions.
Guard us against poisoning of the body
as well as of mind and soul,
and thus be truly a "Blessed" one for us.

983 **Prayer to St. Blase**
Patron of Healthy Throats

D EAR Bishop and lover of souls,
   you willingly bore heavy crosses
in faithful imitation of Jesus.
Similarly, with Christlike compassion
you cured many sufferers.
Then after undergoing horrible tortures
you died as a martyr for Christ.
Obtain a cure for these (. . .) ills
if this is agreeable to God.

984 **Prayer to St. Catherine of Siena**
Patroness against Miscarriages

H UMBLE Virgin and Doctor of the Church,
   in thirty-three years you achieved great perfection
and became the counselor of Popes.

You know the temptations of mothers today
as well as the dangers that await unborn infants.
Intercede for me that I may avoid miscarriage
and bring forth a healthy baby
who will become a true child of God.
Also pray for all mothers,
that they may not resort to abortion
but help bring a new life into the world.

985   Prayer to St. Dymphna
Patroness of the Mentally Ill

O VIRGIN and heroic Martyr,
    we know very little about your origin,
but many have learned to invoke you
and several have claimed to have been helped.
It is said that you remained faithful
to your Divine Bridegroom to the end,
resisting the lusts of your pagan father
and preferring a martyr's death.
Please intercede for this mental patient
that he/she may give glory to God.

986   Prayer to St. Gerard Majella
Patron of Expectant Mothers

D EAR Redemptorist Saint,
    model Priest and Religious,
compassionate toward suffering Mothers
intercede for this expectant Mother.
Let her not be selfish
like those who are willing
to put an end to the life they bear within themselves.
Instead let her remain ever conscious

that she is privileged to be the instrument
through whom God brings another life into the world.
Encourage her for the good of her child
and the glory of the Lord of life.

987   Prayer to St. John of God
Patron of Heart Patients

DEAR Convert, after a sinful life,
    through the power of God's holy Word
you learned to love your fellow human beings.
Self-sacrificing, you founded
the Society of Hospital Brothers.
No wonder the Church made you
the patron of patients and nurses.
That is why we confidently have recourse to you.
Please give assistance to N. . . .
and teach us to be kind like you.

988   Prayer to St. Jude
Patron of Desperate Cases

DEAR Apostle and Martyr for Christ,
    you left us an Epistle in the New Testament.
With good reason many invoke you
when illness is at a desperate stage.
We now recommend to your kindness
N. . . . who is in a critical condition.
May the cure of this patient increase
his/her faith and love for the Lord of Life,
for the glory of our merciful God.

989   **Prayer to St. Lucy**
                Patroness of the Blind

D EAR Sicilian Virgin and Martyr,
    whom the Church recalls in Eucharistic Prayer I,
you valiantly rejected great promises
and resisted several threats
in remaining faithful to your beloved Lord.
For centuries Christians have invoked you
particularly when suffering from eye-trouble.
So now we implore your assistance
on behalf of N. . . .
We also ask you to teach us to imitate you
and to avoid spiritual blindness of any kind.

990   **Prayer to St. Peregrine**
            Patron of Cancer Patients

D EAR Apostle of Emilia
    and member of the Order of Mary,
you spread the Good News by your word
and by your life witnessed to its truth.
In union with Jesus crucified,
you endured excruciating sufferings so patiently
as to be healed miraculously of cancer in the leg.
If it is agreeable to God,
obtain relief and cure for N. . . .
and keep us all from the dread cancer of sin.

991   **Prayer to St. Rita**
         Patroness of Impossible Cases

D EAR Rita, model Wife and Widow,
    you yourself suffered in a long illness

showing patience out of love for God.
Teach us to pray as you did.
Many invoke you for help,
full of confidence in your intercession.
Deign to come now to our aid
for the relief and cure of N. . . .
To God all things are possible;
may this healing give glory to the Lord.

992   **Prayer to St. Roch**
Patron of Invalids

DEAR mendicant Pilgrim,
   you once took care of sufferers from the plague
and were always ready to help others
by kind service and fervent prayers.
You yourself had no home
and you died in a dungeon.
No wonder countless invalids
have confidently invoked your help.
Please grant a cure to this patient
and help us all become spiritually healthy.

993   **Prayer to St. Teresa of Avila**
Patroness of Headache Sufferers

DEAR wonderful Saint,
   model of fidelity to vows,
you gladly carried a heavy cross
following in the steps of Christ
who chose to be crucified for us.
You realized that God like a merciful Father
chastises those whom he loves—
which to worldlings seems silly indeed.

Grant to N. . . . relief from great pains
if this is in line with God's plans.

994   **Prayer to St. Timothy**
Patron of Those with Stomach Disorders

D EAR Saint, well known for your gentleness,
    you were a most faithful disciple of St. Paul
and like him traveled much
to bring the Good News to all people.
The Letters Paul wrote to you reveal your zeal
and inspire us with confidence in you.
You too were cast into prison
and you too gave your life for Christ.
So with confidence we dare to ask:
please obtain relief for N. . . .
if it be God's will.

995   **Prayer to St. Raphael**
Patron of Travelers

D EAR St. Raphael,
    your lovely name means "God heals."
The Lord sent you to young Tobiah
to guide him throughout a long journey.
Upon his return you taught him
how to cure his father's blindness.
How natural, therefore, for Christians
to pray for your powerful help
for safe travel and a happy return.
This is what we ask for ourselves
as well as for all who are far from home.

ST. THOMAS MORE — PATRON OF LAWYERS

As a Chancellor of England and a Martyr of Christ, St. Thomas is the perfect model for lawyers. He combined a love for country and for God that was perfectly ordered—putting God always first. Executed for his steadfast faith, he remained a model of courage and human reason, telling the spectators that he was dying as "the King's good servant—but God's first." He perfectly illustrates what the role of a Patron can be in our society so sorely in need of real heroes.

C) PATRONS OF PROFESSIONS

AS ALREADY mentioned, Vatican II put into per-spective the devotion to the Saints which has been a hallmark of Christians since the foundation of the Church. Among other things it said:

"It is supremely fitting, therefore, that we love those friends and coheirs of Jesus, who are our brothers and sisters and extraordinary benefactors, that we render due thanks to God for them and suppliantly invoke them and have recourse to their prayers, their power and help in obtaining benefits from God through his Son, Jesus Christ, who is our Redeemer and Savior.

"For every genuine testimony of love, shown by us to those in heaven, by its very nature tends toward and terminates in Christ who is the crown of all Saints, and, through him, in God who is wonderful in his Saints and is magnified in them" (Const on the Church, no. 50).

In this section we are invoking the help of those Saints who are known as patrons of certain professions. It is im-portant to note, however, that there are relatively few Patrons "officially" declared by the Church. Most of these Saints have been named patrons of some profession by popular tradition. But the end result of praying to them is the same in either case—we are aided by their intercession with God and brought closer to Christ.

Needless, to say, the prayers contained herein are ex-amples of the way one may pray to the Patron of any profession. In this respect, they are excellent prayer-starters! Prayers to other Patrons of Professions can easily be composed in accord with the models given. Finally, one can use the prayers here with different petitions—al-ways with the provision that they accord with God's will.

996 **Prayer to St. Matthew**
Patron of Accountants

DEAR Levi, now known as Matthew,
you were first a publican, a tax collector,
and then a gatherer of souls for Christ
after immediately following his call.
Later you wrote wonderful accounts
for your Jewish brethren
of what Jesus, descendant of David,
said and did as Teacher and Savior.

Make all accountants imitate your example
in giving careful and honest accounts.

997 **Prayer to St. Genesius**
Patron of Actors

DEAR Genesius,
according to a very ancient story
when you were still a pagan
you once ridiculed Christ while acting on the stage.
But, like Saul on the road to Damascus,
you were floored by Christ's powerful grace.

You rose bearing witness to Jesus
and died a great martyr's death.
Intercede for your fellow actors before God,
that they may faithfully and honestly perform their roles
and so help others to understand their role in life
thus enabling them to attain their end in heaven.

998 **Prayer to St. Bernardine of Siena**
Patron of Advertisers

D EAR Saint of the Franciscan Order,
you were a tireless preacher of God's saving Word.
By your growing love for Jesus
you spread that love all around,
advertising his Holy Name.
Be kind to advertisers in our frantic times.
Make them broadcast only what is true
and what can serve the well-being of humankind,
while doing all for the glory of God.

999 **Prayer to St. John Berchmans**
Patron of Altar Boys

D EAR St. John,
you died at a very young age
but in that short time
you learned to live an exemplary life
as a member of the Society of Jesus.
Directed by your Guardian Angel,
whom you confidently invoked,
you learned to be a most humble server
at the Holy Sacrifice of the Mass.
Help altar boys imitate you
in their service at Eucharistic celebrations
as well as in their conduct with others.

1000 **Prayer to St. Thomas the Apostle**
Patron of Architects

D EAR St. Thomas,
you were once slow in believing
that Christ had gloriously risen;

but later, because you had seen him,
you exclaimed: "My Lord and my God!"
According to an ancient story,
you rendered most powerful assistance
for constructing a church in a place
where pagan priests opposed it.
Please bless architects, builders, and carpenters
that through them the Lord may be honored.

1001   **Prayer to St. Catherine of Bologna**
Patroness of Artists

D EAR saintly Poor Clare,
    so rich in love for Jesus and Mary,
you were endowed with great talents by God
and you left us most inspiring writings
and paintings of wondrous beauty.
You were chosen as Abbess
in the monastery of Poor Clares at Bologna.
You did all for God's greater glory
and in this you are a model for all.
Make artists learn lessons from you
and use their talents to the full.

1002   **Prayer to St. Dominic**
Patron of Astronomers

W ONDERFUL Saintly Founder
    of the eloquent Order of Preachers
and friend of St. Francis of Assisi,
you were a fiery defender of the Faith
and a fighter against the darkness of heresy.

You resembled a great star that shone close to the world
and pointed to the Light which was Christ.
Help astronomers to study the stars
and admire their wonderful Maker,
proclaiming: "Give glory to God in the highest."

1003 **Prayer to St. Sebastian**
Patron of Athletes

DEAR Commander at the Roman Emperor's court,
you chose to be also a soldier of Christ
and dared to spread faith in the King of Kings—
for which you were condemned to die.
Your body, however, proved athletically strong
and the executing arrows extremely weak.
So another means to kill you was chosen
and you gave your life to the Lord.
May athletes be always as strong in their faith
as their Patron Saint so clearly has been.

1004 **Prayer to St. Joseph of Cupertino**
Patron of Aviators

DEAR ecstatic Conventual Saint
who patiently bore calumnies,
your secret was Christ
the crucified Savior who said:
"When I will be lifted up
I will draw all people to myself."
You were always spiritually lifted up.
Give aviators courage and protection,
and may they always keep in mind
your greatly uplifting example.

1005 **Prayer to St. Matthew**
Patron of Bankers and Money Managers

DEAR publican become a Saint,
    after once gathering taxes and tolls
how wonderful was your conversion by grace
when discarding your earthly possessions
you followed the Poor Man of Nazareth.
The Mammon of Money is still worshiped!
Inspire bankers with kindness
and with the desire to help where they can;
for what is done to the least, to the poor,
is done to Jesus, the Son of Man.

1006 **Prayer to St. Charles Borromeo**
Patron of Catechists

O SAINTLY reformer,
    animator of spiritual renewal of priests and religious,
you organized true seminaries
and wrote a standard catechism.
Inspire all religious teachers
and authors of catechetical books.
Move them to love and transmit
only that which can form true followers
of the Teacher who was divine.

1007 **Prayer to St. Maria Goretti**
Patroness of the Children of Mary

CHARMING Saint,
    and true child of Mary, Mother of Jesus,
you were so young but already so strong
in resisting a cruel tempter

and preferring to die a martyr.
How greatly we need today—
when chastity is often discarded—
more models and intercessors like you!
Multiply faithful Children of Mary
for her glory and that of her Son.

1008 **Prayer to St. Dominic Savio**
Patron of Choir Boys

GREAT model for God-loving boys
and cherished pupil of the famous Don Bosco,
you died prematurely, humanly speaking,
but you had already attained mature spiritual wisdom.
Your kindness won you many friends
but your love above all sought the Master
who is present in our tabernacles.
His praises you eucharistically sang.
Make choir boys be singers like you
for the love of Jesus, our most loving Master.

1009 **Prayer to St. Joseph**
Patron of Carpenters

DEAR Saint,
you are the Patron of the family of the Church.
God chose you to be the head and protector
of the Holy Family of Nazareth.
You chose to do a carpenter's work
which made some say about Jesus:
"Is he not the carpenter's son?"
Deign to bless and encourage carpenters
whose work is so much like yours.

1010   Prayer to St. Vincent de Paul
Patron of Charitable Workers

DEAR Saint,
    the mere mention of your name
suggests a litany of your virtues:
humility, zeal, mercy, self-sacrifice.
It also recalls your many foundations:
Works of Mercy, Congregations, Societies.

And the Church gratefully remembers
your promotion of the priesthood.
Inspire all Charitable Workers,
especially those who minister to the poor—
both the spiritually and the materially poor.

1011   Prayer to St. Gabriel
of Our Lady of Sorrows
Patron of Clerics

DEAR Saint,
    your very name recalls your particular devotion
to Christ the Man of Sorrows
and to Mary the Afflicted Mother.

You died young as a Passionist religious
but left to us all an example
of a life of Christlike sacrifice.

Intercede for our seminarians and young religious
who are in desperate need of your patronage
amid today's sensual and selfish world.

1012 **Prayer to St. Vitus**
Patron of Comedians

D EAR Vitus,
the one thing we are certain about
is that you died a martyr's death.
In early times churches were dedicated to you
in important places.

In the Middle Ages your intercession obtained
cures from epilepsy
so that this disease came to be called
"St. Vitus' Dance."
Inspire comedians to make people dance with laughter
and so bear goodwill toward one another.

1013 **Prayer to St. Margaret Mary**
Patroness of Devotees of the Sacred Heart

O HOLY Visitandine,
to hear your name
is to recall the Sacred Heart Devotion,
especially as practiced on First Fridays
and in making reparation for sins.

From early youth you dedicated yourself to Jesus
and you exhibited fervent love for him in the Eucharist.
You became his chosen vessel to spread
the devotion to the Sacred Heart
which has done wonders in modern times.

Make all of us realize ever more Christ's words:
"Behold this Heart that has so greatly loved people."

1014   **Prayer to St. Zita**
Patron of Domestics

DEAR follower of the Son of God,
   you desired to become a servant
and died the death of a slave.
You were not only a faithful maid-servant
but a practical lover of the poor.
Like Mary you could have said:
"Behold the handmaid of the Lord."
Prompt domestics to be just and charitable,
seeing in their employers children of God
and setting an example for them as servants of God.

1015   **Prayer to St. John Bosco**
Patron of Editors

ADMIRABLE apostle of youth,
   founder of religious Congregations,
catechist, educator, writer,
and a light that shone brightly in our time,
you know that one of the greatest powers today
is the power of the Press.
Prompt editors to be always truthful
and to work for the good of human beings,
thus serving the greater glory of God.

1016   **Prayer to St. John Baptist de la Salle**
Patron of Educators

WELL-KNOWN Founder of the Congregation
   of the Brothers of Christian Schools,
orthodox and prayerful theologian,
you realized the very great value
of competent Christian educators.

How great your wholesome influence has been!
Make your followers continue to be
Christlike models for all their students
who in turn will edify others.

1017   **Prayer to St. Paul the Apostle**
Patron of Evangelists

GREAT convert and Apostle of the Gentiles,
you became Christlike and knew only Christ Crucified.
Though extremely learned, you relied completely
on the Wisdom received from the Spirit
and taught from the abundance of your heart.
Instruct modern evangelists—
those who preach Christ to others.
Let them realize that their actions speak louder
than any words they may use.
Teach them to use their talents
in conveying their God-given message
but to rely above all on the promptings of the Spirit.

1018   **Prayer to St. Isidore the Farmer**
Patron of Farmers

DEAR Isidore,
you know how normal it is to cultivate the land
for you were employed as a farm laborer
for the greater part of your life.
Although you received God's help materially
through Angels in the field,
all farmers are aided spiritually
to see the wonders God has strewn on this earth.
Encourage all farmers in their labors
and help them to feed numerous people.

1019   **Prayer to St. Catherine of Siena**
       Patron of Firefighters

DOMINICAN Tertiary and Doctor of the Church,
       you were full of wisdom, the special gift of God,
and you knew how to guide even Pontiffs,
as well as how to extinguish fiery passions
and restore true peace among people.

How inspiring your spiritual writings
and how heroic your abstemious life!
Fires are today unfortunately all too common—
some even caused by criminal persons.
Please protect and encourage firefighters
in their heroic efforts to save lives.

1020   **Prayer to St. Ann**
           Patron of Homemakers

DEAR Saint,
       we know nothing about you except your name.
But you gave us the Mother of God
who called herself handmaid of the Lord.

In your home you raised the Queen of Heaven
and are rightly the model of homemakers.
In your womb came to dwell the new Eve
uniquely conceived without sin.

Intercede for us
that we too may remain free from sin.

1021   **Prayers to St. Frances Xavier Cabrini**
Patroness of Immigrants

HOW much there can be in a name
is most clearly shown in you
who were called Frances Xavier,
thus expressing your wonderful missionary spirit.

An emigrant from Lombardi in Italy,
you in turn took care of immigrants.
You founded the Missionary Sisters
and became the first American citizen
to be canonized a Saint.

Make us dedicated servants of God like yourself
and care for the immigrants who need your help.

1022   **Prayer to St. Thomas More**
Patron of Lawyers

DEAR Scholar and Martyr,
it was not the King of England but you
who were the true Defender of the Faith.
Like Christ unjustly condemned,
neither promises nor threats could make you accept
a civil ruler as head of the Christian Church.

Perfect in your honesty and love of truth,
grant that lawyers and judges may imitate you
and achieve true justice for all people.

1023 **Prayer to St. Frances of Rome**
Patroness of Lay People

DEAR Frances,
    you were an exemplary wife,
ever faithful to your husband.
After his death, you founded and governed
the Congregation of Mount Olivet,
revealing your great devotion to our Lord's Passion.
Your faith in Angels was rewarded
by frequent visions of them.
Please pray for Catholics in our day
that they may be as dedicated to God as you were.

1024 **Prayer to St. Bede the Venerable**
Patron of Lectors

CAREFUL Historian and Doctor of the Church,
    lover of God and of truth,
you are a natural model
for all readers of God's inspired Word.
Move lectors to prepare for public reading
by prayerfully pondering the sacred texts
and invoking the Holy Spirit.
Help them to read in such a way
that those who hear may attain learning and edification.

1025 **Prayer to St. Brendan**
Patron of Mariners

DEAR Saint,
    to mention your name is to recall much traveling.
It was in relation to voyages
that you emerged as a popular Saint.

The Irish became great travelers
thus spreading their faith everywhere.
Protect not only mariners
but also all those who go down to the sea in ships.

1026 **Prayer to St. Francis of Assisi**
Patron of Merchants

MOST lovable and popular Saint,
son of a go-getting and wealthy merchant of Assisi,
you discarded earthly possessions
for the Savior you loved so dearly
and you won innumerable persons for Jesus.

How greatly we need in our day
unselfish and just merchants.
Inspire them with the love of Christ for others
and with the desire for things that endure.

1027 **Prayer to St. Peter Claver**
Patron of Missionaries

DEAR Saint of our modern times,
you were permeated with compassion for the oppressed,
for human beings sold as slaves
and treated as expendable beasts.
While alleviating their natural ills,
you also took away their spiritual ills,
and taught them the surpassing knowledge of Christ.
Inspire many of our contemporaries
to become self-sacrificing missionaries like you.

1028   **Prayer to St. Theresa
of the Child of Jesus**
Patroness of Missionaries

D EAR Little Flower of Lisieux,
how wonderful was the short life you led.
Though cloistered, you went far and wide
through fervent prayers and great sufferings.
You obtained from God
untold helps and graces for his evangelists.
Help all missionaries in their work
and teach all of us to spread Christianity
in our own neighborhoods and family circles.

1029   **Prayer to St. Monica**
Patroness of Mothers

E XEMPLARY Mother of the great Augustine,
you perseveringly pursued your wayward son
not with wild threats
but with prayerful cries to heaven.
Intercede for all mothers in our day
so that they may learn to draw their children to God.
Teach them how to remain close to their children,
even the prodigal sons and daughters
who have sadly gone astray.

1030   **Prayer to St. Christopher**
Patron of Motorists

D EAR Saint,
you have inherited a beautiful name—
Christbearer—as a result of a wonderful legend
that while carrying people across a raging stream

you also carried the Child Jesus.
Teach us to be true Christbearers
to those who do not know him.
Protect all drivers who often transport
those who bear Christ within them.

1031 **Prayer to St. Cecilia**
Patroness of Musicians

DEAR Saint Cecilia,
one thing we know for certain about you
is that you became a heroic martyr
in fidelity to your divine Bridegroom.
We do not know that you were a musician
but we are told that you heard Angels sing.
Inspire musicians to gladden the hearts of people
by filling the air with God's gift of music
and reminding them of the divine Musician
who created all beauty.

1032 **Prayer to St. Gertrude**
Patroness of Cloistered Nuns

MODEL of total fidelity
to the Heavenly Bridegroom
and to your Cistercian Rule,
the Lord was pleased to make available
wonderful private revelations through you.
Help religious to realize that
where there is total generosity
trials are usually not lacking,
but there is also God's infinite love.
Make all religious generous like you.

1033 **Prayer to St. Agatha**
Patroness of Nurses

DEAR Virgin and Martyr,
     whom the Church recalls in her liturgy,
you heroically resisted the temptation
of a degenerate ruler.
Subjected to long and horrible tortures,
you remained faithful to your heavenly Spouse.

St. Peter, we are told, gave you some solace
and so you are invoked by nurses.
Encourage them to see Christ in the sick
and to render true service to them.

1034 **Prayer to St. Camillus of Lellis**
Patron of Nurses and Hospital Workers

MOST wonderful Saint,
     your compassion for the sick and the dying
led you to found the Servants of the Sick.
As the Patron of nurses and hospital workers,
infuse in them your compassionate spirit.

Make hospitals resemble the inn in Christ's Parable
to which the Good Samaritan brought the wounded man
saying: "Take care of him,
and I will repay you for it."

1035 **Prayer to St. Luke**
Patron of Physicians

MOST charming and saintly Physician,
you were animated by the heavenly Spirit of love.
In faithfully detailing the humanity of Jesus,
you also showed his divinity
and his genuine compassion for all human beings.

Inspire our physicians with your professionalism
and with the divine compassion for their patients.
Enable them to cure the ills of both body and spirit
that afflict so many in our day.

1036 **Prayer to St. Michael**
Patron of Police Officers

DEAR St. Michael,
your name means, "Who is like God?"
and it indicates that you remained faithful
when others rebelled against God.

Help police officers in our day
who strive to stem the rebellion and evil
that are rampant on all sides.

Keep them faithful to their God
as well as to their country
and their fellow human beings.

1037 **Prayer to St. John Chrysostom**
Patron of Preachers

DEAR St. John
your oratorical gifts inspired thousands
and earned you the name "golden-mouthed."
Continue to inspire Christians through your writings
and grant us a rebirth of Christian preaching
for the spiritual renewal of the Church.

Obtain from God preachers like yourself
who, animated by the Holy Spirit,
deserve to be called other Christs
and forcefully preach the Good News.

1038 **Prayer to St. John Vianney**
Patron of Priests

SAINTLY Pastor of Ars
and splendid model of all servants of souls,
you were considered not very bright
but you possessed the wisdom of the Saints.

You were a true pontifex, a bridge-builder,
between God and his people
as countless penitents streamed to your confessional.
Inspire all priests to be dedicated mediators
between God and his people in our day.

1039 **Prayer to St. Dismas**
Patron of Prisoners

DEAR St. Dismas,
 you cooperated with the grace that was yours
in suffering the same fate as the Divine Master.
You repented for your sins and believed,
and you heard the Savior say:
"Today you will be with me in paradise."

Obtain for prisoners the same grace
to repent of their wicked ways,
and obtain the same reward—
eternal life with Christ.

1040 **Prayer to St. Basil**
Patron of Reformers

DEAR St. Basil,
 you lived among Saints—
your parents and your best friend, Gregory Nazianzen.
You were an inspirer of true monastic life
and a reformer of priests and laity.

Help all those who work for moral reform
in our turbulent age.
Give them a true knowledge of Jesus
so that they will draw all people to him.

1041   **Prayer to St. Teresa of Avila**
Patroness of Religious

O WONDERFUL daughter of Spain,
    you taught us to walk the way of Christian perfection
which is the way of the Cross.
You inspired innumerable men and women
by your writings as well as your conduct,
deserving the title of Doctor of the Church.
Ever faithful to St. Peter's successors,
inspire fidelity to religious vows
on the part of those who have taken them
and make them ever true to their vocation.

1042   **Prayer to St. Benedict**
Patron of Religious

DEAR St. Benedict,
    you are a "blessing" indeed, as your name indicates.
Practicing what you preached,
you founded the monastic tradition of the West
by joining prayer to labor for God—
both liturgical and private prayer.
Help all religious to follow their Rule
and be true to their vocation.
May they labor and pray for the world
to the greater glory of God.

1043   **Prayer to St. Ignatius of Loyola**
Patron of Retreatants

DEAR Founder of the Society of Jesus,
    a wound you received as a soldier
led to your becoming a spiritual soldier for Christ.

By reading the lives of the Saints,
you changed your life and achieved Sainthood.
You learned to appreciate the value of prayer
and became a master of the Spiritual Exercises,
which greatly fostered retreats.
Help all who make retreats to imitate your example
by becoming true followers of Jesus.

1044 Prayer to St. Albert the Great
Patron of Scientists

DEAR Scientist and Doctor of the Church,
natural science always led you
to the higher science of God.
Though you had an encyclopedic knowledge,
it never made you proud,
for you regarded it as a gift of God.
Inspire scientists to use their gifts well
in studying the wonders of creation,
thus bettering the lot of the human race,
and rendering greater glory to God.

1045 Prayer to St. Jerome
Patron of Scripture Scholars

MASTER of unworldliness and founder of monasteries,
you had a deep love for God's inspired Word
and were a most careful translator
of the Sacred Scriptures.
Your single-mindedness in seeking God's glory
is a perfect model for all exegetes.
Inspire them with respect for the sacred text
as well as for Tradition and the Church's Magisterium.

Help them to impart to all
the true meaning of the Word of God.

1046   **Prayer to St. Genesius**
Patron of Secretaries

DEAR Bishop and Historian,
    faithful to sound doctrine
and fearless defender of the Faith,
you were a careful historian
and preserver of valuable documents.

Imbue secretaries with a sense of your exactitude
and genuine concern for detail.
In carrying out their appointed tasks,
may they also attend to their spiritual duties
and give glory to God in all things.

1047   **Prayer to St. Gregory the Great**
Patron of Singers

GREAT Doctor of the Church,
    you called the Pope
"the servant of the servants of the Lord."
You were outstanding as a moralist and liturgist,
and you introduced the renowned "Gregorian Chant"
into the liturgical celebrations of the Church.

Inspire singers to realize that they have a gift of God
and should use it for the good of others.
Help all Christians to sing joyfully at the Eucharist
and so celebrate it as the community of God.

1048   **Prayer to St. Ephrem**
Patron of Spiritual Leaders

DOCTOR of the Church and Saintly Deacon,
    you were called the "Harp of the Holy Spirit"
because of the power of your mystical works.
Cast out of home by your pagan father,
you met St. Basil, a truly spiritual father,
and became a light in the world
as the instrument of the Holy Spirit.
Endow our spiritual leaders with a little
of your mystical and spiritual sense
so that they may lead us unerringly to Christ.

1049   **Prayer to St. Thomas Aquinas**
Patron of Students

WONDERFUL theologian and Doctor of the
    Church,
you learned more from the Crucifix than from books.
Combining both sources, you left us
the marvelous *Summa* of theology,
broadcasting most glorious enlightenment to all.
You always sought for true light
and studied for God's honor and glory.
Help us all to study our religion
as well as all other subjects needed for life,
without ambition and pride in imitation of you.

1050   **Prayer to Sts. Cosmas and Damian**
Patrons of Surgeons

DEAR twin brothers,
    you both died as witnesses to the Lord you loved.

Sometimes you miraculously healed
the ailing bodies of your fellow human beings.
You also managed to cure the souls
that suffered from unbelief and sin.
Help surgeons in their delicate work,
especially when there exists more danger than usual.
Remind them to invoke often the Lord of Life
while not forgetting to do their part
to save or better the lives of their patients.

1051 **Prayer to St. Valentine**
Patron of Sweethearts

DEAR Saint and glorious Martyr,
 who are so popular with lovers,
be kind to those whom we love and to us.
Teach us to love unselfishly
and to find great joy in giving.
Enable all true lovers
to bring out the best in each other.
Let them love each other in God
and God in each other.

1052 **Prayer to St. John Francis Regis**
Patron of Social Workers

ZEALOUS worker for souls,
 you wrought many miracles
and labored for all classes of people,
but especially to convert the Huguenots.
To you St. John Vianney of Ars attributed
both his vocation and his spiritual successes.
Make social workers go about doing good

not as mere humanitarians
but as messengers of Christ
who have a supernatural love for their clients.

1053 **Prayer to St. Martin of Tours**
Patron of Soldiers

DEAR well-beloved Saint,
   you were first a soldier like your father.
Converted to the Church,
you became a soldier of Christ,
a priest and then Bishop of Tours.

Lover of the poor,
and model for pagans and Christians alike,
protect our soldiers at all times.
Make them strong, just, and charitable,
always aiming at establishing peace on earth.

1054 **Prayer to St. Clare of Assisi**
Patroness of Television Workers

DEAR St. Clare,
   inspired by St. Francis,
you became a poor nun for the sake of Jesus,
and established the "Poor Clares."

We are told how greatly you cherished Christ
present in the Sacrament of the Altar.
Is the Mass not a kind of television
of Christ's sacrifice on the Cross?
Help all television workers to broadcast the truth
and draw away from falsehood and evil.

1055   **Prayer to St. Louis of France**
Patron of Tertiaries

A DMIRABLE Catholic King and devoted family man,
  you raised eleven children of God,
personally served the poor, and respected human rights.
You founded "houses of God"
and provided an example for religious by your fidelity.

Inspire tertiaries to live their vocation
and thereby give an example of Christian love
to others in the world.

1056   **Prayer to St. Augustine**
Patron of Theologians

B ELOVED Saint of our age,
  you were at first wholly human-centered
and attached to false teachings.
Finally converted through God's grace,
you became a praying theologian—
God-centered, God-loving, and God-preaching.

Help theologians in their study of revealed truth.
Let them always follow the Church Magisterium
as they strive to communicate traditional teachings
in a new form that will appeal to our contemporaries.

1057 **Prayer to St. Alphonsus Liguori**
Patron of Moral Theologians

PRECISE and orthodox theologian,
  Master in theology of conduct,
how greatly we need today
theologians who are humble, prayerful,
and eager to spread Christian conduct all around.

You wrote much about the path to perfection
and the means to follow the Teacher of all,
who is the Way, the Truth, and the Life.
Inspire our theologians to help the countless people
who look to them for guidance in life's conduct.

1058 **Prayer to St. Elizabeth of Hungary**
Patroness of Widows

DEAR Saint,
  you were always poor in spirit,
most generous toward the poor,
faithful to your husband,
and fully consecrated to your Divine Bridegroom.

Grant your help to widows
and keep them faithful to their heavenly Lord.
Teach them how to cope with their loss
and to make use of their time in the service of God.

1059   **Prayer to St. Joseph**
          Patron of Workers

DEAR Patron of God's Church,
     you are honored by her as the Worker,
the humble carpenter of Nazareth.
According to St. Teresa of Avila,
you are universal in your intercessions.

Inspire workers of all kinds
to walk ever in your footsteps as faithful servants
coupling charity with justice
and becoming true followers of Jesus.

1060   **Prayer to St. Francis de Sales**
          Patron of Writers

MOST loving and lovable Saint,
     you preached to thousands with the pen,
introducing them to "the devout life."
You wrote sublimely about God's love
and made countless converts by your Christlike kindness.

Make writers realize the power of the Press
and inspire them with your zeal for spreading truth.
Help them to write honestly no matter what the subject,
so that they will really contribute
to bringing about God's Kingdom.

1061 **Prayer to St. Peter Canisius**
Patron of Writers of Catechisms

D EAR Doctor and Defender of the Church,
to you the Master must have said:
"Well done, composer of books
which have taught and inspired
countless persons in many lands."

Help those who compose catechisms
to communicate the true teachings of Christ
in ways that can be understood by our contemporaries
so that they will be moved to follow Jesus.

1062 **Prayer to St. Aloysius**
Patron of Youth

D EAR Christian youth,
you were a faithful follower of Christ
in the Society of Jesus.
You steadily strove for perfection
while generously serving the plague-stricken.

Help our youth today who are faced with a plague
of false cults and false gods.
Show them how to harness their energies
and to use them for their own and others' fulfillment—
which will redound to the greater glory of God.

ST. JOAN OF ARC — PATRONESS OF FRANCE

In her all too brief life on earth, St. Joan lifted up a tottering land and inspired the French people with her courage and devotion. Burned at the stake as a heretic at the tender age of nineteen by a kangaroo English court, this Maid of Orleans was cleared by the Church thirty years later and made a Saint in 1920. She is an excellent example of what a Patron of a Country can do for its people.

D) PATRONS OF COUNTRIES

THE Church is ever solicitous of encouraging Christians to maintain relations with the Saints, for the Church knows that by staying close to the Saints we stay close to Christ. In the words of Vatican II:

"The authentic cult of the Saints consists not so much in the multiplying of external acts, but rather in the greater intensity of our love, whereby, for our own good and that of the whole Church, we seek from the Saints example in their way of life, fellowship in their communion, and aid by their intercession" (Constitution on the Church, no. 50).

One way of insuring that we stay close to the Saints is by assigning a Patron Saint for each country (and each diocese and local Church for that matter). The Church thus holds before the citizens of any country a particular Saint who is their own, so to speak. They can have recourse to him/her in their troubles and celebrate him/her in their joys.

Such a Saint becomes the spiritual spokesperson for the citizenry of that country who place all their faith, hope and love in him/her in return. In this way, the devotion of the people increases and they come closer to God the Father with the Son and in the Holy Spirit.

The prayers contained herein are in no way official. They are, however, indicative of ways in which this patronage of National Saints can be utilized by the people of each country. At the same time, they provide a way of finding one's spiritual roots, so to speak, for people who may have emigrated to other countries which have different Patron Saints.

1063   **Prayer to Our Lady of Guadalupe**
Patroness of the Americas and Mexico

HOW kind you were, O Mary,
    to appear to an Indian convert in Mexico,
leaving on his cloak as credential
a permanent image of yourself.
You thereby won many for Christ
and naturally became the Patroness
of Mexico and the Americas,
and especially of the poor.
May more and more people through your intercession
accept your dear Son as their Lord.

1064   **Prayer to Our Lady, Help of Christians**
Patroness of Australia and New Zealand

AMONG all God's human creatures,
    who possesses greater power to help humankind
than you, O Mary!
While on earth you lived in obscurity
as the devoted wife of a poor carpenter.
But after entering heaven
you have worked countless wonders for humanity,
sometimes healing bodies
but more frequently curing souls.
O Mary, continue to help all Christians!

1065   **Prayer to St. Joseph**
Patron of Belgium

HOW precious to have as a Patron
    the protector of Jesus and Mary,

the Patron of Mother Church,
a man most just and charitable
who was the head of the Holy Family
and who brought up a Child that was God!
Ever humble and obedient St. Joseph,
intercede for us that like you
we may be faithful to our vocation
and true servants of the Lord.

1066 Prayer to St. Ann
Patroness of Canada

FAMILIES that are truly Christian
love the Family of Nazareth
but they also honor the parents of Mary,
especially St. Ann
who bore and gave birth to her.
How glorious to give birth to one
who would be the Mother of God!
May we who have devotion to you, St. Ann,
obtain even more devotion to Mary
and the greatest devotion for Christ, your grandson.

1067 Prayer to St. James the Greater
Patron of Chile and Spain

DEAR brother of John,
who saw our Lord transfigured,
after preaching in Palestine
and then bringing the Good News to Spain,
you became the first Apostle
to die as a witness to Christ.
Witness of Christ's agony in the garden,
teach us to represent Christ in our life,

bearing willingly our cross after him
and working and praying for God's glory.

1068   **Prayer to St. Peter Claver**
                    Patron of Colombia

O MOST compassionate Saint,
    member of the Society of Jesus,
you chose to go to South America
and there as a slave for slaves
you became all things for the blacks—
another Christ in deed!

Inspire us with your zeal
and make us become ever more Christlike,
so that we may hear the words that Jesus promised:
"Well done, good and faithful servant."

1069   **Prayer to St. Wenceslaus**
                    Patron of Czechoslovakia

MODEL governor of Bohemia,
    hated by your pagan mother
and raised by a saintly grandmother,
you vowed to live a celibate life.
You had great respect for priests
and deep love for the Sacrifice of the Mass.

Indeed, it was while you were praying in God's house
that you were slain by your misguided brother.
Help all of us—priests, religious, and laity—
to lead exemplary Christian lives.

1070 **Prayer to St. Canute**
Patron of Denmark

MODEL Catholic King,
like Wenceslaus Duke of Bohemia
you spread belief in the Savior,
and also like him you were slain
by those hostile to the Christian Religion
while you were praying before an altar.
We desperately need civil rulers
who are both just and charitable
like Christ the King of Kings!
Inspire all Presidents and Kings!

1071 **Prayer to St. George**
Patron of England

HEROIC Catholic soldier
and defender of your Faith,
you dared to criticize a tyrannical Emperor
and were subjected to horrible torture.
You could have occupied a high military position
but you preferred to die for your Lord.
Obtain for us the great grace
of heroic Christian courage
that should mark soldiers of Christ.

1072 **Prayer to St. Henry**
Patron of Finland

HEAD of the Roman Empire,
Confessor of the Catholic Faith
and lover of celibacy,

you remained truly humble
even while holding a lofty post.
You thus illustrated how great are the wonders
that God's grace can produce in weak human beings
when they prayerfully follow the Master!
Help us to sanctify ourselves
and thus sanctify many others.

1073   **Prayer to St. Joan of Arc**
Patroness of France

MOST extraordinary soldier,
you insistently proclaimed:
"Let God be served *first!*"
You began by winning many victories
and received the plaudits of princes,
but then you were given to the enemy
and cruelly put to death.
Instill in us the desire to serve God first
and perform our earthly tasks with that idea
ever in our minds.

1074   **Prayer to St. Boniface**
Patron of Germany

DEAR Winfred, a British Benedictine,
you were called Boniface by the Holy Father
who sent you to evangelize Germany.
Aided by many monks
and relying on God's grace
obtained through assiduous prayer,
you made countless converts.
Inbue us with great missionary zeal
and help us in our spiritual renewal,
O Leader who died for the Lord.

1075 **Prayer to St. Nicholas**
Patron of Greece

WONDER-WORKING follower of Christ,
from your early years you practiced fasting
and were outstanding in generosity.
You quickly distributed to the poor
what you had inherited from your parents.
Traveling to Palestine, you became a bishop
and dared to preach the Gospel
for which you were thrown into prison.
As "Santa Claus" you are still loved today.
Teach us to be generous like you!

1076 **Prayer to St. Willibrord**
Patron of Holland

SAINTLY Anglo-Saxon Benedictine,
you became a typical missionary for Frisia
in close relations with the Holy See.
You were later ordained Bishop of Utrecht
and met with great trials.
Missionaries were slain and churches destroyed
but you continued your wonderful work.
Help us to understand that sufferings form part
of the life of any follower of the Crucified Christ.

1077 **Prayer to St. Stephen**
Patron of Hungary

O TRULY Christian King,
you labored long and hard for your people,
caring not only for their material prosperity

but also for their spiritual well-being.
You were attached to fasting, almsgiving, and prayer
and you possessed great devotion to the Queen of heaven.
Help your people in their present affliction,
and teach all Christians to follow your example
by laboring to build up this world
yet not neglecting to take care of their spiritual side.

1078 **Prayer to Our Lady of the Assumption**
Patroness of India, South Africa, and Paraguay

O MARY,
    God's Son became your Son
and you in turn became both our Mother and our Queen.
From your heavenly throne,
intercede for your countless subjects
who are daily confronted with life's trials.
Help us to find comfort in our recourse to you
and to come closer to your Divine Son.
May faith in the glorious Savior be spread
and trust in you, his compassionate Mother.

1079 **Prayer to St. Patrick**
Patron of Ireland

D EAR St. Patrick,
    in your humility you called yourself a sinner,
but you became a most successful missionary
and prompted countless pagans
to follow the Savior.
Many of their descendants in turn
spread the Good News in numerous foreign lands.
Through your powerful intercession with God,

obtain the missionaries we need
to continue the work you began.

1080 **Prayer to St. Francis of Assisi**
Patron of Italy

DEAR Saint, once worldly and vain,
  you became humble and poor for the sake of Jesus
and had an extraordinary love for the Crucified,
which showed itself in your body
by the imprints of Christ's Sacred Wounds.

In our selfish and sensual age,
how greatly we need your secret
that draws countless men and women to imitate you.
Teach us also great love for the poor
and unswerving loyalty to the Vicar of Christ.

1081 **Prayer to St. Peter Baptist**
Patron of Japan

DEAR Franciscan Missionary,
  you were canonized with 25 other Christians
who were slain at Nagasaki
after suffering the horrible torture of crucifixion,
that was suffered also by Simon Peter.

Let us who are followers of the Crucified Christ
take a clear lesson from you.
Teach us to accept every cross,
everything God sends us or permits us to undergo.

1082 **Prayer to St. Paul**
Patron of Malta

A POSTLE of the Nations,
   you took literally our Lord's words:
"Go and teach all nations!"
You journeyed over continents and islands, and said:
"Woe to me if I do not preach the Gospel!"
Help us to realize that the Church is by nature missionary,
that all members must help where they can
to make Christ known and followed.
Enable us to do this by our prayers
and by our Christian lives as well.

1083 **Prayer to St. Olaf**
Patron of Norway

D EAR Norwegian Viking Prince,
   popular in Northern European countries,
after turning Christian you labored hard
to uproot paganism in Norway and Greenland.
Even those responsible for your death
confessed that they had killed a Saint.
Through your intercession
make Christianity flower once more
in Scandinavian peoples.

1084 **Prayer to St. Rose of Lima**
Patroness of Peru

C HARMING spiritual Rose,
   sprung up in Middle America,
you loved virginity and consecrated yourself

to the Divine Bridegroom
as a Dominican of the Third Order.
During your saintly life
you had a wonderful familiarity with Mary and Angels.
Make Americans follow faithfully
in the footsteps of the Divine Master
as you have so wonderfully done.

1085 **Prayer to the Sacred Heart of Mary**
Patroness of the Philippines

O MARY,
    you were consecrated by God
to be a temple of the Holy Spirit
and a tabernacle of the Divine Son.
Blessed among women, you loved God
more than is done by Angels and Saints.
Teach us to love God above all
and make us faithful servants like yourself.
May the Philippine people attain ever greater devotion
to your Sacred Heart.

1086 **Prayer to St. Casimir**
Patron of Poland

S ON of a Polish King,
    combining prayer with mortification
and drawing inspiration from Christ's Passion,
you remained faithful to a vow of celibacy.
You labored to make Ruthenians
faithful followers of Christ.
Most charitable toward the poor,
you became another Francis of Assisi.
Continue to inspire Poland
in its fidelity to Christ the King.

1087 **Prayer to the Immaculate Conception**
Patroness of the United States, Brazil, and Portugal

O MARY,
in virtue of Christ's foreseen merits
you were conceived completely immaculate.
You thus became the new but perfectly obedient Eve,
stainless tabernacle of the Most High,
and exemplary Mother of God.
At Lourdes you revealed immaculateness
and at Fatima you exhorted us to pray.
Protect us against the evil of godlessness,
and remain a Mother and Model for us all.

1088 **Prayer to St. Andrew**
Patron of Russia and Scotland

B ROTHER of Simon Peter,
you heard John the Baptist say:
"Behold the Lamb of God,"
and you chose to follow Jesus.
Leaving your nets,
you became a successful fisher of souls.
Lover of the Crucified Christ,
you too were crucified like him.
Teach us to live and suffer for him
and to win many souls for Christ.

1089 **Prayer to St. Bridget**
Patroness of Sweden

F AITHFUL wife and mother,
you loved to meditate on Christ's Passion
which made you wonderfully patient.

Like Elizabeth of Hungary,
you generously cared for the poor and the sick.
You also founded a monastery
and became a favorite Saint through the centuries.
Help us to be faithful to the vocation
that God intended for us.

1090 Prayer to St. Nicholas of Flue
Patron of Switzerland

SAINTLY head of a large family,
    you later became a devout hermit.
Through your prayerful life of union with God,
you were able to restore and preserve
peace among people.
You see how in our time
we are still threatened by wars.
Teach us how to pray for and obtain true peace
from him who is the Prince of Peace.

1091 Prayer to St. David
Patron of Wales

POPULAR Patron of the Welsh,
    full of missionary zeal,
you realized the value of monasteries.
You were always prayerful and spiritually joyful,
and many churches were dedicated to you in Wales.
You teach us to rely
more on God's inspiration and grace
than on purely human means.
Help us to obtain our spiritual renewal.

1092   **Prayer to St. Gertrude**
Patroness of the West Indies

INSPIRING Nun and genuine Mystic,
    you wholly consecrated yourself to our Lord
whom you loved perfectly.
You showed profound respect and gratitude
to Jesus present in the Eucharist,
and exhibited great courage and consolation
founded on your meditation on Christ's Passion.
Obtain for us a genuine appreciation
of true love and Christian purity
in imitation of you.

9

PRAYERS FOR VARIOUS OCCASIONS

9

825

PRAYER IS CONDUCIVE TO EVERY STATE IN LIFE

No one has a premium on prayer. Whatever our state in life, we must cultivate a solid prayer life, a true dialoguing with God. In this connection, any event or any state will provide reasons of its own for this dialogue.

A) DIFFERENT STATES OF LIFE

CHRISTIANS *are called to pray always, as we have already seen. This is not an easy thing to do, especially in our frenetic times. Hence, over the years many reasons for prayer have evolved and become part of a time-honored mechanics of prayer. This section makes use of the specific states of people's lives as the starting point for praying. The rationale for each prayer is simply a person's membership in a state of life.*

What this actually does is take account of the person's life situation in formulating a prayer life for him/her. Previously, we were asked to pray at morning, midday, and evening—and that is all well and good. However, it was possible to lose sight of these moments in the press of the problems of our daily activities. This section, based on that very life itself, is an apt reminder that our prayer life is not relegated to moments but to our very life. It must continue with our everyday life—no matter what our task.

Indirectly, then, this type of praying has a closer relation to us, affords us a more cogent reason for praying, and reminds us of our ultimate goal even while we are pursuing our everyday goals in life. It gets us in the habit of praying at any time in our daily schedule.

The prayer formulas in this section are not necessarily exclusive. They may be used by persons who are not part of a particular state in life (used in the broad sense) to pray for those who are—for example, religious. This can easily be done by "converting" the prayers through the simple substitution of the pronouns—thus giving us a ready-made set of prayers for common states of life.

1093   **Prayer of the Aging**

MAY Christ keep me ever young
     "to the greater glory of God."
For old age comes from him,
old age leads to him,
and old age will touch me
only insofar as he wills.
To be "young" means to be hopeful,
 energetic, smiling—and clear-sighted.
May I accept death in whatever guise
it may come to me in Christ,
that is, within the process of the development of life.

A smile (inward and outward) means facing
with mildness and gentleness
whatever befalls me.

Jesus, grant me to serve you,
to proclaim you,
to glorify you,
and to manifest you,
to the very end through all the time
that remains to me of life,
and above all through my death.

Lord Jesus,
I commit to your care my last years,
and my death;
do not let them impair or spoil
the work I have so dreamed of achieving for you.

                         Based on Pierre Teilhard de Chardin

1094   **Prayer of Altar Boys**

DEAR Lord Jesus,
     thank you for calling me
to serve you at your holy altar

during the celebration of the Eucharist.
I know that the priest takes your place
when, together with your people
and in the name of the Church,
he makes present again
your Passion, Death, and Resurrection.

Help me to carry out my role
in this memorial of the Last Supper
with dignity and precision
and with full interior participation.
Let me so remain united with you on earth
that I may one day share your glory in heaven.

1095 Prayer of Business Persons

LORD Jesus,
  I am a business person,
engaged in commercial enterprises.
I have to work hard to earn my salary
and I do not always remember
to put my Christianity to work in the market-place.
Please forgive me for this,
and help me in the future
to keep the public interest ever in mind.

I know I cannot change the world by myself,
but I can try in my own little way
to be more honest,
more truthful and more trustworthy
in my business life.
Help me, Lord,
for I cannot do it without you.

1096   **Prayer of Catechists**

ALMIGHTY God,
you have generously made known to human being
the mysteries of your life
through Jesus Christ your Son
in the Holy Spirit.
Enlighten my mind
to know these mysteries
which your Church treasures and teaches.
Move my heart to love them
and my will to live in accord with them.

Give me the ability to teach this Faith
to others
without pride,
without ostentation,
and without personal gain.
Let me realize that I am simply your instrument
for bringing others to the knowledge
of the wonderful things you have done
for all your creatures.
Help me to be faithful to this task
that you have entrusted to me.

1097   **Prayer of Persons Going on a Date**

DEAR God,
you created human beings
and imbued in them a mutual attraction
for one another.
Let me realize that male and female
complement one another in many things,
including sexual love.
Help me to enjoy the many ways
in which young people can fulfill one another—
without falling into selfishness and sin.

Lord,
may my partner and I return from this date
more fulfilled, more human,
and in closer union with you
than before the date.
Grant us the knowledge, the will, and the ability
to have fun in you
and to treat each other as true followers of you.

1098   **Prayer of Doctors**

LORD Jesus Christ,
you are the great Physician of our souls.
During your life on earth, you healed the sick
and even brought the dead back to life.
From your heavenly abode,
continue to be the Divine Physician for your people
and bless the noble work to which you have called me.
Make me truly wise in my medical judgments
and genuinely sympathetic in my dealings with patients.

Dear Lord,
guide my mind and my hands
and inspire me with words of comfort
that I may help those in suffering.
Encourage me in the trials and misery
to which I am daily exposed.
Grant that I may ever use
my power and influence for good,
and let no human respect ever deter me
from the performance of my sacred duty
in accord with your holy law.

1099   **Prayer of Extraordinary Ministers of Communion**

HEAVENLY Father,
    I thank you for calling me
to serve you and your people in this community
as an extraordinary minister of the Eucharist.
You know that I could never be worthy
of such an exalted honor.
Help me to be less unworthy
by remaining free from sin.
Let me nourish your people
with the witness of my life
as I feed them with the Body of Christ.
Grant your strength and holiness
to all your extraordinary ministers
and make them worthy to bring Christ to others.

1100   **Prayer of Farmers**

HEAVENLY Father,
    King of the Universe,
you are the sole source
of growth and abundance.
With your help I plant my crops
and by your power they give forth a harvest.
Grant me the grace always to work
with all my strength and ingenuity
in cultivating the soil
so that it will bring forth fruits
for my benefit
and the benefit of all who will use them.

Make me ever cognizant that without my part
in the work of harnessing the goods of the earth
these particular goods would be lacking
to my brothers and sisters in this world.

Enable me at the same time to realize
that without your part in this process
I would be working in vain.
Accept my thanks for your continuous past help
and your never-failing assistance in the future.

1101   **Prayer of Fathers**

HEAVENLY Father,
you have been pleased to let me be called
by the name that is yours from all eternity.
Help me to be worthy of that name.
May I always be for my children a source of life—
corporal, intellectual, and spiritual.
Enable me to contribute in great part
to their physical growth by my work,
to their mental advancement by good schooling
and to their supernatural life by my prayer and example,
so that they may become complete human beings
and true children of their heavenly Father.

Let me be conscious that my actions
are far more important than my words.
May I always give my children a good example
in all the situations of life.
May I wear my successes modestly,
and may my failures find me undaunted;
may I be temperate in time of joy
and steadfast in time of sorrow.
May I remain humble after doing good
and contrite after doing evil.
Above all, may I scrupulously respect
my children's rights as human persons
and their freedom to follow a rightly-formed conscience,
while at the same time fulfilling my duty to guide them
in the way given us by your Son Jesus.

1102 **Prayer of Fiances**

O LORD,
    we thank you for this wonderful gift of our love
which you have generously granted us
and which allows us to build
a true communion of persons between us—
provided we remain ever open to you,
the source of all love.
Help us to continue to love each other
and accept each other as we are, unconditionally,
as we get to know each other better.
Make us generous in giving
and humble in receiving.

Enable us to communicate to one another
all our joys, sufferings, and desires
and all our hopes, sorrows, and difficulties.
Give us the power of your love
that we may forget self and live for each other
so that we may have truly one spirit,
in preparation for the time
when you will send us children
to add to our union and love.

1103 **Prayer of Grandparents**

H EAVENLY Father,
    I know that every period of our lives
has its responsibilities as well as its joys.
Today, it seems that grandparents have
either too little use
or too much—
either we are shunted aside to do nothing
or we are called upon to do everything.

Help me to know just where my duties lie
in my particular situation
and to carry them out as best I can.
Take care of my family—
my children and their children.
Inspire them all to follow your Son
and lead truly Christian lives.
Keep all of us in your loving care,
never let us turn away from you,
and help us in the end to receive the joy
of entering into your glorious presence forever.

1104   Prayer of Homemakers

DEAR Lord,
in the minds of most people
making a home is a job of little import
and even less talent.
Help me to realize that the opposite is the case—
it is the most important job of all
and it requires a multitude of talents.
Providing a home for living persons
who are made in your image
means helping them inevitably get closer to you.
By my slight efforts
I can influence the members of my family
in hundreds of ways
to become better people and better Christians.

Grant me the grace to know how to handle any situation,
the strength to do the ordinary everyday things,
the love to overcome all animosities,
and the joy to dispel all boredom.
Help me to grow as a person every day,
to fulfill myself in all the areas

that are necessary for a homemaker—
loving relationships, mental effort, manual work.
Give me the strength to bring my family closer to Jesus
not so much by my words as by my actions.

1105   Prayer of Laborers

DEAR heavenly Father,
   I know that all labor likens us to you—
we continue your work of creation.
Without manual labor
the world would ultimately grind to a halt.
So I know that my job is important.
But even more my job is important in forming me
and making me a better person and Christian.
It enables me to give myself to others;
it forces me to be less selfish
and gives me a different outlook on life.
It makes me see that all human beings are in this life
   together
and must work together to get ahead.

Thank you for making it possible for us
to work and to grow.
Grant me the strength to keep working
and to earn a decent wage to take care of my family.
Let me give an honest day's work for a day's pay
and keep me faithful to you every day of my life.

1106   Prayer of Lay People

HEAVENLY Father,
   help me to exercise my lay apostolate
where I work or practice my profession,
or study or reside,

or spend any leisure time
or have my companionships.
Grant that I may become the light of the world
by conforming my life to my faith.
By practicing honesty in all my dealings,
may I attract all whom I meet
to the love of the true and the good,
and ultimately to the Church and to Christ.

Inspire me to share in the living conditions
as well as the labors, sorrows, and aspirations
of my brothers and sisters,
thus preparing their hearts
for the worship of your saving grace.
Enable me to perform
my domestic, social, and professional duties
with such Christian generosity
that my way of acting will penetrate
the world of life and labor.

Teach me to cooperate
with all men and women of goodwill
in promoting whatever is true,
whatever is just,
whatever is holy, and whatever is lovable.
Let me complement the testimony of life
with the testimony of the word,
so that I will proclaim Christ
to those brothers and sisters
who can hear the Gospel
through no one else except me.

1107   **Prayer of Law Enforcers**

HEAVENLY Father,
you have created a marvelous world
which is permeated by a wondrous sense of order.
Yet human beings have a tendency
to war against order on their level.
That is the reason why there are people like me
who work at maintaining order in society.
Help me to use my authority with understanding and
   restraint
and without bias or anger.
Let me remember that in carrying out my function
I am sharing in your divine providence in the universe
so that the people in this world can live full lives
and grow in the knowledge and love of you,
of your Son, and of the Holy Spirit.

1108   **Prayer of Leaders of Song**

DEAR Jesus,
thank you for endowing me with a pleasant voice
and for calling me to use it in your liturgical rites.
Let me never be puffed up by my singing in church
but ever give the credit to your gift.
Help me to lead the singing in such a way
that others will be brought to fuller participation
in the celebration of the Eucharist.
Keep me aware that by helping to celebrate
your Paschal Mystery,
I am helping to bring your redemption to the world
and the world to you in return.

1109 Prayer of Lectors

DEAR Jesus,
thank you for calling me to be a lector
at your eucharistic celebrations.
Let me take this role seriously
and diligently prepare myself for it
by studying the sacred texts before Mass
and by striving to be a better Christian.

By my physical action of reading,
I am the instrument through whom you become present
to the assembly in your Word
and through whom you impart your teachings.
Let nothing in my manner disturb your people
or close their hearts to the action of your Spirit.
Cleanse my heart and my mind
and open my lips that I may worthily proclaim your
   Word.

1110 Prayer of Members of the Armed Forces

O LORD,
you are the God of hosts.
Strengthen us who are members
of our country's armed forces.
Make us prepare so well to defend our country
that we will eliminate the need to do so.
In serving our superiors
may we be rendering service to you.

Make us loyal to our loved ones
in spite of separations of every kind.
Keep us devoted to your Church
in spite of the pressures of our duties.
Help us to lead others to you
by the example we give to our comrades-in-arms.

1111   **Prayer of Mothers**

FATHER in heaven,
    grant me the grace to appreciate the dignity
which you have conferred on me.
Let me realize that not even the Angels
have been blessed with such a privilege—
to share in your creative miracle
and bring new Saints to heaven.

Make me a good mother to all my children
after the example of Mary,
the Mother of your Son.
Through the intercession of Jesus and Mary
I ask your continued blessings on my family.
Let us all be dedicated to your service on earth
and attain the eternal happiness of your kingdom in
    heaven.

1112   **Prayer of Parents for Children**

GOD our Father,
    we want to be true cooperators in grace
and witnesses of faith
for our children.
We know that we have a duty
to educate them in the faith
by word and example.
We also know that we must help them
in choosing a vocation,
carefully promoting any religious vocation
that they may have.

Help us to carry out this sacred trust
all the days of our lives.

Teach us how to dialogue with our children
and share the special benefits
that each generation can offer one another.
Enable us to stimulate them
to take part in the apostolate
by offering them good example,
effective advice, and willing assistance.
May we learn from them how to be open to life
and remain ever young in faith, hope, and love.

1113 **Prayer of Parish Committee Members**

FATHER in heaven,
    you have made me a part of the parish committee
whose members have been brought together by the com-
    munion
created by your Word and the Eucharist.
Let me strive to insure that our committee
will be a true forum of opinion
that will act from a consensus
rather than a plurality or majority of votes.
I am called to represent my co-parishioners
and to be a spokesperson for the community.

Help me to speak truly in the people's name
and express their convictions, ideas, and visions.
As a co-worker with the parish team of ministers,
may I never merely endorse the decisions of that team,
but weigh them carefully and give my honest opinion—
without fear, rancor, or prejudice.
Lastly, let me look beyond parish interests
and consider diocesan and universal ones
as well as civic, national, and human affairs.

1114   **Prayer of Pregnant Women**

HEAVENLY Father,
   Creator of all things,
you have been pleased to enable my husband and me
to collaborate with you in conceiving a child.
Thank you for your gracious gift.
Help me to guard this new life carefully
and do nothing to hurt it in any way.

After my child's birth, let me lavish it with love
and bring him/her up in your love and service,
so that he/she will become a child of yours
and inherit your kingdom.
Be with me, O Lord, in this greatest of tasks
to comfort, strengthen, calm, and enlighten me.

1115   **Prayer of Priests**

DEAR Jesus,
   despite my unworthiness
and through the impulse of your goodness
you have been pleased to raise me to the dignity
of the holy priesthood.
You made me not only your minister
but the voice of your sublime wisdom as well
and the dispenser of your mysteries.

I am filled with joy, love, and gratitude to you
for this singular privilege which I have received,
and I am saddened by my failures to respond as I ought
to your great generositiy.
Grant your light to my mind
that I may daily dispense in greater abundance
the fruits of your redemption of all human beings.
Help me to be a genuine *pontifex*, a bridge-builder,

between you and your people.
and enable me to be truly "another Christ" in the world.

1116 **Prayer of Professional People**

HEAVENLY Father,
I am what is known as a member of a profession—
that is, one which required special training
as well as long years of study.
Most of all, it demanded a talent for understanding
that is your gift to me.
Let me realize that such talent is given
for the good of the whole human race,
not to enrich myself with an overabundance
of the goods of this world.

Grant that I may never abuse my office
nor the knowledge that has been given me.
May I instead so utilize my talents
that others may see in me
the reflection of your infinite perfections.
Then may they be drawn to the surpassing knowledge
of you and your beloved Son
in the unity of the Holy Spirit.

1117 **Prayer of Religious**

LORD Jesus,
I thank you with all my heart
for the privilege of serving you in the religious life.
Let me be convinced that this is the ideal way
in which I can live life to the full.
By taking the vow of poverty,
I did not so much give up all things;
rather I have gained the power to use all things
in your service.

By taking the vow of chastity
I did not so much give up my sexual side
or the ability to love;
rather I am enabled to love you without limit
and all people in you.
By taking the vow of obedience,
binding myself to the will of legitimate authority,
I did not so much give up my own fulfillment;
rather I became free to use my God-given gifts
in ways that ensure my truest self-fulfillment.
In summoning me to be truly Christian,
you have called me to be truly human
and totally involved in building your kingdom on earth.

1118   **Prayer of Scholars**

HEAVENLY Father,
    as we give ourselves to the study
of the various intellectual disciplines
and cultivate the arts,
make us realize that we can do very much
to elevate the human family
to a more sublime understanding
of truth, goodness, and beauty
and to the formation of considered opinions
that will have universal value.
Thus, humankind will be more clearly enlightened
by that marvelous Wisdom
which was before you for all eternity.

Grant that we may be less subjected to material things
and so be drawn more easily
to the worship and contemplation of you, our Creator.
By the impulse of your grace
make us disposed to acknowledge the Word of God,
who before becoming flesh—
in order to save all and sum up all in himself—

was already in the world
as the true Light that enlightens every person.

1119 Prayer of Shut-Ins

DEAR Lord,
because of my difficulty in getting around
I am no longer able to go wherever I please
and am at the mercy of others to be taken out of this
    house.
Let me not withdraw from the outside world
but continue to be interested in it.
For you are there as well as here with me;
you are everywhere in this magnificent world you made.

Enable me to realize that all the different stages of life
are a gift from you;
and each age has its own rewards
as well as its problems.
Let me thank you for each new day's life
and use that day to grow in grace
and in the knowledge and love of you.
Help me when I am tired
and grant me the strength to go on.
And at the end of my journey through life
let me see your glory in heaven.

1120 Prayer of Single People

HEAVENLY Father,
after much prayer and reflection
it is my belief
that I can best serve you in the single state.
Let me be true to my vocation to this life
and never do anything to sully it.
As I freely give up the benefits of married life,

I am aware that I also give up its difficulties
and receive in turn the benefits of the single state.
Enable me to appreciate the freedom at my disposal—
from cares and concerns of spouses and children,
from a highly structured life-style,
and from the legitimate demands of family members.

Help me to make good use
of the added time I have available.
Inspire me to give of myself to others,
to be an example to my married friends
and a comfort to my single friends.
May I ever realize that whether single or married
our one concern should be to serve you each day
and to serve others for your sake.
Grant that I may be so attached to you
that I may never feel lonely in my chosen state.

1121 Prayer of Spouses for One Another

L ORD,
bless this dear person
whom you have chosen to be my spouse.
Make his/her life long and blessed.
May I also become a great blessing to him/her,
a sharer in all his/her sufferings and sorrows,
and a meet helper in all his/her changes and vagaries
in this life.
Make me lovable forever in his/her eyes
and forever dear to him/her.
Keep me from all unreasonableness of passion and
    humor.
Make me humble and giving,
strong, dedicated, appreciative, prudent, and under-
    standing.

May we ever take delight in each other,
according to your blessed Word,
both sharing in your divine love.

1122 **Prayer of Students**

FATHER of Light and Wisdom,
thank you for giving me
a mind that can know
and a heart that can love.
Help me to keep learning every day of my life—
no matter what the subject may be.
Let me be convinced that all knowledge leads to you
and let me know how to find you and love you
in all the things you have made.

Encourage me when the studies are difficult
and when I am tempted to give up.
Enlighten me when my brain is slow
and help me to grasp the truth held out to me.
Grant me the grace to put my knowledge to use
in building the kingdom of God on earth
so that I may enter the Kingdom of God in heaven.

1123 **Prayer of Teachers**

LORD Jesus Christ,
imbue me with the knowledge
of both secular and religious subjects
that is necessary to my task on earth.
Let me be equipped with suitable qualifications
and also with a pedagogical skill
that is in harmony with the discoveries
of the contemporary world.

Help me to be closely united with my students
by the bond of love,
and work in partnership with their parents
to stimulate the students to act for themselves.
Even after their graduation
let me continue to assist them
with advice and friendship.

Bestow on me an apostolic spirit
to bear witness,
both by life and by instruction,
to the unique Teacher—
you, Jesus Christ.

1124   Prayer of Travelers

HEAVENLY Father,
I am presently embarked on a journey
in pursuit of some good.
Grant that I may travel in safety,
without undue disturbance or worry,
and ultimately attain the goal I seek.

Let me also keep in mind
that I am on another and more important journey—
through life.
Keep me ever safe and close to you
as I travel the sometimes hazardous road
toward your kingdom in heaven.

Enable me to follow the guidelines
given us by your Son Jesus
so that I may arrive safely at my eternal destination
with you in heaven.

1125   **Prayer of the Unemployed**

DEAR Lord Jesus Christ,
    you wanted all who are weary
to come to you for support.
Lord, I am worn out
by my inability to find wage-earning work.
Day after day, my worry and fear grows
as the rejections of my applications mount.
I am able and willing to work—
but I cannot find a worthwhile job.
Please help me to obtain one soon
so that I can support myself and my family
in a decent way.

However, if it is your will that I wait longer,
enable me to worry less
and to be able to take advantage of the time available
to get closer to you.
Let me realize that there are other ways
to bring about your kingdom on earth
besides salaried work.
Help me to make use of them for the time being
so that I may continue to grow as a person
for your greater glory.

1126   **Prayer of Widows and Widowers**

LORD Jesus Christ,
    during your earthly life you showed compassion
on those who had lost a loved one.
Turn your compassionate eyes on me
in my sorrow over the loss of my life's partner.
Take him/her into your heavenly kingdom
as a reward for his/her earthly service.

Help me to cope with my loss
by relying on you even more than before.
Teach me to adapt to the new conditions of my life
and to continue doing your will as I see it.
Enable me to avoid withdrawing from life
and make me give myself to others more readily,
so that I may continue to live in your grace
and to do the task that you have laid out for me.

1127   Prayer of Workers

O LORD, our Creator,
   you imposed a duty on all human beings
to work together to build up the world.
Help us to develop the earth
by the work of our hands
and with the aid of technology
in order that it may bear fruit
and become a dwelling worthy of the whole human
   family.

When we do this
or consciously take part in the life of social groups,
we are carrying out your plan
manifested at the beginning of time
that we should subdue the earth,
perfect creation,
and develop ourselves.
Let us realize that
we are also obeying Christ's command
to place ourselves at the service of others
in bringing forth a more human world,
through your Son Jesus Christ
in the unity of the Holy Spirit.

1128 **Prayer of the Young**

L ORD Jesus,
you always showed great love for the young
and the Gospels are filled with incidents about the
young—
children in general and the centurion's son,
the rich young man and Jairus' daughter.

Please pour down your grace to help me
in my growing and formative years.
Enable me to take advantage of all the good things
while avoiding the many pitfalls
of this age.

Grant that I may follow the example of youthful Saints
in remaining devoted to you.
At the same time, let me grow into the adult
that you want me to be,
so that I may carry out my vocation in life
for the good of myself and others
as well as for your honor and glory.

PRAY ALWAYS — IN ANY STATE OF MIND

States of mind provide opportunities for prayer that
are ever fresh. Learning to pray in accord with our
states of mind will give us an inexhaustible source
for prayers and help us stay united to God.

B) DIFFERENT STATES OF MIND

A STATE of mind is something that is always with us as we go through life. At every moment we are in one state of mind or other by the simple nature of being human. This section is intended to show how we can pray in accord with the particular state of mind that may be ours at any given time.

Naturally, the more negative states of mind lend themselves more easily to prayer—for we know that we need help to get out of them. The value of such prayer is that it places us in contact with our God and pulls us out of ourselves—even if only for a few moments. At the same time, it obtains aid for us in a particular and difficult time of our daily schedule. Finally, it sometimes dissipates the negative state of mind at once.

Positive states of mind are also represented in the prayers given below—times of gratitude, joy, mystical insight, serenity, and success. The value of such prayer is that it prevents us from forgetting God when things are going well and reminds us that all we have is only important insofar as God is part of the picture. It keeps us ever aware of our ultimate goal.

Needless to say, many other states of mind could have been represented by the prayers. The ones included herein have been chosen because of their more or less universal appeal. They can act as fitting models for the composition of prayers for other states and they can get us in the habit of praying in any state of mind throughout our lives.

1129 **Prayer in Time of Anger**

LORD Jesus,
     there is anger in my heart
and I cannot root it out.
I know that I should calm down
and offer the hurt and disappointment to you
but my emotion is running away with me.
Help me to overcome this weakness
and give me peace of heart as well as mind.
Let me learn from this experience
and grow into a better human being.

1130 **Prayer in Time of Aridity**

HEAVENLY Father,
     I am enmeshed in a time of spiritual aridity.
You seem so far removed from me
and I cannot even pray.
I am deprived of all sensible consolations
which facilitate prayer and the practice of the virtues.
Yet I want to pray
and I want to remain close to you.

Let me realize the truth of the well-known axiom:
when we think God is furthest away from us
that is when he is closest to us.
Make me increase my efforts at prayer
even if I feel they are useless.
Keep me from being discouraged
and help me remain united with you.
Grant that I may regain my love for prayer
and grow in my relationship with you,
your Son Jesus,
and the Holy Spirit.

1131 **Prayer in a Bad Mood**

HEAVENLY Father,
   I awoke this morning in a bad mood
and I have been unable to shake it so far.
Everything bothers me
and everyone rubs me the wrong way.
I just cannot seem to get my true bearings.
Help me to think of your salvation—
your countless gifts and overwhelming love for me.

Let me relax and forget life's cares
by placing myself wholly in your hands.
Grant that this mood will soon pass
and I will be able to bask in your love
and communicate it to others.

1132 **Prayer in Time of Change**

ETERNAL and ever-living God,
   I am involved in a major change in my life
and it is quite unsettling.
I know that for us creatures
change is an indication of life,
but I still find it hard to accept.

Enable me to see your hand in it,
subtly bringing about your plan for me
and enabling me to come closer to you.
Make me appreciate the many good aspects of change
and learn to live with the bad aspects.
Teach me to be pliable and adaptable to any change,
fully aware that once change stops for me
I will no longer be alive on this earth.

1133   Prayer in Time of Controversy

LORD Jesus Christ,
I am involved in a bitter controversy
in which it is very difficult to tell who is right
and who is wrong.
I cannot understand why these things take place
among people who are trying to live Christian lives,
and I wish I were not involved in it.

Let me realize that controversy is a fact of life
and that even your life was filled with it.
Help me to accept whatever comes in a spirit of resignation
and teach me to be better from this experience.
Grant that I may resolve the controversy
in a Christian manner
and lead others to you because of it.

1134   Prayer in Time of Criticism

HEAVENLY Father,
I am the butt of severe criticism
on the part of others
and I do not know how to react to it.
Help me to know what to do
and to carry it out without fear or hesitation.
Let me fear nothing except to be faithless to you
while avoiding bitterness, defensiveness, or retaliation.

Grant that I may have the moral strength
to keep my poise and my faith in myself
because they are founded on you.
If I deserve the criticism, let me realize it
so that I may change my ways.
If I do not deserve it,

let me be gracious in being vindicated,
in imitation of your Son, our Lord Jesus Christ.

1135   **Prayer in Time of Decision**

LORD God, King of heaven and earth,
    I am facing a difficult decision in my life
and I do not know what road to take.
You have given me the awesome power to choose freely
as well as the intelligence to choose wisely.
Inspire me to make the right decision
no matter what it may be.

Let me carefully weigh the reasons on all sides
from a human point of view
and then rely on your grace for divine help.
When the decision has been reached,
let me not look back,
in the firm knowledge that I have done my part
and have made a right decision in your eyes.

1136   **Prayer in Time of Despair**

HEAVENLY Father,
    I know I am close to despair.
I feel so tempted to give up,
to withdraw from life and religion
and let the world simply carry me along.
Everything seems so meaningless
and nothing appeals to my better instincts.
Help me to remember that Jesus gave meaning
to everything in the world.

Let me bank on that fact
and get over this time of despair,
to really believe in the depths of my being

that there is a reason for living.
Show me the reason for my life
and tell me what I must do.
Bring home to me that I am never alone,
but that you are with me even in the depths of despair.
Remind me that no matter what I may endure now
an unending joy awaits me in the future
if I but cling tightly to you
and your Son Jesus in the unity of the Spirit.

1137   **Prayer in Time of Doubt**

L ORD Jesus,
I believe that you are the Son of God
and the Savior of the world.
Sometimes doubts assail me,
making me confused and frightened.
I know that this is because we still walk
in the shadows of faith while on earth,
relying on the testimony of those who have seen and
    believed.
But I am still affected to some extent
and somewhat shaken by such doubts.

Make me realize that our doubts are the price
which we have to pay
for the fulfillment of the universe in Christ
and the very condition of that fulfillment.
We must be prepared to press on to the end
along a road on which each step makes us more certain,
toward horizons that are ever more shrouded in mists.
All the while we bring forth fruits worthy of our new life
such as charity, joy, and service of others.
In so doing we ourselves become for others
living signs of the power of Christ's resurrection
which the Holy Spirit sets in motion in the Church.

1138 **Prayer before Driving**

DEAR Lord,
   I am about to enter once again
into one of the amazing inventions of the human mind,
which you endowed with so much intelligence.
Yet like all human inventions and advancement
it carries with it a negative side—
the risk of injury and even death
if it is misused whether deliberately or accidentally.

Help me to realize the responsibility that is mine
when I climb behind the wheel.
Let me drive defensively,
obeying the rules with care and alacrity
and avoiding the slightest act of mindlessness.
Curb my anger when I am put in danger
by the carelessness of other drivers
and help me to maintain my balance.
Make my reflexes quick and my sight keen
so that I may react to any situation that may arise
and bring me safely (with my passengers) to my destination.

1139 **Prayer in Time of Economic Hardship**

HEAVENLY Father,
   it is symptomatic of our life today
that economics plays a large part in it.
People labor zealously for a wage
so that they can acquire the needs of life
for themselves and their families.
They also work for the so-called luxuries of life,
for the opportunity to have more leisure
to develop themselves in more ways,
and to keep up with their particular state of life.

Right now I find myself in a bad economic condition.
I just cannot seem to make enough money
to take care of myself and my family.
Please help me in this dangerous situation.
Teach me to live within my means
while at the same time striving to increase those means.
Let me never lose heart but continue to work on.
Most of all, inspire me to seek first your kingdom
in the knowledge that everything else will be given me
together with it.

1140   **Prayer in Time of Failure**

L ORD Jesus Christ,
    I have just experienced the misfortune
of failing in some enterprise,
and I am overwhelmed by it.
Please grant me your grace in this difficult time.
Let me realize that no one who uses all his talents
ever fails in your eyes.

In addition, assist me to see that you utilize our failures
to make us grow into better persons
and more devoted followers of you.
Make me recall that everything good comes from you,
indicating that I must work
as if everything depended on me
but pray as if it all depended on you.
Then if failure comes, there is a reason for it.
Help me to seek and find that reason
and live in accord with it.

1141   **Prayer of a Grateful Heart**

A LMIGHTY and provident Father,
    I thank you from the bottom of my heart
for this wonderful thing that has happened to me

I know it is the result of your goodness toward me
and I pray that I may accept it as I should.
In a world filled with many sufferings and sad occasions
I am fortunate to be blessed in this way.
I offer you my sincere gratitude
and promise to remain united with you
in good times and in bad.

1142   **Prayer in Time of Homesickness**

LORD Jesus Christ,
I am far from home and family today
and afflicted with a bad case of homesickness.
Even though it is important and right for me to be away,
I miss my loved ones and my familiar surroundings.
Help me to realize that true Christians are never alone—
their spiritual family is ever with them:
you, the Father, and the Holy Spirit.
Let me dedicate myself anew to you today
thus overcoming this very human feeling within me.
Then help me to return home
with greater appreciation for my family
and for the things that I have from you.

1143   **Prayer in Time of Irritation**

HEAVENLY Father,
I am filled with irritation
over some occurrences that have taken place,
and it has led to a general impatience with things.
I get very unhappy with my lot
and with those closest to me.
Help me to overcome this feeling
and to cultivate a sense of patience.

Restore to me a sense of prayer
and of total confidence in you,

and enable me to accept whatever comes
with true Christian equanimity.
For after this life
you have reserved for your children
a joy of unimaginable proportions.

1144   Prayer in Time of Jealousy

LORD Jesus Christ,
    I am caught in a web of jealousy
that stays with me night and day.
Help me to put away from me this evil
which your Word tells us rots bones (Prov 14:30)
and even shortens lives (Sir 30:24).
Bring home to me the further evils
to which it leads if left unchecked:
slander, calumny, hatred,
damaged relations, persecutions, and worse things.

Let me dwell constantly on the motives for loving others
rather than being jealous of them.
Remind me of the fleeting character
of all life's attachments and successes
and of the fact that our true happiness
lies in being united closely with you
and with all others in you.

1145   Prayer in Time of Joy

HEAVENLY Father,
    I am overcome with joy at this moment
because of the happy events that have occurred
or simply because of the way you have made us.
The world seems such a glorious place to me
and all the cares of life seem far away.
Thank you for allowing such moments in our lives
and so giving us a glimpse of eternity.

I know that such a grand feeling is sure to pass
and that I will be once again confronted
with the problems and worries of daily life.
Let me realize that all true joy never fades,
for it is the gift of your Spirit
made possible by the saving action of your Son Jesus.
Keep me in your grace
so that I may never lose that inner virtue of joy
even when the outward experience of joy has passed
    away.

1146   **Prayer in Time of Loneliness**

L ORD Jesus Christ,
   I am assailed by a spell of loneliness.
All of a sudden it is as if I am totally alone,
without anyone in the world.
It is a terrifying feeling, Lord;
help me to overcome it.
Let me realize that I am never really alone
if I am united with you—
for you are always with me.

At the same time, remind me that I also have need of
    others,
for I am a social being.
And there are many people whom you have brought into
    my life
to help me on my way to eternity.
Teach me to see that we need one another
if we are to make a go of our lives
and complete the tasks you have given us.

1147   **Prayer for a Loving Attitude**

L ORD Jesus Christ,
   you gave your life out of love for all people

and you encouraged your followers to do good to others.
Over the years many Christians have found this difficult
and I am no exception.
I try, but it is so hard
to have a loving attitude toward all—
and then I feel hypocritical in claiming to follow you.

Help me, dear Lord, to really believe
that Christian love is the greatest energy in the world.
Let me see that this is not an emotion
but a central attitude of one's being—
an attitude of service for others in your Name.
It is the result of your grace,
and prompts us to will only good things for others
as images of God.
Grant that I may always strive to attain this attitude
and so live up to the noble vocation to which I am called

1148 Prayer in Time of Mystical Insight

LORD Jesus Christ,
every once in a while you grant me the great gift
of an inspiring mystical insight
into some aspect of the Christian Faith.
It may happen in church or riding a bus,
walking down the street or sitting at home.
Invariably, it fills me with joy
at the thought of your infinite love for me.

Thank you, dear Lord, for creating me,
redeeming me, and making me a Christian.

1149 Prayer in Time of Natural Disaster

HEAVENLY Father,
a catastrophe happened today
and it has saddened me greatly.

Such evil presents a problem for all people
and I beg you to help me accept it
in the best way that I can.

I know that growth takes place only through risk
and it necessarily entails evils of some kind.
Let me dwell on the good you reserve for us
which will more than make up for the evil we suffer here.
Help me to place myself in your hands
and to accept whatever evils may come
in the firm knowledge that they will lead me
more surely to you.

1150 Prayer for a Sense of Humor

LORD Jesus Christ,
for some reason many Christians seem to lack
a sense of humor.
They become so bogged down in the gravity of things
that they are perpetually tense and serious-minded.
I ask today that I may cultivate a sense of humor
and use it to help others as well as myself.
Let me realize that humor is also a creation of yours
and that a smile is one of the greatest blessings of life.
Teach me to stress the positive side of life
and develop a fine sense of humor.

1151 Prayer in Time of Serenity

ETERNAL Father,
it isn't often but once in a while
I experience a highly refined sense of serenity.
At such times I feel very close to you,
happy with my life
and ready to do anything asked of me.
I realize that these are moments of sensible consolation
and such consolation is never permanent—
still it is very nice to experience.

Grant me the grace to remain just as attached to you
when I am deprived of consolation.
Let me learn to concentrate on what is important
in my relationship with you,
so that I may bear witness to you
in every circumstance of my life.

1152 Prayer in Time of Sleeplessness

LORD Jesus Christ,
during your earthly sojourn
you went sleepless at times
and spent whole nights in prayer.
But there were many other times when you slept.
I cannot seem to get to sleep these nights
and I cannot even pray.

Please help me cure this sickness, Lord,
for I desperately need sleep to do my work
and to behave as a pleasant human being
as well as to act in a Christian manner.
Enable me to get a good night's sleep,
or at least to spend my time in prayer with you.

1153 Prayer in Time of Success

HEAVENLY Father,
you have been gracious enough
to allow me to score a great success.
I humbly thank you for your help
and I hope that I will continue to receive it.
Let me never forget that without you
I would never have been able to achieve anything.
True, I made use of my talents
but they were given to me by you,
and so was the drive that impelled me to use them.

May I always strive to utilize all my talents
to the very best of my ability—
whether I achieve success or not.
For I will in this way be achieving the goal
that you have set out for me in your wisdom
and becoming the person that you want me to be.

1154   Prayer for the Virtue of Temperance

LORD Jesus Christ,
    I have the tendency to over-do almost anything.
When I am involved in something I plunge into it
so that I am oblivious of everything else.
Give me a spirit of temperance
to maintain my balance in all things—
whether it be sleeping, thinking, or working,
playing, visiting, or partying.
Let me realize that whatever I do
I should do for you—and I should do it in moderation!

1155   Prayer in Time of Weariness

HEAVENLY Father,
    I am overcome with weariness and fatigue
both of body and of spirit.
I have been working doubly hard for a long time
and I am beginning to feel the effects.
Let me take this as a sign from myself
that I must slow down,
cut down on pet projects
and eliminate superfluous details.

Help me not to wait till it is too late.
Teach me how to continue to serve you
with a less hectic schedule
and a more sheltered life.

RECOURSE TO PRAYER IN SICKNESS
AND SUFFERING

When all else fails us, we can always count on prayer. For we know that God wants to help us and will always alleviate spiritual evil while sometimes also eliminating material evils. All we need do is ask with faith.

C) IN TIME OF SICKNESS AND SUFFERING

CHRISTIANS *have always regarded sickness and suffering as one of the ways in which we can best imitate our Lord Jesus Christ (see pp. 205-206). When sickness strikes, it uproots us from our everyday life and our customary work schedule and makes us experience solitude and dependence on others as well as the fragile character of life. We are called to live this event too in faith.*

While we struggle against the evil to conquer it, our Lord calls us to join our sufferings with his own in order to collaborate with him on our salvation. Many times he does not free us from the sickness but he does something greater. He gives meaning to suffering and he opens our hearts to hope.

In order to unite themselves with Christ the sick have recourse to reception of the Sacraments (Anointing of the Sick, Penance, and the Eucharist) as well as private prayer. At such times it is difficult to pray, however. That is the reason why this section has been included herein. It provides prayers and ideas for prayers that can be said by the sick persons themselves.

Other prayers of this kind will be found in the section on the Anointing of the Sick (pp. 205-213). The ones found herein are more personal in the hope that they will inspire the sick to make good use of their temporary withdrawal from ordinary life, after the manner of Ignatius Loyola who made use of sickness to change his life and get closer to God, and Margaret of Cortona who made use of suffering to do the same.

869

1156 **Prayer of Resignation in Suffering**

MERCIFUL Lord of life,
   I lift up my heart to you in my suffering
and ask for your comforting help.
I know that you would withhold the thorns of this life
if I could attain eternal life without them.
So I throw myself on your mercy,
resigning myself to this suffering.
Grant me the grace to bear it
and to offer it in union with your sufferings.
No matter what suffering may come my way,
let me always trust in you.

1157 **Prayer to Accept Suffering**

O MY Lord Jesus Christ,
   I believe . . . that nothing great is done
without suffering, without humiliation,
and that all things are possible by means of it.
I believe, O my God,
that poverty is better than riches,
pain better than pleasure,
obscurity and contempt than name,
and ignominy and reproach than honor. . . .

O my dear Lord,
though I am so very weak
that I am not fit to ask for suffering as a gift,
and have not strength to do so,
at least I would beg of your grace
to meet suffering well,
when you in your wisdom lay it upon me.

Cardinal Newman

1158 **Prayer of Offering of Suffering**

HEAVENLY Father,
   you created me

and most lovingly care for me.
I accept all my sufferings most willingly,
and as a truly obedient child I resign myself
to your holy will.
Grant me the strength to accept generously
your loving visitation,
and never let me grieve your faithful heart
by giving in to impatience and discouragement.
I offer you all my pains;
and in order that they may be acceptable to you
and fruitful for my salvation
I unite them with the most bitter pains
of your beloved Son Jesus.

1159 Another Prayer of Offering of Suffering

MY DIVINE Savior, Jesus,
you loved me to such a degree
as to suffer and die for my salvation.
Through the love I have for you,
I most willingly offer to your honor
all that I have ever suffered in the past,
am now suffering,
or will suffer in the future.
This is the basis and motive
of the love which animates me.
Your love enables me to suffer with joy.
I will to suffer because you suffered
and because you want me to suffer,
for I love you more than myself.   St. Gertrude

1160 Prayer to Suffer in Union with Jesus

DEAR Jesus,
for love of you
I desire to suffer all things,

because for love of me
you endured such cruel torments.
O my Jesus,
I unite my pains with the ones which you suffered
and I make an offering of them
to your eternal Father.
O my Jesus,
out of the abundance of your divine goodness
give me the virtues of meekness and patience,
so that I may willingly carry my cross after you.

1161 Prayer to Suffer in Silence

LORD Jesus Christ,
grant me the grace to be kind and gentle
in all the events of my life.
Let me put self aside
and think of the happiness of others.
Teach me to hide my little pains and disappointments
so that I may be the only one who suffers for them.
Let me learn from the suffering that I must endure.
May I so use it as to become
mellow rather than embittered,
patient rather than irritable,
and forgiving rather than overbearing.

1162 Prayer of Acceptance of Sickness

HEAVENLY Father,
I desire to accept this sickness from your hands
and to resign myself to your will,
whether it be for life or for death.
Help me to be faithful to my desire
and give me the courage to carry it out.

1163   **Prayer for Help in Time of Sickness**

LORD Jesus Christ,
    Incarnate Son of God,
for our salvation
you willed to be born in a stable,
to endure poverty, suffering, and sorrow
throughout your life,
and finally to experience the bitter death of the cross.

I beg you to say to your Father on my behalf:
"Father, forgive him/her."
At my death, say to me:
"This day you shall be with me in paradise."
And let me throw myself on your mercy:
"Into your hands I commend my spirit."

1164   **Prayer for the Restoration of Health**

O SACRED Heart of Jesus
    I come to ask you for the gift of restored health
that I may serve you more faithfully
and love you more sincerely than in the past.
I want to be well and strong
if it is your will
and redounds to your glory.

If on the other hand it is your will
that my sickness continue,
I want to bear it with patience.
If in your divine wisdom
I am to be restored to health and strength,
I will strive to show my gratitude
by a constant and faithful service rendered to you.

1165 **Prayer to Love God More Than Health**

ALMIGHTY God,
  you gave me health and I forgot you.
You take it away and I return to you.
How gracious you are to take away the gifts
which I allowed to come between you and me.
Take away everything that hinders my union with you.
Everything is yours—
dispense comforts, success, and health
in accord with my real good.
Take away all the things
that displace my possession of you
so that I may be wholly yours for time and eternity.

1166 **Prayer When Death Approaches**

MOST blessed and glorious Creator,
  you have nourished me all my life
and redeemed me from all evil.
It is your gracious will
to take me out of this fragile life
and to wipe away all tears from my eyes
and all sorrows from my heart.
I humbly consent to your divine plan
and I cast myself into your sacred arms.
I am ready, dear Lord,
and earnestly expect and long for your good pleasure.
Come quickly and receive your servant
who trusts completely in you.

1167 **Prayer of Consolation with God's Word**

DO NOT fear nor be dismayed,
  for the Lord, your God, is with you
wherever you go. (Jos 1:9)

— The Lord is my shepherd; I shall want for nothing....
I fear no evil; for you are at my side. (Ps 23)
— The Lord is my light and my salvation;
whom should I fear?
The Lord is my life's refuge;
of whom should I be afraid? (Ps 27)
— God is our refuge and our strength,
an ever-present help in distress....
The Lord of hosts is with us;
our stronghold is the God of Jacob. (Ps 46)
— Bless the Lord, O my soul;
and forget not all his benefits;
he pardons all your iniquities,
he heals all your ills. (Ps 103)
— They carried to Jesus
all those afflicted and wracked with pain:
the possessed, the lunatics, the paralyzed.
He cured them all. (Mt 4:24)
— Come to me, all you who are weary
and find life burdensome,
and I will refresh you. (Mt 11:28)
— I am with you always,
until the end of the world. (Mt 28:20)
— I myself am the living bread come down from heaven.
If anyone eats this bread he shall live forever;
the bread I will give is my flesh,
for the life of the world. (Jn 6:51)
— I came that they might have life
and have it to the full. (Jn 10:10)
— I am the resurrection and the life:
whoever believes in me,
even though he should die, will come to life;
and whoever is alive and believes in me
will never die. (Jn 11:25f)
— Do not let your hearts be troubled.
Have faith in God and faith in me. (Jn 14:1)

PRAYER DURING HOLIDAYS AND VACATIONS

A dedicated effort to maintain an active prayer life during holidays and vacations will return huge dividends. Our prayers will make our vacations more beneficial and our holidays more meaningful.

D) HOLIDAYS AND VACATIONS

NO MATTER how it may appear at times, the life of every human being is not one long period of unremitting toil and struggle. It is interspersed by our compassionate Creator with periods of rest and recuperation. The rhythm of work-rest-sleep found in our daily experience is also found on a broader scale annually. The longer periods of rest are known as holidays and vacations.

During such times Christians usually have a golden opportunity to become refreshed for the ongoing struggle of life. They are times of new awakening, learning, travel, and leisure that restore our energies and our will to live. It is very important, therefore, that during such times we do not lose our spiritual momentum and neglect our devotional practices.

On holidays and during vacations, we should make a dedicated effort to maintain our prayer life so that we may be spiritually renewed also. Since our schedules at these times will be out of the usual and we may even be in different surroundings, we will find our prayer life difficult to maintain. However, if we set aside a few moments for reflection, we will be greatly blessed and spiritually renewed on our return to ordinary life.

The purpose of this section is to provide themes and ideas for prayers that will accord with holidays and vacations. The underlying point is that our union with the Father and Jesus in the Holy Spirit never takes a vacation. It may change direction and even experience adaptation, but it should remain ever solid and fruitful. Once again, the prayers found herein are only indicative, and can easily give rise to others that will be more in conformity with one's individual circumstances.

1168 Prayer on New Year's Day

JESUS, you are the Lord of history,
and your wonderful redemption comes to us
in a cycle of time—year after year.
Now another year has passed
and a new one is ready to begin.
A backward glance tells us that last year
had its good points as well as its bad.

May the new year hold many more good things
in store for me
and make me a better person:
kinder and more willing to help,
more thoughtful and more loving.
May I fulfill my allotted task in life
and come closer to you
while looking forward to an eternity with you.
Thank you, Lord, for this extended time
that you so graciously allow me
on my journey toward your heavenly kingdom.

1169 Prayer on Lincoln's Birthday

HEAVENLY Father,
today is the birthday of President Lincoln,
a man who was your chosen instrument
in the liberation of the black people.
Like Cyrus of old, Lincoln did not know
that your Spirit was working through him,
yet he cooperated with your grace
and achieved the task you set for him.

Teach me to see that same Spirit's hand working
in any human person, instrument, or experience,
and to be able to use any event to work with you.
Let me strive to eliminate prejudice in myself

and in my circle of friends and acquaintances.
But let me insure that this will be done—
in Lincoln's beautiful phrase—
with malice toward none
and with charity for all.

1170 Prayer on St. Valentine's Day

HEAVENLY Father,
you are known as the God of Love,
and today we are celebrating St. Valentine—
one of the human patrons of love.
Teach me how to make use of the gift of love
that you have given us,
and how to combine it with the supernatural virtue
that you infuse into us.
Let me love you above all
and others in and for you.

Make me faithful to my loved ones,
loyal, dedicated, compassionate, and concerned.
Let me overlook their human failings
and dwell on their good points.
Enable me to love them
not so much for what they can do for me
but for what I can do for them.

1171 Prayer on Washington's Birthday

DEAR Jesus,
today we celebrate the birthday
of the "Father of our country."
Amid many dangers and with much help,
this man forged a motley group into a free people
and left us a legacy of truthfulness.

Help me to realize that I am part of another people,
which you purchased by your blood:
a chosen race, a royal priesthood, a holy nation,
a people of God.
Keep me faithful to this image
and make me relish the truth
after the example of Washington
and even more after your own example,
for you said that "the truth will make you free."

1172   Prayer on Martin Luther King Day

HEAVENLY Father,
today we honor the memory of a Christian minister
who put his Faith into practice
for the good of an oppressed people.
He followed your evangelical counsel of non-violence
to overturn the discriminatory practices
of the ignorant and the misguided.

Teach me to put my Christianity into practice
in the cause of right wherever it may be
and for the freedom of blacks and other minorities.
Let me do what I can to insure that this country,
based on Christian principles,
will remain true to these principles and really be
"the land of the free and the home of the brave."

1173   Prayer on Mother's Day

HEAVENLY Father,
you have been pleased to give all human beings
the joy of having a mother,
one who works with you to give them life
and bring them to human adulthood.

You have given followers of your Son
the added joy of a Christian mother,
who works with you to give supernatural life to a child
and to bring up that child to Christian adulthood.

Over the centuries there have been countless such mothers—
heroic, courageous, loving, dedicated, and unconquerable.
They have given us the Christian Ages and Christian
Saints
and in the final analysis the Christian Faith.
Without them, there would be no Church,
no religious vocation, and no Christian influence in the
world.
Most of these mothers are unsung in the eyes of the
world;
they must be content with little things:
a smile, a thank you, and a token remembrance.

In your eyes, however, they are of inestimable worth.
Your Word in the Bible uses a mother's love
to describe your overwhelming love for your people,
and Jesus uses the image of a mother bird
to indicate his love for his people.
Most of all, when he wants to convey an idea
of the joy of those in heaven
he does so by using the image of a mother's pure joy
in bringing a child into the world.

Dear Lord,
let me honor my mother if she is living
and remember her in prayer if she is dead.
Pour down your grace on her and on all mothers
on this day dedicated to them.

1174 Prayer on Memorial Day

LORD Jesus Christ,
today we honor the memory of those men and women
who have given their lives for their compatriots
in the cause of freedom.
They have worked, fought, and died
for the heritage of freedom, brotherhood, and honor
that they have passed on to us.

Help us to recall that you yourself
gave up your life for all human beings
in the cause of true freedom—
to save us from self-love and sin.
Teach us the true meaning of peace and freedom,
that the real battle must always take place in ourselves
before it will be won in families and nations.
Make us keep your memory in our Eucharistic celebrations
and pray for the peace and freedom of the whole world.

1175 Prayer on Father's Day

HEAVENLY Father,
you have given us the wonderful gift of a father
after your example.
Down through the ages fathers have cared for their children
and most of them have given themselves unstintingly
for their families.
I thank you for my father:
even though he may not agree completely
with my outlook and way of life,
I know that he is genuinely concerned about me.
Keep him well in body and soul

and if he has already come to you
grant him eternal happiness.

Dear Lord,
inspire all fathers to have some of the virtues
toward their children
that you have toward us.
May they watch over their children,
show kindness in their failings,
illumine their ignorance,
and encourage them in their just concerns,
thus leading them to a true Christian adulthood.

1176 Prayer on a National Holiday

HEAVENLY Father,
you created me and made me
a citizen of this country
by birth (or by naturalization).
Let me take part in this holiday
with joy and gratitude.
As I am renewed in mind and body,
may I also be refreshed in spirit.
Make me take this occasion
to rededicate myself to my country
to lovingly uphold its legitimate traditions,
readily obey its decent laws,
and show genuine concern for its people.
At the same time, may I bear uncompromising witness
of my Christian faith to my fellow citizens
and to those who may not be followers of Jesus,

1177 Prayer on Independence Day

HEAVENLY Father,
like the Israelites of old, our ancestors in the faith,
our country has struggled long and hard to be free

and to keep its freedom as a nation.
It too has met with success and failure
in trying to achieve its goals.
Let me take this holiday celebration
to ponder the strengths and weaknesses of my country.
Make me resolve always to do my part to keep it strong
and strive constantly to eliminate its weaknesses:
in the social, political, economic, and religious field.

Teach me to meditate on the teachings of your Son
who brought us a message of peace and freedom
and instructed us to live as brothers and sisters.
His message took form in the vision of our founders
as they fashioned a nation
where people might live as one.
May this message live on in our midst
as a task for people today
and a promise for tomorrow.
Thank you for your past blessings
and for all that, with your help, we will achieve.

1178   Prayer during Vacation Time

HEAVENLY Father,
you have mercifully allowed human beings to have
periods of rest and recuperation
on our long journey through life.
This is my extended period of rest this year—
my vacation from the usual cares of everyday life
and my time to be renewed—
physically, mentally, and spiritually.

Grant that this vacation will bring me
a new awareness of the good things in life,
increased knowledge of your wondrously versatile cre-
    ativity,
delightful travel through fascinating places,

and genuine leisure facilitating revitalization.
Let me be ever mindful of you
and my true goals in life.
And bring me back to carry out my daily tasks
with cheerfulness and goodwill,
and to the best of my strength and ability.

1179   **Prayer on Labor Day**

L ORD Jesus Christ,
    it is the Christian religion based on your teachings
that freed work from its degrading character
and made it into something noble—
so much so that it has become associated
with the so-called "work-ethic,"
symbolized by St. Paul's practical principle:
"If anyone will not work, let him not eat!"
Let me realize that Christians work
in imitation of you and the Father
in accord with your words:
"My Father has been working till now
and I work."

By work we build up the world,
as mentioned by the lines of a classic poem:
"God bless the noble working men
who rear the cities of the plain,
who dig the mines and build the ships,
and drive the commerce of the main.
God bless them! for their swarthy hands
have wrought the glory of our lands."

Let me also understand that work is good
because it builds up your Body in the world
until your second coming in glory.
Thus all human beings are called to work
no matter what type it may be—

from the homemaker to the secretary,
the teacher to the ditch-digger.
And, in reality, there is no difference to the worker—
all work is hard and yet fulfilling,
a burden but at the same time a psychological necessity.
Most of all let me realize that no matter what work I do,
if I fail to do it,
no one else will—
and there will be a setback in building up your Body.

1180   **Prayer on Columbus Day**

G OD of love and majesty,
   today we honor a brave explorer
who followed your inspirations
and opened up a whole new world for all people.
He combined human vision with divine faith,
human daring with Christian hope.
Grant me the grace to share in the virtues of Columbus
just as I share in the benefits of his journey
by living in the land he discovered.
In my own small way let me also conquer new worlds
by leading others to the knowledge of you
through a genuine Christian witness.
just as I share in the benefits of his journey

1181   **Prayer on Election Day**

H EAVENLY Father,
   in your infinite wisdom
you gave human beings the power
to govern themselves in this world.
Those living in a democracy are fortunate
to have the privilege of self-determination
through regular election of leaders.
Help me to take full advantage of this privilege

and never fail to cast my vote
for the best qualified person,
remembering that every vote counts.

Let me diligently analyze the issues and candidates
and then give my vote to the one
who is most in accord with Christian principles,
judging not so much by public utterances of candidates
but by their professional performances in office.

Help me to make the right choices
as I go to the polls today,
and send forth your Spirit
to enlighten and guide those who are elected.

1182   **Prayer on Veterans Day**

DEAR Lord Jesus Christ,
    those whom we honor today
are examples of your words:
"Greater love than this no one has:
that he lay down his life for his friends."
They gave up their lives in the defense of freedom
for their loved ones and their country.

Teach me to appreciate the virtue of patriotism—
a true and Christian love of country.
Let me love my country not to follow it blindly
but to make it the land of goodness
that it should be.
Let my patriotism be such
that it will not exclude the other nations of the world
but include them in a powerful love of country
that has room for all others too.

1183   **Prayer on Thanksgiving Day**

HEAVENLY Father,
   this is the day set aside to give you thanks
for your surpassing goodness to human beings.
You have created us in your own image
and set us over your wonderful creation.
You chose a people to be your own
and to carry your message of salvation to all people.
You carried out your redemption in Jesus your Son,
and his saving fruits are passed on to every generation
to all who believe that by his death and resurrection
Jesus has given them a new freedom in his Spirit.
Let me give you proper thanks for your blessings—
those I am aware of
as well as those that I habitually take for granted.
And let me learn to use them according to your will.

10

PRAYERS
BASED ON
VARIOUS
RELATIONSHIPS

10

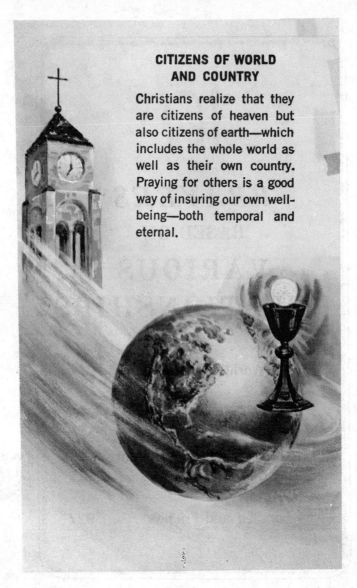

CITIZENS OF WORLD AND COUNTRY

Christians realize that they are citizens of heaven but also citizens of earth—which includes the whole world as well as their own country. Praying for others is a good way of insuring our own well-being—both temporal and eternal.

A) FOR WORLD AND COUNTRY

W E LIVE in an age when the world has become a "global village." As soon as something happens anywhere in the world, it is made known to us through the magic of modern mass communications. Thus our awareness of others is heightened and all human beings are brought closer together.

It is only natural, then, for contemporary Christians to have a genuine interest in all that goes on daily throughout the world. This gives them a better opportunity than their ancestors for putting Christ's command of love into practice—for they have not a few but vast numbers of people to whom they can show love. They possess a golden opportunity to "do good to all men" (Gal 6:10) through their concern and their prayers, for in a certain sense each of us is a citizen of the world.

However, this in no way lessens the attachment of Christians to their country of origin or citizenship. If anything, it solidifies and enlarges that attachment. They have a greater sense of being part of the whole human race—but a very particular part, living in a specific land with its own traditions, laws, customs, and idiosyncracies that can also be of help to others living in other lands.

Hence, Christians can legitimately pray for their country's welfare even as they pray for the welfare of all countries in the world. They can beseech God to make them good citizens of their country as well as upstanding members of the human race. For in the final analysis these two things go hand in hand. That is the whole thrust of the prayers found in this section—to foster a love for the world and for one's country.

1184   Prayer for International Organisms

HEAVENLY Father,
 you created this vast and wonderful universe,
redeemed it in the blood of your Son,
and now guide it by your Holy Spirit.
It is your will that we live as brothers and sisters,
building up the world by the marvelous powers
that you have graciously given us.

Look graciously on the representatives of the nations
who are gathered together today for the good of all.
Enlighten them to put forth wise proposals
in accord with your will.
Teach them to deliberate with honesty
and with genuine respect for one another.
Help them to make just decisions
that will redound to the peace and welfare of all nations.

1185   Prayer for Good International Relations

HEAVENLY Father,
 enlighten the minds and open the hearts
of the statesmen of this world,
that they may make good relations flourish between na-
    tions.

Keep them ever mindful of your guiding principles
to bring about true justice and peace among peoples.
Let your Spirit inspire them in their deliberations
and so lead to genuine harmony in the world.

1186 Prayer for the Full Development of All Peoples as Well as All Individuals

HEAVENLY Father,
in your goodness
you have given human beings
the capacity to better their earthly lot
even as they make their way to you for eternity.
Grant that the true progress made till now
will not stop but be intensified
and eliminate the natural evils that still exist.
Fill the material needs of all who are deprived
even of the basic necessities of life
as well as the moral needs of those steeped in pride.
Let all people be freed from misery
and find subsistence and fulfilling work.
May every human being be able to do, know, and have more
in order to attain the self-fulfillment you desire.

Inspire everyone to know higher values,
to be open to your grace and the gift of faith,
and to live in communion with you and the neighbor.
Prompt all persons to make regular use
of the means required to reach their own full development
as well as the development of others.

1187 Prayer for the Hungry

LORD Jesus Christ,
you urged us to give you food in your hunger
which is visible to us in the starving faces
of other human beings.

Let me realize that there are millions of persons—
children of the same God and our brothers and sisters—
who are dying of hunger
although they do not deserve to do so.

Do not allow me to remain indifferent
to their crying need,
or to soothe my conscience with the thought
that I cannot do anything about this evil.
Help me to do something—
no matter how small—
to alleviate their heart-rending want.
At the very least, let me pray regularly
that these poor starving people will be rewarded
for this terrible suffering they are enduring,
and be relieved of it as soon as possible.

1188   Prayer for Sufferers throughout the World

LORD Jesus Christ,
     during your life you were surrounded by suffering
and you eliminated it whenever you could.
Look down on this suffering world
and alleviate all its suffering.
Help the sick in body, especially those terminally ill,
and the sick at heart who are weary of life.
Come to the aid of those victimized by war
or by their uncaring neighbors.
Encourage those who suffer discrimination
because of race, creed, or color,
because of their poverty, ignorance, or different life-style.
Free those who are oppressed
and feed those who are hungry.
Inspire in me a firm desire to cooperate with you

in this liberation of the downtrodden.
Let me be open to others,
to love them in you
and to share with them what I am and have.

1189 Prayer in Time of Natural Disasters

HEAVENLY Father,
we come to you for comfort
as we do whenever natural disasters occur.
We know that there must be a reason for them
but we do not know what it is.
Teach us to accept them in the light of eternity
and as the by-product of a world in the making.
Help us to cooperate with you in completing the universe,
unlocking its secrets and removing its flaws
while bringing about the fulfillment
of the kingdom of your Son on earth
which is the foreshadowing of your kingdom in heaven.

1190 Prayer for Disarmament

HEAVENLY Father,
you want to save us from the age-old slavery of war.
Yet at the present time we are engaged in an arms race
that seems to be the only deterrent to war.
Inspire leaders of nations to find an alternative method
for—as the Council has said,
it is not a safe way to preserve peace.
Nor is the so-called balance that results from it
a sure and authentic peace.
Enable us to find new approaches
and to restore genuine peace based on your law
thus emancipating the world from its crushing anxiety.

1191   **Prayer for Openness to the World**

LORD Jesus Christ,
    you came into this world as a man
and took part in the customs of your day.
By so doing you showed us
that we can be fully and genuinely human
only by following you.
Help us to be open to the world
in a truly Christian manner.

Let the joys and hopes, sorrows and anxieties
of all who live in this age
be our joys and hopes, sorrows and anxieties
as your disciples.
May nothing that is really human
fail to find an echo in our hearts.
Teach me to apply your principles
to the world events that I encounter each day.
Let me never flee from this world
but bring you into it every day of my life.

1192   **Prayer for the Godless**

O ALMIGHTY God,
    you have given us faith in Christ
as a beacon to light our way
amid the darkness of the world.
Have mercy on all who have strayed
from the path of salvation
even though they may not know it.
Send your message into their hearts
and grant them the grace to receive it
with sincerity and thankfulness.

1193   **Prayer for Our Country**

H EAVENLY Father,
   you are the real foundation of nations,
raising them up to serve and care
for the people dwelling in their boundaries.
I thank you for making me a citizen of this land
of freedom and unlimited opportunity—
which are the result of its Christian base.
Send forth your Spirit to this country
and make it a source of wisdom and strength,
order and integrity throughout the world.

1194   **Prayer for Civil Authority**

L ORD Jesus Christ, King of the universe,
   look with mercy on those who rule over us.
Grant to our President and his administration
the grace to know and do your will.
Let them serve all their subjects
in truth and righteousness.
Inspire our Congressmen with the courage
to make laws for the good of all
rather than the few.
Give our Judges your Spirit of wisdom and understanding
that they may divine the truth
and impartially administer the law.
And let all the people pitch in
to make our way of government continue to work.

1195   **Prayer for the Proper Use of Creation**

ALMIGHTY God, Creator of all things,
you made this earth
with its atmosphere and its myriad living beings
in a marvelous and mind-boggling fashion
so that it could give birth and growth to humans.
You entrusted its environment and its resources to us
to be used in forging a life
that would bring us close to you
and eventually lead us to your heavenly kingdom.

Help us to use these precious resources
with wisdom and restraint,
avoiding waste, pollution, and wanton destruction.
Make us act responsibly so that those who follow us
will also be able to use the earth in your service.

1196   **Prayer for Social Justice**

HEAVENLY Father,
even in the Old Testament
as shown by those marvelous prophets Amos and Hosea
your message stressed the need for your servants
to effect social as well as individual justice in the world.
Your divine Son took the same message even further,
calling for social charity as well.
And your modern Popes have all stressed social justice
if there is to be peace among people and nations.
Grant me the grace to fight social evils and oppression
even as I struggle against evil in myself.
Make me use my freedom according as you will
in the pursuit of justice and peace
for your honor and glory.

1197 **Prayer for Social Service**

L ORD Jesus Christ,
  I know that your call never comes to me in a vacuum
but in the circumstances of my daily life.
Hence, my response cannot be given
only in the privacy of my own mind;
it must overflow into my daily life.
You call me through my family,
through my community or Church,
and through the world.

Teach me to serve others in the knowledge
that those actions of mine which advance true progress
of the Church and the world
are my way of saying yes to your call.
At the same time, let me take the opportunity
to make your Gospel known through my actions
as I work with them to build the temporal order,
directing it to you who are its final goal.

1198 **Prayer for the Advancement of Learning**

H EAVENLY Father,
  your knowledge is infinite
and you have given human beings a wonderful capacity
to learn on every level:
practical, social, cultural, intellectual, and so on.
Bless all institutions of learning
and all teachers as well as all students.
Grant to them all as well as to me
a dedication to true knowledge,
a true love of learning,
and a capacity to continue to learn throughout life,

until they arrive at the knowledge of you,
and your Son, Jesus, in the unity of the Holy Spirit.

1199   Prayer for the Proper Use
of the Means of Communication

HEAVENLY Father,
enable us to make proper use
of the marvelous means of communication
that are constantly being placed at our disposal
so that we will experience no harm,
and, like salt and light,
will give savor to the earth
and brighten the world.

May all men and women of good will
also strive to use them
solely for the good of society
whose fate depends more and more on their proper use.
Grant that, as was the case with ancient works of art,
these discoveries may serve to glorify
the Name of the Lord,
in accord with the words of the Apostle:
"Jesus Christ, yesterday and today,
and the same forever!"

1200   Prayer for Industry

O GOD,
you have called us to cooperate by our daily work
in the immense plan of your creation.
Give all of us a pride in what we do
and a just return for our labor.

Enable us to expand our activity with a Christian spirit,
in the awareness that every person is our brother or sister.
Grant that in the common effort
to build a more just and faithful world
every person may find a place suited to his dignity
to fulfill his own vocation
and to contribute to the progress of all.

MEMBERS OF UNIVERSAL CHURCH
THROUGH LOCAL CHURCH

Christians are members of the universal Church through membership in their local Church—parochial, diocesan, and national. As such, it is fitting that they pray for the whole Church as well as their own community.

902

B) FOR CHURCH AND PARISH

A S ALREADY mentioned, contemporary Christians have a greater awareness of their relationship to the world. They should also possess a corresponding awareness of their relationship to the universal Church and more specifically to the local Church or parish (which is the smallest part of the diocesan and national Church). For in the wake of the Second Vatican Council, we are living in the age of the local Church.

In God's providence it is the Church which has the Holy Spirit in her that puts us in touch with Jesus and the salvation he has achieved. The Church is the sacrament of salvation for the entire world throughout the ages until Christ's final coming in glory.

In the case of individual Christians, it is ordinarily the local Church (the parish) that puts them in touch with Jesus and his saving actions. It is the local Church where they can co-celebrate the Eucharistic celebration in union with their co-parishioners, where they receive the other sacraments, and where they carry out the religious tasks given them by God.

In the aftermath of Vatican II, the local Church has come into its own, bursting with committees and projects in which parishioners can take part and really pull their weight in the Church. The measure of their commitment to such tasks will determine the extent of the Church's influence in their lives.

Thus, Christians should make it a practice to pray for the needs of both the universal and the local Church. In doing so, they will call down God's grace on their Church and increase their own awareness of commitment to that Church.

1201   **Prayer for the Church**

C OME, Holy Spirit, blest Sanctifier,
     mercifully assist your Catholic Church.
By your heavenly power
strengthen and establish her against the assaults
of her enemies.
By your love and grace
renew the spirit of your servants
whom you have anointed.
Grant that they may in you
glorify the Father and his only Son,
Jesus Christ our Lord.

1202   **Alternate Prayer for the Church**

H EAVENLY Father,
     grant that your Church may always find
in the risen Jesus,
who conquered death and sin,
the strength to overcome patiently and lovingly
all afflictions and hardships.
May she thus show forth in the world
the mystery of the Lord
in a faithful though shadowed way,
until at the last it will be revealed in total splendor.

(Based on the Constitution on the Church, no. 8)

1203   **Additional Prayer for the Church**

G OD our Father,
     you willed that the Church should continue
your Son's work in the world.
Help her to imitate Jesus
in laboring for the total salvation

of the poor and the lowly.
May she follow Christ, who took the form of a servant,
and not seek after earthly glory
but be the true instrument of salvation
for the whole world.

1204 **Prayer for the Local Church**

GOD our Father,
    your Second Vatican Council has told us
that the Church of Christ is truly present
in all legitimate local congregations which,
united with their pastors,
are themselves called churches in the New Testament.
Let all such local churches
manifest your univer.al Church—
one, holy, Catholic, and apostolic.
Grant that their members may grow
through the Gospel and the Eucharist
in the unity of the Holy Spirit.
Make them the genuine instrument of Christ's power
in the world.

1205 **Another Prayer for the Local Church**

HEAVENLY Father,
    look graciously on the Church in our country
and keep it faithful to your divine message.
Make it communicate that message in ways
that will be understood by our people
in terms of their culture and customs.
Inspire our religious leaders
with wisdom and courage in this important task.
At the same time enable all members of this Church
to answer your call to spread their faith
among their fellow citizens.

Help us all to keep our Church ever full
of your grace and your teachings
and alive to the needs of all who are in need—
both materially and spiritually—
in imitation of your divine Son
and under the impulse of your Holy Spirit.

1206   **Prayer for the Diocese**

HEAVENLY Father,
in calling us to follow Christ your Son
you have made us members of this Diocese,
which is a local Church.
Teach us to serve you faithfully in its boundaries
and to make it manifest the universal Church for us.
Help both religious and laity who form part of it
to work together in true Christian unity.

May your Word be truly proclaimed and heard here
and may your Sacraments, especially the Eucharist,
be faithfully administered and devoutly received.
Grant that our diocese may provide a fervent example
of the power of your Word and the might of your salva-
    tion
for your honor and glory and our salvation.

1207   **Prayer for the Parish**

HEAVENLY Father,
you have chosen the parish as the vehicle
by which you encounter us in our daily lives.
The parish is the assembly in which
your Word is proclaimed,
your Eucharist is celebrated,
your people are united in a local community
and subdivided into smaller groups

so that they may become the agent of change
for the betterment of the whole Church.

Make our parishioners aware
of the many opportunities and responsibilities
that are theirs as witnesses of you to our age.
Keep us open to our need of your love and fellowship.
Let both religious and laity work together
to serve you in others.

1208 **Prayer for the Pope**

LORD Jesus Christ,
you willed to build your Church on Peter the Rock
and the Popes who have succeeded him through the ages.
Pour forth your grace on our Holy Father
that he may be a living sign and an indefatigable promoter
of the unity of the Church.

Help him to proclaim your message to all people
and to listen to the message that comes to him
from the consensus of all its members
and from the world that you made.
Make him serve others after your example
and in accord with his traditional title:
"Servant of the servants of God."
Unite us closely to him
and make us docile to his teachings.

1209 **Prayer for the Bishop**

LORD Jesus Christ,
you sent your apostles to proclaim the Good News
with Peter at their head
and you strengthened them with the Holy Spirit.
Remind us that our bishops are appointed
by that same Spirit

and are the successors of the Apostles
as pastors of souls.
Together with the Pope and under his authority
they have been sent throughout the world
to continue your work.

Help our bishop to teach all members of his diocese,
to sanctify them in the truth,
and to give them your nourishment.
Make us obey his teachings and love him
as the Church obeys and loves you.
May we remain united with him,
grow in faith and love,
and attain eternal life with you.

1210 Prayer for All Church Leaders

LORD Jesus Christ,
watch over those who are leaders
in your Church.
Keep them faithful to their vocation
and to the proclamation of your message.
Teach them to recognize and interpret
the signs of the times.
Strengthen them with the gifts of the Spirit
and help them to serve their subjects,
especially the poor and lowly.
Give them a vivid sense of your presence
in the world
and a knowledge of how to show it to others.

1211 Prayer for Priests

HEAVENLY Father,
pour out your grace on the priests you have made.

Let them remember that in performing their tasks
they are never alone.
Relying on your almighty power
and believing in Christ
who called them to share in his priesthood,
may they devote themselves to their ministry
with complete trust,
knowing that you can intensify in them
the ability to love.

Let them also be mindful that they have as partners
their brothers in the priesthood
and indeed the faithful of the entire world.
For they cooperate in carrying out the saving plan
of Christ,
which is brought to fulfillment only by degrees,
through the collaboration of many ministries
in the building up of Christ's Body
until the full measure of his manhood is achieved.

(Based on Vatican II)

1212 Prayer for a Parish Council

LORD Jesus Christ,
inspired by the words of your Second Vatican Council,
we have elected some men and women of our parish
to the parish council.
These have the task to represent us
with the parish team
and to work for the good of the entire community.

Help them to carry out their role
with courage and wisdom,
with joy and dedication,
with patience and mutual respect,
and with the conviction that all they do

is done primarily for you
and the honor of the Blessed Trinity.

1213 Prayer for a Spiritual or Pastoral Meeting

LORD Jesus Christ,
we have come together in your name
to work for the good of this parish.
Stay with us with your invisible presence
and pour out the gifts of your Spirit on us.
Make us work in a spirit of trust and love,
as well as a spirit of prudence and understanding,
so that we may experience an abundance
of light, compassion, and peace.
Let harmony reign ever among us
and let us keep our eyes ever fixed upon you.
Enable us to implement your known will for us,
no matter what difficulty it may entail.

1214 Prayer for a Study Group

HEAVENLY Father,
send forth your Spirit
to enlighten our minds and dispose our hearts
to accept your truth.
Help us to listen to one another
with openness and honesty,
eager to learn from the talents and intuitions
that you have given each of us.
Never let differences of opinion
diminish our mutual esteem and love.
May we leave this meeting
with more knowledge and love for you
and your Son in the unity of the Holy Spirit.

1215 **Prayer for the Laity**

HEAVENLY Father,
inspire all lay members of your Church
to know their calling and carry it out.
Let them realize that they are to be witnesses
to Christ in all things
and in the midst of human society.

Help them to bear this witness
by their life and work in their home,
in their social group,
and in their professional circle.
Enable them to do so and thus radiate the new man
created according to God
in justice and true holiness (cf. Eph 4:24),
and so lay the groundwork for the growth
of your kingdom on earth.

1216 **Prayer for Priestly Vocations**

O JESUS, divine Pastor of souls,
you called the apostles
to make them fishers of men.
Continue to draw to you
ardent and generous souls of your people
to make them your followers and ministers;
enable them to share your thirst for universal redemption
through which you daily renew your sacrifice.

O Lord,
always living to make intercession for us,
open the horizons of the whole world
where the mute supplication of so many hearts
begs for the light of truth and warmth of love.
Responding to your call,
may they prolong your mission here below,

build up your mystical Body,
which is the Church,
and be the salt of the earth
and the light of the world.

Pope Paul VI

1217   **Prayer for Religious Vocations**

O GOD,
you bestow gifts on human beings
for the upbuilding of your Church
and the salvation of the whole world.
Pour out your Spirit
to inspire young people
with the desire to follow you more closely
by embracing the evangelical counsels
of poverty, chastity, and obedience.

Grant your powerful and continuing assistance
to all who respond to your call
so that they may remain faithful to their vocation
throughout their lives.
May it lead them to greater fullness
and make them living signs of the new person in Christ,
freed from money, pleasure, and power,
and outstanding witnesses of your kingdom.

1218   **Prayer for Missionaries**

L ORD Jesus Christ,
watch over your missionaries—
priests, religious, and lay people—
who leave everything
to give testimony
to your Word
and your love.

In difficult moments
sustain their energies,
comfort their hearts,
and crown their work
with spiritual achievements.
Let the adorable image
of you crucified on the Cross,
which accompanies them throughout life,
speak to them of heroism,
generosity,
love and peace.

Pope John XXIII

1219 Prayer for the Unity of the Church

HEAVENLY Father,
your blessed Son asked that his Church be one
as you and he are one,
but Christians have not been united as he prayed.
We have isolated ourselves from each other
and failed to listen to each other.
We have misunderstood and ridiculed
and even gone so far as to attack each other.

In so doing we have offended against you,
against all our brothers and sisters in the Church,
and against all who have not believed in you
because of our scandalous disunity.
Forgive us, Father,
and make us fully one.
Blot out our sins,
renew our minds,
enkindle our hearts,
and guide us by your Holy Spirit
into that oneness which is your will.

PRAYERS FOR FAMILY AND NEIGHBORHOOD

Prayer for one's family is so obvious that we tend
to take it for granted most of the time and fail to
use numerous opportunities for prayer that relate
to the family. The same can be said for one's neighborhood. We should strive to remedy this lack.

914

C) FOR FAMILY AND NEIGHBORHOOD

IN ADDITION to their relationship to their country and their Church, all Christians have a close relationship to their families and to their local neighborhoods. In the normal course of things, these relationships also entail responsibilities and privileges as far as prayer is concerned.

The family has been termed a domestic Church, for it is called upon to form Christ in all its members. Indeed, for most Christians it is the place where they first encounter Christ through the prayers and example of their parents. Here too they gain their first experience of human Christian companionship and of the Church. It is only natural then that prayer should come to mind in relation with members of that family and the various occasions of their lives.

The family is also the springboard that gradually introduces human beings into civic partnership with their fellow humans. All Christians form part of a particular local neighborhood with customs and problems of its own. "They must be acquainted with this culture, heal and preserve it. They must develop it in accordance with modern conditions, and finally perfect it in Christ" (Vatican II: Decree on the Missionary Activity of the Church, no. 21). Under such circumstances, it is incumbent on Christians to pray for their immediate neighbors and their local surroundings when occasions arise that call for such prayer.

The prayers found in this section cover only a few such occasions. Many others could be found but they would be too diversified because of the necessarily concrete circumstances that would have to be mentioned. Thus they will have to be left to the ingenuity of each person for composition. The prayers given offer a sufficient variety for such composition as the occasions arise.

1220   **Prayer for a Family**

JESUS, our most loving Redeemer,
    you came to enlighten the world
with your teaching and example.
You willed to spend the greater part of your life
in humble obedience to Mary and Joseph
in the poor home of Nazareth.
In this way you sanctified that family
which was to be an example for all Christian families.

Graciously accept our family
which we dedicate and consecrate to you this day.
Be pleased to protect, guard, and keep it
in holy fear, in peace,
and in the harmony of Christian charity.
By conforming ourselves to the divine model
of your family,
may we all attain to eternal happiness.

1221   **Another Prayer for a Family**

GOD of goodness and mercy,
    to your fatherly protection we recommend our family,
our household, and all that belongs to us.
Fill our home with your blessings
as you filled the holy house of Nazareth
with your presence.
Keep us from sin.
Help each one of us to obey your holy laws,
to love you sincerely, and to imitate your example,
the example of Mary, your mother and ours,
and the example of your holy guardian, St. Joseph.

Lord, preserve us and our home
from all evils and misfortunes.

May we ever be resigned to your divine will
even in the crosses and sorrows
which you allow to come to us.
Finally, give all of us the grace
to live in harmony and love toward our neighbor.
Grant that each of us may deserve by a holy life
the comfort of your Sacraments at the hour of death.

Bless this house,
God the Father, who created us,
God the Son, who suffered for us on the Cross,
and God the Holy Spirit, who sanctified us at Baptism.
May the one God in three divine Persons
preserve our bodies,
purify our minds,
direct our hearts,
and bring us all to everlasting life.

1222 Litany for the Home

O FATHER in heaven,
we thank you for our home and our health;
— we thank you, Father.
For giving us to one another in this family,
for our happy family life together,
and comfort in our common sorrows,
— we thank you, Father.
We ask you to lead us
in the ways of love and service one to another;
— Lord, hear our prayer.
That with honesty and cheerfulness,
with bravery and truth,
we may be quick and ready to help each other
in each day's work and cares,
— Lord, hear our prayer.
That we may with respect and love
avoid quarrels in our home which would threaten unity,

and confine our differences in the home,
—Lord, hear our prayer.
For our life at home now,
and the memories to come,
for making us one and keeping us secure,
—we bless you, O God, our Father.
For the constant support of our holy Church worldwide,
for the assurance of graces given,
and for the promise of eternal peace,
—we thank you, O God, our Father.

1223   Prayer of Parents for Their Children

HEAVENLY Creator of the universe,
   we thank you for the children
that you have entrusted to us.
We want to cooperate with you fully
in helping them grow into free and responsible persons
and mature in the faith received at Baptism.
Grant us the grace to be able to guide them
in the practice of virtue
and the way of your commandments—
by the good example of our lives,
and by the loving observance of your law
and that of your Church.
Most of all, however, guide them with your Spirit
so that they may know the vocation you will for them
and be open to genuine self-giving and true Christian
   love.

1224   Prayer of Children for Their Parents

LORD Jesus Christ,
   you have given me my parents
to bring me into this world
and to help me on my journey to you in the next

by the consoling gift of your holy and generous love.
Fill them with your choicest blessings
and enrich their souls with your grace.

Grant that they may faithfully and constantly imitate
your mystical marriage to the Church
which you imprinted on them on their wedding day.
Inspire them with your wisdom
and enable them to walk in the way of your commandments.
And may I and their other children be ever
their joy in this life
and their crown of glory in the next.
Bring my parents to a ripe old age
in health of mind and body
and grant them a holy death in union with you.

1225 **Prayer of Spouses for One Another**

LORD Jesus Christ,
  help us to love each other
as you love your Immaculate Bride, the Church.
Bestow on us Christian forebearance and patience
in bearing each other's shortcomings.
Let no misunderstanding disturb that harmony
which is the foundation of mutual help
in the many and various hardships of life.

Inspire us to lead truly Christian lives
and cooperate with the sacramental grace given us
on our wedding day.
Give us the grace to live together in peace and happiness,
slow to speak harshly
and quick to forgive each other.
Enable us to rear our children in your love,
assist our neighbor after your example,
shoulder our rightful civic and religious burdens

in union with you,
and bear witness to you before our community.

1226   Prayer of Spouses
on a Wedding Anniversary

HEAVENLY Father,
we thank you from the bottom of our hearts
for your continued blessings on our union
that have enabled us to reach another anniversary.
We thank you for letting our love deepen
and for helping us in time of trial.
We know that without your assistance
we would never have remained so close as we are.

We ask you to continue to watch over us,
over our homes and families.
Help us to renew our vows of love and loyalty
and to strive to remain united with you,
steadfast in our faith and in your service.

1227   Prayer at a Child's Baptism

LORD Jesus Christ,
you have given new birth to our child
by water and your Holy Spirit.
You have made him/her a child of your Father,
a member of your Church,
and an heir of heaven.

We offer you sincere thanks
and promise with the help of your grace
to teach him/her in accord with the baptismal promises
to believe unhesitatingly in your message,
to obey faithfully your commandments,
and to remain ever united with you
in life and in death.

1228   **Prayer for an Unwed Mother**

H EAVENLY Father,
   look graciously on this daughter
who has become a mother out of wedlock.
Grant her and her child your strength
that they may grow in stature, age, and grace.
Inspire others to extend kindness and understanding
to them in their troubled lives,
so that they can live relatively peacefully.
Send them a good man who will be
a loving husband and father.
Teach me to put away all recrimination and condemnation
and be of help and encouragement to them.

1229   **Prayer at a Child's First Communion**

L ORD Jesus Christ,
   in the Sacrament of the Eucharist
you left us the outstanding manifestation
of your limitless love for us.
Thank you for giving our child
the opportunity to experience this love
in receiving the Sacrament for the first time.
May your Eucharistic presence keep him/her
ever free from sin,
fortified in faith,
pervaded by love for God and neighbor,
and fruitful in virtue,
that he/she may continue to receive you throughout life
and attain final union with you at death.

1230   **Prayer at the Confirmation of a Child**

HEAVENLY Father,
    you sent your Spirit to transform the Apostles
into heroes of evangelical strength
on the day of Pentecost.
Thank you for granting that same Spirit
to our child in the Sacrament of Confirmation.
Pour down upon him/her
the sevenfold gifts of the Spirit
that he/she may more closely resemble Jesus
and be an intrepid witness in the world
to you and to your divine Son.

1231   **Prayer at the Marriage of a Son or Daughter**

LORD Jesus Christ,
    you said that on their marriage
grown children would leave father and mother
and cling to their spouse.
Our child has taken this step today,
receiving the wonderful Sacrament of Marriage.

Watch over him/her in this new life.
May this couple find happiness in each other
and in you
as they raise a new family to your honor and glory.
Help me to accept this marriage wholeheartedly
with the realization that I am not losing one child
but gaining another.

1232 Prayer at a Child's Entrance into the Religious Life

HEAVENLY Father,
you have called my son/daughter to be
a priest (or sister or brother),
and he/she has generously responded to that call.
I pray that he/she will be ever faithful
in this new state
and happy with the way of life lying ahead.

Help me to be ever ready to render my assistance
whenever and however it may be needed.
Let me always remember that it is an honor
to give one's child to you
who gave it to us in the first place.

1233 Prayer for a Child's Return to the Faith

DEAR Lord,
you became man, suffered, and died
to win salvation for all souls.
Look graciously on the soul of my child
who has drifted away from you and the Faith.
Grant him/her your grace
to see the error of his/her ways
and return to the fold in your care.
Teach me to stay close to him/her
during this trying time
and strive to convert him/her by action and prayers
more than by words that may antagonize.
Sacred Heart of Jesus, I trust you
to do everything to bring my child back to you.

1234 Prayer for a Neighborhood Civic Association

LORD Jesus Christ,
you praised those who serve the needs of others.
Look graciously on this neighborhood civic association
made up of people of various beliefs
who work for the good of our community.
Prompt them to show genuine respect for all
and to strive to eliminate all injustice
from our area.
Inspire its officers to perform their duties well
and the members to accept their leadership,
so that the people will be relieved of social concerns
and be better able to pursue their spiritual goal.

1235 Prayer for a Neighborhood Problem

HEAVENLY Father,
you know the problem that has arisen in our midst.
Please help those involved to resolve it
with all speed and according to your will.
Watch over us with your grace
so that this community will be a place
where your presence is felt,
true human and Christian friendship reign,
and all work out their salvation in peace.

1236 Prayer for a Declining Neighborhood

LORD Jesus Christ,
our neighborhood was once a thriving area
where people lived peaceful human lives
and fruitful spiritual lives.
Now it is in state of continuous decline,

where peace and harmony have given way
to fear, suspicion, and chaos.
Inspire those who remain to refrain from fleeing
and to work together to build it up again.
Make us all respect one another
as we strive to restore our neighborhood into a place
where people can live in peace
and worship without fear.

1237 Prayer for a Neighborhood School

HEAVENLY Father,
you have made human beings in such a way
that all education is most important for their welfare.
Our neighborhood school is presently in a sad state
and can barely teach our youngsters the essentials
they need in order to live in union with others
and with you, their Creator.
Help us to restore it to its former state
so that our children may receive a good education
and be able to come to the knowledge of you
and of your Son—
which is eternal life.

1238 Prayer for a Neighbor in Difficulty

LORD Jesus Christ,
you taught us to help those in need.
I pray for N. our neighbor who is in difficulty.
Watch over him/her during this time of trial
and enable him/her to rebound from this blow.
Most important of all, keep him/her close to you
no matter what he/she may have to undergo.
Move me to do what I can to help
always respecting his/her privacy
and without in any way diminishing his/her own self-re-
   spect.

PRAYERS FOR SELF AND FRIENDS

There are countless occasions for prayer in our relationship with ourselves and with our friends. All that is needed is an awareness that whatever we may be doing Jesus is with us. We can tune him in at any time and on any occasion.

926

D) FOR SELF AND FRIENDS

IN ADDITION to the relationships already mentioned, Christians also have a relationship to themselves as individuals. Jesus said: "Love your neighbor as yourself." Hence, Christians must do for themselves what they do for others. They must pray for themselves or see to it that their own prayer life does not suffer or become completely non-existent. They must afford spiritual help to themselves even as they do for others.

One of the ways to do this is to have a regular pattern of daily prayer—and that is the reason why we give set-time prayers in this section. Another way is to pray in any situation that may arise during the day. This leads to those prayers that we have already given in the section on states-of-mind prayers, but since there is a little different emphasis in this case we also give here a few such prayers.

Christians also have a relationship with friends and acquaintances. This naturally leads to prayer for such people. It is good for us to do this because it keeps before our eyes our dependence on others and ultimately on our Creator. At the same time it keeps us in touch with him.

By sanctifying our relationships we become better able to cope with them and to live a genuine Christian life. Thus, nothing that we do becomes ordinary or secular. We live in tune with a loving Father who wants to help us at every moment and in every circumstance. By praying we take advantage of that relationship and we uncover the key to our universe.

1239   **Morning Prayer**

MOST holy and adorable Trinity,
    one God in three Persons,
I praise you and give you thanks
for all the favors you have bestowed on me.
Your goodness has preserved me until now.
I offer you my whole being
and in particular all my thoughts, words, and deeds,
together with all the trials I may undergo today.
Give them your blessing.
May your divine Love animate them
and may they serve your greater glory.

I make this morning offering
in union with the divine intentions of Jesus Christ
who offers himself daily in the Sacrifice of the Mass
and in union with Mary, his Virgin Mother and our
    Mother,
who was always the faithful handmaid of the Lord.

See also p. 130 (for Liturgy of the Hours) and p. 709 (Morning Offering).

1240   **Alternate Morning Prayer**

LORD,
    I wake up again today
to your grace,
which is always
your gift.
And I want to value everything today
as your gift of grace.

I thank you, Lord,
for having
passed again today
from sleep to awaking,
from night to day,
from darkness to light,
from the torpidity of me—
which resembles death—
to life,
and with all those who woke up today
in our existence,
to life,

Lord, I am living again
Easter,
the passing
from sin to grace;
Baptism,
Sunday,
all the infinite passages
of my life,
of my day—
going, coming,
getting out, returning home,
moving, walking—
as your journey into the world,
your coming in me,
your coming among us.
Lord, in this awaking
I experience you as Christ again;
I arise in this awaking
suddenly
by your grace
"child of God."

                                        Anna Teresa Ciccolini

1241   **Midafternoon Prayer**

O DIVINE Savior,
     I transport myself in spirit to Mount Calvary
to ask pardon for my sins,
for it was because of humankind's sins
that you chose to offer yourself in sacrifice.
I thank you for your extraordinary generosity
and I am also grateful to you
for making me a child of Mary, your Mother.

Blessed Mother, take me under your protection.
St. John, you took Mary under your care.
Teach me true devotion to Mary, the Mother of God.
May the Father, the Son, and the Holy Spirit
be glorified in all places
through the Immaculate Virgin Mary.

1242   **Evening Prayer**

I ADORE you, my God,
     and thank you for having created me,
for having made me a Christian,
and for having preserved me this day.
I love you with all my heart
and I am sorry for having sinned against you,
because you are infinite Love and infinite Goodness.
Protect me during my rest
and may your love be always with me.

Eternal Father,
I offer you the precious Blood of Jesus Christ
in atonement for my sins
and for all the intentions of our holy Church.

Holy Spirit, Love of the Father and the Son,
purify my heart and fill it with the fire of your Love,

so that I may be a chaste Temple of the Holy Trinity
and be always pleasing to you in all things.

See also p. 140 (Liturgy of the Hours).

1243   **Alternate Evening Prayer**

WHEN it is evening, Lord,
    I place myself before you
to find you again,
because during the day,
long,
cloudy,
tiring,
dull,
lost,
it seems as though I have lost you.

And I find myself again
distracted,
split,
superficial,
selfish,
unhappy:
what am I?
who are you?
what is life?
Or I am
satisfied with myself:
after all I have done,
all I could do,
everything is fine,
people are fond of me,
there is almost nothing I don't have,
I am even engaged in Church doings,
I give courses in updating. . . .

Lord, all this
is nothing

if my goal
is myself and not you.
When it is evening, Lord,
I feel extremely—poor,
empty,
in need
of your Love.
May this, your Love,
become tomorrow, every day,
now,
the soul of my life.

Anna Teresa Ciccolini

1244   Prayer before Meals

BLESS us, O Lord,
    and these your gifts
which we are about to receive
from your bounty
through Christ our Lord.

[370]   Prayer after Meals

See no. 370, p. 278.

1245   Prayer for Jesus' Help in Every Need

IN EVERY need let me come to you with humble trust,
    saying:
Jesus, help me.
In all my doubts, temptations, and troubles of mind,
Jesus, help me.
When I am lonely or tired,
Jesus, help me.
When my plans and hopes have failed,

in all my disappointments and sorrows,
Jesus, help me.
When others let me down,
and your grace alone can assist me,
Jesus, help me.

When my heart is heavy with failure
and when I see no good come from my efforts,
Jesus, help me.
When I feel impatient,
and when my cross is hard to carry,
Jesus, help me.
When I am ill,
and my head and hands cannot work,
Jesus, help me.
Always, always,
in spite of weakness and falls of every kind,
Jesus, help me, and never leave me.

1246   Prayer for the Zest for Living

HEAVENLY Father,
no matter what may befall me,
let me never lose my zest for life
or my appreciation of this beautiful world
that you have created and made available to me.
Keep ever before my eyes the glory of being alive,
the wondrous freshness of each new day,
and the magnificence of the creatures around us
as they sing your praises by their very being.

Do not let me focus on my own troubles
and remain blind to life's wonders.
Teach me how to take time each day
to thank you for all your gifts to us,
singing your glory with all your creatures
in union with your Son Jesus Christ.

1247   **Prayer to Walk with God**

LORD,
    the life of today is frantic and delirious.
I often find myself lost in the crowd,
conditioned by whatever surrounds me,
unable to stop and reflect.

Make me rediscover
and live
the value of walking toward you,
laden and compromised
with all the reality
of today's world;
the consciousness of feeling
constantly
called by name, by you;
the grace of responding freely,
of taking your Word
as light
to all my steps.

1248   **Prayer to Discern God's Plan**
           Made Known in Everyday Life

LORD Jesus Christ,
    you came to earth and had an immeasurable effect
on the lives of those whom you met.
Let me realize that your Father works
through people I meet every day of my life.
In every encounter and in every event,
you are coming to meet me—
if only I can discern your presence.
And by my own life I also become for others
a bearer of God's plan.

Help me to respond to your call gladly
when it comes to me each day in others.

1249 **Prayer to Be Truly Human**

L ORD Jesus Christ,
    you came to earth and embraced our humanity,
thereby teaching us how to be truly human.
Help me to follow your example
and so bring out in myself all that is fully human.
Teach me to appreciate the immense good
that lies in being human,
climaxed by the gift of genuine self-giving.
Enable me to make use of all your gifts
in accord with the purpose for which you gave them
and for the good of others.
Make me realize that only when I am genuinely human
can I be a true follower of you.

1250 **Prayer for Love of God**

M Y GOD and Father,
    I believe that you are Love itself.
Give me a deeper love for you.
I believe that you sent your Son Jesus
to save the world,
and that your enduring love is always
at work among us.

Help me to keep your commandments,
for only then do I truly love you.
Give me a love for you that drives out fear,
a love worthy of a child of God.
Through love may I be incorporated into Jesus Christ,
your Son, the true God and eternal life!

1251   **Prayer for Love of Neighbor**

LORD Jesus,
    you teach me that the greatest of all virtues is love.
I earnestly ask for an increase
of true love for my neighbor.
Give me a love that is long-suffering,
kind not envious,
not self-seeking, and not irritable.

Let my love take no note of injury,
and refuse to rejoice when injustice triumphs
but rather be joyful when truth prevails.
Make it a love that is ready to make allowance,
that always trusts and hopes,
and is ever patient.
May my love be kind, merciful, and forgiving
in imitation of your Father's love for me.

1252   **Prayer to Know and Follow
         One's Vocation**

HEAVENLY Father,
    you have created us in such a way
that each has some state in life to pursue
for the good of the whole human race
and your holy Church.
Help me to know my vocation
and to follow it with joy and dedication.
No matter what problem I may encounter,
let me never lose hope,
aware that you have given me the talents
to succeed in any state to which you call me.

1253 **Prayer of Gratitude for Speech**

L ORD Jesus Christ,
  you said that your words were spirit and life
and your listeners exclaimed
that no one had ever spoken like you before.
I give you thanks for my gift of speech
by which I can praise your goodness and majesty
and communicate with my fellow humans.
Grant that my words may always be such
as to honor you and help others,
and transmit only words leading to eternal life.
And if I fail, please be forgiving
and enable me to start anew.

1254 **Prayer for a Retreat**

L ORD Jesus Christ,
  you told the apostles
to retire to a desert place and rest a while.
I am taking this time to follow your example.
Grant that I may obtain all the fruits
that I can from this retreat.

Enable me to make it in union with you,
to know myself better and to get closer to you.
Help me to listen attentively,
to ponder prayerfully,
and to speak wisely.
Let me emerge from this spiritual renewal
as a more committed Christian,
better equipped to advance along the path
that you have laid out for me.

1255   Prayer for One's Name Day

L ORD Jesus Christ,
     today I celebrate the Saint whose name I bear.
It is a special day for me
and should bring me closer to my Patron
as well as to you and the Father.
Inspire me to strive ever harder
to imitate my Patron's virtues on earth
and come to join him/her in heavenly glory.

1256   Prayer to a Patron Saint

D EAR St. N.,
     I have been honored to bear your name—
a name made famous by your heroic virtues.
Help me never to do anything to besmirch it.
Obtain God's grace for me
that I may grow in faith, hope, and love,
and all the virtues.
Grant that by imitating you
I may imitate your Lord and Master, Jesus Christ.
Watch over me along the way of the rest of my life
and bring me safe to my heavenly home at my death.

1257   Prayer on One's Birthday

H EAVENLY Father,
     today is the anniversary of my birth,
the day on which you allowed me to enter
this magnificent world that you have made.
Let me be convinced that my birth meant something,
despite the very ordinariness of my life.

Make me realize that you set me on this earth
for a reason,
and that I must continue to work
to carry out your plan in every respect.

Thank you for creating me
and for redeeming me.
Teach me the fleetingness of time
and the enduring length of eternity.
Help me to remain close to you until my death,
starting from now,
which is the first day of the rest of my life.

1258 Prayer for Friends

LORD Jesus Christ,
while on earth you had close and devoted friends,
such as John, Lazarus, Martha, and Mary.
You showed in this way
that friendship is one of life's greatest blessings.

Thank you for the friends that you have given me
to love me in spite of my failures and weaknesses,
and to enrich my life after your example.
Let me ever behave toward them
as you behaved toward your friends.
Bind us close together in you
and enable us to help one another on our earthly journey.

1259 Prayer for Relatives

HEAVENLY Father,
you poured out the gifts of charity
into the hearts of your faithful
by the grace of the Holy Spirit.

Grant health of mind and body
to your servants for whom we pray.
Make them love you with all their hearts
and practice with perfect love
only those things which are pleasing to you.
Keep them safe from all harm
and bring them all to your eternal home
after their earthly pilgrimage.

1260   **Prayer for Benefactors**

HEAVENLY Father,
I ask you to pour out your blessings
on all those who have helped me along life's way,
whether I am aware of their contribution or not.
Bless those who taught me in living and in the faith,
those who ministered to my spiritual needs,
those who worked to make my life easier,
those who befriended me along the way,
those who prayed and sacrificed for me,
and those who gave their lives for my welfare.
Grant your blessing to all of them
whether they are living or dead,
and bring them all into the glorious light
of your eternal kingdom.

1261   **Prayer for a Person Disliked**

LORD Jesus Christ,
you told us to love our neighbor.
I know that this does not mean that I must *like* everyone,
but simply that I must wish everyone well
and extend my help to all who need it.
I dislike N.

No matter what I try,
I cannot seem to get along with that person.
The only thing I can do is to ask
that you shower your blessings on him/her.

Let me recall that for our sake
you put up with the infinite weaknesses and imperfections
of the whole world.
Help me then not to be so antagonistic to that person,
but to try to bear with him/her
for your sake.

1262 Prayer to Be a Sign for Others

WHEN I wait for the streetcar,
Lord,
I think of you
and keep looking for you
in the impassive faces of others
who are waiting
like me.
I look for a smile,
a sparkle of love,
but see only
impatience,
boredom,
fatigue,
mad dashes.
There is no personal contact.

Yet they are human
like me,
hallucinated,
in need of love.
I feel a crisis coming.

How can I be for them, too,
a sign of your love?
Lord, I want to measure
all of myself against your love,
because,
accepting
myself as I am,
you teach me
how to be a true "sign"
of your Love.

Anna Teresa Ciccolini

11

PRAYERS
FOR
POPULAR DEVOTIONS

11

943

DEVOTIONS TO JESUS — CENTERED ON SACRED HEART

One of the most important devotions in honor of our Lord is the devotion to his Sacred Heart. This has been highly commended by the Church and is devoutly practiced by countless Catholics.

A) TO JESUS AND THE HOLY SPIRIT

IN THE recent past (until the Second Vatican Council), there was a flourishing type of Catholic devotion known as the Novena. This was the recitation of a prayer or prayers in public or private for an extended period of time—usually nine days or weeks. Contrary to some views, this devotion has not been prohibited; it has just fallen into disuse.

In this part of the book we are providing some updated novenas and other general devotions of the Church. They are based on the four-fold principle set forth by Pope Paul VI as guidelines for all devotions: (1) Biblical basis: our devotions should be based on the bible, our prayerbook par excellence; they should lead the people to listen to that Word and respond to it by prayers and hymns which echo the words of Scripture. (2) Liturgical tone: our devotions should be in harmony with the liturgy and the seasons; they should be inspired by the liturgy and lead back to better liturgical worship. (3) Ecumenical orientation: they should be stripped of any exaggeration and incorrect practices which would hinder Christian unity; they must lead to Christ our Head and the source of unity with one another. (4) Anthropological adaptation: they must not be tied to any particular living conditions but must manifest holiness as coming from hearing God's Word, reflecting on it, and carrying it out in a spirit of love and service; and as human sciences uncover new perspectives, we need to adapt our devotions.

This section gives prayers for novenas and devotions to Jesus and the Holy Spirit with the hope that they will inspire others to be composed. Some of these devotions are more favored than others. For example, the devotion of the Way of Cross is highly approved by the Church as is the novena to the Holy Spirit.

1263   Novena to the Infant of Prague

O CHILD Jesus,
I have recourse to you by your holy Mother.
I implore you to assist me in this need,
for I firmly believe your divinity can assist me.
I confidently hope to obtain your grace.
I love you with my whole heart and my whole soul.
I am heartily sorry for my sins and beg of you,
good Jesus,
to give me strength to overcome them.

I make the resolution of never again offending you,
and of suffering everything rather than displease you.
Henceforth I want to serve you faithfully.
For the love of you, Divine Child,
I will love my neighbor as myself.

Jesus, most powerful Child,
I implore you again to help me:
(mention your request).

Divine Child, great omnipotent God,
I implore you,
through your holy Mother's powerful intercession
and through your boundless mercy as God,
for a favorable answer to my prayer during this Novena.

Grant me the grace of possessing you eternally
with Mary and Joseph
and of adoring you with your holy Angels and Saints.

Novena to the Holy Spirit

1264   INVOCATION

COME, Holy Spirit, fill the hearts of your faithful.
— And enkindle in them the fire of your love.

1265   **HYMN**

COME, Spirit, Lord, Maker of men,
And in our hearts abide again!
Come, give us grace, heaven's bequest,
That we may live, and find our rest.

Comforting Lord, gift from on high,
Seeking your aid, we send our cry!
Fount of all life! Fire of God's love,
Be our anointing from above.

Father on high, God's only Son,
Comforting Spirit, with them one:
Take now our love! And to us send
Gifts of the Spirit—with no end.

1266   **READING**

Rom 8:9-11

BUT you are not in the flesh;
you are in the spirit,
since the Spirit of God dwells in you.
If anyone does not have the Spirit of Christ
he does not belong to Christ.
If Christ is in you the body is dead because of sin,
while the spirit lives because of justice.
If the Spirit of him who raised Jesus from the dead
dwells in you,
then he who raised Christ from the dead
will bring your mortal bodies to life also,
through his Spirit dwelling in you.

1267   **INTERCESSIONS**

LET us pray joyously to the Lord who created his
Church through the Holy Spirit:

℟.   *Lord, renew the face of the earth!*

Lord Jesus, raised up to the right hand of God,
pour out upon your disciples the Holy Spirit
you received from the Father;
— send your Spirit to renew the world.

Since you were glorified by the victory of the cross,
rivers of living water flowed from your side;
— send your life-giving Spirit upon us.

You promised that the Spirit would teach us everything
and remind us of all that you told us,
— send the Spirit to direct our faith.

You promised that you would send the Spirit of truth
to bear witness concerning you,
— send your Spirit upon us to make us faithful witnesses.

1268   **PRAYER**

G OD, by the mystery of today's feast
   you sanctify the whole Church
in every race and nation.
Pour out the gift of the Holy Spirit all over the earth
and diffuse in the hearts of believers
what you caused to spread
at the very beginning of the preaching of the gospel.
We ask this through Christ our Lord.

1269   **The Jesus Prayer**

*One of the most traditional and most common Christian
prayers is the so-called Jesus Prayer, in which the Name of our
Lord is invoked slowly and meditatively. It is an act of deep
faith and self-surrender to the Spirit indwelling in us who will
lead our open minds and hearts where he will.*

L ORD Jesus Christ,
   Son of the living God,
have mercy on me, a sinner.

1269a   ## First Friday Devotions
in Honor of the Sacred Heart

FAITHFUL Catholics conse-
crate to the Sacred Heart of
Jesus, in the spirit of reparation,
the First Friday of each month.
Jesus himself made the following
promises to St. Margaret Mary in
favor of those who practice and
promote this devotion.

1. I will give them all the
graces necessary in their state of
life.

2. I will establish peace in their homes.

3. I will comfort them in all their afflictions.

4. I will be their secure refuge during life, and above
all in death.

5. I will bestow abundant blessings upon all their un-
dertakings.

6. Sinners shall find in my Heart the source and the
infinite ocean of mercy.

7. Tepid souls shall become fervent.

8. Fervent souls shall quickly mount to high perfection.

9. I will bless every place in which an image of my
Heart shall be exposed and honored.

10. I will give the priests the gift of touching the most
hardened hearts.

11. Those who shall promote this devotion shall have
their names written in my Heart, never to be effaced.

12. I promise you in the excessive mercy of my Heart
that my all-powerful love will grant to all those who communicate on the First Friday in nine consecutive months
the grace of final penitence; they shall not die in my dis-

grace nor without receiving their Sacraments. My divine Heart shall be their safe refuge in this last moment.

See nos. 383-384, pp. 283-286, for prayers.

Novena to the Sacred Heart of Jesus

1270 INVOCATION

COME, let us worship Jesus,
—whose Heart was wounded for our sins.

1271 CANTICLE

Rv 4:11; 5:9, 10, 12

O LORD our God, you are worthy
to receive glory and honor and power.

For you have created all things;
by your will they came to be and were made.

Worthy are you, O Lord,
to receive the scroll and break open its seals.

For you were slain;
with your blood you purchased for God
men of every race and tongue,
of every people and nation.

You made of them a kingdom,
and priests to serve our God,
and they shall reign on the earth.

Worthy is the Lamb that was slain
to receive power and riches,
wisdom and strength,
honor and glory and praise.

1272 READING

Rom 5:8-9

IT IS precisely in this that God proves his love for us:
that while we were still sinners, Christ died for us.

Now that we have been justified by his blood,
it is all the more certain
that we shall be saved by him from God's wrath.
He was pierced for our offenses.
— And by his stripes we were healed.

1273   INTERCESSIONS

MY BROTHERS and sisters,
    let us ask Jesus, who is gentle and humble of heart:

℟. *King of love, have mercy on us!*

Jesus, in you resides the fullness of God;
— let us share your divine nature.

Jesus, in you is hidden every treasure of wisdom and
    knowledge;
— reveal to us the wisdom of God
through the many expressions of your Church.

Jesus, favored by the Father,
— enable us who hear your word to persevere in it.

Jesus, from your fullness we have all had a share;
— lavish upon us the grace and truth of the Father.

Jesus, font of life and holiness,
— make us holy and pure in our love.

1274   PRAYER

ALMIGHTY God,
    we glory in the heart of your beloved Son
and recall the principal favors that have come to us
from his love.
Make us worthy to receive superabundant grace
from that heavenly source of gifts.
We ask this through Christ our Lord.

Scriptural Way of the Cross

The Way of the Cross is a devotion in which we meditate on Christ's Passion and Death in order to put their meaning into our lives. This Passion and Death are "revelations" of the love of God the Father for all people and of Christ's love for the Father and all people. The devotion of the Way of the Cross should lead us to do in our lives what Jesus did—we must give our lives in the service of others.

1275   **OPENING PRAYER**

HEAVENLY Father,
grant that we who meditate on the Passion and Death
of your Son, Jesus Christ,
may imitate in our lives
his love and self-giving to you and to others.
We ask this through Christ our Lord.

1276   **1. JESUS IS CONDEMNED TO DEATH**

GOD so loved the world
that he gave his only Son, . . .
that the world might be saved through him (Jn 3:16f).

Though he was harshly treated, he submitted
and opened not his mouth;
like a lamb led to the slaughter
or a sheep before the shearers,
he was silent and opened not his mouth (Is 53:7).

There is no greater love than this:
to lay down one's life for one's friends (Jn 15:13).

Let us pray.
Father,
in the flesh of your Son

you condemned sin.
Grant us the gift of eternal life
in the same Christ our Lord.

1277   2. JESUS BEARS HIS CROSS

I T WAS our infirmities that he bore,
our sufferings that he endured (Is 53:4).

Whoever wishes to be my follower
must deny his very self,
take up his cross each day,
and follow in my steps (Lk 9:23).

Take my yoke upon your shoulders and learn from me, ...
for my yoke is easy and my burden light (Mt 11:28f).
Let us pray.
Father,
your Son Jesus humbled himself
and became obedient to death.
Teach us to glory above all else in the Cross,
in which is our salvation.
Grant this through Christ our Lord.

1278   3. JESUS FALLS THE FIRST TIME

H E has broken my teeth with gravel,
pressed my face in the dust;
my soul is deprived of peace,
I have forgotten what happiness is (Lam 3:16f).

The Lord laid upon him the guilt of us all (Is 53:6).
Look! There is the Lamb of God
who takes away the sin of the world (Jn 1:29).

Let us pray.
Father,
help us to remain irreproachable in your sight,

so that we can offer you our body
as a holy and living offering.
We ask this in the name of Jesus the Lord.

1279   **4. JESUS MEETS HIS MOTHER**

D ID you not know I had to be
in my Father's house? (Lk 2:49).

Come, all you who pass by the way,
look and see
whether there is any suffering like my suffering
(Lam 1:12).

You are sad for a time,
but I shall see you again;
then your hearts will rejoice
with a joy no one can take from you (Jn 16:22).

Let us pray.
Father,
accept the sorrows of the Blessed Virgin Mary,
Mother of your Son.
May they obtain from your mercy
every good for our salvation.
Grant this through Christ our Lord.

1280   **5. JESUS IS HELPED BY SIMON**

A S OFTEN as you did it for one of my least brothers,
you did it for me (Mt 25:40).

Help carry one another's burdens;
in that way you will fulfill the law of Christ (Gal 6:2).

No slave is greater than his master (Jn 13:16).

Let us pray.
Father,
you have first loved us
and you sent your Son to expiate our sins.

Grant that we may love one another
and bear each other's burdens.
We ask this through Christ our Lord.

1281 6. VERONICA WIPES THE FACE OF JESUS

H IS look was marred beyond that of man,
and his appearance beyond that of mortals.
(Is 52:14).

Whoever has seen me has seen the Father (Jn 14:9).

The Son is the reflection of the Father's glory,
the exact representation of the Father's being (Heb 1:3).

Let us pray.
Heavenly Father,
grant that we may reflect your Son's glory
and be transformed into his image
so that we may be configured to him.
We ask this in the name of Jesus.

1282 7. JESUS FALLS A SECOND TIME

I WAS hard pressed and was falling,
but the Lord helped me (Ps 118:3).

We do not have a priest
who is unable to sympathize with our weakness,
but one who was tempted in every way that we are,
yet never sinned (Heb 4:15).

Come to me,
all you who are weary and find life burdensome,
and I will refresh you (Mt 11:28).

Let us pray.
God our Father,
grant that we may walk in the footsteps of Jesus

who suffered for us
and redeemed us not with gold and silver
but with the price of his own blood.
We ask this through Christ our Lord.

1283   **8. JESUS SPEAKS TO THE WOMEN**

D AUGHTERS of Jerusalem, do not weep for me.
Weep for yourselves and for your children (Lk 23:28).

A man who does not live in me
is like a withered, rejected branch (Jn 15:6).

You will all come to the same end
[as some Galileans who perished]
unless you reform (Lk 13:3).

Let us pray.
Heavenly Father,
you desire to show mercy rather than anger
toward all who hope in you.
Grant that we may weep for our sins
and merit the grace of your glory.
We ask this in the name of Jesus the Lord.

1284   **9. JESUS FALLS A THIRD TIME**

I AM like water poured out;
all my bones are racked.
My heart has become like wax.
My throat is dried up like baked clay,
my tongue cleaves to my jaws;
to the dust of death you have brought me down.

(Ps 22:15f)

Your attitude must be that of Christ: . . .
he emptied himself
and took the form of a slave (Phil 2:5-7).

Everyone who exalts himself shall be humbled
and he who humbles himself shall be exalted (Lk 14:11).

Let us pray.
God our Father,
look with pity on us
oppressed by the weight of our sins
and grant us your forgiveness.
Help us to serve you with our whole heart.
We ask this through Christ our Lord.

1285   **10. JESUS IS STRIPPED
OF HIS GARMENTS**

THEY divide my garments among them,
    and for my vesture they cast lots (Ps 22:19).

None of you can be my disciple
if he does not renounce all his possessions (Lk 14:33).

Put on the Lord Jesus Christ
and make no provision for the desires of the flesh.
                                              (Rom 13:14)
Let us pray.
Heavenly Father,
let nothing deprive us of your love—
neither trials nor distress nor persecution.
May we become the wheat of Christ
and be one pure bread.
Grant this through Christ our Lord.

1286   **11. JESUS IS NAILED TO THE CROSS**

THEY have pierced my hands and my feet;
    I can count all my bones (Ps 22:17f).

Father, forgive them;
    they do not know what they are doing (Lk 23:34).
It is not to do my own will
that I have come down from heaven,
but to do the will of him who sent me (Jn 6:38).

Let us pray.
Heavenly Father,
your Son reconciled us to you
and to one another.
Help us to embrace his gift of grace
and remain united with you.
We ask this through Christ our Lord.

1287   **12. JESUS DIES ON THE CROSS**

AND I—once I am lifted up from earth—
will draw all men to myself (Jn 12:32).

Father, into your hands I commend my spirit (Lk 23:46).

He humbled himself,
obediently accepting even death,
death on a cross!
Because of this, God highly exalted him (Phil 2:8-9).

Let us pray.
God our Father,
by his Death your Son has conquered death,
and by his Resurrection he has given us life.
Help us to adore his Death and embrace his Life.
Grant this in the name of Jesus the Lord.

1288   **13. JESUS IS TAKEN DOWN
FROM THE CROSS**

DID not the Messiah have to undergo all of this
so as to enter into his glory? (Lk 24:26).

Those who love your law have great peace (Ps 119:165).
God's love was revealed in our midst in this way:
he sent his only Son to the world. . . .
as an offering for our sins (1 Jn 4:9f).

Let us pray.
God our Father,
grant that we may be associated in Christ's death
so that we may advance toward the resurrection
with great hope.
We ask this through Christ our Lord.

1289   **14. JESUS IS PLACED IN THE TOMB**

UNLESS the grain of wheat falls to the earth and dies,
    it remains just a grain of wheat.
But if it dies,
it produces much fruit (Jn 12:24).

Christ's death was death to sin, once for all;
his life is life for God.
In the same way, you must consider yourselves
dead to sin but alive for God
in Christ Jesus (Rom 6:10-11).

Christ . . . in accordance with the Scriptures
rose on the third day (1 Cor 15:4).

Let us pray.
Heavenly Father,
you raised Jesus from the dead
through your Holy Spirit.
Grant life to our mortal bodies
through that same Spirit who abides in us.
We ask this in the name of Jesus the Lord.

1290   **CONCLUDING PRAYER**

HEAVENLY Father,
    you delivered your Son to the death of the Cross
to save us from evil.
Grant us the grace of the resurrection.
We ask this through Christ our Lord.

DEVOTIONS TO MARY — CENTERED ON
THE ROSARY

Among the many devotions that Catholics practice
in honor of Mary is the devotion of the Holy Rosary.
The Church has enriched it with indulgences and
exhorts her members to make frequent use of it.

B) TO THE BLESSED VIRGIN MARY

W E HAVE *already seen many prayers to the Blessed Virgin Mary (pp. 731ff). This section is concerned with some of the more popular devotions to our Lady. These have been time-tested and found to be very powerful means of keeping Catholics close to Mary and her Divine Son.*

The outstanding devotion is the Rosary. The Scriptural riches of this devotion are of permanent value. After a short lapse into disuse, the Rosary has made a stirring comeback in our day. And in the eyes of the dedicated follower of Mary it is still the devotion par excellence.

Another Marian devotion is the Novena to Our Lady of the Miraculous Medal which is the outgrowth of Mary's appearances to St. Bernadette at Lourdes. It has been a favorite with Catholics since then and can still be used with the necessary updating as found herein.

The appearances of Mary to the three children of Fatima provided the impetus for another devotion—the First Saturdays. Those devoted to Mary cultivate this practice which fosters devotion to Our Lady of the Rosary.

The assigning of months to Mary (October to the Rosary and May to our Lady herself) encourages the faithful to perform these devotions in honor of Mary. The Church desires that Mary be honored in liturgical but also in non-liturgical devotions which may in reality be more familiar to and better appreciated by them. So long as the latter follow the recommendations of Vatican II, they are perfectly proper and should be used with frequency by all Catholics.

The devotions found herein were selected over many others primarily because of their popularity but also because they constitute perfect exemplars for other devotions to the Blessed Virgin.

The Holy Rosary

The devotion of the Holy Rosary has been treasured in the Church for centuries. It is a summary of Christian faith in language and prayers inspired by the Bible. It calls to mind the most important events in the lives of Jesus and Mary. These events are called Mysteries and are divided into three groups of decades. They are: the five Joyful, the five Sorrowful, and the five Glorious Mysteries. Each decade consists of one "Our Father," ten "Hail Marys," and one "Glory be to the Father."

HOW TO SAY THE ROSARY

1. *Begin on the crucifix and say the Apostles' Creed.*
2. *On the 1st bead, say 1 Our Father.*
3. *On the next 3 beads, say Hail Mary.*
4. *Next say 1 Glory Be. Then announce and think of the first Mystery and say 1 Our Father.*
5. *Say 10 Hail Marys and 1 Glory be to the Father.*
6. *Announce the second Mystery and continue in the same way until each of the five Mysteries of the selected group of decades is said.*

THE FIVE JOYFUL MYSTERIES

(Said on Mondays, Thursdays, the Sundays of Advent, and Sundays from Epiphany until Lent)

The Joyful Mysteries direct our mind to the Son of God, Jesus Christ, our Lord and Savior, who took human nature from a human mother, Mary. They also bring to our attention some of the extraordinary events that preceded, accompanied, and followed Christ's birth.

962

1291   **1. The Annunciation**
Lk 1:26-38; Is 7:10-15

MARY, you received with deep humility
    the news of the Angel Gabriel
that you were to be the Mother of God's Son;
obtain for me a similar *humility*.

1292   **2. The Visitation**
Lk 1:41-50

MARY, you showed true charity in visiting Elizabeth
    and remaining with her for three months
before the birth of John the Baptist;
obtain for me the grace to *love my neighbor*.

1293   **3. The Birth of Jesus**
Lk 2:1-14; Mt 2:1-14; Gal 4:1-7

JESUS, you lovingly accepted poverty
    when you were placed in the manger in the stable
although you were our God and Redeemer;
grant that I may have the *spirit of poverty*.

1294   **4. The Presentation in the Temple**
Lk 2:22-40

MARY, you obeyed the law of God
    in presenting the Child Jesus in the Temple;
obtain for me the *virtue of obedience*.

1295   **5. The Finding in the Temple**
Lk 2:42-52

MARY, you were filled with sorrow at the loss of Jesus
    and overwhelmed with joy on finding him
surrounded by Teachers in the Temple;
obtain for me the *virtue of piety*.

THE FIVE SORROWFUL MYSTERIES

(Said on Tuesdays and Fridays throughout the year, and daily from Ash Wednesday until Easter Sunday)

The Sorrowful Mysteries recall to our mind the mysterious events surrounding Christ's sacrifice of his life in order that sinful humanity might be reconciled with God.

1296   1. The Agony in the Garden
Mt 26:36-40

JESUS, in the Garden of Gethsemani,
you suffered a bitter agony because of our sins;
grant me *true contrition.*

1297   2. The Scourging at the Pillar
Mt 27:24-26; 1 Pt 2:21-25

JESUS, you endured a cruel scourging
and your flesh was torn by heavy blows;
help me to have the *virtue of purity.*

1298   3. The Crowning with Thorns
Mt 26:27-31

JESUS, you patiently endured the pain
from the crown of sharp thorns
that was forced upon your head;
grant me the strength to have *moral courage.*

1299   4. The Carrying of the Cross
Mt 27:32

JESUS, you willingly carried your Cross
for love of your Father and all people;
grant me the *virtue of patience.*

1300   **5. The Crucifixion**
Mt 27:33-50; Jn 19:31-37

J ESUS, for love of me
     you endured three hours of torture on the Cross
and gave up your spirit;
grant me the *grace of final perseverance.*

THE FIVE GLORIOUS MYSTERIES
(Said on Wednesdays and Saturdays, and the Sundays from Easter until Advent)

The Glorious Mysteries recall to our mind the ratification of Christ's sacrifice for the redemption of the world, and our sharing in the fruits of his sacrifice.

1301   **1. The Resurrection**
Mk 16:1-7; Jn 20:19-31

J ESUS, you rose from the dead in triumph
     and remained for forty days with your disciples,
instructing and encouraging them;
increase my *faith.*

1302   **2. The Ascension**
Mk 16:14-20; Acts 1:1-11

J ESUS, in the presence of Mary and the disciples
     you ascended to heaven
to sit at the Father's right hand;
increase the *virtue of hope* in me.

1303   **3. The Descent of the Holy Spirit**
Jn 14:23-31; Acts 2:1-11

J ESUS, in fulfillment of your promise
     you sent the Holy Spirit upon Mary and the disciples
under the form of tongues of fire;
increase my *love for God.*

1304   **4. The Assumption**
               Lk 1:41-50; Ps 45; Gn 3:15

MARY, by the power of God you were assumed into
      heaven
and united with your Divine Son;
help me to have *true devotion* to you.

1305   **5. The Crowning of the Blessed Virgin**
               Rv 12:1; Jdt 13:22-25

MARY, you were crowned Queen of heaven
      by your Divine Son
to the great joy of all the Saints;
obtain *eternal happiness* for me.

*At the end of the Rosary, one may add the prayer "Hail,
Holy Queen," no. 410, p. 293, and the following prayer:*

1306   **Prayer after the Rosary**

O GOD,
   whose only-begotten Son,
by his Life, Death, and Resurrection,
has purchased for us the rewards of eternal life;
grant, we beseech you, that,
meditating upon these mysteries
of the Most Holy Rosary of the Blessed Virgin Mary,
we may imitate what they contain
and obtain what they promise,
through the same Christ our Lord.

*The Litany of the Blessed Virgin Mary, no. 389, p. 319, may
also be said.*

1307 **Rosary Novena Prayer**

HOLY Virgin Mary,
Mother of God and our Mother,
accept this Holy Rosary which I offer you
to show my love for you
and my firm confidence in your powerful intercession.
I offer it as an act of faith in the mysteries
of the Incarnation and the Redemption,
as an act of thanksgiving to God
for all his love for me and all mankind,
as an act of atonement for the sins of the world,
especially my own,
and as an act of petition to God
through your intercession
for all the needs of God's people on earth,
but especially for this earnest request.
(Mention your request)

I beg you, dear Mother of God,
present my petition to Jesus, your Son.
I know that you want me to seek God's will
in my request.
If what I ask for should not be God's will,
pray that I may receive that which will be
of greater benefit for my soul.
I put all my confidence in you.

Novena in Honor of Our Lady of the Miraculous Medal

The medal of the Immaculate Conception, known as the Miraculous Medal, was revealed by Mary herself to St. Catherine Labouré in 1830. It bears the words: "O Mary, conceived without sin, pray for us who have recourse to you." Through it and through this Novena many graces have been obtained by Mary for her clients.

[933] **INVOCATION**

O MARY, conceived without sin.
—Pray for us who have recourse to you.

1308 **Hymn**

I MMACULATE Mary, your praises we sing.
You reign now in splendor with Jesus, our King.

Ave, Ave, Ave Maria,
Ave, Ave Maria.

In heaven the blessed your glory proclaim,
On earth we your children invoke your fair name.

We pray for the Church, our true Mother on earth.
And we beg you to watch over the land of our birth.

We pray you, O Mother, may God's will be done;
We pray for his glory, may his kingdom come.

1309 **READING**

Jdt 13:18-19; 15:9

B LESSED are you, daughter,
by the Most High God,
above all the women on earth;
and blessed be the Lord God,
the creator of heaven and earth.
Your deed of hope will never be forgotten
by those who tell of the might of God.
You are the glory of Jerusalem,
the surpassing joy of Israel;
you are the splendid boast of our people.

In your splendor and your beauty,
—triumph and reign, O Virgin Mary.

INTERCESSIONS

M Y BROTHERS and sisters,
let us say to our Savior
who willed to be born of the Virgin Mary:

℟. *Lord, may your mother intercede for us!*

Jesus, while hanging on the cross,
you gave your mother to be the mother of John;
—help us live as her sons.

Savior, your mother stood by the cross;
—through her intercession,
help us welcome a share in your sufferings.

Word eternal, you elected Mary
to be the incorruptible ark of your presence,
—free us from the corruption of sin.

Son of Justice, grant us in the immaculate Virgin,
a guiding light to return to you,
—that we may always walk in your light.

Lord, enable us to imitate Mary your mother
who chose the better portion,
—by seeking the food that remains to life eternal.

King of kings, you willed your mother
to be assumed into heaven with you in body and soul;
—may we always attend to what comes from above.

Lord of heaven and earth,
you made Mary queen at your right hand,
—help us attain a share in the same glory.

Savior of the world, through your redemptive power
you preserved your mother from all stain;
—save us from sin.

Redeemer, you had Mary as the purest dwelling-place
for your presence,

and you made her the holy vehicle of the Spirit;
— make us lasting temples of your Spirit.

1311   **NOVENA PRAYER**

O IMMACULATE Virgin Mary,
    Mother of our Lord Jesus and our Mother,
penetrated with the most lively confidence,
in your all-powerful and never-failing intercession,
manifested so often through the Miraculous Medal,
we your loving and trustful children,
implore you to obtain for us the graces and favors
we ask during this Novena,
if they be beneficial to our immortal souls,
and the souls for whom we pray.
(Here privately mention your petitions.)

You know, O Mary, how often our souls have been
the sanctuaries of your Son, who hates iniquity.
Obtain for us a deep hatred of sin,
and that purity of heart which will attach us
to God alone,
so that our every thought, word, and deed
may tend to his greater glory.
Obtain for us also a spirit of prayer and self-denial,
that we may recover by penance
what we have lost by sin,
and at length attain to that blessed abode
where you are the Queen of Angels and all people.

1312   **CONCLUDING PRAYER**

F ATHER,
    through the Immaculate Conception of the Virgin
you prepared a worthy place for your Son.
In view of the foreseen death of your Son
you preserved her from all sin.

Through her intercession
grant that we may also reach you with clean hearts.
We ask this in the name of Jesus the Lord.

May Devotions

1313   **INVOCATION**

YOU are all pure, O Mary.
—And there is in you no stain of sin.

1314   **READING**

Song 2:10-13

ARISE, my beloved, my beautiful one,
and come!
For see, the winter is past,
the rains are over and gone.
The flowers appear on the earth,
the time of pruning the vines has come,
and the song of the dove is heard in our land.
The fig tree puts forth its figs,
and the vines, in bloom, give forth fragrance.
Arise, my beloved, my beautiful one,
and come!

Blessed are you, O Mary.
—For the world's salvation came forth from you.

1315   **INTERCESSIONS**

LET us implore Mary our Mother for faith
—to walk along the path of righteousness all our lives.
Hail Mary . . .

Let us implore Mary our Mother for the consoling hope
—that enables us to work in this world
but also keep our eyes fixed on the next.
Hail Mary . . .

Let us implore Mary our Mother for the virtue of love
—which is the bond of perfection, unity, and glory.
Hail Mary . . .

Let us offer Mary our Mother the flower
of our love, joy, purity, and hope
—that her joy may be full.

1316   **PRAYER**

HEAVENLY Father,
you chose the Blessed Virgin Mary
to be the Mother of your only Son, Jesus Christ.
Through her intercession
grant us the grace to attain the glory of heaven.
We ask this in the name of Jesus the Lord.

The Five First Saturdays in Honor of the Immaculate Heart of Mary

Mary's Great Promise at Fatima

The observance of the First Saturday in honor of the Immaculate Heart of Mary is intended to console her Immaculate Heart, and to make reparation to it for all the blasphemies and ingratitude of men.

This devotion and the wonderful promises connected with it were revealed by the Blessed Virgin with these words recorded by Lucy, one of the three children to whom the Blessed Virgin appeared at Fatima, Portugal, in 1917:

I promise to help at the hour of death, with the graces needed for salvation, whoever on the First Saturday of five consecutive months shall:

1. *Confess and receive Holy Communion.*
2. *Recite five decades of the Rosary.*
3. *And keep me company for fifteen minutes while meditating on the fifteen Mysteries of the Rosary, with the intention of making reparation to me.*

1317 **ACT OF REPARATION**

O MOST holy Virgin and our Mother,
   we listen with grief to the complaints
of your Immaculate Heart surrounded with the thorns
placed therein at every moment
by the blasphemies and ingratitude
of ungrateful humanity.
We are moved by the ardent desire
of loving you as our Mother
and of promoting a true devotion
to your Immaculate Heart.

We therefore kneel before you
to manifest the sorrow we feel for the grievances
that people cause you,
and to atone by our prayers and sacrifices
for the offenses with which they return your love.
Obtain for them and for us the pardon of so many sins.
Hasten the conversion of sinners
that they may love Jesus
and cease to offend the Lord, already so much offended,
and will not fall into hell.
Turn your eyes of mercy toward us,
that we may love God with all our heart on earth
and enjoy him forever in heaven.

ANGELS AND SAINTS — OUR INTERCESSORS WITH GOD

The majesty of God is so great and above human beings that at times we approach him through intercessors—his friends the Angels and Saints. We ask their help in obtaining our requests from God.

C) TO THE ANGELS AND SAINTS

OVER the years Catholics have developed a host of devotions to the Angels and the Saints. These have varied in form and content but their result was the same —increased confidence in the intercession of a particular Saint, greater appreciation of the mystery of the Communion of Saints which allows them to pray for one another, and closer adherence to Christ the Teacher and Exemplar of all the Saints.

Today, there is a return on the part of Catholics to practice these devotions to the Saints. For they are the perfect complement to the liturgical devotions that have grown by leaps and bounds after Vatican II. Such non-liturgical devotions have much to offer today's Catholic in the area of prayer—as shown by the following principal characteristics which they possess.

(1) They are expression rather than edification; the worshiper is the subject rather than the object of this type of prayer. (2) They are person-oriented rather than theme-oriented; they give the worshiper a lively sense of his association with the Saints and other members of the Mystical Body. (3) They are Christocentric. (4) They are easy to understand and follow, easily identifiable as Catholic prayer. (5) They follow the rhythm of prayer not instruction—utilize the language of intuition rather than logic. (6) They tend to be highly ceremonialized and stylized. (7) Their form is for the most part unvarying.

The devotions found herein are intended to be used as models for the composition of others so that the Faithful will have a large selection of such devotions available for their every need.

Novena to the Angels

1318   **INVOCATION**

COME, let us worship the Lord
in the company of his angels.

1319   **READING**

Ex 23:20-21a

SEE, I am sending an angel before you
to guard you on the way
and bring you to the place I have prepared.
Be attentive to him and heed his voice.

1320   **INTERCESSIONS**

LET us entreat the Lord that,
with the angels who do his will,
we may respond more promptly to the sense of his message:

℟. *With the angels we sing of your glory.*

Lord, you made your angels messengers of your wonders;
—fashion us into heralds of your mighty deeds before all.
The angels ceaselessly proclaim your holiness;
—fashion your Church into a worthy voice for your
praise.
You commanded the angels to protect your servants;
—may they be with us in all our endeavors.
Through the agency of the angels
—may all our petitions rise to you.
May the angels help us in our final hour
—and lead us to the land of paradise.

1321   **PRAYER**

F ATHER,
    with great wisdom you direct the ministry
both of Angels and human beings.
Grant that those who always minister to you in heaven
may also defend us during our life on earth.
We ask this in the Name of Jesus the Lord.

Novena to Our Guardian Angel

1322   **PRAYER**

O MOST faithful companion,
    appointed by God to be my guardian,
and who never leave my side,
how shall I thank you for your faithfulness and love
and for the benefits which you have obtained for me!
You watch over me when I sleep;
you comfort me when I am sad;
you avert the dangers that threaten me
and warn me of those to come;
you withdraw me from sin and inspire me to good;
you exhort me to penance when I fall
and reconcile me to God.

I beg you not to leave me.
Comfort me in adversity,
restrain me in prosperity,
defend me in danger,
and assist me in temptations,
lest at any time I fall beneath them.
Offer up in the sight of the Divine Majesty
my prayers and petitions,
and all my works of piety,
and help me to persevere in grace
until I come to everlasting life.

Novena to St. Joseph

1323   **INVOCATION**

THE just man will blossom like the palm tree
— and flourish forever before the Lord.

1324   **READING**

Col 3:24

WHATEVER you do, work at it with your whole
being.
Do it for the Lord rather than for men,
since you know full well
you will receive an inheritance from him.
Be slaves of Christ the Lord.

I will set him over his household
— and make him lord of his possessions.

1325   **PRAYER TO ST. JOSEPH**

O BLESSED St. Joseph,
loving father and faithful guardian of Jesus,
and devoted spouse of the Mother of God,
I beg you to offer God the Father
his divine Son, bathed in blood on the Cross.
Through the holy Name of Jesus
obtain for us from the Father
the favor we implore.

Appease the divine anger so justly inflamed
by our crimes;
beg of Jesus love for your children.
Amid the splendors of eternity,
forget not the sorrows of those who suffer,
those who pray and those who weep.

Stay the almighty arm which smites us
so that by your prayers and those of your Spouse
the Heart of Jesus may be moved to pity and pardon.

1326   CONCLUDING PRAYER

H EAVENLY Father,
you entrusted to the faithful care of Joseph
the beginnings of the mysteries of our salvation.
Through his intercession
may your Church always be faithful in her service
so that your designs may be fulfilled.
We ask this through Christ our Lord.

Novena to St. Jude

1327   DEDICATION PRAYER

T O YOU, Lord Jesus Christ,
our mediator and brother,
we offer our prayers today.
We acknowledge the special friendship
which your apostle, St. Jude, has with you.
To his love and friendship with you, we unite our prayers.
We praise and thank God
for your supreme love and friendship
for the human family.
We join our prayers intimately
with your generous death on the Cross.
To this enduring act of praise of God,
through which all people are made pleasing to the Father,
we unite our prayers.
We join our prayers today to the Eucharist,
which renews in us the loving act of your death and resur-
    rection,
and expresses most perfectly

the fulfillment of our final union with you.
Be present with us today and each day of our lives.
Deepen our love for our Father and for each other.
May these graces and favors for which we pray
be granted through you,
who live and reign with the Father
in union with the Holy Spirit,
God, forever and ever.

1328   OPENING PRAYER TO ST. JUDE

ST. JUDE, cousin and friend of Jesus
during his life on earth,
chosen by Christ to be his apostle
and to learn directly from him
the message of his redeeming love,
join us now in prayer to day.
We acknowledge your apostolic role
in forming the foundation of Christ's Church
and in taking to many distant places
the message of Christ's love for all people.
We take heart at your generous love
for Christ and humanity,
which ended in martyrdom.
We fully believe
you now rejoice in the happiness of heaven
and have sealed forever your earthly friendship with Jesus.
Perhaps because you share the same name
as the man who betrayed our Lord,
your role as an apostle and friend of Christ
was long forgotten.
But, now, we pray to you
as the patron of hopeless cases and desperate situations.
Now we ask your help.
As sinners we are aware of the complete trust

we must have in God's mercy and love.
Intercede with God to give us the strong faith
to live with our sorrows and trials.
Help us to see in our troubles
God's plan for our salvation.
We ask for your intercession with God
for our present needs.

1329 INVOCATIONS TO ST. JUDE
(For private devotion only)

ST. JUDE, cousin of Jesus, *listen to our prayer!* *

St. Jude, apostle of Christ,

St. Jude, who shared in the love of the Blessed Mother for Christ and his disciples,

St. Jude, who was present at the Last Supper, to celebrate the Holy Eucharist with Christ,

St. Jude, who suffered during the passion and death of Christ,

St. Jude, who rejoiced at seeing Christ risen from the dead,

St. Jude, who witnessed the glorious Ascension of Christ into heaven,

St. Jude, filled with the Holy Spirit on the day of Pentecost,

St. Jude, who preached the Gospel of Christ,

St. Jude, who worked many wonders through the power of the Holy Spirit,

St. Jude, martyr for Christ,

St. Jude, patron of the despairing,

St. Jude, intercessor for difficult cases,

St. Jude, consoler of the distressed,

That God will grant wisdom and prudence to our Holy Father, Pope N., our Bishop, N., to other bishops and priests, and the leaders of all nations, states, and communities, *St. Jude, intercede for us!* **

That the light of the true faith will be brought to all people,

That all people, regardless of race, creed, or personal differences, may live in social harmony,

* Listen to our prayer! *is repeated after each invocation.*

** St Jude, intercede for us, *is repeated after each invocation.*

That all people will be given the mental and emotional strength to live in peace and love under the strain of modern living,

That the ties of love and affection among family members will be strengthened,

That the Church will be strengthened with an abundance of priestly and religious vocations,

That the poor and famished peoples of our earth will find nourishment,

That all people will retain their health and that the sick, especially N., will regain their health, according to God's holy will,

That God will grant us respect for authority and the aged,

That God will grant eternal rest to our departed relatives and friends, N.N. and to all departed souls,

That God will grant us our special intentions, particularly N. and for the intentions of all people devoted to you,

That faith, hope, and charity may increase in our hearts,

That the grace and strength to avoid sin and the occasions of sin will be granted to us,

That we will continually cooperate with God's grace to cleanse ourselves of our sins by sincere sorrow and frequent reception of the sacraments,

That we will prepare ourselves for the merciful judgment of God,

That God will answer the prayers of the people requesting a remembrance in the devotions offered to you at the National Shrine,

1330

Let Us Pray.

GLORIOUS apostle and martyr, St. Jude Thaddeus, whose life and accomplishments we celebrate and who used your gifts and talents to bring Christ's love to many people, pray for us today that the love of Christ in our lives may increase. Pray that we may renounce every sinful habit and refrain from all selfish actions.

May we always know your intercession in danger and difficulty,
and may we safely reach heaven to adore with you the most Holy Trinity,
Father, Son, and Holy Spirit,
forever and ever.

1331 PRAYER FOR PARTICULAR NEEDS

ST. JUDE, apostle of Christ,
the Church honors and prays to you universally
as the patron of hopeless and difficult cases.
Pray for us in our needs.
Make use, we implore you,
of this powerful privilege given to you
to bring visible and speedy help where help is needed.
Pray that we humbly accept
the trials and disappointments and mistakes
which are a part of our human nature.
Help us to see the reflection of the suffering of Christ
in the trials and tribulations of our own lives.
Let us see in a spirit of great faith and hope
the part we even now share in the joy of Christ's resurrection,
and which we long to share fully in heaven.
Intercede that we may again experience this joy
in answer to our present needs
if it is God's desire for us.
(Here make your request.)
We know our prayers will be heard through your intercession.

1332 PRAYER OF THANKSGIVING

LORD Jesus Christ, we thank you
for all the graces and favors which you have given us

through the prayers of your apostle, Jude Thaddeus.
Great apostle, St. Jude, we thank you
for your intercession in response to our prayers.
We will always be grateful to you.
Continue to intercede for our needs and in our difficulties.
Be with us particularly in the hour of death
that we may face that decisive moment with courage and serenity.

Novena to St. Anthony

1333   **INVOCATION**

WHOEVER wonders wants to see
— let him invoke St. Anthony.

1334   **THE RESPONSORY OF ST. ANTHONY
OF PADUA**

IF THEN you ask for a miracle,
    death, error, all calamities,
the leprosy and demons fly,
and health succeeds infirmities.
The sea obeys and fetters break,
and lifeless limbs you do restore;
while treasures lost are found again
when young or old your aid implore.

All dangers vanish at your prayer,
and direst need does quickly flee.
Let those who know your power proclaim,
let Paduans say these are of you.
The sea obeys, and fetters break,
and lifeless limbs you do restore;
while treasures lost are found again,
when young or old your aid implore.

To the Father, Son may glory be,
and Holy Spirit eternally.
The sea obeys and fetters break,
and lifeless limbs you do restore;
while treasures lost are found again,
when young or old your aid implore.

Pray for us, blessed Anthony.
That we may be made worthy of the promises of Christ.

1335 **PRAYER TO ST. ANTHONY**

WE SALUTE you, St. Anthony,
lily of purity, ornament and glory of Christianity.
We rejoice at the favors
God has so liberally bestowed on you.
In humility and confidence we entreat you to help us
for we know that God has given you
charity and pity as well as power.
Then behold our distress,
our anxiety, and our fears concerning
(here mention your intention).

We ask this of you
by the love you felt for the divine Child
when he favored you with caresses.
Tell him of our wants.
Remember your rapture
when you clasped him to your heart,
when you pressed your cheek to his,
and listened to his divine whispers.
One sigh from you whom he honors
will crown our success and fill us with joy.
Think of this and hear our prayer.
Obtain for us all that we desire
and we will publish your greatness

thereby to glorify him
by whom you were so highly favored.

1336 ANOTHER PRAYER TO ST. ANTHONY

O HOLY St. Anthony, gentlest of Saints,
your love for God and charity for his creatures
made you worthy even on earth to possess miraculous
powers.
Miracles waited on your word
which you were ever ready to speak
for those in trouble or anxiety.
Encouraged by this thought,
I implore you to obtain for me my request
(here mention your intention).

The answer to my prayer may require a miracle;
even so, you are the Saint of miracles.
O gentle and loving St. Anthony,
whose heart is ever full of human sympathy,
whisper my petition into the ears
of the sweet Infant Jesus,
who loved to be enfolded in your arms,
and the gratitude of my heart will be ever yours.

1337 INVOCATIONS

S T. ANTHONY, loved and honored by the Child Jesus,
obtain what we ask of you.
St. Anthony, powerful in word and work,
obtain what we ask of you.
St. Anthony, attentive to those who invoke you,
obtain what we ask of you.

1338 **PRAYER TO THE INFANT JESUS IN ST. ANTHONY'S ARMS**

O JESUS my Savior,
  you were pleased to appear to St. Anthony
in the form of an Infant.
I implore you,
through the love you bore to this Saint
when he dwelt on earth,
and which you now bear him in heaven,
graciously hear my prayer
and assist me in my necessities.

1339 **LITANY OF ST. ANTHONY**

(For private devotion only)

LORD, have mercy.
  Christ, have mercy.
Lord, have mercy.
Christ, hear us.
Christ, graciously hear us.
Holy Mary, *pray for us.**
St. Francis,
St. Anthony of Padua,
Glory of the Order of Friars Minor,
Martyr in desiring to die for Christ,
Pillar of the Church,
Worthy priest of God,
Apostolic preacher,
Teacher of truth,
Conqueror of heretics,
Terror of evil spirits,
Comforter of the afflicted,
Helper in necessities,

Guide of the erring,
Restorer of lost things,
Chosen intercessor,
Continuous worker of miracles,
Be merciful to us, *spare us, O Lord!*
Be merciful to us, *hear us, O Lord!*
From all evil, *deliver us, O Lord.***
From all sin,
From all dangers of body and soul,
From the snares of the devil,
From pestilence, famine and war,
From eternal death,
Through the merits of St. Anthony,

* Pray for us *is repeated after each invocation.*
** Deliver us, O Lord *is repeated after each invocation.*

Through his zeal for the conversion of sinners,

Through his desire for the crown of martyrdom,

Through his fatigues and labors,

Through his preaching and teaching,

Through his penitential tears,

Through his patience and humility,

Through his glorious death,

Through the number of his prodigies,

In the day of judgment,

We sinners, *we beseech you, hear us.****

That you would bring us to true penance,

That you would grant us patience in our trials,

That you would assist us in our necessities,

That you would hear our prayers and petitions,

That you would kindle the fires of divine love within us,

That you would grant us the protection and intercession of St. Anthony,

Son of God,

Lamb of God, you take away the sins of the world; *spare us, O Lord.*

Lamb of God, you take away the sins of the world; *hear us, O Lord.*

Lamb of God, you take away the sins of the world; *have mercy on us.*

Christ, hear us.
Christ, graciously hear us.

Pray for us, O blessed St. Anthony.
That we may be made worthy of the promises of Christ.

1339a

LET us pray.
Almighty and eternal God,
you glorified your faithful confessor Anthony
with the perpetual gift of working miracles.
Grant that what we confidently seek through his merits
we may surely receive by his intercession.
We ask this in the Name of Jesus the Lord.

*** We beseech you, hear us *is repeated after each invocation.*

Novena to St. Rita

1340
SUPPLICATIONS
(For private devotion only)

H OLY Patroness of those in need, St. Rita,
  your pleadings before your divine Lord are irresistible.
For your lavishness in granting favors
you have been called the "Advocate of the Hopeless"
and even of the "Impossible."
You are so humble, so mortified, so patient,
and so compassionate in love for your crucified Jesus
that you can obtain from him anything you ask.
Therefore, all confidently have recourse to you
in the hope of comfort or relief.

Be propitious toward your suppliants
and show your power with God in their behalf.
Be lavish of your favors now
as you have been in so many wonderful cases
for the greater glory of God,
the spread of your devotion,
and the consolation of those who trust in you.
We promise, if our petition be granted,
to glorify you by making known your favor,
and to bless you and sing your praises forever.
Relying then on your merits and power
before the Sacred Heart of Jesus,
we ask of you
(here mention your request).

1341   **PRAYER OF INTERCESSION**

B Y THE singular merits of your childhood,
  obtain our request for us (repeated after each invocation).

By your perfect union with the divine Will,
By your heroic suffering during your married life,
By the consolation you experienced
at the conversion of your husband,
By the anguish that filled your heart
at the murder of your husband,
By your sacrifice of your children
rather than see them grievously offend God,
By your miraculous entrance into the convent,
By your severe penance and thrice daily bloody scourging,
By your suffering from the wound received
from the thorn of your Crucified Savior,
By the divine love that consumed your heart,
By your remarkable devotion to the Blessed Sacrament
on which alone you subsisted for years,
By the happiness with which you parted from your trials
to join your divine Spouse,
By the perfect example you gave to people
of every state of life,

Pray for us, St. Rita,
—*That we may be worthy of the promises of Christ.*

1342   **CONCLUDING PRAYER**

O GOD,
in your infinite tenderness you have been pleased
to regard the prayer of your servant Rita,
and to grant to her supplication
that which is impossible to human foresight, skill, and
    effort,
in reward for her compassionate love
and firm reliance on your promises.

Have pity on our adversities
and comfort us in our calamities,
that unbelievers may know that you are

the recompense of the humble,
the defense of the helpless,
and the strength of those who trust in you.
Grant this in the Name of Jesus the Lord.

1343 **Novena of Grace in Honor of St. Francis Xavier**

O VERY dear St. Francis Xavier,
   full of divine charity,
with you I reverently adore the divine Majesty.
Since I greatly rejoice in the singular gifts of grace
that the Lord conferred on you in this life,
and of glory after death,
I return most heartfelt thanks to him,
and I beg of you to obtain for me,
by your powerful intercession,
above all the grace to live well and die holily.

Moreover, I ask you to gain for me
(here insert your petition).
But if that which I suppliantly ask of you
is not for the greater glory of God
and the greater good of my soul,
I beg you to obtain for me
whatever will better promote both these ends.

Our Father, Hail Mary, Glory be, etc.

Novena to Any Saint

1344   INVOCATION

T HE Lord is just and loves justice.
   — The Saints will see his face.

1345   **READING**

Rom 8:28-30

WE KNOW that God makes all things work together
for the good of those who love him,
who have been called according to his decree.
Those whom he foreknew he predestined to share
the image of his Son,
that the Son might be the first-born of many brothers.
Those he predestined he likewise called;
those he called he also justified;
and those he justified he in turn glorified.

The just will rejoice in the presence of the Lord.
— They will exult and be glad.

1346   **INTERCESSIONS**

FATHER, you made all things holy.
    While we meditate on the lives of your Saints
we pray to grow close to you as we recall your words:
℟. *Be holy for I am holy.*

Holy Father, you called us to be your children
and so we are;
— grant that your people throughout the world
may proclaim you as their Father.
Holy Father, you willed that we should live
to please you in all we do;
— grant us the strength to lead good lives.
Holy Father, you made us one with you through Christ;
— teach us to be your children
so that we may be one with each other.
Holy Father, you invited us to the banquet of your kingdom;
— help us to grow in love
as we receive the bread that comes from heaven.

Holy Father, forgive the sins of all your people;
—and bring those who have died into your presence.

1347   **CONCLUDING PRAYER**

L ORD God, you alone are holy
    and no one is good without you.
Through the intercession of St. N. . . .
help us to live in such a way
that we may not be deprived of a share in your glory.
We ask this through Christ our Lord.

PRAYERS FOR THE HOLY SOULS

The Church encourages us to pray for the dead —
either through liturgical prayers (like the Eucharist
and the Liturgy of the Hours) or through private
prayers (like those found in this section). She reminds us that it a holy and wholesome thought to
pray for the dead that they may be loosed from their
sins.

D) FOR THE FAITHFUL DEPARTED

WE CHRISTIANS are aware in faith that beyond death we will be with God. We are also aware that at the moment of death we are not always the kind of persons we should be for all eternity; hence, that a process of purification follows death before we will share life with God, as promised.

The Second Vatican Council upheld the time-honored custom of praying for the dead: "Very much aware of the bonds linking the whole Mystical Body of Jesus Christ, the pilgrim Church from the very first ages of the Christian religion has cultivated with great piety the memory of the dead. Because it is 'a holy and wholesome thought to pray for the dead that they may be loosed from sins' (2 Mc 12:46), she has also offered prayers for them. . . .

"This most sacred Synod accepts with great devotion the venerable faith of our ancestors regarding the vital fellowship with our brethren who are in heavenly glory or who are still being purified after death" (Constitution on the Church, nos. 50-51).

Hence, we who are still able to increase the divine life in us, still able to win God's favor by our cooperation with the grace of Christ, can help the suffering members of God's family, who are in purgatory. They in turn can and do pray for us—although they cannot help themselves.

The prayers in this section are intended to foster this laudable devotion to the holy souls in purgatory and to provide models for other prayers to be drawn up. At the same time, such devotion is an apt reminder of our own death and the need to be ready for it by living in a truly Christian fashion.

General Prayers

1348   **Prayer to the Father
          for All the Faithful Departed**

H EAVENLY Father,
          I believe that in your wisdom and justice
you willed to purify all persons who die
without having attained the state that they need
for all eternity,
all who have still to expiate completely
the sins committed on earth.
I also believe that you have mercifully arranged
that this process of purification can be aided
by the prayers of the living,
and especially by the Eucharist.

Help me to pray for my brothers and sisters
who have departed from this world.
May their time of purification be short
and they be quickly guided into that holy light
promised by our Lord to Abraham and his descendants.
I offer you sacrifices and prayers of praise.
Accept them for all the souls of the faithful departed
and admit them all to the eternal joy of heaven.

1349   **Prayer to Jesus and Mary
          for All the Faithful Departed**

M OST loving Jesus,
          I humbly beg you to offer to your eternal Father,
in behalf of the holy souls in purgatory,
the most Precious Blood which poured forth
from the sacred wounds of your adorable Body,
together with your agony and death.

O sorrowful Virgin Mary,
do you also present to the Father,
together with the dolorous Passion of your Son,
your own sighs and tears
and all the sorrows you suffered in his suffering,
in order that through the merits of the same,
the souls now suffering in purgatory
may receive refreshment and peace.
Delivered from that painful state,
may they be clothed with glory in heaven,
there to sing the glories of God for ever and ever.

1350 Prayer to Jesus for the Suffering Souls

MY JESUS,
by the sorrows you suffered
in your agony in the garden,
in the scourging and crowning with thorns,
in the way to Calvary,
in your crucifixion and death,
have mercy on the souls in purgatory,
especially those who are most forsaken.
Deliver them from the dire torments they endure,
and admit them to your most sweet embrace in paradise.

Our Father. Hail Mary. Eternal rest, etc.

1351 Prayer for a Departed Father and Mother

O GOD,
you commanded us to honor father and mother.
In your goodness,
have mercy on the souls of my father and mother
(*or* the soul of my father, *or* the soul of my mother),
and forgive them their sins
(*or* forgive him his sins, *or* forgive her her sins),

and bring me to see them (*or* him, *or* her)
in the joy of eternal happiness.
We ask this through Christ our Lord.

1352   Prayer for Departed Relatives, Friends and Benefactors

HEAVENLY Father,
accept my prayer for all those in purgatory
for whom I should pray because of ties
of family, gratitude, justice, or charity.
Have mercy on my relatives, friends, and benefactors
as well as those who held positions of authority,
both civil and religious.
Admit them all to your eternal happiness in heaven.
Eternal rest grant to them, O Lord.
And let perpetual light shine upon them.
May they rest in peace.

Prayers of St. Gertrude for the Faithful Departed

1353   INTRODUCTORY PRAYER

HAIL, Jesus Christ, Splendor of the Father;
hail, Prince of peace, Gate of heaven,
Living Bread, Offspring of the Virgin,
and Vessel of the Godhead.
Eternal rest grant to them, O Lord.
And let perpetual light shine upon them.

1354   FIRST PRAYER

I ADORE, greet, and bless you,
O Lord Jesus Christ.
I praise you and give you thanks

with the love of all your creatures
for the infinite love which led you
to become man for us,
to be born and endure hunger and thirst,
toils and sorrows for thirty-three years,
and to bestow yourself upon us
in the Most Holy Sacrament.

I beg you to unite my prayer
with your most holy conversation and life
on behalf of N. departed
(or all the faithful departed).
Supply from the great abundance of your merits
for the things in which he/she is lacking.
Perfectly complete whatever he/she neglected
in your worship and love,
in thanksgiving and prayer,
in virtue and good works,
and all the service due to you,
in all that by your grace he/she might have done
and has not done,
or did from impure motives or carelessly and imperfectly.

1355 SECOND PRAYER

I ADORE, greet, and bless you,
O Lord Jesus Christ.
I give you thanks for that love by which you,
the Creator of all things,
willed for our redemption to be
seized and bound and dragged away to judgment,
trampled upon, buffeted, and spit upon,
scourged and crowned with thorns,
condemned to bear your own cross,
stripped and nailed to the Cross,
die a most bitter death,
and be pierced through with a lance.

In union with that love,
I offer you my unworthy prayers,
begging you to blot out and utterly efface
through the merits of your Passion and Death
whatever this departed person for whom I pray
has ever done against your will
by evil thoughts, or words, or deeds.
I ask that you offer to the Father
all the sorrow and anguish of your torn body
and of your desolated soul,
all your merits and all your actions,
for all that chastisement which he/she has incurred
at the hands of your justice.

1356   THIRD PRAYER

I ADORE, greet, and bless you,
O Lord Jesus Christ.
I give you thanks for all the love and faithfulness
with which you overcame death and rose from the dead,
and glorifed our flesh by ascending in it
to the right hand of the Father.
I beg you to enable the soul for whom I pray
to be a partaker of your triumph and glory.

1357   FOURTH PRAYER

I ADORE, greet, and bless you,
O Lord Jesus Christ.
I render you thanks for all the graces
which you have ever bestowed on your glorious Mother
and on all the elect,
in union with the gratitude
with which all your Saints exult in the bliss
which you have obtained for them

through your holy Incarnation, Passion, and Resurrection.

I beg you to supply to this departed person,

from the merits and prayers of the same glorious Virgin and all your Saints,

whatever is lacking to his/her own.

1358 Litany for the Souls in Purgatory
(For private devotion only)

L ORD, have mercy.
Christ, have mercy.

Lord, have mercy.

Christ, hear us.

Christ, graciously hear us.

God the Father of heaven, *have mercy on the suffering souls.*

God the Son, Redeemer of the world, *have mercy on the suffering souls.*

God the Holy Spirit, *have mercy on the suffering souls.*

Holy Trinity, one God, *have mercy on the suffering souls.*

Holy Mary, *pray for the suffering souls.* *

Holy Mother of God,

Holy Virgin of virgins,

St. Michael,

All you holy Angels and Archangels,

All you holy orders of blessed spirits,

St. John the Baptist,

St. Joseph,

All you holy patriarchs and prophets,

St. Peter,

St. Paul,

St. John,

All you holy apostles and evangelists,

St. Stephen,

St. Lawrence,

All you holy martyrs,

St. Gregory,

St. Ambrose,

St. Augustine,

St. Jerome,

All you holy bishops and confessors,

All you holy doctors,

All you holy priests and levites,

All you holy monks and hermits,

St. Mary Magdalene,

St. Catherine,

St. Barbara,

All you holy virgins and widows,

All you holy men and women, saints of God,

* Pray for the suffering souls *is repeated after each invocation.*

Be merciful to them, *spare them,* O Lord.

Be merciful to them, *graciously hear us,* O Lord.

From all suffering, *deliver them,* O Lord.**

From all delay,

From the rigor of your justice,

From the gnawing pain of conscience,

From fearful darkness,

From their mourning and tears,

Through the mystery of your Incarnation,

Through your coming,

Through your Nativity,

Through your own sweet Name,

Through your baptism and and holy fasting,

Through your most profound humility,

Through your perfect submission,

Through your infinite love,

Through your anguish and torment,

Through your bloody sweat,

Through your bonds and chains,

Through your crown of thorns,

Through your ignominious Death,

Through your sacred Wounds,

Through your Cross and bitter Passion,

Through your glorious Resurrection,

Through your admirable Ascension,

Through your coming of the Holy Spirit, the Paraclete,

In the day of judgment, *we beseech you, hear us.* ***

We sinners,

You who absolved the adultress and pardoned the good thief,

You who save by your grace,

You who have the keys of death and of hell,

That you would deign to deliver our parents, friends, and benefactors from torments,

That you would deign to deliver all the faithful departed,

That you would deign to have mercy on all those who have none in this world to remember or pray for them,

That you would deign to have mercy on all and to deliver them from their pains,

That you would deign to fulfill their desires,

That you would deign to admit them among your elect,

King of dreadful majesty,

Son of God,

** *Deliver them, O Lord is repeated after each invocation.*

*** *We beseech you, hear us, is repeated after each invocation.*

Lamb of God, you take away
the sins of the world; *give
them rest.*
Lamb of God, you take away
the sins of the world; *give
them rest.*
Lamb of God, you take away
the sins of the world; *give*

them eternal rest.
Jesus Christ, hear us.
*Jesus Christ, graciously hear
us.*
From the fate of hell,
*O Lord, you have delivered
them.*

1358a

LET us pray.
O Lord,
the Creator and Redeemer of all the faithful,
grant to the souls of your faithful departed
the remission of all their sins.
By the supplications of your Church
may they obtain the pardon
which they have always desired from your mercy,
who live forever and ever.

1359   Invocations

MY GOD,
pour forth your blessings and your mercies
upon all persons
and upon all souls in purgatory for whom,
by reason of charity, gratitude, and friendship,
I am bound or desire to pray.

1360

JESUS, our Savior,
give us your blessing,
deliver us from everlasting death,

assist your holy Church,
give peace to all nations,
and deliver the holy souls suffering in purgatory.

[405]

ETERNAL rest grant to them,
O Lord,
and let perpetual light shine upon them.
May they rest in peace.

1361

MARY, Mother of God and Mother of mercy,
pray for us and for all who have died
in the embrace of the Lord.

1362

HOLY Mary,
our Lady of Deliverance,
pray for us
and for the holy souls in purgatory.

Prayers for the Faithful Departed for Every Day of the Week

1363 **Sunday**

O LORD God almighty,
  I beg you,
by the Precious Blood which your divine Son shed
in the garden:
deliver the souls in purgatory,
and especially that soul among them
which is most destitute of spiritual aid.

Be pleased to bring that soul into your glory,
there to praise and bless you forever.
Our Father. Hail Mary. Eternal Rest, etc.

1364 **Monday**

O LORD God almighty,
  I beg you,
by the Precious Blood which your divine Son
shed in his cruel scourging:
deliver the souls in purgatory,
and that soul especially among them
which is nearest to its entrance into your glory—
so that it may immediately begin to praise and bless you
and continue to do so forever.
Our Father. Ha'l Mary. Eternal Rest, etc.

1365 **Tuesday**

O Lord God almighty Father,
    I beg you,
by the Precious Blood which your divine Son shed
in his bitter crowning with thorns:
deliver the souls in purgatory,
and in particular the one among them
which would be the last to depart from it—
so that this soul may not tarry so long a time
before coming to praise you in your glory
and bless you forever.

Our Father. Hail Mary. Eternal Rest, etc.

1366 **Wednesday**

O LORD God almighty,
    I beg you,
by the Precious Blood which your divine Son shed
in the streets of Jerusalem
when he carried the Cross upon his sacred shoulders:
deliver the souls in purgatory,
and especially that soul which is richest in merits
in your sight.
May that soul attain the awaiting throne of glory
and magnify and bless you forever.

Our Father. Hail Mary. Eternal Rest, etc.

1367 **Thursday**

O LORD God almighty,
    I beg you,

by the Precious Blood of your divine Son,
which he gave with his own hands
upon the eve of his passion to his beloved Apostles
to be their meat and drink,
and which he left to the whole Church
to be a perpetual sacrifice
and the life-giving food of his own faithful people:
deliver the souls in purgatory,
and especially that one which was most devoted
to this Mystery of infinite love.

May that soul in union with your divine Son
and your Holy Spirit
ever praise you for your love therein
in eternal glory.

Our Father. Hail Mary. Eternal Rest, etc.

1368 **Friday**

O LORD God almighty,
   I beg you,
by the Precious Blood which your divine Son shed
on the wood of the cross on this day,
especially from his sacred hands and feet:
deliver the souls in purgatory,
and in particular that soul
for which I am most bound to pray.
May no neglect of mine ever hinder that soul
from praising you in your glory
and blessing you forever.

Our Father. Hail Mary. Eternal rest, etc.

1369 **Saturday**

O LORD God almighty,
   I beg you,
by the Precious Blood which gushed from the side
of your divine Son
in the sight of and to the extreme pain of
his most holy Mother:
deliver the souls in purgatory,
and especially that one among them
which was most devoted to her.
May that soul soon attain your glory,
there to praise you—and her in you—forever.

Our Father. Hail Mary. Eternal rest, etc.

12

PRAYER-BLESSINGS
for the Laity

12

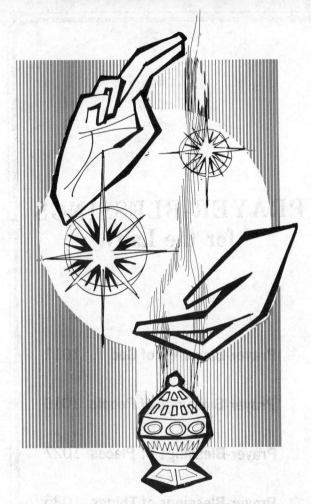

BLESSINGS OF GOD — THANKS FOR
HIS BENEFITS

Our blessings of God consist in offering prayers of
praise and gratitude to him for his many gifts to us.
These gifts are of both the natural and the supernatural order and brighten our lives every day.

1010

A) PRAYER-BLESSINGS OF GOD

(Prayers of Praise and Gratitude)

CHRISTIANS use the word "blessing" in two ways—but in each case it means giving praise and thanksgiving to God as well as asking to use his gifts well. In the first case, we directly bless (that is, praise and thank) God for his greatness in himself and for his gifts to all human beings; at the same time, we indirectly pray to make good use of those gifts.

In the second case, we indirectly bless (that is, praise and thank) God by directly asking him to pour out his grace on persons, places, or things (that is, we ask God to show even greater signs of his love for us). From one point of view, then, we are using blessing in two different senses but from another point of view the end result of both blessings is the same—God is praised and earthly creatures are dedicated to his greater honor and glory while fulfilling their particular function.

The prayers in this first section are cast loosely in the mold of the Jewish berakah, which helps us to thank God first before asking his blessing on us—all through Jesus in the Spirit. It also helps us to pray according to the mind of the Church which has now incorporated the berakah-format in the Eucharistic sacrifice at the preparation of the gifts.

Finally, we might note that the blessings are a form of Sacramental that depend on the Eucharist, the source of all Sacraments and Sacramentals. Their efficacy is derived from the grace and merits of Christ which are made available to us today through the Church in the Eucharist. But this efficacy can be increased by the subjective dispositions of the person who makes use of them.

1370   Blessing for God's Creation

BLESSED are you, Lord God,
    King of the universe,
for creating this wonderful universe (Gn 1:1),
fashioning us in your image (Gn 1:27),
and telling us to fill and subdue the earth (Gn 1:28).
We have immortal souls
and you have destined us to live eternally with you
who are one God in three divine Persons.

Our task now is to sanctify ourselves (1 Thes 4:3)
by serving you and our fellow human beings.
We are helped in this by your grace
and inspired by Christ's example
as we diligently pursue our goal
for your greater glory
and the eternal blessedness of all people.

1371   Blessing for the Redemption

BLESSED are you, Lord God,
    King of the universe,
because you have visited us
and carried out the redemption of your people.
In the house of David your servant,
you have brought us salvation (Lk 1:68f).

How grateful we are to your Son,
our Lord Jesus Christ,
who took the form of a servant,
becoming obedient even to the shameful death
of the Cross (Phil 2:5-8).
May we always be able to say with St. Paul:
I know nothing but Christ crucified (1 Cor 2:2),
and daily accept our crosses
in loving gratitude to our Savior.

1372 **Blessing for God's Living Word**

BLESSED are you, Lord God,
King of the universe,
for giving us your living Word in the Scriptures
that we may be fully competent
and equipped for every good work (2 Tm 3:16).
Your Word is living and effective,
sharper than any two-edged sword;
it judges the thoughts of our heart (Heb 4:12),
and endures forever (1 Pt 1:25).

By the light of faith
and by meditation on your Word,
may we always and everywhere recognize you
in whom we live and move and have our being (Acts 17:
28),
seek your will in every event,
see Christ in all human beings,
and make correct judgments
about the true meaning and value of temporal things
both in themselves and in their relation to our final good.

1373 **Blessing for the Holy Spirit**

BLESSED are you, Lord God,
King of the universe,
for sending us your Holy Spirit.
Substantial Love of Father and Son,
divine Gift of God Most High,
Advocate, Guide, Consoler best,
Spouse of the Virgin Mary,
soul of the Church,
dwelling in us and showing us how to pray!
Teach us gratitude expressed in our Christlike conduct,
as children of God,
because we are led by the Spirit of God (Rom 8:14f).

1374   Blessing for the Church

BLESSED are you, Lord God,
    King of the universe,
who most generously gave us
the one, holy, Catholic, and apostolic Church
as our link with you and your Son in this world.
It has Christ for its founder,
the Holy Spirit as its soul,
and the Blessed Virgin Mary as its Mother.

This wonderful Sacrament of salvation
makes us grow in the knowledge and love of you
and our fellow human beings
by its threefold task of teaching, ruling, and sanctifying.
Grant us the grace to grow in holiness
through our Lord Jesus Christ.

1375   Blessing for Making Us Co-Workers

BLESSED are you, Lord God,
    King of the universe,
who chose to use intruments in your ongoing creation,
particularly human co-workers:
parents, rulers, teachers, prophets, apostles,
farmers, scientists, builders, inventors, and others.
You delight in asking our cooperation
at every possible turn.
You even chose Mary and Joseph
to bring up your own Son
who had also become the Son of Mary.
Help us to continue to work with you,
for the good of humankind
and in a way that is also for your honor and glory.

1376   **Blessing for Making Us Christians**

BLESSED are you, Lord God,
    King of the universe,
who have willed to have your Son
possess meaningful Names!
He had to be called *Jesus* (Lk 1:31),
which means *Yahweh is salvation,*
and he is truly *Christ* (Anointed)
as King with a saving mission.
His followers came to be called *Christians* (Acts 11:25).

What a privilege is ours—
to be members of his Church,
to be animated by his Holy Spirit,
and nourished by his Body.
May we be more and more Christlike every day.

1377   **Blessing for Our Family**

BLESSED are you, Lord God,
    King of the universe,
Triune God, Eternal Holy Family,
represented once so well in Nazareth
and later on in the Catholic Church.
From the beginning you founded the *family*:
father, mother, child.

How greatly today we need your inspiration
when families are breaking down
and parents are abdicating their responsibilities,
and so are the children.
Make our homes small churches, praying Nazareths,
first-grade Christian schools,
O Holy Trinity and undivided Unity!

1378   **Blessing in the Morning**

BLESSED are you, Lord God,
    King of the universe,
for sending us a new day.
Help us to make it a holy day
by seeking to do your will in all things,
accepting whatever crosses come our way.

May it be a day of growth for us
into the likeness of Christ,
under the inspiration of the Holy Spirit,
and with the aid of Mary
who was always a most obedient servant to you.

1379   **Blessing for Midday**

BLESSED are you, Lord God,
    King of the universe,
for the graces you have generously given us
during the morning hours.
How ready we are to make great resolutions
and how quick to forget them.

Some speak of a "Noonday Devil,"
but we know you are always with us,
ever ready to help, strengthen, and console.
Pardon our faults and accept our thanks
for all your many favors.

STAR BANK

THIS IS YOUR RECEIPT

When making a deposit/withdrawal at a tellers window, always obtain an official receipt. Checks and other items are received for deposit subject to the provisions of the Uniform Commercial Code or any applicable collection agreement.

Deposits may not be available for immediate withdrawal.
Bank symbol, transaction number and amount of deposit are shown below.

Deposited / Withdrawn with

```
00192  14104 04/28/97 10:37
DEPOSIT            1514601
        $150.00
```

FORM 4162RB

1380 **Blessing at Day's End**

BLESSED are you, Lord God,
  King of the universe,
for bringing us to the end of another day.
Thank you for your patience
and your continued inspirations.

Thank you also for the crosses which became occasions
for our following your divine Son,
willingly bearing them out of love
both for him and for you.
Enable us to express our gratitude
by following him even more closely tomorrow.

BLESSINGS OF PEOPLE — CONSECRATING THEM TO GOD

Blessings have been used from time immemorial to consecrate people to God. By blessing those we love or come into contact with, we call down God's help on their mission and their needs.

1018

B) PRAYER-BLESSINGS OF PEOPLE

IN THE *final analysis, the use of blessings is only pos-sible because Christians believe in a universe pervaded by God and his power—a universe in which everything speaks of God and leads back to him. It is this type of universe that the Second Vatican Council put before all Christians. In so doing it called all Christians to build up the world until it fulfills its purpose in God's plan.*

In this connection, the Sacred Congregation for Divine Worship discussed blessings in 1972 and concluded among other things: (1) A blessing obtains certain spiritual effects, consecrating people or things to God's service or praying for people and their needs. (2) The first element in a blessing is praise and gratitude toward God who made everything. (3) A blessing reminds us that all creation is good and that God watches over every part of it. When we give thanks to God, we profess that he made all things and gives us all things. (4) The use of blessings should increase in the lives of Christians. We should continue to be conscious of God and his providence over the universe. Accordingly, it is good for lay people to make use of blessings, especially those which refer to their daily lives and activities.

The prayers for God's blessings in this part of the book are all intended to be prayed by lay people. They aim to get people in the habit of calling upon God at every moment of their lives and to impart the conviction to them that everything has a role to play in the working out of their supernatural destiny.

1381   Blessing of a Family

FATHER in heaven,
   we give you thanks and praise
for instituting the human family
to multiply and fill the earth (Gn 1:28),
thus making husband and wife your cooperators.
Bless this family
and keep them one in heart and mind (Acts 2:31).

May they take as their model
the holy Family of Nazareth in which
the Child Jesus was obedient,
Mary and Joseph were ever devoted to their tasks,
and all prayed together and stayed together.
We ask this in the name of Jesus.

1382   Blessing of a Woman before Childbirth

HEAVENLY Father and Author of life,
   you are the Creator of every human soul,
but you enable a woman to conceive
and give birth to a child
which can become forever a blessed child of yours.
We praise and thank you for this privilege.

Bless this Mother and her unborn child.
Give her courage.
Make her grateful for her privilege,
repeating with the Blessed Virgin Mary:
"God, who is mighty, has done great things for me.
Holy is his Name!" (Lk 1:49).
Grant this through Christ our Lord.

1383 **Blessing of a Woman after Childbirth**

F ATHER, your blessings pervade the universe.
   Bless this Woman who has given birth to a child.
Jesus said that a mother after childbirth
no longer remembers her pain
because of her joy
that a person has been born into the world (Jn 16:21).
Like Mary, she now magnifies the Lord
and rejoices in God her Savior (Lk 1:46f).

May this mother—
through prayer and good example—
raise a true child of God,
for what we learn at a mother's knee makes many faithful
to the Lord until death.
We ask this through Jesus the Lord.

1384 **Blessing of an Engaged Couple**

H EAVENLY Father,
   we praise you for your wisdom
in arranging that man should not be alone
but should unite himself to another
to form a living cell or unit,
bringing forth new members for your kingdom (Mt 19:5f).

Bless this Couple who have manifested their intention
to unite in marriage in the future.
Keep them close to you and to one another,
deepen their spirit of prayer and love,
and lead them to receive the Sacrament of Marriage
with joy and happiness.
We ask this in the Name of Jesus the Lord.

1385   Blessing for a Wedding Anniversary

HEAVENLY Father,
Lord of the universe,
we praise you for your goodness
in providing helpmates for human beings
that they may comfort and encourage one another
in their journey through life.
We thank you for the years together
that you have granted this Couple.

May they continue to find joy and companionship
in each other
and in union with you.
May their children revere them,
their friends esteem them,
and all human beings respect them
for their devotion to you and to one another.
We ask this through Jesus Christ our Lord.

1386   Blessing of an Adult

HEAVENLY Father,
we praise and thank you
for sending your only Son into the world
to save us and to instruct us in the way
to become your children forever.
Jesus, we know, is the Way.
In Nazareth he set the example
for our proper development.
He was obedient to Mary and Joseph, his creatures,
and progressed steadily in wisdom, age, and grace
before God and human beings (Lk 2:51).

Grant to this Person
an ever greater desire to be more Christlike,
an exemplary lover of God and neighbor,

and eventually a member of the divine Family
in heaven.
We ask this through Christ our Lord.

1387   Blessing of a Sick Adult

GOD of Love,
   your Son became man
and acted not only as a physician of souls
but also as a healer of physical and mental illnesses.
We ask you to cure this Sick Person
if it is in accord with your plan for him/her.

Enable him/her to serve you
with a healthy body and mind.
May he/she strive for Christian perfection,
helped by your grace,
for your greater glory and honor
and for the advantage of his/her neighbor.

1388   Blessing of an Aged Person

MERCIFUL Lord,
   we know that with its many good aspects,
such as wisdom and serenity,
old age also brings various ailments.
Teach this Person to meditate often
on the sufferings of your innocent Son.

Sustain and encourage him/her to accept the crosses,
in the realization that sufferings can be offered
for the good of souls,
for conversions,
for vocations to the priesthood and the religious life.
Enable him/her to entrust himself/herself
to your Holy Spirit, the Spirit of love,
who is of all consolers the very best.
Grant this through our Lord Jesus Christ.

1389   Blessing of a Pilgrim

HEAVENLY Father,
we thank you for making it possible for us
to travel to your sanctuaries all over the world.
In our day there are still many pilgrimages,
to the Holy Land,
to Guadalupe, Lourdes, St. Anne de Beaupre, Fatima.

Help this Pilgrim to make a holy pilgrimage,
to obtain a cure perhaps,
but above all one that is truly sanctifying
for him/her.
May he/she accept your crosses,
and turn everything to your greater glory.
Make his/her life one long pilgrimage to you
in union with your Son and the power of the Spirit.

1390   Blessing of a Child

DEAR Lord Jesus,
eternal Son of God,
you chose to become a little child
although you could have taken on
a fully developed nature of an adult.
You loved children for their innocence and said:
"The Reign of God belongs to such as these' (Lk 18:16).

Bless this Child and give it abundant grace,
that it may be true joy for the parents
and as it becomes more Christlike
it may give you ever greater glory
and serve as an example for both young and old.

1391 **Blessing of a Sick Child**

COMPASSIONATE Lord and Savior,
you know well how profound a grief is suffered
by normal mothers when their child is sick.
Good mothers are truly "compassionate,"
that is, they suffer with their children.
Please bless this Sick Child
and bring consolation to the parents.
This we ask through the intercession of Mary, our Mother,
who on Calvary became the Mother of Sorrows.

1392 **Blessing of Any Person**

HEAVENLY Father,
from all eternity you foreknew and willed
the existence of this person
whom you endowed with an immortal soul.
You had a particular vocation for him/her.

Bless this Person, granting him/her the graces
to carry out perfectly the design you have in mind.
May he/she strive for Christian perfection
for your own glory
and for his/her eternal happiness with you
and the Son in the unity of the Holy Spirit.

BLESSINGS OF PLACES — CENTERING
THE WORLD ON GOD

We bless places to remind ourselves of God's presence in them and of the use they can be to our salvation. Thus, our whole world can be centered on God and everything we do can redound to his greater glory.

C) PRAYER-BLESSINGS OF PLACES

N O ONE of us lives in a vacuum. We always live in some place or other—a home, a school, a neighborhood, etc. Thus, it is altogether natural that after providing prayers for God's blessings for people we should add blessings for the places in which people carry out their existence.

By asking God's blessing on the places that touch our lives—our work, our leisure, our rest—we can furnish a vivid reminder for ourselves that no matter what we do, no matter how secular it may seem or how trifling it may be, we can do it for the Lord. When we visit the places that have been blessed, Christ is there in a presence that is more grace-laden than his usual presence in creation. As a result the activities we carry out there will be more open to his grace and more beneficial for our salvation and that of the whole world.

The subjects chosen for the blessings in this section are the most usual places in which our lives unfold in the normal course of events. The blessings can thus serve as models for blessings of other places in our experience. The most important thing to remember is that no place on earth is devoid of God's powerful presence and no place is outside the pale of the salvation wrought by Christ through the power of the Spirit.

1393   **Blessing of a Home**

HEAVENLY Father,
    your divine Son came to this earth
and lived for many years in a home at Nazareth (Lk 2:5)
which was sanctified by the holy Family:
Jesus, Mary, and Joseph.
Bless this Home
and all who live or come to visit herein.
May it always breathe forth the true Christian spirit,
the spirit of your Son who said:
"Seek first [God's] kingship over you, his way of holiness,
and all else will be given you besides" (Mt 6:33).

At the same time, may all members of this home
also be fully human,
fully committed to their vocation
—whether secular or religious—
so that they may continue to build up
the Body of Christ here below
until he returns in glory at the end of time.

1394   **Blessing of a School**

FATHER of truth and wisdom,
    we thank you for making human beings so wonder-
       fully
and for endowing them with the limitless capacity
for intellectual, experiential, and moral learning.
We thank you for sending your Son
as the Teacher par excellence
to teach us the way to you.
He instructed a group of unlettered disciples
and sent them out to teach all nations (Mt 28:19).
He taught them so well

that they eloquently spread his teaching
throughout the world of their day.

Bless this School
and all who pass through its halls of learning.
May its teachers be filled with love
and skilled in imparting true knowledge.
May its students be open-minded
and imbibe the teachings with joy and eagerness.
May this School always be the home of truth and wisdom,
faith and good will toward all,
helping to build up our community
and your kingdom of justice, love, and peace.
We ask this in the Name of Jesus the Lord.

1395   Blessing of a Hospital

L ORD God,
you are the compassionate Father of your people,
comforting us in our afflictions
and healing our maladies.
You sent your only Son, the Good Samaritan,
to heal our physical and spiritual sickness.
He does so by bringing us to his Church, saying:
Look after them and I will repay you
on my way back (cf. Lk 10:25ff).

Bless this Hospital which is an extension
of the divine mercy and compassion.
May your Spirit comfort all who come here in pain
and enable them to leave in joy.
May that same Spirit prompt all who care for the sick
to carry out their duties and ministry
in true Christian love and service,
ever mindful of the words of Jesus:
"As long as you did it
for one of the least of my brothers,
you did it for me" (Mt 25:40).

1396   Blessing of a Library

FATHER in heaven,
    in your presence all human knowledge is as nothing
    (Jb 38),
yet you have given us a marvelous mind
that strives to plumb the universe in its mysteries
and even your own most inner Triune life.
Bless this Library stocked with books and materials
that store the knowledge of the ages.
Grant that all who come herein
may be enlightened by the Spirit of truth (Jn 14:17)
so that they may know the truth
and the truth may make them free (Jn 8:32).

Let them neither be puffed up with nor despise
the knowledge of the world.
Rather may they learn to use it
in conjunction with the knowledge of you,
so that they may come ever more
to know you and your Son whom you have sent—
for this is eternal life.
We ask this through Jesus Christ our Lord.

1397   Blessing of a Place of Business

HEAVENLY Father,
    Lord and organizer of the universe,
you gave us the task of subduing the earth
as your privileged co-workers (Gn 1:28).
In carrying out this task
human beings have become engaged
in all types of business,
aided by their mental and physical prowess
as well as the capacities of the machines they build.

Bless this Place of Business.
May its products serve to enhance human life
and so contribute to a deeper spiritual life for all.
May those who work here in any manner
always act with justice and practice charity.
May they never forget that our principal business on
  earth
is to love and serve you
and our fellow human beings.

1398　Blessing of a Place of Recreation

COMPASSIONATE Lord Jesus Christ,
  you bid your disciples one day
to come apart for a while and rest (Mk 6:31).
In so doing, you taught us
that the bow should not always be bent,
but that we have a very human need
for genuine diversion, relaxation, and recreation.

Bless this Place of Recreation.
May it provide wholesome relaxation,
the kind that is good for the body
and good for the soul,
the kind that in no way leads to anything
which is offensive to you.
May all who come here attain relaxation
and return to their daily activities
better able to fulfill the tasks you have set for them.

1399　Blessing of a Place of Entertainment

DIVINE Master,
  some of the entertainments offered to the public
in your day were abominations—
in the form of torture and murder of the innocent.
Today there are gross types of entertainment

that can scandalize the young
and foster the immoral conduct of some adults.

Bless this Place of Entertainment.
May what is offered herein be always decent,
something that will raise people's minds to higher things
and make them enjoy what is truly noble and beautiful.

1400   **Blessing of a Meeting Place**

D IVINE Savior Jesus Christ,
you said that where two or three gather in your Name
you are in their midst (Mt 18:20).
Bless this Place of Meeting.
May the meetings it houses
be held in a spirit of justice and charity,
for the material and spiritual advantage of many
and for your greater glory.
In our world where there is so much division,
may meetings begin and end with prayer
and thereby obtain your blessing.

1401   **Blessing of a Neighborhood**

L ORD God,
you made us social beings
and destined us for family life in heaven.
Your Son, who chose to die for all human beings,
told us to love our neighbor as ourselves (Mt 19:19).
All were made after your image.
That is the reason why we now ask you
to bless our Neighbors and our Neighborhood.
May we strive to preserve loving union among us,
always ready to help one another in time of need.
May we resemble the first Christians
who after Pentecost were of one heart and one mind
   (Acts 4:32).

1402 **Blessing of Any Place**

ALMIGHTY and eternal God,
you are present everywhere in your creation,
sustaining existence, preserving life, granting grace,
and even giving us the very Body and Blood
of your only Son.
Certain places, namely, our churches,
enjoy your special presence
on the altar and in the tabernacle.
In all places, however, we can unite with you
in loving prayer of adoration, thanksgiving, and petition.
Bless this place.
Help with your grace
those who dwell in it and those who come to visit.

BLESSINGS OF THINGS — CHRISTIFYING
THE UNIVERSE

Through the power of Christ's saving Mystery all things in the world can be renewed and supernaturalized. Everything can be made to work for the greater glory of God and the salvation of all human beings. By a judicious use of blessings we can Christify the entire universe.

D) PRAYER-BLESSINGS OF THINGS

CHRISTIANS are aware that by the proper use of created things we are working with Christ to bring creation to its fulfillment under God's plan. However, by asking God's blessing on creation, we can consecrate everything in it to God's service in a special way through our prayer. We are working even more closely with God and helping to restore all things in Christ.

Thus, as we pray for God's blessing on other persons, we can also pray for his blessing on things that we use in our daily lives. By doing so, we render ourselves better equipped to carry out St. Paul's injunction: "Whatever you do, whether in speech or in action, do it in the name of the Lord Jesus. Give thanks to God the Father through him" (Col 3:17).

By praying for God's blessing on the things that we use daily, we remind ourselves that no task is too demeaning or too secular or too alien to the spiritual life— provided we know how to bring God into it.

It is rather fitting to conclude this prayer book with the section dedicated to blessing things and bringing them into accord with the divine redemption. The prayers found herein show how we can sanctify the whole world of things, both animate and inanimate, dedicating them to the use of God's people. May we so use them as to truly restore all things in Christ.

Blessing of an Airplane

A LMIGHTY Creator,
your wisdom and power are evident in your creatures.
When we watch the ease of flight of birds
and see their swiftness and precision,
we marvel that anyone could believe such wonders
to be the product of lifeless and mindless matter.
Inspired by the freedom of your birds,
human beings made use of the reason you gave them
and invented flying machines.

Bless this Airplane.
May it never meet with accidents,
but always provide safe, speedy and pleasant transportation
for those who will make use of it.
May it serve at the same time to remind them
of the majesty and greatness of their Creator
who made the sky through which they fly
and the birds whom they imitate in their flight.
We ask this through Jesus Christ our Lord.

1404 **Blessing of an Ambulance**

L ORD Jesus Christ,
you noted how in your day sick and injured people
were taken to a place of solace by a beast of burden (Lk
10:33).
Today many lives are saved
when sick and wounded are rushed to a hospital
by ambulances—
insuring that such people will possess more time
in which to give glory to you
and work out their salvation.
Bless this Ambulance and make it a true life-saver.
May it be used with proper speed,

never endangering the lives of travelers on the same road.
Endow its drivers with compassion and resourcefulness
as well as genuine Christian charity toward their passengers.

1405 **Blessing of an Animal**

A LMIGHTY and generous Providence,
   how great the variety of living things
you have put at our disposal!
You told our first parents:
"I give you all animals of the land" (Gn 1:30).
Some can be used as food,
or for labor or transportation,
but also for our companionship and recreation.

Bless this Animal.
May it carry out the function it has been given
and may it aid us to think of you its Creator
and give praise and thanks to you forever.
We ask this in the Name of Jesus our Lord.

1406 **Blessing of a Pet**

L ORD God,
   you have made all living things
and you are even more wonderful
than the things you have made.
We thank you for giving us our pets
who are our friends
and who give us so much joy in life.

Bless this Pet.
May it give us joy and remind us of your power.
May we realize that
as our pets trust us to take care of them,
so we should trust you to take care of us,

and in taking care of them
we share in your love for all your creatures.
Grant this through Christ our Lord.

1407   Blessing of an Automobile

MERCIFUL God,
our age has seen the invention
of many new means of transportation.
Automobiles now transport multitudes every day
and there is also a multiplication of accidents
for those who make use of them.

Bless this Automobile.
May your Angels guard those who use it.
May its drivers proceed carefully at a proper speed,
always conscious of their great responsibility.
And may all who reach their earthly destination in it
also enjoy a safe journey to their heavenly home.
We ask this through Christ our Lord.

1408   Blessing of a Boat

LORD Jesus Christ,
you are the supreme Fisherman of souls.
You frequently travelled by boat on the Lake of Gene-
    sareth
and from a boat you sometimes preached to crowds (Mt
    13:2).
You chose fishermen to be your disciples (Mk 1:16f)
and calmed the storm for their safety (Mk 4:39).

Bless this Boat.
May it always be used for good purposes,
and ever ferry its passengers to their proper port.
May it remind them of the great blessing
of belonging to the Church,
sometimes called the Bark of Peter.

1409 **Blessing of a Book**

LORD Jesus Christ,
you have made us in such a way
that we can learn from others
and transmit what we know to others in turn.
Books are the great instruments for imparting knowledge
as well as for forming us in truly human ways.

Bless this Book.
May all who use it grow in wisdom and grace,
and in turn communicate their knowledge to others.
We ask this through Jesus your Son,
whose Life was a living Book that has inspired the ages.

1410 **Blessing of a Christmas Tree**

HEAVENLY Father,
in your goodness you did not abandon us to our sins
but sent your only Son to redeem us (Jn 3:16f).
The birth of Jesus is a manifestation
of his great love for all human beings
as well as your infinite compassion toward us.

Bless this Christmas Tree which we have set up
as a symbol of Christ's birth by its lights
and a symbol of our joy by its decorations.
May this remind us to accept Christ more deeply into
our lives
and bring us closer to you every passing day.

1411 **Blessing of Crops**

HEAVENLY Father and Lord of the universe,
you are Providence and Supreme Provider,
but you desire our cooperation.
Accordingly, we sow, plant, water, and watch—
and ultimately bring in the harvest.

Be pleased to bless these Crops.
May they bring wholesome nourishment or other benefit
to many people.
But we do not live on bread alone (Mt 4:4).
We need food for our souls.
And speaking of a spiritual harvest,
your Son told his disciples:
"The harvest is rich but the workers are few.
Ask the harvest-master to send workers
into his harvest" (Lk 10:2).
As we harvest these crops, may we also be concerned
about our spiritual life
and those who care for it—the harvesters of souls.
Grant this through Christ our Lord.

1412   Blessing of Seed

DIVINE Master,
how frequently you spoke about seed in your teaching
and how often the seed of your Word
was received on stony ground (Mt 13:20).
Wonderful are the promises contained in the smallest
seeds.

Bless this Seed
and grant it full development and rich fruitfulness.
Let us not forget that the most important seed
is the Word of God (Lk 9:11)
and that you expect us to make it most fruitful
for time and for eternity.

1413   Blessing of a Train

LORD Jesus Christ,
how different are our ways of travel
from yours and those of your apostles!

How much we have gained in comfort and also in speed!
But speed is also a cause of accidents.

Bless this Train.
May it give good service to travelers.
May the engineer always keep in mind
his great responsibility with regard to the passengers.
May he be prayerful and rely on your divine protection,
and may all who ride herein entrust themselves to you
for time and for eternity.

1414   Blessing of a Typewriter

FATHER in heaven,
    you have given human beings some of your wisdom
  (Sir 1:1)
so that by their proper use of it
you can renew the face of the earth (Ps 104:30).

Bless this Typewriter,
which is a product of human ingenuity,
that it may always be used for good
and not for evil,
to give life rather than death (Dt 30:15).
Let it be a wonderful source of communication between
    people,
a conveyor of truth not falsehood,
a promoter of the common good,
an aid to the betterment of life,
and a mark of your Spirit in us.
We ask this in the Name of Jesus our Lord.

INDEX OF PRAYERS

BIBLICAL INDEX

OTHER OUTSTANDING CATHOLIC BOOKS

Jesus, Mary, and Joseph,
assist us all during life
that we may be united
with you forever in heaven.